WOMEN
AND
SPORT

Continuing a Journey of Liberation and Celebration

Ellen J. Staurowsky, EdD

Drexel University

Editor

Human Kinetics

Library of Congress Cataloging-in-Publication Data

Names: Staurowsky, Ellen J., 1955- author.
Title: Women and sport : continuing a journey of liberation and celebration / Ellen J. Staurowsky, Ed.D., Drexel University, editor.
Description: Champaign, IL : Human Kinetics, [2016] | Includes bibliographical references and index.
Identifiers: LCCN 2015030635 | ISBN 9781450417594 (print)
Subjects: LCSH: Sports for women. | Sports for women--Social aspects. | Women athletes.
Classification: LCC GV709 .W568 2016 | DDC 796.082--dc23 LC record available at http://lccn.loc.gov/2015030635

ISBN: 978-1-4504-1759-4 (print)

The web addresses cited in this text were current as of January 2016, unless otherwise noted.

Senior Acquisitions Editor: Myles Schrag; **Developmental Editor:** Ragen E. Sanner; **Managing Editors:** Carly S. O'Connor and Karla Walsh; **Copyeditor:** Joy Wotherspoon Hoppenot; **Indexer:** Sharon Duffy; **Permissions Manager:** Dalene Reeder; **Senior Graphic Designer:** Joe Buck; **Graphic Designer:** Kathleen Boudreau-Fuoss; **Cover Designer:** Keith Blomberg; **Photograph (cover):** Scott W. Grau/Icon Sportswire; **Photographs (interior):** © Human Kinetics, unless otherwise noted; **Photo Asset Manager:** Laura Fitch; **Visual Production Assistant:** Joyce Brumfield; **Photo Production Manager:** Jason Allen; **Senior Art Manager:** Kelly Hendren; **Associate Art Manager:** Alan L. Wilborn; **Illustrations:** © Human Kinetics, unless otherwise noted; **Printer:** Sheridan Books

Printed in the United States of America   10 9 8 7 6 5 4 3 2 1

The paper in this book is certified under a sustainable forestry program.

Human Kinetics
Website: www.HumanKinetics.com

United States: Human Kinetics
P.O. Box 5076
Champaign, IL 61825-5076
800-747-4457
e-mail: info@hkusa.com

Canada: Human Kinetics
475 Devonshire Road Unit 100
Windsor, ON N8Y 2L5
800-465-7301 (in Canada only)
e-mail: info@hkcanada.com

Europe: Human Kinetics
107 Bradford Road
Stanningley
Leeds LS28 6AT, United Kingdom
+44 (0) 113 255 5665
e-mail: hk@hkeurope.com

Australia: Human Kinetics
57A Price Avenue
Lower Mitcham, South Australia 5062
08 8372 0999
e-mail: info@hkaustralia.com

New Zealand: Human Kinetics
P.O. Box 80
Mitcham Shopping Centre, South Australia 5062
0800 222 062

E5580

Contents

Part I   Women's Sport in Context: Connecting Past and Present   1

Foreword

Donna Orender

I never wanted to be on the sidelines. The things happening on the field and on the court were far too compelling. I wanted to be right there on the baseline, on first base or the free throw line with my own ball in hand. The opportunity to compete in athletics—from youth to the professional level—provided me the background, the backbone, and the vitally required confidence to blaze a trail, rather ill-defined at the time, in the male-dominated sport industry.

The power of the ball, the game, the field, and the court is such a powerful vehicle through which to learn about leadership, teamwork, diligence, and perseverance—not to mention how to compete and how to win. All of these are critical lessons for the development of our youth, especially for girls and young women, who historically have not had the sustained exposure and benefits accorded to my male friends and colleagues through sports.

Not until I became the president of the WNBA, an iconic brand that was all about strong women, did the all-important mission of validating women as full and valued participants in sports—as athletes, fans, administrators, business colleagues, and consumers—crystallize for me. I first had to recover from the culture shock. I suppose I should have expected it, but I truly did not anticipate the disparity when leaving the highly regarded, well-funded PGA TOUR, the pinnacle of global men's professional golf, to take up the lead of the oft-dismissed yet hugely valuable WNBA. I often joked that I went from negotiating billion-dollar business deals to dialing for dollars. It was telling and

continues to be so. We saw yet another very visible example when the USA women's national soccer team wowed the world on their march to winning the 2015 World Cup. Record-setting television ratings, some that even exceeded those of the NBA finals, provided ample evidence of mainstream interest in the women's game. And yet, when it came time for FIFA to disburse the champion's purse, the women's shares were a pittance compared to the men's purse awarded the previous year.

It is about time that a thoughtful and thoroughly researched text has been written that addresses the comprehensive influence and purview of sport from a woman's perspective. The dearth of research, content, and stories about women and by women has been a significant gap on all of our resource shelves. Dr. Ellen Staurowsky, a professor of sport management at Drexel University who is an accomplished and lauded educator in addition to being a well-versed student of the collegiate sport arena, at long last and most welcomely contributes a book that is both scholarly and motivational. Her myriad personal experiences as a varsity coach of both men's and women's collegiate teams, as a collegiate athletic director, and as an expert on issues pertaining to gender equity give her a unique vantage point for cohesively pulling this wide-ranging material together. She has curated a deep and rich text with the assistance of experienced and erudite contributors. It will be a touchstone for change in an industry that will greatly benefit from its insights and new perspectives. The comprehensive coverage of the touch points for women and sports goes beyond just the historical context of participation to include issues of access, participatory barriers and benefits, the media, leadership, and business.

This book embodies a long and ongoing road that female athletes have taken from liberation to celebration. The need to better understand the complete marketplace is an imperative for all who want to maximize their success in the sport industry, women and men alike. Men who want to be in the industry: Ignore this book's content at our collective peril. In a changing world where the population continues to diversify and where success metrics are increasingly tied to leadership teams that emulate that of their consumer base, a consumer base where women influence or make over 85 percent of the purchasing decisions, it is absolutely vital that we embrace the value and values that gender equality brings to business.

The book on women in sports is an active, ongoing story of strength, influence, growth, and perseverance. The authors have done a remarkable job of not only documenting the starting point but motivating the jumping-off point. This is an action adventure in the making. Thanks to Dr. Staurowsky for giving us the foundation for understanding.

Happy reading.

Donna Orender is CEO of Orender Unlimited, a company focused on working with companies, both established and start-up, by implementing innovative sales, marketing, media, and diversity strategies to help companies grow and prosper. She is founder of Generation W, a women's leadership platform that has made significant progress in elevating the voice and platform for women and girls. Previously she was president of the WNBA for six years and senior vice president of strategic development for the PGA TOUR in the Office of the Commissioner. Orender also played for three years, and was an All-Star, in the Women's Professional Basketball League (WBL). She has been elected to several halls of fame. She has been recognized as one of the top 10 most powerful women in sports and has been a recipient of the March of Dimes Sports Leadership award. She currently serves as an operating executive for Solera Capital and is on the boards of PowerIce, Vardama Inc., and Gudpod. With a strong belief in giving back, Donna proudly serves as cochair of the UJA Sports for Youth Initiative and vice president of Maccabi USA and contributes on the boards of the Monique Burr Foundation for Children, the V Foundation for Cancer research, Jacksonville Public Education Foundation, the Brooks College of Health, and W.O.M.E.N., a mentoring organization.

Preface

In a photo taken at the 1936 Olympic Games held in Berlin, two athletes sit side by side. It is not merely the smiling expressions on the faces of the athletes that command interest, but the easy camaraderie between the two as they sit engaged in conversation between events. In an infield strewn with track and field athletes from around the world, two brilliant runners who brought glory to their homeland and won gold in world record–breaking performances share this most intimate moment as friends, peers, teammates, and citizens of the United States. Their uniforms are exactly the same—sweatshirts with USA sewn on the front, towels tucked in at the collar, sweatpants, and cleats. Within the narrow confines of the photo's frame, the image suggests that they are equals in every respect.

Perhaps in that moment they were equals, to themselves and to some within the Berlin Olympic Stadium. However, the games of the XI Olympiad would assume the dimensions of a visible struggle over political and ideological worldviews, with host country Nazi Germany seeking to showcase the racial superiority of White athletes. And thus, in revisiting the photo, we encounter the greatness of Jesse Owens, who won gold in the 100- and 200-meter dashes, the long jump, and 4 × 100-meter relay, a feat that would stand for nearly five decades. While achieving the stature of a national hero, Owens returned to an America that had not resolved its own issues with race, offering second-class citizenship to the very same favorite son who had upheld the country's honor overseas. Poignantly, after the Games, he observed, "The battles that count aren't the ones for gold medals" (Spence, 2009).

Sport has often served as the site where social struggles around race, ethnicity, religion, sexuality, and gender have played out in both overtly public and subtly private ways. If we consider the fate of the woman in the photo, Helen Stephens, we see just how subtle those struggles have been at times. Although she was as famous as Owens in her day, how many are familiar

Runners Helen Stephens and Jesse Owens at the 1936 Olympics in Berlin.

with her name today? At one time, she inspired sportswriters to nickname her The Missouri Express and The Fulton Flash because of her great speed as a sprinter. Stephens' performance in the 100-meter dash at the 1936 Olympics would not be beaten for 24 years. However, as a leading figure in sport she was no mere flash, as her nickname implied. The breadth of her record-setting talents went well beyond running events to include broad jump and discus. Why is it that so few know about Helen Stephens, the first woman to create, own, and manage a semiprofessional basketball team in 1938?

Some insight in this regard can be found in the sports pages of the *Cleveland Plain Dealer* from November of 1937, a year after Stephens owned the headlines. In an article titled "Says Sports Ruins Feminine Figures," writer Bob Considine reports on the views of Miss Rebecca Dean, characterized as a leading expert in women's physical culture. Waging a "campaign against muscles" and advocating for swimming and golf as the only two acceptable sports for girls, Miss Dean's mission in life was to argue against the violent aspects of American women's sport that threatened femininity, marriageability, and the capacity to have children, as embodied in female athletes like Babe Didrikson and Helen Stephens, the greatest female athletes of their generation. At the time Considine was writing, neither were married.

This tension around matters of equality and what happens to great female athletes in U.S. culture serves as a starting point for appreciating how far we have come in American society in admiring the accomplishments of female athletes and understanding the importance of sport in the overall lives of girls and women. At the same time, female athletes continue today to navigate a tenuous tightrope, as seen in controversies around their representation in the media, appropriate training levels and safe techniques, barriers to participation, and the subtle cues that suggest that female athletes remain second-class citizens (see chapters 1 and 2). While this book is not a history of women's sport in the United States, it is advised by events,

beliefs, and attitudes that have served to shape our current national conversation about what it means to be a female athlete and a woman working in sport. By acknowledging the influence of the past, we can better understand the pressing questions of our day.

While U.S. educational, economic, and political structures have arguably come to terms with the idea that boys and girls and men and women are going to learn together, work side by side, and lead as equals organizations as disparate as Little Leagues, Fortune 500 companies, professional football franchises, and the U.S. House of Representatives, the structure of sport remains largely segregated. As a result, the forces that allowed Helen Stephens' heroic achievements to disappear from collective memory remain intact today. These same forces manifest in the suspicions raised about female athletes like Brittney Griner, whose sexuality and temperament were questioned frequently during her college basketball career at Baylor University as she became stronger and more powerful. And while each generation is much more in tune with the events and personalities of their own time that take over collective memory, the fact remains that male sport superstars are remembered much longer than their female counterparts (see chapter 11). In another 20 years, will we find that Brittney Griner, quite possibly one of the greatest female basketball players to ever play the game, remains in the American memory any more than Helen Stephens? We cannot know the answer to that question but we know the implication. We know that when these great women are rendered invisible, generations of both men and women are robbed of the opportunity to envision possibilities for themselves and the women in their lives. We can use that question to explore the support systems that allow female athletes to fulfill their dreams and promise, as well as the barriers to their success. This book will explore the connections between sport as liberation and as celebration by focusing on women winning access to the playing field as well as the front office and making their own way to greatness.

Photo Credits

CHAPTER OPENER PHOTOS

Chapter 1: © The Rucker Archive/Icon Sportswire; **Chapter 2:** © Brand X Pictures; **Chapter 3:** © Press Association via AP Images; **Chapter 6:** © serge simo/fotolia.com; **Chapter 7:** AP Photo/Elaine Thompson; **Chapter 8:** © Colin Anderson/Blend Images/Age Fotostock; **Chapter 9:** © Steve Nagy/Design Pics/Age Fotostock; **Chapter 10:** © Digital Vision; **Chapter 11:** © Ric Tapia/Icon Sportswire; **Chapter 12:** © AP Photo/Kathy Willens; **Chapter 15:** © AP Photo/Jim Mone

ADDITIONAL PHOTOS

p. xi: Photo courtesy of Jesse Owens family; **pp. 5, 10, 14, 25:** Courtesy of Drexel University Archives; **p. 38:** © Casey Rodgers/Invision for Ubisoft/AP Images; **p. 47:** J.P. Wilson/Icon Sportswire; **p. 85:** © Bananastock; **p. 102:** Courtesy of Special Collections, The College of Wooster Libraries. Contact there: Denise D. Monbarren DMONBARREN@wooster.edu; **p. 103:** Gian Mattia D'Alberto/LaPresse/Icon Sportswire; **p. 108:** AP Photo/Hassan Ammar; **figure 8.2:** © AP Photo/Marion Curtis, StarPix; **p. 140:** © Darryl Dennis/Icon Sportswire; **p. 152:** GEPA/Imago/Icon Sportswire; **p. 157:** © Mary A. Hums; **p. 165:** © Andres Rodriguez/ fotolia.com; **p. 185:** © AP Photo/RFS; **p. 186:** Ray Carlin/Icon Sportswire; **p. 198:** © Anthony J Causi/Icon Sportswire; **p. 202:** © AP Photo/ Andrew Parsons, Pool; **p. 213:** © Darrell Walker/ Icon Sportswire; **p. 237:** © Cynthia Lum/Icon Sportswire; **p. 249:** © AP Photo/B.K. Bangash; **p. 260:** © Xinhua/Imago/Icon Sportswire; **p. 311:** Photo courtesy of Drexel University Media Relations; **p. 313 (Antunovic):** Photo courtesy of Steve Sampsell, College of Communications, Pennsylvania State University; **p. 313 (Carter-Francique):** Photo courtesy of Texas A&M University; **p. 313 (Daniels):** Photo courtesy of the University of Lethbridge; **p. 313 (Farneti):** Photo courtesy of Richard J. Bolte, Sr. School of Business, Mount St. Mary's University; **p. 314 (Hardin):** Photo courtesy of John Beale, College of Communications, Pennsylvania State University; **p. 314 (Hums):** Photo courtesy of University of Louisville College of Education and Human Development; **p. 314 (Krane):** Photo courtesy of Vikki Krane; **p. 314 (McDowell):** Photo courtesy of Jacqueline McDowell; **p. 315 (Oglesby):** © Ginny Naumann; **p. 315 (Phillips):** Photo courtesy of University of Waikato, Media Relations; **p. 315 (Sell):** Photo courtesy of Hofstra University Media Relations; **p. 315 (Smith):** Photo courtesy of Maureen Smith

Introduction
Becoming a Female Athlete

Dayna B. Daniels, PhD, Emeritus Professor, University of Lethbridge

When I was a young girl—one who loved sports and wanted to play all the time—opportunities for joining organized sports teams were nearly nonexistent. Depending on where they lived, the ethnic diversity of the area, and the social class of their parents, girls could access a number of activities. There was dance, figure skating, equestrian events, some tennis, and swimming. At the time, these were all considered appropriate physical activities for girls, ones that for the most part did not include much competition. Notice, as well, that none of these were team sports or activities that were seen to be appropriate for boys—rough and tumble, head-to-head sports that generally were played in teams and often included physical contact. If this sounds very Victorian, it was. Not that I am *that* old, but prior to Title IX, Victorian ideals of gender-appropriate behaviors were deeply ensconced in the play and sporting activities of girls, particularly for middle-class Caucasian girls. The attitudes regarding appropriate physical activities for African American girls and other ethnic and religious groups (regardless of socioeconomic class) were different based on historically different social experiences in the United States. For example, African American girls were encouraged to be strong and to participate in a variety of activities such as track and field events and team sports, including baseball and basketball. Native American girls were often excellent horsewomen and active participants in cultural sporting activities that mainstream Americans knew nothing about.

The historical realities of the participation of girls and women in sport and physical activity had much more to do with race and class than with sex. Even during the Victorian era, young aristocratic girls participated in numerous activities behind the protective walls of estates and private equestrian, golf, tennis, or swimming clubs. Girls from the working class and rural areas participated in activities that built the strength and agility required for work on farms or in factories. The rise of a middle class during the Industrial Revolution set forth a common sensibility that became the public face of American society. This included rules about what girls and boys ought and ought not to do. Team sports, such as basketball and baseball, came to be considered unladylike, and girls were discouraged from playing them, even though girls and women had been participating in these games since their inventions in the 1800s (Cahn, 1994).

For me and for many girls in my generation, there were some school programs once we got to junior high or high school. These were limited and did not offer the perks that boys' teams received (no uniforms, no leagues, limited competition). We had access to gyms and fields after the boys' teams were finished with them. Often, our coaches were overworked female physical education teachers who were not paid to coach. Even in college, although there were many more options for teams and activities for girls, there were no scholarships, and coaches for girls' teams were paid significantly less than their male counterparts, if they were paid to coach at all.

I received my personal introduction to the rules of becoming an athlete when I was about 8 years old and showed up for an initial Little League meeting. I was told, "You can't play, you're a girl." Skill, desire, and love of the game had nothing to do with playing. Many of the boys likely did not want to be there—not all boys like sports! They were sent to sign up by parents for any number of reasons. But, ultimately, regardless of who really wanted to be there, only the boys could join up.

Since the inception of Title IX (see chapter 2), the reasoning that girls can't play has mostly vanished from the North American landscape. From data by the Women's Sport Foundation, Kane reported that prior to Title IX, approximately 300,000 girls participated in high school sports in the United States. By 2011, that number had grown to over 3 million (Kane, 2013). However, other reasons for attempting to keep girls out of some sports have taken the place of the traditional "you're a girl" excuse.

Perhaps, then, it takes a historian to observe the obvious—namely, that the theories, methods, and sensibilities of Western science have, for four centuries, been under the control of an exclusively male guild. For the greater part of that period, the society that shaped every scientist, great and minor, was male dominated through and through. And society took all that was male to be normal, whether in politics, art, the economy, scholarship, social ethics, or philosophy. As Londa Schiebinger has argued, "at the core of modern science lies a self-reinforcing system whereby the findings of science (crafted by institutions from which women were excluded) have been used to justify their continued absence" (Rozsak, 1999, p. 14).

BEING A FEMALE ATHLETE IN THE 21ST CENTURY

Human beings have an innate need to move—to be physically active. Movement is essential for developing the motor skills needed to successfully navigate life. For centuries, these movements and skills were directed primarily for survival, not recreation. Competitions of various kinds added to the enjoyment of life, but were often based on these work-essential activities. Women, men, and children all participated in various games. What does being female have to do with being an athlete? The simple answer to the question is, essentially, nothing.

Unfortunately, the reality of the world of sport in the 21st century is a bit more complex. Following World War II, the social tapestry of the United States went through a significant social shift. The economic, political, and human upheavals of the first half of the 20th century and the beginning of the Cold War caused instability and uncertainty in American life. There was a need to stabilize the family and grow the population. Women were encouraged to go back into the home and men to become the single breadwinner of the middle-class family. Men and boys became the public face of American

culture while women and girls became relegated to the private, and primarily invisible, sector.

Organized sport in the amateur and professional realms became important in building a national spirit. Men's team sports took front and center stage. Even though women and girls continued to participate in almost all sports and activities, their endeavors were not celebrated. The dichotomous state of public and private deemed the sporting activities of girls frivolous or inappropriate. Television added to this division as the broadcasting and reporting of men's sporting lives became part of the daily fabric of life. Women were no longer seen to be athletes or even regular participants in sports. The realities of women's sporting history disappeared. But the reality of women's ability to be athletes did not.

Being female is a biological designation that is tied to having two X chromosomes in the 23rd pair of the human genetic makeup, and even that is not a completely universal reality. Biological differences between women and men (as well as among women and among men) are a matter of degree. According to Fausto-Sterling (1993), there are five sexes that can be placed on a continuum. These are female, female pseudo-hermaphrodite, hermaphrodite, male pseudo-hermaphrodite, and male. Most people who are intersex cannot be distinguished through casual observation while they are clothed; thus the female–male designation will continue to be used throughout this introduction. The recognition of intersex and trans people cannot be minimized within this discussion (see chapter 7 for more discussion on this subject). But even if femaleness were straightforward, there is nothing about this condition that has any limiting factors to becoming an athlete. Some men may be stronger than all women, but many women are stronger than some men. The person with the greatest flexibility is likely to be female, but many men have excellent flexibility. There is nothing inherently male or masculine in strength, nor anything female or feminine in flexibility. Try being a successful athlete without both of these characteristics. All people have some degree of all physical characteristics, but through training and practice, these necessary sport components can be changed, increased, and improved in everyone (see chapter 5 for more discussion).

Being an athlete in the 21st century has nothing to do with a person's sex. The barriers that girls and women face are remnants of a social structure that separated female and male athletes into discrete categories with strict socially constructed rules of behavior.

Differences in athletic ability between and among women and men and girls and boys can be traced to differences in opportunities, quality of coaching and equipment, practice time, and levels of competition (Sokolove, 2008). Since the dissolution of discrimination based on sex in school programs became a reality (as contentious as Title IX has been in the realm of sport), the success rates of women in almost every sporting activity have soared. Most barriers to females' becoming athletes remain in the social realm.

The realities of women's sport history and the struggles that women undertook to reclaim their place in sports can be illustrated in the two films *American Masters: Billie Jean King* (Erskine & Gregory, 2013) and *Shooting Stars* (Stein, 1987). In *American Masters: Billie Jean King*, viewers learn about the legendary sports icon who has had a profound effect on democratizing sport and creating a fairer society that is more inclusive and just. *Shooting Stars* tells the 25-year history of the Edmonton Grads, a women's basketball team that competed all over the world from 1915 to 1940. This team won the North American Championship series in 1934, 1935, and 1936.

Certainly not all girls and women will be able to reach their desired level of success in their chosen sport. This is true for all people, but the reason cannot be attributed to the sex of the athlete, only to the various biological and social factors that make up the individual and our culture.

MYTHS AND MISCONCEPTIONS ABOUT FEMALE AND MALE DIFFERENCES

Essentially, there is no magic combination of physical characteristics that can be identified as creating an athlete—whether female, male, intersex, or transgender. Every sport and physical activity requires its own ratio of performance characteristics. Age, skill level, and levels of intensity of participation and competition can alter these ratios as well. Certainly, some characteristics are needed for athletic performance in general. Strength, flexibility, power (aerobic and anaerobic), agility, speed, rhythm, and coordination are all needed to some extent in all human movements. But if we look at specific sports, individual positions in team sports, or various events within multi-event sports, we can see that each of these requires a specific combination of physical characteristics for successfully executing the required biomechanical and physiological (not to mention, at this point, psychological) demands of the activity or event. Being short may be a disadvantage for playing volleyball or basketball at the highest of levels, but it does not prevent a person—female or male—from developing the basic skills to play the game, even to a very high degree. Even though being short does provide an advantage to athletes in gymnastics and diving, being tall does not prevent a person from learning the skills of the sport and executing them well. Interest in the activity is a greater motivator for learning skills and executing them successfully than body type or the sex of the performer.

Very few of us will be endowed with the exact combination of physical and psychological characteristics needed to reach the highest levels of our chosen sports. But that does not mean that we should be prevented from trying our best and maximizing whatever potential we have. Besides, look at any Olympic or professional team in any sport or activity. There is a lot of variation in the size and shape, amounts of strength and flexibility, levels of intelligence, and psychological fortitude of all the athletes on a team or in a sport. Of course, there are some similarities as well, but why should the characteristics needed to be an Olympic or professional athlete keep anyone from learning a sport and participating to any level that is worthy of being designated an athlete? One of the ways that we can think about this further is by considering several facts and fallacies about male and female athletes.

Fact: In general, size and strength favors untrained males over untrained females.

Fallacy: All males are bigger and stronger than all females.

A 350-pound (159 kg) defensive lineman may be a good example in attempting to prove this fallacy, but a horse racing jockey will not. To assume that an athlete with the physical characteristics of a jockey will be able to play NFL football just because he is a male is as fallacious as stating that a woman will never be able to play in the NFL, or that the 350-pound defensive lineman could never make it as a wide receiver . . . not to mention as a jockey.

Counterarguments

1. You cannot use the physical characteristics of athletes at the highest professional level to prove that someone else cannot or should not play that sport. Parents ought to look only one or two levels above the entry level that their child will participate in to assess the skill level needed to play and the average size of the players.

2. The use of examples of male strength and size to keep girls from participating in certain sports is further compounded by the fact that it is primarily professional team sports that are given as examples. If you look at myriad professional individual sports, you will see that female athletes participate at the highest levels of these activities. Women and men generally do compete only against others of their sex, but many sports have mixed competitions (tennis, badminton, curling). In equestrian sports, women and men compete head to head. The lack of media coverage, especially on television, of non-team sports, women's team sports, Paralympic events, master's events, Gay Games, and Special Olympics adds to the arguments supporting male-only participation (see chapter 14).

3. Where head-to-head competition between males would pose an extremely lopsided competition due to differences in size and strength, sport structures adapt by utilizing weight classes. It is easy to understand why a heavyweight boxer never fights a flyweight. This structural compromise could be expanded to any number of differences in athletes to provide greater participation and success for women as well as men. Girls and women very successfully compete in all of the sports that use weight classes, including judo, tae kwon do, boxing, and wrestling. It is the ersatz masculinity factor (discussed later in this introduction) that frames the arguments against female athletes participating in these head-to-head contact sports.

Fact: Males have greater amounts of testosterone than females.

Fallacy: Women can never be as strong as males.

As exercise physiologists Katie Sell and Sharon Phillips point out in chapter 5, for preadolescent boys and girls, there is little evidence to support a conclusion of difference that is statistically meaningful on measures of strength, endurance, or skill. Girls are even muscularly stronger than boys until age 12. Due to increase in size and levels of testosterone, boys on average do surpass girls in strength during puberty. Denying difference serves no purpose. However, making too much of it is even more problematic. As Epstein wrote (2014, para. 18),

> If we wanted to simply see the fastest runners, we would have cheetahs race instead of humans. But sports are the ultimate contrivances: Take agreed-upon rules, add meaning. We must be vigilant to ensure all women who want to compete have the opportunity to do so, but the idea that women's athletic performances must be equivalent to men's in order to be deemed remarkable belittles the achievements of female competitors.

Counterarguments

1. Although it is true that males have greater amounts of naturally occurring testosterone in their bodies than do females, what exercise physiologists are learning is that females recruit different hormones than males to develop muscular strength (McArdle, Katch, & Katch, 2007).

2. Discussing strength as a singular and complete characteristic is not a good representation of the various measurements of strength. Total body strength can be measured as absolute or relative. Absolute strength is measured by the total amount of weight that a person can lift or push. A male Olympic weightlifter can manipulate a clean and jerk of more than 400 pounds (181 kg). A female gymnast could never be expected to manipulate that kind of weight. However, if strength is calculated relative to body weight, the gymnast, who has to control five to six times her body weight in tumbling moves or landings (with no steps or loss of balance), is significantly stronger than that male weightlifter.

3. Comparisons of strength vary by body parts or regions. When absolute total body strength is measured, the overlap of average strength of males and females is about 85 percent. However, when lower body strength is considered, the gap between females and males closes significantly. If flexibility were to be used as the comparative component, women would excel over most men. This is just one reason that strength, and not flexibility, is often used to make the argument to keep females out of sport. Without flexibility, however, the amount of injuries to all athletes would keep the majority of people out of many high-performance activities!

Fact: Men and women receive the same number of injuries when playing sports.

Fallacy: Women are more injury prone than men.

Research shows that female athletes who are well trained and coached, who develop all the necessary physical components and skills of their sports, and who have access to the newest and best equipment have statistically no more injuries nor more serious injuries than male athletes (Sokolove, 2008).

Counterargument

1. Boys are often coached to "suck it up" if they get injured in practice or games. If they are benched or sent to a doctor, they are often forced to return to play far too soon in the healing process of their injury. Because the domain of sport is considered a masculine one, and this masculine angle is often the excuse used to keep females out of sport, girls are often coached to respond to injuries in the same ways boys are. The difference for girls and boys is that injuries to girls are often more serious or career ending than they are for boys. This is not because the athletes are female, but rather because they may be getting less or poorer training and skill development than their male counterparts, leaving their bodies at greater risk of injury.

Where female–male differences in anatomy and physiology do exist, it is important to develop training methods and performance skills that will enhance the play of female athletes and not put them at risk for injury because they are not male. Being female is not an excuse that should keep anyone out of sport.

Fact: Opportunities should be available for anyone healthy enough who wants to play.

Fallacy: Only people who look like the professionals currently playing should play sports.

Using the highest level of sporting excellence as a benchmark for entry into a sport or activity creates barriers for many people. Based on this comparison, Paralympic athletes, a relatively new class of athletes to enter public awareness, and other people with physical (including visual and aural impairments) or cognitive disabilities might assume that a sport is not for them at any level (see chapter 9). For both younger athletes and those who are more mature, age might be seen as a challenge when entry-level opportunities are directed primarily to young children or when only the highest levels of sport and advantageous body types are used as the benchmark for participation. Race and ethnicity may be a barrier (see chapter 6) if, at the professional level, there are no athletes of a particular race or ethnicity playing the sport or particular positions in a team sport (this is often a result of a racially biased process known as *stacking*).

Children and parents may think that there is a legitimate reason for the lack of participants and role models. Finally, sex is a huge barrier. Professional sports (and these examples come primarily from the big four: football, baseball, basketball, and hockey) have few, if any, females to highlight as athletes. Does that mean girls ought not play? This is another false argument.

Counterarguments

1. It isn't wise to put a 6-year-old into Pee Wee football as the gateway to the NFL or a 4-year-old into gymnastics so he or she can make an Olympic team because you think your child will eventually grow to match the body types seen in professional or Olympic athletes. Instead, parents should have realistic (or even better, *no*) expectations other than that their child will learn new skills and hopefully get some enjoyment out of the activity. According to coaches Bruce Brown and Rob Miller, the thing children need to hear from parents in order to feel supported and encouraged is "I love to watch you play" (Henson, 2012).

2. If one looks to almost all sports and activities other than the big four North American professional team sports, girls and women are participating in growing numbers. In some activities, these equal or even exceed the numbers of boys and men participating. American soccer has had a very difficult time getting a foothold at the professional level. Many attempts for men's professional leagues have tried and failed, and these leagues are only now cementing their professional presence in North America. But since the 1999 U.S. women's victory in the World Cup, girls have been flocking to soccer. Professional women's soccer is a direct outcome of the great enthusiasm for the game even as resistance to soccer as a men's sport has very slowly dissipated in many locales.

Fact: Opportunities should be available for anyone healthy enough who wants to play.

Fallacy: What has historically been a men's sport should stay a sport just for men.

Even though cultural spaces reflect the erosion of the notion that certain sports are to be protected as all-male preserves, certain sports in the United States continue to be viewed or encoded as male activities. The continuing practice of advertising fall youth sport leagues with sign-ups for football and cheerleading advertised next to each other continues to convey a message that football is an activity to be played by boys and men and cheerleading is for girls and women.

Counterargument

1. Sports that are already entrenched in the Olympic program can cause entry difficulties for females at that level, but not necessarily at entry levels and other competitive levels. These sports were added to the Olympics at a time when Victorian ideas about female–male differences and false assumptions about risks of athletics to women's reproductive capacities were used to justify keeping females and males from participating in the same activities and most females from engaging in a majority of sports (see chapter 1).

A recent example of the struggles of women to participate in an Olympic sport traditionally closed to them is ski jumping, even though women's ski jumping has held a world championship for many years. A worldwide protest to the IOC and the Supreme Court of Canada did not open ski jumping to women competitors in Vancouver, Canada, in 2010, but they did compete in Sochi, Russia, in 2014. The initial restriction regarding women's ski jumping was based on erroneous Victorian notions of female frailty and the fear of damage to the reproductive system through heavy landings. This unjustified position was used to prohibit girls and women from participating in many activities until late in the 20th century (Daniels, 2009). The true barrier was false and outdated social concerns.

The International Olympic Committee has changed its requirements for new sport entry into the Summer and Winter Olympic Games. Every new sport accepted into the Games must be open to female and male competitors. There are even clearly defined guidelines for transsexual athletes to compete at this level. At entry, all of these sports had high performance levels among all competitors. This illustrates that equal opportunity and training for all participants result in equally high performance outcomes for all participants.

Fact: The media doesn't cover women's sports, even though the competitors are just as good as male athletes.

Fallacy: No one wants to watch women's sports because men are better athletes.

Media coverage is one of the worst offenders in promoting and sustaining the fallacy that men are better athletes than women or that no one is interested in women's sports. The majority of print and broadcast coverage of sport is overwhelmingly of U.S. professional men's football, basketball, baseball, and hockey. Women's sport is nearly invisible outside of Olympic coverage or some major golf, tennis, or figure skating competitions. Specialty channels may have coverage of other women's events, but these are costly to acquire, which limits their exposure and influence.

Counterarguments

1. According to Kane, there is a "symbiotic relationship between sport media and hegemonic masculinity" (2013, p. 232). Broadcast coverage of women's sports is less than 2 percent, which "actively perpetuates a *false narrative*" (Kane, 2013, p. 232) that women are not interested in sport, that women are not good enough in sport to be included in broadcast schedules, or that if women's sports were televised, no one would watch. None of these arguments can be supported.

2. As evidence of Kane's assertion, consider the response to ESPN's coverage of the NCAA Division I women's softball championship, known as the WCWS (Women's College World Series). Between May 22 and 25, 2014, games aired across ESPN platforms (ESPN, ESPN2, ESPNU, and ESPNNEWS) generated a viewership of 26,347,000 viewers. That represented an increase of 30 percent in audience from the previous year. When women's sports are cov-

ered, the possibility for interest can be shown and grown (Volner, 2014).

SOCIAL CONSTRUCTS OF FEMININITY

As a social construction, femininity represents a set of understandings that develop as people interact with the world and encounter the social dynamics of power and ideology. More often than not, we are not aware that our reality and viewpoints are being shaped—sometimes subtly, sometimes not so subtly—by those around us. The primary reason that girls and women are considered less able to be athletes is a social one (Bem, 1993). Various beliefs about gender (the proper designation of the subcategories of femininity and masculinity) form the foundation of the barriers that have been accepted in the belief that girls and women cannot be athletes even though they have always been active in physical activities.

The terms *sports* and *athlete*, as we have come to understand them, are relatively modern interpretations. They have come to represent realms that are highly organized, highly specialized and competitive, professional (as in full-time or nearly full-time endeavors regardless of remuneration), public, and gendered. The largest culprit in modern understandings of sports and athletes that define sport as a male domain (i.e., athletes ought to be males and masculine) is gender. At its root, gender is a linguistic categorization, not a biological one. Throughout Western history—due to power, whether social, political, or physical—what is desirable and of greater value to a culture became labeled as masculine. However, not all males were granted the same masculinity status. Social status and wealth, citizenship, religion, and race have all been used to stratify the cultural position of certain men over others. Regardless of the level of strength or power of these males, the privileges of masculinity were not afforded to them.

Desirable characteristics of femininity, although never equal to the social status of those deemed desirable, were also restricted to certain females. Traits and abilities attributed to wives (and women suitable to be wives) and daughters of the elite of a society that were viewed as signifiers of femininity were rarely applied to women of lower or less desirable classes. Demure, refined, restrained, deferential to men, and attendant to those around them, women of the upper and middle classes were thought of as frail. A counterpoint to her husband who went out into the world as a breadwinner, a woman of substance was to devote her life to him and to hearth and home.

Early in the 20th century, sexologists and psychiatrists started to study gender as an academic pursuit. Although gender was defined as traits, interests, and abilities that might be possessed by any person—female or male—traditional designations of some of these characteristics as feminine, masculine, and neutral caused gender to be looked at as a continuum, with feminine at one end, masculine at the other, and neutral spread across the center.

Some of the early research into gender was attempting to classify people into feminine or masculine personalities depending on the distribution of characteristics with which they identified (Terman & Miles, 1936). A problem arose, however, when some researchers, regardless of the results of their studies, were unwilling to designate "healthy/normal" females as having masculine personalities and males as having feminine personalities. The significant number of neutral characteristics seemed to have gotten lost in this interpretation. The lasting effect of this misinterpretation of research findings is twofold: (1) Gender (femininity and masculinity) is attached to the sex of the individual (female and male), and (2) it is linked to biology, therefore assumed to be naturally occurring. In other words, this false link between sex and gender results in the fallacy that females *are* feminine and males *are* masculine.

Rather than being seen as a continuum with various human traits and interests spread across it and with neutral characteristics that were neither feminine nor masculine, gender morphed into a binary designation that linked gender to the sex of an individual. Even more problematic to the linking of sex with a specific gender was a moral interpretation of cross-sex possession of gender traits. In other words, a female who demonstrated masculine characteristics (and vice versa) was determined to be ill, unnatu-ral, potentially dangerous, or possessing other "undesirable" designations such as lesbian.

If we put this definition of gender into a historical analysis of the place of women in sport, we can ascertain how the negative associations of women and sport came to be applied and accepted (an extensive explanation and analysis of this interpretation of gender can be found in Daniels, 2009). If sport is designated a masculine domain, then females who want to engage in sports become suspect as feminine girls and women in a number of ways (Messner, 2002). It is important to remember, however, that this interpretation and explanation of gender was seen to apply only to people of the dominant race, class, religion, and ethnicity of the time—in other words, White, middle class, Anglo-Saxon, and Christian. People who did not fit into this group were essentially ignored. Thus, girls and women of both the upper classes and the working classes were freer to engage in many sports and activities in their diverse environments. The lack of visibility of this sporting involvement in the greater population made its reality moot.

CONTEMPORARY IMPORTANCE OF ROLE MODELS

We hear a lot about role models for young girls and teens today—both good and bad. This is often a focus directed outside of the family to actors, rock stars, and athletes, or to teachers, coaches, and clergy. The most important role models in a child's life exist inside the family. Parents or guardians, siblings, and other close relatives are the most important and influential role models. Mothers, grandmothers, aunts, older sisters, female cousins, and other women who participate in sport and physical activities who are close to the family and who encourage girls and teens to be active will have the greatest effect on the current and future involvement of female children in sport and physical activity. This in no way means that only women can be effective role models. To the contrary, men in the family and friends of the family can be excellent role models for young girls and teens. However, it is important for girls to see other girls and women being active and competitive and challenging themselves physically. This sends a message that it is appropriate and desirable for them to do these things as well (Eime et al., 2013). The same is true for bad role models! Children are easily influenced. Undesirable behaviors can be imprinted and practiced just as easily as healthy ones.

Who makes a good role model for sport and physical activity involvement? This can be a slippery slope, especially when we consider all the media attention regarding girls' bodies and bullying behavior for girls who may not have the *de rigueur* figure currently deemed desirable by popular culture. Even girls and young women who are active and successful athletes surveil their bodies constantly, and can have great anxiety about how they look both within their sporting arena and outside of it. We must tell girls that what they can do athletically with their bodies is more important than having a body that fits into an artificial and socially mediated standard. Still, this dialogue can only go so far in stemming the peer and media pressures with which girls and women are constantly bombarded.

Many highly successful female athletes who are excellent role models from an athletic perspective have media profiles that focus almost exclusively on their bodies and looks rather than their performance as athletes. It can be a challenge to find media images of female athletes participating in their sports. Yet, it is very easy to find images of these athletes in poses that resemble soft porn, scantily clad or nude. These images give no indication of the athletic excellence of the girl or woman. The two-edged sword of this type of media presentation—athlete versus sexy persona—may not promote the woman as an athletic role model as strongly as we might like (Daniels, 2012; Knight & Guiliano, 2003).

As role models, family members can also present mixed messages. Many moms, aunts, grandmothers, and big sisters are physically active in their gyms and fitness clubs. At first glance, this appears to be sending a strong message to younger girls about being physically active. Let's look more closely at a typical session at the gym for many college-aged women who are not athletes: 30 to 45 minutes of cardio training

(elliptical, treadmill, stationary bike), some ball work or yoga, and some stretches. There is often no resistance training and certainly no motor skill development that will enhance athletic performance, as likely would be seen in the training sessions of female athletes. Training for fitness exclusively is not being an athlete. This type of limited workout can send a poor message to girls about working out strictly for the benefits of exercise. The majority of women who join a gym or fitness center work out to lose weight. Again, we have a focus on how the body looks rather than how it can perform in an athletic environment (Chalk, Miller, Roach, & Schultheis, 2013).

There is no problem at all with using the elliptical as long as the user is increasing her general fitness or training for cross-country skiing or hiking. Stationary bikes are good warm-ups for going cycling with friends or family. The important part of being a role model is showing girls that skill development and participation in athletic events is the follow-up to the cardio workouts at the gym. Resistance training, aerobic and anaerobic power training, balance and agility exercises, and hand–eye or foot–eye coordination drills have the same goal.

Time needs to be budgeted for healthy play for all members of the family. Playing as a family has a huge influence on children. Even 30 minutes a few times a week as a family can have positive lifelong effects. Certainly, sports can be expensive, and putting children into organized activities may be problematic for many families. Subsidies and scholarships are often available to lower-income families from service agencies and sport organizations in many communities. If you find that assistance is primarily directed to boys, talk to the head of the sponsoring group (or get help from the YWCA or local women's center) and advocate for support for girls.

One way to increase the potential of females' taking up sports is to participate with them. Take tennis lessons with your daughter, go skiing or snowboarding as a family, put up a basketball hoop on the garage or go a local playground to shoot hoops, or throw or kick a ball around. Learn to ice skate and play hockey or ringette. Join a curling or golf league. Rather than sitting on the sidelines watching your daughter at soccer practice, grab some of the other moms and play pickup games yourselves. Learning new sports and activities with your family is a great way to increase family fun time and to show your girls (and boys) that sports is about learning; having fun; possibly competing in a sport inside or outside of school; getting an athletic scholarship to college; competing at a regional, national, or world level; or maybe even becoming an Olympian or professional athlete. Or just participate in sport for the fun and health of it. Having good role models is an important part of this journey.

PEOPLE LIVE WITHIN MULTIPLE SOCIAL CONSTRUCTS

As you read the previous paragraph, you may be thinking, What about families that do not have the time or money to put their girls, let alone adult female family members, into sports and physical activities? What about girls who live in small communities where there just are not a lot of choices of activities or opportunities for girls? What about religious restrictions that affect how girls may dress or the days of the week that they cannot participate? What about girls and young women with physical or cognitive disabilities? What about immigrant girls whose parents do not understand that in our culture, sport and physical activities for girls are an appropriate way to spend time? And what if all of these situations were combined into the life of a single girl?

The intersectionality of many socially defined categories, or social constructs, when added to sex, creates myriad barriers for a great number of girls and women who want to be athletes and who deserve the right to pursue this goal. Intersectionality can become a very complex matrix of domination that causes girls and women to be treated differently for reasons beyond sex, but also added to sex.

Social attributes that can be included with sex in this matrix are age, social class, race, religion, sexual orientation, educational achievement, physical (dis)abilities, cognitive (dis)abilities, indigenous or immigrant status, geographic locale, and language. Each of these attributes may have unique barriers that can negatively affect the sporting involvement of girls and women. When two (or three or four, and so on) of these attributes are part of an individual woman's life, the barriers that get set up to prevent her from becoming an athlete may seem insurmountable.

Simply being female has traditionally been at the forefront of restrictions and limitations to girls' and women's participation in many aspects of society, including being allowed to get an education, own property, run for political office, or even vote. As play became more organized into formal games, sports were contested in schools and public settings and international competitive structures were created. Eventually, professional sports and leagues gained local, national, and international media attention. Girls and women were systematically blocked from participating in this cultural form even though many had been active before public and private structures began to control large aspects of sporting involvement.

Focusing on the barrier of sex is the most important point of analysis and development of solutions for all girls and women in becoming athletes, but we need to be reminded of how and why other social attributes affect this goal differently.

Beginning with the Victorian era of the late 1800s, some Western societies began to extend social privileges to certain women (see chapter 1). Many benchmarks can be identified that illustrate the opening up of society to specific women or groups of women. Women's entry into institutions of higher learning was a major breakthrough for women's social advancement. Students in colleges and universities that were predominantly or all female began to demand the same opportunities that their brothers had in their schools, including physical education training and competitive sports. In reaction to myriad social conditions, women began to demand the right to vote. Once enfranchised, women began to seek the right to run for public office and the right to own property (Munkwitz, 2012).

At first glance, these advancements for women seem to represent groundbreaking social reform and integration of women into all aspects of society. What must be remembered was that only certain women were afforded these privileges. University education was available only to women who came from wealthy families. Racial and religious restrictions for entry were limited primarily to White Protestant Christian women. People of color, immigrants, Jews, and Catholics often had to create and fund their own postsecondary institutions for their young women.

It is interesting to note that many poor and working class females, girls and women of color, and members of numerous immigrant groups had many more opportunities to participate in games and sports. The dismissal of these women in general society and their overall second-class status made them invisible to mainstream cultural observation. Thus, they could participate in many activities that middle-class girls were not able to access. The focus of the middle class was upward—toward the social graces and wealth of the aristocratic, not downward to the lower classes. This gave girls and women from these classes and races much more freedom to play and compete in activities and sports on playgrounds, in union-based leagues, and even in some professional sporting activities that were used for entertainment by the middle and upper classes.

Throughout the 20th century, numerous social and political events were responsible for major changes for girls and women in general and for specific groups in particular. The two world wars brought many women out of their homes and into schools and factories where they learned skills that could be turned into careers outside the home. Because of their military training, women became pilots and drivers. Many turned these skills into sporting or daredevil careers. Between the wars, many women remained in the public sector and participated in basketball, baseball, and track and field competitions organized by the factories for which they worked. Keeping girls fit became a goal of educators and recreational leaders. Physical education classes were taught in schools and certain competitive sports were added to public school curricula.

The increasing visibility of female athletes in limited sports and media programming was used to further the women's movement of the late 1960s and early 1970s. The civil rights, gay rights, and lesser known American Indian rights movements of this same time period in the United States helped to establish a mind-set regarding civil rights and equality in general. This convergence of activisms helped to create acceptance of the need for and passing of Title IX (see chapter 2).

Being female played differing roles in all of these civil rights movements, but it was seen as a challenge to freedom and equality in all of them.

SYSTEMIC BARRIERS IN SPORT ORGANIZATIONS

Academic research and literature is filled with accounts of the misogynistic attitudes (among other biases), structures, and actions of sporting organizations from local to international levels. This systemic matrix of bias against female athletes created a strong foundation, keeping barriers in place that still exist today in many organizations. Although Title IX has brought about significant changes to the opportunities that have arisen for girls and women in sport, it must be remembered that Title IX is an education act. In and of itself, it affects only what is done in schools. The effects of Title IX may go well beyond school structures, but there may be no legal means to change many of the sport delivery systems that exist outside of schools, possibly allowing many organizations to keep biased practices—even unintended ones—in place.

It is important for female athletes and those who care about them (parents and family members, teachers, coaches, partners, friends) to ask questions about the sporting organizations they are interested in joining. What is the structure of the local, regional, national, or international sport governing body? Is the CEO or executive director male or female? Who is on the board of directors? Do they support and train female coaches and officials? Do they offer equitable structures for female and male athletes or mixed participation? Is their financial support equal for female and male athletes? This is not to say that the predominance of men in a sport organization makes it de facto biased against women, but the presence of women in all levels of decision making, program creation, and delivery, including all paid and volunteer positions, may be an indicator of a more female-friendly organization (see chapters 12 and 13).

Sport organizations that have an exclusively upward focus (i.e., they look to world and professional levels of structure and performance) may be less friendly to children and recreational participants. Sports governing bodies that are willing to modify rules and equipment and provide coaching and officiating methods that are more appropriate to each performance level are likely to be more welcoming to nontraditional participants, including all girls and women, people with disabilities, and others who have had difficulty in accessing the sport in the past.

Learning Aids

Summary

This introduction explores what it takes to be a female athlete. It looks at historical barriers, contemporary confusion regarding the realities of gender, myths of female and male biological differences, the effects of intersectionalities, and the structures of some sports governing bodies. All of these factors have, to some extent, been complicit in the difficulties that girls and women have faced in accessing sport and becoming athletes, simply because they are female.

Discussion Questions

1. Discuss how an analysis of race and class differences could paint a more realistic picture of the involvement of girls and women in sport and physical activities since the Victorian era.

2. How does the contemporary belief that femininity is connected biologically to female bodies serve a barrier to the open access of all sports to all girls and women?

3. How might your sporting involvement been different if you had been born into a different social class? Racial or ethnic background? Rural rather than urban or suburban geographical locale? Religion? Explore these and any other socially constructed attribute.

4. Sport performance requires a mixture of numerous physical components such as flexibility, strength, power, and agility, regardless of the sport being played or the person playing it. How can we educate girls and boys to accept that all of these components are necessary for all athletes and that it is time to remove any gendered assignment to these human characteristics?

5. What can you do to become a positive role model to girls and women in your life?

Learning Exercises

1. Get a group of your female and male friends or classmates together in a gymnasium or a field where there is a lot of room. Measure out a distance that you think the best thrower in the group can cover. Collect a bunch of balls to throw. From a standing (rather than running) approach, using an overhand pattern, throw a ball as far as you can. Mark the landing spot for each member of the group. Now, repeat this exercise throwing the ball with your nondominant hand. Discuss why there might be differences in dominant and nondominant side performance. Is it simply biological, or are their other reasons for cross-

lateral differences and for sex differences? Discuss how our beliefs about female–male performance differences might have developed.

2. Using library resources and the Internet, research at least three female U.S. athletes, from different sports or activities, from the first six decades of the 20th century. Using the theory of intersectionality, analyze why these female athletes might have been included in historical and media records. Who might be omitted? Why?

PART I

Women's Sport in Context
Connecting Past and Present

You may be familiar with the expression "we stand on the shoulders of those who came before us." This section serves as a reminder that much of what we know and understand about women's sport today has precedent: Many have come before us to prepare the way. The seeds of events that occur (the 2015 FIFA Women's World Cup), the questions we ask (Why is the high school baseball field better than the softball field?), the controversies that arise (Should soccer superstar Hope Solo have been permitted to represent the United States as a member of the national team when she was charged with domestic violence?), the sports we recognize (Are cheerleading and dance sports?), and the victories we witness (tennis player Serena Williams' 20th Grand Slam singles win at the 2015 French Open) were sown decades, sometimes centuries, ago. An awareness of the historical forces that shape us today provides important perspective in assessing progress, recognizing when progress stalls, and deciding how to keep moving forward.

Chapter 1 introduces the social, political, and economic arguments rooted in Victorian ideals of femininity and masculinity that have historically characterized women as the weaker sex. The chapter explores the influence of these historical ideas on views about women playing sport. An emphasis on femininity and expectations regarding women's roles as wives and mothers barred many women from participating in sport. When the window of opportunity was available through schools like Smith College, where basketball was first introduced to women

in 1892, rules were developed in accordance with fears regarding women's health and over-exertion. One sidebar illustrates the obsession in the late 1800s and early 1900s with women's frailty; another demonstrates the disconnection between those ideas and how women were living their lives, as revealed in the story of the Fort Shaw Indian School girls' basketball team, which became the 1904 champions of the World's Fair.

Fast-forwarding to the decades of the 1950s through 1970s, chapter 2 offers an overview of the effect of the civil rights and women's movements on women's sport in the United States, focusing primarily on the story behind the passage of Title IX (the law that requires that students be treated fairly and equitably regardless of sex) and how the law is applied in the present to federally funded, school-based athletic programs. Attention is given to key features of the law that citizens should know in order to understand what Title IX requires, and what it does not require. And consideration is given to what the future holds for Title IX, and for women's sport.

A set of paradoxes or contradictions that female athletes face in the 21st century forms the basis for the final chapter in the part I trilogy, connecting past and present. As women have entered the U.S. sport system in record numbers, many barriers to participation have been challenged and overcome. Still, assumptions about women formulated in previous ages still resonate in modern women's sport experience. How strong can a woman be and still be viewed as a woman? In a culture where small female bodies are deemed beautiful, how do women embrace athletic demands that call for bigger, faster, and stronger? In sport systems that are structurally set up to separate men and women, and often value men more both socially and economically, how is equality to be achieved? And while there is evidence of equality in sport, does it exist across the board for all women or just for some?

While part I is intended to anchor your reading of the entire book through the lens of history, it is not an exhaustive consideration of women's sport history, which is far too complex and multidimensional to be addressed in just a few short chapters. Knowing that all of the topics and issues covered in the book have a backstory, ask yourself what pieces of the puzzle may be missing when we think about these issues. Look beyond the obvious to gain a deeper appreciation of what is at stake for men and women in discussions about women's sport and gender equality.

CHAPTER 1

Women's Sport Through the Lens of History

Ellen J. Staurowsky, EdD, Drexel University

Learning Objectives

In this chapter, you will learn about the following:

- How Victorian ideals of female inferiority and male superiority have shaped sport in the present day
- How the lived experiences of women and girls in sport often do not match the popular medical and scientific narratives that have been used to justify the limited participation of female athletes in formal sport activities
- How the past continues to influence opportunities available to women in sport

On June 26, 2014, Alysia Montaño, defending champion in the 800-meter event who had won a total of five national titles, joined a field of top runners on the track at Hornet Stadium in Sacramento, California, during the U.S. National Track and Field Championship. What a difference a year had made in her performance, however. Montaño, known as the Flying Flower because of the signature flower she wore in her hair when she competed, had dominated the 800-meter race the previous year. This time around, she was destined for a last place finish in her preliminary heat. Then again, when she won the championship in 2013, she wasn't 34 weeks pregnant.

Just six weeks away from giving birth to her first child, Montaño's time of 2 minutes and 32.13 seconds was slow for the field and about a half a minute slower than her personal best time. Even though her time was slower, her joy in racing, the shared experience with her child, and the reception of the crowd (who gave her a rousing standing ovation) rendered her laps around the track triumphant.

When contemplating the training she would be doing for the race and wondering if it might harm both her and her baby, Montaño consulted her medical team. Because she was an elite-level athlete who had trained most of her life, she could continue to train, being watchful of signs that might suggest that she slow down or stop and adjusting to her pregnancy by cutting back on intensity as she got closer to the birthing date. "My midwives and doctors were so encouraging. You are a professional runner. Your threshold, your lactate levels are going to be completely different than anybody else's. That took away any fear of what the outside world might think about a woman running during her pregnancy," Montaño said (Cox, 2014, para. 5). She also learned that exercising as a general rule is good for expectant mothers, a growing number of whom have been athletes most of their lives.

Like Montaño, female athletes in various stages of pregnancy have challenged the public perception of what a woman is capable of doing when she is with child. Famed basketball player Sheryl Swoopes, who had a record-breaking collegiate career at Texas Tech and competed on three U.S. teams that won gold in the 1996,

2000, and 2004 Olympic Games, is credited with making the road a bit easier for pregnant athletes after her first year in the Women's National Basketball Association (WNBA) was delayed due to her pregnancy in 1997 (Ohikaure, 2013). She returned to the court for the Houston Comets six weeks after she gave birth to her son, contributing to a team that won the WNBA championship that year.

After the 2012 London Olympic Games, Kerri Walsh Jennings revealed that she had won her gold medal in beach volleyball with U.S. teammate Misty May-Treanor while five weeks pregnant with her third child. She was not the only pregnant athlete at the Games. Nur Suryani Mohamed Taibi, the first woman to participate in an Olympics for the country of Malaysia, was eight months pregnant when she competed in the sport of shooting. While her husband was supportive of her participation, traveling with her to London, some of Taibi's friends and relatives were not. About her desire to continue with her sport during pregnancy, Taibi commented, "Most people said I was crazy and selfish because they think I am jeopardizing my baby's health. My husband said grab it as this is a rare chance which might not come again. Also, I am the mother. I know what I can do. I am a stubborn person" (Pickup, 2012, para. 6).

Fears around women's involvement in sport and risks to reproductive health have endured since the Victorian era of the 1800s to the present, emanating from gender stereotypical notions of feminine inferiority and weakness.[1] Hoffmann, Jette, and Vertinsky noted,

> A central problem with organized sport has been the way sport-related policies—particularly those enforcing sex segregation—have codified historical myths about female physical inferiority, fostering a system which, while offering women more opportunities than ever before, has kept them from being perceived as equal athletes to men. (2009, p. 26)

The warm reception Alysia Montaño received at the U.S. Track and Field Championships signaled a level of public understanding and acceptance that athleticism and womanhood in all of its variations need not be contradictory or oppositional. Still, women's sport participation and concerns about potential damage to a woman's capacity to conceive and bear children remains a consideration in the minds of some who seek to guard access to sport from women.

Just a few months before Montaño ran at Hornet Stadium, a historic event was taking place half a world away at the 2014 Winter Olympics in Sochi, Russia. Amid the figure skating and half-pipe snowboarding, curling and ice hockey, luge and downhill skiing, women's ski jumping had finally appeared in the Olympic program.

As Travers pointed out, for female ski jumpers and their advocates, "ski jumping itself is not a new event at all; it is simply an event from which women have been excluded due to sexist discrimination" (2011, p. 127).

As a matter of historical accuracy, for more than 100 years women have taken to the slopes and sought the exhilaration that comes from being airborne on skis and striving to stay aloft a big longer and go a bit farther. Women's access to the sport at the highest level had been barred due to concerns about their reproduction. The International Ski Federation (ISF), the governing body that held the authority to request that women's ski jumping be considered for inclusion by the International Olympic Committee (IOC), failed to do so for many years. In a 2005 interview with National Public Radio, Gian-Franco Kasper, the ISF president at that time, said that women's ski jumping was not supported by the ISF because not many women were good at the sport, adding that "it's like jumping down from, let's say, about two meters on the ground about a thousand times a year, which seems not to be appropriate for ladies from a medical point of view" (Mann, 2005).

In 2009, as female ski jumpers challenged the Vancouver Olympic Committee to have the sport included in the 2010 Games, feminist scholars wrote, "Women's current position of subordination within the sporting realm does not reflect that natural gender order, but is a legacy of long-standing patriarchal and patronizing views about female bodies and women's participation in sport" (Hoffmann et al., 2009, p. 27). The dispute over women's place in the sport of ski jumping in the 21st century is part of a much larger and ongoing dispute that some have suggested emanates from the gendered

The separation of the sexes into boys' and girls' sports teams that continues to this day began in the mid-to-late 1800s and may contribute to a belief that female athletes aren't equal to their male peers in athletic prowess.

arrangements that have structurally locked female athletes into certain roles for nearly two centuries.

The foundation for those arrangements, which form the basis for sex segregation in sport, is intimately tied to ideas that emerged in the mid-to-late 1800s. During the Victorian era, for the upper and middle classes, the march of time and progress resulted in economic and family conditions that cast men in the role of breadwinners who ventured out into the public domain to make a living for themselves and their families. In their turn, women were confined to hearth and home, expected to fulfill their roles as wives, mothers, and caregivers. The lasting legacy of those influences remains in the present.

The activism of female ski jumpers to pursue their sport and to do so at the highest levels of competition illustrates the connections and intersections that exist between women's access to and control of education (women's empowerment through knowledge and status), the political system (women's suffrage), their own history (representation of women's sport as a series of "historic firsts" when women have been participating for hundreds of years), and their own health and well-being (public policy and medical beliefs). Over the span of history, a woman's right to move is connected to her right to vote, to exercise her free will, and to set a course for herself unencumbered by roles imposed on her by a system of laws and social mores that demanded female subservience, denied women right to property, limited opportunities to earn a living, and offered few avenues of escape from abuse.

The assertion of a woman's right to move in sport, to exert her own sense of self and expression in physical ways, is intimately tied to education, politics, medicine, economics, family, religion, and myriad other social institutions that have served as vehicles to enact social scripts based on prevailing values and beliefs. The time period from roughly 1830 through 1920 is marked by a transition from the Victorian Era to the **suffrage movement**, culminating in women's gaining the right to vote. During that time period, ground rules would be established that would be used to shape sport for girls and women and to rationalize the involvement of girls and women in some forms of physical activity, while also denying them opportunities to compete freely and on their own terms.

This chapter examines the importance of women gaining entry into educational institutions, where physical education became an avenue for women to take up sporting activities, as well as medical views of female inferiority and the complications of women's lives. It also considers how these views became integrated into the rules that governed women's sport. Finally, it concludes with thoughts on how the past continues to influence the present.

WOMEN'S EDUCATION IN THE LATE 1800s

During the late 1800s, significant changes were occurring as a result of the **Industrial Revolution**. The dawn of the machine age had begun, bringing with it massive changes in how people made a living, where they lived, and how their communities were organized. An economy once based primarily in agriculture gave way to manufacturing. The world became more accessible as mechanized transportation systems—automobiles and trains—overtook horse-drawn buggies and wagons. And as the world became more accessible, with social and economic centers shifting from close-knit farm and small rural communities to more populated urban settings, families once bound to the land and to neighbors a short distance away were being uprooted and moved. The distance between work and home also shifted, resulting in a division of labor that mirrored societal expectations about men and women, locating more firmly men in the public sphere and women in the domestic sphere. Women from the working class did take jobs outside of the home, serving as factory workers, mill hands, and teachers, for example. Upper-class women, who represented the ideal, were expected to devote themselves to family and children and serve as an object of display as testament to their husband's success by wearing fashionable clothing and expensive jewels. Regardless of class or circumstance, however, motherhood came first (Gerber, Felshin, Berlin, & Wyrick, 1974; Kimmel, 2012; Sack & Staurowsky, 1998).

Within this space, a supportive rationale grew for some women in the upper and middle classes to be educated. Through the lens of womanly obligation, education became an avenue that prepared women for their roles in supporting their husbands and in raising virtuous children who would become good citizens. The responsibilities women were expected to shoulder became the link between home and school.

Fears about what would happen to women who became educated spoke to an ideal of femininity and inspired wild conjecture about what would happen to the carefully constructed gender order if women became too educated.

Historical Conjectures and Beliefs About Women

- Some medical authorities believed that if a woman simply got pregnant, her illness would be cured. In Victorian America, fulfillment of the feminine ideal was found in a woman who was a mother. Pregnant women were also the visible signs of male sexual potency (Wood, 1973).

- Women who were outwardly intellectual were perceived as threatening to the world order. To be a "bluestocking" (a woman who was too bright) might signal a life as a spinster, a woman who was deemed unmarriageable.

- In some parts of the United States, only unmarried women could teach. This was the case with Senda Berenson, who had to give up her role as physical training director at Smith College when she married Herbert Abbott, the chair of the English department there (Melnick, 2007). According to the Frontier Life Project, "as late as the 1930s, nearly 80% of American school districts employed no married women, and more than 60% required female teachers to resign if they married" (Czajka, n.d.).

- Similar societal inhibitions to women receiving education would influence views about women participating in sport. The freedom to be enjoyed by riding a newfangled contraption called the bicycle, for example, was subject to interpretation from medical authorities and social commentators:
  - Women in the late 1890s and early 1900s were warned against the potential dangers of riding a bicycle. The physical demands of balancing while pedaling a bicycle were thought to give women an unattractive appearance called a **bicycle face,** which was considered a medical condition (Fee & Brown, 2003).
  - In an 1895 article that appeared in the *New York World*, women who rode bicycles were presented with 41 things to avoid in order to maintain their dignity and decorum. Part satire and social commentary, the list included advice on fashion ("don't wear a man's hat"; "don't try to ride wearing your brother's clothes 'to see how it feels'"); proper conduct ("don't use bicycle slang, leave that to the boys"; "don't go out after dark without a male escort"; racing is unladylike and should be left to the "scorchers"); and bicycle safety (e.g., don't refuse help when riding uphill; coasting is dangerous). The list ends with an admonition that women riding bicycles not "appear to be up on 'records' and 'record smashing'" because "that is sporty" (Popova, n.d.).

Thus, leading educators of the day, like Mary Lyon, who founded Mount Holyoke College in 1837, were confronted on a regular basis with easing fears that the process of education would make women unfit for fulfilling their roles, "rendering them manly, indelicate, and unsexed" (Sack & Staurowsky, 1998, p. 52).

In a time when an ideal woman was entrusted with raising children to be functioning adults who could take care of themselves and lead productive lives, women who questioned those around them, most particularly the men who controlled their lives, posed a threat. Before women won the right to vote, the very idea of their speaking in public was controversial. Progressive schools that were open minded enough to allow women to enroll found it difficult to overcome the societal prohibition against women speaking in public, often having male authorities read commencement addresses written by female students at the end of their college careers. The prohibition in this regard was so strong that even a liberal school like Oberlin College, where both female and Black students had been admitted since 1833, waited more than two decades before permitting a woman to speak at commencement.

The perceived negative effects of education on women were well chronicled by several leading educators. In his 1873 work *Sex in Education*, Harvard medical school professor Edward Clarke reported that brainwork eroded women's health, causing a litany of illnesses including neuralgia, dyspepsia, hysteria, and other derangements of the nervous system. Charles Eliot, president of Harvard from 1869 to 1909, predicted an array of social disappointments that would befall women who subscribed to what he called "impracticable theories" that led them to believe that they could support themselves economically and forgo the necessities of marriage.

In typical prose of the day, Eliot cautioned that "if brain education is what woman now seeks . . . she must only sink to a lower level. We all blunder, and we all sin and suffer through ignorance, and woman more than man, because she is weaker and can bear less" (Sack & Staurowsky, 1998, p. 43). To all of this handwringing, Bryn Mawr president M. Carey Thomas had

only one response, speculation that President Eliot may have been suffering from "sunspots" on his brain when it came to what he knew about educating women.

FEMALE COMPLAINTS AND THE SUSPECT SCIENCE OF FEMALE WEAKNESS

However true Thomas' responses were, the science of the time that Eliot and others espoused had resiliency, feeding beliefs regarding the sensitive nature of women's constitutions. Popular medical opinion in the late 19th century held that women were born with a limited amount of vital energy and that the reproductive functions of puberty, menstruation, and especially childbirth required a significant amount of this energy reserve. Because a woman's primary function in life was motherhood, she needed to conserve her energy to fulfill her reproductive destiny, which meant forgoing strain deemed unnecessary, such as rigorous physical activity and higher education (Hoffman et al., 2009).

These ideas, as confounding as they appear in a contemporary context, were the products of very real concerns about health risks that were affecting both men and women. Poor nutrition, bad sanitation, air pollution, overcrowded living conditions, and unsafe workplaces produced public health problems that led to a rise in a number of life-threatening illnesses (e.g., cholera, influenza, small pox, tuberculosis, and typhoid). Endemics from airborne diseases that struck with little warning and devastating effect left lasting impressions on the psyche of the survivors, resulting in a public preoccupation and anxiety about health.

Medical opinions about women's health were based in part on social practices that gravely limited women's choices of behavior and avenues for self-protection. Married women swore a vow of obedience to their husbands (a vow their husbands did not take), meaning that they might have to perform what was called the "wifely duty" (have sex with their husbands) whether they were well enough or wanted to do so. The historical perception of women as the weaker sex takes on a whole new meaning within this context. On one hand, the physical toll of bearing numerous children could be quite great. Unreliable birth control offered few options for women who might need a respite during the period between giving birth to one child and conceiving another. A strategy for women, then, was to feign or employ the symptomology of weakness as a way of protecting herself (Smith-Rosenberg, 1972). Even as women sought to take control of their bodies, the strategies of feeling faint, having "sick headaches," and having general malaise contributed to a public perception of women as the weaker sex, so much so that the condition itself became the source of great ambivalence. A certain glamour was associated with flighty, breathless women who were prone to bouts of a generalized neuralgia or hysteria.

Of course, beyond the calculated expressions of weakness that women used at times in order to resist having to do things that were not in their best interests, obvious causes of women's perceived weakness were often misinterpreted or completely overlooked. As a case in point, the fashion of the age dictated that women wear an undergarment called a corset.[2] The corset was a girdle that was laced up to create an hourglass figure (tiny waist, uplifted chest, and accentuated posterior). Small wonder that some women felt a bit dizzy, perhaps suffered from a stomach ailment, or experienced back and pelvic problems.

About the corset, sociologist Thorstein Veblen (1899) described it as a "mutilation" designed to lower a woman's vitality while visually and physically reinforcing the fact that high-class women were not to be engaged in productive employment. The corset was both a social and fashion statement that reflected the financial largess of the leisure class, a class that could afford to avoid any obvious signs of physical work. For example, there was emphasis on women's hands being well manicured, without calluses or traces of the wear and tear that could come from manual labor. High-class women also focused on fine fashion, wearing French heels that made it difficult for them to walk, layers of clothing made of expensive fabric that weighed them down, and corsets that led some women to the fainting couch, a piece of furniture with a high back that allowed women to lounge

because corset designs prevented them from sitting upright.

A woman struggling with her own identity, suffering with depression or exhaustion from the oppressive nature of her upbringing or the strain of reigning in her own thoughts and spirit, would be subjected to medical treatment that could be harsh and punishing. Doctors viewed general malaise or high-strung ways among female patients as failures of their commitment to feminine standards. They prescribed the so-called rest cure, which confined women for months and sometimes years to locked rooms with barred windows, where their sole occupation was lying in bed and eating. Under the theory that women's energy reserve was limited and needed to be directed toward a compliant personality and the demands of home and husband, the rest cure was thought to allow the female patient to reorient her outlook and embrace the standard of femininity put before her.

> Since her disease was unconsciously viewed as a failure in femininity, its remedy was designed both as a punishment and an agent of regeneration, for it forced her to acknowledge her womanhood and made her totally dependent on the professional prowess of her doctor. (Wood, 1973, p. 37)

As writer Charlotte Perkins Gilman so artfully described in her 1892 short story *The Yellow Wallpaper*, the curative value of the rest prescription, which isolated women from social contact and amounted to a form of solitary confinement controlled by physicians, was much in question, revealed as contributing to some women descending into madness.

WOMEN'S PHYSICAL EDUCATION AND THE FAIR BUT WEAKER SEX

Women's physical education developed within women's colleges in response to public suspicion that women would collapse under the pressure of academic work. Smith College's president from 1873 to 1910, L. Clark Seelye, spoke directly to the public anticipation of the harm that might come to women in college when he said during his inaugural address, "we admit it would be an insuperable objection to the higher education of women, if it seriously endangered her health" (1875, p. 27). Like Seelye, other presidents and founders of women's colleges saw the merits in having a physical education curriculum that could offer assurances that attention was being paid to the health of the students entrusted to them. And they sought out medical philosophies that contradicted the doom-and-gloom scenarios that discouraged active participation of women, turning to the work of the few women in medicine at the time to help support their cause.

Elizabeth Blackwell, the first female doctor in the United States, believed firmly in the value of physical activity for girls and women. In a series of lectures about women's health in 1859, Blackwell identified exercise as being the first law of life. The board of trustees at Vassar College in 1865 identified physical training as an aspect of women's education that was "if not first, intrinsically considered . . . as fundamental to all the rest" and recognized good health as an essential component of success for the female student. President Seelye at Smith College noted, "with gymnastic training wisely adapted to

their [women's] peculiar organization, we see no reason why young ladies cannot pursue study as safely as they do ordinary employments" (1875, p. 28).

As more women became college students, the demand for female physical educators grew. By 1900, the Sargent School and the Boston Normal School of gymnastics had begun to fill the void by preparing women as instructors in physical education. The emphasis on monitoring the health of female students while acknowledging women's societal role as mother was reflected in the curriculum, where a wide range of activities addressed an array of health concerns, from activities that strengthened the body to parenthood lectures. Female physical educators along with medical personnel conducted health exams of each female student while keeping careful records of their diet, weight, sleep habits, exercise behavior, and menstrual cycles.

Although physical education in women's colleges was focused on the very serious work of ensuring the health of the students in their care, the fun in physical education would come in the slow but steady inclusion of sports over time. A survey of sports in physical education programs at private women's colleges, coed colleges, state

Early physical education courses for women focused on health benefits and slowly began adding sports to the curriculum.

universities, and state normal schools between 1833 and 1900 found 14 sports, from long-distance walking to field hockey. Despite efforts to maintain restrained and subdued forms of physical activity, women found ways to play things that they liked. In the end, "sports held an appeal for women that gymnastics and regulated exercises did not" (Sack & Staurowsky, 1998, p. 56).

Creating the Athletic Woman's Uniform

As the academic discipline of women's physical education became integrated as a necessary component of a responsible women's education model, the costume women wore to play became an issue. As a practical matter, fashionable dress for women restricted movement and undermined the ability of female physical educators to teach in an environment that supported, rather than created, problems for their students.

A fashionable woman dressed in accordance with "the gospel of good clothes," typically wearing up to 15 layers of petticoats and crinolines under skirts that skimmed the floor over their laced corsets. Bodices described as all the rage in fashion magazines of the late 1800s were tight fitting, with collars 2 to 4 inches (5-10 cm) high made of "absolutely unbendable aluminum-plated watch spring steel collar supports" (Sack & Staurowsky, 1998, p. 56). These were worn over starched camisoles and undershirts. Other contrivances, such as hoops and bustles, gave distinctive shapes to the drape of cloth cascading over women's bodies but added bulk to the entire balancing act. When fully outfitted, a high-fashion woman of the late 1800s might have been wearing as much as 20 pounds (9 kg) of clothing (Lebing, 1987).

Liberating women from their fashionable prisons spawned the **dress reform movement**, a movement that women's physical educators were aligned with either out of a philosophical sensibility that women's clothes were trapping them in lives of ill health, passivity, and overt dependence, or out of the practical necessity that women simply could not pursue a health agenda encumbered by the constrictions of the corset and the weight of their own clothing (Baker, 2013). The freeing **bloomers** costume,

usually consisting of a tunic worn over a set of pantaloons, became the preferred uniform for women in their athletic and physical education pursuits (Lannin, 2000; Marks, 1990).

Introducing Women to Basketball

When Smith College's women's physical education director Senda Berenson introduced the new sport of basketball (originally referred to as *basket ball*) in the 1890s, "women in college appeared ready for a game that allowed them to express the freedom they were slowly beginning to realize through their education" (Sack & Staurowsky, 1998, p. 57).

Adapting rules of the game invented by James Naismith for sportsmen at the Young Men's Christian Association (YMCA) to meet standards of womanliness, Berenson was careful to carve out a space for women's basketball that was distinct from that of men's. Berenson made adjustments to the game because "conventional wisdom taught that women tired easily, were unable to deal emotionally or physically with the rigors of competitive team sport, and needed to have guidelines in terms of womanly court behavior to protect against trauma to the reproductive organs" (Sack & Staurowsky, 1998, p. 57). The possibility of women becoming winded or experiencing overexertion was avoided by dividing the court into three sections. Restriction in the number of dribbles, length of time players were allowed to hold the ball, and rules against aggressive play were all incorporated to customize the game according to the genteel standards of womanhood in the 1890s.

At Sophie Newcomb College in Louisiana, Clara Baer encountered an even more stringent set of expectations about female gentility. After writing to Naismith seeking permission to make alterations to the game, Baer created a version of basketball that she called *basquette*. The court was again sectioned off, but this time into 9 to 11 distinct sections or boxes. This game allowed 18 to 22 women on the court at one time, but required them to stay within their assigned boxes. Limiting play further to make sure that women did not become too overworked, the game emphasized passing, not scoring. In basquette, there was to be no dribbling, no guarding, no falling down, and no talking.

These new forms of women's basketball did not question societal notions of female inferiority, but they were "revolutionary in the liberating effect [they] had on students" (Sack & Staurowsky, 1998, p. 57). A revolutionary tone is found in Berenson's assessment of the importance of the game. She believed that true womanhood was based on the development of both the mind and body. And she appeared to have little patience for societal preferences for weak women, criticizing the perception of women as "small waisted, small footed, small brained damsel, who prided herself on her delicate health, who thought feinting interesting, and hysterics fascinating" (as quoted in Ikard, 2005, p. 10).

In the late 1800s, civil rivalries in a refined atmosphere became commonplace among women for the first time (Sack & Staurowsky, 1998). In the residential confines of college campuses where entertainment was student generated, women's basketball games provided an outlet for exuberant students to gather, cheer on their friends, and feel connected to their community. Often inspired by their teachers, extensive interclass basketball programs flourished as contestants and the students who witnessed them saw a change in the way women related to each other and the world around them. Historian Reet Howell conveys the excitement that could be generated by one these events:

Inside the gymnasium all was turmoil and excitement. Crowds blocked the hallways and stairs. Girls here, girls there, everywhere talking, laughing, shouting, and singing their class songs. In the balconies . . . there were almost 1,100 young ladies anxiously watching the entrance from the dressing room on either side of the stage. Both balconies were splendidly decorated with class colors. (as quoted in Sack & Staurowsky, 1998, p. 58)

Fort Shaw Indian School Girls' Basketball Team, 1904 Champions of the World's Fair

While disputes over rules and the regulation of how much energy and effort women could exert while playing form the basis for much of what we know about women's basketball history, certain revealing and important chapters have been overlooked or covered over, resurfacing periodically to remind us that there were multiple realities for female athletes in every era. The story of the 1904 Fort Shaw Indian School girls' basketball team illustrates the point. During a time when official U.S. policy regarding American Indians resulted in Native children being taken from their homes and educated in government-run Indian schools, a group of 10 young women representing seven Indian tribes came together on a basketball court at the Fort Shaw Indian School. Playing full court, the Fort Shaw "aboriginal maidens" debuted against a boys' team that they had to travel more than 50 miles (80 km) by horse-drawn wagon to beat. They would go on to beat other men's teams from the University of Montana and Montana State by scores of 25-1 and 22-0, respectively. Accomplished musicians and dancers, they would perform artistic pieces during halftime, confronting racial and gender prejudices (being sneered at, called "squaws," and knowing that they were being used as exhibits for governmental purposes) with the weight of their grace, personalities, and talent. Playing before crowds at the Louisiana Purchase Exposition in St. Louis, the Fort Shaw team would defeat the Missouri All-Stars to emerge, as Montana journalists referred to them, as "the undisputed . . . world champions" (Peavy & Smith, 2008, p. 330).

I felt a strong relationship to Minnie. . . . She was a natural, tall like me, and strong. She was a full-blood Indian. They were not just winners, but gracious about it. They kept winning and every time the hate became less . . . began transforming into respect. I believe that team had influence on the popularity of basketball into tribal culture that lasts to this day.

Paulette Jordan on playing Minnie Burton from the Fort Shaw Indian School girls' basketball team in the movie *Shoot, Minnie, Shoot*

Creating a Cultural Script for Women's Enjoyment of Sport

As a hallmark of women's sport, the constant tension between how fervently women could play or how much passion they could exhibit while competing and the sense that women's participation in sport was somehow unnatural carried forward through numerous discussions regarding the terms and conditions under which women could play.

As a case in point, in 1929, Ohio State physical educator Gladys Palmer published a book titled *Baseball for Girls and Women.* From Palmer's perspective, the book was necessary because up to that point in time, there had been no rules available for girls and women to play the outdoor game of baseball, despite the fact that the modified indoor version had been very popular among girls and women since the late 1800s. Seemingly progressive in outlook, Palmer marked the changes that had occurred in attitudes toward girls and women playing the national pastime. She used the views of former professional baseball player turned sport manufacturing entrepreneur Albert Spalding as something of a baseline, so to speak, in measuring how far girls and women had come in the game.

Conceding that women had begun to establish a tenuous presence in the sports of cricket, lawn tennis, basketball, and golf, Spalding adhered to a position that "neither our wives, our sisters, our daughters, nor our sweethearts may play Base Ball on the field" because the game was simply

too strenuous (as cited in Palmer, 1929, p. 10). He wrote that a woman should not be found on the diamond but,

She may take part in grandstand, with applause for the brilliant play, with waving kerchief to the hero of the three-bagger, and since she is ever a loyal partisan of the home team, with smiles of derision for the umpire when he gives us the worst of it.

It is clear, given the purpose of the book, that neither Palmer nor some of her physical education colleagues around the country subscribed to Spalding's narrow vision of women's role in the sport of baseball. She argues in the book that baseball offers similar lessons for both girls and boys, teaching them to make quick judgments and think on their feet, to develop coordination that translates thought into action, and to cultivate a capacity to anticipate what others might do in advance. She also argues that playing baseball helps encourage qualities such as loyalty, self-confidence, responsibility, and sportsmanship in both boys and girls.

This progressiveness, however, gives way to Palmer's sense that a guiding principle in the development of outdoor baseball rules for girls and women would need to meet what she called the "particular requirements of girls and women," noting that boys are naturally born to play the game and to throw overhand, while girls are not equipped physically or psychologically for the rigors of the game. She does not challenge four long-held reasons about the unsuitability of the game for girls and women, presenting them as factual (1929, p. 11):

- The intricate technique of the game is too difficult for the average girl to master.
- The throwing distances are too great.
- There is no advantage which cannot be enjoyed through participation in a more simple and well-planned, but less strenuous game, based on the men's game.
- The danger of injuries is unnecessarily great with the use of the small, hard ball.

Introducing sports within the women's physical education curriculum allowed students to understand and enjoy team sporting events in new and exciting ways.

What unfolds in *Baseball for Girls and Women* is a carefully crafted set of arguments grounded in the science and education of the time, which communicated that something like baseball was acceptable for girls and women to play as long as they did not aspire to play the real game, the game with the hard ball. And while Palmer and her peers recognized the value of playing the game, they were careful to argue that the rule adaptations made to accommodate girls and women in the game were being made for two reasons: so that women could play the game only in recreational settings and so that their exposure to the game would allow them to serve as spectators for men's games.

As a text, Palmer's rulebook passed along not only rules, but also the arguments put forward by political, social, educational, and medical authorities about the proper role for women in the society. One can wonder in retrospect how female physical educators could object to Spalding's outright prohibition of women from the game but then turn around and embrace ideas about women's frailty and weakness. No one answer adequately addresses such a complicated question, but *Baseball for Girls and Women* provides a window into the deliberations and the delicate balancing act that women's physical educators were engaged in as they tried to open up opportunities for girls and women to play while living within the confines of beliefs that relegated women to subservient roles. This hesitancy to just let girls play baseball, to learn the game as it was developed for boys, reveals how strong the pressure to not violate certain gender boundaries was.

While Palmer wrote at the end of the flapper era, an age when social mores became more relaxed, medical opinions regarding women as the weaker sex were very much still influencing the general understanding about the capability of girls and women to participate in sport. Palmer, an advocate for women, wrote, "because they do not have a natural aptitude for throwing, which all boys have from early childhood, many girls when in the act of throwing a ball, tend to lob it or attempt to throw it with a weak forearm snap, failing to bring into play the shoulder and back muscles and to transfer the weight of the body from the right to the left foot, both of which are so indispensable in acquiring speed, distance and accuracy" (1929, p. 17).

Era by era, from the 1800s forward, there is evidence of important changes in expectations for women, important victories won for women to be able to fulfill their promise and potential as human beings. And yet, era by era, there were setbacks, reversals, and opposition to allowing women to simply play and compete as athletes in their own right, without their femininity being questioned, their moral character maligned, and their athletic accomplishments scrutinized as possible evidence that they were not real women.

> *I throw my curveball like Clayton Kershaw and my fastball like Mo'ne Davis.*
>
> Mo'ne Davis

Learning Aids

Summary

In August of 2014, pitcher Mo'ne Davis of the Taney Dragons became the first girl in the history of the Little League World Series to throw a no-hitter, an accomplishment that would land her on the cover of *Sports Illustrated* and result in a groundswell of admiration and support from baseball players and fans across the United States. Major league baseball players offered their congratulations and acknowledged the skill and talent Davis exhibited on the mound.

Davis' example contests the essential flaw in the science that was passed on in texts like Palmer's *Baseball for Girls and Women* that suggested that throwing overhand was something boys did naturally and girls could not do. And yet, even with Davis and the 18 other girls who have played in the Little League World Series over the years, the fact that baseball remains male dominated speaks to how ideas become embedded in structures that become self-reinforcing. Baseball continues to be a sport primarily for boys and men, while girls and women are tracked into the sport of softball. One is left to wonder how many more Mo'ne Davises there are in the world whose talents have been overlooked because they are either not playing baseball at all or are playing softball instead. Emblematic of how resilient these gendered expectations are, during an interview with Davis after her pitching performances had become national news, Eric Bolling, a host on the morning television show *Fox & Friends*, asked Davis, "What about [playing] a, you know, typically . . . more female-friendly sport, like soccer?" (Ley, 2014).

The residue from the science of the 19th and 20th centuries continues to echo in the present. The first two decades of the 21st century offer a moment similar to the previous eras of women's sport where progress is clear. As Alysia Montaño demonstrates, athletic participation and motherhood are not exclusionary, and women have the capacity to be athletes and mothers. At the same time, confronted with the reality of Montaño and so many other female athletes like her, many remain hesitant to allow women quite literally to soar under their own power, as illustrated in the fight that was waged over the sport of ski jumping and its inclusion as a sport for women in the Olympics. This is part of the paradox of women's sport: It offers so much to celebrate, but there is still so much to anticipate and more work to be done.

Discussion Questions

1. In the 21st century, are women liberated from the corset?

2. In her analysis of the movement to include women's ski jumping as part of the Olympic program, Travers (2011) asked several questions about the reaction to women not being allowed to ski jump in the Olympics, noting that significant race and class issues are regularly ignored in terms of the Winter Olympics, with sponsored sports reflecting the tastes and preferences of a governing body that is primarily White and from the moneyed classes. What are your thoughts after reading the following passage from her article? "So why should we care that 15 young and White female ski jumpers were excluded when the Olympics themselves are so exclusive? What makes the exclusion of *this* group of individuals a significant moment in the struggle for social justice in sport and beyond?" (p. 129).

3. Research the history of girls and women in the sport of baseball. How many more Mo'ne Davises are there in the world? Given her success in the sport of baseball, should we expect to see more girls pitching on coed teams in the future? What is the likelihood that the number of women's baseball teams will increase as a result of the public attention Davis has brought to the position of girls and women in the sport?

Learning Activities

1. Ask the class to collect some basic research related to the size of men's and women's hands. Encourage them to go into the dining hall, residence hall, library, fraternity or sorority house, or stadium and randomly ask men and women, aged 18 and older, to touch hands, thumb to thumb, and palm to palm, noting which of the two in each pair have the larger hand and tallying up the results. Each student or student research team is instructed to bring their results to class. When the tally has been reported, present the class with two items: a baseball and a softball. Ask them to consider which one is more uniquely suited to men and women, given the data they have collected. Allow the students to reflect on the reasons why girls are tracked into playing softball while boys are tracked into playing baseball during their school years. Ask the students to consider what would happen if softball were no longer an option and the only sport out of the tandem to be played is baseball. Alternatively, ask students what would happen if baseball were no longer an option and the only sport out of the tandem to be played were softball.

2. Organize a women's basketball game where participants are asked to play by rules written by Smith College's Senda Berenson in 1892 or the rules governing the game of basquette developed by Clara Baer at Sophie Newcomb College. Take these considerations into account as you prepare for the game: What type of uniforms would players be wearing in the 1800s, what was the configuration of the court, how many players would be on the court at one time for each team, and how much publicity would the game have gotten? After playing, contemplate the importance of games representing exciting

occasions for the women who participated, and reflect on the rules themselves. What do the rules reveal about the expectations for women in the late 1800s?

Glossary

bicycle face—A medical condition identified in the 1800s by physicians who believed that the strain of balancing on a bicycle could threaten the health of women. The condition was characterized by tension around the eyes and a general expression of weariness.

bloomers—Baggy trousers or pants that were associated with the women's rights movement of the 1850s and the health movement that helped to foster physical education for girls and women in the late 1800s and early 1900s. Controversial because of a belief that men should be the ones to wear the pants in a family, disputes about girls and women wearing pants would continue well into the 1970s.

corset—A garment associated primarily with women that created or accentuated an hourglass figure (small waist, full breasts and hips). Described as "the most controversial garment in the entire history of fashion," it was an element of fashionable dress for nearly 500 years. Early forms of corsets required that wearers be laced into them. Men have at times also worn corsets (Steele, 2001).

Industrial Revolution—The time period between the 17th and 18th centuries that marked a change from agrarian to industrial societies in Europe and America. The age of mechanization transformed the way that people live, with population shifts from rural communities to urban centers.

suffrage movement—A movement to gain women the right to vote. Supporters of this movement were called *suffragists*.

Notes

1. Beliefs about the power of a woman's uterus to cause hysteria and other forms of mental imbalance date back before the Victorian era. More information on how long these ideas have had a hold on the way that we think about women's health, sexuality, physical prowess, and mental state, either through attribution or interpretation, can be found in chapter 1 of Gilman and colleagues (1993).

2. The history of the corset is elaborate, and researchers offer numerous perspectives on the degree to which women went to adhere to a fashionable image that emphasized a tiny waist. Although stories abound of women who trained their waists to be 14 or 15 inches (35-38 cm) in diameter, historians speculate that this feat would have been rare. Different designs of corsets (not all resulted in an hourglass shape) would have had different effects on a woman's body. For more details on the range of work that has been done on this topic, see Davis (2014).

CHAPTER 2

Title IX and Beyond

The Influence of the Civil Rights and Women's Movements on Women's Sports

Ellen J. Staurowsky, EdD, Drexel University

Learning Objectives

In this chapter, you will learn about the following:

- The story behind Title IX, the piece of federal legislation passed in the United States providing for equitable treatment in schools
- Title IX's application to athletics
- Title IX's effect on athletics
- Title IX and the future

While working at my computer on the Fourth of July in 2012, I glanced up to a see a 20-something mother jogging past my house accompanied by her 5-year-old daughter. Mother was turned somewhat protectively toward daughter, gauging her pace to match that of the little legs beside her. With blond curls bouncing and floating in rhythm with their progress, the daughter smiled brightly up at her mother, head high. She looked so proud to be embarking on a journey, the destination of which she likely will not understand for years to come.

Beautiful and true and joyous, the moment demonstrated in a way that no amount of rhetoric or research can that the opportunity for girls to run and play and claim their place in the world is a fulfillment of their possibility. They get to discover what they are capable of, what they excel at, what they like doing, who they like doing things with, and what it takes to be good at something. This discovery of self is not exclusive to sport, but it is elemental. Human existence is about movement—the beating of the heart, the taken-for-granted intake and exhalation of breathing, the firing of brain synapses, the coursing of life-giving blood through veins.

The story unfolding on the tree-lined lane in front of my house was at once deeply personal and broadly political. In its simplest form, it is the story about a young athlete just getting her first taste of what a life in sport might entail. At the same time, it is part of a tapestry of women's experience in the United States that is built on hard-won victories for equality.

The story of a mother introducing her daughter to sport in such a casual and public way represents the breaking of a cycle of oppression that had once rendered such an act socially unacceptable and politically revolutionary. It bears testament to the success of multiple women's movements spanning nearly two centuries, connecting all women in the United States to the struggle for the right to vote, the right to own property, and the right to life, liberty, and the pursuit of happiness.

The moment itself was powerful because it was devoid of social inhibitors that would have raised doubts about the mother and fears for the girl. There were no voices of authority saying that a girl or woman who ran risked threats to

> I couldn't really imagine growing up in a world where someone said, "No, you can't play basketball because you're a female," or can't do something else. It's important for us to take a minute and appreciate [the changes].
>
> Maya Moore, two-time NCAA champion at Connecticut, where she is the Huskies' all-time leading scorer

her future womanhood, her essential femaleness, her social standing, and her health.

On the 40th anniversary of Title IX, the law passed in 1972 that bans sex discrimination in U.S. schools, espnW referred to such stories as being part of a mosaic, a mosaic that included another story about a parent and his daughters. This one, however, happened to be that of president of the United States, Barack Obama. Describing the fulfillment he experienced coaching his daughter Sasha's basketball team, he wrote,

> Any parent knows there are few things more fulfilling than watching your child discover a passion for something. And as a parent, you'll do anything to make sure he or she grows up believing she can take that ambition as far as she wants; that your child will embrace that quintessentially American idea that she can go as far as her talents will take her. (Obama, 2012, para. 2)

Noting that the barriers to equal opportunity had not all been dismantled and that there was more work to be done in enforcing the mandates of Title IX, President Obama pledged his commitment to "keep Title IX strong and vibrant and maintain our schools as doorways of opportunity so every child has a fair shot at success" (2012, para. 9). That pledge is an important one, especially given the fact that few people actually know what Title IX is and what it requires.

Speaking at the screening of *Sporting Chance*, a documentary on the influence of Title IX on women's sport, three-time Olympic track and field gold medalist Jackie Joyner-Kersee said, "A lot of people don't even know what Title IX is.

And we can't let that happen" (Simpson, 2012, para. 9). Similarly, gymnast Shawn Johnson, who won gold for the United States in the Beijing Olympics in 2008 when she was 16, has said that she didn't learn about Title IX until after she made the Olympic team. She observed, "I don't think it's something that's really taught as you're growing up" (Simpson, 2012, para. 13).

> *[W]e all need to be reminded that since Title IX was put in place by a legislative body, it can be taken away by a legislative body.*
>
> Patsy Matsu Takemoto Mink,
> American politician known as the
> mother of Title IX

In order to fully appreciate women's sport and what it means to have moments of liberation to celebration, we need to know the story behind Title IX, the effect it had and continues to have not only on women's sport but on the place of women throughout American society, the basics of how it applies to athletics, and what Title IX means for the future.

THE STORY BEHIND TITLE IX

As a young woman with a passion for education, Bernice Sandler (known to her friends as Bunny) entered the University of Maryland in the 1960s with an expectation of earning her doctoral degree and teaching. Smart, motivated, and committed, Dr. Sandler had done well in her PhD program, and she was excited about the prospects of what lay ahead as she approached graduation. What she had not seen coming after teaching part time while earning her degree was a consistent rejection of her qualifications when she applied for jobs. Puzzled by the fact that although multiple positions were available in her own department, no effort was made to extend her a job offer, Dr. Sandler asked her department chair. He told her bluntly that she was being passed over because she came on "too strong for a woman" (Sandler, 1997).

The expression "too strong for a woman" was code for the reluctance male faculty and administrators felt in terms of hiring women in the 1960s. Viewing female candidates as less qualified and committed, prone to putting marriage and family before job, and disruptive to all-male faculties, the routine dismissal of female applicants for positions in higher education was a standard practice. It was this rejection that led Dr. Sandler to become the country's leading authority on sex discrimination in schools.

Working at a time when there were few reports on the status of women in education, she built the initial case for why this form of discrimination was damaging to the women involved and to society overall. This concept of sex discrimination was so new, in fact, that the culture had yet to develop a vocabulary to adequately convey that women were being accorded second-class status in a democracy that prided itself on fair and equal treatment of its citizens. As historian Susan Ware points out, "phrases like sexism and sexual harassment were not even in common usage" (2011, p. 46).

What strikes us as unbelievable today in the United States and other Western cultures was accepted practice in the years leading up to the passage of Title IX. Girls were required to meet higher grade and test score thresholds in order to get into colleges and professional schools than boys. Colleges and universities maintained admission quotas to ensure that only so many women would receive a higher education. Greater amounts of financial aid were awarded to men regardless of whether women were more qualified. Women were disqualified as applicants for jobs in education simply because they were women.

Connecting with members of a newly formed organization called the Women's Equity Action League, Dr. Sandler found a sympathetic ally in Representative Edith Green (R-OR), who had devoted her life of public service to issues that improved the nation's schools, thus earning her the nickname Mrs. Education (Blumenthal, 2012). Motivated out of concern for the injustices done to girls by educators, Green conducted seven days of Congressional hearings on the barriers women faced in higher education during the summer of 1970. About the testimony she heard, Green said, "our educational institutions have not proven to be bastions of democracy" (Tolchin, 1976, p. 32). Dr. Sandler was hired to compile the written record of the hearings, resulting in a two-volume, 1,300-page document refuting denials from higher education leaders that women were not being treated fairly in schools. Some of the findings that emerged from the hearings included the following (Blumenthal, 2005; Sandler, 2002):

- State universities in Virginia had turned away 21,000 women in the early 1960s; during the same time period not a single man was turned away.

- A brochure from the University of North Carolina declared that admission of women—but not men—was "restricted to those who are especially well-qualified." As a result, the 1970 freshman class had nearly 1,900 men and only 426 women.

- At the University of Michigan, more qualified female students applied than male students. So the school adjusted its requirements to keep girls to less than half of the freshmen class. Officials didn't want an "over-balance" of women.

- Quotas at many medical and law schools limited women to just 5 or 10 students out of every 100. Consequently, just 7 percent of the doctors in the United States at the end of the 1960s were women.

- Even though most teachers from grade school through high school were women, they were rarely promoted. Most principals were men. (See table 2.1 to see how Title IX influenced enrollments in college, law, and medical schools as well as athletic program participation.)

According to Sandler, "the hearings probably did more than anything else to make sex discrimination in education a legitimate issue" (Ware, 2011, p. 46). And the hearings set the stage for Title IX to be enacted two years later, as Green worked alongside of U.S. Representative Patsy Mink (D-HA; see sidebar) and Senator Birch Bayh (D-IN) to navigate the halls of Congress and move the bill through to final passage. When it was passed, few anticipated the dramatic effect that it would have on every aspect of American society.

Title IX was part of the Education Amendments of 1972, a piece of omnibus legislation signed into law by President Richard M. Nixon just days before news of the Watergate scandal broke, shaking his presidency to the core. At the time, other provisions from that bill captivated the attention of news makers, "including a major appropriation for higher education and student loans, money to improve education for Native Americans, and most controversially, a provision

Table 2.1 Comparisons of Representation of Boys and Girls and Men and Women in Educational Programs and Settings, 1971-1972 to 2013-2014

Program or setting	Sex of participants	PARTICIPATION BY YEAR	
		1971-1972	2013-2014
High school varsity sports participation	Boys	3,666,917	4,527,940
	Girls	294,015	3,267,664
NCAA varsity sports programs	Men	170,384	267,604
	Women	29,977	205,021
Receiving bachelor's degrees	Men	500,590	787,231*
	Women	386,683	1,052,933*
Entering medical school	Men	10,435	9,499
	Women	1,653	8,579
Attending law school	Men	85,554	73,668
	Women	8,914	65,387

*National Center for Educational Statistics, 2014

Data from American Bar Association (2013), Irick (2014), National Federation of State High School Associations (2014).

postponing the implementation of court orders related to racial desegregation" (Buzuvis, 2012, para. 1).

It took longer for the implications of Title IX to begin to penetrate the consciousness of law-makers and education officials. Title IX's day, however, would soon come. And when that day arrived, the American approach to the education of boys and girls and men and women would never be the same. It earned a reputation as "the little statute that could," a reference to the fact that Title IX consists of only 37 words. Title IX has been credited with having an enduring effect on American education for more than four decades, shaping and reshaping opportunities

to be accessed and realized within educational systems that receive federal financial support (Blumenthal, 2012; Buzuvis, 2012).

A BRIEF OVERVIEW OF TITLE IX'S LEGISLATIVE HISTORY

At the time of its passage, Title IX was generally considered a modest bill that did not possess the "historical gravitas of the civil rights legislation of the 1960s" (Ware, 2011, p. 47). Regardless of the weight given to it at the time it became law, the connection between Title IX and civil

Patsy Mink, the Mother of Title IX

Among the 25 senators in the official portrait of the 1958 legislature of the ter-ritorial senate in Hawaii, only one is a woman. Her name is Patsy Matsu Take-moto Mink. That photo symbolizes the firsts that would become a hallmark of Mink's life and legacy. She became the first girl to be elected president of a the student body at Maui High School and the first Asian American and woman of color to serve in the United States Congress.

Elected in 1964, Mink served the people of Hawaii in Congress from 1965 to 1977 and again from 1990 until her death in 2002. In the intervening years between her terms of service in the U.S. House of Representatives, she served in the Jimmy Carter administration as an assistant secretary of state for oceans and international, environmental, and scientific affairs (1977-1978). She was president of Americans for Democratic Action (1978-1981), and she served on the Honolulu City Council (1983-1987), maintained a private law practice (1987-1990), and founded the *Public Reporter* (1989-1991), an organization that monitored and publicized the activities of the Hawaii state legislature.

Known as "a vigorous and tireless champion of women's rights, an early and vocal opponent to the Vietnam War, and a leader on issues involving education, the environment, welfare, and civil rights" (Ruth, 2008, para. 2), Mink was one of the principal authors of Title IX, a bill that would eventually be named in her honor. Describing the influence of both the legislation and Mink herself, U.S. senator Mazie Hirono said, "Patsy's legacy lives on in every female student and athlete in America who's been given a fair shot to compete in the classroom and on the playing field" (Wang, 2014, para. 6).

Mink said,

What you endure is who you are. And if you just accept and do nothing, then life goes on. But if you see it as a way for change, life doesn't have to be so unfair. It can be better. Maybe not for me, I can't change the past, but I can certainly help somebody else in the future so they don't have to go through what I did. (Wang, 2014, para 5) rights legislation from the 1960s is important to understand in order to appreciate its meaning and influence (Anderson, 2012). When Title IX was first introduced, Senator Birch Bayh noted that the language of the statute mirrored that of Title VI, which prohibited discrimination on the basis of race, color, or national origin. Stating that Title IX was designed to close a loophole, Bayh said, "our national policy should prohibit sex discrimination at all levels of education" (1972, p. 5807).

As enacted, Title IX reads as follows:

No person in the United States, shall, on the basis of sex, be excluded from participation in, be denied the benefits of, or be subjected to discrimination under any education program or activity receiving Federal financial assistance. (20 U.S.C. Section 1681 (a), 2011)

Over the years, many have noted that the statute itself does not expressly refer to sports or athletics. Few questions were raised at the time Congress considered the law. At one point, Senator Bayh was asked about whether Title IX would require schools to offer coed teams (mixed gender teams). He responded (1971, p. 407),

I do not read this as . . . mandat[ing] the desegregation of football fields. What we are trying to do is provide equal access for women and men students to the educational process and the extracurricular activities in a school, where there is not a unique facet such as football involved. We are not requiring that intercollegiate football be desegregated, nor that the men's locker room be desegregated.

The brief interchanges on the floor of the Congress about Title IX's applicability to athletics hardly hinted at the controversies that unfolded once leaders within the National Collegiate Athletic Association (NCAA), which was then all male, became aware of the law. Mobilizing the assistance of key legislators in Congress, most notably Senator John Tower (R-TX), the NCAA sought to have an amendment (which came to be known as the Tower Amendment) passed that would remove athletics altogether from Title IX consideration. Unsuccessful in that effort, they

then attempted to carve out an exemption that would leave the men's revenue-producing sports (primarily football and to a lesser degree men's basketball) free of Title IX's reach.

Once again, that effort failed, but the Javits Amendment was passed in its wake. This amendment charged the U.S. Department of Health, Education, and Welfare (HEW) with the task of preparing and publishing regulations to help schools implement the provisions of Title IX in athletic departments, giving due consideration to "the nature of particular sports" (NCWGE, 2007). That expression, "the nature of particular sports," eased tensions that had grown out of the football powers' fear that Title IX would require that women's sports receive exactly the same amount of money that men's sports did. Clarifying expectations, the regulations acknowledged that not all sports operated the same way and required the same amount of financial investment. Rosters for cross country teams could be smaller than those for football teams. The amount of money necessary to outfit an ice hockey player was different than what it might cost to outfit a swimmer. The notion of equality under Title IX took those differences between sports into account while avoiding a hard and fast rule that for every dollar spent on a male athlete, a dollar needed to be spent on a female athlete.

The charge to HEW staffers to develop regulations was a routine request that spoke to the system of checks and balances in place within the U.S. government as represented by the three branches of government. Identifying a need for a law that prohibited sex discrimination in schools, Congress in its capacity as a legislative body passed Title IX. Once the bill became law, it was then up to the executive branch, through the appropriate government agency of HEW, to develop guidelines for how Title IX applied to schools and to create a means of enforcing the law. When disputes have arisen over the meaning of specific language of the law and its constitutionality, the judicial branch (the federal court system) has come into play when lawsuits are filed.

When it came to Title IX's application, however, the response was a bit more than routine. In the drafting process for the regulations, more than 10,000 comments were submitted from lobbyists, lawyers, educational administrators, athletics directors, coaches, teachers, and parents (Carpenter & Acosta, 2005). The balance of comments, over 90 percent, were directed toward the application of Title IX to athletics, despite the fact that athletics was only one small part of the areas in schools that the law covered. Title IX had struck a nerve within the athletic community. At the time the law was passed, there was an expectation that schools would be in compliance by 1978. However, the challenges Title IX faced from the men's athletic community guaranteed that compliance would be postponed throughout the 1970s until the mid-1990s, with uneven commitment to providing fair and equitable treatment for female athletes.

For example, the NCAA's wish for athletic departments to be exempt from Title IX was

The fight for girls and women to have equal access to sports during their school years has taken decades to implement through Title IX. These women playing for Drexel University in 1979 played as the rules for Title IX were still being established.

granted briefly between the years 1984 and 1988 as a result of a U.S. Supreme Court ruling in *Grove City College v. Bell*. In this case, a small private Christian school located in western Pennsylvania took the position that it need not comply with Title IX because it did not directly receive any federal funding. And while the Supreme Court disagreed, pointing out that students at Grove City did receive financial support through a federally funded grant program, it nevertheless ruled that the only department on campus where Title IX applied was the financial aid office.

The *Grove City* decision set a precedent that athletic departments did not need to worry about complying with Title IX unless the departments themselves received direct federal funding in some form. In the immediate aftermath of this ruling, courts dismissed Title IX claims against athletic departments and other university departments. The effect of the Grove City decision, however, "significantly narrowed the scope of four civil rights statutes, and . . . the basic civil rights of women, minorities, the elderly and the disabled, have been threatened, denied, and ignored with no redress" (Anderson, 2012, p. 343). In response to this, Congress enacted the Civil Rights Restoration Act of 1988, making clear that the scope of Title IX's coverage was institution-wide.

Ambiguities and areas of confusion would be addressed over time by an increasing array of Title IX resources furnished by the federal government, including the *Intercollegiate Athletics Policy Interpretation* issued in December of 1978, the *Title IX Athletics Investigators Manual* released in 1990, and several memorandums and letters of clarification provided by the U.S. Department of Education's **Office for Civil Rights (OCR)**, formerly HEW (Ali, 2010; Ali, 2011; Cantu, 1996; Cantu, 1998; Monroe, 2007; Monroe, 2008; Reynolds, 2003). Despite these ongoing efforts, by Title IX's 20th anniversary in 1992, few schools were in compliance with the law in the area of athletics, a record reflecting the degree of resistance that girls and women faced in accessing equal access and opportunity in the realm of sport.

At some level, the casual pace of compliance was a product of the amount of time it took to negotiate the regulations and interpretations and put a policy manual together. The provision within civil rights enforcement guidelines that allows schools to put together a plan to achieve compliance in what was called a "reasonable period of time" without setting an exact time period for compliance to occur also contributed to the slow pace. But administrators also decided that they would not go out of their way to comply unless they were sued, an expensive prospect for the aggrieved plaintiffs. Some administrators were willing to endure the legal process rather than cooperate and engage in good faith to ensure the rights of female students (Pemberton, 2012).

The decade of the 1990s served as a turning point in terms of Title IX compliance efforts. First, there was the element of public embarrassment when the NCAA Gender Equity Task Force reported widespread and massive inequities in college and university athletic programs, with male students representing nearly 70 percent of intercollegiate athletics participants. From a financial perspective, men's programs at the time were receiving nearly 77 percent of operating budgets, 70 percent of scholarship funds, and 83 percent of recruiting dollars (Hosick, 2007).

Second, higher education officials took notice of the U.S. Supreme Court's decision in *Franklin v. Gwinnett County Public Schools*, which established that successful Title IX plaintiffs could recover monetary damages and attorney fees for intentional discrimination. In effect, administrators realized for the first time that there would be a penalty if they intentionally failed to fix sex discrimination in their schools. After this decision, "Title IX saw its first large spike in litigation with 24 decisions from the end of 1992 until 1995" (Anderson & Osborne, 2008, p. 150).

Third, in the landmark case of *Cohen v. Brown University*, the regulatory scheme that had been put in place for Title IX was tested. The outcome of the case was that schools were obligated to abide by the regulations as developed.

Fourth, a number of lawsuits filed by male plaintiffs alleging that Title IX served to create "reverse discrimination" when men's teams were cut all failed. Courts determined that while some men's programs were cut by administra-

tors, male athletes as a group were benefitting more because of receiving more opportunities, greater financial investment in their programs, and greater scholarship assistance. These cases demonstrated that the Title IX enforcement scheme did not mandate what sports schools could or should offer and that decisions regarding specific sport offerings were to be left up to individual institutions.

Fifth, the Equity in Athletics Disclosure Act (EADA) was passed in 1996. This act required colleges and universities receiving federal funds to publicly report on an annual basis how much money was spent on men's and women's athletics. As a result, anyone who wants to learn more about what is happening in terms of gender equity within a particular school can now go online and find the report. And while there are deficiencies in how athletic finances are accounted for, the report at least provides a starting point that allows citizens to raise questions about what their school is doing to comply with Title IX.

Even though all that ground had been covered, more delays regarding compliance occurred in the early 2000s under President George W. Bush, who charged the U.S. Department of Education with the task of putting together a commission to review Title IX and its effect on athletic opportunities. Politically charged, the review raised concern for a time that Title IX might be radically altered. As awareness grew about the potential damage that could be done to the progress made under Title IX, controversy surrounded the deliberations of the commission. In the end, the Office for Civil Rights controversially issued an additional clarification in 2005 regarding female interest in athletics and how it would be measured. Without public notice or input, the new policy effectively lowered the standards schools needed to meet in providing equitable athletic opportunities to female and male students. Schools were allowed "to show compliance with the law simply by sending an email survey to all female students and then claiming that failure to respond indicates a lack of interest in playing sports" (Save Title IX, 2006, p.1). That clarification would be rescinded, however, by the Obama administration in 2010 (Hosick, 2010).

GROWTH IN ATHLETIC PROGRAMS SINCE TITLE IX

At the time Title IX was passed in 1972, fewer than 32,000 women were playing sports at the college level, 2 percent of athletics budgets were allocated to women's sports, and athletic scholarships for women were nearly nonexistent (National Women's Law Center, 2012). In the decades following the passage of Title IX, women's sports participation at the college level increased by 584 percent, with the number of participation opportunities rising to 205,021 in 2013-2014. At the high school level, female participation in sport increased by 1,011 percent, with the number of playing opportunities for girls on high school teams jumping from 294,015 in 1971-1972 to 3,267,664 in 2013-2014 (National Federation of State High School Associations, 2014; see table 2.2). While there have been fluctuations in school enrollments between 1965 and 2012, with several more million children attending in those later years, enrollment tends to hover just under or around 50 million (high school enrollments around 15 million), so the increase in female sports participants cannot be attributed merely to a growth in the female high school student population (National Center for Education Statistics, 2013, 2015). Instead, the difference can be attributed to greater access to sports for female athletes. It is not surprising that there would be less growth in boys' sports because they were already much farther along in development in 1971-1972 than girls' sports.

The fears of Title IX destroying men's sports are not borne out in the numbers for boys' and men's sport participation. Male athletes continue to participate in higher rates in school sports compared to female athletes. In 2013-2014, boys' high school sport participation surpassed 4.5 million (an increase of 22%; NFSHA, 2014). At the college level, men's sport participation has grown by 57 percent since the early 1970s, with 267,604 opportunities available for men to play on NCAA varsity teams in 2013-2014 (Irick, 2014; see table 2.3).

According to the National Women's Law Center (2012), at the high school level there are large gaps in participation rates between female and male athletes, suggestive of large patterns of inequitable treatment. Arthur Bryant, a lawyer who has represented female athletes in some of the most important Title IX cases, including *Cohen v. Brown University*, pointed out that in the most elite NCAA programs (Division I-FBS), school funding for female athletes represented only 28 percent of their overall allocations, 31 percent of their recruiting dollars, and 42 percent of their athletic scholarship dollars (Bryant, 2012).

WHAT EVERY CITIZEN SHOULD KNOW ABOUT TITLE IX

For a law that has had such a profound effect on our educational system, Title IX presents an interesting paradox. Although Title IX is nearly as important to our nation's history as the 19th Amendment, which gave women the right to

Table 2.2 High School Sport Participation

Year	1971-1972	2013-2014	Percent increase
Female	294,015	3,267,664	1,011%
Male	3,666,917	4,527,940	23.46%

Data from National Federation of State High School Associations (2014).

Table 2.3 NCAA Varsity Sport Participation Opportunities

Year	1971-1972	2013-2014	Percent increase
Female	29,977	205,021	584%
Male	170,384	267,604	57%

Data from Irick (2014).

vote, there is very little concerted effort to introduce students to it. According to one study, less than 50 percent of educators understand what Title IX covers (Nash, Klein, & Bitters, 2007). Further, "only a miniscule percent of students and parents are aware of their rights under Title IX" (Nash et al., 2007, p. 89). Similar results occurred in a 2007 phone interview survey of 1,000 randomly selected adults in the United States. Over 80 percent of those surveyed indicated that they were "strongly supportive" of Title IX; however, approximately 60 percent of respondents did not know what steps to take to enforce compliance (Mellman Group, 2007). In a *New York Times*/CBS News poll conducted in March of 2011, 64 percent of 1,266 adults indicated that didn't know much or knew nothing about Title IX (2011).

Recent research targeting how much those working in athletics know about Title IX has shown that they too know very little about the law. In the first comprehensive study of NCAA coaches of men's and women's teams ever done, Staurowsky and Weight (2011) found that less than half knew enough to pass a test dealing with basic Title IX information, while 83.4 percent of coaches reported that they had never received any formal education about Title IX. In a study of athletics administrators charged with Title IX oversight, results indicated that only 25 percent received Title IX education as part of their training as administrators and that there is a significant gap in the level of Title IX comprehension that may contribute to a lack of Title IX–compliant decision making among administrators (Staurowsky & Weight, 2013).

This generally hazy idea of the law and void in Title IX knowledge may be attributed in part to a failure in the Title IX enforcement mechanism. At the time that the Title IX regulations were passed, attention was given to creating a mechanism to make sure that citizens understood what the law is, what it requires, and what their rights are under it. Contained within the regulations was a requirement that each school designate an employee who was to serve as a Title IX coordinator. The coordinator was expected to conduct compliance reviews, hear grievances, oversee correction and remedial actions, and educate constituents whose lives were affected by the law. Despite this requirement, some schools either ignored it all together, or they simply were not aware that there was an obligation to do this (Carpenter & Acosta, 2005; Pemberton, 2012).

Administrators' seriousness in considering Title IX's role has been questioned over the years. As Carpenter and Acosta pointed out, "other than posting a name and title on the back-corridor bulletin board, many schools did little to disseminate to the campus community information about the requirements of Title IX" (2005, p. 8). Significantly, the designated coordinators were supposed to develop preventive activities "such as the periodic assessment of the awareness of employees and students regarding Title IX requirements . . . and updating services to staff regarding compliance responsibilities" (Matthews & McCune, 1975, p. 51).

This dysfunctional link in the Title IX enforcement chain may explain why only a third of NCAA coaches were aware of who their Title IX coordinator was, while 42.5 percent indicated that they were not sure and another 25.8 percent reported that their institution did not have a Title IX coordinator. "While there was an expectation that education would be handled directly within each school, which would have then resulted in generations of students understanding the requirements of the law, compliance efforts have often been inconsistent and haphazard" (Staurowsky & Weight, 2011, p. 198).

Moving into the fifth decade of Title IX, there has been an increasing call for ongoing and regular Title IX education that creates a network of informed citizens conversant in baseline understandings of how the law is applied to athletic programs (Staurowsky & Weight, 2011, 2013). As a civil rights law, Title IX provides for two things: equal access to athletic programs and equitable treatment of athletes in those programs. Equal access is assessed through a consideration of how well an institution is accommodating the interests and abilities of athletes of the underrepresented sex, most often female athletes. The **three-part test** is the measure of whether a school has provided equal athletic opportunity for male and female athletes. Schools need to satisfy only one of the three parts of the test, which include **substantial**

proportionality, a **history and continuing practice of program expansion**, or **accommodating interests and abilities**. Thus, an institution must demonstrate one of the following (Office for Civil Rights, 1979):

- Substantial proportionality: intercollegiate level participation opportunities for male and female students are provided in numbers substantially proportionate to their respective enrollments

- A history and continuing practice of program expansion responsive to the developing interests and abilities of the members of the underrepresented group of athletes

- Full and effective accommodation of the interests and abilities of the members of the underrepresented sex by the program already in place

Under Title IX, the question of what constitutes a sport is considered. In a letter to the Minnesota State High School League, the Office for Civil Rights noted that "certain school activities in which students are engaged may be activities that require a considerable amount of athleticism, but not every athletic activity qualifies as a sport" (*Biediger v. Quinnipiac University*, 2013, p. 46). Several factors are taken into account when determining if a particular activity qualifies as a varsity sport under Title IX (see table 2.4), including an activity's structure and administration, team preparation, and competition (Monroe, 2008).

Intended to be flexible, the means by which institutional compliance can be achieved affords higher education administrators considerable latitude for developing plans that best reflect the missions of their respective institutions, the composition of their undergraduate full time enrollment, and their economic circumstances. While Title IX generally requires schools to treat men and women equally throughout their athletic programs, it does not require that male and female athletes be treated exactly the same in every instance (Cohen, 2005). Program components that substantially affect the quality of the experience for athletes, and are subjected to Title IX analysis, include athletic training facilities and services, equipment and supplies, housing and dining services, locker rooms and facilities, opportunities to receive coaching and academic assistance, publicity, scheduling of games and practices, and equivalent travel and per diem expenses (Staurowsky et al., 2007). Further, schools are expected to distribute athletic scholarship dollars equitably as well (Bonnette, 2004; Carpenter & Acosta, 2005; Cohen, 2005; National Women's Law Center & Piper, 2007).

Table 2.4 Examples of Factors Used in Determining Which Activities Are Sports Under Title IX

Factor	Elements considered
Consistent program structure and administration	• Operating budget • Support services (sports medicine, academic, strength and conditioning) • Coaching staff • Recruiting practices similar to those of established sports • Opportunity for athletic scholarships • Opportunity for awards
Team preparation and competition	• Practices (number, length, quality) • Competitive opportunities quantitatively and qualitatively similar to other varsity sports • Consistent set of competition guidelines, regulations, and rules • Primary purpose of activity—to provide opportunities to compete or to provide support in marketing and promoting other team • Resources consistent with competitive level (staffing, coaching, travel funding to support competition level) • Postseason competition—dependent on regular season competition

Title IX Compliance

How do you know if your school's athletic department is in compliance with Title IX? As a best practice, school administrators are required by law to designate a Title IX coordinator who is responsible for overseeing compliance efforts, including education of administrators, coaches, athletes, families, and citizens in the local area about the requirements of Title IX. Schools are also encouraged to conduct ongoing evaluations of their athletic departments to determine whether the following requirements are being met:

- Athletic opportunities are being offered equitably using the three-part test.
- Athletics-related financial aid is being awarded proportional to the participation of males and females in the athletic program.
- Female and male athletes are being afforded equal treatment in the allocation of resources in 11 benefit areas: equipment and supplies, scheduling of games and practice times, travel and daily allowance or per diem, access to tutoring, coaching, locker rooms and practice and competitive facilities, medical and training facilities and services, housing and dining facilities and services, publicity and promotions, support services, and recruitment of student-athletes.

Some schools have gender equity committees that take responsibility for creating Title IX compliance plans and implementing changes when called for.

When internal mechanisms within schools fail to assess the degree to which athletic department policies and practices meet Title IX expectations, the magnitude of the lack of Title IX compliance is so great, or there are simply no other alternatives, those harmed by sex discrimination may decide to register a complaint with the federal agency responsible for the enforcement of Title IX, the OCR at the U.S. Department of Education. They may also get a lawyer and file a lawsuit.

Filing a Title IX complaint with the OCR can be a relatively accessible avenue for bringing attention to unfair treatment. Any citizen who observes what they believe to be sex discrimination in an athletic department sponsored by a school that receives federal financial assistance can submit a complaint using an electronic online form, writing an e-mail to ocr@gov.edu, or sending a letter or fax to the OCR. Sending a detailed complaint (with facts and information that will help guide OCR investigators to key people to interview and the identification of the problems that may exist within a particular program) will increase the likelihood that the complaint will be moved forward.

Pros and cons exist for each approach to Title IX enforcement. Ideally, since Title IX is reflective of a moral mandate to provide equal treatment to students, regardless of sex, schools who proactively monitor their Title IX status and appreciate the benefits of compliance create win–win situations for themselves and their students. Internal mechanisms have conflicts, though. Some school administrators operate under stereotypical ideas about female and male athletes and resist complying with the law, or they simply don't take the time to learn what is expected under Title IX. Seeking relief through the OCR or the courts can create tensions between plaintiffs and their communities at times. Plaintiffs alleging discrimination under Title IX have often had success in court; however, the legal process can be time consuming, stressful, and expensive if not done on a pro bono basis. According to a 2015 report issued by the OCR, nearly 40 percent of the 9,000 Title IX complaints received were related to athletics (Lhamon, 2015).

THE FUTURE OF TITLE IX

As the years have gone by, the standard excuses that educational administrators have historically used to explain noncompliance have lost their power to persuade. With a full array of Title IX resources in place after years of debate and discussion, pressure is building on schools to fulfill the requirements of Title IX. As Cynthia Pemberton, an associate dean at Idaho University who lost her job as a coach because she advocated for Title IX, observes, "nearly half of the U.S. population has come of age since we were to have achieved educational equity and Title IX compliance" (2012, p. 609). Title IX, during its 40th anniversary year in 2012, received more attention than it ever had before.

U.S. culture has also become more accustomed to the idea of women participating in sport and being an integral part of the sports scene. During the buildup to Title IX's 40th anniversary, *Sports Illustrated* featured the legislation itself on its cover. ESPN, the self-proclaimed worldwide leader in entertainment and sports, devoted coverage to the anniversary across multiple platforms, including a microsite on espnW, a special issue of *ESPN the Magazine,* and a commitment to developing a year-long series of documentaries on women's sport through the ESPN 30 for 30 program. Organizations such as the National Association of Collegiate Women Athletics Administrators (NACWAA) hosted a video project urging members to record the histories of how Title IX influenced the lives of female athletes, coaches, and administrators on college and university campuses across the country. Local newspapers across the nation reported on women's sport pioneers who made a difference in high school sports and on Title IX fathers and mothers who advocated on behalf of their daughters. Seventy-one of the 80 lawmakers in the California Assembly, from both sides of the aisle, sought to cosponsor a resolution commemorating Title IX's passage in May of 2012. This unprecedented coverage signals a continuing shift in attitudes toward women's sport that bodes well for the future.

In many ways, however, the real work to be done in integrating girls and women into the existing sport system is just starting. Title IX has allowed the concept of sex segregation to remain intact. As such, it requires attention and thoughtful consideration of what equality means and how to achieve it. And the door remains open for further discussion down the road in terms of whether the sport system should always separate boys and girls and men and women, or whether there will come a day when mixed teams will represent the norm. In the meantime, there is much work to be done in realizing the promise of Title IX in athletics.

Many questions remain for the implementation and continuation of Title IX, but the results should be clear: more girls and women having the opportunity to participate in sport.

Learning Aids

Summary

The history of Title IX provides a window into the complexities of social change, allowing us to see how ideas that were once feared or forbidden yet speak to the truth of human existence cannot be denied or suppressed forever. When those ideas are challenged and space is provided to offer proof of the misguided thinking behind stereotypical perspectives, attitudes shift. Women's sport from the 1970s to the present offers testament to the importance of waking up members of society and examining the prevailing views that rob individuals of their full potential and society of opportunities for greatness.

Advocates for Title IX have long maintained that old notions that girls and women are not interested in sport and are not physiologically or emotionally able to participate with boys and men on an even playing field would be laid to rest if opportunities were offered. Their sensibility in this regard is borne out in the numbers and in a reimagined American landscape that no longer finds female athleticism to be outside of the norm.

The influence of Title IX has been felt across every sector of society, from the workplace to the boardroom to the locker room. And while that effect has been transformative, not all girls and women have benefitted equally. As law professor Deborah Brake pointed out, while girls and women of color have also accessed some of the benefits made available by Title IX in terms of athletic scholarships and participation opportunities,

> they remain under-represented in girls' and women's sports, and the women's sports that have seen the biggest gains in the post-Title IX era are sports with very little participation by women of color. Getting at the root of this problem is very difficult—it has less to do with Title IX and more to do with the deeply embedded racial stratification that is a core feature of our Nation's educational system. (Golden, 2011)

And there remains the paradox that even as progress has been made, there are clear patterns of noncompliance and of the need for massive education regarding the law and what it requires. Nancy Hogshead-Makar, CEO of Champion Women, noted the following when her organization launched a campaign to contact NCAA Division I institutions that were not offering athletic scholarships in accordance with Title IX requirements: "Every year, college women receive $190 *million* less in athletic scholarships. If schools provided men and women with equal opportunities to participate in sports, 134,528 more would have a varsity sports experience" (2015, para. 1). There is much to marvel at in terms of the pathways to success and promise opened as a result of Title IX. But basic rights to participate in school sport in environments that value equal treatment are still denied to female athletes on a regular basis. And so the work continues, and the story is still being written.

Discussion Questions

1. In 1971, a Connecticut judge stated, "athletic competition builds character in our boys. We do not need that kind of character in our girls, the women of tomorrow" (Weitkamp, 2012). That quote frames the beginning to the film *A Sporting Chance*. Watch the film and reflect on its opening quote and the circumstances

that existed at the time where few formal opportunities for girls and women to compete in varsity sports existed and where athleticism in women was discouraged. Can you imagine that world? Does it still exist today? www.youtube.com/watch?v=iqmOp-R_itI&list=PL7B5FC65092DB7223

2. Under Title IX, how is a sport defined? Among the controversies that surround Title IX is an issue that arose when athletic officials at Quinnipiac University cut their established women's volleyball program with the intention of substituting a less-established cheerleading program in its stead. In this case, the issue of how a sport is defined under Title IX came up. The federal judge who heard the case ruled that cheerleading, while clearly a physical activity, did not satisfy the requirements to be designated as a varsity sport under Title IX and therefore was not an acceptable substitute. Compare and contrast two readings about this case: the first, a statement issued by the Women's Sports Foundation (2013) and the second, a piece written for *Law 360* by Rick Meyer and Joe Nahra (2012). Which side of the argument do you find more persuasive?

3. Nearly 45 years have passed since Title IX was passed, and many schools remain out of compliance with the law. What are the implications of this kind of noncompliance? Can you think of any other law where publicly paid officials (school principals and athletic directors, for example) seem to ignore their obligations? What might this say about the forces at work? What kind of a strategy would you develop to address this issue?

Learning Activities

1. Conduct your own Title IX audit of your school or another school of your choosing. The National Women's Law Center provides a tool that leads you through the questions and fact-finding that mirror what school officials should be doing in terms of assessing compliance with Title IX. When you've completed your review, write up a summary of your results. Go to the resource at the following website and begin your audit: www.nwlc.org/resource/check-it-out-playing-field-level-women-and-girls-your-school

2. Earlier in the chapter, you were introduced to the idea that any citizen can file a Title IX complaint. Go to the United States Department of Education Office for Civil Rights website and go through the process of how to file a discrimination complaint: www2.ed.gov/about/offices/list/ocr/docs/howto.html. Review the electronic complaint form as part of your work on the site (found at www.ed.gov/about/offices/list/ocr/complaintintro.html). Based on your experience, what is your view of how accessible the complaint process is?

Glossary

accommodating interests and abilities—Part of the three-part test that examines where the interests of athletes in the underrepresented group have been fairly accommodated in the athletic program. Factors used in assessing interests and abilities include (but are not limited to) sport offerings at the regional and national level, sport offerings at the conference level, high school participation sport patterns, and campus participation in physical education, club, and intramural programs.

Cohen v. Brown University—When Brown University sought to balance its athletic budget by cutting two women's sports (gymnastics and volleyball), exacerbating existing gender disparities that favored male athletes and disadvantaged female athletes, it was sued by several female athletes. Although the university originally cut the teams and then argued that the athletic program met Title IX requirements, a federal judge determined that Brown had violated Title IX. The court dismissed Brown's assertion that the cuts were justified because male athletes were more interested in sport, an argument that the court found to be stereotypical and discriminatory.

Franklin v. Gwinnett County Public Schools—After experiencing repeated sexual harassment and abuse from her high school teacher, the female plaintiff in this case sought relief in the form of damages for the harm done to her. The U.S. Supreme Court ruled that when school administrators and teachers are deliberately indifferent to sex discrimination, and fail to intercede on behalf of the victim once told of the abuse, they may have to pay compensatory damages (compensation to the victim for the harm done).

Grove City College v. Bell—This lawsuit, won by Grove City, raised the issue of whether Title IX applied to athletic programs if those programs were not direct recipients of federal financial aid, a connection that must be in place in order for Title IX to apply to an educational institution. The Supreme Court ruled in favor of Grove City, the result being that compliance with Title IX in school-based athletic programs slowed between 1984 and 1988. In 1988, Congress stepped in to pass the Civil Rights Restoration Act, which reset Title IX's application to mean that receipt of federal funds by an institution, regardless of whether that money went directly to a particular program or not (like an athletic department), was sufficient to require all areas of an institution to be compliant with Title IX.

history and continuing practice of program expansion—The first part of the three-part test of Title IX compliance. This test asks schools to demonstrate that they have, over a span of years, made affirmative efforts to address the needs of athletes in the underrepresented group by adding participation opportunities.

Javits Amendment—When the Title IX regulations were being considered by the U.S. Congress, this amendment sought to clarify that the standard to determine if equitable spending on female and male athletes has occurred should be based on the nature of the sport. This means that differences between sports and funding needs must be taken into account. Title IX does not require that a dollar must be spent on a female athlete or women's sport for every dollar spent a male athlete or men's sport.

Office for Civil Rights (OCR)—Located within the U.S. Department of Education, the OCR is charged with enforcement of Title IX.

substantial proportionality—One part of the three-part test of Title IX compliance. In order to determine if an athletic department meets this standard, the proportion of female and male full-time undergraduate students is compared to the proportion of female and male athletes enrolled at an institution. Schools may receive a bit of leeway if the proportions between those groups (female students to female athletes) do not match up, and reasons for any existing gaps may be unrelated to sex discrimination. That said, a difference of one to three percentage points may signal that a school is not in compliance with Title IX.

three-part test—Assesses equitable participation opportunities for female and male athletes. A school must pass only one part of the three-part test. The test includes a history and continuing practice of program expansion, substantial proportionality, and accommodation of the interests and abilities of athletes who are part of a class that is underrepresented.

Tower Amendment—Amendment proposed by John Tower, a Republican senator from Texas, to remove athletics from Title IX's reach. When his first amendment to Title IX failed, Tower proposed a second one that attempted to exempt football from the application of Title IX. That too failed.

CHAPTER 3

Women's Sport in the 21st Century

Ellen J. Staurowsky, EdD, Drexel University

Learning Objectives

In this chapter, you will learn about the following:

- Changes in baseline data from the 1970s to the present
- The concept of the female athlete paradox
- The paradox of the female athlete warrior
- The paradox of strong female athletes feeling like they need to apologize for being strong
- The paradox of femininity and muscularity
- Female athletes who transcend the female athlete paradox
- Female athletes in a separate but equal sport system

During the summer of 2014, if you had tuned into the NBC show *American Ninja Warrior*, an American television show that challenges athletes in top physical condition to test their strength, agility, timing, flexibility, wits, and nerve against extreme obstacles, you would have seen women successfully competing alongside men. About the success of women in the 2014 season, host Matt Iseman said, "This has been the year of the women. . . . We've had three women complete the qualifying course where none have ever done it before" (Bickel, 2014). Kacy Catanzaro, a 5-foot, 100-pound (152 cm, 45 kg) former gymnast, acquired the name Mighty Kacy as she powered through the qualifying course to become the first woman to prevail in the extended course, earning her a spot in the finals and a chance to win the $500,000 prize ("Catanzaro Makes History," 2014).

For those unfamiliar with the show, the course itself appears to be an elaborate jungle gym or child's play set with a dash of military boot camp thrown in. Competitors who succeed in earlier rounds face more difficult challenges as they proceed through various stages. For those who complete each course, time then becomes an issue, since the athlete who finishes in the shortest amount of time is declared the winner. With catchy names like the Salmon Ladder, Warped Wall, the Quad Steps, and the Spider Climb, the obstacles require contestants to hang suspended in midair while moving forward or upward using only their upper bodies, to navigate steps that are placed at awkward angles and require leaping from one to other, to traverse walls that are curved, and to scale walls that offer few opportunities for leverage.[1] A misstep or miscalculation results in competitors falling into a pool of water, their run to glory at an end.

Describing her fascination with the show, Catanzaro said, "After I graduated from Towson and completed my gymnastics career, I knew I needed something else to put all of my time and effort into" ("Catanzaro Makes History," 2014). Connecting with one of the show's veterans (who would eventually become her boyfriend), she set out to unlock the mysteries of the course, meeting challenges with optimism and determination. Although she did well as a first-time competitor in 2013, she failed to make it out of the qualifying round. Setting her sights high after that, Catanzaro said, "I knew I had to come back and really make my mark this season. Making history by being the first female in the six seasons of American Ninja Warrior to make it up the warped wall and finish the qualifying course was a dream come true."

A measure of how far women have come in sport, the might of Kacy Catanzaro is revealed for what it is—the power of a strong, quick-think-

Kacy Catanzaro celebrating the completion of the parkour course at Ubisoft's Assassin's Creed Experience during Comic-Con.

ing, determined fighter whose accomplishments inspire awe and respect. Although the overwhelming majority of other contestants were men, she held her own on her own merits; her fate rested quite literally on her own shoulders. In the *American Ninja* venue, where the relationship between the athlete and the course is so exposed, attributing her accomplishments to anything other than her talent and skill would be transparently sexist. Thus, although the media coverage was not devoid of observations about her femininity (see chapter 11 for more on media coverage of female athletes), commentary about her performances were routinely complimentary of her athletic talents.

Interestingly, Catanzaro is a product of a sport system that often separates male and female athletes through a sex-segregated system. Her main training ground was the sport of gymnastics, a sport dominated by girls and women in the United States. Of the 102,295 total competitive American gymnasts in 2013, 72 percent were female (not counting those involved in acrobatics, rhythmic, and tumbling, which would elevate that figure to as much as 83%; USA Gymnastics, 2013).

Whether Catanzaro represents an athletic figure who transcends gender in the 21st century is a question worth pondering. Other women from the beginning of time have been the athletic equal to men. Still, in a world where the effects of Title IX have played out now for more than 40 years, contributing to the mass acceptance of female athletes within the culture, Catanzaro's ability to envision an athletic life unencumbered by social prohibitions against participating with and against men as an equal may offer one more bit of evidence that the ever-emerging path for girls and women in sport continues to be more inclusive.

The journey, however, to get to this moment has been a long one. As so often happens on long journeys, the question of whether we are there yet, whether we have reached a destination where girls and women are fully accepted as athletes, remains an open one. Baseline data from the 1970s to the present, as you will read in this chapter, show just how much change has occurred and where girls and women in sport are positioned in the 21st century.

The remainder of this chapter focuses on considering the changes in that baseline data from the perspective of several paradoxes that exist for girls and women in sport, including the paradox of the female athlete warrior, the paradox of strong female athletes feeling like they need to apologize for being strong, and the paradox of femininity and muscularity. Attention will also be directed to whether female athletes can reconcile these paradoxes and whether the sport systems organization around a concept of separate but equal helps to remove or reinforce paradoxes that affect female athletes.

> *Women's sport has never been as emancipated and accepted as it is today. . . . In our grandmother's day, sport for women was frowned on and sometimes even prohibited.*
>
> Sybele Miller

SPORT INVOLVEMENT FOR WOMEN AND GIRLS: CHANGES IN BASELINE DATA

Despite all of the growth that has occurred for girls and women in the area of sport, issues associated with equal sport involvement remain. Girls continue to start their engagement in sport behind boys, as evidenced by the age at which children first get involved in sport. According to a study conducted by researchers for the Women's Sports Foundation, parents reported that 60 percent of their sons and 47 percent of their daughters were playing on their first team by age six. When asked about the importance of sport to them, 60 percent of boys in all elementary and secondary grades believed that sport was a big part of who they were. In contrast, only 37 percent of girls believed that sport was a big part of who they were (Kelley & Carchia, 2013).

Female athletes may also experience higher incidences of burnout, leaving their sport because of a reduced sense of accomplishment or because of physical or emotional exhaustion (Holden, Keshock, Forester, Pugh, & Pugh, 2014). Reasons often cited for female athletes deciding to end their college careers included lack of free time, a feeling of being overextended due to all their activities and obligations, lack of playing time, injuries, and the feeling that participation had ceased to be fun (Bradford & Keshock, 2010).

Recognizing a need to get more children participating in sport, and understanding that opportunities available for girls are not as great as for boys, in January of 2014, the Aspen Institute Sport & Society Program brought together 250 national leaders from the areas of sport, health, and coaching as part of an initiative called Project Play: Reimaging Youth Sports in America. The purpose of the meeting was to focus on barriers faced by populations with the lowest sport participation in the United States and to develop strategies to address the needs of those populations. One of the key groups of underserved children were girls.

Focusing on girls from racially and economically diverse backgrounds reveals that sport access is uneven among girls and uneven compared to boys. Rarely do girls who are involved in at least one organized sport play more than boys. Looking at boys and girls participating by grade level (3 to 5; 6 to 8; 9 to 12) and geographic setting (urban, suburban, or rural), there was only one occasion in which girls had greater sport involvement than boys: in grades 3 to 5 in rural schools. Girls' opportunities in that one category outpaced those of boys by 4 percent (Sabo & Veliz, 2008).

In a 2011 study titled Progress Without Equity, similar patterns in terms of girls' involvement in high school sports were reported (Sabo & Veliz, 2011). The key findings from that study were the following:

- While high schools gradually increased their allocations of athletic participation opportunities between 1993-1994 and 2005-2006, progress toward closing the gender gap slowed after 2000.

- Boys received a larger proportion of funds for athletic participation opportunities than girls did for each school year in all communities (i.e., urban, suburban, town, and rural).

- The lowest percentages of athletic participation opportunities occurred in urban schools, whereas the highest percentages were issued in rural schools.

- Schools with greater economic resources provided more athletic participation opportunities for their students—both girls and boys—than their less fiscally sound counterparts.

- Girls were provided proportionately fewer athletic participation opportunities than boys during each school year and in all geographic regions (i.e., Northeast, Midwest, South and West).

In broad terms, the influx of girls and women into sport since the passage of Title IX has been remarkable, as reflected in the historic number of female athletes participating in high school and college sport. As demonstrated in figure 3.1, opportunities for girls to participate in high school sports between 1971-1972 and 2012-2013 increased nearly a thousandfold, while opportunities for women to compete on NCAA varsity teams grew by 570 percent.

At the Olympic level, steady growth in women's sport is seen in the number of sports offered, the number of female participants, and the percentage of women who compete in the Winter and Summer Olympic Games. The 11 women who participated in the 1924 Winter Olympics in Chamonix, France, comprised 4.3 percent of the athletes competing in those Games. In contrast, by the time the 2014 Winter Games were hosted in Sochi, Russia, women made up over 40.3 percent of the athletes, numbering more than 1,100 in total. The Summer Olympic Games has evidenced even greater participation from women, who made up over 44 percent of participants in the 2012 London Games, a sharp contrast to the 2.2 percent of women who participated in 1900 (International Olympic Committee, 2014). In 2012, there were more women than men on the U.S. Olympic team for the first time in history, with women winning more gold medals than their male teammates (Burke, 2014).

Even as progress can be mapped through increases in sport participation for girls and women, their involvement in sport continues to be affected by gendered expectations that have historically situated sport activity as a prerequisite for demonstrating masculinity and

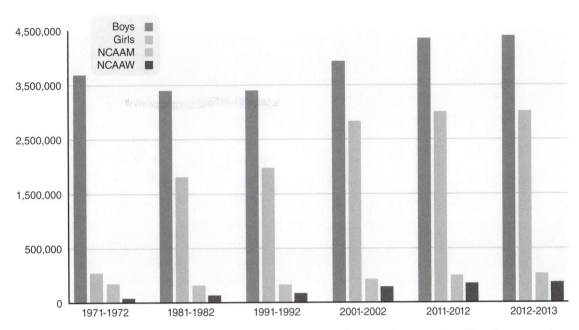

Figure 3.1 Interscholastic and intercollegiate varsity sport opportunities by gender, 1971-1972 through 2012-2013.

Created with participation data from the National Federation of State High School Associations (2013) and the National Collegiate Athletic Association (2013).

a contradiction to femininity. These expectations influence decisions made about funding athletic programs for males and females, the types of sports offered to male and females or viewed as more acceptable for one or the other, the amount of media coverage devoted to male and female athletes, and ultimately the way male and female athletes experience their sport participation. In this chapter, we'll try to explore the dimensions of these gendered expectations through three paradoxes: the paradox of the female athlete warrior, the paradox of strong female athletes feeling like they need to apologize, and the paradox of femininity and muscularity.

THE CONCEPT OF THE FEMALE ATHLETE PARADOX

A **paradox** is a situation, person, or thing that combines contradictory features or qualities. Each generation of girls and women in sport has challenged stereotypes that hold them back and navigated contradictory messages about what they can do, be, or feel. They have effectively lived what gender studies scholar Vikki Krane and her colleagues (Krane, Choi, Baird, Aimar,

& Kauer, 2004) refer to as "the female athlete paradox," a circumstance where being an athlete and being a woman are thought to be in contradiction to each other.

The female athlete paradox is given voice and expression on a routine basis. As a case in point, consider an interview with *HuffPo Live* on May 11, 2015: Skylar Diggins, a professional basketball player for the WNBA's Tulsa Shock told the show's host that she "operates on a beauty and beast mentality" (Brekke, 2015). She observed that female athletes "battle" with reconciling the strength and toughness required in their sports with their femininity. In other words, they live the paradox. And as more girls and women participate in sport, female athletes confront a variety of contradictions:

- With social prohibitions against fighting by women, how do female athlete warriors make sense of their experience?

- In a society where prevailing standards of female beauty value slenderness and a thin physique, how do female athletes reconcile muscularity and strength with those standards? And can muscularity be seen as a symbol of desirable femininity?

Ultimately, we are then left to consider whether, in a sport system that is largely organized around the separation of female and male athletes, it is possible that female athletes can be viewed as equal to male athletes.

PARADOX OF THE FEMALE ATHLETE WARRIOR

The image of an athlete warrior has long been associated with male athletes and men's sports. From the gridiron football hero to the boxing champion, the physically tough, hard-nosed, unyielding, and dominating image of the male athlete warrior is celebrated in sports coverage every day. Female athlete warriors, while not wholly absent from the sport scene, have been fewer and farther between. By virtue of sports that have been primarily or exclusively male for a long time—football and baseball—or versions of sports that allow full body contact and hitting for male athletes but not for female athletes—ice hockey and lacrosse—the notion of the female athlete warrior is not as visible or as understood. Just as athleticism itself has had an uneasy relationship with femininity, a further layer of complexity is added when female athletes engage in sports that require outright physical confrontation or where fighting actually occurs, as in the sports of boxing, wrestling, and martial arts. That contradiction in how females are expected to behave and what it takes to be a female athlete warrior also presents a paradox.

There have been waves of progress for girls and women in sport. Societal restrictions first got released around sports that could be seen as more socially acceptable and less threatening to prevailing notions of femininity, such as archery, golf, swimming, tennis, and track. Over time, greater access was granted to girls and women in team sports, as long as rules were adopted to restrict physical contact and limit physical exertion. In the sports in which the image of the male warrior is strongest, progress for girls and women has taken more time. A look at data reveals that high school sports in which there were no girls participating in 1971-1972 had thousands of female athletes by 2012-2013: in baseball (1,259), football (1,531), ice hockey (9,447), weightlifting (7,790), and wrestling (8,727) (National Federation of State High School Associations, 2013).

Interestingly, the gates of access to those sports were not opened by Title IX. Due to a provision in the Title IX regulations called the Contact Sports Exception, which carved out a protected space for male contact sports, girls and women seeking to participate had to take their cause to the courts under a different law, asserting their rights to be free from discrimination under the Equal Protection Clause of the 14th Amendment. Battles for girls to be able to compete in the sports of boxing, baseball, football, wrestling, and a host of other sports were waged one at a time, pushing those gates open a bit farther each time (Caggiano, 2010; Fields, 2008).

Arguably, we can see how the vistas of athletic opportunity and for societal acceptance for female athletes have become more expansive over time in ESPN's decision to honor Ronda Rousey, a professional mixed martial arts (MMA) fighter, as Best Female Athlete of the Year in 2014.[2] Rousey had won acclaim in the sport of judo, representing the United States at the Beijing Olympics and winning a bronze medal there. Like many of her male peers in the sport of MMA, she sought an outlet to continue her sport in a professional setting. The Ultimate Fighting Championship (UFC) became that vehicle.

Rousey is credited with persuading Dana White, the CEO of the UFC who nurtured the growth of MMA as an industry, to rescind his vow to never promote women fighters. After White relented and agreed to include women as part of the UFC, Rousey became one of its most bankable, successful, and controversial stars.[3]

The gendered discourse around Rousey is evocative of long-standing ambivalences about powerful women. She has been alternately celebrated as a figure of imposing physical skill (as evidenced by her dominance in the cage,[4] where opponents rarely last past the first round), disliked for her role as an antihero who is overly intense, and sexualized for her blonde good looks. Some see her as fearsome and menacing, others simply as a splendid fighter. Others admire her savvy entrepreneurship and her ability to leverage her celebrity and persona into a Hollywood film career.[5]

Katniss and Other Accomplished Female Archers

The fictional heroine of *The Hunger Games*, Katniss Everdeen, inspired a resurgence of interest in the sport of archery in the United States. While film historians point out that the storyline may fade over time, the influence that it has had on this generation of girls and boys will take decades to fully understand. In the meantime, a tale of two female archers offers food for thought.

In the state of South Carolina, an inquisitive Ella Kokinda picked up the sport when she was in seventh grade. She and her coach of four years started an archery team at her high school, pointing out that the South Carolina Department of Natural Resources provides support for such programs (Goyanes, 2012). She went on to place second in the United States at the National Archery in the Schools Program tournament in 2012.

A half a world away, Dolly Shivani Cherukuri from India made history by becoming the youngest archer in the country to score 200 points across distances of 5 and 7 meters. She was just nine days short of celebrating her third birthday. Considered by some to be a prodigy whose talents have been cultivated by her father, Dolly has been described as the future of the Volga Archery Academy, the same academy where her brother, a world-class archer and Indian national team coach, had trained. The family legacy in the sport is being carried on by Dolly, who received her first bow and arrow set at the time of her birth (Boren, 2015).

Rousey herself articulates cultural suspicions about female athleticism and womanhood, harboring disdain for a would-be challenger named Cyborg (Brazilian Cristiane Justino) who was suspended, and possibly banned, from the sport because of her discovered use of performance-enhancing drugs. Arguing that Cyborg should not be permitted to continue in the sport, Rousey has questioned Cyborg's femininity, commenting, "This girl has been on steroids for so long that's she's not even a woman anymore" (Thomas, 2014).

Regardless of the dialogue around Rousey and her own contribution to it, the fact that a female fighter could be viewed as female athlete of the year speaks to the degree to which women's prospects in sport have continued to transcend boundaries.

Rousey may be a reflection of a larger societal shift in values and expectations that exist for girls. A succession of female warriors have made their way into the lives of girls and their families through literature and movies, including Katniss from *The Hunger Games*,[6] the Black Widow from *The Avengers*, Merida from *Brave*, and Tris from *Divergent*. They share qualities that distinguish them as strong willed, in control of their lives, and willing to risk great things for causes beyond themselves. The conception of girlhood poised on womanhood is reshaped, as demonstrated by Merida, described as a "bold, daring, courageous, rebellious, and headstrong girl who does not fit the stereotypical princess role" (Disney, 2012). Much like the 21st-century princess Catherine, Duchess of Cambridge, who is well known for her athletic prowess,[7] Merida overthrows the notion of a damsel in distress, being known throughout the kingdom as the best archer in the land.

Toy manufacturers have adjusted course in responding to these themes, developing and marketing combat-themed lines, such as bows and arrows and toy guns. While the toy store aisles continue to be filled with makeup and hair sets, baby dolls, and homemaking and craft items, room has been made in all of that pink, purple, and glitter for toy weapons (Stout & Harris, 2014).[8]

Friedman (2013a), in her book *Playing to Win: Raising Children in a Competitive Culture,* pointed

Popular fiction with female warriors as lead characters, such as *The Hunger Games*, allowed girls to imagine themselves as skilled and athletic heroes.

out that parents and children are more tolerant of the expression of multiple forms of femininity. Based on interviews with nearly 200 parents, children, teachers, and coaches about activities girls are involved in, such as dance, soccer, and chess, Friedman found that parents discussed expectations regarding their daughters in terms of three main scripts: the graceful girl, the aggressive girl, and the pink warrior girl. Notably, these terms were used by the parents in discussing their reasons for encouraging their daughters to choose certain activities or their responses to their daughters' desires to do certain activities.

> *I like sports because I'm able to escape from the stress of school or distractions at home with friends. When I play sports, all of my energy is dedicated to focusing on the present moment, and it feels refreshing to not have to think about anything else.*
>
> Girl archer and athlete, quoted in *Graceful Girls, Aggressive Girls, and Pink Warrior Girls*

Friedman found that parents who supported their daughters in dance sensed that it was important for girls to be in activities that taught them how to be graceful, instilled social etiquette, and focused on relationships. They also appreciated activities that cultivated attractiveness as measured by the male gaze. Competition, while present, was carefully managed to be indirect in that the dancers' efforts were judged by an outsider, which led the dancers to be supportive of one another.

Parents in Friedman's study who encouraged their daughters to participate in sports like soccer appeared very aware of raising daughters who are not girly girls (a reference to the dance girls). One father described his hope for his daughter in this way:

> I encourage her to be more aggressive because she's a cute little girl, but I don't like her to be a girly girl. . . . You know, I don't want her to be a cheerleader—nothing against that—but I want her to prepare to have the option, if she wants to be an executive in a company, that she can play on that turf. (Friedman, 2013b, p. 135)

Misty Copeland and Under Armour's "I Will What I Want" Campaign

In 2014, leading athletic shoe and apparel company Under Armour announced the launch of a new campaign to attract female athletes, whether they compete in high-level sport or participate in the rigors of demanding workout programs from Pilates to kickboxing to spin classes. The campaign—designed with social media in mind—featured six accomplished women, among them Olympic skier Lindsey Vonn, discussing their take on the challenges they confront, the views others have of them as women, and the dreams they have for their lives.

The first one released was of Misty Copeland, a dancer with the American Ballet Theater. As the camera scans Copeland's body as she begins to dance, viewers hear a girl's voice reading a letter of rejection: "Dear Candidate . . . Unfortunately, you have not been accepted. You lack the right feet, Achilles tendons, turnout, torso length, and bust. You have the wrong body for ballet. And at 13 you are too old to be considered." The camera follows Copeland gracefully flying through the air. The commercial ends by listing Copeland's name and job title at the time, ballerina soloist with the American Ballet Theatre, followed by the advertising tagline, "I will what I want." Copeland's persistence resonated with an audience who could relate. The video went viral and picked up more than 4 million views in the first week. On June 30, 2015, Copeland made history when she was promoted to principle dancer for the American Ballet Theater, their first African American principal dancer.

To view Misty Copeland's Under Armour commercial, visit www.youtube.com/watch?v=ZY0cdXr_1MA.

According to Friedman, every parent of a soccer-playing daughter used the terms *aggressive* or *assertive* during the interview.

Among parents who envisioned the possibilities of what chess offers their daughters, Friedman found a greater latitude for developing *pink warriors*, girls who may subscribe if they wish to societal pressures to be feminine while competing head to head with boys and beating them. Enthusiasts have argued for years whether chess is a sport (McClain, 2011). Chess master Susan Pulgar, author of a book on gender and chess, suggested that chess is a perfect game for girls to learn how to compete with boys on an equal footing. She observed,

I think girls need to understand that, yes, they have equal potential to boys. I think that chess is wonderful too as an intellectual activity, where girls can prove that unlike in physical sports, because by nature maybe boys are stronger or faster, in chess women can prove equal. (Friedman, 2013b)

Looking past the terminology of girly, aggressive, and pink warrior to the structures underneath these activities—dance, soccer, and chess—one is coded as female dominant and the other two as male dominant. According to Chessmaniac.com (2012), 7 percent of chess players in the United States are women, and the U.S. Chess Federation (2014) reports that less than 25 percent of the top chess players holding the title of grand master are women.[9] Chess prodigy Carissa Yip became the youngest American to achieve expert level, doing so at the age of 9. She aspires to one day be the overall champion, not just in the female category (Associated Press, 2013).

In each of these settings and situations, we see the performance of gender, a parental investment in how girls are either different from boys or similar to them and in the kind of activities that will help equip their daughters to become successful women. Parents who advocated soccer and chess for their daughters were more likely to come from the upper-middle and upper classes, with well-educated backgrounds. Dance parents were more likely to come from middle and working-class backgrounds (Friedman, 2013a).

This performance of gender, affected as it is by cultural messages about the ideal female body and feminine behavior, plays out in the social spheres surrounding young girls, contributing to the people girls are influenced by and who girls wish to become. While the child's rhyme that girls are made of sugar and spice and everything nice while boys are made of snakes and snails and puppy dog tails does not quite hold to the degree it once did, the stereotypes about girls being kind, polite, neat, pretty, and deferential remain uncontested. Research focusing on girls' attitudes toward physical activity has shown that girls worry about ruining their appearance when they participate, expressing concerns about their hair and makeup getting messed up (American Psychological Association, 2013).

As much as sport feminism has sought to unlock the hold that fears regarding appearance have on female athletes, a reminder of the scrutiny that female athletes receive occurred when U.S. gymnast Gabby Douglas rocketed to stardom following her all-around gold medal performance in the 2012 London Games. In the aftermath of her victory, social media channels were filled with commentary about her hair. In women's sport, this struggle for the identity of female athletes has been depicted at times through an understanding of something called the female apologetic.

PARADOX OF THE STRONG FEMALE ATHLETE WHO FEELS THE NEED TO APOLOGIZE FOR BEING STRONG

A concept coined by Felshin (1974) around the time that Title IX was passed, the *female apologetic* recognized that the place of female athletes within U.S. society was tenuously balanced and that a woman's athleticism was not easily reconciled with societal expectations of femininity. These two factors result in women apologizing for their accomplishments and their strength. The image of the strong, independent, and fierce woman who competed with abandon on the athletic field, who cared about winning, who was a force to be reckoned with, and who

had the potential to beat men did not necessarily fit with conventional ideals of femininity at that time. Thus, female athletes were thought to engage in behaviors to soften their images, growing concerned about their appearance and feminine beauty ideals (hair, makeup, and clothes), downplaying their athletic accomplishments and minimizing their strength, elevating the importance of men's sports and male athlete accomplishments, and projecting heterosexual behavior by being seen in the company of men and avoiding suspicions about their sexuality given the prohibitions of the time (Davis-Delano, Pollock, & Vose, 2009).[10] Felshin believed that as conceptions about gender and the role of women became more expansive, apologetic behavior would diminish.

In keeping with that idea, some studies have found that female athletes do not feminize their own sport participation, but are inclined to engage in apologetic behaviors outside of sport, especially when it comes to appearance and socializing (Ezzell, 2009; Festle, 1996; Ross & Shinew, 2008). While apologetic behavior has diminished over time, it is not wholly gone, and female athletes continue to be affected by social forces that inspire some types of apologetic behaviors. Some female athletes still evidence concerns about feminine appearance, downplay aggressive behavior, and continue to mark themselves as heterosexual.

In a study of NCAA Division II and III basketball, softball, and soccer players ($N = 40$), more than half engaged in some kind of apologetic behavior at least on an occasional basis. Softball players were reported to be most inclined to engage in a variety of behaviors to manage their public perception, including avoiding physical contact with other women in public (47%), apologizing for aggression or physical force (47%), and making a concerted effort to look feminine (50%; Davis-Delano et al., 2009). In a study of softball media guides (Riemer & Wainwright, 2011), careful attention to hair and makeup was a prominent feature in the representation of collegiate softball players.

The tensions around the ideal female can be seen in the multiple expressions of femininity circulating throughout the female athlete experience and how girls and women view female athletes. When confronted with images of female

Women should be seen for their talent and accomplishments. Still, sportswomen will sometimes make concerted efforts to appear feminine. Here, the University of Florida team wore flowers in their hair during the 2015 Women's College World Series.

athletes competing in their sports, adolescent girls aged 13 to 17 and college women aged 18 to 22 responded with appreciation for the athletes' talent, accomplishments, determination, focus, and commitment to something they were passionate about. When those girls and women viewed sexualized images of female athletes, they reacted with commentary about the women's bodies and their sexiness. The athlete herself (her agency) was lost in translation in that kind of imagery. When faced with sexualized images of an athlete, female viewers may envy her face and figure and admire her waistline, but their comments did not value her capacity for independent action (Riemer & Visio, 2003).

The appearance of female athletes and conformity to traditional forms of femininity appear to be more valued by men than by women. In a study of attitudes toward female athletes held by 267 undergraduate students, men responded more favorably to female athletes who conformed to gender stereotypes, while women were more supportive and appreciative of the power female athletes demonstrate when they are playing (Jones & Greer, 2011).

PARADOX OF FEMININITY AND MUSCULARITY

Within the athletic environment, where there is value in strength and muscularity, it seems reasonable that athletes, regardless of gender, would have a comfort level with their own power and their ability to use that power to achieve high performance. However, how female athletes relate to the requirement that they get stronger in their sports and develop some level of muscularity reflects concerns about conformity to feminine standards of appearance.

In a comparison of attitudes about muscularity, male athletes evidenced the highest motivation to become muscular. Female athletes scored higher than female students from the general population, but less than their male counterparts. Interviews with female athletes showed that 45 percent considered functionality (the ability to better play their sport) was the most compelling reason to become more muscular. Forty-two percent valued getting stronger because of health reasons. Just over 20 percent of the female athletes interviewed enjoyed the attention they received from others who admired their muscles, and 18 percent found it personally gratifying to become stronger and more developed. Unlike male athletes, all of whom wanted to be muscular, 16 percent of female athletes would prefer to find a way to get strong without becoming muscular (Steinfeldt, Carter, Benton, & Steinfeldt, 2011).

A taken-for-granted aspect of sport participation is the uniforms that athletes wear. Often form-fitting, sometimes skintight, and engineered for efficiency, uniforms may present female athletes with a particular set of stressors related to appearance and their bodies. In some sports, for example, beach volleyball and track and field, standard uniforms are much more revealing for female athletes than for male athletes (bikini bottoms, bare midriffs). In a culture where body consciousness already runs high, some female athletes feel that their uniforms uncomfortably expose their size and muscularity, leaving them vulnerable to public scrutiny and sexualized attitudes from male fans (Thompson & Sherman, 2010).

As a case in point, in a study of NCAA Division I volleyball players, the women were proud of and confident in their athletic bodies while playing, enjoying the feeling of their own strength. They were, however, conflicted about their bodies in social settings, expressing worry about how their bodies looked, particularly when they were wearing their uniforms. They also worried about how they would attract fans to come to their games. There was a sense among the players that promotions needed to involve a sexualized element, noting that an angle to get heterosexual male fans out to the games would be to offer them an opportunity to see a bunch of girls in spandex. The women reported humiliating experiences when fans specifically caricatured intimate parts of their bodies and held them up for public display (Steinfeldt, Zakrajsek, Bodey, Middendorf, & Martin, 2013).

Female athletes whose bodies are a source of self-esteem and satisfaction also experience triggers in the athletic and social environments that undermine their ability to engage in their sports with full confidence and commitment. Becoming stronger means getting bigger muscles in a society where bigger is not always viewed as better for women. That kind of conflict can lead to disordered eating and ambivalence about training. Some girls and women may not even attempt a sport because of fears about how they will look wearing a uniform. And while there is evidence to show that some female athletes persist in spite of their concerns and eventually get used to wearing uniforms they are not comfortable in, developing coping strategies because they want to continue to play, the residue of that concern appears to carry over outside of the athletic environment (Krane et al., 2004).

TRANSCENDING THE PARADOX: THE FEMALE ATHLETE WHO IS UNAPOLOGETIC

As much as pressures to conform to limited feminine appearance standards fuel the continuing existence of the female athlete apologetic, in her work with female rugby players, Broad (2001) identified female athletes who were unapologetic in their preferences for sports that flaunted those standards. Other studies of female rugby players have affirmed this sensibility that the aggression and raw physicality to be found in contact sports encourages its players to transcend gender stereotypes (Chase, 2006; Fields & Comstock, 2008; Lawler, 2002).

Responding to a belief that society still expected women to sacrifice a part of themselves as wives and mothers, female rugby players found comfort in the sport because it allowed them to be who they were. The sport of rugby was viewed by female athletes as a vehicle of female empowerment, a place where women who wanted to compete on the field in a highly physical way could tackle with abandon, get bruised in the process, feel the pleasure of engaging in sanctioned aggression and violence, and offer no apologies to other players who were similarly engaged (Chase, 2006; Fields & Comstock, 2008; Lawler, 2002).

In her study of female rugby players, Broad described women who were "aggressive by nature" and "rugby players by choice" (2001, p. 199). When invited to give voice to her experience playing rugby, one woman described the opportunity to make an open field tackle as awesome.

For female rugby players, bruises are sites of particular pride. Some players looked forward to being bruised, and others regarded black eyes as badges of honor. The way those badges are viewed by others outside of the context of the game reveals concerns about female vulnerability, victimhood, and the complications associated with hitting a woman. One of the women reported that an old man, seeing her black eye, jokingly commented that she must have had to listen only once, a reference to women being beaten by men for some provocation. Others were inclined to show off their bruises in social settings, knowing that people would wonder how they got them. Some of the women she interviewed were not averse to being confrontational, whether on the field of play or in other settings, if such behavior was warranted. They saw fighting outside of rugby as acceptable.

The **female unapologetic** has been regarded at times as a new form of femininity, a disruption of dominant notions of gender, sexuality, and identity. Martin (2012), however, has described rugby as a place of sexual indifference, where female and male participants are both defined in male terms. She further argues that the rationale that if men can play contact sports, women should be able to do so as well is insufficient. Martin suggests that it is not enough for female athletes to interrupt or disrupt dichotomies that place masculine and feminine in opposition to one another and that work to maintain boundaries around sexuality (heterosexual versus homosexual). She makes the point that these boundaries need to be displaced entirely. Martin cautions that "creating affirmative femininities in rugby should not just focus on trying to reverse the power of the male gender order" (2012, p. 196); rather, it should test the boundaries of what it means to be authentically female as rugby players.

SEPARATE BUT EQUAL: DOES IT REMOVE OR REINFORCE THE PARADOXES THAT AFFECT FEMALE ATHLETES?

As discussed in chapter 2, as important as Title IX has been in fostering the development of girls and women's sport, it allowed to go unchallenged the concept of separate but equal, leaving the sex-segregated athletic structure largely intact. Arguments in support of this kind of arrangement have recognized the general physical differences that exist between girls and boys and men and women, as well as the fact that girls and women in male-dominated sport had to catch up with an advanced system of athletics that had developed over many years. Thus, a single-sex environment in sport has been thought to be most beneficial for girls and women to grow as athletes and to reach their full potential.

While many of those arguments continue to have validity in the 21st century, there are limitations to a separate but equal sport system. Assumptions associated with inherent male superiority and female inferiority, directly or indirectly, go unchallenged. A sex-segregated athletic system reinforces ideas about difference, and has an investment in maintaining those differences. Within a sex-segregated system, conditions are ripe for inequities between groups to occur. And finally, opportunities are rare for male and female athletes to compete together, to experience what life would be like if they shared athletic spaces as genuine teammates rather than as members of separate groups competing against each other for resources, facilities, and support.

Some have argued that in the athletic context, separate is not equal. According to McDonagh and Pappano (2012), keeping male and female athletes contained within a sex-segregated system fuels the false assumption that female athletes are inherently inferior. As a result, female athletes are assigned the status of second-class citizens.

Noticeably, sex integration does happen at various levels for a variety of reasons throughout sport. In the early years, girls and boys may play on the same tee ball team (tee ball is a precursor to the sport of baseball). Recreational and intramural leagues have mixed teams with provisions on the number of female and male participants.

A growing list of scholars have advocated for the value of sex-integrated sport activities. Messner (2002) identified coed sport participation as having the capacity to not only level the playing field between female and male athletes but also

Where Does Female Athletic Excellence Fit in a Sex-Segregated Sport System?

Can you imagine being so good that your coach doesn't know what to do with you? That's what happened to Mary Cain, a 1,500-meter runner who won the New York State high school girls championship at age 14, setting the freshman record at the time. By her sophomore year, she was on her way to the Junior World Championships in Barcelona, setting a new American record after running a 4.11.01 in the 1,500. Cain's talent so surpassed what her coach was accustomed to that he stopped coaching her entirely, leaving her on her own to map a course for herself. In an interview with the *New York Times*, Cain's father said, "She'd show up to practice and do her own thing. It was heartbreaking to be a parent of a kid who has all this potential and see her not getting any coaching at all." The high school and the New York State system didn't quite know what to do either. For a time, Cain ran with the boys' team. However, she was moved back to the girls' team because of a New York State rule that indicated that if a girl ran with boys in meets during the competitive season, she would need to race with boys in the championship. Concerned about whether that scenario would help or hinder her, Cain returned to competing against an all-girl field. Eventually she would receive a call from another great American runner, Alberto Salazar, who invited her to train with him in Oregon.

While her talent would come to the attention of those who could nurture it, this case raises a question to ponder. When was the last time that a male athlete who had remarkable talent was left on his own to figure out what to do with it? And does Cain's case suggest that there are other female athletes who may not be fulfilling their full potential because of the organization of the sport system itself? What should happen to a girl like Mary Cain?

See Weil (2015) for more of Mary Cain's story.

provide a place where participants could learn about a more just and equitable world. While coed sport has the capacity to do those things, some scholars have noted that even in these supposedly sex-integrated settings, there is still a bias against female participants. Perceptions of male superiority have led to rules in sports like coed flag football, where female players are required to pass or catch once every four downs. Wachs has found that female participants in coed softball may be relegated to the role of helper positions, circumscribing the roles that girls and women can play on coed teams (2002, 2005). A review of coed intramural leagues found that goals scored by female players counted double, and slide tackles were removed from the game out of fear that female participants would get hurt (Henry & Comeaux, 1999). They also found that despite claims by participants that they wanted the team to be inclusive, male athletes continued to dominate play.

As coed sports have evolved, they have often been designed around sex-segregation within sex-integration. The sport of korfball, thought to be the first sport to be truly gender mixed, has rules that require that male participants match up with other male participants and female participants match up with other female participants (Cohen, Melton, & Peachey, 2014).

While these experiments in integrating female and male athletes within the same team have prompted a variety of rule structures and accommodations, some evidence shows that working with female athletes toward a common goal can create a substantive change in the way that male athletes view their female peers (Fink & Maxwell, 2010; Voepel, 2006). The practice of using male practice players in women's basketball has generated controversy over the years for reducing playing opportunities for female athletes. After ESPN reporter Mechelle Voepel wrote about a movement to ban male practice players from NCAA Division I women's basketball programs, several male practice players wrote to her about their roles as support players to some of the finest collegiate women basketball players in NCAA Division I. One wrote, "I know that it thoroughly enhanced my college experience and allowed me to appreciate women's athletics so much more than I had before" (Voepel, 2006, para. 11). Another male practice player described the women's basketball coach as one of the most influential women in his life. He went on to write, "Because of my opportunity to practice with the young women on the team, I grew to respect the women's game as a whole and greatly admire the dedication and effort that it takes to be a collegiate athlete. . . . It made me a better person" (para. 17). And yet a third had this to say:

> [The women] commanded my respect with their heart, their love of the game . . . they took charges, threw the occasional elbow, were more vocal than most guys on my high school team. I spent three years in awe. They showed me a lot about how women should be treated (not just on the court). They whipped me into shape in more ways than one. (para. 25)

A space where the possibility of genuine sex integration may occur is in the sport of quidditch. Drawn from the pages of the popular *Harry Potter* book series, the International Quidditch Association has expressly put forward the sport as truly coed. The rulebook offers no special accommodations to female participants, simply encouraging quidditch enthusiasts to play and compete as chasers, seekers, beaters, and keepers alike. In a study of the influence of the sport's conscious devotion to inclusivity has had on participants' attitudes toward players of the opposite sex, participants believed that quidditch did offer a positive coed experience for women and men. Because it was a positive experience to play a sport where the tensions around gender were not as obvious and where the purpose of the sport was to be inclusive, participants expressed a desire to persist with similar sport experiences. Both genders evidenced a reduction in gender stereotypes, and women reported increases in self-confidence and pride. Although the sport does much to challenge prevailing assumptions about women and men in sport, underlying prejudices toward women athletes were still found among participants. A fully inclusive atmosphere takes time to develop. Overall, however, researchers found that quidditch is laying the groundwork for a different future for sport, where men and women are equal as teammates and competitors (Cohen et al., 2014). Although quidditch and other coed sport forms continue to emerge, the sex-segregated sport system remains a place where equal access is illusory for some girls.

Learning Aids

Summary

Using the years just after Title IX's passage as a baseline for how girls and women in sport have changed over time, it is clear that the sport system has become more inclusive. Not only are female athletes competing in larger numbers, they are also making inroads in sports that were once thought of as off limits, most particularly in the contact sports of football, ice hockey, and mixed martial arts.

The effect of parental expectations on the prospects that girls envision for themselves has facilitated this change. This is seen nowhere more directly than in case of Ronda Rousey. Her pathway to being named ESPN Female Athlete of Year was paved in part by her mother, Dr. AnnMaria De Mars. An accomplished athlete in her own right, Dr. De Mars became a sixth-degree black belt in judo and the first American to win a gold medal at the World Judo Championship in 1984. Reflecting on her mother's influence and what her own legacy may be, Rousey said,

> I don't want little girls to have the same ambitions as me. But I want them to know that it is OK to be ambitious, and I don't want them to say the same things that I do, but I want them to know it's OK to say whatever it is that is on their mind. (Dolan, 2014)

While Rousey was given the opportunity to pursue her athletic talents in an aggressive sport, the imprint of societal expectations regarding feminine standards of appearance and behavior have influenced her journey, as they do for the vast majority of female athletes.

Unapologetic of her own choice to break taboos around women being fighters, she holds to certain expectations of womanhood, as reflected in her view of competitor Cyborg.

In that contradiction, we have a window for viewing the multiple paradoxes that female athletes live within. Despite historic highs in terms of female participation in sport, there lingers a tendency to engage in apologetic behaviors to soften female athletes, especially in terms of appearance and the visible signs of power and strength as evidenced in female muscularity. So, too, do barriers exist relative to whom girls and women compete against, with social prohibitions favoring keeping male and female athletes separate from one another.

The exclusionary aspects of sex segregation in sport are the subject of discussions around equal access. To illustrate, the increase in the number of girls participating on high school baseball teams (1,259 in 2012-2013) (National Federation of State High School Associations, 2013) is a promising indicator that change has occurred. However, that number pales in comparison to the nearly 475,000 million boys who play high school baseball. And while softball is offered up as the alternative for girls, the plain fact of the matter is the two are not the same and do not lead to the same possibilities. The chances of a girl succeeding in an attempt to try out for a professional baseball team are slim if she has played softball for the bulk of her career. Legions of girl softball players will not help to provide the pool of talent needed to elevate a girl to the professional ranks in baseball. While USA Baseball sponsors a women's national team, it is largely unknown. The notion that women in the 21st century somehow lack the mental acuity and physical skill to pitch overhand and hit balls that have been pitched overhand is difficult to sustain at an objective level. And yet Title IX offers no relief in challenging this systemic problem. The equal protection clause of the 14th Amendment does, but change requires female athletes to take up these issues one at a time, largely on their own in their local communities. We do not yet know what a world where boys and girls have played on the same baseball team throughout their school years and into adulthood would look like.

Sex segregation by itself, however, is not the only thing that can hold a female athlete back in sport. As Sabo and Veliz (2008, 2011) demonstrated, female athletes still have fewer opportunities to participate in sport , with girls from lower income situations and urban and rural environments having the fewest sport opportunities.

As Rousey's stories and others attest, there is much to celebrate about women's prospects in sport. The work, however, continues to ease the burdens of the paradoxes that female athletes face.

Discussion Questions

1. Among the issues discussed in this chapter is the response of toy manufacturers to the popularity of female warriors in films and books like *The Hunger Games* by developing and selling toy weapons specifically designed for girls. This is not the first time that toy manufacturers have attempted to sell toys that had once been exclusively marketed to boys (science sets and construction sets have been redesigned and marketed with girls in mind in recent years). The marketing of toy weapons to girls does appear to have taken hold, however, in a way that has not often been seen. This raises the question of whether the marketing of toy weapons to girls is really a positive development or something that shouldn't be done for either boys or girls. Further, given that the toys continue to be heavily coded as female, with heavy emphasis on pink, are these toys, as Monique Conrod (2014) of *Teaching Kids News* noted, too violent or too girly? Watch *The Hunger Games* and reflect on these developments. How would you answer these questions? Are these even the right questions to ask?

2. Watch the ESPN Films and ESPNW *Nine for IX* short film titled *Rowdy Ronda Rousey* (Mundo & Croshere, 2014) and consider Rousey's story in light of the concept of the female apologetic/unapologetic dynamic. How do you think that concept applies to Rousey's story? What kind of a role did her mother play in Rousey's success? Has she contributed to the creation of a new form of femininity?

3. In the Under Armour ad campaign, "I Will What I Want," one of the women selected as an athlete was supermodel Gisele Bündchen (who is also the wife of Boston Patriots quarterback Tom Brady). View the video and debate whether she should have been chosen as one of the female athletes in the campaign: www.huffingtonpost.ca/2015/07/15/under-armour-gisele-misty-copeland-lindsey-vonn_n_7801270.html

Learning Activities

1. Jessica Caggiano (2010) provides an excellent overview of Title IX's contact sports exception and asks a very interesting question: Is the contact sports exception something to stand behind or hide behind? Read her article and offer your thoughts on that question.

2. Research rules pertaining to coed intramural and recreational leagues in your school, hometown, or campus. Assess how fair those rules are and how well they foster an equal playing field for all participants.

Glossary

female apologetic—Any behavior by female athletes that emphasizes a female athlete's femininity. This behavior is in response to the masculine or lesbian stereotypes associated with female sport participation.

female unapologetic—New form of femininity; a disruption of dominant notions of gender, sexuality, and identity.

paradox—A situation, person, or thing that combines contradictory features or qualities.

Notes

1. For a visual of the obstacles competitors face on *American Ninja Warrior*, go to www.nbc.com/american-ninja-warrior.

2. Other nominees for the ESPY Female Athlete of the Year Award included Mikaela Shiffrin, a U.S. skier who won a gold medal in the slalom at the 2014 Winter Olympics; Breanna Stewart, a University of Connecticut women's basketball player who was honored as the Associated Press National Player of the Year in 2014 for her role in helping UCONN to an undefeated season; and Maya Moore, a professional women's basketball player for the Minnesota Lynx who played on the WNBA First Team and assisted her team in winning the WNBA championship and was named the WNBA Finals MVP (Zucker, 2014).

3. Mixed martial arts fighters come from an array of sport disciplines, including boxing, judo, jujitsu, karate, and wrestling.

4. In boxing and other combat sports, fighters compete in a ring. The ring has ropes as barriers. MMA fighters in the UFC compete in a cage, an enclosed ring. The walls of the ring are made of material that looks like a chain link fence.

5. In 2014, Rousey made her film debut as an action hero in *The Expendables 3*, a project starring established action hero stars Arnold Schwarzenegger and Sylvester Stallone.

6. Since December of 2011, USA Archery reported that the number of clubs in the United States nearly doubled, from 279 to 540, as momentum built around Collins' trilogy of books (*The Hunger Games*, *Catching Fire*, and *Mockingjay*) and the upcoming movies, the first of which was released in early 2012 (Rubin, 2012).

7. Princess Catherine played field hockey when she was in school.

8. In a study conducted by the National Sporting Goods Association (Ryan & Schwartz, 2013), participation in hunting with firearms increased by 18 percent in 2013, with a sharper increase reported for females, which was up nearly 29 percent compared to 2011.

9. There has been wide speculation that girls and women have not been as successful in chess because they are not as intellectually strong as male competitors. Bilalic and colleagues (Bilalic, Smaldone, McLeod, & Gobet, 2008) laid that theory to rest, demonstrating that male dominance of the activity is accounted for simply by the fact that there are more boys and men playing.

10. Davis-Delano, Pollock, and Vose (2009) provide a comprehensive overview of the female apologetic in sport and the work of many scholars, some of whom noted that some female athletes reported engaging in apologetic behavior and others did not evidence apologetic behavior. Hardy defined female apologetic behavior in sport to include "any behaviour by female athletes that emphasizes a female athlete's femininity. This behaviour is in response to the masculine and/or lesbian stereotypes associated with female sport participation. Female apologetic behaviour is commonly found in the media as an attempt to reinforce gender hierarchies" (2015, p. 155).

PART II

Strong Girls, Strong Women

Sport participation is generally encouraged as a way for people to become physically stronger and mentally resilient, to problem solve when presented with obstacles and disappointments, and to take positive steps to reach their full potential. While progress has been made in creating equitable access to sport opportunities for girls and women, the need remains to educate the public about the loss of opportunities to play for female athletes and the consequences of these losses. Gender consciousness allows for a greater appreciation of the benefits of sport participation for girls and women, and it also helps in identifying and dealing with the risks and vulnerabilities that come along with playing a sport.

The fourth chapter offers an expansive overview of the benefits of sport for girls and women, including the influence of sport participation on educational attainment and academic performance as well as physical and mental health benefits. Research over the span of many years shows that women who play sport and are physically active in their early years are less likely to suffer from heart ailments, diabetes, and overweight, and have reduced rates of certain forms of cancer.

As positive as sport participation may be for the overall health of girls and women, it is not a panacea. Some research shows that female athletes in some sports may exhibit concerning rates of binge drinking, eating disorders and disordered eating, and excessive exercising. Finally, chapter 4 also looks at the topic of female athletes and injuries, focusing on two of the most talked about ones—knee injuries and concussions.

Looking at the issue of whether biology is destiny, chapter 5 examines the nature of physiological differences between female and male athletes. Noting when and where physiological differences exist between female and male athletes, the authors help us interpret what those differences mean. Finally, the chapter offers insight regarding how an understanding of female athlete physiology translates into appropriate approaches to training.

CHAPTER 4

Benefits and Risks of Sport Participation by Women and Girls

Ellen J. Staurowsky, EdD, Drexel University

Learning Objectives

In this chapter, you will learn about the following:

- Sport participation, educational attainment, and the female athlete
- Physical benefits of sport participation for girls and women
- Female athletes, mental toughness, and depression
- Female athletes and substance abuse (use of alcohol, tobacco, and other illicit drugs, including steroids)
- Sexual risk prevention and female athletes
- Female athletes and injuries, specifically ACL injuries and concussions
- The female athlete triad

There are good athletes and then there are remarkable athletes. Kim Chiarelli is one of the remarkable ones. A standout girls' soccer player at Bishop Eustace Preparatory School (New Jersey; 2004-2007), she made her mark in her youth by being chosen for the Select South Jersey Girls Soccer League all four years for which she was eligible (1999-2002) and playing as a member of the Jersey Devils (travel squad) from 2003-2007. She was so good coming out of high school that she was drafted to play for the Atlantic City Diablos in what was then the Women's Professional Soccer League (WPSL). Although her time as a professional women's soccer player would end soon after it started when the WPSL folded, her athletic talents were far too great to go unnoticed.

She was recruited to play for the Drexel University women's soccer team, where her combination of outright athleticism, competitive spirit, leadership qualities, and academic achievements made her a sought-after player. From the moment she arrived on campus, she had an impact, becoming the Colonial Athletic Association (CAA) Rookie of the Year. During her tenure on the Dragon women's soccer team, she became a mainstay, an inspiring teammate who commanded respect and elevated the level of play of those around her.

Her career as a varsity athlete at Drexel would not end with soccer, however. After being granted a fifth year of eligibility, Kim did something quite rare. She took up a new sport and a new position, joining the field hockey team as a goalkeeper. Notably, in soccer, she had been a midfielder. Prior to learning the sport of field hockey for the first time, she had never played in goal.

Describing his lack of surprise at Kim's ease in switching from soccer to field hockey, her former soccer coach Ray Goon said, "Kim was a fierce competitor and became a tremendous leader for our program. She wanted to win at everything. Not just games, but every drill or training competition, even if it was rock-paper-scissors, she wanted to come out on top" (Ciminera, 2011). Denise Zelenak, one of the most accomplished field hockey coaches in the world, was serving at the time as the U.S. women's indoor field hockey coach as well as Drexel's head coach.

She observed, "Kim works hard at practice and has done everything she can to learn this new position—a real team player. As for fitting in with the team, it was a seamless transition. She is a field hockey player" (Ciminera, 2011). Within weeks of taking up the game, she was chosen as the starting goalkeeper, earning a reputation in the CAA as a player whom opposing teams feared going up against.

As much as Kim exemplified many of the qualities that are celebrated in really great athletes—athletic talent, adaptability, courage, risk taking, leadership, and a commanding presence—she was also attending to the rest of her life even as she competed fiercely on two different college teams. As an undergraduate communications major, Kim worked as a communication and media assistant with the Philadelphia Electric Company and as a communication and editing assistant with the Children's Hospital of Philadelphia in fulfillment of degree requirements to complete two cooperative learning experiences. She was eventually hired by the Drexel Sports Information Office to serve as an assistant, covering numerous sports. While in that role, she worked to complete her master's degree in sport management (Kim Chiarelli, personal communication, May 15, 2014).

Kim, like generations of female athletes, embraced her athleticism and gave expression to the power within her as an impact player on the field, an accomplished worker off the field, and a valued friend along the way. Kim's story is a thread in the larger narrative that so many girls and women live. Their lives are vibrant in possibility, brave in outlook, and dynamic in execution.

As rich in scale as women's sport is for so many, the narrative is not always perfect and is sometimes haunting. Just a few short blocks from where Kim's playing and school days unfolded at Drexel, another female athlete was competing and striving for her dreams as well. Another Jersey girl who had made her way to Philadelphia, Madison Holleran seemed to be on a trajectory similar to Kim's. She, too, was a remarkable athlete. She received scholarship offers for soccer but decided instead to accept Penn's invitation to participate on the track team. The young woman described by a teammate as "one of those people who had an effortless glow about her," who did "everything with elegance and grace," had struggled in her first semester at college as a philosophy and political science major (Volk, 2014). Although she was quite strong academically, having earned a 3.5 grade point average in her first semester, she had started to harbor doubts about her intellectual abilities, surrounded as she was by high-achieving students. Balancing the demands of her athletic life along with the rigors of the academic environment and a new social scene was stressful, so much so that she sought the

How Might You Know if a Teammate Is Depressed?

A teammate may give signals that they are struggling with feelings of depression.

WARNING SIGNS OF DEPRESSION

- General feeling of fatigue or a change in sleep habits (trouble sleeping, not being able to get to sleep, sleeping for long periods of time)
- Skipping meals, not being hungry, or eating too much
- Alcohol and drug use
- Loss of interest in what is going on around them (increasing isolation)
- General lack of energy or energy level has gone down
- Contemplation of death and suicide
- Persistent feeling of sadness
- Feelings of helplessness and hopelessness (a sense that no matter what there isn't a solution to problems)
- Difficulty focusing and concentrating (not being able to get coursework done, having trouble getting assignments done, forgetting practice times)
- Crying and experiencing feelings of anxiety
- Aches and pains that don't go away and recurring injuries and illness

WAYS TO HELP A DEPRESSED TEAMMATE

- Create a safe environment for your teammate (no judgment zone).
- Let them know that you care.
- Encourage your teammate to seek help from those who can help most.

MORE RESOURCES ON ATHLETES AND MENTAL HEALTH

- The National Athletic Trainer's statements on mental health for college and high school athletes: www.nata.org/NR03032015
- NCAA article "Mind, Body, and Sport": www.ncaa.org/health-and-safety/sport-science-institute/mind-body-and-sport-depression-and-anxiety-prevalence-student-athletes

NATIONAL SUICIDE PREVENTION HOTLINE

Are you in crisis? Please take the first step in getting help by calling 1-800-273-TALK (8255). The call is free within the United States, and you will be connected to a skilled, trained counselor at a crisis center in your area.

services of a counselor. She was supported in doing so by her parents. The transition to college proved too much, and she committed suicide. The abrupt end to Madison's life leaves many questions to be answered and a heavy burden on the heart. Some of the answers rest with her alone, and others are related to the challenging path girls and young women must navigate in making their way to adulthood. Her story is also an important part of the women and sport narrative.[2]

In this chapter, both Kim and Madison's stories are situated within the broader range of research about sport and physical activity participation for girls and women, and the benefits to be realized in terms of educational attainment as well as physical and mental health. While the evidence strongly supports that sport participation is good for girls and women, female athletes are, at times, negatively affected by their sport participation.[3] As a consequence, this chapter also examines substance use and abuse among female athletes, the **female athlete triad**, and how female athletes are affected by certain injuries.

EDUCATIONAL ATTAINMENT AND SPORT PARTICIPATION

Research studies conducted over the past few decades have generally found a positive association between high school sport participation and different educational outcomes (Farb & Matjasko, 2012; Feldman & Matjasko, 2005). Some studies suggest that among high school–age students who participate in sport programs, girls may realize an additional academic advantage when compared to boys (Hanson & Kraus, 1998; 1999; Pearson, Crissey, & Riegle-Crumb, 2009; Veliz & Shakib, 2014).

Researchers have also found a connection between girls' athletic participation and their success in what have historically been viewed as male-dominated academic areas, such as math and science. One theory on the reason for this connection is that sport presents a unique cultural environment where girls learn non stereotypical assumptions about femininity. As such, girls become accustomed to challenging common views about what they can and cannot

do (Hanson & Kraus, 1998; 1999; Pearson et al., 2009; Veliz & Shakib, 2014).

In a nationally representative sample of 4,644 public high schools for the academic school year of 2009-2010, the advanced placement (AP) enrollment rates were modestly or much higher for girls than boys in math (4.32% to 4.22%), science (4.91% to 4.09%), foreign language (3.29% to 1.93%), and at least one AP course (18.9% to 13.53%). For schools where there was a one-to-one gender ratio between female and male athletes, there was a higher representation of female students in AP science courses (Veliz & Shakib, 2014).

Sport participation may have a favorable influence on girls' aspirations to attend college and to complete an undergraduate degree. According to Lipscomb (2006), girls who participated in sport at the high school level were 5 percent more likely to aspire to college compared to their peers who did not play sports. Troutman and Dufur (2007) found that girls who played sports were also more likely to earn a degree, although that effect was lessened when other factors were taken into consideration (parents' education, family income, type of school, student expectations, family size, race, high school test scores, college grades, and whether the student continued her athletic career at college).

Based on federal graduation rate (FGR) data, NCAA female athletes appear to exhibit higher graduation rates than male athletes and the general student body. There is, however, a racial dimension to this. For athletes entering college in the 2006 class year, White female athletes reported FGRs that were 11 percent above the general student body, while African American female athletes graduated at a rate slightly below that of the general student body (62% compared to 64%) (National Collegiate Athletic Association, 2013).

The determination of whether athletes as a group have more favorable graduation rates than the general student body has been questioned in recent years as a fuller understanding of the FGR has come to light. Noting that the FGR does not take into account a transfer bias, Southall and colleagues (2014) reported that graduation rates for NCAA athletes may be less than those

As a result of sport participation, girls receive a 5 percent boost in terms of their likelihood of attending college (Lipscomb, 2006).

of the general student body. Using a statistic called the adjusted graduation gap (representing the gap between the FGR and the adjusted figure that removes the transfer bias), NCAA women's basketball players in major conferences had a −13.6 adjusted graduation gap.

When taken in the aggregate, girls' and women's involvement in sport can complement academic development and aid in opening up vistas of educational opportunity. There is still more work to be done, in light of Southall and colleagues' findings, to better understand the nuances of this relationship.

PHYSICAL HEALTH BENEFITS OF FEMALE SPORT PARTICIPATION

Research over the span of decades confirms that participation in sport and regular physical activity, in no small part, provides a critical foundation for girls and women to lead healthy, strong, and fulfilled lives. With benefits that include the development of physical strength

to deal with the demands and rigors of daily living, the cultivation of psychological health that helps in meeting the challenges of each day with a positive outlook, and the social benefits to be realized through the friendships forged with teammates or exercise class, it is an understatement to say that physical activity does a body good.

Combined with a balanced approach to nutrition, ample sleep, and moderation in the use of alcohol, physical activity and sport involvement have been shown to offer girls and women a better quality of life in the present and well into their futures. In a study of 65,838 post-menopausal women who were assessed using American Cancer Society (ACS) prevention guidelines and awarded scores between 0 and 8 on a combined measure of diet, physical activity, body mass index (current and at the age of 18), and alcohol consumption, women with the highest ACS scores had a 17 percent lower risk of any cancer, 22 percent lower risk of breast cancer, a 52 percent lower risk of colorectal cancer, 27 percent lower risk of all-cause mortality, and 20 percent lower risk of cancer-specific mortality (Thomson et al., 2014).

Regular physical exercise and diet can also have a dramatic effect on reducing the risk of heart disease among women, a disease that has been identified as a leading cause of death among women in the United States. According to the U.S. Department of Health and Human Services' Office on Women's Health (2012), women of color are a particularly vulnerable population in terms of susceptibility to coronary heart disease, exhibiting multiple risk factors for heart disease, including high blood pressure, diabetes, and obesity. In a study reported in the *Journal of Women's Health* (Giardina et al., 2011), 57 percent of Latina women, 40 percent of African American women, and 32 percent of White women had three or more risk factors for having a heart attack. Those women also were unaware of the warning signs of a heart attack.

Beyond the reduction in cancer risks and increased heart health, women benefit physically in many ways from engagement in physical activity. Moderate levels of exercise have been found to be positively associated with helping

> *Swimmers must have the mental ability to let go of what their body feels and focus on the race, their stroke, or anything else that helps them finish the race.*
>
> Sally Anderson, Women's Swimming and Diving, Penn State

women retain mental acuity and maintain strong bones, alleviating symptoms associated with dementia, maintaining body weight and core muscle strength that affect balance and movement, and combating the acquisition of diseases associated with sedentary lifestyles, such as diabetes and sleep disorders. For women, these overall effects spell a better quality of life as they age (see chapter 8 for more details).

FEMALE ATHLETES, MENTAL TOUGHNESS, AND DEPRESSION

Those who study the science of exercise have known for years that regular participation in physical activity, whether dance or soccer or weightlifting or yoga, produces positive results by elevating mood states. The capacity for exercise to influence mood occurs primarily through two ways. Chemicals (dopamine, endorphins, epinephrine, and serotonin) released during exercise can help manage stress and fatigue, make you feel good, and regulate sleep. Exercise also has the capacity to stimulate the creation of brain-derived neurotrophic factor in the brain, which aids in the repair of neurons and the generation of new neurons (Craft & Perna, 2004; Warren, 2013).

Much is often made about sport involvement and physical activity providing opportunities for athletes to manifest and develop mental toughness. Think of those highly emotional sport moments when a female athlete has come through in the clinch, and you know what mental toughness is. One need only recall watching U.S. women's soccer star Abby Wambach turn around a key game with an electrifying goal against a Brazilian team that seemed destined to dismiss the U.S. team early in the

Women's World Cup in 2011 to appreciate the concept. Mental toughness is thought to consist of four dimensions (Kaufman, 2014):

- **Hope:** The unshakeable self-belief in one's ability to achieve competition goals ("I can think of many ways to get out of a jam.")

- **Optimism:** A general expectancy that good things will happen ("In uncertain times, I usually expect the best.")

- **Perseverance:** Consistency in achieving one's goals and not giving up easily when facing adversity of difficulties ("I am often so determined that I continue working long after other people have given up.")

- **Resilience:** The ability to adapt to challenges in the environment ("I do not dwell on things that I can't do anything about.")

Athletes are believed to have these qualities in abundant measure compared to nonathletes.

A number of studies have suggested that participation in sport is associated with psychological benefits and that it acts as a buffer against various sources of stress (Proctor & Boan-Lenzo, 2010). This leads athletes to present an *iceberg profile*, meaning that they possess high levels of vigor along with low levels of anger, depression, tension, fatigue, and confusion (Morgan, 1980; Morgan & Pollock, 1977; Puffer & McShane, 1992; Terry, 1995). Compared with other populations, athletes overall demonstrate decreased levels of depression (Terry, 1995).

While it is uncontested that physical activity, whether at the recreational or elite level, contributes to a greater sense of self-worth and confidence, awareness is growing that depression among athletes may be underreported because of social prohibitions against admitting to weakness or needing help. The athletic culture presents challenges that can feel overwhelming, especially if other areas of an athlete's life, including school and family, involve stressors. The pressures that accompany high-level training and competing have been found to create difficulties for athletes, with risk for depression being higher among female athletes than male athletes (Donohue et al., 2004; Storch, Storch, Killiany & Roberti, 2005). Injured athletes experience short-term and long-term depression as a result of the interruption to their playing careers and the rehabilitation that follows (Sabo, Miller, Melnick, Farrell, & Barnes, 2005), which is often accompanied by a sense of withdrawal or separation from the support of a team, and female athletes exhibit higher levels of depression following injury compared to their male counterparts (Appaneal, Levine, Perna, & Roh, 2009).

By virtue of their involvement in sport, collegiate athletes may experience depression as a result of a number of factors. The sheer stress of competing overtime leads most athletes to contemplate quitting when the strain of daily workouts, the demands of time and expense, the looming prospect of retirement, and the toll of injury become too great. In a study examining depression levels among athletes before and after competition, 68 percent of athletes studied met the criteria for experiencing a major depressive episode before competition, with more female athletes experiencing depression compared to their male peers. After competition, more than a third of the athletes met the criteria, with 26 percent reporting mild to moderate symptoms of depression. The more elite the athlete, the greater likelihood of depression; performance failure was significantly associated with depression in that group (Hammond, Gialloreto, Kubas, & Hap Davis, 2013).

Fears about disappointing or provoking disapproval from family members, teammates, coaches, and friends who supported them throughout their athletic careers become obstacles that prevent athletes from leaving their sports. The ongoing expectation to exceed performance goals, day in and day out, year in and year out can be daunting—especially if an athlete is receiving an athletic scholarship and runs the risk of losing it if they let up (Gill, 2008; Proctor & Boan-Lenzo, 2010; Yang et al., 2007).

In a study conducted by researchers at Georgetown University Medical Center (Mallet,

> You can become strong, and powerful, and beautiful.
>
> Serena Williams

2013), college athletes were found to be twice as likely to report feelings consistent with diagnostic levels of depression compared to athletes who had graduated from college. The results suggested that participation in intercollegiate athletics was more stressful than what common understanding would suggest.

In 2007, the NCAA published a resource titled *Managing Student-Athletes' Mental Health Issues* (National Collegiate Athletic Association, 2007). Depression, with the potential for suicide, was described as a critical disorder. Encouraging greater awareness among athletic department personnel about the mental health issues of college athletes, the handbook notes (p. 8),

> Coaches sometimes want to assume that student-athletes are healthy simply because they are athletes. Coaches must remember that they are not just student-athletes. They are human beings with the same frailties as non-athletes. They are young people attempting to deal with the complexities of life, the demands of college life and the pressures that sometimes accompany performance.

Increasingly, sports medicine personnel are directing greater attention to the mental health concerns of athletes. Described as a silent injury, suicide was found to be the third leading cause of death among college athletes between the years 2004 and 2008, according to NCAA data (Noren, 2014). In the fall of 2013, the National Athletic Trainers' Association (NATA) issued recommendations for college athletic departments to develop plans to recognize and refer athletes with psychological concerns. Addressing the state of responsiveness within the college sport community to mental health issues, Tim Neal, an assistant athletic director for sports medicine at Syracuse University and one of the leaders of the NATA effort, said, "I liken the awareness and management of mental health issues in student-athletes to where we were with concussion awareness and management 10 to 15 years ago. The landscape, in my opinion, is a little behind" (Noren, 2014, para. 11). Education is key for addressing the important issue of female athlete health and well-being. NATA has suggested that the following behaviors, although not a comprehensive list, may reflect that an athlete is in distress and needs professional assistance (Neal et al., 2013):

Behaviors to Monitor That May Reflect Psychological Concerns

- Changes in eating or sleeping habits
- Unexplained weight loss or gain
- Drug or alcohol abuse
- Gambling issues
- Withdrawing from social contact
- Decreased interest
- Taking up risky behaviors
- Loss of emotion or sudden emotional changes
- Irresponsibility or lying
- Talking about death or dying
- Problems concentrating or focusing
- Negative self-talk
- Frequent fatigue, illness, or injury
- Increased irritability or anger problems
- Feeling out of control
- Unexplained wounds or evidence of deliberate harm
- Legal problems or fighting
- Mood swings
- All-or-nothing thinking
- Excessive worry or fear
- Agitation
- Shaking or trembling
- Stomach problems or headaches
- Persistent injury

For more information, access the National Alliance for Mental Illness and the National Suicide Prevention Lifeline.

FEMALE ATHLETES AND SUBSTANCE USE AND ABUSE

While conventional wisdom has created the impression that athletic experience may serve to moderate substance use and abuse, in the report *Her Life Depends on It III* (Staurowsky et al., 2015), the authors noted,

Empirical research shows that the relationship between sports participation and substance use is complex. The playing field may help to buffer against some kinds of substance use, such as tobacco or illicit "hard" drugs, while exacerbating the risk of others such as smokeless tobacco, alcohol, and anabolic-androgenic steroids. Gender further complicates the equation. Traditionally girls have tended to have lower rates of substance use than boys, but the long-standing gender gap is narrowing—especially for those substances that have most typically been closely linked to sports. (p. 62)

Female Athletes and Alcohol Consumption

For girls and women who participate in sport at some point in their lives, the relationship between alcohol consumption and their engagement in sport offers a mixed picture. Research indicates for the most part that female athletes in high school and college are more likely to engage in problem drinking, such as binge drinking (events where female athletes may drink excessively), than their nonathletic peers (Diehl et al., 2012; Kwan, Bobko, Faulkner, Donnelly, & Cairney, 2014; Lisha & Sussman, 2010; Turrisi, Mallett, Mastroleo, & Larimer, 2006). Those results, however, are not written in stone. Other research shows that female athletes may engage in excessive alcohol consumption at lower rates than other students or that athletic participation by itself may have no effect on alcohol consumption one way or another (Mays & Thompson, 2009; Yusko, Buckman, White, & Pandina, 2008).

The influence of peers, sport-related identities, and sport subcultures may all serve as mediating factors in complicating the relationship between athletic participation and drinking behavior. The College Alcohol Survey "established that male student-athletes may drink 16 percent more and female athletes may drink in excess of 19 percent more alcohol and experience greater drinking-related consequences than their peers who do not participate in college athletic programs" (Isaac, 2010, p. 34). According to a

How to Help an Athlete Exhibiting Signs of Substance Abuse

Extending a helping hand to an athlete with a substance abuse issue can be challenging. Experts recommend simply laying out facts for the athlete about their behavior, expressing care and concern, and offering information about support available. Examples of specific behaviors that may suggest a problem with drug or alcohol abuse include the following:

- Moments when athletes are out of control socially (not remembering what they did the night before)
- Passing out and waking up in a different location with no memory of how they got there
- Indiscriminate and unprotected sex
- Doing things that would ordinarily be out of character (getting into fights, engaging in confrontations, threatening other people)
- Deterioration in relationships with friends, family, and teammates
- Engaging in criminal acts (property damage, stealing, driving while under the influence, being arrested)
- Experiencing damaging health effects (taking longer to physically recover after use, vomiting or feeling nauseated)
- Being overly hyper and anxious (unable to sleep, disruptive, unable to listen or be around other people)
- Unable to stop using, which negatively affects their athletic skills and performance (shooting percentages going down, not able to get back on defense, timing is off, not as strong, coach and teammates noticing that contributions are not what they once were)
- Effects on academics (missing classes and assignments, failing to show up for exams, grades falling)

For substance abusers, denial is particularly strong. Interventions can be challenging because they threaten the abuser's desire to continue using. Prohibitions around disclosure may be particularly strong for athletes. Because of team conduct codes, athletes may feel that they will be removed from the team if they admit a substance abuse issue to a coach or team captain. It may be helpful for teams to regularly explore questions around what is recreational use versus abuse.

For more information, see Hainline, Bell, and Wilfert (n.d.).

study by the National Collegiate Athletic Association (2014), one-third of female college students self-report patterns of drinking that fit the criteria for binge drinking. This represents a decline from previously reported data from 2005, when 41 percent of college female athletes reported drinking four or more drinks in one sitting.

There may be many reasons why female athletes engage in excessive drinking. Within the athletic culture, it is not uncommon for athletes to self-medicate in order to handle the stress and anxiety that comes along with competition and injuries. Team sport subcultures, such as those found in field hockey, soccer, and lacrosse, may promote drinking. College athletes may also have exaggerated perceptions of their teammates' alcohol use due to an overestimation of drinking, heavy episodic drinking, and rumors of teammates' breaking training rules (Dams-O'Connor, Martin, & Martens, 2007; Perkins & Craig, 2012). Comparisons between female and male athletes suggest that reasons for drinking may vary by gender: Female athletes may be more susceptible to using drinking as a coping mechanism, and male athletes may be more inclined to drink for social reasons (Wilson, Pritchard, & Schaeffer, 2004).

Smoking and Female Athletic Participation

Based on available research, athletic participation appears to protect girls against smoking. The longer girls are in sport, the less likely they are to smoke. Sports involvement itself and more general physical activity have been found to lower rates of cigarette use, especially among girls (Kaczynski, Mannell, & Manske, 2008; Kaczynski, Manske, Mannell, & Grewal, 2008). When female college athletes were compared to undergraduate female students who did not participate in sport, the female college athletes were two to three times less likely to engage in smoking, both in and out of the competitive season for their sport (Yusko et al., 2008). As a practical matter, lower rates of smoking among female athletes may be due to a desire on their part to avoid behaviors that make it difficult to breathe, which would jeopardize athletic performance (Wichstrom & Wichstrom, 2009).

Team rules barring smoking may also provide the external support that female athletes need to resist peer pressure and turn down opportunities to smoke. The prospect of being suspended or dismissed from a team because of smoking could potentially be a persuasive deterrent. According to Miller, Sabo, Melnick, Farrell, and Barnes (2001), girls who are more engaged in sport than casual athletes are less likely to smoke. Girls who participate on three or more teams are the least likely group to report ever using cigarettes. The connection between the level of sport participation and female athlete smoking behavior may be due to something that researchers call a "physically active concept" (Rodriguez & Audrain-McGovern, 2004; Verkooijen, Nielsen, & Kremers, 2008), meaning that using cigarettes simply does not fit with the self-concept of a physically active girl or woman. Sport participation, with its potential to reduce stress, elevate mood, and enhance social status, may eliminate the need for female athletes to smoke (Audrain-McGovern, Rodriguez, Cuevas, & Sass, 2013).

Although smoking is encoded as a negative behavior for athletes, because of its potential to reduce physical performance and its sanctions from coaches, the sport culture has a different relationship with smokeless or spit tobacco (also called dipping or chewing tobacco). For those unfamiliar with the drug, tobacco is sold in loose form in small canisters or pouches. Users take a wad of tobacco and put it into their mouths. The habit is as addictive as smoking. Athletes may find the need to chew and spit as a way of relaxing. In the sport of baseball, for example, the use of smokeless tobacco by coaches and players is a cultural feature of the game, and it is imitated by younger athletes (Severson, Klein, Lichtensein, Kaufman, & Orleans, 2005). Despite the serious health effects (e.g., various cancers of the mouth and jaw), both male and female athletes indulge. According to the National Collegiate Athletic Association (2009), 29 percent of male athletes and 2 percent of female athletes used smokeless tobacco during the previous year for which they were reporting their behavior. While NCAA softball players reported higher rates than other female athletes at 6 percent, in comparison, 52 percent of baseball players used smokeless tobacco (National Collegiate Athletic Association, 2012).

Female Athletes and Illicit Drug Use

As an overall trend, female athletes exhibit lower rates of drug use than their nonathletic peers, which indicates that sport participation may provide protective cover for girls against illicit drug use. Based on available research, female high school athletes and high school girls who exercise are significantly less likely to use marijuana, cocaine, or most other illicit drugs, with White girls seeming to be most open to the protective effects against drug use that sport participation provides (Miller et al., 2001; Pate, Trost, Levin, & Dowda, 2000). Female college athletes have been found to abuse nonmedical prescription tranquilizers and opiates significantly less than other female undergraduates (Ford, 2007).

In the area of marijuana use, the data is equivocal. Although college athletes are less likely to use marijuana than undergraduate nonathletes, 18 percent of NCAA female college athletes reported using marijuana during the past year (National Collegiate Athletic Association, 2012). Higher rates were reported among players of ice hockey (36%), lacrosse (30%), and soccer (23%). Lower rates were reported in the sports of tennis (15%), basketball (15%), and track (9%).

Interpreting what these statistics reflect about the connection between sport participation and female athlete use of marijuana is complicated. Because NCAA athletes are required to agree to drug testing in order to maintain their eligibility, and marijuana is a type of drug that remains in the system for a relatively long period of time, the threat of potential exposure may discourage this kind of behavior. Still, if 25 to 40 percent of female athletes in NCAA institutions in select sports report using marijuana, the deterrent effect may not be that strong.

A number of factors likely affect the decisions of female athletes regarding drug use. The desire to excel in her sport of choice and strive to meet performance goals may encourage a female athlete to abstain from drug use. The enhanced self-esteem female athletes experience from playing may inoculate them from the pressures to use illicit drugs. The fact that female athletes have little time that is not supervised might be a realistic reason as well. Access to prosocial networks composed of teammates, coaches, and health care professionals (sports medicine personnel, athletic trainers, nutritionists, counselors) may create spaces where illicit drug use is less tolerated.

Use of Steroids and Performance Enhancement Drugs

Citing numerous studies, sport psychologist Joel Fish (2012) estimated that 5.9 percent of boys and 4.6 percent of girls have used steroids at one point in order to build muscle. As a group, athletes are a high-risk population for steroid use and abuse. Further, girls and women, whether they are athletes or not, are motivated by contemporary standards of attractiveness that emphasize a lean, sleek, and fit body (think washboard or six-pack abs). For some absorbed with body issues, steroid use may be part of a larger pattern of disordered eating, poor body image, and an obsession with weight (Elliot et al., 2006; Gruber & Pope, 2000). For those who are prone to taking health risks, a predisposition to using steroids may also signal a susceptibility to elevated risk for use of alcohol, tobacco, and other illicit drugs, as well as risk of sexual risk-taking, violence, suicidality, pathogenic weight control, and other unhealthy behaviors (Elliot, Cheong, Moe, & Goldberg, 2007; Harmer, 2009; Miller, Melnick, Barnes, Farrell, & Sabo, 2005; Wichstrom & Pedersen, 2001). However, there appear to be differences between athletic and nonathletic steroid users; athletic participation is associated with less risk of engagement with other risky behaviors (Miller et al., 2005). While steroid use is found in organized sports or body-building, female adolescents in these sports may actually be less likely than female nonathletes to use steroids. When data on female steroid use is adjusted to remove girls who simply experimented, meaning they tried steroids once or twice but didn't persist in use, use among female athletes drops below that for female nonathletes (Harmer, 2009). Interestingly, among health club members who were asked about their attitudes regarding steroid use, there was less tolerance for use for performance enhancement than use to improve appearance (Dawes, Dukes, Elder, Melrose, & Ocker, 2013).

SEXUAL RISK PREVENTION AND THE FEMALE ATHLETE

For adolescent girls, under certain conditions, athletic participation is linked to a reduction in risky sexual behaviors, such as early sexual initiation, multiple sex partners, or unprotected sex (Dodge & Jaccard, 2002; Eitle & Eitle, 2002; Erkut & Tracy, 2000; Lehman & Koerner, 2004; Miller, Miller, Verhegge, Linville, & Pumariega, 2002).

Although one study of middle and high school–age girls found that athletes were more likely to engage in oral sex and sexual intercourse than their nonathletic peers (Habel, Dittus, DeRosa, Chung, & Kerndt, 2010), sexually active athletes may be more likely to practice safe sex than their peers. Among sexually active girls, those in organized team sports were more likely to use condoms, discuss sexual histories with partners, and seek out information and services related to sexual health (Lehman & Koerner, 2004). Explanations for why young female athletes engage in less risky sexual behavior include the following:

- Adolescent female athletes may have more inner resources for handling sexual situations, including greater self-esteem, coping skills, a sense of self-empowerment, and physical strength.

- Adolescent female athletes have an incentive to avoid risky behaviors that would result in interference with their training and opportunity to play (i.e., avoid getting pregnant).

- Adolescent female athletes simply have fewer opportunities to confront issues of sexual experimentation because they have less time after school as a result of their participation in sport activities that are organized and supervised.

For female athletes, the protective effects of sport participation actually lessen as they get older and move on to college. The connections between college sport participation, unsafe sex, and excessive drinking have been reported in several studies (Faurie, Pontier, & Raymond, 2004; Grossbard, Lee, Neighbors, Hendershot, & Larimer, 2007), which "found that female college athletes are actually at higher risk than their nonathlete peers for some forms of unsafe sex, particularly in the context of heavy drinking" (Staurowsky et al., 2015, p. 76). In a recent nationally representative study of more than 20,000 college athletes, 8 percent of female college athletes reported having unprotected sex during the past year and 9 percent reported having had multiple sex partners (Huang, Jacobs, & Derevensky, 2010).

While it was assumed at one time that female athletes were less likely to be sexually assaulted, research has offered equivocal findings here as well. One study that tested the sport protection hypothesis found that female athletes were less likely to be sexually victimized (Fasting, Brackenridge, Miller, & Sabo, 2008). A later study reported that female athletes reported higher incidences of rape and attempted rape. By way of explanation, authors of that study speculated that female athletes were in situations where there was greater situational risk. The combination of female athletes drinking heavily and socializing with male athletes created conditions where sexual assault was more likely (Brown, Spiller, Stiles, & Kilgore, 2013).

FEMALE ATHLETE TRIAD: DISORDERED EATING, AMENORRHEA, AND BONE HEALTH

Many girls and women benefit in myriad ways from participating in regular physical activity over a period of time. Still, some percentage may experience one or more serious medical conditions that are referred to as the *female athlete triad.* The three interrelated conditions that make up the female athlete triad include, in their most severe forms, eating disorders (starving, binging, or purging), amenorrhea (a disruption or disappearance of a woman's menstrual cycle), and osteoporosis (loss of bone mass that weakens bones). "Although any one of these problems can occur in isolation, nutrition inadequate for a woman's level of physical activity often begins a cycle in which all three occur in sequence" (IOC Medical Commission Working Group Women in Sport, 2006, p. 2).

Female athletes are susceptible to triggers that prompt disordered eating behaviors, which fall somewhere on a continuum between healthy and pathological eating patterns (Sundot-Borgen & Torstveit, 2010). As the body adjusts to working without proper nutrition, a female athlete faces the loss of several or more consecutive menstrual periods. Calcium and bone loss potentially follow as the body searches for ways to compensate for not having the nutrients and fuel it needs to function. This loss increases risk of stress fractures of the bones.

While any female athlete can develop the triad, adolescent girls are most at risk because of the active biological changes and growth spurts, peer and social pressures, and rapidly changing life circumstances that go along with the teenage years. In a study reported in the *Archives of Pediatric and Adolescent Medicine*, twenty percent of female high school athletes in the state of California were found to exhibit at least one symptom of the female athlete triad (Nichols, Rauh, Lawson, Ji, & Barkai, 2006).

A propensity to worry about body weight, body shape and figure, and food is something that female athletes share with many other women. "The prevalence of disordered eating ranges from 0% to 27% in female athletes and ranges from 0% to 21% in the general population" (Coelho, Gomes, Ribeiro, & Soares, 2014, p. 106). The connection between disordered eating and eating disorders may be stronger in elite female athletes compared to female nonathletes. In a study of women with disordered eating behaviors, 18 percent of the elite athletes and 5 percent of the nonathletes were diagnosed with eating disorders following clinical interviews (Sundot-Bergot, 1993).

Abnormal eating behaviors along with weight-loss strategies fill in the continuum of disordered eating. For a female athlete affected by disordered eating, healthy eating habits give way to efforts to lose weight, lose body fat, become more fit, and look better by resorting to idiosyncratic food selections (such as choosing only low-fat foods and limiting food intake) and adopting strategies to lose water weight through excessive exercise while wearing layers of clothing. Decisions around food become more and more extreme, leading to eating disorders such as anorexia nervosa (starvation) or bulimia nervosa (binging and purging). Among the female athlete population, another syndrome, known as anorexia athletica, may manifest. A female athlete with this kind of disorder will eat just enough to keep herself going in terms of her sport, but her energy expenditure far outpaces her energy intake. Female athletes may also be prone to orthorexia nervosa, an obsession with healthy

eating behaviors that potentially becomes disruptive in and of itself.

The athletic setting, with its emphasis on the body, human performance, and competitive advantage, creates an environment where athletes are at risk for developing abnormal eating behaviors and eating disorders. While athletes in all sports are affected by these influences, sports that are structured around weight classes (e.g., wrestling, boxing, martial arts), aesthetic sports (e.g., diving, gymnastics, figure skating, water ballet), endurance sports (e.g., distance running, swimming, cross-country skiing, and cycling), and the flying sports or sports that oppose gravity (e.g., the high jump, ski jumping, and pole vaulting) lend themselves to preoccupations about food and weight (Coelho et al., 2014).

Among athletes who compete in weight-class sports, 94 percent indicate that they rely on extreme weight-loss strategies to make weight in order to compete. Estimates of the prevalence of disordered eating among female athletes is 40 percent in aesthetic sports, 30 percent in weight-class sports, and 15 percent in team sports (basketball, field hockey, lacrosse, soccer, softball; Coelho et al., 2014). While female athletes have greater body satisfaction than girls and women in the general population, in studies of collegiate athletes, 40.7 percent of female athletes exercised one or more hours a day to burn calories, and 15.6 percent had fasted or engaged in strict dieting two or more times in the past year (Greenleaf, Petrie, Carter, & Reel, 2009; Petrie, Greenleaf, Reel, & Carter, 2008). Among the female college athlete population, between 6.2 and 16.2 percent have been found to binge eat (Carter & Rudd, 2005; Johnson, Powers, & Dick, 1999).

Because of the vulnerability of female athletes to disordered eating, eating disorders, and the physiological implications resulting in bone loss and disruptions to the reproductive cycle, "eating disorder prevention should be a mandatory part of the educational curriculum for coaches and athletes across all sports" (Coelho et al., 2014, p. 110). Beyond sharing information with coaches and athletes about risk factors, nutrition, effect on performance, and long-term health consequences, numerous organizations—including the American Academy of Pediatrics,

Signs of Eating Disorders to Watch for in Female Athletes

Eating disorders affect the body in different ways and may manifest in physical conditions and changes in behaviors. Signs that a female athlete may be suffering from an eating disorder include the following (National Eating Disorders Association, 2011):

- **Attitude changes**: being impatient, cranky, unhappy, or obsessed or preoccupied about food (restricting food, not eating, eating only selected items); avoiding drinking water because of concerns about weight gain and water retention; exhibiting excessive concerns about appearance or perfectionism
- **Concerns about performance**: decreased energy, longer recovery times after practices and workouts, decreased coordination, slower speeds, muscle cramping, overtraining
- **Physical issues**: increased fatigue, decreased concentration, feeling cold, feeling faint or lightheaded, experiencing stomach pains and injuries, muscle tears, or joint sprains
- **Social issues**: becoming isolated and reluctant to spend time around other people, being unable to enjoy a day of rest or not working out, tensions with teammates and coaches

the International Olympic Committee Medical Commission, and the American College of Sports Medicine—advocate that international and national sport organizations and federations put forward policies and procedures that discourage risky weight-loss practices. Studies where educational programs have been used as prevention strategies have been found to be effective in educating female athletes about the risks of eating disorders, but research has not yet shown whether these programs have changed behaviors.

FEMALE ATHLETES AND INJURIES

Like all athletes, female athletes risk injury and pay the price for participating and competing. While the practical limits of this chapter prevent us from delving into an expansive discussion of the physical injuries that female athletes may sustain in their playing careers, the two most reported and discussed injuries that female athletes experience are anterior cruciate ligament (ACL) tears and concussions. Awareness of gender-specific treatment and recovery strategies have been found to be important in fully understanding why these injuries occur within female athlete populations and how female athletes recover from them.

According to Dr. Pietro Tonino, director of sports medicine at Loyola University Medical Center, the more girls who enter the sport system, the more likely it is that ACL injuries will occur (Loyola University Health System, 2014). The American Orthopaedic Society for Sports Medicine reports that female basketball and soccer players are two to eight times more likely than male athletes to experience an ACL injury. Greater female athlete susceptibility to ACL injuries peaks during adolescence and then declines (Dharamsi & LaBella, 2013).

Among the reasons cited for the great incidence of ACL injuries in female athletes compared to male athletes include hormonal and neuromuscular factors (Dharamsi & LaBella, 2013). The onset of puberty, with changes in hormonal levels leading to growth spurts and variable muscle development in female athletes leading to subsequent changes in the center of gravity, appears to account for the higher incidence of ACL tears in female athletes.

At a neuromuscular level, compared to male athletes, female athletes exert less control of knee motion during training, relying more on quadriceps muscles than their hamstrings. Girls also tend to exhibit greater prevalence of asymmetry in muscle strength, with one leg being stronger than the other. This kind of imbalance creates a situation in which the ACL is under greater strain. Girls tend to have less core strength, which results in shifts away from the center of support (Zazzali, 2013). And girls employ different mechanisms when landing from jumps, relying on bones and ligaments (Dharamsi & LaBella, 2013). When female athletes land in a bent-knee position, they are more likely to rely more on the quadriceps (muscles in front of the thigh) to stabilize the knee and balance. Male athletes, in contrast, are more likely to mobilize hamstring muscles (the muscles behind the thigh), which are typically stronger (Brody, 2010).

Expressing concern for the rise in the number of female athletes he sees in his practice, Tonino noted that "many of these injuries could be prevented with a simple warm-up program that could be done in minutes" (Loyola University Health System, 2014, para. 3). One such program is the Federation International Football Association's (FIFA) 11+, a warm-up that takes about 20 minutes to complete. In teams who did the warm-up twice a week, FIFA found a 30 to 50 percent reduction in the rate of ACL injuries among players (Loyola University Health System, 2014). See chapter 5 for a more in-depth discussion of ACL injuries in female athletes.

As a result of news coverage and lawsuits, there has been an increasing awareness in the past decade regarding athletes' vulnerability to concussions. In simplest terms, a concussion is an injury to the brain, regarded in scientific circles as a type of mild traumatic brain injury. As such, athletes who suffer from them potentially face an array of serious short- and long-term health consequences. Headaches and dizziness are the two most commonly reported symptoms. While loss of consciousness occurs in about 10 percent of athletes who experience concussions, other symptoms include nausea along with vomiting and headache, which may signal acute gastroenteritis. Dizziness is associated with the possibility that the heart is not functioning properly (acute cardiac compromise). Athletes who have been concussed could

Women in high-collision sports are at risk for concussions.

Do Headbands Provide Concussion Protection for Soccer Players?

In June of 2015, the Women's World Cup was hosted in Canada. During a first-round game against Australia, Ali Krieger, a member of the U.S. women's soccer team, was wearing a headband called the Unequal Halo, a device designed to provide protection for a player's head. After suffering the second concussion of her career a few weeks before the World Cup, Krieger opted for the perceived protection offered by the headband. According to the manufacturer, the headband is made of material used in the clothing and equipment for military and law enforcement personnel that absorbs and disperses forceful impact. Translated to a sport setting, that means that the headband reduces the force of the impact from heading the ball.

The need for and the appeal of the promise of such equipment is obvious. According to pediatricians, however, there are limits to what the headgear will do for soccer players. They point out that the sport of soccer is categorized as a mild- to high-collision sport. As a result, players may experience concussions from blows to the body or falls to the ground. Female athletes, who tend to have long recovery times and more severe effects of concussions, must be clear about what a headband will and will not do when developing strategies for protection and prevention.

To read more about this headband, go to www.sporttechie.com/2015/06/10/u-s-womens-soccer-player-wears-hi-tech-headband-prevent-concussions

also experience amnesia, distorted vision, lack of balance, sleep disturbances, depression, and attention deficit disorder (Eichelberger, 2013; Harmon et al., 2013).

Among college athletes with no history of concussion who underwent baseline testing, 59 percent reported concussion-like symptoms in the prior year. At the high school level, 50 to 84 percent of athletes with no history of concussion reported concussion-like symptoms in the prior year (Harmon et al., 2013).

Among individuals of high school and college age (15 to 25 years), motor vehicle crashes are the leading cause of concussions, followed by sport-related hits and injuries. In the United States, approximately 300,000 sport-related concussions are reported each year. Athletes are more likely to experience concussions when they are competing in a game rather than at practice. And while football reports the highest concussion rate among high school athletes, girls' soccer reports the second highest incidence (8.2%), followed by boys' wrestling (5.8%) and girls' basketball (5.5%). In gender-comparable

sports, girls had a higher concussion rate (1.7 per 10,000 athlete exposures) than boys (1.0 per 10,000 exposures; Marar, McIlvain, Fields, & Comstock, 2012). Concussion prevalence among high school athletes in Maine who completed baseline preseason testing using a program called ImPACT revealed that out of 2,312 female athletes, 14 percent reported a history of one or more concussions, 3.8 percent reported a history of two or more, and 1.0 percent reported a history of three or more concussions (Iverson, Gerrard, Atkins, Zafonte, & Berkner, 2014).

Comparisons between male and female athletes who compete in sports with similar rules (i.e., soccer, basketball, softball/baseball, wrestling) reveal that female athletes experience a higher number of symptoms than male athletes. Further, the concussion symptoms last longer for female athletes, and it takes girls and women longer to recover (Harmon et al., 2013).

A number of reasons have been offered to explain why female athletes may suffer symptoms longer and experience symptoms with greater severity. First, there is some speculation that the neck muscles for female athletes are not as well developed or as large as those of male athletes. Second, estrogen and differences in terms of the flow of blood to the brain may contribute to more severe symptoms among female athletes and the length of their recovery from concussion. Third, core strength for female athletes may also be a consideration (Franks, 2013; Harmon et al., 2013).

Learning Aids

Summary

Kim Chiarelli's story shows the benefits of sport participation for girls and women. Sport became a vehicle to allow Chiarelli to realize her considerable athletic and leadership talents and to build social networks. She found ways to blend her interest in athletics with her academic interests that led to a career opportunity in sports media relations. Strong and confident, Chiarelli takes on challenges that others would not dare risk. Described as a mentally tough competitor, Chiarelli has the outlook to succeed and prevail when challenged. Her commitment to being physically strong and healthy through exercise and balanced nutrition and to taking good care of herself set the foundation for good health in the present, and anticipates a good quality of life in the future.

Madison Holleran's story, in turn, reminds us that female athletes face challenges that are sometimes so great that when they need help, safety nets need to be in place to catch them. For all of the good that sport does, it can also present female athletes with a set of stressors that are difficult to manage.

Discussion Questions

1. Explore the efforts made within your team or athletic department in terms of educating athletes about eating disorders, alcohol and substance issues, sexual risks, and mental health issues. Assess how effective those efforts are. Do those efforts effectively address the concerns of female athletes? Are coaches sensitive to the issues that female athletes confront and responsive to their needs? Are there things that could be improved about the approaches taken to female athlete health issues? What resources exist within your community, school, or on your campus to address these issues?

2. How do female athletes respond to injuries when they occur? Interview a female athlete who has suffered an ACL injury, concussion, or some other injury that sidelined her for a time. Develop a question protocol before interviewing her.

3. Explore the team or athletic department code of conduct or training rules at your school. Discuss the purpose of those rules or codes. Are they designed to deter athletes from engaging in risky health behaviors or manage their risky behaviors around their athletic participation? Do the training rules differ by gender?

Learning Activities

1. The Tucker Center for Research on Girls and Women in Sport produced a documentary in collaboration with Saint Paul–Minneapolis public television titled *Concussions and Female Athletes: The Untold Story*. Watch the video and

write a two-page reaction to it. The video is at www.mnvideovault.org/index .php?id=22775&select_index=0&popup=yes.

2. View the lecture *Prevention of Female Athlete Triad*, presented by the sports medicine division of the Boston's Children's Hospital, and summarize the key points. The video is at www.youtube.com/watch?v=P95PSPqYbls.

Glossary

anorexia athletica—Eating just enough to keep going but not enough to keep up with the amount of energy expended as a result of training.

female athlete triad—Some female athletes may experience one or more serious medical conditions as a result of training and nutrition. The three interrelated conditions that make up the female athlete triad include, in their most severe forms, eating disorders (starving, binging, or purging), amenorrhea (a disruption or disappearance of a woman's menstrual cycle), and osteoporosis (loss of bone mass that weakens bones).

hope—The unshakeable self-belief in one's ability to achieve competition goals. ("I can think of many ways to get out of a jam.")

optimism—A general expectancy that good things will happen. ("In uncertain times, I usually expect the best.")

orthorexia nervosa—An obsession or fixation with healthy eating habits.

perseverance—Consistency in achieving one's goals and not giving up easily when facing adversity of difficulties. ("I am often so determined that I continue working long after other people have given up.")

resilience—The ability to adapt to challenges in the environment ("I do not dwell on things that I can't do anything about.")

Notes

1. The Colonial Athletic Association (CAA) has borne witness to many remarkable female athletes, including Elena Delle Donne from the University of Delaware, who was the recipient of the Honda Sports Award for Basketball in 2012-2013.

2. On May 7, 2015, ESPN ran a story titled "Split Image" covering Holleran's story (Fagan, 2015). Some thought the piece served an important purpose in encouraging conversation about mental health. Editors at the *Huffington Post*, however, cautioned that the story may have violated the National Institute of Mental Health's guidelines regarding coverage of suicide (Holmes & Turgeon, 2015). The author notes here this concern about how and in what ways these issues are covered and encourages discernment on how to engage classes in these kinds of conversation.

3. Both female and male athletes receive benefits and encounter risks associated with sport participation. Because this is a book about women and sport, the focus in this chapter is on the benefits and risks that girls and women in sport encounter.

CHAPTER 5

Physiology and the Female Athlete: Is Biology Destiny?

Katie Sell, PhD, Hofstra University
Sharon Phillips, PhD, Hofstra University

Learning Objectives

In this chapter, you will learn about the following:

- Important considerations for children and intensive training
- Differences and similarities between prepubescent boys and girls related to the development and training of athletes
- Differences between pubescent boys' and girls' development related to their fitness levels and abilities
- The influence of reaching puberty at an early age as it relates to athletic performance
- The role of girls' perceptions and how they can influence training practices
- Postpubertal physiological and structural differences between men and women that influence athletic performance
- Implications of menstrual cycle fluctuations and hormonal contraceptives on athletic performance
- Training recommendations for female athletes
- The role of the media on female athletes' self-perception

A headline in the *Indianapolis Star* in the fall of 2014 asked, Could high school sports be coed? It is a question that has endured over decades, arising every year as incursions across gender boundaries occur when an athlete, female or male, becomes a member of an opposite-sex team. While in some communities and states, those moments come and go with little notice (the girl who competes on the boys' golf team, the boy who finds his way onto the girls' field hockey team), others protest loudly at the prospect of boys and girls playing on the same team. In 1976, Ben Davis High School (Indiana) won the state volleyball championship with three boys on its roster. Within a month of that win, the Indiana State High School Athletic Association passed a rule barring male athletes from competing on girls' teams, a rule that remains in place today. The rationale for the ban is the belief that having boys on girls' teams "creates unfair competition through an overbalance of strength and ability of male contestants on teams designed for girls" (Benbow, 2014, para. 7).

Are the physiological differences between the sexes so great that the prospect of coed sport as the norm rather than the exception is unthinkable to support and impractical in reality? During the course of 2014, stories regarding girls participating in sport on an equal playing field with boys were more than just an accidental occurrence. Mo'ne Davis, the now famous youth league baseball pitcher, made history in the Little League World Series, throwing a fastball at 70 miles (112 km) an hour at the age of 13. Football player Shelby Osborne became the first female defensive back to be signed at the college level, playing on the roster of the Campbellsville University (Kentucky) team in the fall of 2014. Are these female athletes statistical outliers or indicators that assumptions about what physiological differences mean may underestimate the capacity of female athletes to compete alongside of male athletes?

This chapter focuses on research designed to understand the physiological differences between men and women in terms of sport. It seeks to understand misconceptions about female athletes and the injury prevalence and risk factors for injury that female athletes sustain that may differ from their male counterparts. This chapter also prescribes population-specific training programs. And while the question of whether the sport system should be coed will continue to be debated for some time to come, this chapter sheds some light on these topics so we can better prepare to support all girls as they gear up for the next season.

Over the last two decades, evidence-based research that dispels many training misconceptions related to female athletes has grown and the number of certified fitness professionals (personal trainers and strength and conditioning coaches) has increased. Consequently, strength and conditioning practices for female athletes have become as extensive as those used with male athletes. However, according to the American College of Sports Medicine (Thompson, 2013), the third and fourth top fitness trends worldwide for 2014 were strength training and the continued education, certification, and growth of experience for fitness professionals. This suggests that the application of training programs for female athletes is not standardized and is influenced by many individual factors that include, *but are not limited to*, sex- and sport-specific variables.

Misconceptions about how the physiology of women may affect their athletic development, adaptations to training, and performance capabilities relative to men are common. Although there are several key differences in the physiology of men and women, the comparative athletic performance capabilities of either sex are often influenced by additional factors related to training exposure, psychological readiness and motivation, and other personal factors (e.g., form and skill set required to play a sport). Research has suggested that sex-related physiological differences may influence the magnitude of specific training adaptations that are possible for female athletes (at least without significant supplementation), but may not restrict the rate of adaptations relative to men (Chandler & Brown, 2013). However, many of the sex-related differences in physiology and their consequent influences on aptitude for training adaptations and athletic performance are generally more prominent after puberty.

PREPUBESCENT TRAINING DIFFERENCES IN BOYS AND GIRLS

Boys and girls, guys and gals, gentlemen and ladies, men and women. Call them anything you like, but at the end of the day, these two sexes are inherently different in many ways, not the least of which is physical. These physical differences are not only anatomical and structural; they also play a role in the development of the athlete. This section discusses the time before puberty and how differently, or perhaps similarly, boys and girls should approach physical training.

Before talking about differences between sexes, it is important to discuss the role of training for children. Awareness and concern are growing among coaches, physical education teachers, and parents about the physical and psychological effects on children who participate at a progressively younger age and with increased intensity in sports originally designed for a post-

Overly ambitious or focused training at too young an age might affect an athlete's overall skill set later on in life.

adolescent population (American Academy of Pediatrics, 1976; Borms, 1986). The "catch them young" philosophy created a consensus that is it important to start intense athletic training before puberty (Baxter-Jones and Mundt, 2007). Due to this philosophy, many children have been trained at exhaustingly high levels, and it is has been assumed that they can handle the physical and psychological pressures that participation in elite sport can entail (Borms, 1986; Kentta, Hassmen, & Raglin, 2001; Matos & Winsley, 2007). In fact, up to the age of 8, it is recommended that both boys and girls enjoy an array of activities that will stimulate them and help them develop a generalized base of physical and movement skills followed by more specific skill instruction guised in a general setting. It has been suggested that children who specialize in a particular sport early will lack the abilities to be as widely skilled as they get older and begin engaging with more intensity (Borms, 1986) and that the athletic abilities shown by prepubescent children are not a solid indicator in predicting postpubescent athletic abilities (Williams, Armstrong, Kirby, & Welsman, 1995).

While the age of children for beginning sport needs to be taken into consideration, the next logical question is about training-related differences between male and female children. At this point, little evidence supports statistically significant differences (and the few differences found are slight) between prepubescent boys' and girls' height, weight, fitness (strength or endurance), or skill levels (Blanksby, Bloomfield, Elliott, Ackland, & Morton, 1986; Borms, 1986; Courteix et al., 1998; Faigenbaum, Westcott, Loud, & Long, 1999; Marta, Marinho, Barbosa, Izquierdo, & Marques, 2013). It has been suggested that concurrent training methods can be used to improve the conditioning and strength performance of prepubescent athletes of both sexes (Marta et al., 2013).

DIFFERENCES IN PUBESCENT FITNESS DEVELOPMENT FOR BOYS AND GIRLS

Unlike in the prepubescent stage, there are many training differences for boys and girls during and after puberty based on their physiological differences. This section discusses various physiological differences between boys and girls during puberty and how these affect aspects of their physical fitness. Understanding the basic physiological differences between male and female sexes can help in prescribing training that is tailored to individual athletes, partially based on their sex.

Girls hardly differ from boys in aerobic power during the prepubescent period; however, after the age of 14, their aerobic power is significantly lower than their male counterparts (15%). Interestingly, this maximum aerobic power in girls reaches a plateau around age 14, whereas in boys it can increase until the age of 18 (Borms, 1986). Of course, aerobic power can increase from training and decrease with age; however, this is highly individualized (Bouchard et al., 1999). The reason for continuation in aerobic power for boys and not girls is due to the variation in growth. Girls tend to have a growth spurt approximately two years prior to boys and grow to their adult height much faster. Therefore, boys are still experiencing growth factors, such as larger levers, which affect the mechanics and efficiency of aerobic activities, into their later teen years. Continuing into adulthood, for example, at the elite level male runners have a higher **maximal oxygen consumption** ($\dot{V}O_2$max) than female runners (Noakes, 2002).

The muscle weight for a prepubescent child is approximately 27 percent of their total body weight, whereas after puberty the percentage of muscle weight increases to 40 percent (Borms, 1986). Up to age 12, girls tend to be muscularly stronger than boys (Maffulli, King, & Helms, 1994). However, due to the increase in testosterone being higher during puberty in boys than in girls, boys tend to become stronger at a more rapid rate than girls, and ultimately develop greater muscular strength.

Speed is an important aspect of success in many sports. Children from 1.5 to 10 years of age have been suggested to improve in running speed (Roberton & Halverson, 1984). Boys tend to increase in their sprint velocity between the ages of 5 to 16; girls increase velocity from 5 to an average age of 14 (Borms, 1986). This

development seems to happen in two phases. Probable reasons for this are the development of the nervous system and improved coordination of arm and leg muscles. Another velocity increase occurs around 12 years of age for girls and between 12 and 15 years of age for boys. This happens because of the increase in body size with age along with the increase in muscular strength, power, and endurance. Boys have slightly higher performance levels after puberty.

INFLUENCE OF EARLY MATURATION ON ATHLETIC PERFORMANCE

Many recruitment programs have a "catch them young" mentality, fueled by the belief that in order to experience performance success in college or beyond, training and competition must begin early, and the earlier the better (Baxter-Jones, 1995). This belief has not yet been supported by research. The notion has consistently been refuted by both physical educators and medical professionals, who have proposed that participation should be the goal for prepubescent children, both boys and girls.

Many will argue that because improvements in physical fitness among young children are due to growth and maturation, it is not appropriate to use the physical characteristics of an adult, even if the criteria have been validated for a particular sport, as selection or identification criteria for future sport performance. These criteria are inaccurate, and they also discriminate against late developers (Baxter-Jones, 1995). In fact, young athletes who experience success primarily because of their size and early maturation have been found to leave top-level sport participation once when they come across athletes who have developed more slowly.

> There's a sense that the NCAA doesn't want to address this topic at all.
>
> Dom Starsia, the men's lacrosse coach at Virginia, regarding curtailing early recruitment of high school athletes

This brings up another question regarding whether or not competition levels should be organized by age. Perhaps we could replace it with the question, At what age should youth competitions use adult rules? Nevertheless, the concern about age-related competitions stays on the forefront. It is directly related to the "catch them young" mentality. For children who hope to be recruited for college, or an even higher level, competitive sport, the question as to whether they should be organized by chronological age (CA) is critical.

The identification of talent tends to be defined by the success of the athlete in CA-grouped competitions. The existing research suggests that size and overall physique are very important factors in CA competitions (Baxter-Jones, 1995). The concern with CA competitions is that using CA to categorize competitive levels does not consider maturational age (MA). MA is defined by growth and development. Growth refers to size increases in the body. Development is defined as the stage of progress toward a postpubescent state. This is particularly important during puberty because there are maturity-related differences in strength, speed, and endurance in children of the same CA.

A large number of the physiological components used to evaluate sport and fitness performance change with growth; therefore, MA should be taken into consideration when assessing levels of performance (Crampton, 1908).

Notice the year on the reference in the preceding sentence; even more than 100 years ago, it was suggested that CA is not the best determinant of sport performance. In fact, skeletal age has been found to be a more reliable predictor of sport performance than CA (Baxter-Jones, 1995). Advanced maturation positively influences aerobic power, muscular strength, and muscular endurance as well as motor proficiency and intelligence. Children differ in both physical and psychological maturity.

Sports in which weight, height, strength, and power are necessary (e.g., alpine skiing, field events in track and field, and swimming) favor those who experience early maturation (Borms, 1986). Although getting to puberty early is an advantage in many sports, the opposite can occasionally apply to girls. Interestingly, there seems to be an advantage in certain sports for girls who have not yet reached puberty and still have a prepubescent physique (e.g., diving, figure skating, and gymnastics) (Carter, 1981).

CA-grouped competition not only typically gives advantages to athletes who have matured at an earlier age, but even favors the time of year the athlete was born. The time of year depends on sport, but those who are a few months older are often favored, since a few months can mean major differences during competition. Sports in which size matters tend to have a strong tendency to recruit children whose birthdays are earlier in the year. In sports where size is not

Debunked Myths Regarding Strength Training and Physiological Adaptation in Female Athletes

Several of the most common misconceptions regarding strength training in female athletes are that weight training will lead to bulky muscles that appear masculine, chest size increases significantly following training, and heavy weights should not be lifted because this may damage connective tissue and other physiological function. Research has consistently demonstrated a lack of support for these beliefs because most female athletes do not have naturally circulating testosterone and their strength training does not involve lifting the heavier resistance needed to activate Type II muscle fibers (Baechle & Earle, 2008; Zatsiorsky & Kraemer, 2006). However, these myths are still common among the general population, so fitness professionals should be prepared to discuss these reasons with anyone experiencing initial hesitation to engaging in a resistance training program.

an advantage, the birth dates of selected athletes are distributed more evenly throughout the year (Barnett & Dobson, 2010). Once an athlete has been selected for additional training, based on height, this training begins to separate those athletes even further from children who are late to experience puberty. Once again, this reverts back to the question, Does recruitment based on the talent discovered in CA-organized competitions reward MA more than skill?

The trend of being recruited for high-level sports at a prepubescent age can have detrimental effects. The emotional health of athletes is just as important as their physicality. Girls who reach puberty early tend to experience a socialization process that does not motivate them to excel in physical exercise any longer. On the other hand, girls who experience puberty at an older age tend to be socialized into sport participation, and it is suggested that they are more able to cope with the social pressures related to competitive sports (Borms, 1986).

MENSTRUATION AND ATHLETIC PERFORMANCE

The onset of menstruation is a challenging time for young female athletes as a result of the physiological and emotional changes that may accompany **menarche**. The increased release of estrogen promotes an increase in body fat accumulation throughout the body as well as an increase in rate of bone growth. A predictable pattern of hormonal fluctuations continues during menstrual cycles throughout a woman's reproductive years.

Progestins, like estrogens, are also released in varying magnitudes throughout the menstrual cycle. These hormones may have androgenic and anti-estrogenic effects on the body; in addition to their estrous cycle responsibilities, they may also promote increased body temperature, ventilation rate, bloating (as a result of increased salt and water retention through the kidneys), and possibly increased submaximal heart rate and perceived exertion (England & Farhi, 1976; Fortney, Turner, Steinmann, Driscoll, & Alfrey, 1994; Schoene, Robertson, Pierson, & Peterson, 1981). However, the magnitude of body temperature and respiratory changes is influenced by training status or the presence of a pulmonary condition (e.g., asthma; Tan, McFarlane, & Lipworth, 1997). Training is thought to offer a compensatory effect, as shown by lower respiratory stress or impairment during athletic performance in those with higher fitness levels. However, given the potential for body temperature fluctuations during the menstrual cycle, research has suggested that athletic performance, especially endurance activities, may be more significantly affected in women when exposed to additional stressors such as extreme heat (Frankovich & Lebrun, 2000).

Hormonal fluctuations that accompany the menstrual cycle throughout adulthood may cause mood swings, as well as symptoms such as nausea, fluid retention, abdominal pain, and cramping (independent of, but further magnified by, exercise). Blood loss that accompanies menstruation can decrease hemoglobin concentrations, stimulating an increase in heart rate and ventilation rate to maintain cardiac output at rest and during exercise. Heavy periods may result in levels of iron and blood loss significant enough to develop anemia (increasing risk of fatigue and lightheadedness, as well as caloric expenditure). Blood flow through muscle tissue may also decrease due to a decreased blood volume and dilation of blood vessels (resulting also from increased salt and water retention that may accompany certain phases of the menstrual cycle), potentially impairing gas exchange mechanisms and the delivery of nutrients and oxygen to working tissue (Lebrun, 1994; Lebrun, Petit, McKenzie, Taunton, & Prior, 2003). However, during certain phases of the menstrual cycle, blood lactate production also decreases (higher during the follicular versus the luteal phase), but the research on whether this will increase endurance capacity is not well supported (Lebrun et al., 2003).

These hormonal fluctuations may also influence exercise capacity, as well as joint laxity. Consequently, knee joint laxity may be altered over the menstrual cycle (coinciding with variations in estrogen levels), leading to variations in joint mechanics and joint load for certain sport-related movements (Park, Stefanyshyn, Ramage, Hart, & Ronsky, 2009; Shultz, Sander, Kirk, & Perrin, 2005). However, despite the fact that estrogen and progesterone receptors are found in the synovial lining of the knee and cells within ligaments (Liu, Al-Shaikh, Panossian, & Finerman, 1996), research has not strongly supported a correlation between hormonal fluctuations during the menstrual cycle and susceptibility to ACL injury risk (Wojtys, Huston, Boynton, Spindler, & Lindenfeld, 2002), nor length or tendon tightness of the Achilles tendon (Burgess, Pearson, & Onambele, 2009).

Despite the potential for lower bone mineral density, research does not strongly support the increased prevalence of stress fractures in female athletes with menstrual irregularities (Ristolainen, Heinonen, Waller, Kujala, & Kettunen, 2009), but female athletes experiencing amenorrhea or menstrual irregularities are believed to be at greater risk of osteopenia and osteoporosis (which may lead to increased risk of stress fractures later in life; Brunet, 2010; Goodman & Warren, 2005). A more extensive discussion of the effects of the menstrual cycle on athletic performance can be found in an excellent summary by Frankovich and Lebrun (2000).

The debate concerning the benefits and drawbacks to female athletes using hormonal contraception (e.g., the Pill, NuvaRing, Depo-Provera) is often inconclusive. Limited research has suggested there may be a slight decrease in oxygen utilization in female athletes taking hormonal contraception (which may affect elite level performance; Lebrun, 1994; Lebrun et al., 2003), but this is not well supported, and further research into the influence of hormonal contraceptives on athletic performance is needed. The addition of extraneous hormones, particularly estrogen, was thought to impede athletic development in response to training; however, research does not support the notion that such contraception is beneficial to athletic performance or has side effects that considerably affect training capacity (Chandler & Brown, 2013; Nichols, Hetzler, Villanueva, Stickley, & Kimura, 2008; Rechichi & Dawson, 2009). As long as female athletes have been approved to take such medication (Hannaford & Webb, 1996), hormonal contraception may help lessen the severity of symptoms associated with menstruation, such as bleeding, bloating, and pain, that may also affect athletic performance (either helping physical performance or providing psychological and emotional comfort; Chandler & Brown, 2013). Hormonal contraceptive use may also help preserve bone density and decrease the thermogenic influence of progesterone (Frankovich & Lebrun, 2000; Grucza, Pekkarinen, Titov, Kononoff, & Hänninenet, 1993).

Coaches should be aware of the signs and symptoms that may accompany a female athlete's menstrual cycle so that they can monitor any decrease in performance and adjusted training programs appropriately to avoid excessive fatigue or unnecessary physiological stress. However, this may be complicated by the sensitivity of this situation (which can be difficult for strength and conditioning or sport coaches to address). Recommendations on working with female athletes and developing strategies for acknowledging and communicating about issues related to menstrual cycles and athletic performance can be found elsewhere (Women's Sport and Fitness Foundation, n.d.). However, these hormonal changes may not always necessitate modification of a training program for female athletes because the performance of many female athletes may not be significantly affected during their menstrual cycle. The magnitude of the physiological (as well as perceived social and psychological) effect that menstruation may vary considerably for different athletes, since it may be influenced by training status, magnitude of menstrual bleeding, and possibly hormonal contraceptive use (Lebrun, McKenzie, Prior, & Taunton, 1995).

Methodological differences and the influence of confounding factors (e.g., nutrition, training status) have prevented the current research from providing consistent conclusions regarding the effect of menstruation on athletic performance (maximal or submaximal aerobic capacity or muscular strength; Chandler & Brown, 2013; Frankovich & Lebrun, 2000).

POSTPUBERTAL PHYSIOLOGICAL DIFFERENCES AND PERFORMANCE VARIABILITY

After puberty, physiological training adaptations in men and women are thought to be related to a number of factors, including training program variables (e.g., intensity, frequency, volume of training), age, and sex-related differences in circulating serum testosterone and estrogen (Vingren et al., 2010). Testosterone is an androgenic-anabolic hormone that is naturally produced by the body. It interacts with intracellular androgen receptors to help increase protein synthesis within muscle and inhibit protein breakdown. Collectively, these functions facilitate muscle growth and hypertrophy when stimulated. Estrogens are a group of steroid hormones in the body that moderate the menstrual and estrous reproductive cycles in women and behave in an androgenic manner in fat and muscle tissue. Estrogens may also be involved in moderating blood clotting processes, metabolism (increasing fat metabolism to preserve and increase intramuscular and hepatic carbohydrate uptake and storage), and salt retention through the kidneys (which may increase weight gain), as well as facilitating calcium uptake into bone to increase bone mineral density (Fragala et al., 2011; Frankovich & Lebrun, 2000).

Sex-specific differences in joint-specific laxity and fat deposits throughout the body and the relatively greater accumulation of fat in women compared to men are thought to be related to significantly higher levels of estrogen and lower levels of testosterone in women (Frankovich & Lebrun, 2000). Specifically, women have additional fat deposits in the pelvic, buttock, and thigh regions and essential (lower limit) body fat percentages of around 12 percent (versus men at 3%). Research has suggested that physical activity does not alter estrogen metabolites even though improved fitness may result in greater lean body mass and altered estrogen metabolite ratios (Campbell, Westerlind, Harber, Friedenreich, & Courneya, 2005). Any changes in estrogen levels that occur in conjunction with a training program are thought to result from additional healthful behaviors (e.g., nutrition, minimal alcohol consumption, no smoking) also often observed in regular exercisers.

Body weight is a predictor of bone mass in both men and women. Peak bone mass occurs around age 20 to 30 for men and women; it starts decreasing at approximately age 50 and gradually continues decreasing with increasing age (Arabi et al., 2004; Lin et al., 2003). In women, bone mass decreases after all the following decrease: estrogen's regulation of osteoblast and osteoclast activity, mediation of skeletal response to biomechanical strain, and influence on the behavior of parathyroid hormone and calcitonin (Riggs, Khosla, & Melton, 2002). Greater levels of circulating estrogens in women are thought to contribute to quicker bone mineral loss, especially in those with delayed menarche or amenorrhea, which may affect bone health late in life (including risk of osteoporosis) (Brunet, 2010). Generally, men have greater bone diameter and cortical thickness than women, even when corrected for height. On average, women tend to be shorter than men, and they have greater relative torso length, shorter leg length, greater bitrochanteric and bicristal (hip) width, higher percentage of body fat, and smaller bone mass or thickness (Chandler & Brown, 2013). The relatively longer torso, shorter legs and arms, wider pelvis, and lower center of gravity, as well as tendency of the hips to sway when moving with increased intensity, may decrease women's efficiency of running and jumping mechanics compared to men. However, the ratio of hip strength (e.g., flexion and extension behaviors of the hamstring and quadriceps muscles) is similar for men and women (Harput, Soylu, Ertan, Ergun, & Mattacola, 2014), even though female athletes may tend to rely more on quadriceps strength during isokinetic anterior tibial translation compared to men, who may show greater reliance on hamstring strength for knee stabilization (Huston & Wojtys, 1996). Consequently, the aforementioned morphological and structural differences may help explain research findings that suggest women have better flexibility and agility, as well as increased accuracy and precision of movement (Kibler, Chandler, Uhi, & Maddus, 1989; McHugh, Magnusson, Gleim, & Nicholas, 1992).

Potential for muscle mass growth, age, training experience, fitness level, and changes in body composition in male versus female athletes may affect mechanism and magnitude of possible physiological adaptations. Men have higher levels of circulating testosterone than women and significantly higher testosterone release following resistance training compared to women, for whom research has often been equivocal in the magnitude of posttraining serum testosterone release (Vingren et al., 2010). Although men and women do not differ in the level of muscular force generation per muscle unit or the capacity of active muscle to generate ATP aerobically, the greater testosterone release in response to training stimulus may allow for greater potential for intramuscular protein synthesis in men (Haff & Triplett, 2015; Kvorning, Andersen, Brixen, & Madsen, 2006). However, recent research has questioned whether physiological changes in anabolic hormones after exercise promote muscle protein synthesis or if other intramuscular factors (e.g., increases in skeletal muscle androgen receptor protein) are responsible since increases in myofibrillar protein synthesis have been shown in the absence of postexercise testosterone increases (Mitchell et al., 2013; West et al., 2012). In both men and women, the training program and the age and experience level of the individual may influence which physiological mechanisms signal increases in muscle-related metabolism (e.g., protein synthesis, muscle hypertrophy, strength and power in response to training stimulus; Haff & Triplett, 2015; West et al., 2012).

Lower testosterone levels are also related to lower hemoglobin levels and subsequent decreased oxygen-carrying capacity. Coupled with relatively smaller hearts and higher body fat, women typically average 15 to 30 percent lower maximal aerobic capacity than men (Hutchinson, Cureton, Outz, & Wilson, 1991; Juhas, 2011). This difference in hemoglobin levels (men typically have 10-14% greater levels of Hb) is consistent across trained and untrained individuals. The lower hemoglobin levels also helps explain higher resting heart rates in women and the larger cardiac output in teenage girls and women compared to their male counterparts, but this is removed when body size and fitness status are similar (Dewey, Rosenthal, Murphy, Froelicher, & Ashley, 2008; Malczewska-Lenczowska, Sitkowski, Orysiak, Pokrywka, & Szygula, 2013). The small sex difference in oxygen-carrying capacity is compensated for by a proportionate increase in cardiac output during submaximal exercise.

Consequently, female athletes may experience increased energy expenditure and perceived exertion compared to men engaged in an exercise bout of the same absolute intensity. However, oxygen-carrying capacity is also influenced by physical activity levels, physical fitness, body composition, resting metabolism, and other physiological adaptations.

TRAINING IMPLICATIONS FOR FEMALE ATHLETES

Despite structural and physiological differences, the rate and type of adaptation to comparable training stimulus are similar for both male and female athletes. The NSCA position statement on strength training for female athletes (National Strength and Conditioning Association, 1989, p. 30) suggests the following:

> Due to similar physiological responses, it seems that men and women should train for strength in the same way, employing similar methodologies, programs and types of exercises. Coaches should assess the needs of each athlete, male or female, individually, and train that athlete accordingly. Coaches should keep in mind that there are more differences between individuals of the same gender than between men and women. Still there are many psychological and/or physiological considerations that should be taken into account in training female athletes.

Although this position statement was written more than 20 years ago, current research still supports this notion. Men and women undergo similar neurological adaptations that facilitate initial increases in strength early on in a training program, such as increased motor unit recruitment and neuromuscular firing rate. However, the complexity of the exercise movement (e.g., simple, single-joint versus complex, multi-joint exercises) within a given program may continue to influence magnitude and rate of muscle growth beyond early anatomical neuromuscular adaptations. More complex exercises may have a longer learning curve, requiring greater time for neural adaptations, thus slowing the rate of muscle growth in the respective muscle groups (Chilibeck, Calder, Sale, & Webber, 1998; Haff & Triplett, 2015). Additional adaptations exhibited by both men and women include potential decreases in blood pressure, resting and submaximal heart rate, and body fat, as well as increases in muscular strength, endurance, and aerobic capacity (Carter, Banister, & Blaber, 2003; Frankovich & Lebrun, 2000). Men and women of a similar training status also have similar muscle-fiber distributions, and athletes with more fast-twitch fibers have shown a larger increase in cross-sectional area of trained muscle than people with lower proportion of these fibers, regardless of sex (Chandler & Brown, 2013). Research has suggested that muscle protein, cross-sectional area of the quadriceps vastus lateralis, and neurological adaptations in men and women after four weeks of high-intensity training were similar (Multer, 2001).

Although estrogen differences may affect bone mineral density, men and women experience similar rates of strength, power, hypertrophic, and muscle endurance responses to resistance training. Overall adaptations per unit of muscle are also similar in response to comparable intensity and volume of training. Consequently, for both men and women, functional training benefits from resistance training are highly influenced by initial performance capacity and health status, appropriate nutritional intake, and exercise selection, frequency, duration, intensity, volume, and rest intervals (Deschenes & Kraemer, 2002; West et al., 2012).

Differences in hormonal responses to training stimulus, body composition (and fat-free mass distribution), and anthropometric attributes may help explain sex differences in the absolute magnitude of hypertrophic muscle adaptation, power, and strength (Haff & Triplett, 2015). Women have significantly lower absolute upper body and lower body strength than men (Janssen, Heymsfield, Wang, & Ross, 2000; McArdle, Katch, & Katch, 2016). Research has suggested that women have approximately half the abso-

> My coach said I run like a girl, and I said if he ran a little faster, he could, too.
>
> Mia Hamm

lute upper body strength of men (largely due to less muscle mass in the upper torso), and close to two-thirds the absolute lower body strength, although these comparisons vary depending on the specific muscle group (Fleck & Kraemer, 2004; Janssen et al., 2000; McArdle, Katch, & Katch, 2016). Comparative to absolute strength, differences in lower body strength relative to body weight or fat-free mass between men and women are minimal, as is the difference for upper body strength relative to fat-free mass (Holloway, 1998). Kell (2011) showed that both trained men and women demonstrated significant increases (above that of a nonexercising control group) in back squat, bench press, lateral pull-down, and dumbbell shoulder press following a 12-week periodized resistance training program. Although the men exhibited higher absolute strength and women showed a greater overall percentage increase for the dumbbell shoulder press (which was attributed by the researchers to differences in training experience and familiarity), similar training responses for both men and women were observed. Consequently, priority may need to be placed on increasing upper body strength and coordination in the training or strength and conditioning program of a female athlete, especially if her ongoing training or sport performance depends on multijoint, whole-body movements. Weakness in the upper torso may delay whole-body development; therefore, by prioritizing development of upper body strength and endurance, the female athlete will increase the likelihood that her "body is proportionally strong to perform complex exercises" (Juhas, 2011, p. 44).

Individuals with larger muscle cross-sectional area have a greater capacity for force production—this is consistent across men and women (McArdle, Katch, & Katch, 2016). Trends in absolute muscular power (e.g., performance on the vertical jump assessment) between men and women are thought to follow the same trend as absolute strength. According to recent research, differences in anaerobic power capacity are not fully explained by sex differences in body composition, physique, muscular strength, or neuromuscular factors (similar trend in children and adolescents; McArdle, Katch, & Katch, 2016). Trainability, genetic disposition, and volume

Women and men can perform the same strength training programs and exercises.

and manner of training are thought to strongly influence the development of anaerobic power (Baechle & Earle, 2008; Harris, Stone, O'Bryant, Proulx, & Johnson, 2000). This is supported by research that has suggested there may be a genotype disposition to sensitivity regarding responsiveness of training stimulus across both men and women (Maffulli et al., 2013; Yang et al., 2003).

For men and women, a strong enough training stimulus (e.g., high volume or high intensity/high metabolic demand) is thought to be necessary to elicit a neuromuscular, endocrine, or related physiological response to stimulate protein synthesis and increase muscle mass (Nunes et al., 2011; Uchida et al., 2009). Although this response may include postexercise fluctuations in hormones (e.g., testosterone, growth hormone, IGF-1), recent research has suggested potential intramuscular changes (e.g., upregulation of androgen receptors) versus transient increases in circulating hormones are responsible for the

physiological stimulus that promotes muscle development and that signaling responses may differ in men and women (Gonzalez et al., 2015; West et al., 2012). For example, West and colleagues (2012) found increases in rates of protein synthesis in women who had ingested 25 grams of whey protein before and 26 hours after a high-intensity resistance training session, independent of increases in postexercise testosterone. Research has consistently shown elevated testosterone release in men following heavy resistance training, but has shown equivocal results with women, as have other endocrine responses that affect metabolic and muscle adaptation. However, estradiol (one of the most common estrogens) may also serve a protective role for women in response to exercise by serving as an antioxidant and stabilizing oxidative stress or damage, often marked by increases in creatine kinase or lactate dehydrogenase release. This protective effect is also observed when looking at the inflammatory response to muscle damage following exercise, and it is consistent with the effect of testosterone and estrogen levels on varying susceptibility for men and women to specific diseases (Fragala et al., 2011). In one study (Kraemer et al., 1998), blood profiles collected during the first week of training, after six weeks, and again at the end of an eight-week heavy resistance training program incorporating primarily lower body multijoint exercises showed higher testosterone at all phases in men versus women, and showed an overall increase in men after six weeks. Women showed an increase in pre-exercise growth hormone levels compared to men at all time points, but both showed an increase in resting testosterone after the six-week point. This delay in testosterone response in women was also observed with pre-exercise cortisol. Cortisol production increased above pre-exercise levels for both men and women after weeks 1 and 6, respectively. Exercise-induced lactate production increased above resting levels for both men and women, but did not significantly alter throughout the training program (Kraemer et al., 1998). Acute hormonal responses may also differ for men and women. Following a high-intensity, short-interval resistance training session consisting of back squat, bench press, and deadlift

(75% 1RM, descending pyramid scheme), lactate and cortisol levels increased in both men and women. A greater lactate response was observed in men, which was attributed to the greater total work completed relative to the trained women, even though no significant differences were observed in time to completion, average relative intensity, perceived exertion, or heart rate. Researchers attributed the unexpected insignificance of difference in cortisol release following the exercise bout to the magnitude of adrenal stress generated by the intensity of the exercise (Szivak et al., 2013).

Further research has suggested that resistance training may increase bioactive growth hormone in women (but with minimal change in resting growth hormone levels), and higher concentrations have been observed in women with higher levels of muscular strength (Kraemer et al., 2003). Resistance training has also been shown to increase insulin-like growth factor I in women; but as with adaptations related to growth hormone, further research is still needed to more fully understand how these hormones interact with other anabolic hormones and what mechanisms related to transportation and receptor interaction actually help these responses with facilitating muscle development in women (Haff & Triplett, 2015).

Research suggests that sex differences in the endocrine responses to exercise may affect potential mechanisms and magnitude for muscle mass growth and physiological adaptation that will benefit athletic performance. Women who have higher amounts of testosterone or an elevated response following resistance training are more readily able to exhibit adaptations to resistance training similar to men, but those with fiber composition and endocrine responses more common to their sex, a greater training stimulus may be necessary to generate these responses (e.g., considerable activation of fast-twitch muscle fibers; Häkkinen et al., 1990). Research has suggested that fast-twitch-fiber recruitment and significant testosterone release will occur predominantly at higher intensity efforts. Given that women's muscle fibers are smaller, heavy loads (~3 to 5RM > 90%) may be necessary to evoke sufficient physiological stimulus to help increase maximal strength or power (Baechle &

> *Many female athletes are afraid that picking up any weight over a 10-pound dumbbell will instantaneously give them the physique of a professional bodybuilder. This stigma must be overcome by explaining the different styles for specific outcomes.*
>
> **Anne Tamporello, head strength and conditioning coach of Olympic sports, Duke University (Bennett, 2007)**

Earle, 2008; Zatsiorsky & Kraemer, 2006). This may necessitate higher loads than some female athletes are accustomed to lifting or are traditionally encouraged to lift, given misconceptions regarding excessive hypertrophy (Juhas, 2011). However, as long as the appropriate prerequisite competencies are fulfilled, female athletes can apply the same training approaches and relative intensities as men.

Training capacity may be influenced by small differences in fuel metabolism. Women are possibly less reliant on glycogen during exercise, and they have a decreased response to carbohydrate-mediated glycogen synthesis during recovery. Estrogen may promote fat metabolism to preserve carbohydrates, thus decreasing reliance on insulin and possibly increasing blood glucose levels (Ruby & Roberg, 1994; Volek, Forsythe, & Kraemer, 2006), but this trend is also affected by variables such as pre-exercise nutritional status and muscle glycogen stores (Frankovich & Lebrun, 2000). Therefore, although protein requirements for female and male athletes are similar, carbohydrate recommendations for men are slightly higher (>7 grams CHO per kilogram for women, ~8 grams for men; Tarnopolsky, 2008). However, consistent with many of the aforementioned adaptations, short-term resistance training program adaptations concerning substrate utilization (and power output) are similar in men and women with comparable aerobic fitness and activity levels (Astorino et al., 2011). As with muscular strength and power, the rate of aerobic conditioning in response to training stimulus (e.g., long slow distance training, intervals, sport-specific training) is similar for female and male athletes (Buskirk & Hodgson, 1987; Elosua et al., 2003). However, as a result of the attenuated inflammatory response and possible differences in fuel metabolism, women fatigue more slowly and recover more quickly than men when matched for strength (Fulco et al., 1999; Hunter & Enoka, 2003). In an analysis of elite-level Ironman performance, body fat levels were significantly related to men's performance, whereas the amount of training was a more significant factor for female Ironman athletes (Knechtle et al., 2010). Given the increased reliance on fat metabolism and attenuated muscle damage in response to training, female athletes have become an increasingly prominent presence at ultramarathon events (>42.2 kilometers), even outperforming their equally trained male counterparts (Bam, Noakes, Juritz, & Dennis, 1997). However, female endurance athletes may need longer to acclimatize to training in hot external environments because they may be more susceptible to the detrimental effects of ambient heat stress due to their increased body fat levels (which may not be as much a factor in elite-level endurance athletes), fewer sweat glands, lower overall volume of sweat, and decreased capacity for capillary blood flow to the muscles (Hazelhurst & Claassen, 2006; Juhas, 2011; Marsh & Jenkins, 2002).

The manner and magnitude of training necessary for promoting or maintaining bone mineral content depends on the availability of testosterone and estrogen. Given the influence of estrogen on bone mineral balance, research has consistently supported including weight-bearing exercise or training in the strength and conditioning programs of female athletes, even those engaging in non-weight-bearing activities (e.g., swimming), and monitoring for overtraining because it may lead to decreases in bone mineral (Chandler & Brown, 2013). However, the bone mass benefits of combining hormonal contraceptive use with weight-bearing exercise are thought to be influenced by the woman's age, onset of contraceptive use, and potency of the contraceptive (Frankovich & Lebrun, 2000).

Athletes may exhibit different sex-related (e.g., Q-angle, increased laxity), sport-related (e.g., unilateral dominance), or age-related (e.g.,

sarcopenia, lower bone mineral density) predispositions or inadequacies that may need to be corrected through prehabilitation or corrective exercise programs. These programs should be individualized based on the needs of the athlete, male or female, to prepare them for a training program. However, similar prerequisite competencies for training are required (Juhas, 2011). For example, prior to engaging in resistance training or loaded movement patterns, correct form and biomechanics should be demonstrated for that specific movement pattern. This may involve correcting instabilities, immobilities, or muscle imbalances, or demonstrating minimal strength or explosive power competencies (e.g., back squat 1.5 times body weight prior to engaging in moderate- to high-level lower body plyometrics) (Baechle & Earle, 2008).

PHYSIOLOGICAL DIFFERENCES AND INJURY RISK

Comprehensive comparisons of the physiological differences and similarities between men and women have been conducted (Brunet, 2010). However, there are trends in structural and anatomical differences that are not well understood or researched, and the influence of these sex-related possible differences on athletic development or performance is not always consistent. However, several structural predispositions are present in female athletes that may affect injury risk, and understanding these may help guide corrective exercise programs (the athlete's sport will also have a significant effect on program development). For example, the carrying angle of the elbow is greater in women (cubital valgus) as a result of hormonal influences. This increased angle is thought to elevate the risk of overuse injury through friction around the elbow (Paraskevas et al., 2004).

Previous research (Ristolainen et al., 2009) has indicated no sex-based differences in the rate of acute and overuse injuries in 15- to 35-year-olds over a span of one year. However, injury type and location did differ when adjusting for sport, with men exhibiting a higher rate of injury as a result of posterior thigh (hamstring) overuse, and women showing an increased disposition to ankle overuse injury and risk for ACL injury.

Addressing the Inconsistencies in Physiological Trends and Differences in Current Research

Many of the limitations with using current research to help guide professional practice related to training female athletes result from gaps in the literature or a lack of consistency in research findings. These issues are thought to result from various methodological inconsistencies or small sample sizes used by researchers, including (but not limited to) the following (Juhas, 2011):

- Dominant inclusion of male samples and either untrained or non–elite level athletes in research exploring effectiveness of training programs or magnitude of adaptation
- Research primarily limited to basic training adaptations—does not explore more subtle changes that may affect elite-level performance
- Different measurement tools and approaches used to evaluate outcome measures
- Different training program designs used as training interventions (lack of replication across different samples)
- Need for greater diversity of athletic populations addressed in research (e.g., more sports, larger age range—youth through adults and master's athletes)
- Short-term training intervention studies (<12 weeks)

Although the volume of research exploring the benefits and precautions associated with using an increasingly diverse number of training approaches in both men and women has grown considerably (along with the volume of distribution through publications and advocacy by various governing bodies), there is still a high demand for applied, intervention-based long-term research studies that address some of the aforementioned limitations in current research.

More absolute overuse and acute injuries were observed in men, but a higher proportion of female soccer players compared to male soccer players had combined acute and overuse injuries in the knee and ankle. Researchers concluded that differences may have largely been accounted for by differences in volume of training and exposure time, but acknowledged that increased joint-specific laxity in the ankle and knee in women may predispose them in certain sports (e.g., soccer, basketball) to a higher risk of ACL injury. Research has consistently reported a higher rate of ACL injury in women compared to men involved in the same sport (with ratios differing between sports; Arendt & Dick, 1995; Chandler & Brown, 2013; Hewett, Ford, & Myer, 2006; Ireland & Ott, 2004; Wojtys et al., 2002).

Research looking at sex-related differences in laxity of joints other than knee, shoulder, and ankle is sparse, and lean-tissue mass and training volume are thought to explain a large portion of the discrepancy between individuals (Ristolainen et al., 2009).

Anterior pelvic tilt is typically greater in women than in men, and it may contribute to increased risk of lordosis and lumbopelvic instability; however, very little research has examined these trends in men or women. Greater genu recurvatum (hyperextension of the knee) may be a secondary compensation exhibited as a result of excessive anterior pelvic tilt and greater laxity at the knee joint (Shultz, Schmidt, & Nguyen, 2008), but given the ambiguity and sparseness of current research examining sex differences in these structural trends, conclusions about specific issues with pelvic tilt and hip injuries in female athletes cannot be made (Ristolainen et al., 2009). Women typically experience a greater posterior tibial slope and Q-angle than men (although this is not consistently related to a wider pelvis), and this angle is further magnified if femoral anteversion and knee valgus are present (Hvid & Andersen, 1982). A greater Q-angle increases the risk of abnormal tracking of the knee during lower extremity movement, and this may further increase risk of patellofemoral joint dysfunctions (Brunet, 2010). Women also have smaller notch widths and ACL cross-sectional area, although any relationship between these does not appear to affect ACL injury risk (Sutton & Montgomery Bullock, 2013). However, these structural differences must be appreciated so that any detrimental influence they may have on patellofemoral tracking and movement patterns can be corrected and the risk of ACL injury minimized. Female hip and knee structure increases chances of knee separation during jumping movement patterns (e.g., a drop-jump test). Although hormonal fluctuations may be a risk factor for non-contact ACL injury (Shultz et al., 2010), research has consistently recommended that additional attention be paid to jumping technique and corrective jump training programs in female athletes, particularly for those in sports that require explosive movements, since ACL injury commonly occurs during movements involving landing, cutting, or deceleration (Renstrom et al., 2008). Additional training (e.g., protocols that focus on alignment, muscle balance, and neuromuscular firing patterns) in female athletes resulted in decreased (good) knee separation (Noyes, Barber-Westin, Fleckenstein, Walsh, & West, 2005) and decreased risk of ACL injury (Renstrom et al., 2008; Sutton & Montgomery Bullock, 2013). Although research suggests that female athletes are at increased risk of injury to the contralateral ACL, both male and female athletes are at equal risk of rerupturing previously injured ACLs (Sutton & Montgomery Bullock, 2013). The increased risk of ACL injuries in women suggests that female athletes should implement strength and proprioceptive or stabilization training early on

(implemented preseason and possibly revisited on a regular basis) to promote and maintain early anatomical adaptations that strengthen and support vulnerable joints such as the knees and ankles (Juhas, 2011). A comprehensive description of knee and lower extremity physiology in women as it relates to ACL injury risk can be found elsewhere (Chandler & Brown, 2013; Lipps, Oh, Ashton-Miller, & Wojtys, 2012; Sutton & Montgomery Bullock, 2013).

However, the prevention and return-to-play management of acute ankle and knee injuries (e.g., use of orthotics, external joint supports, multi-intervention training programs to correct improper movement patterns and imbalances) have been recommended for both male and female athletes (Sutton & Montgomery Bullock, 2013). Additional examination of hip structure and function has helped develop corrective exercise training interventions to promote optimal jump mechanics and stabilize and decrease stress on the hip, knee, and ankle joints; these are specific to female athletes, especially those at risk for patellofemoral pain syndrome or other patellar tracking issues (Chandler & Brown, 2013).

Sex-based differences in lower extremity anatomy may place increased demands on core musculature in women. Furthermore, female athletes tend to have lower overall total strength, decreased proximal strength, and possibly a less stable base from which to generate force production than men. Coupled with a lack of core stability, which may be a factor in lower extremity injury, there is a strong argument for incorporating a hip and core stability and strength-based training emphasis in the strength and conditioning program for female athletes. However, muscle weakness or imbalance, poor gluteal activation, and poor core health are prominent risk factors for lower back and lower extremity injury in both men *and* women (Brunet, 2010; Croisier, 2004; Kibler, Herring, Press, & Lee, 1998). Not surprisingly, current recommendations based on evidence-based research for lower extremity injury risk reduction include building a combination of plyometric, stability, balance, strength, and neuromuscular exercise interventions that target the core, shoulder, and hip regions, and the lower extremity through an individualized training program (Kibler, Press, & Sciascia, 2006; Tse, McManus, & Masters, 2005). Previous hamstring strains and age have also been identified as independent risk factors for new hamstring strains as opposed to sex- or sport-specific risk factors. Injuries may also be explained by fatigue, high training intensity, poor mechanics, muscle imbalance, insufficient warm-up, and prior tightness (Chandler & Brown, 2013; Knapik, Bauman, Jones, Harris, & Vaughan, 1991; Wang & Cochrane, 2001).

Furthermore, the mechanism of many injuries to the torso, lower back, and upper back does not appear to be specific to sex. Scapular winging or rounded shoulders (tight pectorals, weak rhomboids and trapezius muscles) have been found to be more related to poor postural habits than sex-related structural differences. Anatomical dispositions that are a result of regular sport participation may influence movement patterns and landing or swinging mechanics. The mechanisms often linked to lower back injury are similar for men and women, with the effects of physical activity or sport-related stress, type of training, fitness, and training volume often overriding sex-based differences in physiology or anatomical structure.

WOMEN, THE MEDIA, AND PERCEPTION

Some barriers to sport performance and participation for women lie outside of the physical arena and with perceptions connected to society's opinion and view of female athletes. One such example is weight or resistance training. It has been suggested that female athletes do not train with weights for as long a time period, nor do they seemingly put out the same effort and drive, as their male counterparts (Fischer, 2005; Poiss, Sullivan, Paup, & Westerman, 2004). While many female athletes understand the importance of weight training and participate willingly, a larger group of female athletes are driven away from weight training by their perceived negative social outcomes of the activity (Gill, 2000). These perceptions have in great part been created and continued by the media.

Since Title IX came into effect, there has been an increase in female sport participation. Yet despite the 3.17 million American high school girls in 2009-2010, who made up 42 percent of all high school athletes (National Federation of State High School Associations, 2010), the media coverage of female sports equated to only 1.6 percent in 2009 (Messner & Cooky, 2010). The manner in which this small percentage of media coverage has been conducted and how female athletes have been portrayed in the media and society has affected girls and their attitudes and perceptions of many aspects of sport participation, including training practices (i.e., weight training; Heywood & Dworkin, 2003).

The media is a major contributing factor toward female perceptions of both of themselves and of other athletes. The media has influential ways of portraying female athletes: performance focused (i.e., action pictures during sport) or sexualized (i.e., scantily clad in nonathletic apparel). The second is the more commonly used portrayal (American Psychological Association, 2007). Take, for instance, Mia Hamm and Anna Kournikova. Hamm has been widely recognized for her athletic feats, whereas Kournikova has been glorified for her sex appeal.

Interestingly, research strongly suggests that both boys and girls respond well to performance-focused images, reporting that these women are talented and powerful (Heywood & Dworkin, 2003). Girls and women viewed female athletes portrayed as sex symbols as being more attractive, more sexually experienced, more feminine, and more desirable than the women in the more athletic images, but less capable, less strong, less intelligent, less determined, and with less self-respect (Gurung & Chrouser, 2007). Girls' reactions to these images are related to their own self-images. Both types of images promoted girls to focus on themselves. The performance-focused images created a focus on their own athleticism, whereas the sexualized images caused the girls to focus on their appearance (Daniels, 2009; Thomsen, Bower, & Barnes, 2004). Performance-focused images have evoked a feeling from girls and women that allows them to think about what their bodies can do, and these act as a counterweight to the overly thin, standard portrayal of women, which is all too frequently overwhelming among media images (Daniels, 2012).

Documentary: *Twisted Sisters*

Twisted Sisters is a documentary by Chuck and Marilyn Braverman that shadows three female athletes as they engage in training and preparation to compete as professional bodybuilders. The documentary discusses the physical, psychological, and emotional changes that the women underwent to compete at the elite level, including how they challenged and attempted to overcome the biological obstacles that influence physiological adaptation and growth. This documentary raises several interesting questions for discussion:

1. What practices did these female athletes engage in that enabled such extreme muscle adaptation and definition? Which of these practices is frowned on by society and why?

2. What physiological effects did steroids have on the athletes in this documentary? Were all of these changes beneficial to performance and body image?

3. How does society view the sport of professional bodybuilding for men and women?

Learning Aids

Summary

The biology of female athletes may influence certain predispositions to injury or physiological adaptation, but it does not necessarily predefine their capacity for athletic performance or magnitude of potential adaptation in response to training. Training program individualization is imperative, particularly since Juhas (2011) points out that it is not necessarily common for an athlete to display the purely female physiological and anatomical characteristics presented in this chapter. Research examining anatomical and physiological trends and differences between men and women may be misleading when nonathletic populations are included. For example, a female athlete may have atypical fat distribution, narrower hips, and wider shoulders, and may have experienced morphological or physiological changes in muscle-fiber makeup as a result of regular exercise or sport play. Furthermore, some female athletes may have the genetic (or have a slight training-induced) disposition for greater hypertrophic development as a result of a stronger hormonal response to training and an improved ability to engage in high-intensity resistance training (Fleck & Kraemer, 2004). More consistent measurement tools and research methodologies are needed for examining anatomical and physiological differences in men and women across different ages within athletic populations. Discussion on the influence of nutritional supplements or ergogenic aids (e.g., supplemental hormones) on training outcomes (rate and magnitude of adaptation) for female athletes is beyond the scope of this chapter, but a more extensive discussion of this topic can be found elsewhere (Campbell & Spano, 2011; Kersey et al., 2012; Mueller & Hingst, 2013).

It is important that the female athlete or the athlete's coaching staff understand where the particular athlete may have an increased risk of injury due to her anatomical structure, sport-specific demands, and physiological and current fitness status, rather than relying solely on sex-based differences identified in the current literature. Physiological adaptations depend on many factors, including biological or genetic disposition, psychological readiness and maturity, and appropriate training approaches based on fulfillment of prerequisite competencies and understanding of correct lifting technique and program development. Research has consistently supported the premise that female athletes can train using the same training approaches and relative intensities as men, but for both sexes, the choice of training approach should be based on physiological and psychological readiness to engage in such training (especially high-intensity programs).

Discussion Questions

1. What are the implications of menstrual cycle fluctuation on athletic performance?
2. How can injuries in female athletes that are primarily based on anatomy be prevented?
3. Why is upper body conditioning based on resistance training important for female athletes?
4. Discuss the misconceptions you had about women and their athletic abilities in relation to men.
5. Discuss the role of society in predetermining athletic ability in prepubescent children.

Learning Activities

1. What are two important safety considerations for children and intensive training?
2. Why is there a debate over the benefits or disadvantages of female athletes using hormonal contraceptives during intensive training or competition?
3. What is the role of the media on self-perception of female athletic capabilities?
4. Can you find two advertisements or commercials that promote physical conditioning for female athletes? Discuss what type of training or image the advertisement or commercial is trying to portray or promote.
5. What are five training recommendations you would provide for a strength and conditioning coach working with collegiate female athletes to optimize adherence to a training program?

Glossary

maximal oxygen consumption ($\dot{V}O_2max$)—Measurement used to determine aerobic power, or the ability of the heart and lungs to provide oxygen to working muscles to produce energy.

menarche—A girl's first menstrual cycle.

PART III

Women, Sport, and Social Location

A social location is the characteristics and qualities that shape the way we see ourselves and how others see us. All of us, by virtue of who we are—our age, physical ability or disability, ethnicity, gender, gender identity, nationality, political affiliation, race, religion, socioeconomic status, and sexual orientation—are socially situated. This section explores various social locations that female athletes and women working in sport occupy and how those affect access to participation and opportunity.

Chapter 6 discusses the experiences of women of color in sport using feminist and critical race theories. Touching on the sociohistorical realities of racism and sexism and the social processes grounded in those realities, the authors explore how women of color in sport are marginalized as a result of being positioned as the "other" within a patriarchal power structure (not White, not male). While Title IX is assumed to promote equality for women, its single-axis framework (which considers sex in isolation from intersections with other factors that affect social location) has offered limited support to women from racial and ethnic minorities. This chapter offers a fuller understanding of pathways to achieving equitable treatment for all women in the U.S. sport system.

In an examination of the issues of inclusion and prejudice as they are experienced by sexual minorities in sport, chapter 7 focuses on transgender athletes and historical and current experiences of heteronormativity, homonegativism, and transnegativism in sport culture.

An introduction to appropriate language to use when talking about transgender athletes is followed by a consideration of the physical changes that occur for transsexual athletes and the effect this may have on their athletic performance. The chapter concludes with an overview of how LGBT athletes have been viewed and treated in sport culture, as well as how coaches and athletes can foster a climate that optimally encourages athletes to be their most authentic selves and express who they are without fear of retribution.

Chapter 8 reflects on the experiences of older women in sport. While some may still assume that women in mid- and later life are no longer interested in sport, evidence shows older women's enthusiasm for sport. The array of sport interests older women pursue and the success they have as athletes are serving to reshape the way they are viewed in U.S. society. Women into their 90s are running marathons, taking up sport interests for the first time in later life, and enjoying the health benefits to be realized from remaining active. Like their younger female counterparts, older female athletes serve as inspiration.

Chapter 9 provides an overview of the issues that women with disabilities in sport encounter, situating them within the context of the broader disability rights movement and both the mainstream sport system and the sport system for persons with disabilities. The chapter begins with a brief introduction of the development of sport for people with disabilities. It next explores the legal avenues that challenged the sport system status quo and opened up opportunities for people with disabilities to play and compete. The chapter features the stories of selected women working on behalf of athletes with disabilities and concludes with thoughts on what the future holds.

This section also presents a final chapter on women, sport, and sexual violence (chapter 10). Girls and women in sport are affected by sexual violence in myriad ways, at the hands of teammates, coworkers, and authority fig-

ures (coaches and bosses). The uniqueness of the coach–athlete relationship is presented as an area of special concern due to the power dynamics that exist and the intimacy of the coaching setting. This chapter explores the prevalence of sexual victimization of female athletes and the effects of sexual violence on girls and women in the sport system. It also presents legal avenues under Title IX for holding perpetrators accountable and safeguarding female athletes in school sport settings, along with education and prevention programs.

CHAPTER 6

Experiences of Female Athletes of Color

Jacqueline McDowell, PhD, George Mason University
Akilah Carter-Francique, PhD, Texas A&M University

Learning Objectives

In this chapter, you will learn about the following:

- Differential experiences that female athletes of color face on the court and field
- Barriers that female athletes of color encounter
- Strategies that female athletes of color use to overcome marginalized experiences
- Intersectionality theory and the three forms of intersectionality
- Sport participation rates and patterns of women of color

In her book *So Much to Live For*, Althea Gibson, the African American[1] athlete credited with breaking the color barrier at two of the most prestigious tennis events in the world, Wimbledon and the United States National Tournament (later to be called the U.S. Open), wrote, "Most of us who aspire to be tops in our fields don't really consider the amount of work required to stay tops" (Gibson & Curtis, 1968, p. 59).[2] While Gibson's quotation was in reference to the work ethic and practice involved in maintaining champion status, we cannot help but wonder how her identity as an African American woman in the White, upper-class sport of tennis may have influenced her perspective. Years later, Venus and Serena Williams, also African American, would grace the same courts as Gibson with a stature, strength, and flair that were outside the conservative norm of tennis.

The coverage of the careers of these two women is demarked by positive experiences like Venus' successful fight for pay equality at Wimbledon to the negative experiences that Serena, Venus, and their father Richard described in 2001 at the Indian Wells tournament (known currently as the BNP Paribas Open)[3] (Drucker, 2009; Williams & Paisner, 2009). In a scene described by veteran sportswriter Bruce Jenkins (2013) as "one of the ugliest scenes in sports history," the Indian Wells crowd of nearly 16,000 maligned Serena when she entered the stadium to warm up for her final with Kim Clijsters by booing loudly and then turning their attention to her father and Venus when they settled into their seats to watch the match.

Throughout the match, the crowd continued to taunt Serena and cheered when she made errors. After beating Clijsters, a White Belgian tennis athlete, the crowd continued to express their disapproval by booing during the awards ceremony. Media reports indicate that the backlash against Serena was a result of speculations that the Williams sisters, at the bidding of their father, had fixed the semifinal match. The atmosphere was fueled by a perception that Venus had feigned an injury, backing out of the semifinal match with her sister the day before to clear the way for Serena to advance to the final. These claims were unsubstantiated, and despite Richard's allegations that racial slurs had been

directed at him ("Off-Court Distractions," 2001), their experiences were not deemed by the media or tournament director as being racially motivated (Douglas, 2005). After a 14-year boycott of the event, Serena finally returned to Indian Wells in March 2015; however, just as her sister had done in 2001, Serena also withdrew from the semifinals because of a knee injury.

Throughout the years, Venus and Serena have continued to dominate tennis with numerous Grand Slam and WTA titles. Instead of receiving constant accolades for their success, fellow tennis players viewed "all Williams" Grand Slam finals as "a little bit sad for women's tennis" and questioned whether the William sisters were good or bad for tennis (Nichols, 2002; Philip, 2002; Roberts, 2002). Serena would face similar taunts and boos at the 2003 French Open—and similar to the Indian Wells discourse, the role of race was discounted in that event as well (Douglas, 2005).

Specifically, during her semifinal match in Paris, Serena's performance was derailed when opponent Justine Henin-Hardenne, a White Belgian, put up her hand while Serena was in the midst of her first serve (in tennis, you get two chances to serve a ball into the court). Serena backed off of her serve because Justine had signaled that she was not ready, and the ball went into the net. The expected protocol would have been for the server to receive another first serve. The chair umpire, however, did not see that Justine had gestured that she was not ready. Etiquette generally requires that players offer information to clarify a situation like that; however, Justine remained silent. Serena lost the serve, the next four points, and eventually the match in front of a partisan crowd who clearly wanted the Belgian to win. Eight years later, after Justine retired, she admitted that she had intentionally withheld information that day as a way of countering what she described as the Williams' sisters capacity to "intimidate" their opponents (Chase, 2011). The lone voice in the media to acknowledge the role of race came from Serena's mom, Oracene Price, who explicitly asserted, "They wanted a blonde and a ponytail" (Vecsey, 2003).

Concerns about racism and sexism were, however, explicitly raised about Venus and Serena's recurrent placement on the No. 2 Court in the Wimbledon tournament. The sisters, along with many prominent players, questioned the reasons for these decisions. Greg Couch, a reporter for *Sporting News,* boldly asserted, "They still want players in white, and are stuck in a time when tennis was exclusive. Whatever their real intentions and reasons, the club looks like a walking stereotype when it deals with the Williams sisters" (Couch, 2011, para. 17). In fact, in 2010, the club spokesman acknowledged that physical attractiveness was taken into consideration while assigning players to Centre Court (Andrews, 2009). Serena and Venus have been noted for being beautiful women, but in the tennis world their beauty is denigrated because they do not "fit the typical white tennis ideal: tall, blonde and rail thin" (Couch, 2011, para. 25). In a failed attempt to be complimentary, *Rolling Stone Magazine* described Serena as "black, beautiful and built like one of those monster trucks that crushes Volkswagens at sports arenas" (Rodrick, 2013, para. 2).

Douglas' (2005) use of critical race scholarship and Whiteness offers a great counter narrative to Venus and Serena's purportedly raceless experiences in professional tennis and highlights the role that overt and hidden systemic racism and discrimination played in defining their experiences. One might ponder: Is Serena encountering racialized hostility or simply hostility? If tennis players such as Ashley Harkleroad, Anna Kournikova, Maria Sharapova, or Ana Ivanovic (all racially categorized as White) had repeatedly won Grand Slam and WTA titles,[4] would they have been treated similarly and told that it is about time they give others a chance ("The Story," 2003), or that it is "a little bit sad for women's tennis" (Philip, 2002, p. 10)?

As exemplified by Venus and Serena's experiences, female athletes of color[5] encounter challenges—positive and negative—that shape their athletic endeavors and affect their life experiences. While these challenges are significant, not all are known, and many are framed in a manner that reduces the athletes' contribution and dehumanizes their existence.

This chapter highlights additional experiences that collegiate and professional female athletes of color have faced while participating in sports in the United States and abroad. Highlighting sport participation experiences for women of color in the United States and abroad is beneficial for all women to understand the differential experiences and social realities at the intersection of marginalized race, sex, class, religion, and sexual orientation identities. A delineation of the experiences of female athletes of color serves to exemplify some of the successes and adverse treatment that they experience in their quest to succeed; however, their experiences and challenges should not be interpreted as representative of those of all female athletes of color (Collins, 2000).

LIVING ON THE MARGINS: WOMEN OF COLOR

Women of color have a range of poignant experiences, both individually and collectively, in the sport context (Bruening, 2005; Corbett & Johnson, 2000; Green, Oglesby, Alexander, & Franke, 1981; Smith, 1992; 2000). However, in sport *and* society, those experiences have been marginalized by sociohistorical realities (e.g., racism, sexism) and systemic processes (i.e., White supremacy, patriarchy) that often isolate and silence them (Crenshaw, 1991; hooks, 2000). Historical marginalization for women of color resides in the social construction and hierarchical traditions of race and gender that classify them as the "other" (Collins, 2000).

The notion of the "other" is rooted in dominant ideologies and binary categorization to justify the treatment of people and groups (Collins, 2000). More specifically, Collins connotes that classification as the "other" is maintained by the concept of oppositional differences, or binaries, in which the classification does not have meaning without its converse (e.g., black/white, male/female, and strong/weak). These pairings have oppositional differences that have meaning and significance when placed in relation with each other. Thus, women of color represent an oppositional difference to White heterosexual men that are the dominant group within the U.S. context and within its institutions. As a result, women of color are subjugated and placed on the margins (Giddings, 1984; hooks, 2000). In the context of sport, this often results in women of

Suggested Films and Documentaries About Female Athletes of Color

- ESPN's *Nine for IX* series, which includes the following:
  - *Venus vs.*—a documentary about Venus Williams' struggles with gender pay equity in women's professional tennis
  - *Swoopes*—a documentary that chronicles Sheryl Swoopes, a professional basketball player known as the female Michael Jordan, and her struggles with love, money, and personal identity
- *The Boxing Girls of Kabul*—a documentary film that follows female boxers from Afghanistan in their quest to qualify for the 2012 Olympic Games
- *Victoire Terminus*—a French documentary about women's boxing in Kinshasa, Republic of Congo
- *Bend It Like Beckham*—a film that follows an Indian girl who was raised in the traditional culture as she explores her desire to play professional soccer
- *The Gabby Douglas Story*—a film about Gabrielle Douglas, the first American artistic gymnast to win gold in both the individual all-around and team gymnastic Olympic competition in one year
- *The Longshots*—a film about Jasmine Plummer, the first African American girl and first girl in general to play quarterback in the Pop Warner youth football tournament
- *Run for the Dream: The Gail Devers Story*—a film about the struggles and triumphant return of Gail Devers, a track and field athlete who was diagnosed with Graves' disease
- *Amazing Grace: Black Women in Sport*—a documentary film that highlights the accomplishments of many African American female athletes, such as Florence Griffith Joyner, Althea Gibson, Wilma Rudolph, Zina Garrison, Jackie Joyner-Kersee, Debi Thomas, and Dominique Dawes
- *Nadia*—a film on the life of Romanian Olympic gymnast and five-time gold medalist Nadia Comaneci
- *On Thin Ice: The Tai Babilonia Story*—a film on the life of the African American Olympic champion and pairs figure skater
- *Edge of America*—a film based on a true story about the cultural challenges of a high school girls basketball team on a Native American reservation and their journey to playing an all-White girls high school team
- *Girlfight*—a film about a Hispanic young woman who trains to become a successful boxer, despite her father's disapproval and reluctance from her would-be trainers in the male-dominated sport
- *Parting the Waters*—a documentary film about the experiences and challenges of Maritza Correia, the first Puerto Rican of African descent to swim on the U.S. Olympic team, and Cullen Jones, an African American world record holder in the Olympic 50-meter freestyle

> *These women are injured, but when the race ambulance and the gender ambulance arrive at the scene, they see these women of color lying in the intersection and they say, "Well, we can't figure out if this was just race or just sex discrimination. And unless they can show us which one it was, we can't help them."*
>
> Kimberlé Crenshaw, American scholar of critical race theory

color having limited opportunities and access to positions of leadership, less pay for equal work (Abney, 2007; Lapchick et al., 2011; McDowell & Cunningham, 2009), and decreased rates of sport participation (Sabo & Veliz, 2008).

Women of color living on the margins in sport is not a new phenomenon (Cahn, 1994; Green et al., 1981). Existing as women of color, living with their intersecting oppressions, and experiencing the constant reaffirmation that they are the subjugated "other" necessitate a critical elucidation of the nature of their experiences. Thus, while famed biographies, filmed documentaries, and oral narratives capture the nature of the lives of women of color, their experiences are rarely presented within an intersectional framework. The intersectional framework, or **intersectionality theory**, is rooted in the notion of the "other" and the expression of bias, domination, and social power. The term *intersectionality* was coined by Kimberlé Crenshaw in the 1980s to explain how different forms of **discrimination** (e.g., **race**, **ethnicity**, gender, social class, sexual orientation, religion) are interrelated and how they interact (e.g., **anticategorical complexity**, **intercategorical complexity**, **intracategorical complexity**; see McCall, 2005), as well as how that interaction results in multiple, and often simultaneous, forms of social inequalities within larger systems of oppressions (Hancock, 2007). Crenshaw purports that "because of their intersectional identity as both women *and* of color within discourses that are shaped to respond to one *or* the other, women of color are marginalized within both" (1991, p. 1244). Therefore, scholarship that focuses on gender or

issues based in race or ethnicity tend to present one marginalization or the other; rarely are these issues presented as layered experiences. Thus, throughout this chapter, we will employ the concept of intersectionality to describe the diverse ways that gender, class, race, and ethnicity intersect to shape sport participation experiences for women of color.

It is within this space that the conception of intersectionality is essential for articulating the experiences of women of color, since intersectionality attempts to encapsulate multiple and contradictory experiences of marginalization (McCall, 2005). Intersectionality acknowledges that there are multiple truths and that knowledge is a socially constructed thought process that associates contemporary issues with postmodern theoretical notions. Therefore, when understanding the realities of intersectionality, it is necessary to consider the multilevel effects of oppression and identity politics, particularly the structural, political, and representation intersectionalities (Crenshaw, 1991, 1993). Structural intersectionality examines how power structures based on race, gender, social class, sexual orientation, religion, and other categorical dimensions create differential treatment and experiences (e.g., receipt of services such as health care or housing assistance) for subordinate people and groups. Political intersectionality examines how policies and practices marginalize issues (e.g., sexual harassment, domestic abuse, hiring and firing) or place one categorical oppression over another for subordinate people and groups, and thus often fail to fully articulate the nature of discrimination. Finally, representational intersectionality examines how historical and contemporary productions of images situate subordinate people and groups negatively and how any critique of such images can further marginalize or objectify these people and groups. The three levels of intersectionality also differentiate the ways in which the experiences for women of color are shaped and examine how their social categorization can foreshadow their identity and often trivialize their experiences of discrimination. Therefore, by centering on women of color and their intersectionalities, we hope to illuminate the multitude of their experiences and to demonstrate the valuable contributions they experience and provide through their sport participation.

SPORTING EXPERIENCES OF WOMEN OF COLOR IN THE UNITED STATES

In the United States, women of color have a history of sport participation; however, due to the structural, political, and representational notion of the "other," most experiences referencing female athletes of color are about Black women. Ergo, this chapter places Black women's experiences at the center, but also highlights the limited scholarship on Asian, Hispanic, and Native American women's experiences in sport.

After segregation and following **Title IX of the Education Amendments of 1972** (Title IX), women of color continue to achieve athletically; however, time and legislation have not diminished the marginalized effects of the "othered" categorization. As noted by Tina Sloan Green, cofounder of the Black Women in Sports Foundation, Title IX has had many successes, but it is limited by effective implementation. It has opened doors, but it has yet to allow for "access on all levels, ranging from skill acquisition to full professional representation" (2007, p. 26).

One of the reasons for this limited access is that Title IX focuses solely on sex discrimination, not fully addressing the needs of women of color. A legal precedent was set in *DeGraffenreid v. General Motors Assembly Division* (1977), which established that claims for single-axis-based antidiscrimination laws could be brought up for "race discrimination, sex discrimination,

> If Title IX is to fulfill its goal of sex equality in a way that benefits all women, Title IX advocacy must go beyond a male–female comparison to challenge the systemic inequalities that have given some girls and women steeper obstacles to playing sports than others.
>
> Deborah L. Brake, author of *Getting in the Game*

or alternatively either, but not a combination of both." This single-discrimination focus is problematic for women of color because it is impossible to successfully separate racial oppression from gender discrimination from their experiences (Combahee River Collective, 1995). Therefore, Black, Asian, Hispanic/Latina, Native American, and other women of color remain on the margins.

Participation Rates for Women of Color

As highlighted in chapter 2, Title IX has resulted in many successes, but these successes are usually discussed without mention of race. For instance, Drs. Acosta and Carpenter's biennial *Women in Intercollegiate Sport* reports have provided significant historic documentation of the growth of women's sports since 1977, but they present women as a homogeneous group—failing to acknowledge racial differences and disparities. In 1999, the NCAA began to collect data on its student-athletes' race and ethnicity, but historical data of trends for collegiate athletic participation of athletes of color in NCAA institutions was not highlighted until 2003 by the Women's Sports Foundation (Butler & Lopiano, 2003). The report noted that between 1971 and 2001, female athletes of color obtained a substantial increase in scholarship assistance (shifting from less than $100,000 to $82 million), and their participation rate increased from 2,137 to 22,541.[6]

In the 2013-2014 *Racial and Gender Report Card on College Sport*, Lapchick, Fox, Guiao, and Simpson's 2015 research approximated 20.6 percent of female collegiate athletes in NCAA Division I, II, and III institutions as women of color compared to 72.5 percent White women. Disaggregating women of color, 10.9 percent self-identified as Black, followed by 4.5 percent Hispanic, 2.2 percent Asian/Pacific Islander, 0.4 percent American Indian/Alaskan Native, 2.6 percent two or more races, and 6.8 percent as other or nonresident aliens. Examining the participation and affiliation of sport teams at the NCAA Division I level, women of color embody the largest percentages in the sports of basketball (59.4%) and outdoor track and field (36.2%), with Black women representing the

Soccer is the fastest-growing sport for girls in the United States; however, African American girls continue to be significantly underrepresented.

greatest number of participants in each (51.1% basketball, 26.8% outdoor track and field). The continual sponsorship of **emerging sports** by NCAA institutions have increased women's sport opportunities, but these increases have primarily been witnessed for White women and thus have resulted in limited increases in participation rates for women of color (Irick, 2014; Suggs, 2005). Sports that are currently or were previously identified as emerging sports include ice hockey, water polo, rowing, rugby, bowling, archery, badminton, synchronized swimming, team handball, and sand volleyball ("NCAA Emerging Sports Timeline," n.d.). With bowling as an exception, female athletes of color are grossly absent from most emerging sports and from other highly sponsored sports such as lacrosse, golf, swimming, field hockey, softball, tennis, and even soccer—the sport that has seen the greatest increase in participation and sponsorship since Title IX was implemented.

In secondary education, participation data from the National Federation of State High School Association (NFHS) shows that in 1971, 3,666,917 boys and 294,015 girls participated in high school athletics. During the 2014-2015 school year, these figures had increased to 4,519,312 boys and 3,287,735 high school girls participating in sports. The NFHS, however,

does not designate racial breakdowns. Similarly, at the professional and Olympic sports level, highly successful female athletes of color (e.g., Nicole Lyons, a premier female professional racecar driver; Gabrielle Douglas, a gold medal gymnast; and Venus and Serena Williams) are highlighted in the media, but systematic documentation of the number of female athletes of color participating at these levels is not available. Dr. Richard Lapchick, director of The Institute for Diversity and Ethics in Sport provides reports for the WNBA, but demographic reports on other women's professional leagues and Olympic participation are not available. This limited documentation is problematic when attempting to address inequities and create equality because without baseline data or statistics, schools, organizations, and associations remain unaware of the disproportional representation in terms of sport participation by girls of color (Women's Sports Foundation, 2011).

We need leadership that thinks about the future and asks us to invest in ourselves.

Anita DeFrantz, Olympic rower and International Olympic Committee board member

Growing Up Without Title IX

Alpha Alexander, Fitness Director at Walters State Community College, Chair of the Morristown Committee on Diversity

Can you imagine being a Black woman involved with sports in the 1960s and 1970s before the Title IX bill was passed by the U.S. Congress in 1972? Here are a few instances to consider:

I was born in Nashville, Tennessee. My father moved the family from the South to the North to supposedly avoid racism. In the meantime, while I was up North, my cousins down South had an opportunity to play basketball on the high school level. They may have not dealt with racism on the court, but, of course, they had to deal with the racism that was going on off the court in the South. My cousin told me they were going to play a school in another state and on their way to the other high school, they had to stop at a gas station. The girls needed some water and got out of the van to go to the gas station to get some. Not only did the gas station attendants make them go to the back of the station to drink the water, the attendants made the girls drink out of the same glass. When the girls finished drinking the water, the gas station attendant threw the glass away.

In another instance, one of my cousins went to Stillman College in Alabama, and people were amazed that she could play basketball. Can you imagine that women's basketball was outlawed in the state of Alabama at that time?

And finally, as a Black woman in the North, there were no sports available to me at the high school level. Therefore, I did not experience sports until I reached The College of Wooster in Wooster, Ohio. Outside of school, a friend of my mother's was teaching his sons how to play tennis, and he took me under his wing and taught me the game. In 1972, my freshman year, The College of Wooster had 13 sports for women. This was also the year Title IX became a law. I can remember wondering what this law was about. One of my coaches at Wooster took a group of young ladies to nearby Oberlin College to hear what this law was all about. Who would have known the impact that this law would have in the development of women in sport in this country? It had an impact for women, but to a certain extent, Black women did not benefit from the law.

In 2006, Alpha Alexander was named one of the 100 most influential NCAA student-athletes of the century. She is a former athletic director of Lane College, and has served in leadership positions at Temple University, the Young Women's Christian Association (YWCA), the Arthur Ashe Athletic Association, and the United States Olympic Committee (USOC). She also cofounded the Black Women in Sport Foundation (BWSF).

Barriers to Participation and Representation

Documentation of participation rates of female athletes of color provides an important account of their underrepresentation in many sports, but does not provide a full picture of their experiences in sport. An analysis of these numbers and participation trends reveals highly segregated participation patterns for women of color in sport. Therefore, an important question to answer is, What factors contribute to these inequities?

The Women's Sports Foundation's (WSF) 2003 report on female athletes of color highlighted the presence of racial clustering in five sports (bowling, badminton, basketball, and indoor and outdoor track). This clustering was surmised to be caused by "continuing racism and the disparate impacts of economic inequality on populations of color" (Butler & Lopiano, 2003, p. 6). The inequitable representation of female athletes of color in certain sports has also been attributed to socialization, inequitable education opportunities, and lack of role models at the playing level and in athletic leadership positions. For instance, in 2015, only 8 athletic directors at the NCAA Division I level were identified as women of color, and 10 and 9 women were identified at the Division II and III levels, respectively (National Collegiate Athletic Association, 2015). Furthermore, approximately 14 percent of head coaches of women's teams at all NCAA divisions were women of color. The low representation of women of color as role models and mentors has far-reaching consequences in terms of developing future female players and leaders; hence, to address participation inequities in sport, we have to address inequities in leadership at the youth, interscholastic, and college levels.

The racial clustering and low representation of women of color in nontraditional sports at the college level is also correlated to limited opportunities for girls of color to participate in these sports at the youth and high school levels. An analysis of national educational data sets (e.g., National Longitudinal Study, High School and Beyond Survey, National Educational Longitudinal Survey, and Educational Longitudinal Survey) revealed that "interscholastic athletic access and participation opportunities for females are unevenly distributed along racial lines" (Pickett, 2009, p. 163). Pickett's study also showed that in 1972, African American girls had higher high school participation rates than White girls, but by 2002, African American,

Media coverage of highly successful female athletes of color give the perception that participation rates for women of color are high, but rates are still disproportionate.

Asian, and Hispanic high school girls were 20 to 30 percent less likely to participate in sports than their White female peers. Moreover, the analysis revealed that public schools attended predominately by Black girls and boys offer African American girls fewer opportunities to participate in softball, basketball, soccer, ice hockey, volleyball, tennis, cross country, track, golf, and gymnastics. Hence, limited sponsorship of emerging sports at the high school level and increased sponsorship of these sports at the college level have reduced sport opportunities for girls and women of color (Dees, 2008; Evans, 1998).

While race, gender, and socioeconomic factors play a role in decreased participation, they also may shape the positive and negative experiences girls and women of color face in sport. For instance, in college sport, limited research has found that female student-athletes graduate from high school and college in higher numbers than nonathletes and generally report positive academic and athletic experiences (Bruening, Armstrong, & Pastore, 2005; Butler & Lopiano, 2003; Sellers, Kuperminc & Damas, 1997). However, research also suggests that "African American women student athletes' college life experiences differ in meaningful ways from both White women student athletes and African American men student athletes" (Sellers et al., 1997, p. 715). The historical, structural, and political notions of racism at the collegiate level (e.g., recruitment and retention, position placement, hiring and promotion practices), especially at predominantly White institutions of higher education, can cultivate an environment that maintains discriminatory practices and patterns of participation. The cyclical and systemic pattern of discrimination subsequently creates additional barriers to participation and representation in sport at all levels (Women's Sports Foundation, 2011).

In 2011, the Women's Sports Foundation issued another report on the state of sport participation among women of color. In the *Foundation's Position on Race and Sport*, the WSF reiterated findings similar to the 2003 report; the report noted that structural and political manifestations of racism and discrimination remain barriers to equal representation and

identified four specific barriers that affect sport participation for women of color. Mainly, in addition to the aforementioned lack of baseline data, intersecting experiential factors and barriers related to culture, stereotypes, and economic status have been identified as prominent factors affecting the number of women of color who participate in sport.

Socioeconomic Challenges

Through Title IX legislation, the U.S. Department of Education ensures that no person can be excluded or discriminated against in his or her participation in educational programs and activities, including sports, based on their sex (see chapter 2). However, as aforementioned, the law's **single-axis framework** negates discrimination based on intersecting identities. Sex intersects with race, class, and other identities to produce differential life experiences and opportunities. As a result of a racial history characterized by oppression and servitude in the United States and many countries abroad, race and class are inextricably intertwined categories. As such, people of color have a higher representation in lower social classes due to their racial categorization. Again, race and racial categorization pervade societies and institutions to include politics, education, and economics; therefore, the hierarchical categorization of race reflects economic inequalities within communities, neighborhoods, places of employment, and schools.

To delineate the influence of intersecting identities on sport participation, Sabo and Veliz (2008) analyzed various aggregate participation rates to include race, gender, **socioeconomic status**, and school type (e.g., urban, suburban, rural). They found that the participation rate for girls of color in the United States was 15 percent for those who came from families with household incomes of $35,000 and less. When examining the participation rates for girls of color with household income at the $35,001 to $50,000 level, we see a one-point percentage increase to 16 percent participation; but when comparing this to participation rates for White boys (27%), White girls (18%), and boys of color (38%), we see a disparity. Interestingly, Sabo and

Veliz's (2008) analysis found that in general, participation rates increased for children residing in households with higher income levels; but for girls of color, there is a decline in participation and a stark disparity when compared to White boys, White girls, and boys of color. See table 6.1 for more detail.

Young girls *and* boys of color from households with lower disposable and discretionary incomes, especially in Hispanic families, often work part-time jobs or care for younger siblings after school, rather than participating in extracurricular activities such as sport (Sylwester, 2005). Children of color from lower socioeconomic classes who do have the opportunity to participate in sport may be deterred due to additional costs (e.g., uniforms, equipment, and transportation) associated with sport participation (Women's Sports Foundation, 2011). For example, a 2013 *Huffington Post* article affirms the rising cost associated with youth sport:

> In the United States, parents spend $671 on average per year to cover the costs of uniforms and the hefty fees charged for registration, lessons and coaching, and at least 1 in 5 ends up spending over $1,000 per child, every year. The result . . . is that youth sports are no longer an excellent opportunity for social involvement determined by passion and skill, but by the family's financial resources, sustaining a $5 billion-a-year industry. ("High Cost of Youth Sports," 2013)

In addition, the article highlights the most and least expensive sports (according to parents). At the top of the list are football (27%) and baseball and softball (12%). The least expensive sports were identified as track and field (4%), volleyball (3%), swimming and diving (3%) ("High Cost of Youth Sports," 2013). While the percentages ascertained from the aforementioned report are based on parental perceptions, the article is noteworthy because parents ultimately determine whether their children can participate in sport, particularly when participation involves additional costs.

Socioeconomic status, often associated with household income and school type, affects sport opportunities. For example, many urban schools with high concentrations of children of color (e.g., Black, Hispanic/Latina) lack the financial and physical resources to offer adequate and diverse sport opportunities (Brake, 2010; Sabo & Veliz, 2008). *Cohen v. Brown University* held that athletes' interests and abilities "rarely develop in a vacuum; they evolve as a function of opportunity and experience . . . and women's lower rate of participation in athletics reflects women's historical lack of opportunities to participate in sports" (1996, section 179). Moreover, sociologist Don Sabo similarly noted that "dreams, aspirations and interests are influenced by the kinds of opportunities and perceived realities that inhabit their world. If there were more programs out there, girls would play" (Murphy, 2009, para. 23). Hence, because interests are cultivated through socialization, disparities in sport opportunities limit chances for women of color to explore and develop a range of diverse athletic abilities (Sloan Green, 2007).

The "severe inequalities between school districts combined with the reality of racial stratification in schools and neighborhoods contribute to a stubborn racial gap in girls' sport participation" (Brake, 2010, p. 117). In particular,

Table 6.1   Athletic Participation Based on Race, Gender, and Economic Income

Income level (USD)	CHILDREN OF COLOR		WHITE	
	Girls	Boys	Girls	Boys
$35,000 and lower	15%	25%	9%	20%
$35,001-$50, 000	16%	38%	18%	27%
$50,001-$65,000	7%	18%	23%	36%
$65,001 and higher	13%	34%	38%	40%

Sabo, D., & Veliz, P., 2008, *Go out and play: Youth sports in America.* East Meadow, NY: Women's Sports Foundation.

many women of color from lower socioeconomic backgrounds do not have opportunities to participate in many of the NCAA-identified emerging sports, such as lacrosse, rowing, ice hockey, and water polo, which are played primarily by "girls from suburban, largely white communities" (Brake, 2010). Moreover, many of these sports are being offered and recruited out of private clubs (Suggs, 2001, 2005; Wiggins, 2008), which not only limits exposure to diverse sport opportunities, but decreases scholarship opportunities that would allow female athletes of color to compete at higher levels of sport.

Stereotyping

Stereotypes are rooted in race, class, and gender ideologies that perpetuate negative, often unfounded information about people or groups. Haslam, Oakes, Reynolds, and Turner explicate that stereotypes become common because they are "shared with social groups for the simple reason that members of those groups were exposed to similar patterns of social information" (1999, p. 810). Therefore, stereotypes are the resultant process of imposing characteristics on people or groups based on their social categorization (Haslam, Oakes, Reynolds, & Turner, 1999; Oakes, Haslam, & Turner, 1994). When stereotypes are based on limited information and fallacy, they become problematic and are often linked to prejudice and discrimination.

Stereotypes, particularly those that maintain hegemonic notions of race and gender, can have a profound influence on how women of color are socialized in society by parents, the media, schools, and other institutional contexts about sport (Bruening, 2005; Davis & Harris, 1998). More specifically, negative stereotypes can influence which sports women choose to participate in and can also inhibit and discourage girls and women from sport participation (Coakley, 2007; Csizma, Wittig, & Schurr, 1988). Stereotypes can affect how much funding schools and parents provide women (Sabo & Veliz, 2008; Women's Sports Foundation, 2011), as well as how women (as athletes) are characterized and framed in the media (i.e., lack of coverage for women, lack of representative women of color/role models; Cunningham, 2011) and discussed by others (e.g., racial-gender slurs; Gill, 2011).

Gendered stereotypes in sport present challenges regardless of racial or ethnic background; however, women of color face additional challenges to participate in sport due to the hegemonic and culturally specific gender roles that undergird the stereotypes (Smith, 1992; Women's Sports Foundation, 2011). To expound, gender roles and corresponding ideologies of femininity influence how women perceive sport participation; however, when gender intersects with race in the context of sport, a multiplicative effect takes place (Smith, 1992). Thus, women of color experience sexism and racism because their cultural norms, traditions, and socialization patterns are often outside of the norms for dominant society.

For example, hegemonic notions of femininity and masculinity are used to categorize sports as masculine or feminine. Feminine sports exude delicacy, flexibility, and artistry (e.g., gymnastics and synchronized swimming), while masculine sports exude strength, power, and aggressiveness (e.g., football and basketball). These categorizations often place women of color on the margins because the sports defined as feminine are also more expensive (e.g., require a specialized coach, expensive equipment, or facility) and, as noted in the previous sections, are often supported by private clubs or suburban schools with a low representation of racial and ethnic minorities. Cahn (1994) noted that due to the categorization of feminine sports and White women's abandonment of the "masculine" sports such as basketball and track and field, African American women found a place to occupy, and in doing so persevered. Consequently, the success of African American women in these sports reaffirmed racial and gender stereotypes of African American women as emasculating, racial and gendered hegemonic notions of their intellectual inferiority and athletic superiority (Bruening, 2005; Vertinsky & Captain, 1998), and perceptions of them as amazons or lesbians (Cahn, 1994). Additionally, in the institution of sport, prevalent stereotypes about African Americans having innate running and jumping abilities have been identified as reasons why African American women are overrepresented in basketball and track and field (Bruening et al., 2005).

Althea Gibson stated that "in the field of sports you are more or less accepted for what you do rather than what you are" (2000, p. 344), but unfortunately these words do not ring true for all athletes. Limited research investigating the influence of stereotypes on sport experiences for women of color has found that racial- and gender-based stereotypes, discrimination, and **microaggressions** (subtle insults directed toward people of color, often automatically) have tainted Black college female athletes' participation experiences (Bruening et al., 2005), athletic achievement (Foster, 2003; Gill, 2011), and psychosocial development (Carter & Hawkins, 2011; Singer & Carter-Francique, 2012). Research has also found that African American female student-athletes have been stereotyped as sexual objects and have had to contend with racist and sexist comments from male athletes in the weight room (Bruening et al., 2005). Hence, as the framework of intersectionality indicates, multiple categorization can often overshadow a person's identity (i.e., race, sexual orientation) and subsequently limit the fullness of her experiences.

Stereotypes also create barriers for women of color. Being subjected to personal and public scrutiny based on race, gender, and other marginalizing factors can sour the desire of current and younger generations to participate due to possible negative experiences. Consider for example, *Jennifer E. Harris v. Maureen T. Portland and Pennsylvania State University* (2006), a U.S. lawsuit between a student-athlete and coach in which the intersection of race, gender, and sexual orientation were at the fore of the legal case. Harris, an African American female athlete attending Pennsylvania State University, was dismissed from the women's basketball team by her coach, Maureen Portland. The dismissal was the result of Portland's antigay team policy and her public proclamation of not allowing lesbian players on her team. Although Harris, to date, had not publicly identified as a lesbian, her demeanor and appearance (e.g., cornrow hair style, masculine dress) were associated with lesbianism and deemed a "bad influence" by Portland. Harris and two of her teammates, also African American, were released from the team, leaving the team with an all-White female

roster. None of the dismissed players had violated any rules at the institutional, conference, or NCAA level. These factors led Harris to feel that she was discriminated against based on her presumed sexual orientation as well as her race. To further this, the case was mediated in such a manner that reaffirmed stereotypical notions of Black/African American women. Issues of sexual orientation are generally salient, but the influence of race in Portland's decisions was implicitly evidenced in her dismissal patterns.

Cultural Barriers

Religion and gendered cultural norms and expectations inhibit girls and women from different racial and ethnic backgrounds from participating in sport. For instance, in many Native American and Hispanic homes, cultural traditions dictate that girls help with family childcare responsibilities after school, thus limiting their opportunities to participate in after-school sport activities (Eyler et al., 1998; Sylwester, 2005). Also, similar to their male counterparts, Native American female athletes have struggled for acceptance and opportunities in a predominately White sport system when they tried to move from the reservation to a more competitive or college level (Staurowsky, 2005). Also, in many Asian countries (e.g., China, Taiwan, Korea, Japan), lingering Confucian beliefs of women's inferiority to men have remained influential, resulting in limited female participation and Asian female athletes' being under the "conventional patriarchal control of coaches" (Jinxia, 2003, p. 207). Moreover, Jinxia wrote that female athletes from highly collectivistic cultures in Asia, Africa, and Latin America are often faced with a difficult choice: "whether to end their athletic career [which is associated with individualism] at a relatively early age or delay marriage and family life" (p. 207). This is because athletic career responsibilities are perceived as competing with family obligations.

The cultural significance of basketball and track and field to the African American community can also function as a barrier to participation for female athletes of color in an array of sports. Because of cultural traditions and stereotypes, African American girls are highly exposed to basketball and track through family, friends, coaches, and the media, but they are not socialized to pursue other sports nontraditional to the African American community (Bruening, 2000, 2005). Research has also found that hair can serve as a possible cultural or dermatologic barrier to participation by African American women in water activities and aerobic or gym activities that involve high sweating (Gathers & Mahan, 2014; Hall et al., 2013; Versey, 2014).

Many female athletes also face challenges with negotiating conflicting religious and sport identities in response to political, social, and cultural pressures (Benn & Dagkas, 2013). Chapter 15 focuses on the role that religion plays in defining female athletes' experiences and opportunities, but a brief discussion of religion is included in this chapter because race, gender, and religion are highly intertwined in many countries. Therefore, conversations about religion are also conversations about race and sex. In this chapter, however, we limit our discussion to the Muslim faith.

Muslim women of various races and ethnicities face constraints to participating in sports, including dress codes, exercise during Ramadan, and coed classes and sports (Dagkas & Benn, 2006). Examples include many dress code policies, such as the International Volleyball Association's requirement of shorts or a bathing suit for beach volleyball, the International Judo Federation prohibition of "any kind of head caps and cover," or the FIFA requirement that players' uniforms cannot have "any political, religious, or personal statements." These uniform policies have a disparate influence on Muslim women because they are in contrast to their religious requirements of modesty and the wearing of a hijab, or head covering (Benn & Dagkas, 2013; de Tarczynski, 2010). The importance of modesty to the Muslim faith was evidenced when Sania Mirza, an Indian tennis player, received criticism for wearing traditional tennis attire ("Muslim Group Slams," 2005).

Muslims are not a homogeneous group. Muslim people live in different "political, linguistic, economic and sociocultural situations" (Benn & Dagkas, 2013, p. 284); hence, women's experiences and challenges in sport will differ based on country of residence, social class, and family support. For instance, in countries such as Iran, Oman, and Saudi Arabia, Muslims live under Sharia law, which severely hinders women's participation in sport and physical activity, because sport is viewed as a predominately male arena (Alsharif, 2012; Carter-Francique & Regan, 2012). Many of these countries dis-

This Saudi women's soccer team must practice in secret.

courage and preclude women from competing in sports, and some female athletes have faced "political, cultural and religious resistance to participation, with negative sanctions such as exile and vilification by male Islamist clerics" (Benn & Dagkas, 2013, p. 282). For example, in 2012, Wojdan Shaherkani and Sarah Attar, the first Saudi Arabian female athletes to compete in the Olympics, were vilified on Twitter as "prostitutes of the Olympics" ("Saudi Female Athletes," 2012). In 2013, Saudi Arabian girls in private schools were allowed to participate in sport and physical education if they were in compliance with Sharia law; but as of March 2015, a ban still prevents girls in public schools from participating in physical education, and women are not allowed to spectate at public sporting events (Laboy, 2015). Other Muslim women in secular but highly Muslim countries such as Turkey or in non-Muslim Western countries may face opposition, but they have increased opportunities and support to participate in sports (Benn & Dagkas, 2013).

CREATING POSITIVE SPORTING EXPERIENCES FOR WOMEN OF COLOR

Each of the aforementioned barriers poses challenges for girls and women of color, but they can be overcome. The conclusion of the 2011 WSF report provides ways to advance athletic opportunities for women of color. The scholars and advisors suggested a multilevel approach to eradicating inequitable factors, with interventions that include grassroots participation, baseline data, financial incentives, recruitment in employment of coaches and staff, public education and imagery, media representation, and service on standing committees. Employing intersectionality theory as a guide for accomplishing each factor may be beneficial. Accordingly, this section highlights these factors and their significance within the structural, political, and representational intersectionality levels. Ultimately, each of these levels and their subsequent ways to increase participation for women of color can either directly or indirectly affect the experiences for women of color.

Structural Intersectionality

Intersectionality as a method examines the multilevel discriminatory practices that serve as structural barriers for women of color. More plainly, Crenshaw suggests, "women of color are differently situated in the economic, social, and political worlds. When reform efforts undertaken on behalf of women neglect this fact, women of color are less likely to have their needs met than women who are racially privileged" (1991, p. 1250). Therefore, it is necessary to highlight the numerical realities regarding baseline data, or rates of participation and representation of women of color, at all levels (i.e., athletes, coaches, administrators) and in all areas (i.e., schools, sport clubs, recreation, media). For example, in 2014, Mo'ne Davis made the cover of *Sports Illustrated*, making her the third African American female to appear on the cover since 2000 (Sinha, 2014). These statistics have the ability to illuminate the social realities of when and where women of color enter (e.g., *Racial and Gender Report Card*, NCAA Race and Gender Demographics).

Once the baseline data have been obtained, communities and organizations should create opportunities at the grassroots level for girls and women of color. Grassroots efforts often occur at the community or local level and serve as political gestures aimed at addressing groups that have been marginalized and overlooked within their local community and greater society. The Women's Sports Foundation (2011) contends that participation begins in grassroots programs and that greater access and opportunity are often the result of education (e.g., learning how to play the sport, gaining the skill sets to obtain the position). However, while these efforts may begin on the community level with community resources (e.g., people, finances), they warrant additional support (e.g., stakeholders, financial, political) to provide ongoing opportunities.

Thus, there is a need to garner financial support. The WSF encourages current organizations and associations that provide grants and financial aid to address issues of racial and ethnic marginalization and to strive to create programs and opportunities specifically for women of color, including sponsorship for girls and women of color to participate in sports that exceed their socioeconomic means, such as figure skating, golf, gymnastics, and tennis. Promoting financial support and providing organizations and associations with financial incentives is one way to reduce the economic barrier for girls and women of color. A number of organizations in the United States and abroad are working to dispel myths and stereotypes, reduce economic and sociocultural barriers, and create policies and positions to advocate for women of color.

For example, the Black Women in Sport Foundation (BWSF) was founded in 1992 by Tina Sloan Green, Alpha Alexander, Nikki Franke, and Linda Greene as a nonprofit organization dedicated to "increas[ing] the involvement of black women and girls in all aspects of sport, including athletics, coaching, and administration" (Black Women in Sport Foundation, n.d.). The BWSF is resolute in "facilitat[ing] the involvement of women of color in every aspect of sport in the United States and around the world, through 'hands-on' development and management of grass roots level outreach programs."

While the BWSF has enjoyed over two decades of successful development of young women through programs and outreach, still, there is much more to do. Young women in urban and rural areas continue to lack the financial, emotional, and spiritual support necessary to rise to the level of their own brilliance. Hence, the BWSF's future focus is to reach out to more of these young women and girls and provide soft and hard skills through sport, workshops, and mentoring to help them establish a strong foundation and pursue their individual personal and career goals. See table 6.2 for a list of other organizations and associations in the United States that address issues pertaining to women of color in sport.

Political Intersectionality

Experiences for women of color under the conception of intersectionality often place these women in a bind based on their race and gender in society and sport (Abney, 2007; Bruening, 2005; Carter, 2008; Carter-Francique & Flowers, 2013; Corbett & Johnson, 2000; Smith, 1992,

2000). This bind, called different names by scholars—"double bind" (Smith, 1992), "double jeopardy" (St. Jean & Feagin, 1998), and "multiple jeopardy" (King, 2007)—reifies the need for intersectionality, since women of color find themselves on the margins of equity efforts because of their overlapping oppressions of race and gender. As a result, women of color are often left out of equity initiatives that benefit men of color and White women.

In addition to promoting efforts that recruit and employ women of color in sport, there is a need to promote the engagement and representation of women of color serving on committees (i.e., hiring, standing, governance). Membership on committees can help to ensure that plans and programs serve the interest for women of color as participants, staff, coaches, and administrators and also promote a practice of inclusive excellence. Therefore, baseline data should be maintained to ensure that plans, policies, and programs are increasing access and opportunities for women of color and other marginalized groups.

Representational Intersectionality

The social categorization for women of color is intertwined with how they are culturally constructed and represented in society (Crenshaw, 1991; McCall, 2005). Crenshaw concludes that cultural imagery affects how women of color are perceived within and throughout society and its institutions; it therefore influences the interactions of racial and gender hierarchies. More plainly, the sociohistorical and sociocultural representations for women of color more often than not use negative and stereotypical conceptions (e.g., angry Black woman, sexually promiscuous) to justify practices of marginalization (e.g., glass ceiling effect, old boys' network). Education and representation will provide organizations, associations, employers, and employees with an opportunity to combat these barriers through familiarity and understanding.

The WSF advocates educating organizations, associations, and the public about the lack of women of color in sport and of positive portrayals for women *and* men of color. Organizations

Table 6.2 Associations and Organizations That Address Issues Pertaining to Women of Color in Sport in the United States

Association or organization	Platform	Website
National Association for Coaching Equity & Development (NACED)	The NACED focuses on "empowering, developing and advancing the professional careers of racial and ethnic minority coaches in athletics."	www.nafced.org
Black Women in Sports Foundation (BWSF)	The BWSF is dedicated to "increasing the involvement of Black women and girls in all aspects of sport, including athletics, coaching and administration" through grassroots-level outreach programs.	www.blackwomeninsport.org
Feminist Majority Foundation (FMF)	Founded in 1987, the FMF is focused on addressing issues for equality, reproductive health, and nonviolence. Additionally, through forums and advocacy, the foundation strives to empower women through economic, social, and political initiatives.	www.feminist.org • Gender equity in athletics and sports: www.feminist.org/sports/index.asp
National Association of Collegiate Women Athletics Administrators (NACWAA)	NACWAA coordinates a program to educate and provide strategies for women of color pursuing careers in intercollegiate athletics.	www.nacwaa.org
National Coalition for Women & Girls in Education (NCWGE)	NCWGE is a nonprofit organization dedicated to improving girls and women's educational opportunities by developing educational policies, providing strategies for equity, and interpreting and implementing issues surrounding Title IX.	http://ncwge.org • Report: Title IX at 40: Working to Ensure Gender Equity in Education: www.ncwge.org/PDF/TitleIXat40.pdf
Advocates for Athletic Equity (AAE)	The Advocates for Athletic Equity, in partnership with the NCAA, "advocate and promote ethnic minority coaches for positions of leadership at all levels of sport." The AAE's Achieving Coaching Excellence (ACE) programs work to reduce barriers through the ongoing recruitment and employment of coaches and staff. In addition, this program prepares racial and ethnic women and men for careers in intercollegiate coaching with the specific goal of acquiring a head coaching position.	http://aaesports.org • ACE women's basketball program: http://aaesports.org/sports/2015/8/3/GEN_0803150955.aspx • *Race and Gender Demographics* report: www.ncaapublications.com/p-4220-2009-2010-race-and-gender-demographics-member-institutions-report.aspx
Women's Sports Foundation (WSF)	The WSF is focused on advancing issues of gender equity and equality for girls and women in sport and physical activity. Numerous research reports and grant funding opportunities exist to assist schools and grassroots organizations with providing opportunities for sport and physical activity.	www.womenssportsfoundation.org

and associations should take the time to review marketing and promotion materials to ensure all groups are represented in positive regard. The benefits of equitable image representation include increasing sport participation, recruitment, and retention and providing role models for women of color. In addition to imagery, media representations for women of color should also be addressed. There is a charge to media and sports media entities to depict positive portrayals (i.e., images, narratives) for women of color in sport. Positive media images and narratives can encourage girls and women of color to explore a variety of sports and can educate the public that women of color do exist (Bruening et al., 2005).

Learning Aids

Summary

As highlighted in the introduction of this chapter, Venus and Serena Williams' success in the tennis world is characterized by triumphs and trials. Serena Williams' return to Indian Wells after a 14-year boycott was inspired by South African Nobel prize winner and humanitarian Nelson Mandela. In the 2015 issue of *Vogue* magazine, Serena stated that after reading Mandela's autobiography *Long Walk to Freedom*, "That's when I realized I had to go back . . . I always talk about forgiveness, but I needed to actually show it. It was time to move on" (Johnston, 2015, p. 244). Similar to Serena Williams, other women of color athletes have continued to move on despite challenges. Through determination and persistence, athletes such as Althea Gibson, Alice Coachman, Wilma Rudolph, and Rosemary Casals paved the way on the field and court for current female athletes of color. Their legacies continue to inspire other athletes to pursue social change and social justice in sport and society. Notable achievements have been made at all levels of competition, but female athletes of color continue to experience marginalization and face structural, political, and representational constraints to participation.

For female athletes of color, participation on the field and court has increased substantially since the integration of public schools and the passage of Title IX, but these increases have primarily been seen in a few sports such as badminton, basketball, bowling, and track and field. Inequities in participation have been attributed to racism, economic inequalities, socialization, lack of role models, and limited diverse sport offerings in educational institutions with higher racial minority enrollments. Moreover, the lack of baseline data at all levels of competition, cultural barriers, stereotypes, and socioeconomic constraints serve to limit opportunities for women of color in sport.

Title IX legislation has helped address many of these inequities, but as noted by professors Nancy Hogshead-Maker and Andrew Zimbalist in *Equal Play: Title IX and Social Change*, "the strength of civil-rights laws hinges on the ability and willingness of our citizens to prevent and expose violations and bring the goal of equality to fruition" (2007, p. 187). Hence, to advance women of color in sports, grassroots efforts are needed, and people in positions to effectuate policy changes and practices must address the low rates of female athletes of color participating in nontraditional sports; the limited number of staff, coaches, and administrators of color; and the limited representation of women of color. Moreover, organizations, associations, and the public need to be educated on how intersecting oppressions marginalize women of color to produce differential experiences and opportunities.

Discussion Questions

1. In 2007, Don Imus, a radio jock, referred to the African American women on the Rutgers University women's basketball team as "nappy-headed hoes." Discuss this incident from an intersectionality position.

2. This chapter identified associations and programs, such as the Black Women in Sports Foundation, that work to generate interest in nontraditional sports among girls and women of color. Discuss other ways that interest and opportunities in NCAA-emerging sports can be generated among girls of color.

3. What are some ways in which cultural barriers (e.g., religion, childcare responsibilities) can be overcome in order to include more women in sport without compromising their cultural beliefs or traditions?

4. Venus Williams was fighting for pay equity not just as a prominent athlete, but as a prominent Black female athlete in a historically White sport. How is race interrelated with gender in the fight for equity in women's sports, both in the predominantly White sport of women' tennis as well as other sports (for instance, the Don Imus and Rutgers women's basketball incident)?

5. Discuss how intersections of race and sexual orientation play a role in media portrayal and coverage of women's basketball.

Learning Exercises

1. Without looking at print or electronic media (e.g., social media), create a list of female athletes of color, along with their sport. How many athletes were you able to identify? Next, compare your list to those of your classmates. Were you and your classmates knowledgeable about a lot of female athletes of color?

2. *Check It Out: Is the Playing Field Level for Women and Girls at Your School?* This resource (www.nwlc.org/resource/check-it-out-playing-field-level-women-and-girls-your-school) can be used to determine whether male and female athletes are being afforded equal opportunities, benefits, services, and financial resources. In accordance with Title IX, the checklist, however, does not take race into account. Review the checklist and provide recommendations for additional questions that should be added to provide baseline data for female athletes of color.

3. Compare and contrast images and descriptions found in print media (e.g., newspapers, magazines) and electronic media (e.g., blogs, websites) of female athletes of color with White females in the same sport (e.g., Gabrielle Douglas and Jordyn Wieber, Venus Williams and Maria Sharapova). Discuss any similarities and differences in how they are portrayed and characterized.

Glossary

anticategorical complexity—A methodological approach of intersectionality that does acknowledge social inequalities, but does not acknowledge the role that social categories have on a person's experience.

discrimination—Actions or policies that deny a person or group equal access and treatment.

emerging sports—Up-and-coming varsity sports recognized by intercollegiate athletic governing bodies for the purpose of increasing women's athletic opportunities and meeting institutional sport sponsorship requirements.

ethnicity—A person's cultural affiliation, often based on shared history, values, norms, and patterns of behavior.

intercategorical complexity—A methodological approach of intersectionality that acknowledges the existence of social inequalities based on social categorizations.

intersectionality theory—A theoretical framework that illuminates how different forms of discrimination are interrelated and interact, as well as how that interaction results in multiple and often simultaneous forms of social inequalities.

intracategorical complexity—A methodological approach of intersectionality that reflects notions of anticategorical and intercategorical complexities. Thus, it acknowledges social categories, the challenges of social categories, and how people with intersecting categories and subjugated identities are affected.

microaggression—An unconscious, subtle, and denigrating behavior or insult—verbal or nonverbal—targeted toward individuals based on their social identity group or groups (e.g., a white woman clutching her purse if a black man approaches, telling an Asian American she speaks English very well).

political intersectionality—Examines how policies and practices function to marginalize issues or place one categorical oppression (e.g., race) over another (e.g., sex), thereby failing to fully articulate the nature of discrimination.

race—A socially constructed category based on a person's biological characteristics and traits.

representational intersectionality—Examines how historical and contemporary productions of images marginalize and objectify individuals and groups.

single-axis framework—Defined by American law, requires a claimant to identify the category to which they claim protection from discrimination; therefore, the single-axis framework, or single-axis-based discrimination, further expresses this idea of unjust discrimination due to this classification.

socioeconomic status—A class-based categorical approach that focuses on a person's material goods and economic resources; includes income, education, and occupation.

stereotype—A widely held oversimplified generalization about a person or group of people based on race, gender, sexual orientation, social class, and/or other identity markers.

structural intersectionality—Examines how hierarchical power structures based on social categorizations create differential treatment and experiences for subordinate people and groups.

Title IX of the Education Amendments of 1972—A federal law prohibiting gender discrimination in institutions that receive federal funding. It states, "No person in the United States shall, on the basis of sex, be excluded from participation in, be denied benefits of, or be subjected to discrimination under any education program or activity receiving Federal financial assistance."

Notes

1. The terms *Black* and *African American* are used interchangeably in this chapter. *Black* is used to represent the socially constructed category of a racial group, which is attributed to persons of African descent, whereas *African American* is used to represent an ethnic group of persons with shared cultural experiences and social history (Davis, 1991; Smith, 2000).

2. Gibson became the first Black woman to hold a card with the Ladies Professional Golf Association (LPGA). She is credited with breaking the color barrier in women's professional golf as well as in tennis. She served as the New Jersey state commissioner of athletes from 1975 through 1985 ("Gibson Served as . . .," 2003).

3. Indian Wells, now BNP, is one of the five major tournaments players are expected to play on the Women's Tennis Association (WTA) tour.

4. In fact, before Venus and Serena's debut in professional tennis, players such as Martina Navratilova, Christine "Chris" Evert, and Stefanie "Steffi" Graf dominated women's tennis with extended winning streaks.

5. The expression *people of color* has recently emerged as a preference over using *non-White* and *minority* to refer to Native Americans and Americans of African, Asian, or Hispanic descent. In this chapter we have chosen to use this expression because it is more inclusive; the expression *non-White* defines people by what they are not, whereas the term *minority* can convey inferiority and subordination (Clark & Arboleda, 1999; Safire, 1988).

6. During the same time period, White female athletes increased from 27,840 to 116,918. Successes of women of color are commonly attributed to Title IX, but Dees (2008) argued that *Brown v. Board of Education*, the landmark U.S. legislation that stated "separate educational facilities are inherently unequal" and unconstitutional, had more of an influence than Title IX on increasing Black women's opportunities in sport.

CHAPTER 7

Gender Identity and Sexual Orientation

Inclusion and Prejudice in Sport

Vikki Krane, PhD, Bowling Green State University

Learning Objectives

In this chapter, you will learn about the following:

- The appropriate language for talking about transgender athletes (e.g., define and distinguish the terms *sex*, *gender*, *gender identity*, *gender expression*, *affirmed female*, and *cisgender*)

- The bodily changes a transsexual athlete may undergo and the effects these changes can have on athletic performance

- Heteronormativity, homonegativism, and transnegativism and why they are problematic

- The characteristics of a sport climate in which athletes are likely to feel comfortable expressing any sexual or gender identity compared to climates in which they may feel the need to conceal diverse identities

- Allies and ally programs, and examples of them

As a volunteer with the city recreation center, you are working the desk during registration for the summer youth tee ball program. Your routine is fairly simple: Have a parent or legal guardian complete the registration form, check that everything is filled in completely and correctly, look at a birth certificate or passport to see that the age matches the registration form, collect the fee, and file the form. It's been busy, and you have registered about 30 children in the past hour. As you are quickly glancing at one child's birth certificate, the answer for gender is different from how the child appears. Thinking that you must be getting tired, you slow down and read more carefully. Sex: male. This does not match your vision of the young girl in front of you. You think to yourself that there must be some mistake. "I'm sorry, did you hand me your son's birth certificate by accident?" Her dad responds, "No, my daughter is transgender; she is a girl." Now you wonder, How do I proceed?

As we learn more about transgender children and the parents who support their child's gender inclinations, scenarios like the preceding example will present themselves more often. Some sport organizations are being proactive and developing guidelines and policies for inclusion of transgender athletes in youth sport programs. However, before diving into policy decisions, it is prudent to understand the facts and dispel misinformation and stereotypes about transgender athletes.

Let's begin by focusing on prepubescent children. Consider two 6-year-old tee ball players. Both wear the same uniform and have similar skills, and they are about the same height and weight, yet one is a girl and the other a boy. Given their similar size and ability, there seems to be no reason that they cannot be on the same team. Within sport, however, there is a strong tradition of separating boys and girls, starting at very young ages, onto different teams and leagues. This example begins to point out how sex and gender differences are socially constructed. Physically (size and skill), young children do not differ based on sex. While there may be a wide range of height, weight, and skill among 6-year-olds, for example, there is as much variability within a sex as between the sexes.

However, social conventions in sport mandate that they be divided by sex (i.e., girls' teams and boys' teams), which leads to social expectations that boys and girls will differ.

Because humans are made up of physical, cultural, social, and behavioral elements, social scientists use different terms to refer to these aspects of us. That is, "males and females have a recognizable and distinct chromosomal, hormonal, physiological and anatomical make up (i.e., **sex**), and corresponding culturally shaped **gender** (i.e., masculinity and femininity) and **gender expression** (i.e., the display of gender through dress, movement, speech and action)" (Krane & Symons, 2014, p. 120). For most people, sex, gender, and gender expression align predictably; for example, a female child is feminine, and expresses herself as female. However, some children recognize at a very early age that their body (sex) does not match what is a comfortable gender and gender expression for them (Stieglitz, 2010). These children are transgender; their gender identity is incongruent with their physical sex and their gender expression may be what is considered **gender nonconforming**. In other words, their mannerisms, hairstyle, speech, or attire are unconventional for someone of their sex (e.g., a male child who wears a dress and acts in a feminine manner). **Gender identity** refers to an internal sense of being female, male, both female and male, neither female nor male, or transgender (Enke, 2012). **Transgender** people (sometimes referred to as *trans*) have a gender identity that differs from the sex assigned to them at birth.

Equipped with a better understanding of language and terminology, the remainder of this chapter focuses on the experiences of

> Teams that operate more on inclusion always have a better chance to succeed. In the end, we all want to be athletes that are respected. It is my hope that . . . we can spread the word on celebrating our differences off the field, so we can all enjoy winning on the field.
>
> Abby Wambach, U.S. women's national soccer team

transgender athletes, both children and adults. It also explores how people with varied sexual orientations are treated in women's sport as well as the effects of prejudice based on gender identity and sexual orientation. Finally, this chapter highlights the effects of accepting and affirming sport climates.

TRANSGENDER YOUTH SPORT PARTICIPANTS

When considering youth sport, should it matter what sex a child was assigned at birth? Or should sport administrators recognize a child's gender identity when registering her or him for a girls' or boys' team? What would you do if faced with the example at the beginning of the chapter? When talking about prepubescent children, there are no physical reasons that support banning a transgender child from participating with **cisgender**[1] children (whose gender identity is consistent with their birth sex) ("Understanding Gender," 2013). The Transgender Law & Policy Institute points out that hormone levels in pre-adolescent children do not differ significantly between the sexes:

> Therefore, no hormone-based advantage or disadvantage between girls and boys exists. Prior to puberty, boys do not have any physical advantages over girls because of their physiology. Gender segregation in children's sports is purely social. It is not based on any significant physiological differences. (2009, p. 2)

Only bias and discrimination support separating trans youth from their cisgender peers. Alternatively, there are myriad benefits of supporting inclusive sport for trans youth.

Some transgender children recognize their nonconforming gender identity as young as 2 or 3 years of age (Stieglitz, 2010). When these children are forced to live contrary to their gender identity, they often become very unhappy, distant, angry, and depressed. As they get older, they may engage in self-harming behaviors (e.g., cutting) or substance abuse, develop behavioral and emotional problems, or attempt suicide

Jazz, a Transgender Youth Soccer Player

Jazz appears to be a typical 9-year-old who loves playing soccer. Because her skills have excelled, she set out to join the local all-girls' travel team in the Florida Youth Soccer Association (FYSA).

Jazz was born a male, and has the physical body of a young boy. When she was 3 years old, she was diagnosed with gender identity disorder (the formal psychological diagnosis when gender identity and the sex assigned at birth do not match). At age 5, Jazz began living as a girl. Now she looks and acts like any other girl her age and, by all accounts, she is happy and well adjusted.

When administrators realized that Jazz's birth certificate and passport both indicated her gender as male, the FYSA refused to allow her to join the girls' team. Over the next two years, Jazz's parents appealed to every administrative level in the FYSA. Eventually, the complaint was brought in front of the U.S. Soccer Federation (USSF) board of directors, who unanimously supported Jazz's right to participate on the girls' team. The USSF subsequently developed a task force to learn more about transgender athletes. This resulted in an inclusive policy that applies to soccer players at all age groups and competitive levels within USA Soccer (except the national and Olympic teams, which must abide by international rules). The policy is one of *self-determination*—players identify their own gender. Should there be a challenge concerning a player's gender, it is directed to a committee appointed by the USSF and is not addressed at the local club, state, or regional level (Torre & Epstein, 2012; Woog, 2013).

(Edwards-Stout, 2012; Spack et al., 2012; Wallien & Cohen-Kettenis, 2008). When families support their children's gender expression and recognize them as transgender, the children are far happier and better adjusted (e.g., Drescher & Byne, 2012). As in the tee ball example, the girl's parents affirm their child's expressed gender identity and support her participation in activities consistent with that gender identity. Yet even with supportive families, transgender youth are vulnerable to harassment and discrimination by other adults as well as by peers. For example, in 2013, the parents of transgender children had to fight to allow their children to use the school bathroom associated with their gender identity (Banda, 2013), attend a school dance in clothes consistent with their gender identity ("Tony Zamazal," 2013), and participate on the sport team consistent with their gender identity (Woog, 2013). Trans youth and adolescents also may experience high rates of harassment from peers at school (D'Augelli, Grossman, & Starks, 2006; Grossman & D'Augelli, 2006). Yet, when supportive adults (teachers or administrators) intervene and stop harassment, transgender children feel safe, and all students have a better experience (McGuire, Anderson, Toomey, & Russell, 2010). When transgender youth have social support, high self-esteem, and a high sense of personal mastery, they are resilient and are less affected by negative experiences (Grossman, D'Augelli, & Frank, 2011). Sport has the potential to support transgender children and help them achieve high self-esteem and personal mastery, as well as educate cisgender children and their parents.

POSTPUBESCENT AND ADULT TRANSGENDER ATHLETES

Prior to puberty, there are no sex differences between boys and girls that should prevent transgender children from playing on a sport team consistent with their expressed gender identity. But what happens after puberty? Is it fair to let a transgender teenage girl participate in a girls' league? To begin to answer this question, we must distinguish between transgender and transsexual people as well as delve into some basic physiology and endocrinology (the study of hormones).

Because sports are traditionally separated into men's and women's teams, there are sometimes questions about team placement for an athlete who is transgender.

After puberty, hormonal changes in bodies generally lead most boys to grow taller and bigger than most girls. Boys also develop more musculature, strength, and speed compared to most girls. Because the average postpubescent boy is bigger and stronger than the average postpubescent girl, our society assumes that all male athletes have a competitive advantage over their female peers. As such, questions arise, in particular, if a transgender girl or woman (who was born with a male body) wants to compete on a female team. While transgender people may not make any changes to their bodies, someone who is **transsexual** wants to "live and be accepted as a member of the other gender" (Edwards-Leeper & Spack, 2012, p. 322). They plan to, have begun, or have completed making changes to their body chemistry or anatomy to bring their physicality in alignment with their gender identity (Krane & Symons, 2014). Once a transsexual person decides to make changes to the body, she or he enters a period called transitioning. During this time, that person may change outward gender expression by, for example, altering hairstyle, changing the type of clothes worn, and becoming more masculine or feminine. Also at this time, hormone therapy often begins. **Affirmed males** (i.e., female sex assigned at birth; also called a *trans-man* or *female-to-male* [FTM]) will begin taking testosterone, which will lead to gains in lean body mass, muscle mass, strength, and bone density, as well as loss of body fat (Van Caenegem et al., 2012). They also will gain facial hair and other male secondary sex characteristics. **Affirmed females** (i.e., male sex assigned at birth; also called a *trans-woman* or a *male-to-female* [MTF]) will undergo hormone therapy that suppresses testosterone and increases estrogen in their bodies. Affirmed female athletes will experience a decline in lean body mass, muscle mass, strength, bone mineral content, and bone density, and will gain body fat (Lapauw et al., 2008; Mueller et al., 2011). It is generally accepted that after one year, affirmed male and affirmed female athletes on hormone therapy will have body physiology (i.e., hormonal balance) consistent with their desired sex. Additionally, some transsexual people will choose to have **sex reassignment surgery (SRS)**, in which changes are made to their anatomy and outward appearance.

 变性手术

The process of SRS may include multiple surgeries, in which changes are made to the breasts and genitals, as well as cosmetic procedures. Prior to SRS, medical standards of care require transsexuals to undergo at least one year of hormone therapy (Coleman et al., 2011). Thus, by the time a transsexual athlete completes SRS and related rehabilitation, her or his body (anatomically and physiologically) is similar to cisgender women or men. Research consistently supports that postoperative transsexuals have no advantage over cisgender athletes and should be able to compete as their current sex (e.g., Ljungqvist & Genel, 2005; Lucas-Carr & Krane, 2011).

Taylor Edelmann, Transgender College Volleyball Player

In 2013, Taylor Edelmann graduated from Purchase College, where he played varsity volleyball—on both the women's and men's teams. Taylor identifies as transgender. At 4 years of age, Taylor questioned his body: He wanted to know why he didn't look like his brothers. He didn't understand what he was feeling until his first year of high school when he learned about transgender people while doing research online. At that time, he did not tell anyone, and volleyball became his sanctuary. In college, Taylor continued to play volleyball on the women's team. After his first semester, he began telling friends that he was transgender and he then told his parents, all of whom were accepting and supportive.

Although volleyball had been his release in the past, once he came to terms with his gender identity, Taylor felt out of place on the women's team. "I had fun playing (on the women's team), but at the same time, I did feel like an outsider . . . I felt like I was infiltrating a female space" (DeFrancesco, 2013, para. 31). At the end of the summer, Taylor began taking testosterone. Within six months, his voice deepened, facial hair appeared, and his body fat shifted.

Taylor e-mailed the men's volleyball coach about his transition. In the winter of 2012, he joined the men's team. The transition to the men's game was challenging. The pace was faster, and Taylor was not able to score kills with the ease he'd had while on the women's team. So Taylor focused on strength workouts and gained 30 pounds of muscle to improve his game. After his junior year season, his teammates voted him as team captain (DeFrancesco, 2013; Zeigler, 2013).

Returning to the issue of transgender and transsexual sport participation, if a postpubescent athlete has completed SRS or has been on hormone therapy for one year, that athlete should be allowed to compete as his or her current sex. Many sport policies support similar stances, including those by the National Collegiate Athletic Association (National Collegiate Athletic Association, 2009) and International Olympic Committee (2003).[2] Rules often mandate that a postpubescent affirmed female athlete (who has not made any body changes) who practices sport at highly competitive levels must participate as the sex assigned at birth (i.e., on a male team); affirmed male athletes typically can compete in either gender category. Some high school associations, however, allow athletes to compete in the sex category consistent with their gender identity (Lovett, 2013).

Another consideration regarding transgender athletes is the use of a puberty-blocking intervention. Medical intervention can delay puberty so that transgender youths can avoid bodily changes that may be highly distressing for them (e.g., developing breasts for an affirmed boy), and medical professionals can delay introducing cross-sex steroids and potential surgeries until the child is able to fully understand their implications, which may include infertility (Edwards-Leeper & Spack, 2012). If an affirmed female (i.e., biological male) has puberty suppressed, she will not gain any of the sport advantages connected to increased testosterone that her cisgender male peers gain. One may argue that she should be eligible to compete with other girls her age. In all, research supports that transgender youth or those undergoing a puberty suppression intervention should be able to compete on a team consistent with their gender identity. By one year after beginning hormone therapy or SRS, transsexual athletes can compete fairly with their affirmed gender.

SEXUAL ORIENTATION AND WOMEN'S SPORT

As a high school basketball player, Susan was ecstatic when she learned that the coach of State University wanted to meet with her and her parents. Now she is listening intently to Coach Smith as she explains, "We have a family atmosphere on our team. We welcome players' boyfriends at our events. I recruit young ladies, not women of an alternate lifestyle. Other schools, like University of State, may accept that on their team, but we maintain a high level of decorum, and our athletes are exceptional people."

This scenario is common in women's sport. In the past, discrimination against women, especially lesbian women, in sport was the norm. Today, we see wide ranging levels of acceptance. On one hand, more athletes than ever before now openly reveal lesbian identities. On the other hand, we also see flagrant discrimination. In the previous scenario, why might a coach talk like this to recruits? What is the hidden message? Through veiled (and sometimes blatant) language, some coaches engage in **negative recruiting**, an unethical strategy based on myth and misconception that sometimes occurs within women's collegiate sports in which school recruiters suggest to potential students "that a rival college or university's coach is gay, or that an opposing team is 'full of lesbians'" (Women's Sport Foundation, 2011, p. 1). Negative recruiting is unethical and contrary to NCAA policy, yet it also is a common form of bias based on sexual orientation specifically aimed at college coaches (Ionnatta & Kane, 2002; Kauer, 2009; Krane & Barber, 2005). The goal is to discourage athletes from attending rival programs by supposedly besmirching the rival coaches or athletes by labeling them as lesbians.

Negative recruiting is an attack based on one's (perceived) sexual orientation and sexual identity. **Sexual orientation** refers to one's emotional and sexual attractions. Typically, in Western societies, sexual orientation is designated as heterosexual, attraction to people of the opposite sex or gender; as lesbian or gay, attraction to people of the same sex or gender; or as bisexual, which includes an attraction to both men and women (Krane & Symons, 2014). **Sexual identity** reflects a person's sense of self based on sexual orientation as well as feelings of connection to a community of others who share this orientation (American Psychological Association, 2008). Negative recruiting also is grounded in negative stereotypes about lesbians in sport, and it plays on the fears of some athletes and parents "that a gay coach or gay players might negatively influence the sexual orientation of potential recruits" (Women's Sport Foundation, 2011, p. 1).

Stereotypes about lesbians in sport are plentiful! You may hear that most female athletes are lesbian or that playing certain sports will make a girl a lesbian. There also are misplaced concerns that lesbians in the locker room will make unwanted passes at teammates or ogle them in a sexual manner. In truth, yes, there are lesbian athletes and coaches, just like we can find lesbian women in every other corridor of life. However, the other concerns are not based in fact. Still, these stereotypes affect coaches' and athletes' beliefs and actions.

> As a gay water polo player, I did everything I could to hide my sexuality from my teammates, especially in a sport that is so physical. I desperately did not want them to know the secret that I was hiding, because I didn't want them to think I was touching them inappropriately or looking at them in the locker room.
>
> Nikki, a water polo player at Cal State Monterey Bay who shared her story on the website Go! Athletes

Until relatively recently, most lesbian and bisexual athletes chose to conceal their sexual identity. As is evident from Nikki's story, this hiding still occurs. When athletes feel compelled to conceal lesbian and bisexual identities (i.e., they perceive that it is not safe to come out), stereotypes, accusations, labeling, and discriminatory treatment are fueled. It is much easier to aim bigotry at an invisible and unknown entity than at someone you know and like. No longer is it unusual to read about a high-profile female athlete acknowledging that she is lesbian. In today's media world, these women rarely make a big announcement; rather within an interview or in social media, they may nonchalantly mention a partner or their sexuality. For example, Rutgers' former athletic director Julie Hermann included the following on her official bio on the athletics department website: "Hermann and her partner Dr. Leslie Danehy are the proud

parents of a 7-year-old son, Aidan" (Buzinski, 2013). Meleana Shim of the National Women's Soccer League described herself as lesbian on her Athlete Ally profile (Athlete Ally, 2013b). But in some places today, being a lesbian or even talking about it is still taboo and fraught with bigotry. The story of Coach Rene Portland and Penn State Basketball (see the sidebar Homonegative Discrimination: Rene Portland, Jennifer Harris, and Penn State Basketball) exemplifies the worst in women's sport.

Many signs show that society in general has become much more accepting and inclusive of lesbian, gay, bisexual, and transgender (LGBT) people (e.g., the normalness of lesbian and gay characters on television shows and legalization of same-sex marriage). In 2011, the Gay, Lesbian, and Straight Education Network (GLSEN) National School Climate Survey (which has been documenting middle- and high-school climates for LGBT students since 1999) showed for the first time that a national sample of LGBT students reported "decreases in negative indicators of school climate (biased remarks and victimization) and continued increases in most LGBT-related school resources and supports" (GLSEN, 2011, pp. xvii-xviii). While this is promising, at the same time sport seems to lag behind when it comes to reducing prejudice against lesbian and bisexual athletes. The same GLSEN data, looking at only LGBT student-athletes, showed high levels of bullying and harassment in school sports and open hostility toward athletes who are not heterosexual (GLSEN, 2013). In many places, high school locker rooms are perceived as unsafe areas, and bullying is common there (Birkett, Espelage, & Koenig, 2009; GLSEN, 2011).

Negative treatment, discrimination, and bigotry toward lesbian and bisexual people are referred to as **homonegativism.** I prefer not to use the often-used term *homophobia* (defined as an irrational fear of LGBT people). When beliefs are irrational, they tend to be treated as an illness or something one cannot control. Homonegativism, however, is purposeful, and use of this term holds people accountable for their attitudes and behaviors toward LGBT sportspeople. Hostility "based on gender identity and aimed at trans people, is trans prejudice or transnegativism" (Krane & Symons,

Homonegative Discrimination: Rene Portland, Jennifer Harris, and Penn State Basketball

Jennifer Harris dreamed of going to Penn State and playing basketball for Coach Rene Portland. During a recruiting visit, Harris recalled, "I mentioned that I'd already visited Virginia and liked it a lot. She said that if that was the case, I probably wouldn't like Penn State because 'at Virginia they date women, and at Penn State they date men.' It was a strange thing to say, but at the time I was so focused on becoming a part of such a respected basketball program that her comment didn't really register with me. Penn State offered me an athletic scholarship, and I accepted" (Blatt, 2006).

Harris played for Penn State for only two years. During that time, Coach Portland accused her of being a lesbian. On two occasions, Harris was accused of dating a teammate and truthfully responded that they were friends. Coach Portland made it clear that this was unacceptable on her team and threatened to kick her off the team if she found out Harris was a lesbian.

During her sophomore year, Harris became a starter and significantly contributed to the team's success. Still, Coach Portland continued to question Harris and also began focusing on her appearance; Harris was told "to dress in more feminine clothing and wear her hair in a more feminine style instead of the cornrows [she] preferred" (Osborne, 2007, p. 482).

Soon after, Harris lost her starting position. "Because Coach Portland thought that I was gay, I was treated in a very demeaning manner. . . . Coach Portland created an offensive, hostile and intimidating learning environment for players she believed were gay. She created divisiveness on the team by instructing players not to associate with other players she believed to be gay, or they would be kicked off the team also" (NCLR, 2005). Eventually Harris was kicked off the team.

Although Portland's ill treatment of lesbian players spanned decades (in 1986 Portland was quoted stating she had a "no-alcohol, no-drugs, no-lesbians policy"), Jennifer Harris was the first to stand up to the coach. "I struggled with whether I should just walk away and try to forget what happened. I finally realized that I could never put this incident behind me as long as other students were being subjected to the same sort of humiliation and discrimination I experienced from Coach Portland. In the end, I knew I had to speak out" (Buzinski, 2005).

Represented by the National Center for Lesbian Rights, Harris filed a lawsuit for discrimination based on race, gender, and sexual orientation. The parties ultimately came to a confidential settlement, and shortly afterwards Rene Portland retired from coaching (NCLR, 2005).

2014, pp. 125-126). Homonegativism and **transnegativism** are overtly discriminatory actions. More often, in today's social climate, sport settings may be considered **heteronormative**. "Heteronormativity reflects an ever-present cultural bias in favor of heterosexuality and the omission of other forms of sexuality" (Krane & Symons, 2014, p. 125). These climates often are referred to as "don't ask, don't tell," the former U.S. policy in which LGBT people could join the military as long as their sexual orientation was not obvious through their speech or actions. Heteronormativity creates an air of superficial acceptance. That is, explicit discrimination is not present, yet LGBT people are expected to conform to heterosexual expectations or not talk about or act as if they are not heterosexual. While seemingly innocuous, heteronormative sport environments can be very frustrating or stressful for LGBT athletes.

CONSEQUENCES OF HETERONORMATIVITY, HOMONEGATIVISM, AND TRANSNEGATIVISM

Sadly, lesbian, bisexual, and transgender youths commit suicide at a higher rate than their heterosexual peers (Haas et al., 2011; Zhao, Montoro, Igartua, & Thombs, 2010). Experiences of discrimination, continued harassment, and bullying often underscore suicidal ideation and attempts. This negative treatment also may be associated with depression, stress and anxiety, and decreased self-confidence and self-esteem (Krane, Surface, & Alexander, 2005; Mustanski, Garofalo, & Emerson, 2010; Russell, Ryan, Toomey, Diaz, & Sanchez, 2011). Some athletes may turn to alcohol or forms of substance abuse or engage in cutting or self-injury in reaction to experienced discrimination.

Much homonegativism and transnegativism is aimed at gender nonconformity. Research consistently supports that gender nonconformity is related to high levels of harassment (e.g., D'Augelli, Grossman, & Starks, 2006; Grossman, D'Augelli, & Frank, 2011). What this means is that athletes who do not adhere to valued gender-role expectations (e.g., girls must appear and act feminine) are most at risk of negative treatment. This finding illustrates how sexual orientation and gender expression often are confounded. When female athletes appear or act too masculine, they are labeled lesbian. Needless to say,

I feel like there are a lot of gay women in soccer . . . but not very many of us openly talk about it. . . . I think the silence sends a message that it's not okay to be a lesbian in sports, or that it's a taboo topic. . . . Whenever I hear the statistics about kids killing themselves because of their sexuality, or they're being bullied at school, it makes me want to do something about it.

Meleana Shim, midfielder, National Women's Soccer League

this creates a conundrum for most female athletes, especially those in sports where there is a lot of physical contact or where being muscular and powerful is an asset. Regardless of actual sexual orientation or gender identity, being perceived as different regarding gender role expectations puts many sportswomen at risk of homo- or transnegativism and the concomitant psychological and emotional consequences. Further, athletes who are questioning their sexuality may have more negative reactions to bullying and harassment aimed at sexual orientation (Espelage, Aragon, Birkett, & Koenig, 2008). Often, these athletes have not talked about their feelings with others. They may question their feelings, fear disclosure, or feel embarrassed because they are working to understand their identity. As such, they have not developed social support networks that can assist in coping with the negative treatment. Once LBT (lesbian, bisexual, or trans) athletes come out (tell others of their sexual identity), they are able to seek out allies and support.

Further, living with constant discrimination, or fear of it, can negatively affect sport

Transgender High School Basketball Player, Tony Bias

Tony Bias was a high school basketball player in California. At age 15, Tony came out as transgender and gave up his dream of playing professional basketball. Bullies often targeted Tony, calling him "he-she." To avoid more abuse, he simply quit the sport rather than trying out for the boys' team. "I miss it so much. To be who I am, I've had to give up something that's really big in my life" (Haywood, 2013; Lovett, 2013).

performance and participation. Harassment by teammates or coaches can lead to low motivation, which can result in burnout or dropping out of sport (see sidebar about Tony Bias). Fear of harassment leads some LBT athletes to conceal their identities, which can be very stressful. Imagine hanging out with teammates and trying not to use pronouns for the person you are dating or not disclosing where you went over the weekend. Focusing on concealing one's sexual identity, experiencing harassment, or working to avoid harassment distracts athletes and diverts mental energy away from athletic performance. Further, high stress can interfere with athletic skill performance. Team dynamics also suffer on teams with homonegative and transnegative climates. Cliques or divisiveness may form. Some players may fear becoming a target, in which case they will not challenge discriminatory actions. These athletes may feel guilty or experience other negative emotional reactions. In all, heteronormativity, homonegativism, and transnegativism create unhealthy and unproductive sport environments.

ACCEPTING AND AFFIRMING SPORT CLIMATES

More and more, athletes are coming out to teammates, and their teammates are responding positively (Fink, Burton, Farrell, & Parker, 2012; Kauer & Krane, 2006; Stoelting, 2011). Not surprisingly, when joining a team, LBT athletes often will judge the team climate before disclosing their sexual or gender identities. When coaches are LBT inclusive, other teammates are openly LBT, or the athlete has least one ally in the athletic administration, players perceive the climate as safe, and are more likely to come out. Additionally, some athletes who already are open about their sexuality will continue to be open when joining a new team. For example, openly lesbian high school athletes will not want to become closeted for a college coach.

In interviews about why lesbian athletes decided to come out to their teammates, the athletes noted that they did not want to hide an important part of their identity (Stoelting, 2011). Also, given the amount of time players spend

> *There are not many athletes who are out. And I think it's something that's important. It felt important to me. . . . I guess it seems like a weight off my shoulders, because I've been playing a lot better than I've ever played before. I think I'm just enjoying myself and I'm happy.*
>
> Megan Rapinoe, U.S. women's national soccer team

with teammates, these athletes wanted to be real with them; they did not want to lie to their friends. When athletes can be open about their sexual identity, positive things happen within the team as well (Kauer & Krane, 2006). Teammates learn about each other's experiences. Previous biases and stereotypes are challenged and changed. All athletes begin to challenge discrimination aimed at their teammates. Also, diverse identities become normalized. That is, regardless of whether one is heterosexual, lesbian, bisexual, or transgender, all sexual and gender identities are treated in a similar respectful manner. People talk about who they are dating or attracted to, no matter the gender of that person. Everyone's partners are included in social activities, and it just seems normal. Learning about the struggles other people have gone through can lead to better understanding and a desire to challenge discrimination. This is the foundation for the current **ally movement** in sport, which includes programs created by heterosexual **allies** (advocates) with the goals of creating social change and social justice in sport, fighting discrimination based on sexual and gender identity, and making sport safe for LGBT athletes (Kauer & Krane, 2013).

> Through sports, we learn so much about ourselves, others, and what it means to be part of a team. One of my biggest takeaways from team sports is that everyone brings different gifts and tools to the table, which is awesome! Diversity should be accepted, respected and celebrated. That's why I am an athlete ally. Because at the end of the day, we aren't so different after all. We all want to play, compete and live while being ourselves. I

A supportive team environment can allow players to be open and true to themselves, removing the pressure of secrecy and allowing athletes to better focus on competition.

want women's soccer and the entire sports community to be a landscape of inclusion (Athlete Ally, 2013).

Websites such as Go! Athletes (www.go athletes.org) provide LBT athletes with support and role models. There they can get peer support, read the stories of other LGBT athletes, and even submit their own stories. Importantly, websites also provide support and crisis intervention that were not easily available for LGBT athletes of earlier generations. Examples of these programs include the following:

- Athlete Ally (www.athleteally.org)
- Br{ache the Silence (www.freedom sounds.org)
- It Gets Better Campaign (www.itgets better.org)
- Step Up! Speak Out! (www.stepupspeak out.ca)
- TRANS*ATHLETE (www.transathlete .com)
- The Trevor Project (www.thetrevor project.org)
- You Can Play Project (http://youcanplay project.org)

Prior to the emergence of these ally programs, several educational programs led the way in fighting LGBT discrimination in sport. In 1996, the Women's Sport Foundation, with the assistance of Martina Navratilova, launched the It Takes a Team program and spearheaded the campaign against homonegativism in sport. Unfortunately, It Takes a Team became a victim of budget cuts in 2009. However, Pat Griffin, who was the director of the program its final five years, continued her advocacy with Changing the Game: The GLSEN Sports Project (http://sports.glsen.org), which debuted in 2011 under Griffin's leadership. The Sports Project, as described on the GLSEN website, "is an education and advocacy program focused on addressing LGBT issues in K-12 school-based athletic and physical education programs" (GLSEN, n.d.). Another pioneering program is the National Center for Lesbian Rights (NCLR) Sports Project, which began in 2001 with Helen Carroll as the project director. The Sports Project provides legal support and engages in litigation and policy work to fight LGBT discrimination in sport. The GLSEN and NCLR programs still are at the forefront of fighting discrimination and providing educational materials.

Sport should be a place where athletes can learn skills, have fun, and enjoy the camaraderie of the team. Many social and health benefits of sport participation exist, and many life lessons can be learned on the field and in the gym. Homonegativism and transnegativism unfairly rob some athletes of these benefits. The good news is that the resources mentioned in this section provide support for LGBT athletes so they do not need to feel alone and vulnerable. All of these programs also provide educational materials for coaches and parents who want to support their athletes and create safe, supportive, and inclusive sport settings. The emergence of these programs also makes it chic to now support LGBT people in sport. Athlete leaders are expected to step up and intervene when they hear trans- or homonegative language or see prejudiced actions. Public service announcements exist that educate us on how to approach our peers when they use unacceptable language (e.g., see Think B4 You Speak on www.glsen.org). Compassion and inclusion are becoming the new normal in sport.

Learning Aids

Summary

Inclusive sport settings recognize the needs of LGBT athletes as well as discourage discrimination. Specific to transgender and transsexual athletes, it is important to be able to understand athletes' gender identity and their physicality. Prepubescent children have similar bodies regardless of gender or gender identity. Athletes who choose to take hormones to change their physical bodies will have hormone levels and concomitant physicality similar to their cisgender teammates after one year of continued hormone therapy. It also is important to recognize that some athletes may have puberty suppressed, in which case their bodies will not undergo any hormonal and related changes that their peers will experience. Perhaps most important to consider is the psychological and social consequences of inclusion or exclusion from sport and the effects of transnegativism within a team. Safe and inclusive sport for transgender athletes provides them with opportunities to develop skills, friendships, and life lessons that all athletes gain.

Historically, sport has been unwelcoming toward lesbian and bisexual female athletes. Today, we see a wide range of climates: Some are highly inclusive, others highly homonegative, and many are somewhere in between. In homonegative sport settings, overtly prejudicial actions are aimed at lesbian and bisexual athletes. In heteronormative settings, bias is more subtle, creating a "don't ask, don't tell" environment (i.e., "we'll accept you if you don't act lesbian or bisexual"). Heteronormative, homonegative, and transnegative sport can lead to increased stress, anxiety, and depression; decreased self-esteem; decreased sport performance; and increased thoughts of or attempts at suicide. LBT and heterosexual coaches and athletes can participate in one of many ally programs that will help reduce discrimination, educate athletes, gain support, and create inclusive sport settings. Creating affirming and inclusive team environments will be educational and beneficial for all team members.

Discussion Questions

1. Should an affirmed female athlete be able to complete on the girls' middle school basketball team? Provide a rationale for why or why not.

2. Create a policy for a high school athletics department regarding transgender participation on sport teams. Because parents are likely to have lots of questions, also include the justification for why this policy is fair.

3. What is negative recruiting and why do some coaches engage in this action? If you were a high school athlete being negatively recruited, how might you respond?

4. As the parent of an LGBT college athlete, you have heard that the coach often uses homonegative language. Discuss the potential consequences of the coach's actions and why this behavior concerns you.

5. How can you encourage your team or a university team to participate in an ally program? Select a program and develop the steps needed to get full team involvement.

Learning Activities

1. See the resources for supporting transgender student-athletes on the GLSEN Sports Project webpage (http://sports.glsen.org/resources/resources-for-supporting-transgender-student-athletes). Develop a list of 8 to 10 strategies that administrators, coaches, and athletes can use to create a trans-inclusive sport climate.

2. Complete the school athletic climate checklist that is on the GLSEN Sports Project website (http://sports.glsen.org/the-school-athletic-climate-check-list). Think about a team you are on currently or have recently played for as you mark your responses. For any items you marked "don't know" or "no," look at the other resources on this website and develop strategies that can turn these responses to yes.

3. Go to the website www.outsports.com. Read through the headlines on the first page. Follow at least one story all the way through. Consider the concepts discussed in this chapter and apply them to what you learn in the articles:

   a. Describe any examples of homo- or transnegativism.

   b. Describe any actions of allies.

   c. What are the consequences of these prejudiced or supportive actions?

   d. What are your reactions to the stories and issues communicated on the website?

4. Watch the video of the ESPNW interview with Brittney Griner (http://espn.go.com/video/clip?id=9309516). Then answer the following questions:

   a. How does Griner talk about her gender identity?

   b. Describe the atmosphere at Baylor for athletes like Griner.

   c. What did you learn about Griner's coming out experiences?

   d. What are some of her negative experiences related to sexual orientation? Gender identity?

   e. How would you describe Griner's attitude toward her critics? Did she always feel this way?

   f. Would you consider Griner a role model for young athletes? Why or why not?

Glossary

affirmed female—A person who was assigned the male sex at birth yet whose gender identity and gender expression are female; also called a trans-woman or a male-to-female (MTF).

affirmed male—A person who was assigned the female sex at birth yet whose gender identity and gender expression are male; also called a trans-man or female-to-male (FTM).

allies—Heterosexual people who advocate for and support lesbian, gay, bisexual, and transgender people.

ally movement—Programs created by heterosexual allies with the goals of creating social change and social justice in sport, fighting discrimination in sport based on sexual and gender identity, and making sport safe for LGBT athletes.

cisgender—An individual whose gender identity is consistent with the sex assigned at birth.

gender—Socially and culturally constructed attitudes, expectations, roles, and behaviors that have been associated with masculinity and femininity.

gender expression—How an individual displays gender through dress, movement, speech, behavior, and actions.

gender identity—An internal sense of being female, male, both female and male, neither female nor male, or transgender.

gender nonconforming—Self-presentation in which mannerisms, hairstyle, speech, or attire are unconventional for someone of their sex.

heteronormativity—A pervasive cultural bias that favors heterosexuality and omits consideration of other forms of sexuality.

homonegativism—Negative treatment, discrimination, and bigotry toward lesbian and bisexual people.

negative recruiting—An unethical recruitment strategy in which one coach implies that players or coaches from a rival university are lesbian, with the goal of dissuading athletes from wanting to attend that rival university.

sex—A person's chromosomal, hormonal, physiological, and anatomical makeup.

sex reassignment surgery (SRS)—Surgical procedures in which changes are made to anatomy and outward appearance; the process may include multiple surgeries in which changes are made to the breasts and genitals as well as cosmetic procedures.

sexual identity—A person's sense of self based on sexual orientation as well as feeling connected to a community of others who share this orientation.

sexual orientation—One's emotional and sexual attractions; in Western societies, typically labelled as heterosexual, lesbian or gay, or bisexual.

transgender—A person whose gender identity and gender expression is not consistent with the physical sex that was assigned at birth.

transitioning—The time during which trans people change outward gender expression (e.g., hairstyle, type of clothes worn) and become more masculine or feminine consistent with their gender identity. During this time, hormone therapy often begins, and some trans people may have sex reassignment surgeries.

transnegativism—Negative treatment, discrimination, and bigotry based on gender identity and aimed at trans people; also called trans prejudice.

transsexual—A person who plans to, has begun, or has completed making changes to their body chemistry, anatomy, or both to bring their physicality in alignment with their gender identity.

Notes

1. The term *cisgender* is more appropriate than *non-transgender* because the latter implies that being transgender is abnormal, while being non-transgender is normal. Further, use of *cisgender* reminds us that all people have a gender identity, not only people who navigate an unconventional gender identity.

2. The IOC policy allows eligibility two years after sex reassignment surgery and continued hormone therapy, whereas the NCAA allows eligibility after one year of hormone therapy.

CHAPTER 8

Women's Sport and Aging

Ellen J. Staurowsky, EdD, Drexel University

Learning Objectives

In this chapter, you will learn about the following:

- The degree to which older women participate in sport and physical activity
- The culture of aging and its influence on women participating in sport in mid- and later life
- Competitive sport opportunities for older female athletes
- Benefits of participation in sport and physical activity for older women
- The factors that encourage older women to participate in sport and physical activity or prevent them from doing so

What is it that inspires a woman of 60-plus years to envision the possibility of swimming 103 miles (166 km) in the open ocean in the turbulent and unpredictable Straits of Florida? Surely it cannot be the prospect of swimming nonstop for two and a half days through shark-infested open water where a shoreline is not visible for hour after hour and touching bottom for a little rest is out of the question.

For ultramarathon swimmer Diana Nyad, the reason may be as obvious as the fact that she is a rare and remarkable athlete. An Olympic hopeful whose wish to compete in the 1968 Mexico City Games was derailed by a three-month bout with a heart infection that drained her of the speed she once had, she eventually redirected her considerable talents into long-distance swimming (Nyad, 1978). By her mid-20s, she had accomplished feats that no other woman, and only a handful of men, had done. In 1974, she set a women's record in a race around the Bay of Naples with a time of 8 hours, 11 minutes. A year later she would make national headlines by swimming the distance around the island of Manhattan in less than 8 hours. And in a flourish that was to be the last record-breaking effort of her career, she set a world record in distance swimming in 1979 when she completed a 102.5-mile course from the Bahamas to Florida. Her performance that day set a mark that no swimmer, male or female, had ever done before (Howard, 2010; Weil, 2011).

For 30 years, Nyad pursued other interests. At one point, she was ranked among the top 30 women's squash players in the United States. A career in broadcast journalism placed her behind the microphone and in front of the camera, reporting on world-class athletes. When she turned 60 years of age in 2009, however, her thoughts returned to unfinished business, a dream she had pursued but failed to achieve at the height of her career: to swim the distance between Havana, Cuba, and Key West, Florida. To pursue the dream was not so much an exercise in what could have been for Nyad, but more about "looking into that mirror of yourself and finding the soul" (Howard, 2010). After a three-decade hiatus in which she did not swim a lap, Nyad reentered the water, experimenting at first to see if she could begin to regain a level of

physical fitness that would allow her to endure the rigors of powering her way through the high seas, incrementally increasing her workouts as the months passed. Following a 24-hour training swim when she realized that she still had more she could do, she committed to the project to swim from Cuba.

This project was a dangerous undertaking that placed the body at risk for many reasons, not least of which was the physical toll wrought after prolonged exposure to the elements. Nyad opted for an open swim format without aids such as fins. Due to the threat of sharks, kayaks accompanied her on either side outfitted with electronic shark shield protection, devices that send out electronic signals that drive sharks away. No such protections existed, however, from winds that make navigation difficult and can easily add more distance and time to a swim that was calculated to take approximately 60 hours to complete. Nyad would also be vulnerable to contact with jellyfish. The poisonous stings that they inflict when they encounter other life-forms can temporarily paralyze a swimmer, leaving her numb, nauseous, and disoriented.

Nyad made her second attempt at the swim from Cuba in 2011 (her first had been in 1978) without success, and tried two more times in 2011 and 2012, yet failed to reach her goal. To some commentators, Nyad's quest to achieve what few in the world have ever done and to do it on her own terms seemed, at best, courageous (Clift, 2011; Stein, 2011) but also quixotic (Franks, 2012; Weil, 2011) and at times perhaps overindulgent and maybe even scary, given the potential for things to go wrong (Smith, 2012). For Nyad, however, to aspire to such a challenge was to assert a belief that "you can dream at any age. . . . We are far from irrelevant as we grow older" (Nyad, 2011). In June of 2013, Nyad announced that she would make a fifth attempt

> *Attempting this swim has become an emblem of never giving up, not only to me and my life spirit, but to millions of people who are rooting for me to show them that we can all, at any age, live large.*
>
> Diana Nyad

at the swim from Cuba. In September of 2013, Nyad triumphantly made history, successfully conquering the currents and completing a 103-mile swim from Cuba to Florida (see figure 8.1) in 53 hours (Sloane, Hanna, & Ford, 2013).

While Diana Nyad's aspiration of swimming 103 miles may be epic, she is not alone in rewriting the script on what female athletes can accomplish later in their lives. In the months leading up to the 2008 Beijing Games, photos published by the *New York Times* featured then 41-year-old five-time U.S. Olympian, Dara Torres, whose sculpted, sleek, strong, and muscular body challenged societal notions of what the mother of a 2-year-old looked like. Torres' much-discussed body is shown in figure 8.2.

While some thought that Torres looked too thin ("Dara Torres," 2008)—a concern that might not have been misplaced given that Torres had publicly acknowledged over the years that, like many female athletes (see chapter 4), she'd had to come to terms with an eating disorder—her performance in Beijing confirmed that she remained a world-class competitor whose times were still going down. In the 2008 Olympics, she served as the anchor for the U.S. women's 4 × 100 medley relay, where she had a split time of 52.27 seconds. Because the U.S. team came in second to the Australians in that race, few were aware that Torres' time was the fastest ever in a women's medley relay up to that point (Anderson, 2008).

Like Nyad, Torres has talked about how age presents its issues and its advantages. As the careers of both of these female athletes attest, competing in mid- and later life presents a new set of issues. Bodies take longer to heal and recover. As veteran athletes who know training and how their bodies respond to it, neither Nyad nor Torres do the same kind of workouts that they did when they were younger. They have learned that training differently and training smarter yielded results that allowed them to not just participate in their sports but continue to excel.

They have both also figured out a way to pay the high financial price it can take to train at such a high level later in life. For Nyad, her 2012 attempt to swim from Cuba to Florida required an investment of $300,000 (Weil, 2011), while the expense associated with the team of coaches, masseuses, stretchers, and a chiropractor cost Torres approximately $100,000 a year in 2008 (Weil, 2008). And then, of course, there is also the time commitment. For each, pursuit of their athletic goals amounted to full-time jobs.

Figure 8.1   Map of swimmer Diana Nyad's route from Cuba to Florida that she would follow five times until she achieved success, at the age of 64, in September of 2013.

Figure 8.2 The physique of 41-year-old Olympic-bound swimmer Dara Torres was the subject of much attention and earned her an appearance in the Got Milk? ad campaign.

While Nyad and Torres offer examples of how athletes who have competed at the top of their sports and set course through the various passages of their lives as athletes and women, the remainder of this chapter situates their stories within the broader expanse of U.S. population trends and participation levels of aging women in sport and physical activity, cultural expectations about women and aging, competitive sport opportunities for women, competitive sport

> *The water doesn't know how old you are.*
>
> Dara Torres, U.S. swimmer who competed in five Olympic Games (1984, 1988, 1992, 2000, and 2008)

opportunities for older women, benefits older women receive as a result of that participation, and barriers to participation.

WOMEN, AGING, AND U.S. SPORT PARTICIPATION TRENDS

In the United States, Canada, and other countries around the world, people are living longer as a result of better health care and quality of life. The magnitude of what that means for women and their long-term health is reflected in some basic population statistics. According to the U.S. Administration on Aging (2013), the older population has increased by 21 percent since 2002, with older Americans in 2012 numbering 43.1 million, which translates into one in every seven members of the population being an older American. Life expectancy continues to increase, with people who reach the age of 65 expected to live an additional 20.4 years if female and 17.8 years if male. Women outnumber men, and older men are much more likely to be married than older women (71% of men vs. 45% of women). Fewer than 40 percent of older women are widows. Almost half of older women age 75 or older live alone. More than half a million grandparents aged 65 and over serve as the primary caregiver for the grandchildren who live with them, and approximately 10 percent of the older U.S. population is living in poverty.

Similar trends are happening worldwide:

> In 2009, 14% of Canada's 32 million people were aged 65 years or older. This proportion is expected to rise to between 23 and 25% by 2036, effectively doubling the number of seniors observed in 2009, placing increased demand on the health care system and the nation's workforce. (Smith, Carr, Wiseman, Calhoun, McNevin, & Weir, 2012)

Geoghegan (2011) reported that women around the world are outliving men in the United States, United Kingdom, Canada, Australia, and Japan.

A report titled *Healthy People 2020* that presents 10-year goals and objectives for health promotion and disease prevention for citizens of the United States showed that "more than 80%

of adults do not meet the guidelines for both aerobic and muscle-strengthening activities" (U.S. Department of Health & Human Services, 2010, p. 1). While 37.6 percent of the male adult population in the United States was engaging in at least moderate or vigorous intensity aerobic activity, only 28.6 percent of females were meeting the standard. The gap between men and women for participating in activities that increase muscle strength was similar (28.4% to 20.1%).

While women make up the largest sector of the older population, they are less likely to engage in physical activity. In 2010, only 8.4 percent of women aged 65 and older were likely to have participated in physical activity at a level that would result in health benefits (Women's Health USA, 2010). "Moreover, fewer older women achieve recommended levels of PA, compared to men of similar age groups" (Stephan, Boiché, & Le Scanff, 2010, p. 339).

Broad population statistics about older women participating in physical activity and sport are scant, but the few areas where sport-specific data are available about older women's participation contribute to a greater understanding of women's sport experience. According to Running USA (2013), whose annual reports document women's participation in a variety of running events, out of 8,699,000 race finishers in 2012, 16 percent were women aged 45 to 54, 6 percent women aged 55 to 64, and 1 percent were 65 and up. In 2013, women made up a record high 43 percent of those who finished one of the 1,100 marathons sponsored around the United States. Broken down by age, half or more than half of the women who finished the marathon (55%), half-marathon (53%), and timed events (50%) were 35 years of age or older (Harsbarger & Jacobsen, 2013). According to the National Runner Survey 2013, of the 30,425 respondents, 56.4 percent were female. The survey data showed that the typical female was 39.3 years of age. Among the female runners, 60.7 percent were married, 77.8 percent were college educated, and 70.8 percent earned incomes of $75,000 or more.

While it is still more common for younger rather than older women to engage in athletic competition, the participation of older women is growing, with over 50 countries sponsoring master athlete events. In masters swimming, the influence of women has been present literally from its inception. June Krauser, a powerhouse of a leader who is regarded as the mother of masters swimming in the United States, worked alongside male and female colleagues to promote swimming as a form of fitness to adults over 25 years of age in the 1970s, a time when research was just beginning to challenge perceptions that competing in athletics in adulthood could be harmful (Dunbar, Beach, Spannuth, & Wilson, 2012). An International Swimming Hall of Fame inductee, Krauser participated in national masters events continuously over three decades starting in 1971, being named Masters Swimmer of the Year in 2001, a year in which she set 13 new world records and 27 number-one rankings in the 70 to 74 and 75 to 79 age groups (House, 2003).

In a 2011 U.S. Masters Swimming (USMS) membership survey, out of 7,180 responding, 48 percent (3,473) were women (Daughtery, Vowels, & Black, 2011). In a demographic study of USMS annual membership, Boyd (2006) reported that roughly half of the 45,000 masters swimmers in the United States were women (49.5% female compared to 51.5% male).

In contrast, in the sport of golf, women have consistently constituted under 25 percent of all those who play. Findings from the National Golf Foundation indicate that of the 25.3 million golfers in the United States, 4.4 million were adult females 18 years and older (Berkley, 2013).

In certain team sports, adult women dominate. For example, USA Volleyball (2013) reports that while women (18 years and older) make up only 13 percent of all members, they constitute 62 percent of all adult members of USVBA. As awareness grows that women are increasingly involved in sport and physical activity later in life, more documentation of their activities is warranted.

The picture of older women participating in sport is incomplete, however, because of the absence of comprehensive data that take into account the broad array of things that older women can participate in to play competitively, stay fit and healthy, and improve their quality of life. This lack of attention may speak to low cultural expectations about older women being active and involved in sport. The next section explores some of the cultural beliefs that affect older women, as well as how older women's participation in sport can change the way we think about what they can achieve as athletes and active women.

CULTURE, AGING, AND THE OLDER WOMAN

While celebrity athletes like Nyad and Torres offer examples of how some female athletes navigate the aging process, offering their own challenges to cultural expectations about women and aging, perhaps the more powerful examples reside in the myriad women who pursue their sports largely outside of the public spotlight, enacting scripts that they choose to write for their own lives within their own communities. Social historian and gender scholar Patricia Vertinsky (2002, p. 58) said,

> If history, aging and popular culture tell us anything, it is that all three, like the images they retail, are socially constructed. And there is certainly no shortage of images of old age on which the non-aged draw—though the dominant ones still tend to be held up as mirrors of mortality, forcing more attention to the biological processes of decline than the possibilities of sustaining vigour and sporting prowess. Since sport is one of the major contemporary sites where youthful physical displays are paramount and physiological requirements important, it is hardly surprising that aging sportsmen and sportswomen are not abundantly evident in the public gaze.

Women, who live longer than men, are built for what Vertinsky called the "marathon of life" (2000). And yet, there is a paucity of imagery of older athletes in general, and of older female athletes in particular, fueling perceptions of aging that focus on decline, loss of function and productivity, and unattractiveness, associations that run counter to engagement in sport at any age. Pointing out the contradiction between the mythical spaces older

women are thought to inhabit compared to their reality, Vertinsky observed, "though it seems increasingly in our power to intervene directly in the processes of aging and the environments in which older women live, negative imagery and distortions concerning their aging bodies are difficult to dislodge" (2002, p. 61).

When interventions occur, they rewrite the way in which older women engage with sport and the expectations they hold for themselves, and they offer alternative ways to approach aging countering the narratives of decline (Oghene, 2013). A case in point is the marathon, a 26.2-mile (42 km) endurance event that women had been barred from participating in out of fears of overexertion, ruination of reproductive organs, and collapse. Those fears were so powerful that it would take until 1984 before the women's marathon was included in the Olympic Games.

Significantly, the first official marathon in the United States that permitted women to run was held in 1962. Running the course on Pikes Peak in Manitou Springs, Colorado, 61-year-old Katherine Heard placed second (Cooper, 1998; Vertinsky, 2002). "Marathon Madge" Sharples (1989), born in 1916, took up the sport in her sixties, competing in 50 marathons worldwide and writing a book urging others that if she could do it, they could too. In May 2015, Harriette Thompson crossed the finish line of the Suja Rock 'n' Roll marathon in San Diego, California, becoming the oldest woman to complete a marathon at the age of 92, having finished 17 marathons previously (Associated Press, 2015).

Even as these stories begin to fill in the picture of what it means to be an older female athlete, "the knowledge base about the participation of middle-aged and older women in sport, particularly from the perspectives of women themselves, is embryonic" (Litchfield & Dionigi, 2013, abstract).

In their work on culture, aging, and sport participation, Tahmaseb-McConatha, Volkwein-Caplan, and DiGregorio note that "the spectre of old age has a cultural dimension that associates old age with mental and physical decline" (2011, p. 48). Cultural definitions of old age are manifest in prevailing images of the elderly as dependent and physically weak. Across cultures, older adults are often subjected to multiple sources of discrimination. For women, who have historically encountered discrimination and imposed limitations on their ability to participate in sport, the added effect of ageism (the process of stereotyping and prejudice directed toward older people) compounds already sensitive territory relative to physical strength, appearance, and perceived vulnerability. As Kirby and Kluge put it, "gender shapes lived experience, intersects with age, and can result in older women, in particular, thinking they are too old and too unfit to become physically active or try something new later in life" (2013, p. 291).

According to interviews conducted with female athletes who competed in the 2001 Australian Masters ($N = 70$; aged 55 to 82 years) and the 2009 World Games ($N = 2$; aged 56 to 82), the participation of older female athletes in sport is an exercise in both resistance and conformity. By virtue of their participation, older female athletes are aware that they are challenging traditional stereotypes about gender and aging. Their sport participation of the women interviewed was a source of personal empowerment that affected their identity, feeling of belonging, engagement with others and their communities, and their bodily competence. While older female athletes defy some stereotypes and help to sweep away limiting perceptions about what older women can do, they are not immune to the dominant cultural ideals that place a higher priority on youthfulness.

COMPETITIVE SPORT OPPORTUNITIES FOR OLDER WOMEN

For older women who wish to pursue their sports and compete at a high level, several different avenues are available. Arguably, one of the most established of these is the masters division of U.S. track and field. For athletes 30 years and older, competition at the masters level allows athletes to compete in five-year age groups (30 to 34, 35 to 39, 40 to 44, 45 to 49, and so on). Women compete against women and men compete against men in track and field, long-distance running, and race walking in both indoor and outdoor venues.

Women's participation in organized team sport leagues has also seen a steady rise over previous decades. The National Sporting Goods Association conducts annual surveys, and their results show that the number of women ages 55 and up who play basketball at least 50 times a year increased substantially between 1995 and 2005, growing from 16,000 to nearly 131,000 (Syeed, 2007). According to sport studies professor Michael Rogers, "You see more and more senior women's teams participating in state and national competitions and more recreational leagues. In the future it will be commonplace to have leagues like this" (as quoted in Syeed, 2007, para. 5).

The phenomenon of the Granny Basketball League (GBL) reflects this history. The league

Susan Ershler, Summits to Climb in Midlife and Beyond

For some, midlife might be a time to think that what is ahead is downhill. Not so for Susan Ershler, a motivational speaker who tackled the challenge of climbing Mount Everest in her mid-40s. In 2002 when she reached the summit of Everest, she was one of only 12 women in the world to have done so. She is the fourth American woman to scale the Seven Summits (the tallest mountains on each of the seven continents) and the first to do so with her husband. To prepare for the rigors of the Everest climb, she spent her lunch breaks climbing the 35 flights of stairs in her office building while wearing a 40-pound (18 kg) backpack.

With a clear disposition for taking on challenges, Ershler decided to enter her first body sculpting competition after she turned 50. When not training for a major challenge, Ershler works out on a daily basis, engaging in a combination of strength training and cardio workouts (Julian, 2015).

Getting older does not have to mean an end to athletic interests. Clubs and leagues are available to those who want to find them. And if nothing is available in a given area, interested athletes can always start a club themselves.

was started in 2005 by women in Iowa who played six-on-six basketball when they were in high school (Borzi, 2007). Focusing on their members' desire to play but acknowledging the limits of aging, the league adopted women's basketball rules from the 1920s, along with attire to match the era. Thus, the court is divided into three sections. Running, jumping, and physical contact are forbidden. Players are required to dribble twice before shooting, and a shot made underhand results in three points. In 2014, the GBL had 25 registered teams with more than 200 women over age 50 participating (Staton, 2014).

Women's leagues reflect the diversity of their players. The legacy of limited opportunity still plays out for women later in life, with leagues accommodating skill and experience levels "from older women who haven't hit the court in decades to women who have led their teams to tournaments in the post-Title IX era" (Syeed, 2007, p. 2). While the Granny Leagues offer a

retro approach to aging women who want to participate in sport, the limits imposed on women in the pre–Title IX generation has served as a motivator for some to reenter the athletic arena unencumbered by rules that assumed female frailty and weakness. For Kathy Moffitt, who graduated from high school in 1955, the experience of playing six-on-six basketball made her feel like she hadn't really played sports. Her involvement in track and field as a senior athlete allowed her to savor true competition in her view, to press her limits in ways that her early sport experiences did not (Valade, 2013).

Regional leagues, such as the Senior Women's Basketball Association of San Diego, send teams along to the National Senior Games (NSG). Of the 250 basketball teams that competed in the 2013 Games, 104 were women's teams. In some NSG sports, women's teams numbered more than men's. Women's senior softball teams numbered 56 compared to 48 for the men; in the sport of volleyball, 78 women's teams participated as opposed to 57 men's teams. In terms of overall participation in the NSG, women made up 40.5 percent (4,416) of all participants, surpassing participation by men between the ages of 50 and 59. After age 60, however, women's participation declined at a much faster pace when compared to men (National Senior Games Association, 2013).

For women who have been playing catch-up in terms of sport participation, these sectors of senior participation where women dominate may foretell a future where women will be as, or more, active than men in their later years. Research support for such speculation is borne out in a study tracking the activity patterns of women who competed on teams in college during the 1960s and 1970s. As those women grew older, they remained engaged in moderate or strenuous activity at least three times per week (Strawbridge, 2001).

BENEFITS OF SPORT PARTICIPATION FOR OLDER WOMEN

Across the spectrum of health and well-being indicators—cognitive functioning (memory, retention), weight, flexibility, strength, psychological outlook, and social connectedness—the more active a woman, the more likely she will experience an increase in life expectancy and quality of life. The effects of chronic illnesses that affect older women, such as breast cancer, diabetes, dementia, heart disease, high blood pressure, obesity, and osteoporosis, are mediated by physical activity (Staurowsky et al., 2015).

As a case in point, "total leisure time physical activity, walking pace, and amount of walking in mid-life were all independent predictors of exceptional health and function in women aged about 70 years" (Sun et al., 2010, abstract). More specifically, among 13,535 healthy women, midlife physical activity was found to be associated with greater likelihood of successful survival to age 70; while some activity was good, more activity was better for these women. High habitual physical activity is associated with less weight gain in younger postmenopausal women and less weight loss in older postmenopausal women. These findings suggest that promoting physical activity among postmenopausal women may be important for managing body weight changes that accompany aging (Sims et al., 2012).

SUCCESSFUL AGING THROUGH CONTINUED SPORT PARTICIPATION

Female athletes who continue to pursue athletic careers as they grow older are believed to have a greater likelihood of **successfully aging**. This term, which is used by a number of researchers, refers to the results that accrue from older adults participating in meaningful activities while maintaining physical and cognitive functions that yield benefits in terms of life satisfaction, mental and physical well-being, and a robust quality of life (Heo, Culp, Yamada, & Won, 2013). "Facilitating ways for older adults to be active as they age can be important related to distinguishing and transforming their aging identities, offering a collective social experience, and as a means to set goals relative to aging" (Kelley, Little, Lee, Birenda, & Henderson, 2014, p. 63).

Athletic women who train on a regular basis are also more likely to exhibit characteristics associated with successful aging, experiencing fewer chronic health conditions and diseases associated with the aging process. Older trained female athletes have been shown to have 30 to 50 percent higher $\dot{V}O_2$max capacity than sedentary women (they can process oxygen better, and are aerobically in better shape). They also maintain lower percentages of total and central body fat compared to healthy sedentary women. Reduced body fat and maintenance of muscle mass may contribute to enhanced glucose uptake and insulin action in highly trained female athletes (Serra, McMillin, & Ryan, 2012).

Interviews with women who participated in the Senior Games revealed that they were engaged in what Heo and colleagues (2013) described as serious leisure, realizing an array of positive outcomes that tested their resolve, allowed them to move through developmental phases from novice to master, and resulted in connections to important personal and social support systems. As is the case for women at any age, this group of competitors had to deal with the demands of physical training. They faced fatigue, anxiety, and injury in the course of pursuing their sports, necessitating responses to adversity, maintaining focus on goals, and cultivating mind-sets that they would overcome pain, inconvenience, and setbacks in order to achieve. The camaraderie of the competitive environment and the companionship of like-minded athletes and coaches were sources of solace and inspiration for older female athletes who were still interested in pursuing excellence, reaching for personal bests, and working to get better, faster, and stronger. The status of being a senior female athlete was considered a valuable social identity for these women, an identity that was not short lived or temporary, but inherent to the core of how they saw themselves as women and people.

Similar patterns were found among veteran field hockey players aged 45 and older (Litchfield & Dionigi, 2013). With developed identities as field hockey players, these older female athletes connected with the rituals that they had known throughout their experience playing over many years. The tournament itself served as a milestone and a goal to be prepared for each year. Attendant cultural norms—practical jokes, comedic mascots, and friendly rivalries—served to connect the women to their sporting experience and to each other. The championship dinner, with its formal dress, dancing, and feel of a night out on the town, created a space for enjoying each other's company and building relationships.

BARRIERS TO OLDER WOMEN'S SPORT PARTICIPATION

Across their life span, girls and women encounter barriers to participation in physical activity and sport. As Pfister noted (2012), the lasting imprint of cultural expectations that places greater value on female youthfulness shapes the sporting possibilities for women as they age. So, too, do practical issues associated with access, including financial means to participate, safe places to play and engage in physical activity, and transportation considerations. For women in mid- and later life, responsibilities associated with work and caregiving have been identified as problematic, but they also offer potential opportunities.

Influence of Work

According to Carmichael, Duberley, and Szmigin (2014), paid employment serves as a "double-edged sword" for women in their 50s, 60s, and 70s in terms of participation in physical activity. As women live longer and remain longer in the workforce, a complex set of factors affects their health and activity levels, including competing demands between work and family, income level, individual health status, previous participation in sport and physical activity, and an array of psychological and social concerns.

Carving out time in a day already filled with responsibilities and obligations can be particularly challenging. As Carmichael and colleagues noted (2014, p. 14),

> While such factors are not exclusively relevant to older women, constraints on time are a feature of the double burden of work and home shouldered by women who are

Income level may affect an elderly woman's ability to take part in health and fitness programs available at fitness clubs, but senior centers can help to offset this problem by offering active programs of their own.

more often than not the main carers for children, older relatives and husbands at different stages in their lives.

For some older women who have paying jobs outside of the home, workplace fitness and wellness programs help them find the time to exercise. Memberships to fitness clubs and fees associated with working out and competing are also more available to working women.

Stability and Falling

As women get older, a generalized concern that affects participation in physical activity is fear of falling. A strong psychological deterrent to even high-functioning older women, the fear of falling has been found to reduce participation in physical activity (PA) (Bruce, Devine, & Prince, 2002). Among 262 older women, PA levels were affected by fear of falling. In cases where there were fall histories and medication use was higher, women had lower levels of physical activity as measured by a pedometer (Doi et al., 2012). Physical exercises recommended

for this population include yoga to increase flexibility and strengthen muscles, tai chi to improve muscle strength, and gait and coordination training. Increased core strength, flexibility, and balance among elderly women can lead to a reduction in fear of falling, greater confidence in moving, and greater control when walking (Harvard Health Publications, 2014).

Older Women's Reasons for Participation and Nonparticipation in Sport and Physical Activity

For women who do have a regular workout regimen or training program, motivation can vary widely from one woman to the next. A one-size-fits-all motivational approach to encourage older women to participate in PA does not seem to be the answer. Persistence seems to be key. Research to see who persisted and who dropped out of an organized PA program demonstrated that women's motives for participating are varied, individualized, and multidimensional. Although the serious health benefits of PA may

Track and Field Icon, Olga Kotelko

Olga Kotelko was a retired school teacher who took an interest in track and field when she was in her seventies (Grierson, 2010). Although she enjoyed softball in her youth, she put her athletic pursuits on hold as other life events—marriage, children, divorce, single-parenthood—exacted demands on her time, attention, and energies. When she retired, softball beckoned, at least for a while. A suggestion from a teammate that she might like track and field led her to connect with a local coach and a Hungarian trainer who pushed her to get stronger. At 77, she was working out up to three hours at a time, pushing her body with exercises such as planks, Roman chairs, bench presses, and squats. Tellingly, she professed that she wished to be "a young-at-heart athlete rather than an old woman" (Palowski, 2014, para. 3). Among masters athletes, Kotelko became an icon, winning more than 750 gold medals and setting 27 records in international competition in running, jumping, shot putting, and hammer throwing (Stewart, 2014).

Described by her daughter as "a fearless competitor who tackled each new adventure with passion and determination," Kotelko was on pace to continue her winning ways in her 95th year (Ha, 2014, para. 7). Just a week before she passed away in June of 2014, she competed, taking gold, in three events at the Langley Pacific Invitational meet (the weight throw, javelin throw, and hammer throw), having participated in what would be her last World Masters Championships the preceding March in Budapest.

be motivating, such information by itself may not be enough to keep women participating over time. Women who dropped out of the program "attributed lower personal importance to the activity, felt less personally pressured to do the activity, and could not express their reasons for participation" compared to the women who stayed with the program. Importantly, differences between women who remained involved and those who dropped out were not dramatic (Stephan et al., 2010).

For older women, beliefs about risks associated with physical activities can serve as deterrents or motivators. When women aged 70 and older (N = 143) were interviewed about their beliefs regarding benefits and risks associated with six different fitness activities (brisk walking, aquacizing, riding a bike or cycling, stretching slowly to touch the toes, doing modified push-ups, and doing supine curl-ups), there was general agreement that exercise and physical activity offered broad health benefits. However, some of the women revealed strong, even sensational, beliefs about risks that effectively served to limit their involvement even when they were capable of participating. Fear of overexertion, of being hurt, and of being physically vulnerable, as well as a general lack of confidence were identified (Cousins, 2000).

While these fears provide insight as to what holds some older women back from participating, insight can be gained from older women who participate in activities like the Senior Games. Engagement in a regular exercise or training program motivated women to be more physically active. Fun, health benefits, the opportunity to meet new people and be around friends in a social setting, competition, creative expression, and doctor's recommendation were all identified as factors that motivated older women to get out and move (Henderson, 2010).

Learning Aids

Summary

In her 2012 book *Aging With Strength*, 60-year-old Lorenn Walker presents the stories of 10 senior female athletes who have pursued rich lives in their sports of choice. Each has a unique message to share about their enduring love of sport, the seamlessness of who they are as women and athletes, and the strength they draw from their own inner reserves and those who inspire them. Among the women featured in the book is Audrey Sutherland, a solo kayak paddler who set out when she was 60 to explore the coast of Alaska on her own. Over the course of her career, she paddled more than 8,000 miles (13,000 km) of the southeast Alaska and British Columbia shorelines. At 91 (her age at the time the book was published), she was still focused on achieving her goals, taking incremental steps that led her to her dreams.

When taken as collective wisdom about the lives of senior female athletes, these stories offer compelling testament to the powerful connection between engagement in physical activity and sport and life fulfillment, as well as the remarkable capacity that women have to conquer fear, to make midcourse adjustments in order to search for understanding that comes only after the journey has been undertaken, to envision possibilities for themselves and those around them, to develop attitudes of excellence that embrace change, to foster positivism, to resist defeat, and to savor what life has to offer.

Discussion Questions

1. In the introduction to this chapter, you were introduced to ultramarathon swimmer Diana Nyad. In a 2012 video titled *Diana: A Documentary*, Nyad talks about

her journey and why she decided to take on the challenge of swimming from Cuba to Florida. To access the video, go to www.youtube.com/watch?v=eFh9Wq_FAjI. After viewing the video, what is your reaction to Diana's decision to devote her energies to this challenge? Does she challenge prevailing ideas about older women as athletes? (An alternative video to watch is *Diana Nyad: Xtreme Dream,* which aired on CNN on September 19, 2011. View it at www.cnn.com/video/data/2.0/video/health/2011/09/19/sgmd-diana-nyad-xtreme-dream.cnn.html.)

2. The 2012 documentary *Granny's Got Game* follows a senior women's basketball team for a year leading up into their participation in the National Senior Games. To watch the film, go to http://grannysgotgame.com.Listen carefully to the commentary throughout the film. How are the women in the film depicted? What is emphasized most: their athleticism, their age, or their status as women? What do you learn about these women and why their participation on the team is important to them? What surprised you about the film?

3. In the documentary *The Secret Lives of Seniors*, Lisa Ling explores the new realities of a growing population of Americans who are breaking the mold of what it means to age. After watching the film (www.youtube.com/watch?v=Z7_X-Gu51xs), interview an older woman in your life about her sport experiences, how her attitudes toward sport and physical activity have evolved over time, and her expectations to maintain an active lifestyle.

Learning Activities

1. Research the senior women's leagues in your area and interview at least one of the women who plays on the team.

2. The National Senior Games Association has a list of senior games in the United States. Locate the games in your state or area and volunteer to work at those or at a qualifying event for the games.

Glossary

successfully aging—A term used by a number of researchers that pertains to the results that accrue from older adults participating in meaningful activities while maintaining physical and cognitive functions that yield benefits in terms of life satisfaction, mental and physical well-being, and a robust quality of life.

CHAPTER 9

Women With Disabilities in Sport

Mary A. Hums, PhD, University of Louisville

Learning Objectives

In this chapter, you will learn about the following:

- History of sport for people with disabilities
- Different levels of sport opportunities for athletes with disabilities, including the Paralympic Games, Special Olympics, and grassroots opportunities
- Legal aspects that apply to athletes with disabilities, including Section 504 of the Rehabilitation Act of 1973, the Americans with Disabilities Act, the United Nations Convention on the Rights of Persons with Disabilities, and Dear Colleague Letter of 2013
- Participation by female athletes with disabilities at various levels
- Perspectives of women who are leaders in sport for people with disabilities
- Future for women with disabilities in sport

It's the situation you dream about. Runners on second and third, two outs in the late innings of a scoreless game. Walking in from the on-deck circle for your at bat, you hear the stadium announcer's voice: "Now batting, the shortstop—number 5—Mary Hums." As you step into the box, the umpire says, "Batter up! The count is 0-2." "Time out!" you say to the ump as you back out of the box. "I just stepped in! How can I have two strikes against me before I even get a chance to swing the bat?" The ump looks at you, points to the pitcher, and barks, "Play ball!"

As we all know, being a woman in sport can be challenging. Being a person with a disability in sport can be challenging as well. A woman with a disability entering the sporting arena faces twice the challenges. It's like having two strikes against you when you step into the batter's box. So what are we to learn from this situation? Over the years, we have come to learn that women with disabilities are pretty darn good two-strike hitters—they swing and watch a line drive sail over the pitcher's head into center field.

A Special Olympian holds her medal aloft. A blind marathon runner completes a grueling race. A wheelchair racer spins around the Paralympic Games track. A hearing-impaired basketball player guides her WNBA team to the championship. A cheerleader with a prosthetic leg leads the crowd at a college bowl game. An amputee golfer sinks a putt. Each of these athletes with disabilities is active and part of her sport. Yet according to Ian Brittain on the blog *Paralympicanorak*, "gender appears to play a key role in participation rates amongst persons with disabilities" (2012, para. 1). Before specifically examining women with disabilities in sport, it is important to have an idea of how opportunities for people with disabilities in sport[1] have evolved.

> *Disability is not a "brave struggle" or "courage in the face of adversity." Disability is an art. It's an ingenious way to live.*
>
> Neal Marcus in *Making an Entrance: Theory and Practice for Disabled and Non-Disabled Dancers*

According to the United Nations, approximately 15 percent of the world's population has a disability (United Nations Enable, n.d.). Opportunities for people with disabilities exist on all different levels. How have these opportunities evolved, and what influences have helped shape them? This chapter provides a brief overview of the general development of sport for people with disabilities, including some of the legal avenues that have helped open up participation opportunities. We will also hear from some women currently working in sport for people with disabilities, who provide their perspectives on the topic. The chapter concludes with some reflections on the future of women in sport for people with disabilities.

HISTORY OF SPORT FOR PEOPLE WITH DISABILITIES

It is a mistake to think that people with disabilities are not interested in sport! Research indicates that people with disabilities are very interested in sport and physical activity, if the opportunities are available to them. People with disabilities have been active in sport and physical activities over the years. According to Sportanddev.org, "there is evidence of people with a disability participating in sport as early as the 18th and 19th centuries and sport activities were instrumental in the rehabilitation of people with a disability" ("Milestones in APA," n.d., para. 1). Sport clubs for the deaf existed in Berlin in 1888 (International Paralympic Committee, n.d.-a). The first Silent Games were held in 1924, and World Games for the Deaf have been held every four years since then. While the documented history of sport for people with disabilities is sparse, it is evident that opportunities are continuing to grow due to legislation and increased visibility of major events.

PARTICIPATION OF FEMALE ATHLETES WITH DISABILITIES

Girls and women with disabilities want to participate or compete in sport at whatever level is appropriate for them. Yet girls and women with disabilities face a double discrimination—

being disabled and being a woman. Girls and women with disabilities can participate at the grassroots level or in more organized settings. Two major multisport events that illustrate the continued development of sport for people with disabilities are the Paralympic Games and the Special Olympics. The following sections talk about these three levels of opportunity: grassroots, Special Olympics, and the Paralympic Games.

Grassroots Opportunities

Getting the general population up and moving is always a challenge, particularly in this day and age of video games and mobile devices. People with disabilities face more hurdles to being active and are three times more likely to be sedentary than their able-bodied peers (Women's Sports Foundation, 2007). Yet girls and women with disabilities want to be active and healthy. Not everyone has the skills, abilities, resources, or access to training to be an elite athlete. Some girls and women with disabilities just want to be able to get out and move and feel as if they are making strides to stay healthy. This may mean heading to the pool to swim or exercise in the water, taking a yoga class, playing in a city softball league, teeing off for a round of golf, or visiting a local park to take advantage of an accessible nature trail. The White House Task Force on Childhood Obesity reports (2010, p. 67):

> There is growing awareness that many activity and health disparities reported among children and adults with disabilities are not necessarily a direct result of the disability, but rather a result of the challenges these individuals face in accessing community services and programs. Such challenges include poor accessibility of facilities, services, and programs, as well as environmental barriers such as lack of accessible equipment or transportation.

While it may be difficult for people with disabilities to access these types of activities, some organizations work particularly with young people with disabilities to help them be active. In the United States, organizations such as Blaze

Sports America as well as the National Center on Health, Physical Activity and Disability, the National Ability Center, and the Inclusive Sports Initiative with the Institute for Human Centered Design all provide information on promoting sport and physical activity for people with disabilities. The U.S. National Park Service has a free access pass for people with disabilities, and many state parks and local park systems offer similar packages. Numerous cities play host to a Miracle Baseball League, where girls and boys with disabilities of all types play baseball on special fields designed for safe use of wheelchairs, walkers, and scooters. (The author of this chapter had the honor of throwing out the first pitch on opening day 2013 for the Toyota Bluegrass Miracle League in Lexington, Kentucky. As a lifelong baseball fan, softball player, and a woman with a disability, it was a highlight beyond compare!)

We must also keep in mind that the need for people with disabilities to be active is not limited to North America, but is a global issue. When looking at developing nations, people with disabilities, and particularly girls and women, face an even greater uphill battle. Organizations like Sport 4 Socialisation in Zimbabwe, Handicap International, and Survivor Corps (formerly the Landmine Survivors Network) use sport as a means to facilitate healthy living for people with disabilities.

Many local and national organizations provide sport and physical activities for people with disabilities. The United States Olympic Committee (USOC) established U.S. Paralympics to oversee the development of Paralympic sport in the United States. The USOC's Paralympic Military Program and the Wounded Warrior Project provide sport and recreational opportunities for wounded U.S. veterans who served in recent military conflicts and occupations. Other organizational examples that provide grassroots participation opportunities include the National Ability Center in Park City, Utah; TOP Soccer with state organizations around the United States; the Lakeshore Foundation in Birmingham, Alabama; and Disabled Sports USA, with chapters in all 50 states.

Blaze Sports America provides sport opportunities that bring with them life lessons. The goals of Blaze Sports are as follows (Blaze Sports America, 2013, para. 4):

- To provide sport, recreation and physical activity opportunities for people with physical disability in sport comparable to those provided [to] nondisabled [participants], nationally and internationally.
- To foster character development, productive lives, healthy lifestyles and self-sufficiency for people with physical disability through sport.
- To use cutting-edge training, distance learning opportunities, and fresh ideas as a vehicle to build the capacity of local service providers.
- To build positive perceptions of people with physical disability.
- To promote peace building, human rights and equity through sport.

Sometimes people with disabilities want to participate on their own, and other times they wish to be a part of a greater organization. One such organization for people with intellectual disabilities is Special Olympics.

Special Olympics

Special Olympics is a well-known organization that provides sporting opportunities for people with cognitive disabilities. Its beginnings grew from the interest of Eunice Kennedy Shriver. Mrs. Kennedy Shriver had observed how unjustly people with intellectual disabilities

> *Courage can be contagious. For girls, especially girls who are also in the minority in some other way, sport can be the vehicle to develop courage. When you are a double or triple or quadruple minority, we must consciously teach the development of courage in order to instill confidence and to ensure one's view of self is positive. Sport, by its very nature, helps to do this.*
>
> Anjali Forber-Pratt, PhD, U.S. Paralympian—Beijing 2008 and London 2012

were treated, and decided to take personal action to change things through sport and physical activity. In the late 1950s and early 1960s, she developed a series of summer day camps for young people with disabilities. Her summer camp concept spread across the country until literally thousands of people with intellectual disabilities were active, moving, and participating. On the 50th anniversary of the founding of Special Olympics, *Sports Illustrated* honored Mrs. Kennedy Shriver with its inaugural Sportsman of the Year Legacy Award. In his tribute to her, Jack McCallum wrote,

> You watch and what you see is nothing less than a transformation, the passage of someone who has been labeled unfortunate, handicapped, disabled or challenged to something else: athlete. Eunice Kennedy Shriver knew this could happen. Fifty years ago she saw it all. For that, we recognize her as one of those revolutionaries who saw opportunity where others saw barriers, someone who started a movement and changed a world. (2008, p. 5)

This courageous woman's early work blossomed into the Special Olympics we know today.

In 2012, Special Olympics hit a milestone, registering more than 4 million athletes worldwide in its programs. In addition to local and state events, the Special Olympics World Games take place every two years, alternating in a cycle similar to the Olympic Games, with both Summer and Winter Games. Host cities have included Dublin, Ireland; Shanghai, China; and Athens, Greece. In 2015, the Summer Games were held in Los Angeles, California. Special Olympics has also been in the forefront of leading the campaign against use of "the R word," *retarded*, as an insult to describe someone as less intelligent or less skillful (Grinberg, 2012).

Special Olympics offers 30-plus Olympic-style individual and team sports on its program, and women are active participants. As of 2013, almost 40 percent of Special Olympics athletes were female (Special Olympics, n.d.-b).

The gender ratio between male and female athletes changed in 2008, signaling a trend toward greater participation among female athletes. It is currently 1.6:1 with 1.6 male athletes for every female athlete. There are some interesting regional variations regarding athletes and gender. In 2008, Asia-Pacific reported the highest level of female participation of all seven regions, followed by Africa. In these regions, female participation constitutes more than 42 and 41 percent of the total, respectively. (Special Olympics, n.d.-a., para. 6)

With Special Olympics, participants learn social skills, healthy living habits, and sport fundamentals. No doubt many of you reading this have at one time or another volunteered to help at a Special Olympics event. Maybe you were a finish line hugger, a coach, an event organizer, or part of a Unified Team, where people with and without disabilities play on the same team. Special Olympics continues to provide opportunities for people with disabilities in local communities around the world.

While the focus in Special Olympics is primarily on participation and developing social skills, some female athletes with disabilities are highly skilled and want to compete at elite national and international levels. For them, the prize is representing their countries on a global stage—the Paralympic Games.

Paralympic Games

The first major competition for people with disabilities took place at Stoke Mandeville Hospital in Great Britain in 1948. There, Dr. Ludwig Guttmann, who worked at the hospital, incorporated sport and physical activity into the rehabilitation of soldiers injured in World War II, organizing "the first competition for wheelchair athletes which he named the Stoke Mandeville Games. They involved 16 injured servicemen and women who took part in Archery" (International Paralympic Committee, n.d.-a, para. 4). Interestingly, women were among these first competitors, and their numbers have grown slowly and steadily in the Paralympic Movement over the years. From humble beginnings, the competitions expanded to include more events and competitors (including women) and eventually evolved into the Paralympic Games.

The first Summer Paralympic Games took place in Rome, Italy, in 1960, and the first Winter Paralympic Games were in Sweden in 1976. Just like the Olympic Games, the Paralympic Games take place every four years. Held two weeks after the Olympic Games end, the Paralympic Games are held in the same cities and venues as the Olympic Games. The most recent Summer Paralympic Games, hosted in London in 2012, featured more than 4,200 athletes representing 164 countries (International Paralympic Committee, n.d.-b), while the 2014 Sochi Winter Paralympic Games showcased close to 550 competitors from 45 countries. In Rio de Janeiro in 2016, the Paralympic Games program is scheduled to include 526 medal events in 22 sports. The athletes and teams competing in the Paralympic Games reached that status by meeting a required standard at a sanctioned qualifying event or by placing at a certain rank at international team competitions. Competitors have specific physical disabilities, including athletes with visual impairments, amputees, those who have cerebral palsy, or those who are short in stature. Some athletes with intellectual disabilities compete, but on a very limited basis.

Women are more visible now at the Paralympic Games, but it has been a long road for them. Women were among the very first competitors at Stoke Mandeville in the 1940s. Forty-four women competed in the first Summer Paralympic Games and 37 at the first Winter Paralympic Games. While the numbers would slowly increase, an organizational plan was needed to make that happen.

In an effort to address the shortage of women as athletes, coaches, officials, and leaders, the International Paralympic Committee (IPC) established the Women in Sport Commission (WISC) in 2003. Specifically, the purposes of the WISC are to "advocate for the full inclusion of girls and women at all levels of Paralympic sport, identify barriers that restrict participation, recommend policies and initiatives that address these barriers, and oversee the implementation of initiatives to increase participation" (International Paralympic Committee, 2010, p. 4).

In 2010, the IPC issued its Women in Sport Leadership toolkit. In that document, the organization expressed its desire to increase women's participation:

Athletes with disabilities compete year-round in a variety of sports.

The IPC views gender equity and more specifically the participation of girls and women in Paralympic Sport as a priority. It believes it is important for girls and women to have the opportunity to participate in sport from a recreational to an elite level. Therefore, the IPC is dedicated to addressing the actual and perceived barriers. (International Paralympic Committee, 2010, p. 4)

The IPC has made participation by women a priority, including the following goal in its strategic plan: "to develop opportunities for female athletes and athletes with a severe impairment in sport at all levels and in all structures" (International Paralympic Committee, 2013, p. 7). The IPC has also sponsored regional summits for women with disabilities in sport.

So, how have the IPC's efforts played out? At London 2012, a record 1,501 female athletes competed across 18 sports, more than twice the number who participated in the Barcelona Games in 1992.

The number of women taking part in the Paralympic Games has enjoyed great growth in recent times. At the Atlanta 1996 Games, 790 female athletes took part, followed by 990 at Sydney 2000, 1,165 at Athens 2004, and 1,383 at Beijing 2008. (International Paralympic Committee, n.d.-c., para. 3)

On the higher levels, efforts are in place to increase the number of women in leadership positions in Paralympic sport. As of 2013, three women were members of the IPC's governing board: Ann Cody of the United States, Rita van Driel of the Netherlands, and Kyung-won Na of South Korea. A limitation that women face in reaching this level is that they must move up through the ranks of their national Paralympic committees first. In some countries, men hold many of the upper level positions and so women cannot break through that glass ceiling. In addition, these women often face barriers similar to those faced by women working in other sport organizations, such as dealing with work–life balance (see chapters 12 and 13).

The women who have ascended to positions of influence and power within the Paralympic movement are tremendous role models as leaders. Later sections of this chapter include some of their stories—stories of athletes, coaches, and advocates.

The influence of sport on the lives of people with disabilities is immeasurably positive. Although you might think these opportunities have always been readily available and abundant, this is not the case. Over the years, people with disabilities have had to fight for acceptance and access. One major method for doing this has been through the legal system. The next section discusses important legal mechanisms people with disabilities have used to gain access to sport and physical activities.

LEGAL SYSTEM AS AN ACCESS TOOL

These days, when you go to a mall, school, or airport, curb cuts and accessible parking spaces seem to be the norm. This was not always the case, however. For many years, people with disabilities were limited in where they could shop, learn, or travel, among other activities able-bodied people took for granted. During the Civil Rights movement in the United States during the 1960s and '70s, laws were passed to limit discrimination against people based on demographics such as race, gender (think Title IX), age, and disability. These laws helped open up access for people with disabilities in commerce, travel, and education. At times, opportunities for people with disabilities to participate in sport and physical activity have come about due to impetus from the legal system. This section discusses some legal documents that have opened up the world of sport to people with disabilities.

Section 504 of the Rehabilitation Act of 1973

The first major piece of legislation that dealt with discrimination against people with disabilities was Section 504 of the Rehabilitation Act of 1973. In a nutshell, this piece of legislation commonly referred to as *Section 504* opened up educational opportunities for people with disabilities.

Section 504 states that "no qualified individual with a disability in the United States shall be excluded from, denied the benefits of, or be subjected to discrimination under" any program or activity that either receives Federal financial assistance or is conducted by any Executive agency. (U.S. Department of Justice, 2009, Rehabilitation Act section)

Triathlon and Canoe: Two New Paralympic Sports

The Paralympic Games are constantly updating the program of sports offered. In 2016 in Rio de Janeiro, triathlon will make its Paralympic debut, and female competitors will be part of those very first competitions. Women are competing in triathlon in increasing numbers around the world, so it only makes sense that women with disabilities should be included in this inaugural event. Competitors will qualify by placement at recognized IPC-sanctioned world qualifying events.

In canoeing, the athletes will compete in the same events as their able-bodied counterparts do in the Olympic Games. Governed by the International Canoe Federation, paracanoe gives paddlers of differing abilities the chance to compete at their highest level. Women will be represented in this new event, which debuts in Rio de Janeiro in 2016 as well. The competitors are classified based on their functional ability in paddling and in applying force to the foot board or seat to propel the boat.

Which sports will debut next? That remains to be seen, but women with disabilities are eager to compete in as many different sports and events at the Paralympic Games as possible. These elite athletes are truly role models to young athletes around the world, and the Paralympic light will shine brightly on them in Brazil!

Basically, Section 504 makes it illegal for any program receiving federal funds to discriminate against someone because he or she has a disability. Regarding sport and physical activity specifically,

> A recipient of federal funds cannot discriminate on the basis of disability in providing physical education courses and athletics programs. A recipient that offers P.E. courses or intramural athletics must provide to qualified students with disabilities an equal opportunity for participation in these activities. This may require a reasonable accommodation. . . . Also, you cannot be denied the opportunity to compete for regular teams or to participate in regular courses. Most students with disabilities are able to participate in one or more regular physical education and athletic activities. A reasonable accommodation may have to be given. (Illinois Legal Aid, 2005, Physical Education and Athletics section)

Section 504 remains the law, but in 2013, the U.S. Office of Civil Rights issued a set of guidelines referred to as a *Dear Colleague Letter* that offered more specific information on the application of Section 504 to sport in schools.

Dear Colleague Letter of 2013

The Dear Colleague Letter provided further guidance for the implementation of Section 504. The letter was not a new law, but rather served to provide additional clarification for existing regulations and policies established by Section 504.

According to Active Policy Solutions (2013, p. 2):

> Section 504 of the Rehabilitation Act of 1973 requires that schools provide students with disabilities equal opportunities to participate in schools' extracurricular activities—including club, varsity and intramural sport programs. To allow students with disabilities to participate in athletics to the greatest extent possible, schools can provide the following participation opportunities:
>
> - **Mainstream programs**—school-based activities that are developed and offered to all students
> - **Adapted physical education and athletic programs**—programs that are specifically developed for students with disabilities
> - **Allied or unified sports**—programs that are specifically designed to combine groups of students with and without disabilities together in physical activity.

These guidelines make it very clear that high school and university students with disabilities need to have access to appropriate athletic opportunities (Moorman & Hums, 2013; Stau-

The Impact of Policy on Students With Disabilities

Terri Lakowski, CEO of Active Policy Solutions

The Dear Colleague Letter is a landmark moment for individuals with disabilities, and will do for students with disabilities what Title IX did for women. The landscape of leadership that governs sports is changing. Educational institutions are responding to the resonating message that students with disabilities must be provided opportunities for physical activity and sports equal to those afforded to students without disabilities.

Students with disabilities are entitled to enjoy the benefits that involvement in sports can provide, including a teaching environment for self-discipline, teamwork, and confidence. The actions of the Office for Civil Rights will pave the way for more individuals with disabilities to follow, resulting in happier, healthier future generations, regardless of disability.

rowsky, 2013). Schools need to meet the interest of their students with disabilities—remember, it is incorrect to assume people with disabilities are not interested in sport and physical activity. Actually, that sounds a little bit like the outdated pre–Title IX notions (see chapter 2) that girls were not interested in sport! Increasing offerings that are open to students with disabilities will not reduce opportunities for able-bodied students. Remember also that just because a student with a disability tries out for a team, there is no guarantee of a roster spot on a team unless the student has sufficient skill levels to warrant a place on the team. These students are entitled to a fair tryout, however. This Dear Colleague Letter benefits students both with and without disabilities. The students with disabilities have an opportunity to contribute to a team and the able-bodied students earn a greater appreciation for the abilities of their fellow athletes who happen to have a disability.

Section 504 and its updated guidelines in the Dear Colleague Letter are just part of the current legal landscape applicable to people with disabilities. The landmark Americans with Disabilities Act also lays out the legal framework of opportunities.

Americans With Disabilities Act

Twenty years after Section 504 became law, many parts of the language needed to be revisited. As a result, Congress passed the Americans with Disabilities Act (ADA) into law in 1990. This piece of legislation extended the rights of people with disabilities. "The ADA prohibits discrimination on the basis of disability in employment, State and local government, public accommodations, commercial facilities, transportation, and telecommunications. It also applies to the United States Congress" (U.S. Department of Justice, 2009, ADA section). Sport and physical activity are included under this law since access to places of public accommodation such as recreation facilities, arenas, stadiums, and fitness clubs all fall under the reach of the ADA.

Many people became aware of the ADA and its relationship to sport through the landmark Supreme Court case involving PGA golfer Casey Martin. Martin, a professional golfer with a pro-

nounced mobility disability, sought to use a cart while competing in PGA events. Although it had to go all the way to the Supreme Court before succeeding, the Martin case was a victory for people with disabilities generally, and it shone a spotlight on people with disabilities and sport (Moorman & Masteralexis, 2001).

While the focus so far in this chapter has been on the U.S. legal system, access for people with disabilities is a global concern. In order to ensure that people with disabilities around the world are treated with dignity and respect, the United Nations has weighed in on the issue.

United Nations Convention on the Rights of Persons With Disabilities

While numerous legal actions in the United States have resulted in gains for people with disabilities, the same could not always be uniformly said across nations around the world. The major international organization that sets the tone globally in the area of promoting human rights and equality is the United Nations. Over the years, the United Nations has addressed the treatment of numerous groups, including women, refugees, religious minorities, children, and, in the first human rights treaty of the 21st century, people with disabilities. In an effort to raise the status of people with disabilities, the United Nations General Assembly approved the Convention on the Rights of Persons with Disabilities in 2006, and it was ratified (took the force of law) in 2008.

The following provides a little background on the meaning of *convention* in the context of the United Nations:

> The generic term "convention" is generically synonymous with the generic term "treaty". . . Whereas in the last century the term "convention" was regularly employed for bilateral agreements, it now is generally used for formal multilateral treaties with a broad number of parties. Conventions are normally open for participation by the international community as a whole, or by a large number of states. (United Nations, 2006, para. 13-14)

In addition, "through ratification of international human rights treaties, Governments undertake to put into place domestic measures and legislation compatible with their treaty obligations and duties" (United Nations Human Rights, 2013, para. 4). In other words, when a required number of countries ratify (approve) a convention, the convention takes the power of international law, and governments must work to implement the convention into their own countries' domestic laws.

The United Nations has ratified numerous human rights conventions and treaties that mention sport or physical activity, including the Convention on the Elimination of All Forms of Discrimination Against Women, the International Convention Against Apartheid in Sports, and the Convention on the Rights of the Child. The convention with the most well-defined language regarding sport is the Convention on the Rights of Persons with Disabilities (CRPD). Article 30.5 (Participation in Cultural Life, Recreation, Leisure, and Sport) of this Convention contains the following language (United Nations, 2006, p. 23):

5. With a view to enabling persons with disabilities to participate on an equal basis with others in recreational, leisure and sporting activities, States Parties shall take appropriate measures:

a. To encourage and promote the participation, to the fullest extent possible, of persons with disabilities in mainstream sporting activities at all levels;

b. To ensure that persons with disabilities have an opportunity to organize, develop and participate in disability-specific sporting and recreational activities and, to this end, encourage the provision, on an equal basis with others, of appropriate instruction, training and resources;

c. To ensure that persons with disabilities have access to sporting, recreational and tourism venues;

d. To ensure that children with disabilities have equal access with other children to participation in play, recreation and leisure and sporting activities, including those activities in the school system;

e. To ensure that persons with disabilities have access to services from those involved in the organization of recreational, tourism, leisure and sporting activities.

Sport and Human Rights

The United Nations and sport may seem like an odd pairing. When we think of human rights, we generally think of issues such as access to safe drinking water, sufficient health care, or the ability to be free from religious or political discrimination. However, sport has a place in this discussion as well in two ways. First, the practice of sport is a human right, and it has been recognized as such by organizations such as the United Nations and the International Olympic Committee, which has such language in its governing document, the Olympic Charter. Similar to art or music, participation in sport makes us more fully human. Second, sport can be used to promote human rights. This was seen, for example, at the 1968 Olympic Games when Tommie Smith and John Carlos stood on the medal stand with black-gloved fists raised aloft in protest of treatment of African Americans in the United States and again at the 2014 Olympic Games in Sochi when athletes such as Martina Navratilova and Greg Louganis spoke out against the oppressive anti-LGBT laws in Russia. Sport offers a platform for the discussion of human rights in many ways, and athletes and sport managers can serve as leaders in the discussion.

Laws like Section 504 of the Rehabilitation Act, the Americans with Disabilities Act, and the United Nations' Convention on the Rights of Persons with Disabilities work to allow equal access to athletes of all abilities.

The national and international influence of the CRPD is still being assessed (Clifford, 2011; Harpur & Bales, 2010; Hums, Wolff, & Morris, 2009; Moorman & Hums, 2010). Hopefully, this international document will soon begin to affect sport and physical activity opportunities for people with disabilities around the globe. There is no question, however, that the CRPD applies to sport and to the work of sport managers as well. While the majority of leaders in the sport industry are men, the number of women in leadership positions continues to rise. This is also true in the realm of sport for people with disabilities, where we see a number of prominent women in leadership positions.

WOMEN AS LEADERS IN SPORT FOR PEOPLE WITH DISABILITIES

Although women with disabilities face challenges as athletes, some do manage to rise above those challenges and become leaders in sport for people with disabilities. These women bring with them interesting stories and strong leadership skills. This section profiles a few women with disabilities who have risen to the top and continue to advocate for women with disabilities in sport.

- *Ann Cody.* Ann Cody, who hails from tiny Homer, New York, represented the United States in three Paralympic Games: 1984 (basketball), 1988, and 1992 (athletics). A gold medalist in athletics, she has been around Paralympic sport for many years. Like so many other elite athletes with disabilities, she earned her degrees from the University of Illinois. Currently, she is the director of policy and global outreach for Blaze Sports America. In addition, Cody is one of only three women serving on the IPC's governing board, making her one of the most powerful women in international sport.

- *Linda Mastandrea.* A Paralympian and native of Chicago, Illinois, Linda Mastandrea has devoted her life to promoting the cause of people with disabilities in sport. She represented the United States in two Paralympic Games in athletics, setting numerous national, world, and Paralympic records along the way. After earning her undergraduate degree at the University of Illinois, Mastandrea went on to become a practicing attorney, specializing in disability and civil rights. When Chicago cast its bid to host the 2016 Olympic and Paralympic Games, Mastandrea provided a strong voice for the Paralympic aspects of the bid. A tireless campaigner for people with disabilities, she serves on the boards of a number of disability advocacy organizations ("About Linda," n.d.).

- *Stephanie Wheeler.* Stephanie Wheeler established herself as a wheelchair basketball star, winning three national championships while competing for the University of Illinois and also being part of two USA Paralympic gold medal winning teams, in Athens and again in Beijing (Division of Disability Resources & Educational Services, n.d.; United States Olympic Committee, n.d.). The native of Norlina, North Carolina, has now moved up the ranks to be the head coach of the team she once led to the medal stand. She will lead the team into the 2016 Summer Paralympic Games in Rio de Janeiro, Brazil. She is one of just a handful of female Paralympic sport coaches with a disability.

- *Tatyana McFadden.* Born in Russia and adopted by a family in the United States, Tatyana McFadden is widely known for her fight to be allowed to compete on the track with her teammates when she was a student at Atholton High School in Columbia, Maryland. Her legal battle resulted in the state legislature passing the Fitness and Athletics Equity for Students with Disability Act, "the first law in the country to allow, and encourage, students with disabilities to participate in their schools' sports programs" ("Equity in Sport," n.d.). McFadden, another University of Illinois athlete, medaled in three Paralympic Games in athletics ("About Tatyana," n.d.), but her biggest victory came off the track as an advocate who successfully challenged the law in Maryland and opened up opportunities in sport and physical activity for people with disabilities.

- *Aimee Mullins.* Athlete, advocate, fashion model—how many times are these three words used to describe the same person? All these would be included in any introduction of Aimee Mullins. A native of Allentown, Pennsylvania, Mullins represented the United States in the Paralympic Games and has since gone on to be an outstanding advocate for

women and people with disabilities in sport. A past president of the Women's Sports Foundation; a model who has been featured in fashion publications such as *Elle, Cosmopolitan, Harper's Bazaar, W,* and *Glamour;* and an advocate seen on TED ("Biography: Aimee Mullins," n.d.), Mullins actively seeks to change people's definition of the word *disabled.*

> There's an important difference and distinction between the objective medical fact of my being an amputee and the subjective societal opinion of whether or not I'm disabled. Truthfully, the only real and consistent disability I've had to confront is the world ever thinking that I could be described by those definitions. ("Paralympic Record Breaker," 2012, para. 3)

THE FUTURE FOR GIRLS AND WOMEN WITH DISABILITIES IN SPORT

Girls and women with disabilities are gradually seeing more opportunities open up for them, but progress is at times painfully slow. What needs to be done into the future to help girls and women with disabilities access sport and physical activities? Cody (n.d.) makes the following suggestions:

Signs of Progress

Ann Cody

In 2009, the International Paralympic Committee General Assembly elected three women (and nine men) to its governing board—the most women ever to serve. The 2012 Paralympic Games saw more women athletes enter and compete in more events than at any time in history. These are all quite positive signs of progress. More work remains if we are to achieve gender equity in this domain, however. In disability sport, we are keenly aware of the detrimental effects of marginalization; therefore, we must hold ourselves to a higher standard of inclusivity. It is imperative that we continue to encourage women coaches, athletes, officials, and sport administrators to seek leadership positions in sport. When equal numbers of women and men are elected to sport decision-making bodies, we will have made progress.

Ann Cody is the director of policy and global outreach for Blaze Sports America and a member of the International Paralympic Committee Board of Governors.

- Increase participation of women and girls with disabilities at the local level at YMCAs, local road races, and high school sport.
- Provide women with disabilities more competitive sport opportunities.
- Showcase female athletes with disabilities and sports, as BOSTON 2024 has done by naming Paralympian and Boston Marathon champion Cheri Blauwet to its board of directors.
- Involve women and men with and without disabilities and organizations ranging from the Women's Sports Foundation to state high school athletic associations in outreach programs to recruit more female athletes with disabilities.
- Train more female coaches to work with athletes with disabilities.

These suggestions make good sense, and they require people willing to believe in girls and women with disabilities in order to come to fruition. In this effort, people with disabilities and their able-bodied allies will need to partner together to create change. A notion that is implied in these suggestions is the need for more female role models and mentors in the forms of athletes and coaches. The idea of "If I can see one, I can be one" is very powerful. More media coverage of our athletes with disabilities in the Paralympic Games will certainly help create interest in young athletes with disabilities. The issuance of the Dear Colleague Letter will definitely affect opportunities for girls in high school and college sport. The sooner girls with disabilities can see other girls and women with disabilities being active, the better chance their interest will be sparked.

Learning Aids

Summary

People with disabilities want to participate in sport just like their able-bodied peers. This is just as true for girls and women as it is for boys and men. Opportunities for participation and competition can take various forms, from local to international and from recreational to elite. Organizations like the International Paralympic Committee and Special Olympics are leading the way to open the doors for girls and women with disabilities to be more active. Local organizations serve people with disabilities in their communities by offering sport and recreation opportunities at different levels.

According to the International Olympic Committee, "the practice of sport is a human right" (2011, p. 10). This means for *everyone*—men and women, people who are able-bodied and people with disabilities. Sport in and of itself is neither positive nor negative, but it has the power to transform us and make us more fully human. Don't we all deserve that?

Remember that batter in the opening scenario stepping into the box with two strikes against her? Listen to Stephanie Wheeler's words: "The future for women with disabilities in sport is bright! Sport will serve as an incredible vehicle for inclusion and social justice" (personal communication, August 1, 2013). The world she envisions is one where sport can serve as a means for inclusion of girls and women with disabilities, one where the playing field will be level and women with disabilities in sport will earn their two-strike counts like any other batter. In that world, when the umpire says, "Play ball!" we all win.

Discussion Questions

1. This chapter presented the stories of five influential women in sport for people with disabilities. Research similar information on five more women who have influenced sport for people with disabilities.

2. You have been given the opportunity to intern with U.S. Paralympics. As part of your internship, you will be working with different national governing bodies that oversee sports for athletes with disabilities, including a new Paralympic sport, paratriathlon, which will be on the Paralympic program for the first time in Rio in 2016. One of your responsibilities is to help increase the number of female athletes with disabilities in this emerging Paralympic sport. What strategies will you use?

3. Think back to your experience as a high school athlete. Did you ever compete with or against an athlete with a disability? What did that experience teach you about people with disabilities? What did it teach you about your personal status as either *(a)* an able-bodied person or *(b)* a person with a disability?

Learning Exercises

1. As soon as the opportunity presents itself, volunteer at a local Special Olympics event. After doing so, reflect on the following:
   a. Describe the event and your responsibilities at the event.
   b. How did you feel about your contribution to the event?
   c. Describe any interactions you had with the athletes and their families.
   d. After this experience, are you likely to volunteer at a similar event in the future? Why or why not?
   e. What did you learn about people with disabilities and their experience of sport? How was it similar or different from your experiences with sport?

2. Visit the International Paralympic Committee website (www.paralympic.org) and then follow the links to watch video highlights of two different men's and two different women's sports from any recent Paralympic Games. After watching, answer the following questions:
   a. Describe the look of the Games (e.g., colors, flags, venues, uniforms).
   b. How were the athletes from different countries depicted? How did athletes from different countries approach the sport differently? Were any fans from different countries covered or discussed? If so, what did you see?
   c. During the time you watched, explain any major issues that came up during the competition or that the announcers discussed.
   d. What are two things you especially liked about watching the Paralympic sports you chose to watch? What are two questions you would now like to have answered about these sports?
   e. What were your impressions of the female athletes who competed and their sports?

Glossary

adapted physical education and athletic programs—Programs that are specifically developed for students with disabilities.

allied or unified sports—Programs specifically designed to combine groups of students with and without disabilities together in physical activity.

mainstream programs—School-based activities that are developed and offered to all students.

Note

1. Various terminology exists when people discuss this topic. In this chapter, the author will use the phrase *sport for people with disabilities* because it is more inclusive than *disability sport*, which refers to sport specifically designed for people with disabilities. Although the chosen term can include sport where only people with disabilities participate, it also includes sport where people with disabilities participate with and against able-bodied counterparts. People-first language will also be used throughout the chapter, such as *people with disabilities* or *athletes with disabilities*.

CHAPTER 10

Women, Sport, and Sexual Violence

Ellen J. Staurowsky, EdD, Drexel University

Learning Objectives

In this chapter, you will learn about the following:

- Terms associated with sexual violence, including *bystander intervention, rape, rape myth, sexual abuse, sexual assault,* and *sexual harassment*
- The prevalence of sexual violence that affects girls and women in sport
- The blurred boundaries that exist in coach–athlete relationships
- Legal remedies that may be sought when sexual violence against women in sport occurs in education and the workplace
- Approaches to education and prevention

Before you begin reading this chapter. There is no easy way to talk about sexual violence. What we know is that it is the rare person who will not eventually be affected by it in some way. Even if you never personally experience sexual violence, someone around you has, and is living with the consequences, whether you know it or not. Some of the content to follow may trigger emotions for you. Use your own emotional barometer to determine how in depth your reading will be. If this material triggers unpleasant memories and reactions, consider speaking with your instructor to explore alternatives.

On a warm evening in late summer, a 16-year-old girl who was an honor student and athlete set out for a night of partying in a neighboring community. With the start of the school year approaching, young people by the dozens—academics, jocks, nice kids, snobs, stoners, troublemakers—converged at the home of a volunteer football coach to take advantage of one more night of glorious freedom before classes, practices, volunteer service, church, and part-time jobs consumed their lives in the months ahead. Earlier in the day, the girl thought about what she was going to wear, rehearsed the story she was going to tell her parents about what she was doing that night, made arrangements to get a ride to the party from a girlfriend, and wondered whom she might meet.

Arriving to the sounds of "Party Rock" by LMFAO, the wave of energy in the first room she entered pulled her along into the house, past kids dancing, the random guy trying too hard to hit on the pretty girl, a couple in the corner having a fight. She got a blue slushie in a red plastic cup. It was spiked with vodka and tasted good. A nice way to start the evening, she thought, or so it seemed.

In the days following the party, the girl really couldn't say exactly when things began to unravel. To be honest, she really couldn't remember. The slushie followed by a shot of vodka straight up and then another drink left her weaving and uncertain on her feet. She remembers feeling drunk, wanting to get some air, and heading outside holding hands with the star quarterback of the high school football team. That would be her last recollection before waking up the next morning, naked and lying on the floor of a stranger's house. While the events of that night eluded her, others at the party were recording what happened to her on social media through photos, tweets, and video, a documentary history eventually shared with millions. Throughout the night, bystanders witnessed her sexual violation but chose to mock her instead of attempting to stop the crimes committed against her by the football players she met at the party.

After a friend picked her up the next morning, the girl pieced together what had happened to her as she tuned in to Facebook, Twitter, and her local newspaper, realizing that she was being described as a "slut" and a "drunken whore." The dawn of a new day offered an explanation for the physical discomfort she felt as the details of her rape played out in public view, a view that her parents would inevitably see as well, as graphic photos were posted to Instagram. She found the image of her unconscious body carried by the quarterback and wide receiver like a potato sack, photographed by a third football player, posted to Facebook and held up for public comment. Although she was unaware while at the party that she had been an object of ridicule, she learned in the aftermath that a baseball player, at the urging of other partygoers, had urinated on her.[1] She harbored a fear afterward that she had been drugged, a fear that many dismissed as untrue. However, this fear had a foundation in the symptoms she exhibited, including her physical collapse, nausea and vomiting, and blackout.

As disturbing as we find this story, based in large part on what came to be known as the Steubenville High School football rape case (Macur & Schweber, 2012; Noveck, 2013; Welsh-Huggins, 2013; Wetzel, 2013), its elements speak to the underlying belief structures held by many that misinterpret what sexual violence against women and girls is or that wrongly justify it, belief structures experts refer to as **rape myths**. Misunderstandings about the nature of sexual violence are reflected in some people's inability to recognize what happened to the girl as a rape and in the actions of others that fed into the incident's occurrence.

To illustrate, one of the players who stood by and watched what happened to the 16-year-old victim, unmoved to do anything other than use his cell phone to video the event, explained afterward that he did not see what his teammates were doing to the girl, who could barely speak or move, as a crime (Ove, 2013; Wetzel, 2013). The inability of perpetrators and bystanders to empathize with the harms done to victims was further demonstrated in this case by victim blaming, where the girl who was violated became the object of public humiliation because she had been drinking and may have been flirting with the players. None of her accomplishments as a student or athlete nor her relationships with friends protected her that night. A party hosted

One in five women has reported rape. You might never know, when talking to a group of people or friends, that one of them could be the "one" part of the statistic.

by a volunteer coach where underage drinking occurred and where two players from his team targeted a vulnerable girl reflects the troubling issue that coaches may knowingly or unknowingly contribute to a climate where these kinds of behaviors are acceptable (Macur & Schweber, 2012).

As high profile as the Steubenville case became, the fact that a high school girl was raped and subjected to ridicule is not a new story by itself. According to the U.S. Centers for Disease Control and Prevention, 10.5 percent of high school–age girls have been sexually assaulted (Gregoire, 2012). In the United States, 1 of every 5 women (18.3%) and 1 in 71 men (1.4%) report being raped at some point. Should the Steubenville victim go to college, she will share the experience of having been through an attempted or completed **sexual assault** with 20 percent of her female undergraduate classmates (Krebs, Lindquist, Warner, Fisher, & Martin, 2007).

The conduct of the male perpetrators in this case conforms to patterns that have been well established in the research as well (Crosset, Ptacek, McDonald, & Benedict, 1996; Forbes,

Adams-Curtis, Pakalka, & White, 2006; Humphrey & Kahn, 2000; McMahon, 2010; Moynihan, Banyard, Arnold, Eckstein, & Stapleton, 2010; Sawyer, Thompson, & Chicorelli, 2002). Similar to those involved with fraternity and sorority life, male athletes are more likely to subscribe to rape myths, believing that women either ask for this kind of treatment or deserve to be treated in this manner. In an analysis of factors that affected the degree to which athletes subscribed to rape myths, younger college male athletes (first years and sophomores compared to juniors and seniors) held more tightly to beliefs that women who reported being raped were lying about being raped. Female athletes as a whole generally part ways with their male counterparts in their attitudes about rape; however, the most elite female athletes in Division I sports evidence patterns similar to their brethren (McMahon, 2010).

This chapter focuses on the intersections between women, sport, and sexual violence, starting with an overview of the prevalence of sexual violence that girls and women encounter in the sport world, including **sexual harassment**, sexual assault, and **interpersonal**

It could have been much worse. She's lucky. Obviously, I don't know, maybe she wasn't a virgin, but she shouldn't have put herself in that position, unless they slipped her something, then that's different.

Serena Williams

When you have somebody as prominent as Serena, and you have as many girls that look up to her as a role model, that's what bothers me. Because, in essence, what she is telling these girls is, "If you are drunk, it is your fault, and you shouldn't report anything, and this is what's to be expected."

Kathy Redmond, founder of the National Coalition Against Violent Athletes

relationship violence (intimate partner abuse). The overview is followed by a section regarding the unique nature of the coach–athlete relationship. The chapter concludes with information regarding efforts to address sexual violence in sport through the application of legal remedies in schools and workplaces, educational programs, and public policy.

PREVALENCE OF THE SEXUAL VICTIMIZATION OF GIRLS AND WOMEN IN SPORT

Commenting on the Steubenville rape case in *Rolling Stone Magazine*, tennis great Serena Williams focused her comments on the female victim in a manner that appeared to be blaming the girl, taking the victim and her parents to task for her apparent drunken behavior while describing the conduct of the boys as being "stupid" (Distant, 2013). While Williams sought to clarify her remarks once they became public, offering sympathy and support to the victim, a general confusion regarding sexual violence directed toward women is evidenced in her remarks, a confusion that is more likely to exist among males as a group and among certain portions of the population, including those involved in fraternity or sorority life and in athletics (McMahon, 2010).

Regardless of the confusion around these issues, what is very clear is the regularity with which sex is used as a tool by peers and people in positions of authority to control others, often with significant and long-lasting health consequences. Sexual victimization of girls and boys, defined by the Women's Law Project as "behavior ranging from sexual comments and inappropriate touching to rape" (2012, p. 151), occurs throughout their lives in school, from elementary through college. According to a survey conducted by the American Association of University Women (AAUW), 50 percent of students in grades 7 through 12 reported experiencing some form of sexual victimization during the 2010-2011 academic year (Hill & Kearl, 2011). In seventh grade, the pattern of sexual victimization is similar for boys and girls but, as children hit puberty, the gender gap becomes more pronounced. By 12th grade, girls report higher rates of sexual victimization compared to boys (62% to 39%). Sexist jokes, comments, and gestures are the most common form of sexual victimization, followed by the use of homophobic slurs, display of sexual pictures, and unwelcome sexual touch. With the rise of social media, the incidence of cyber harassment has also increased, with one-third of girls and almost one-quarter of boys reporting having been targeted during their school years (Hill & Kearl, 2011). Student-to-student misconduct is the most frequent form of sexual victimization in school; however, almost 10 percent of the students in the AAUW study reported that educators engaged in sexual misconduct with them sometime during their time in school (Hill & Kearl, 2011).

Due to definitional issues, studies seeking to focus on sexual victimization among athletes and within athletic communities offer somewhat less clarity in terms of the prevalence of coach and sport official misconduct. Brake writes, "At this stage of the research, there is no clear picture of how often coaches become sexually involved with athletes" (2012, p. 399). Further, unlike the ongoing work that has been done to chronicle sexual victimization in U.S. schools, the most comprehensive work on issues associated with sexual victimization in sport has been undertaken outside of the United States. Brake speculates that this reflects "an ideology that idealizes coaches and overlooks or minimizes the harmful aspects of sports" (p. 399).

Other challenges are associated with gathering data due to the fact that abusive behaviors are not always recognized for what they are. Sexist behaviors in sport are common currency, tolerated by athletes and perceived to be part of the game (Rodriguez & Gill, 2011). As a result, reported prevalence rates may not reflect the actual level of sexual victimization in sport because "athletes do not always (or even most of the time) recognize harassing and abusive behavior when they experience it" (Brake, 2012, p. 400).

Existing studies indicate that a range of 15 to 48 percent of female athletes reported being subjected to sexual harassment in a sport context (Fasting, Brackenridge, & Sundgot-Borgen, 2000; Fasting & Knorre, 2005; Kirby, Greaves, & Hankivsky, 2000; Toftegaard Nielsen, 2001; Volkwein, Schnell, Sherwood, & Livezey, 1997). According to Brackenridge, Bishop, Moussali, and Tapp (2008), the prevalence rate for **sexual abuse** in sport based on available research falls between 2 and 22 percent.

In one of the most comprehensive studies of sex abuse in sport, Canadian Olympic athletes were asked about their experiences in the sport system. Of the 266 respondents, one-fifth reported having had sexual intercourse with an authority figure in sport. Detailed descriptions of verbal bullying and physical assault led researchers to conclude that out of that group, 15 (11 females and 4 males) had been coerced, with 5 (2 females and 3 males) reporting forced sexual intercourse before the age of 16 (Kirby et al., 2000).

With a lack of local and national reporting mechanisms to help establish the frequency with which sexual abuse is perpetrated by coaches and sport officials, news accounts and the public announcements of specific sport organizations lend support to the assertion that sexual victimization in sport is a serious concern. In 2013, 85 coaches were listed on the USA Swimming website as having received a lifetime ban from the organization, resigned their membership, or been deemed ineligible for membership, the majority having violated the code of conduct.

According to USA Gymnastics, 89 coaches were similarly barred from membership as a result of "conduct . . . determined to be inconsistent with the best interest of the sport of gymnastics and the athletes we are servicing" (2013, para. 1). In a report from the *Seattle Times*, between 1993 and 2003, "159 coaches in the state of Washington were fired or reprimanded for sexual misconduct ranging from harassment to rape. Nearly all were male coaches victimizing girls. At least 98 of these coaches continued to coach or teach" (Willmsen & O'Hagan, 2003, para. 9).

To bring the picture of the sexual victimization of girls and women in sport into sharper focus, more needs to be understood about the relationships that exist for female athletes, not just with coaches but also with other sport officials, peers, athletic training and sports medicine personnel, spectators, and the array of other individuals who constitute the village of sport for individual participants. In interviews with 25 athletes done by Fasting, Brackenridge, and Walseth (2007), the perpetrators of sexual harassment were authority figures, primarily male coaches along with a sport manager and a coach. The women in the study indicated that they were subjected to sexual harassment from male peer athletes as well (Fasting et al., 2007). For athletes from southern Nigerian universities reporting on the various types of sexual harassment they have experienced, peer athletes were responsible for 96.5 percent of **gender harassment**, 86.35 percent of unwanted sexual attention, and 79.74 percent of sexual coercion (Elendu & Umeakuka, 2011). Whether in Norway, Canada, the United States, or Nigeria, female athletes experience a range of sexual violence.

Within athletic departments, the incidents of athlete-to-athlete sexual victimization are not captured adequately by research statistics. The complications of sexual assaults that occur among athletes are evidenced in a recent case. For Beckett Brennan, a women's basketball player at the University of the Pacific, attendance at a campus party led to acquaintance rape by two players from the men's team. The athletic department responded to Brennan's allegations that she had been raped by creating a rule that restricted female basketball players from socializing with male basketball players. Brennan filed a lawsuit against the University of the Pacific complaining that the rule violated her rights under Title IX (for more information on Title IX, see chapter 2 and the section Title IX and Sexual Harassment in this chapter).

Less is known about the degree to which women working in sport experience sexual harassment. In one of the few studies of a specific group of female sport workers, sport print media professionals, half of the 112 respondents indicated that they had been sexually harassed during the 12 months previous to participating in the study (Pedersen, Lim, Osborne, & Whisenant, 2009). Controversy following complaints of inappropriate conduct on the part of players from the New York Jets towards broadcaster Inés Sainz led the National Football League (NFL) to "reaffirm publicly that 'all employees and associates of the NFL have a right to work in a positive work environment' free from all harassment, intimidation, and discrimination" (Schulman & Clifton, 2011, p. 1). In one of the most widely publicized cases, former National Basketball Association (NBA) executive Anucha Browne Sanders received an $11.5 million settlement in 2007 from Madison Square Garden and then coach of the New York Knicks Isiah Thomas, after alleging she had been fired for filing a sexual harassment claim against Thomas (Diamond, 2011).

From the time girls and boys enter the sport world, they are given messages that reinforce long-standing stereotypes about women as subservient and as sex objects. The call for football players and cheerleaders at the elementary school level every June in local communities is put forward with every intention that the boys will be the football players and the girls will be on the sidelines cheering them on. This idea carries forward into men's college teams, which use women (sometimes known as hostesses) to recruit top players (Christiansen, Hubbell, Lee, O'Brien, & Staurowsky, 2010). That worldview remains intact through every level of schooling and into the professional ranks, with men's professional sport teams marketing boys night out promotions with the incentive of spending time with the cheerleaders who pose in bikinis for team calendars. Part of the fun of sport is

encoded with a generalized practice of sexualizing women. Into that world, girls and women enter to navigate as best they can. To complicate the situation further, the unique aspect of the athletic environment, as it plays out in coach–athlete relationships, reveals why researchers refer to athletic teams and athletic environments as being at-risk locations for sexual violence to occur.

BLURRING OF BOUNDARIES IN COACH–ATHLETE RELATIONSHIPS

For athletes with talent and dreams to succeed, they often must allow coaches to occupy a central role in their lives. Charged with developing athletes at critical moments in their careers, coaches operate as trusted authorities who inspire confidence through their professional achievements and associations, specialized knowledge, and ability to motivate and to communicate, sometimes assuming the status of gods and father figures (Brake, 2012).

Because of the public nature of sport and its emphasis on quantifiable performance, the notion that the person who is most responsible for the health, safety, and welfare of athletes may pose the greatest threat to them seems counterintuitive. And yet, for decades, sport insiders and sport scientists have known that the boundaries between coaches and athletes often become blurred, with coaches exploiting the trust given to them and exercising power in ways that are abusive to athletes, both mentally and physically (Brackenridge, 1997). In one of the troubling outcomes following the highly publicized case of former Penn State football coach Jerry Sandusky, who used the platform of his notoriety with a famed football program to create a child welfare agency through which he identified and preyed on young boys, there is greater awareness that the sport system presents conditions for coaches to abuse athletes sexually and in other ways. However, as Hartill wrote, "the concealment of CSA [child sex abuse] is an historical feature of organized sport" (2013, p. 241).

As a case in point, USA Swimming, the national governing body (NGB) for swimming in the United States, has been engulfed in issues associated with the sexual exploitation of female athletes for years precisely because of the willingness of authorities to ignore the signs of improper or illegal relationships between coaches and athletes, allowing coaches dismissed at one club or program to continue coaching elsewhere. In a 2010 *ABC News* investigation, it was reported that USA Swimming had banned at least 36 coaches for molesting, fondling, and abusing dozens of swimmers (Chuchmach & Patel, 2010). Coaches like Andy King and Rick Curl, long protected by the silence of numerous parties (other coaches, athletics officials, parents, and athletes) to their abuse and the vulnerability of their victims, have been brought to justice recently, receiving jail sentences of 40 and 7 years, respectively. However, the fact that coaches who have perpetrated crimes against athletes continue to work in the sport of swimming has prompted calls for U.S. Congressional oversight. Since USA Swimming is a national sports governing body funded by taxpayer dollars, there is a growing sense that the swimming community has abdicated its responsibility to hold abusive coaches accountable and that the problem requires the intervention of the U.S. government.

While the swimming community has been under increased scrutiny because of the painful and slow process of unlocking the vault of silence around these cases and moving some to prosecution, sexual misconduct by coaches and sport officials is not confined to the sport of swimming, but can occur anywhere there is a coach–athlete relationship. The athletic environment offers unique opportunities for coaches to exert outright or coercive power over the athletes they work with and, by extension, over those who love those athletes. The control coaches have over athletes extends far beyond the limits of the playing field or performance venue. The boundaries between an athlete's personal and playing lives are porous, prone to intrusion by the coach under the pretext of pushing athletes to become better and stronger. From dietary choices to dress and conduct codes to sleep regimens to daily routines related to when an athlete wakes up and goes to bed, a coach's influence reverberates across almost every dimension of an athlete's life. As gatekeepers to opportunities, coaches have considerable leverage to manipulate athletes with threats of withholding instruction, playing or practice time, recommendations for scholarships

Athletes who can trust that they are safe under their coaches' care and tutelage will perform better.

and award nominations, and places on all-star, regional, or national teams.

The fate of coaches and athletes are interconnected and intertwined in physical and emotional ways, creating conditions for the abuse of female athletes to go relatively unnoticed and unchecked. As Volkwein and colleagues (1997) pointed out, the disintegration of personal boundaries may occur so subtly over time that female athletes may not even be aware that the sexist remarks, suggestive touches, or more overt forms of sexual abuse are inappropriate.

Coaching has historically been viewed as a touching profession where physical contact with athletes is believed to be a necessary part of the instruction and learning process. Athletic injuries require physical assessment and treatment, and coaches have often administered aids to athletes' physical recuperation, such as massages. The physical and emotional connections athletes and coaches build over time often occur within a family atmosphere created by long hours spent together in informal situations, shared travel to contests, overnight stays at hotels, and team dinners. The more intimate the connections become, the less objective the position of the coach. Benign territory for the collaborative, nurturing, and supportive coach, this shared physical space between coach and athlete can serve as a convenient avenue for coaches to groom potential targets, to press boundaries, gain trust, and cultivate a level of interdependence where female athletes are unable or unwilling to challenge the coach.

While sexual violence is not restricted to any one group or social institution, the fact that sport is a gendered institution dominated by male athletes and men in leadership creates a situation where male sport officials can easily commit sexual misconduct and abuse against female athletes and coworkers. As a practical reality, men make up 57 percent of head coaches of women's college teams, 80 percent of all head coaches of college teams (both men's and women's teams), and 80 percent of athletic directors at the college level (Acosta & Carpenter, 2012). At the high school level, female coaches are represented in somewhat higher percentages, with men holding 73 percent of all head coaching positions (LaVoi,

2013). Even in the WNBA, 58 percent of head coaches are men.

The internalization of a patriarchal system that values male privilege to the detriment of female students and athletes is revealed in individual and focus group interviews with male high school coaches and administrators regarding their attitudes about sexual aggression against girls and women (Lyndon, Duffy, Smith, & White, 2011). The authors concluded that the male coaches interviewed "may be transmitting values and beliefs that support and condone the sexual aggression of their athletes" (Lyndon et al., 2011, p. 1) given the degree to which they minimized the problem of sexual aggression, expressed supportive views of rape myths, and evidenced a lack of education about the serious consequences of sexual aggression.

According to Lyndon and colleagues (2011, pp. 8-9), the high school male coaches "held a narrow and rather simplistic view of sexual assault, expressing beliefs that girls who consent to any sexual activity are consenting to all sexual activity and that 'promiscuous' girls are to blame for being or putting themselves in bad situations." They further reported that male coaches stated that "once girls engage in some sexuality they give up their right to say 'no'."

Sexual harassment from coaches is not solely an American problem. In a study asking U.S. and Israeli athletes and Israeli coaches to assess the behaviors that coaches exhibit toward athletes, athletes were more likely to agree that the following behaviors from coaches were considered sexual harassment: making physical and verbal advances toward female athletes, showing a sexual interest in an athlete, proposing a sexual encounter, asking an athlete about her sex life, pinching an athlete on the bottom, staring at an athlete's breasts, telling an athlete about their own sex life, or caressing an athlete (Fejgin & Hanegby, 2001).

Twenty-five Norwegian female athletes who recalled recent experiences where their coaches had sexually harassed them reported emotional reactions that included anger, disgust, fear, and irritation (Fasting et al., 2007). Despite these reactions, female athletes were reluctant to formally report their coaches because "they [did] not want to hurt the harasser and they fear[ed] complaining might negatively affect his job or family" (Fasting et al., 2007, p. 428). Rodriguez and Gill speculated that "it is possible that female athletes have to deal with persistent unwanted sexist and sexual behaviors in order to maintain their sport participation while camouflaging or tolerating the complexity of the societal gender expectations and cultural values (e.g., respect and dignity)" (2011, p. 325). In their study of elite Puerto Rican female athletes, they described a love–hate relationship with the coach who harassed them. One athlete put it this way (Rodriguez & Gill, 2011, p. 330):

> He was a person with a split personality. The part of him related to his knowledge was the part that I needed to reach my goals. That was the part that I wanted! But there was the other part . . . and that part is the one that I had to battle with.

LEGAL AVENUES

For girls and women in sport who have been hurt by sexual violence, numerous laws are in place at the state and local level that might allow them to seek justice for the wrongs done to them by perpetrators. As the Women's Law Project notes, "sexual assault is a crime" (2012, p. 156). As such, when sexual assaults are reported to local law enforcement (police and prosecutors), the criminal justice system becomes an avenue for those harmed to seek redress.

Two federal laws that have been used by plaintiffs include Title IX of the Education Amendments Act of 1972, which applies in school settings that receive federal financial assistance, and Title VII, whose prohibition of discrimination based on sex addresses sexual violence in the workplace.

Title IX and Sexual Harassment

Title IX's application to sexual harassment that occurs in school settings begins with two key premises. First, sexual harassment is a form of sex discrimination. And second, sexual assault is considered under Title IX to be a form of sexual harassment.

For a female athlete who experiences sexual harassment, the effect on her life can be profound. She may become depressed, engage in alcohol and other drug use, have difficulty sleeping or concentrating, struggle with anxiety disorders, and develop a range of physical health issues from eating disorders to pregnancy to sexually transmitted diseases. In an attempt to prevent her from speaking up, her harasser may threaten her with further harm, undermining her ability to continue to participate on her team, achieve in the classroom, and feel comfortable just being in school. In reporting that she has been sexually harassed, she may become a social pariah. The end result for a female athlete who has been sexually violated by another student or athlete, coach, or athletic administrator is that her access to an education is no longer equal to that of others in her school. Her opportunities to participate in her education and succeed are more limited as a result of the harassment she has endured.

Title IX helps to protect students from hostile environments, which lets them focus on the sport they wish to play.

What Can You Do About Sexual Assault in the Sport Setting?

Student activists and advocates started the Know Your Title IX (KYIX) campaign in 2013 to do two things: educate students in the United States about their rights under Title IX and empower students on college campuses to stop sexual violence. Their website offers accounts of students who have gone through the experience of sexual violence, highlights challenges that survivors on campus face when attempting to hold perpetrators and institutions accountable, and identifies positive steps that can be taken to improve the lives of students, one campus at a time.

KYIX has developed resources to help students deal with the array of issues that arise after an assault has occurred. It also provides prevention strategies. Issues addressed include the following:

- Practical considerations (how to find a lawyer, the economic costs of gender-based violence, implications for student loans if the student decides to leave school or change schools in the aftermath of an assault)
- Emotional support (how to build a support network and how to handle lack of support from those around you)
- Media issues (what to do if your case becomes public, how you are treated by the media, what to do if you are misrepresented by the media)
- What your school should and should not be doing (administrators should not retaliate against you for coming forward)
- Considerations for women who are members of racial and sexual minorities or who subscribe to various faiths and religious traditions

As a result of KYIX's work to deliver a petition with 100,000 signatures to U.S Department of Education Secretary Arne Duncan and other government officials in July of 2013, President Barack Obama created the White House Task Force to Protect Students from Sexual Assault in January of 2014. The task force issued a report the following April calling for greater transparency around enforcement of Title IX. Within days of the April report being released, the Department of Education published a list of colleges and universities that were under investigation for the way in which they handled incidents related to sexual violence under Title IX. For more information regarding KYIX, go to http://knowyourix.org/dealing-with.

Title IX's prohibition against unfair treatment is designed to offer protection and relief for a female athlete who has endured sexual harassment. Guidance provided by the OCR at the U.S. Department of Education requires schools to recognize and respond when sexual harassment occurs so as to ease the **hostile environment** for the student who has been mistreated. Under Title IX, "if a school knows or reasonably should know about student-on-student harassment that creates a hostile environment, Title IX requires the school to take immediate action to eliminate the harassment, prevent its recurrence, and address its effects" (Ali, 2011, p. 4).

A female athlete who files a complaint of sexual harassment, or being subjected to **harassing conduct**, should expect that the complaint will be handled promptly by school administrators, who are obligated to conduct an investigation. School officials are expected to use a preponderance of the evidence standard in reaching a finding about a sexual harassment complaint, meaning that it is more likely than not that sexual harassment did occur. Appropriate steps are expected to be taken before the investigation is completed to eliminate the hostile environment for the complainant. Even when the sexual harassment has occurred outside of the school setting, administrators remain obligated to provide support and to take appropriate action because of a spillover effect (where the harassment follows the victim to school, so to speak). For example, a female athlete may be targeted by fans from another institution (Ali, 2011; Women's Law Project, 2012).

Title VII and Sexual Harassment

Women working in sport can pursue recourse under Title VII of the Civil Rights Act of 1964, which outlines two types of **sexual harassment** (Shulman & Clifton, 2011). The first is **quid pro quo**, where an employee is promised some kind of job benefit in exchange for a sexual favor. In effect, an employee will receive a promotion or raise or be permitted to keep her job if she agrees to go to dinner with her boss or engage in other forms of sexual activity. The second is **a hostile environment**, where the unwelcome sexual attention is so severe and pervasive that it pervades the work atmosphere and makes it difficult for the employee to remain unaffected by it. A hostile environment is one in which the behavior is severe, pervasive, and objectively offensive by the standards of a reasonable person. The standard established under Title VII has been used to shape analyses under Title IX (Buchwald, 2008).

EDUCATION AND PREVENTION PROGRAMS

From the IOC to the NCAA to the NFL, sport organizations in the United States and around the globe recognize that sport, while providing opportunities for the fulfillment of human potential and achievement, is a place where girls and women can be subjected to trauma from trusted coaches, their own teammates or players they compete against, sport officials and administrators, and spectators. Compelled by both moral and legal obligations, advocates are undertaking numerous efforts to educate people throughout the sport system about what constitutes sexual violence and to foster a safe and healthy environment for athletes and those who work in sport.

Among the approaches used to create awareness and to combat the silence that often allows sexual violence to occur in sport is **bystander intervention** programs. In reading the opening scenario about the Steubenville football rape case, you might have wondered why so many people who watched what happened to the rape victim did nothing to stop it. The bystander approach takes the perspective that everyone is a potential witness to sexual violence and invites everyone to consider the stake they have in protecting members of their community. This approach is thought to fit in well with the emphasis athletic departments place on leadership training for athletes (Moynihan et al., 2010).

Safe4Athletes is a group formed by Katherine Starr, a former Olympic swimmer who turned the pain of the sexual abuse she endured by her coach into a passion for making change within club-level sport organizations where children have the least amount of advocacy. In a comprehensive handbook that outlines policies and procedures that club officials should have in place to "create a safe and positive environment free of sexual abuse, bullying, and harassment, Safe4Athletes provides recommendations that call for coaches to be vetted through background checks, mechanisms [put] in place to receive complaints about abuse, and processes in place to investigate complaints when they arise" (Starr, 2013).

In 2012, the NCAA put forward a model policy for preventing inappropriate relationships between college athletes and athletic department personnel in a report titled *Staying in Bounds* (Burton Nelson & Brake, 2012). One of the first concerted efforts of its kind, the policy urges athletic departments to forbid relationships between college athletes and athletic department personnel, regardless of whether

Safe4Athletes

Founded by Katherine Starr in 2012 to provide a safe space for athletes, parents, and coaches to get information regarding sexual abuse in sport, Safe4Athletes serves as a comprehensive educational resource with the express purpose of preventing coach abuse of athletes. Safe4Athletes advocates for sport organizations at all levels to adopt and maintain policies and procedures that raise awareness regarding bullying, sexual misconduct, and other forms of inappropriate interaction between coaches and athletes. The organization helps athletes who have been the victims of abuse to connect with others who have had similar experiences. It also provides suggestions regarding professional counselors and advice on how to handle issues that arise when an athlete is mistreated (how to approach administrators and club officials with concerns, how to seek the dismissal of an abusive coach, how to go about getting legal assistance). Model policy and procedure templates are available for adoption. For those harmed by coaches, Safe4Athletes investigates reports of abuse. The website provides a list of coaches banned or suspended due to misconduct for selected sports (Steinbach, 2012). For more information, go to www.safe4athletes.org.

the athlete is of age and whether mutual consent exists between both parties. According to Burton Nelson and Brake, the power differential between an athlete and those who run athletic departments is sufficient to jeopardize the validity of the consent that is given (2012, p. 6):

Whether the student-athlete is 17, 18, 19, 20, or 21, or older, she or he is significantly less powerful than a head coach, assistant coach, athletics trainer, sport psychologist, athletics director, or other athletics department staff with supervisory control or authority over student-athletes. It is this power differential that makes such relationships inherently unequal, and when relationships are unequal, the concept of "mutual consent" becomes problematic.

The National Coalition Against Violent Athletes (NCAVA), an organization founded by Kathy Redmond, works to hold athletes and those around them accountable for the sexual violence they perpetrate. Through a program called INTERCEPT, the program focuses on leadership development and accountability.

NCAVA also provides continual education and guidance in helping victims as well as educating coaches and athletes (www.ncava.org).

A Colby College football player named Connor Clancy started a Change.org petition with Carmen Rios through the SPARK Movement to approach NFHS to "instate an optional sexual assault prevention course for coaches as part of coaches' annual accreditation requirements" (Rios & Clancy, 2013). With the help of a coalition that included the Ohio Alliance to End Sexual Violence, Futures Without Violence, Mentors in Violence Prevention, the California Coalition Against Sexual Assault, the National Sexual Violence Resource Center, and the Pennsylvania Coalition Against Rape, they created a curriculum to empower coaches to take on the work of sexual violence education with their own teams. Rios and Clancy write, "as local 'heroes' and role models, we need athletes to lead their communities toward a rape-free climate, and we expect coaches to be prepared to initiate and foster dialogue with their athletes around issues of sexual violence that is productive and educational" (2013, para. 3).

Learning Aids

Summary

This chapter reviews the prevalence of sexual violence against women and girls along with the unique aspects of coach–athlete relationships that provide insight into why sexual violence in sport occurs. It examines legal avenues to hold perpetrators and school administrators accountable, most specifically Title IX and Title VII, and provides an overview of the some of the education and prevention efforts being undertaken to address issues associated with sexual violence in sport.

Discussion Questions

1. What limitations should be placed on the physical contact coaches have with athletes? Is it practical to expect that coaches would never touch an athlete physically?

2. In the case of Beckett Brennan (*Jane Doe v. the University of the Pacific*) the athletic department responded to the allegations that she had been raped by two men's basketball players by creating a rule that restricted female basketball players from socializing with male basketball players. Brennan filed a lawsuit against the University of the Pacific complaining that the rule violated her rights under Title IX (see chapter 2 and the section Title IX and Sexual Harassment in this chapter for more details). Read the complaint as well as the judge's ruling. Do you think that Brennan was treated fairly by the school? If you were the athletic director, how would you have handled this situation? The complaint can be found here: www.nacua.org/documents/doe_v_upacific.pdf. The decision can be found here: www.leagle.com/decision/In%20FCO%2020120131180/DOE%20 v.%20UNIVERSITY%20OF%20PACIFIC.

3. Read Harvey Araton's *New York Times* article about Kathy Redmond found at www.nytimes.com/2012/12/02/sports/ncaafootball/kathy-redmonds-journey-of-reconciliation-with-the-university-of-nebraska.html?pagewanted=all&_r=0. After reading her story, write a two-page reaction paper. What are the key points that you take away from the article?

Learning Exercises

1. Create an opportunity for students to think through their own understandings of what constitutes rape. This might be done through a quiz regarding rape myths or through an assignment where students are asked to read about rape myths and offer a reaction along the lines of "what would you say to someone who believes this myth?" An example of a guide to reference regarding rape myths is the Southern Arizona Center Against Sexual Assault Rape Myths and Assault Fact Sheet, which can be retrieved at http://azrapeprevention.org/sites/azrapeprevention.org/files/07-SACASA.pdf. Students might also be encouraged to develop a presentation refuting rape myths. An example of one of these can be located at http://prezi.com/ x6frttbl1n74/copy-of-rape-myths/?utm_source=website&utm_medium=prezi_ landing_related_solr&utm_campaign=prezi_landing_related_author

2. In the spring of 2013, an unidentified female student filed a Title IX lawsuit against administrators at Forest Hill Central High School in Michigan. In the suit, the plaintiff (listed as Jane Doe) alleged that after she reported that she

had been raped by a boys' basketball player who was a top NCAA Division I prospect, school officials discouraged her from pursuing the case because of what that would do to her assailant's future. Once word got out that Jane Doe had filed a complaint against the player, she claims to have been the target of cyberbullying from her classmates and of physical threats from her assailant and his friends. Read the complaint at www.nwlc.org/sites/default/files/pdfs/doe_v._forest_hills_complaint_no._13-428.pdf and consider, based on what you know about Title IX's application to sexual harassment cases, whether the school complied with the requirements of Title IX (Ressler, 2013).

Glossary

bystander intervention—When someone takes steps to prevent or stop sexual violence when it is happening.

gender harassment—The range of insulting and offensive attitudes against women (gender-based hazing).

harassing conduct—May take many forms, including verbal acts and name-calling; graphic and written statements, which may include use of cell phones or the Internet; or other conduct that may be physically threatening, harmful, or humiliating. Harassment does not have to include intent to harm or involve repeated incidents. It may not even be directed at a specific target. Harassment creates a hostile environment when the conduct is sufficiently severe, pervasive, or persistent so as to interfere with or limit a student's ability to participate in or benefit from the services, activities, or opportunities offered by a school. When such harassment is based on race, color, national origin, sex, or disability, it violates the civil rights laws that OCR enforces (Ali, 2010).

hostile environment—Unwelcome sexual attention is so severe and pervasive that it pervades the work atmosphere and makes it difficult for the recipient to remain unaffected by it.

interpersonal relationship violence (intimate partner abuse)—Pattern of controlling behavior with a current or former dating partner or spouse. Characteristics of this type of behavior include isolation, jealousy, threats, or name-calling and may include emotional, sexual, or verbal abuse. Physical violence may or may not be part of this pattern.

quid pro quo—Harassment wherein an employee is promised some kind of job benefit in exchange for a sexual favor. In effect, an employee will receive a promotion or raise or be permitted to keep their job if they agree to go to dinner with their boss or engage in other forms of sexual activity.

rape myth—Beliefs that either legitimize or deny that sexual assault occurs. Blaming the victim (she deserved it), making excuses (they were drinking), or minimizing the trauma of the assault (doesn't occur often, not a big deal) all deflect accountability and perpetuate the cycle of violence that is underneath this behavior.

sexual abuse—Unlike sexual harassment, which is demonstrably unwelcome, sexual abuse often involves a slow seduction (or "grooming") whereby one person gradually prepares another to accept special attention, and then proceeds with sexual activity. The term *sexual abuse* is often used in reference to sexual activity between an adult and a minor, but adults can also sexually abuse other adults in contexts where one adult holds power over another.

sexual assault—Sexual conduct or behavior that is not consensual. The wide range of behaviors that fall under this definition can include intimidation to various forms of touching to penetration or rape.

sexual harassment—Unwelcome conduct of a sexual nature, which can include unwelcome sexual advances, requests for sexual favors, or other verbal, nonverbal, or physical conduct of a sexual nature. Thus, sexual harassment prohibited by Title IX can include conduct such as touching of a sexual nature; making sexual comments, jokes, or gestures; writing graffiti or displaying or distributing sexually explicit drawings, pictures, or written materials; calling students sexually charged names; spreading sexual rumors; rating students on sexual activity or performance; or circulating, showing, or creating e-mails or websites of a sexual nature.

Note

1. This scenario is based on details from the Steubenville football players rape case. There are two versions of this part of the story. One is represented as told here and contained in a *New York Times* report (Macur & Schweber, 2012). YahooSports! writer Dan Wetzel would report in April of 2013 that a player never urinated on the victim, but that a bystander, who did nothing else, offered to pay someone $3 if they did so.

PART IV

Women in the Sport Industry

This section documents the richness of girls' and women's sport participation, along with the expansive range of roles women play in the sport industry. Chapter 11 deals with the effect of media on the experiences of girls and women competing and working in the sport system. Following a historical overview of women in sports media, it explores the challenges for women in sports media. It also considers the parallels that exist between women covering sport and the way in which women are represented as serious athletes and competitors, concluding with thoughts on the limitations and possibilities of media and its influence on public understandings of women and sport.

Chapter 12 highlights the prospects of female leaders and their associations with sport. The chapter begins with a discussion of the influence of sport on female executives working in non-sport industries and shifts to the gendered dynamics at play in the sport workplace for women that affect the identification of women as leaders and the hiring, promotion, and retention of women in sport organizations. It reviews reasons behind the general trend of women being underrepresented in positions of authority within professional and national and international sport organizations, along with strategies to advance women into leadership ranks in both professional and international sport. The chapter concludes with a discussion of the importance of sharing stories about female leaders in sport.

Similar to the previous chapter, chapter 13 describes the lives and experiences of women working in the gendered environment of sport, but shifts the focus from professional and national and international sport organizations to high school and college sport settings. Its overview of the roles women play within these workplaces, along with documentation demonstrating that women are minorities as workers within school-based athletic departments, provides the backdrop for a consideration of pay inequities and unequal treatment.

Beyond making contributions to sport as workers, women form a significant demographic that influences the financial status of the sport industry. Chapter 14 presents a profile of women as sport consumers and fans and describes the efforts that are made to target female consumers in terms of sport merchandise and sporting goods sales. It considers efforts undertaken to market women's sport and sport marketing tactics that take gender into account as well as the opportunities that sport marketers miss by overlooking or underestimating women's sport.

Chapter 15 examines the ways in which political traditions, influenced by religion at times, are brought to bear in support of an international sport governance system that resists the inclusion of female leaders. Pointing out that organizations like the International Olympic Committee (IOC) and national sports governing bodies around the world have developed gender equity policies but have never implemented them fully despite the passage of decades, the authors encourage readers to fully understand the international sport system so they can make change on behalf of women.

CHAPTER 11

Women, Media, and Sport

Marie Hardin, PhD, Pennsylvania State University
Dunja Antunovic, PhD, Bradley University/Pennsylvania State University

Learning Objectives

In this chapter, you will learn about the following:

- Role of women in sports media in a historical context
- Issues that affect women's status in the sports media industry
- Connection between the status of female media professionals and female athletes in media depictions

It was a packed house at a movie theater in downtown Washington, D.C., even though it was a Monday night. Hundreds of people—including one of the authors of this chapter—had shown up to watch the premiere of a new ESPN documentary, *Let Them Wear Towels.* The documentary was part of the network's 2013 *Nine for IX* series, created in recognition of the 40th anniversary of Title IX (see chapter 2).

The stories that unfolded on the big screen might have been surprising to many in the crowd of mostly college-aged students. They were stories of discrimination and struggle. Of women being barred from, pushed out of, and sometimes even *carried* out of U.S. men's major-league locker rooms as they tried to do their jobs. They included the stories of Melissa Ludtke, a *Sports Illustrated* writer who filed a lawsuit for Major League Baseball locker room access during the 1970s; Robin Herman, the first female sportswriter for the *New York Times*; and Claire Smith, one of the very few African American women covering sports, who was physically removed from the San Diego Padres clubhouse during the 1984 National League Championship Series (Riley, 2013).

After the screening, Ludtke was joined by *USA Today* columnist and television commentator Christine Brennan (also featured in the film) and Laura Gentile, vice president of the ESPN enterprise that focuses on women's sports, *espnW*, to talk about the video. Ludtke described herself as a quiet negotiator who wouldn't call her editor after getting kicked out of a locker room but would instead steel herself to get the story. A national advocacy group for women covering sports, the Association for Women in Sports Media (AWSM), wouldn't form until the late 1980s. "We were just determined that no one was going to stop us," Ludtke said. "Each of us was working out there on our own."

Brennan suggested that although women still have barriers to address, the progress for women covering sports since the 1970s is notable. And on locker room access, Brennan noted that there have been thousands of uneventful postgame locker room entries in recent years by female reporters. "We're there. It's done," she added.

Ludtke wasn't so sure. She pointed to television, where relatively few women have made it into the booth for play-by-play and commentating for men's marquee sports. "We're in a position today that we were in the 1970s," she observed. Almost as if on cue—to underscore her point—a 9-year-old girl at the event raised her hand. She told the panelists about the "wide gender gap" in her elementary school. "I'm the only girl playing with the boys at recess," she said. Gentile, from *espnW*, asked whether the girl felt she was accepted by the boys. "Not

Films About Women and Sports Media

- *Let Them Wear Towels* (2013): An ESPN *Nine for IX* production, this film brings visibility to the barriers women face in the sports journalism industry. Through interviews with female journalists, directors Annie Sundberg and Ricki Stern present a historical perspective on workplace discrimination and the role of women in sports journalism.

- *Branded* (2013): An ESPN *Nine for IX* film that explores the sexualization of female athletes in sports media. Directors Heidi Ewing and Rachel Grady examine the marketing strategies, sponsorship, and business decisions behind the promotion of female athletes on an international scale.

- *Playing Unfair* (2002): This film, produced by the Media Education Foundation, focuses on patterns and problems in media representations of female athletes. With commentary from scholars and activists, it critically examines the underrepresentation and sexualization of women in sports media.

really," the girl replied. "I get upset at times at how much hasn't changed," Ludtke said. "Let's keep telling the stories."

The exchange after the movie screening leads us to ask, Where *are* women in sports journalism today? Is the work done, or have times really *not* changed that much for women who want to pursue sports media careers? And how is their trajectory tied to that of female athletes, in terms of media visibility and coverage? (It is no accident that women in sports media began making serious inroads—and seeing serious resistance—during the same years that Title IX began changing the landscape for female athletes.)

In order to fully appreciate and understand the status of women in the world of mediated sports, we need to know more about the history of women in the sports department and the barriers they have confronted—and cleared—along the way. Understanding the reasons for their historic and ongoing struggles in the newsroom and the locker room is helpful as we consider the future for women in the field. Further, as we think about the role of women in *covering* sports, we will also think about how women in sports *are covered.* We will explore how the two are related.

HISTORY OF WOMEN IN SPORTS MEDIA

As long as sports have been covered in the mass media, through magazine, radio, newspapers, television, or digital platforms, women have been helping to produce that coverage (Creedon, 1994a, 1994b). For instance, in the United States, women wrote about sports and physical activity in popular periodicals during the 1800s, such as *The Lily*, edited and published by Amelia Bloomer, who wore and advocated for "bifurcated trousers" instead of dresses for the active woman (Creedon, 1994a, p. 113).

Women were also writing sports-related stories in the late 1800s, when the penny press fueled the rise of newspapers and sports sections. They sometimes wrote using pseudonyms or initials instead of their names, effectively disguising their gender identities. An example is Nan O'Reilly, who started a golf column for the *New York Evening Post* in 1916 and was a frequent

contributor to *The Professional Golfer* magazine (Creedon, 1994b). Women were, however, largely absent from the sports pages until the 1920s, when public interest in sports was elevated; women were more welcome in newsrooms (after suffrage), and they were also seen as possessing special attributes enabling them to do the kinds of feature stories considered well-suited for sports heroes of the day (Kaszuba, 2003). Among the most active and prominent were Margaret Goss, who often wrote about women in sports for the *New York Herald Tribune*; Lorena Hickok, who wrote for the *Minneapolis Tribune*, and was considered the most famous female reporter in the United States in the early 1930s; and the *New York Telegram*'s Jane Dixon, who wrote about boxing and other sports from a so-called woman's angle (Kaszuba, 2003).

The number of female bylines on sports pages dropped with the Great Depression, but began to climb again during World War II, when newsroom vacancies allowed women easier entry. Perhaps the most famous female sportswriter and editor during the decades between the war and the early 1970s was Mary Garber, sometimes called the "dean of women sportswriters" (Creedon, 1994b, p. 80). When she started covering sports in 1946, "her craft was essentially a man's domain. Coaches often treated her with condescension, fellow sportswriters ignored her and professional associations kept her out" (Goldstein, 2008, para. 3). She worked full time covering high school and college sports for 40 years, as her editors persuaded sports organizations to give her press-box access.

It was the 1970s, however. At the same time that Title IX was forcing the doors of opportunity open for female athletes, women who wanted to cover sports moved into a higher profile and often ran into hostility, discrimination, and harassment in the process. Most (but not all) of the public controversies surrounded the right of access by female reporters to postgame locker room interviews with male athletes. Without them, they were at a competitive disadvantage with their male peers, who were able to stride into the locker room, gather comments, and file on deadline. After the lawsuit filed by Melissa Ludtke (*Sports Illustrated*), a U.S. federal judge ruled that all reporters, regardless of sex, should have equal access to the locker room. The matter of access and equitable treatment was not settled there, however, as players sometimes harassed female reporters and teams and leagues sought to cut off their access. Perhaps the most famous incident of harassment in American sports journalism is that of Lisa Olson, who was harassed in an NFL locker room in 1990. After she com-

Covering Sport as a Woman in South Africa

Interview with Romy Titus

Were you encouraged by any family members or friends to pursue this career?

To be honest, there was not much encouragement from my family members to pursue a career where men prevailed.

How often do you encounter other women doing the same kind of work as you?

I could probably count on one hand the women who are credible, respected, and followed. I think there is the perception that women in sport are "easy," for a lack of a better word, because we work in a male-dominated industry. There is also the notion that to get into broadcasting, all you need is a pretty face.

Why do you think there are few women covering sports in South Africa?

I guess it's just not a place for a woman. Women in traditional South Africa should not have an opinion, should have a secretarial job, should be at home pregnant and in the kitchen cooking and looking after their families. My generation, I think, are only starting to follow our dreams.

Do you think that your status as a woman in a male-dominated field brings you any advantages?

I do think so. At times my male counterparts would pose certain questions and they would get no answers—and when I ask the question and perhaps phrase it differently I would get an answer.

When you talk to women who want to follow your path, what advice do you give them?

Study! If you want to pursue journalism and you want to venture into broadcasting, then study, study, study, so that you have the foundation and groundwork to fall back on.

What needs to happen to change the status of women in sports broadcasting?

Men's attitudes need to change. At times I do feel we're judged by the way we look and not by the ability we have to deliver the best on the sport that we specialize in, and this at times makes me very weary of where I'm heading as a journalist, the older I get.

At the time of this interview, in August 2013, Romy Titus was a broadcaster with the South African Broadcasting Corporation. Prior to that, she covered soccer for Supersport International in South Africa. She has more than a decade of experience as a television journalist, covering news and sports.

plained, the public hostility—including the form of obscene phone calls, hate mail, and death threats—was so great that Olson left the United States, working as a journalist in Australia for six years before returning.

In the late 1980s, a handful of women covering U.S. sports, including Christine Brennan, founded the AWSM. The organization celebrated its 25th anniversary in 2013. Although many women who work in the industry believe that things have markedly improved, at least in the United States, Ludtke and others point to sports broadcasting as a part of the field where progress has stalled. Although women as sportscasters appeared on television relatively early—hosting a weekly 15-minute NBC segment on female athletes, *Sportswoman of the Week,* for instance—women were generally absent from sport broadcasts until the 1970s (Creedon, 1994a). Since then, they have steadily become more visible, but generally through the sideline role, which can ultimately garner just seconds of airtime during a typical game, and is considered more dispensable than the roles of play-by-play commentator or analyst.

In a column for *espnW* titled "How Far Have We Really Come?" pioneering *New York Times* reporter Robin Herman observed,

> If kicking open the locker room door was heavy with social meaning in the 1970s, being on the sideline of the playing field is socially significant now. We see that the top male sports broadcasters can do their work above the fray, assessing the athletes' performance in an anchor booth or TV studio, while women are almost always dealt a supplicant's role, on the field, holding a mike out for players to comment. (2013, para. 8)

CHALLENGES FOR WOMEN IN SPORTS MEDIA

Don Cherry said in 2013, "I don't believe, and I really believe this, I don't believe that women should be in the male dressing room" (Fitz-Gerald, 2013, para. 6). Based on the progress female journalists have made in the past decades, it might be tempting to believe that such comments would

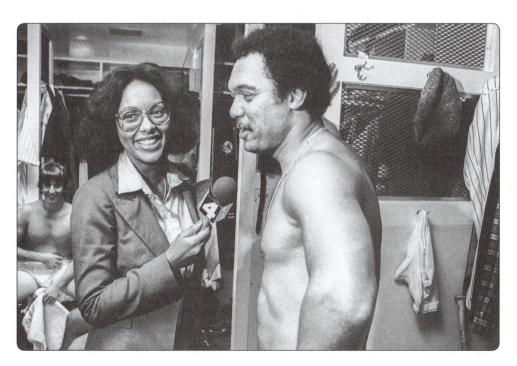

Women who work as sports reporters today stand with the activism of women over the past century behind them. Female sportscasters and sportswriters were allowed into locker rooms for the first time for postgame interviews on September 26, 1978.

at least fade, and even disappear. But they have not.

The ways women can respond, however, have changed. In contrast to the 1970s, when Melissa Ludtke and others were on their own, professional organizations now exist to respond to discriminatory comments against women in the industry. When Cherry, a Canadian Broadcasting Corporation hockey broadcaster, made the argument that women did not belong in the locker room (thus, they essentially could not cover games), the AWSM issued a statement that read as follows:

> Cherry's stance that women should not be allowed in hockey locker rooms is as sexist as it is outdated. Professional female sports journalists and media relations personnel have been working alongside their male counterparts in NHL locker rooms for nearly 40 years. (Association for Women in Sports Media, 2013)

The challenges are not only in locker room access. Despite the efforts to normalize women's place in the sports media industry, sports departments remain a predominantly male domain. Because of the historic exclusion of women from sports and from news production, women who enter a career in sports journalism face unique challenges, many of which do not apply to their male counterparts. The issue of locker room access has received substantial media coverage, but numerous other barriers continue to prevent women's advancement in sports journalism. We address three main issues that scholars observed:

- Bumping against the glass ceiling
- Workplace constraints
- Masculine gender norms

Women may face any or all of these issues during their careers in sports journalism, which may explain why we do not see more women covering sports. In the United States, the percentage of women in sports media across outlets, including newspapers, broadcasting, radio, sport information, and even blogging, does not exceed the 15 percent threshold (Hardin & Whiteside, 2006; Hardin & Whiteside, 2009; Whiteside & Hardin, 2010). Even lower are the percentages of

women who are in positions of leadership, such as editors or news directors. For example, a 2012 report indicated that 90.4 percent of newspaper sport editors were male (Lapchick et al., 2013). Hardly encouraging is that these percentages are consistent with global trends. An international survey of 80 newspapers in 22 countries found that "sports journalism in international print media is a man's world," with more than 90 percent of the writers being male (Horky & Nieland, 2011, p. 6). Women in other sectors of the media industry also remain minorities in leadership positions, but nowhere is the gender discrepancy as drastic as in sport.

Glass Ceiling in Sports Media

To explain why women's advancement to leadership positions occurs slowly, scholars coined the term **glass ceiling** to refer to "an invisible but seemingly unbreakable barrier preventing women from breaking through the top echelons of industry and business" (Chambers, Steiner & Fleming, 2004, p. 83). In the case of sports

Access for women who are sports reporters has come a long way, but barriers such as a glass ceiling, workplace constraints such as being seen as tokens within the organization, and the need to work around masculine gender norms still exist.

media industry, the glass ceiling is even more pronounced because despite women's entrance into other traditionally male-dominated fields, sport newsrooms failed to recruit and retain female journalists, which contributes to the continued lack of diversity in this sector (Hardin & Shain, 2005a). In other words, women may enter sports journalism, but with little opportunity to advance due to gender-related barriers, many leave after just a few years. This pattern is referred to as the **revolving door** of sports journalism, whereby as younger women enter, others leave, which keeps female sport journalists from reaching a critical mass (Hardin, Shain, & Shultz-Poniatowski, 2008).

Both structural and cultural factors form the glass ceiling. In many ways, these structural and cultural factors that create artificial barriers for women derive from the beliefs we hold about gender. Newsrooms, especially sport newsrooms, often operate under **masculine standards**, which then render certain behaviors and norms acceptable and even desired.

Workplace Constraints for Women in Sports Media

Within the structure of the sport newsroom, women face particular workplace constraints. Even though women who enter the industry initially express enthusiasm and find their work satisfying, high levels of job satisfaction are compromised by time demands that conflict with family responsibilities (Hardin & Shain, 2005b). Studies have found that women often lack a support system at their job that would allow them necessary flexibility to handle both work and family obligations (Whiteside & Hardin, 2012). Some younger women even believed that a romantic relationship would disrupt their careers in sports journalism (Hardin & Whiteside, 2009). Even though these are problems that derive from gender-based workplace discrimination, women—particularly women with children—often blamed themselves for not being able to advance in their careers, and therefore were more likely to consider leaving the profession than their male counterparts (Whiteside & Hardin, 2010). Women in sports departments may also be treated like **tokens**,

meaning that they are identified more in terms of gender (and its presumed limitations, in the sport context) than by individual merit. This kind of treatment often leads to limited opportunities for advancement.

Influence of Gender Norms on Women in Sports Media

Other issues that women face derive from our cultural understandings about gender norms. As mentioned earlier, the sport newsroom is a heavily masculine space. Masculine newsroom cultures where sexist attitudes toward women are normalized manifest in a number of ways. Women, thus, face the following:

- Sexual harassment
- Pressure to be one of the boys
- Discrimination in job assignments

Sexual harassment of women in the workplace is a global issue. It begins with a lack of policies about sexual harassment and resources on how to report sexual harassment. A study conducted by the International Women's Media Foundation found, based on a survey of 522 companies in 59 nations, that many organizations had no policies on gender equity and gender-related issues such as sexual harassment. This included countries where such policies are required by law (Byerly, 2011).

In the United States, sexual harassment is prohibited by law, yet researchers observed that, particularly for women under 30, it is a significant and serious problem—one women in sports media were subjected to most frequently by sources and sometimes by coworkers (Walsh-Childers, Chance, & Herzog, 1996). Similarly, younger female sports media professionals were more likely to experience sexual harassment, most likely from coworkers and athletes or coaches they encountered through their job (Pedersen, Lim, Osborne, & Whisenant, 2009).

Some women report unwelcome sexual advances or become targets of sexually charged comments. These are the stories we hear in the media. But many—in order to manage their jobs—choose to ignore such behavior and, instead, tolerate it (North, 2007). Because women

Telling Her Story: Sportswriter's Challenges Serve Future Journalists

Lori Shontz

When I'm teaching journalism to aspiring sportswriters, I always tell the story of the time I got patted on the head. I was covering a golf tournament, and I'd come directly from another assignment. The tournament was well under way, and as I checked a bulletin board to see what I'd missed, a man asked what I was doing. I explained that I was a reporter, and he said, "You'll figure it out." Which was fine—and true—except that he punctuated his encouragement by rubbing my hair as if I were a 7-year-old puzzling over math homework.

I explain how hard it was to watch a male colleague win an award for a story I had wanted to write about a convicted rapist playing on a local team; my male editors said I wasn't qualified, but they gave it to a man who had no more experience with police reporting than I. (Not long after, I requested a temporary assignment to the cops beat.) And I repeat my joke about how I'll know women have achieved equality when I can answer the phone, "Hello, sports," and not have the caller respond, "Um, could I talk to someone in the sports department?"

I don't usually tell "war stories" in the classroom. I focus on what makes good reporting, writing, and editing and ethical decisions, and I let guest speakers spin tales of life in the press box. But by telling my story, I give students context they wouldn't otherwise learn. Unlike some other women sport journalists, I was never sexually harassed. But enduring sexist slights and condescension were part of the job, part of how society viewed women who participated in any part of athletic culture.

I want the young men whose mothers and sisters and girlfriends play sports to know how valuable their support is—and how not long ago, even their acceptance would have been unusual. I want the young women who grew up idolizing Mia Hamm and the U.S. women's soccer team to appreciate an important part of their own history. And so I tell how when I took over the high school wrestling beat at a medium-sized paper in northeastern Pennsylvania, the coaches gave me the cold shoulder. Frustrated and angry, I finally dropped into conversation with Coach No. 7 that I'd covered the Penn State wrestling team—including an Olympian and a national champion—for three years. I followed up with a technical question about takedown technique. The answer was useless for my story, but asking the question allowed me to prove I knew my stuff. Within a week, thanks to the grapevine, coaches were happy to see me.

Twenty years ago, the male reporter I followed on the wrestling beat didn't need to do that. Today, most of the young women in my classes won't encounter that blatant sexism. But everyone will encounter sources who are skeptical for one reason or another, and I hope they'll remember my technique for combating it.

And the larger point of the story.

Lori Shontz was a newspaper reporter and editor, mostly covering sports, for 18 years. She still covers sports as a freelance writer. She is now a faculty member in the School of Journalism and Communication at the University of Oregon, where she is adviser to the campus chapter of the Association for Women in Sports Media.

have not moved out of the token status in sport newsrooms, they frequently opt to adapt to the locker room mentality in order to meet the masculine standards of the newsroom. Such a newsroom environment urges women to act, so to speak, despite their gender, to display toughness under pressure to prove themselves, and to become one of the boys in order to succeed (Whiteside & Hardin, 2012).

In sum, it is clear that sport newsrooms remain a male domain. The organization of the newsroom, manifest in the low percentage of women, and the processes that normalize masculine values attest that we have to be attentive to the ways in which sports departments are gendered. These values pertain not only to newsroom dynamics, but also to coverage. Thus, we may wonder if masculine values that influence opportunities for women in sports media can be linked to how female athletes and women's sports are represented.

PARALLELS: WOMEN COVERING, WOMEN COMPETING

As we noted, the percentage of women working in the sports media industry is low. But does male domination in the newsroom affect media coverage? Or, in other words, would an increase of women in the sports media industry make a difference in terms of the coverage of women's sports? We suggest that it could, indeed. Although it is difficult to answer this question because of the underrepresentation of women in the industry, evidence suggests that women's presence may lead to change in newsroom norms because female journalists—similarly to female athletes—are better located to recognize and question the treatment of women's sports. As feminist scholars note,

> Sports news is home to one of the most intense and most historically enduring gender divisions in journalism, in terms of who is permitted to cover which sports as journalists, how athletes are covered as well as in terms of which genders are served as audiences. (Chambers et al., 2004, pp. 111-112)

Simply put, women who *cover* sports, and the female athletes who should expect to *be covered* by the media, share a similarly marginal status. In other words, "both are *not male*, and, as such, are *not valued* within the sports/media complex because they do not and can never meet the masculine standards on which it is built" (Hardin & Shain, 2005b, p. 816).

Because women's sports are deemed less important than men's sports (across Western culture) for many reasons, women who cover women's sports may have fewer opportunities for advancement, which in turn leads to lower levels of job satisfaction and higher chances that they will leave their careers (Whiteside & Hardin, 2012). The second-class status of female athletes and women's sports, then, make that story assignment less desirable, encouraging female sport journalists to accept and reproduce the lower-class treatment of women's sports, and thus accept the standards by which women's sports and their importance are judged.

Finally, commonly adopted (and seldom questioned) journalistic standards also discourage coverage of women's sports. One of the most frequently cited reasons as to why women's sports do not receive more coverage is that readers and audiences—predominantly men—are just not interested. Because audiences are presumably not interested in women's sports, and men's sports bring the big money, the journalistic standard of **objectivity** dictates that men's sports receive the majority of the coverage. For women to show that they adhere to standards of objectivity means that they need to focus on men's sports, because covering women's sports would be considered promotional journalism (Knoppers & Elling, 2004). What is often missed in this logic is that journalistic coverage of *men's* sports, especially in the United States, was built on the idea that it *should* be promotional. Promotion of men's leagues, teams, and players was foundational to the development of American sports journalism (Bruce & Hardin, 2014).

ESPN's 2010 launch of *espnW* for female fans may have been a step in the right direction. The site has received mixed reviews from scholars, who on the one hand praise it for highlighting women's accomplishments, but on the other hand critique it for reinforcing stereotypical roles for women (Barnett, 2013). The site, however, has been praised for its coverage, and female writers provide the bulk of stories on the site. For example, in 2012, *espnW* commemorated the 40th anniversary of Title IX through stories about historical milestones and personal anecdotes on how Title IX benefited girls and women, and even a critical analysis on how minority girls remain excluded from participation. The films in the recent documentary series *Nine for IX* are directed and produced by women, and the spotlight is on women's sports. While segregating women who love sport (as *espnW* markets) may further marginalize women's sports, this effort provides an example of how a site with women as the majority in production roles corresponds with more coverage and even advocacy.

Women have not yet reached a percentage in the sports media industry that would allow them to significantly challenge existing masculine norms. In fact, many sport newsrooms do not employ even one female staffer. Because of women's low numbers and because of the journalistic norms that privilege men's sports, it is difficult to tell the extent to which women may be able to change the newsroom culture and the treatment of women's sports. However, we would contend that women's presence in the newsroom contributes to the necessary diversity that can ultimately make a positive difference in coverage of women's sports.

FEMALE ATHLETES AND THE MEDIA

Since the implementation of Title IX, the number of girls and women who participate in sports has exponentially grown. Yet female athletes and women's sports have not seen a transformative change in media coverage, which continues to trivialize them in many ways (Cooky & LaVoi, 2012). In this section, we address three dimensions of female athletes' relationship to the media:

- Issues in representation of female athletes and women's sports in the media

- Female athletes' interpretations of media text

- Openings toward more equitable coverage of women's sports

These three issues are important to address because not only is the coverage of women's sports slim, but female athletes often appear in **gender stereotypical** ways. Even though female athletes often voluntarily agree to be photographed and covered, these depictions may not signify how they actually would *prefer* to be represented. As such, we offer examples of media images that may indicate a positive change toward social acceptance of female athletes.

Issues in Representation of Female Athletes

Media scholars and sport sociologists have documented, and concurred, that female athletes remain marginalized across media outlets, including newspapers (Rowe, 2007), television (Messner & Cooky, 2010), radio (Nylund, 2007), and even blogging (Clavio & Eagleman, 2011). In the United States, specifically in the Los Angeles market, television time appears to be the worst among the measures of women's sports coverage, barely reaching 2 percent in regular time, excluding during the Olympics. National coverage of women's sports is also very low, and it has not improved over the past 15 years (see figure 11.1). Sports media do not accurately reflect the gender division in sport: The ratio between men's and women's participation far exceeds the ratio of men's and women's media representation.

But underrepresentation is not the only problem. When female athletes do garner media attention, they are often depicted in gender stereotypical ways that serve to undermine their accomplishments and render them as less athletic, less competent, and thereby less significant than male athletes. A number of strategies exist that contribute to such cultural ideals about gender. One way in which coverage takes away from female athletes' accomplishments is by depicting them as *dependent on their family*—especially on men. Even when women's accomplishments are cited, these are often attributed to their coaches or their fathers, suggesting that female athletes lack independence (Knoppers &

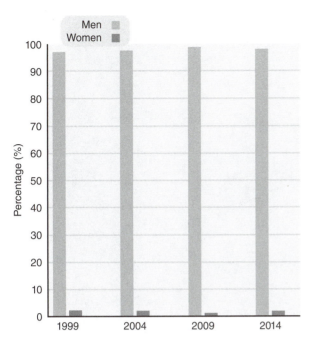

Figure 11.1 Coverage of women's sports on *SportsCenter,* the most popular sports highlight program in the United States.

Created from data from Cooky, Messner, & Musto (2015).

Elling, 2004). Additionally, women tend to be portrayed in traditional family roles, such as wife or mother. One example might be the coverage of acclaimed professional basketball player Candace Parker, who was featured on a 2009 *ESPN the Magazine* cover during her pregnancy, with an accompanying article that went as far as to provide her bra cup size. While providing information about an athlete outside of the sporting word may not in itself be an issue, such representations do become problematic within the context of how little coverage female athletes receive and how poorly, as discussed earlier in the chapter, women's sports are regarded in sport newsrooms. Because women's sports hold secondary cultural status in comparison to men's sports, coverage that further diminishes their competence—such as focus on looks or husbands—only reinforces the stereotype that female athletes are athletically inferior to men.

Newspaper articles and television broadcasts, especially, frequently emphasize female athletes' looks (Jones, Murrell, & Jackson, 1999; Billings, Angelini, & Eastman, 2005). Cameras or photographs focus on female athletes' body parts,

such as buttocks, breasts, or thighs, thereby positioning them as eye candy for the viewers (Jones, 2011). Scholars have pointed out that endeavors such as ESPN's *Body Issue,* which presents soft-pornographic images of both male and female athletes, ultimately also hurt female athletes because they provide yet another outlet where female athletes are sexualized for male audiences (Kane, LaVoi, & Fink, 2013; Krane et al., 2010). Even though one could argue that both male and female athletes are sexualized in that instance, such equal opportunity objectification may not ultimately help promote women's sports; rather, it just offers much of the same image (Hatton & Trautner, 2011).

The assumption behind these representations, and the reason for their widespread utilization, is the common notion that female athletes' sex appeal sells (Kane et al., 2013). The assumption is based on the common practice of **sexualization** of women in media for the purpose of increasing ratings by appealing to the (heterosexual) male viewers. This practice transfers into sports because advertisers continue to target men. Ignored from this equation is that such sexualized representations of female athletes may actually deter readers. Additionally, these images hardly build respect for women's sports. As Kane wrote, "sex sells sex, not women's sports" (2011, para. 9). But what do female athletes think about such representations?

Female Athletes' Interpretation of Media Texts

Thus far, we have found out much about women in sports news production, and women's representations in the media, but female athletes' perspectives on their media representation have been missing from research. Scholars have recently begun asking women to evaluate these images, and their findings offer a complex picture. To examine female athletes' relationship to representations, researchers invited athletes to a photo shoot and gave them full control of how they wanted to be portrayed (see Krane et al., 2010) or showed them photographs and asked them which representation they preferred (see Kane et al., 2013). This approach, consistent with other perspectives presented in this chapter,

When given a choice, female athletes preferred being seen in a realistic sport setting to being sexualized in print media.

considers that sports media are a social structure that shape ideas about gender.

Even though female athletes acknowledged that sexually inviting images may appeal to audiences, particularly to male audiences, they assertively did not want to be portrayed in such ways—they wanted to be seen as legitimate athletes. One athlete summed up the overall sentiments when she said, "most of us want to be respected as an athlete and not just a [pretty] image" (Kane et al., 2013, p. 286). Athletes therefore asked to be photographed in their natural habitat, the athletic environment, where they appeared in athletic poses, as if they were at practice or competition (Krane et al., 2010).

If elite female athletes, indeed, prefer to be portrayed in ways that accentuate their competence—an image we do not see enough—then why are there so many sexy depictions? To answer this question, ESPN's *Body Issue* serves as an excellent example. Women's sport advocates tend to vehemently oppose the magazine because, they argue, it perpetuates sexualization rather than athleticism. However, female athletes who pose for the magazine express that, in fact, they feel proud of their bodies. For instance, Hope Solo, goalkeeper of the U.S.

National Women's Soccer team, proclaimed, "I didn't have an issue posing nude, because now I see my body as empowering" (Ain, 2012, para. 2). Such contradiction may be a positive, since both approaches have merit. Perhaps then, the "central issue is not the *act* but the *motive*" (Hardin & Whiteside, 2014, p. 15): Does the female athlete feel empowered and does she think she is communicating a positive message about women's sports in these media images? Even if the answer to this question is yes, it is important to continue to critically examine how such depictions serve to reinforce the gender hierarchy that positions male athletes as superior.

Potential for Change

Even though the media coverage of female athletes and women's sports continues to raise concern, there has been some progress in isolated pockets. Scholars have found that female athletes receive more equitable treatment during international sporting events, such as the Olympics. The 1996 Olympics in Atlanta earned the title of "Olympics of the Women," while the mainstream media celebrated Title IX as the U.S. women outnumbered the men in medal

> *I still don't buy the idea that I'm a "sex symbol." It's amazing that there are so many beautiful bodies out there on the female athletic side, and it's great that they are starting to get attention.*
>
> **Hope Solo, goalkeeper of the U.S. National Women's Soccer team**

count at the London 2012 Olympics (Brennan, 2012; Eastman & Billings, 2000). During the Olympics, women's sports were more likely to receive airtime, and the blatant bias against female athletes also shifted toward a focus on competence (Fink & Kensicki, 2002). Sexualizing images are far from gone (Jones, 2011), but these examples illustrate that nationalism may overpower gender norms and serve as a vehicle through which women's sports gain respect. Yet, this is hardly enough to challenge the secondary status of female athletes in the media. For women's sports to gain social acceptance, media representations need to significantly improve.

Learning Aids

Summary

The documentary mentioned at the beginning of this chapter, *Let Them Wear Towels*, presents struggles of U.S. women covering sports several decades ago. The documentary does not bring us up to the present day, letting us fill in that gap. What the research and the experiences of women who cover sports globally tell us is that although conditions and opportunities may have improved in some ways, women who dare to enter sports media fields—and who hope to stay there—will face gender-related challenges. Those challenges are cultural and structural. We also suggest that *who* covers sports makes a difference in *what* sports are covered and *how* they are covered. In other words, the problems in how high-level female athletes are covered in the United States and around the world (in terms of quantity and quality) are related to the relatively low numbers of women in the industry and the challenges they have faced in moving up and making a difference.

Discussion Questions

1. What does it mean for female journalists to have equal access to the athletes?
2. In the conversation after the film premier of *Let Them Wear Towels*, two pioneer female journalists, Christine Brennan and Melissa Ludtke, disagreed on the progress of women in sports journalism. How are female media professionals viewed today in society? Are they accepted?
3. In your view, how has the coverage of women's sports changed over time?
4. How do you see the relationship between the status of women as sport journalists and the coverage of women's sports?

Learning Exercises

1. Explore the website of the Association for Women in Sports Media (http://awsmonline.org). What does the organization do? Which resources did you find most helpful?
2. Visit ESPN's site (http://espn.go.com) and compare it to *espnW* (http://espnW.com). Who writes the stories? Are the journalists men or women? Which sports are

covered? How are women's sports covered? Do you see any patterns in coverage addressed in the chapter?

Glossary

gender stereotypical—Representations that accentuate and emphasize traits based on simplistic and overgeneralized assumptions about the roles of men and women in society. In relation to coverage of women's sports, this term refers to the media's representing female athletes in traditional roles, such as mothers, or emphasizing their womanhood.

glass ceiling—An invisible barrier in workplace settings that prevents women (as a group) from advancing in their careers, thus making women's entrance into leadership positions virtually impossible.

masculine standards—Norms and practices that position values associated with gendered assumptions of being a man. The male-as-norm standards render women as outsiders and often lead to discriminatory practices against women.

objectivity—A principle in journalism that news reporting ought to be factual and unbiased. Within the context of sports journalism, the standard of objectivity has been used to justify the exclusion of women from coverage.

revolving door—A term used to describe the pattern in sports journalism whereby women leave the industry after only a few years. As younger women enter the industry, more experienced women leave. This pattern sustains the lack of diversity in the workplace and the lack of women in leadership positions.

sexual harassment—A legal term describing discrimination based on sex, including but not limited to unwelcome sexual advances and verbal and physical harassment of sexual nature, leading to a hostile work environment.

sexualization—Representation that focuses on women's sexual appeal, emphasizing her clothing, body parts, and physical attributes. Sexualized images of female athletes closely resemble soft pornography.

token—A term used to describe a group that occupies a minority position, generally less than 15 percent, in an organization. Those in token status (in this case, women) are often considered representatives of their entire social group, and become defined based on that one social identity rather than individual merit.

CHAPTER 12

Female Leaders in Corporate Sport

Ellen J. Staurowsky, EdD, Drexel University
Maureen Smith, PhD, University of California Sacramento

Learning Objectives

In this chapter, you will learn about the following:

- The influence of sport on female executives working in non-sport industries
- Gender and the sport workplace
- Patterns of gendered hiring in professional sport
- Opportunities for female leaders in international sport
- Experiences of women working in the sport industry
- Strategies for advancing women into leadership ranks in both professional and international sport
- The importance of stories about female leaders in sport

How would your worldview change if you were the youngest woman to compete in your sport at the Olympic Games? Donna de Varona had the opportunity to answer that question. A teenage swimming phenomenon who started to make headlines at the age of 13, she would go on to break 18 world records as a senior in high school and win two gold medals at the 1964 Tokyo Olympics along the way.[1] A glimpse at de Varona's own sense of her future was revealed in a *Sports Illustrated* interview two years before her stunning performance in Tokyo, a performance that would win her acclaim at home in the United States as Female Athlete of the Year by two press associations. Contemplating a time when she would no longer be the best at her sport, she said, "Maybe I could go abroad and do something to promote good will" (Heilman, 1962).

Promoting goodwill on behalf of women in sport has proven to be a life work for de Varona. After she stopped competing in the sport of swimming, de Varona directed that laser-sharp focus and competitive spirit into shaping the national and international dialogue about female athletes and what women could do in the sport industry. Her penchant for being the first would lead her to become the first female broadcaster for ABC's *Wide World of Sport* (Espinosa, 2012). Of de Varona's role in transforming national views about girls and women in sport, Espinosa notes, "Behind the scenes, she worked tirelessly for the passage of Title IX of the Education Act of 1974 . . . and helped found, with Billie Jean King, the Women's Sports Foundation" (2012, para. 5).

As a sport executive with considerable political and economic influence, she has been a driving force behind some of the most significant changes that have occurred in women's sport. In every decade since she surfaced in an Olympic pool and made headlines in *Sports Illustrated,* de Varona has contributed in tangible ways to opening doors for women as athletes and leaders. During the 1970s, she worked in the U.S. Senate as a consultant not only to help facilitate the passage of Title IX but to contribute to the restructuring of the USOC. The 1980s would find her launching a campaign to oppose the U.S. boycott of the Moscow Olympics while lending her energies to the development of the first IOC Athletes' Commission during the IOC Congress in Baden-Baden in 1981 (Riley, 1999). She served as a consultant on the 1984 Los Angeles Olympic Games, a role she would reprise as the city of Chicago put forward a bid to host the Games in 2016.

It was de Varona who served as chair for the FIFA Women's World Cup in 1999, an event hosted in the United States that led to arguably one of the most exciting women's sports events ever played, when the U.S. team battled with China in an epic game that was watched around the world (see chapter 14 for details). In 2013, in an effort to help elite female athletes realize the power of their position to transition into myriad careers in business, education, government, medicine, and politics, she collaborated with other female executives to create the Women Athlete Global Leadership Network (Rossingh, 2013).

De Varona has been a central figure in ushering in a whole new era of women's sport and pushing the boundaries in terms of career opportunities for women in corporate sport. As influential and successful as de Varona has been, her career has not been insulated from some of the trials women encounter when seeking their rightful place within sport. In 2000, de Varona was honored by the American Women in Radio and Broadcasting for her work. Just a week before that ceremony, she filed a $50 million lawsuit against ABC for engaging in age and sex discrimination by firing her (Rogers, 2000).

In an interview about the lawsuit, de Varona commented that she would have preferred to simply walk away from ABC without public acknowledgment of what had happened, but she felt an obligation to contest her dismissal because she had been viewed for so many years as a role model. In de Varona's story, we see themes that are consistent with what is known about women working in the sport industry. While progress has been made, and there are fewer firsts when it comes to women serving in key leadership positions, the foothold that women have is at times tenuous. Even as the expanse of jobs available to women in sport have increased, much still needs to be done to create a work environment that is supportive of women's success. And as women move into

> *We've made incredible inroads. The future is more of the same—carving out a niche for ourselves. We have to build alliances as women. We have to fight for our place in this brave new world of women's sports.*
>
> **Donna de Varona, Olympic athlete and sports executive**

expanding roles, there is more to learn about their experiences.

In other chapters, the focus is on the roles women play in high school and college athletics and in sports media. Here our attention shifts to women as power players in the most elite level of sport, primarily at the professional and international levels, in the sector that falls under the umbrella of corporate sport. Thus, the remainder of this chapter looks at the connections between sport participation and women as executives, gender and the sport workplace, the representation of women in the realms of professional and international sport, and strategies to foster continuing access for women in these sectors of the sport industry.

MAPPING GENDER AND THE SPORT WORKPLACE

The purpose of this section is to provide context for this chapter by creating within the bounds of available information a map of gender and the sport workplace. The sport industry landscape includes terra firma, meaning information that has been firmly established about certain sectors of the sport industry, and terra incognita, meaning that there are certain sectors of the sport industry that have not yet been explored relative to gender, hiring practices, and work climate. Thus, this section highlights existing information on women in two key corporate sport sectors: professional sport enterprises (MLB, NBA, NFL, and WNBA) and international sport and governing bodies. As research continues to be done on women in the sport industry, especially those working in event management, facilities management, sport marketing firms, sporting goods, sports commissions, and many others, there is little doubt that the boundaries

will shift. Whole landmasses may emerge, and a more complete appreciation of the terrain will follow. In the meantime, this is generally what researchers know.

For two decades, scholars have written about sport as a site for gender relations that privileges maleness at the expense of femaleness (Burstyn, 1999; Disch & Kane, 1996; Hall, 1996; Messner, 2002; Messner & Sabo, 1990; Messner & Solomon, 2007; Shaw & Hoeber, 2003). In an analysis of gendered sports programming as manifest in the 1992 Barcelona Olympic Summer Games, Daddario (1997) described the administration of sport as a generic preserve of men.

In a nuanced discussion regarding the connections and intersections between gender, sport, and management, Knoppers and Anthonissen (2005) explored the ways in which male athletic and management masculinities conform to one another and form an interlocking set of values and expectations that become problematic for women entering the sport management workplace. Describing the male culture of sport, they noted that as the popularity and influence of sport in Western society has steadily increased from the early 1970s to the present: "Management continues to be numerically dominated by men, especially in the senior ranks" (p. 123).

In turn, Shaw and Hoeber reported that "senior management roles were heavily dominated by discourses of masculinity that are linked to men and are highly valued in sport organizations" (2003, p. 347). Further, if women in the sport industry are anything like women in other male-dominated professions, and Sartore and Cunningham's (2007) work offers limited evidence that this may be so, women also internalize stereotype threat and limit themselves (Bergeron, Block, & Echtenkamp, 2006). As a result, "females within sport organizations may fail to view themselves as adequate and appropriate leaders . . . preventing them from acting as such" (Sartore & Cunningham, 2007, p. 244).

Whereas it is clear that women are in the minority as employees in the sport industry, no central resource or clearinghouse is available at the present time that tracks the representation of women working in the sport industry across the array of job categories that generally fall under the terms *sport administration*, *management*,

Billie Jean King launched a Leadership Initiative in 2014 to address inclusion and diversity issues in workplaces.

marketing, or *media*. Information gathered from research studies narrowly focusing on specific sectors of the industry and watchdog groups, however, provides statistical support for the assertion that the sport industry is dominated by male employees, whether on the playing field or in the boardroom, broadcast booth, marketing department, press box, front office, or television studio. As Hardin and Whiteside (2006) point out, tracking the statistical representation of women in the industry may well be a rudimentary means of assessing the progress women have made in securing jobs in the sport industry. At the same time, this kind of monitoring serves as one of the most basic indicators of progress that should be evaluated on a periodic basis.

Considering that women constitute almost 50 percent of the working population and 43 percent of college athletes nationwide (BLS Reports, 2013; National Collegiate Athletic Association, 2014), the sport industry workforce is not reflective of either population as evidenced in the sectors examined here. Opportunities across job categories and sectors indicate that women's access to work in the sport industry is localized in lower-level positions. Further, women's access to positions of power and decision making is severely limited. In other words, the map reveals that the terrain women must travel to get into the sport industry is uneven, not clearly marked, and often unsafe, with few welcoming places where career momentum can be achieved. The next two sections elaborate on the connections between sport participation, women, and executive leadership followed by explanations regarding the scarcity of women working in the sport industry.

Women, Executive Leadership, and Sport Participation

In 2013, Ernst & Young released a report revealing the perspectives of global business leaders about the value of sport participation for women and about the connection between sport and working in high-performing teams (N = 328 female, 493 male).[2] Women at the executive level were found to have participated in university sport more frequently than women who were in manager positions (55% to 39%, respectively). Large majorities of female executives in this study (nearly 70%) indicated a belief that a background in sport was helpful to career advancement, because involvement in sport prepares people to work better in teams. Many others (76%) believed that the performance of work teams can be improved by applying behaviors and techniques from sport to what goes on in the corporate environment (Ernst & Young, 2013).

In a follow-up study that surveyed 400 female executives from around the world (Brazil, Canada, China, the United Kingdom, and the United States), there was widespread agreement that a sport background is viewed favorably by employers. Seventy-four percent of respondents expressed a belief that sport participation has the potential to help accelerate a woman's career, while 61 percent thought that their own sport involvement contributed positively to their own career success (Ernst & Young, 2014).

The findings from the Ernst & Young reports (2013, 2014) are consistent with others linking sports participation to women's success in business. In a study of female executives conducted by research firm Catalyst (Tahmincioglu, 2012), 82 percent were found to have participated in organized sports beyond the elementary school level. Sixty percent expressed a belief that their sports participation helped to give them a competitive edge in working with others in the business world. In a 1992 Oppenheimer Funds study of more than 400 senior female business executives who had an annual income of $75,000 or more, 81 percent reported being physically active or having been involved in organized team sports when they were growing up. They also credited their sport involvement with helping them to become more disciplined (86%), develop leadership skills and achieve professional success (69%), deal with failure (65%), and gain a competitive edge (59%; Di Giorgio, n.d.).

In one of the few studies not conducted by a corporation, Wentworth (2009) interviewed 11 women who held executive-level positions in higher education, the corporate sector, and, in one case, the military to assess how participation in intercollegiate athletics contributed to their preparation to assume leadership positions. Female executives in this study believed that their sport participation provided an opportunity to develop as leaders through competing, working as a member of a team, and receiving opportunities to be in charge. In terms of the benefits to be realized from competition, the women who were interviewed indicated that through engaging in competition, they gained confidence, the capacity to persist in the face of disappointment and loss, and an appreciation for challenges set out for them to overcome. Practice and preparation were identified as foundational skills that were transferable to other work settings, as were the necessity of conflict resolution and communication when working with other people in team settings.

While the corporate sector recognizes that women with athletic background have transferable skill sets and leadership qualities that are assets in the world of business, the sport business sector has been slow to recognize women as leaders who have come through the sport system.

Corporate Sport: Professional Sector

The Racial and Gender Report Card published through the Institute for Diversity and Ethics in Sport at the University of Central Florida is the only longitudinal study series that provides information regarding hiring practices and trends in select major professional leagues. Since the 1980s, the Report Card has graded MLB (Major League Baseball), the NBA, and the NFL on their demonstrated record of hiring women and minorities in leadership positions. The Report Card later expanded its scope to include MLS (Major League Soccer) and the WNBA.

According to Lapchick, Johnson, and Yacaman (2014), the WNBA surpasses any other professional sport entity in hiring women and racial minorities (see table 12.1). From the top down, the WNBA has distinguished itself as a forward-looking and forward-thinking organization. It

> In order to achieve gender equity [in sports], we need to talk about transformative thinking and strategies. In order to take meaningful steps, we have to recognize our hidden biases, what I like to call "purple elephants."
>
> Donna Orender, CEO, Orender Unlimited

Table 12.1 2014 Gender Hiring Grades From the Racial and Gender Report Card

Professional league	Gender hiring grade
WNBA	A+
NBA	B+
MLB	C/C+
MLS	C+
NFL	C–

The Racial and Gender Report Card issued in April of 2015 has some data for 2014 and some for 2015.

Orender Unlimited

A business executive with an enviable sport pedigree, Donna Orender has done much in her career in the sport industry. In college, she pursued a bachelor's degree in psychology while competing on a nationally ranked women's basketball team at Queens College in New York. With considerable talent and the right timing, she holds the distinction of being one of only 20 women to compete all three years in the Women's Professional Basketball League, which ran from 1979 to 1981. A life course adjustment during graduate school would take her away from social work and land her a production assistant position with ABC Sports, doing research for the legendary sports broadcaster Jim McKay. From there, she moved on to the PGA Tour, where she stayed for 17 years, moving up the ranks and earning the title of Senior Vice President of Strategic Development in the Office of the Commissioner in 2001. It would be the combination of professional experiences (pro basketball experience, television production background, and negotiating skills) that would position her to become the president of the WNBA in 2005, a position she held for five years (Kuttler, 2014; Mathis, 2015).

To read about Orender is to be inspired, not only by her accomplishments but by the wisdom she exhibits in her approach to professional life. Now founder and CEO of Orender Unlimited (a company name that reflects her vision of the world as unlimited), she provides strategic advice to companies for bettering their performance and outcomes. Discussing the lessons she learned about strategy from her roles as a player and WNBA executive, she said in an interview, "The game really is about outthinking your opponent, out-moving your opponent. There's this strategic interaction of people on the court and it actually elevates itself to this rhythmic poetry" (Mathis, 2015, para. 10).

Orender places great value on relationship building, and she is motivated, in part, by gratitude. She is mindful of how fortunate she is:

> It's that gratefulness that drives me to make sure that when anyone calls me, I constantly say yes to everything. There have always been people that have said yes to me, and I feel like my life moving forward is a constant saying thank you to them for that. (Mathis, 2015, para. 31)

is led by the first woman of color to become president of a professional sports league, Laurel J. Richie. The workforce within the WNBA is predominated by women, with 79 percent holding a variety of staff positions (Lapchick, Johnson, & Yacaman, 2014). The increasing role of women in executive positions in the league can be seen over time. Over a 10-year period, women's participation as majority owners in the league has been on an upward trajectory, going from 18 percent in 2004 to 40 percent in 2012 and 33 percent in 2014.[3]

However, even within the WNBA, a league known for its commitment to women and women's leadership, women do not necessarily have a stronghold on administrative positions. The representation of women in senior administration roles has fluctuated from a high of 52 percent in 2012 to 37 percent in 2014. Women in positions as chief executive officers and presidents have fluctuated from a high of 40 percent in 2010 to 13 percent in 2012, rebounding a bit to 20 percent in 2014. In some significant job categories, including head coaching, general manager, and athletic trainer, the representation of women has fallen by nearly 40 percent or more over time. Between 1998 and 2014, female head coaches have gone from 70 percent to 50 percent, female general managers from 77 percent to 40 percent, and female athletic trainers from 100 percent to 54 percent (Lapchick, Johnson, & Yacaman, 2014). These percentages are tempered somewhat by the relatively small number of teams that comprise the WNBA, which is 12. Within such a small pool, when changes occur, the percentage shifts are more noticeable. That said, the facts that the WNBA has only a dozen teams and that there is kind of volatility around women's positions raise questions regarding job stability for women.

Whereas the majority of WNBA employees throughout the league are women, this situation is a clear anomaly when compared to the industry overall. The WNBA's brother league, the NBA, has a record of hiring women that has historically placed it well ahead of other professional leagues. During the 2013-2014 NBA season, the representation of female minority owners declined from 12.7 percent in 2011-2012 to 5.6 percent;[4] less than 8 percent of chief executives were women, while women constituted 16.6 percent of team vice presidents, 21.4 percent of senior-level administrators, and 35 percent of professional administration (i.e., managers, supervisors, or coordinators in areas such as marketing, promotions, and publications; Lapchick, Donovan, Loomer, & Martinez, 2014).

MLS has had a mixed history of hiring women, with more women represented in league office positions and fewer in team professional administration roles (Lapchick, Domingues, Haldane, Loomer, & Pelts, 2014). In 2012, MLS was awarded a failing grade for exhibiting little progress in hiring women in the area of senior administration. While their grade improved in 2014 to a C+, there continue to be no women in positions of ownership and no women working as general managers; 14.3 percent serve as vice presidents and 19.5 percent in senior administration. The highest representation of women (37.4%) was found in the league office among professional employees.

MLB and the NFL have shown similarly slow progress in hiring women. For the 2014 season, women made up 29.4 percent of the total workforce in MLB, a slight decrease from the previous year that is reflective of a slow decline over the past four years. At the senior executive level, women held 22.6 percent of those positions and 26.8 percent of director and managerial positions, while women made up 16.3 percent of majority owners. The pattern of employment for women in positions of power and authority within MLB included 17.3 percent of team vice presidents and 27.2 percent of senior team administrators (i.e., senior advisors, assistant general managers, legal counsels). Women also held 28 percent of the professional administration positions as managers, supervisors, or coordinators in MLB (Lapchick & Salas, 2015). Similarly, Lapchick, Donovan, Rogers, and Johnson (2014) determined that 9 percent of NFL majority owners were women serving at the chief executive officer/president level; 15 percent at the vice-president level were women. Women constituted 19 percent of senior administrators and 27 percent of professional team administrators.

Corporate Sport: Elite International Sector

The Olympic Games are the pinnacle sporting event for athletes, with more than 10,500 athletes competing in the Summer Games and just over 2,500 athletes in the Winter Games. At the most recent Summer Games in London, women constituted their highest percentage of participants ever, with 44.3 percent (4,751) competing for 205 national Olympic committees (NOCs; Smith & Wrynn, 2010; 2013). Despite the efforts to achieve gender equity among the athletes, the leadership of women at the Olympic Games as members of the IOC, NOCs, and International Federations (IFs) is nowhere near the equity achieved by female athletes. Female sport leaders at the Olympic level continue to struggle in terms of overall numbers and positions of power. This section assesses female sport leadership at three levels: IOC, NOC, and IF. Additionally, it evaluates similar parallel structures in the Paralympic Games organization.

The IOC is a male-dominated organization at every level. Founded in 1894 with 13 members, all male, the IOC governs the Summer and Winter Olympic Games and serves as the stewards of the Olympic movement. IOC membership bestows a great deal of power to its exclusive 106 members, making decisions ranging from which sports to include in the Games and the location of the Games to distribution of funding to NOCs. To address the gender imbalance in sport leadership in the IOC, in 2000, the organization established a 20 percent minimum threshold for the inclusion of women in administrative structures to be achieved by 2005 (Smith & Wrynn, 2013). Despite setting the 20 percent threshold (a figure that falls well short of 50%), the IOC and its various structures struggled to meet their own minimum standard. In 2012, for the first time in the IOC's history, they achieved their 20 percent goal, with 22 women accounting for 20.8 percent of total membership (an increase from 2008, when women made up 14.9 percent of the membership). Equally important was the historic inclusion of three women (Claudia Bokel from Germany, Nawal El Moutawakel from Morocco, and Gunilla Lindberg from Sweden) on the 15-member executive board, including El Moutawakel as one of four vice presidents.[5] To date, there has never been a female president in the IOC's history. To address the role and status of women in the Olympic movement, the IOC has established the Women and Sport Commission and has hosted five world conferences on women and sport.[6] There are a total of 29 IOC Commissions with women accounting for 84 of the 442 positions (19%). Of the 29 commissions,

Although Nawal El Moutawakel of Morocco and select other women have made it to the executive level of the IOC, there has never been a female president in the IOC's history.

11 meet or exceed the IOC's 20 percent standard (this is up from 4 of 31 in 2008). Six of the 29 commissions are chaired by women: the Women and Sport Commission (Anita DeFrantz), the Athletes Commission (Claudia Bokel), the Evaluation Commission (Gunilla Lindberg), the PyeongChang 2018 Coordination Commission (Gunilla Lindberg), the Rio 2016 Commission (Nawal El Moutawakel), and the Youth Olympic Games Coordination 2016 Commission (Angela Ruggiero). Despite this progress, 6 of the 29 commissions have less than 10 percent female participation and 4 commissions have no female members (Smith & Wrynn, 2009, 2010, 2013).

The decision by the IOC to establish the 20 percent threshold goal for the inclusion of women in leadership roles extends to NOCs, IFs, and NGBs, though these bodies have also struggled to meet the minimum threshold. Women have few opportunities to serve in leadership capacities within national and international sports structures. NOCs, of which there were 205 at the 2012 Summer Olympic Games, also represent sport leadership opportunities. The two major positions of leadership within each NOC are the president and secretary general. After the London 2012 Summer Games, only eight NOCs have female presidents (3.9%), with 22 women holding the role of secretary general (10.8%), both slight increases from the previous Olympiad (4th IOC World Conference on Women and Sport, 2008). Of the 205 NOCs, 175 (85.4%) had all-male leadership teams, with 29 (14.1%) NOCs having coed representation. Zambia is the only NOC with a women-only leadership team. Henry and Robinson (2010), in their examination of women in leadership positions in the Olympic movement, concluded that NOCs had failed to meet the IOC's 20 percent minimum threshold (Smith & Wrynn, 2013).

International Federations, which govern the various Olympic sports, also provide women with unique leadership positions, though only 2 of the 28 IFs (7.1%) in the 2012 Summer Olympic Games had a female president: the Federation Equestrian Internationale and the International Triathlon Union. Six of the 28 IFs have executive boards that meet the IOC's 20 percent threshold. Ten IFs include only one woman or none at all. There are seven Winter IFs, and none of these is led by a woman. Two of the seven IFs have female secretary generals, and of the 17 vice presidents, 2 are women (11.8%).

The Paralympic Games are governed by the International Paralympic Committee (IPC). The president and vice president of the IPC are both men. The IPC has a goal of 30 percent female representation in its leadership structures; currently, 3 of the 15 members of the IPC are female (20%). Seven of the 23 (30.3%) Sport Representatives to the Sport Councils of the Paralympic Games are female. Just as the IOC is making some efforts to include women in its leadership structure, the IPC has made the inclusion of women part of its mission, including a video on their website that details their efforts (titled "Being a Woman at the International Paralympic Committee"). Like the IOC, the IPC has a Women in Sport committee, which is chaired by a woman. Of the remaining 10 committees, 2 others are chaired by women: the Classification committee, Development committee, and the Education committee. Of the 55 members of the 11 IPC committees, there are 21 women, accounting for 38.2 percent of the overall committee membership and exceeding the IPC's 30 percent standard (Smith & Wrynn, 2009, 2010, 2013).

There are 175 National Paralympic Committees (NPCs), and each is led by a president and secretary general or main contact. Sometimes these two positions are held by one person. At the 2012 Summer Games, there were 19 NPCs led by a female president (10.9%) and 42 with women in the position of main contact (24%), which may be a point for slight optimism. Eleven countries (Austria, Brunei Darussalam, Democratic Republic of Congo, Indonesia, Mozambique, Namibia, Romania, San Marino, Uzbekistan, Venezuela, and Virgin Islands) have all-female leadership teams—the majority of which are all female due to the fact that one person serves as both the president and the main contact for the NPC (Smith & Wrynn, 2013).

In looking at the representation of women in Olympic and Paralympic leadership in the United States, women continue to face barriers. The United States Olympic Committee is the governing body of all Olympic sports in the United States. The USOC is headed by Scott

Blackmun, and 37.5 percent of members on the Board of Directors are female, exceeding the IOC's 20 percent threshold. The leadership of the USOC is comprised of 17 people, including 6 women (35.3%). Anita DeFrantz and Angela Ruggiero are members of the USOC and serve as representatives to the IOC. Both are former Olympic athletes, a familiar path for women in advancing to positions of leadership in sport. At the 2012 Olympic Games, no NGBs had all-female leadership, while 23 NGBs had all-male leadership (79.3%). Sixteen of the 29 NGBs met the IOC's standard of 20 percent female membership, with five NGBs including only one woman, and judo having no women on their executive board (Smith & Wrynn, 2010, 2013).

It is important to note the structural efforts by the IOC and IPC to ensure the inclusion of women in sport leadership positions at all levels. However, standards of equity set at 20 percent by the IOC and at 30 percent by the IPC indicate that much work needs to be done. The number of committees, commissions, and governing bodies that fail to achieve having women as 20 percent of their members remind us that women still face imposing and seemingly impenetrable barriers when it comes to some of the most important and powerful positions in international sport organizations.

In an examination of the role of women in British sports governing bodies, White and Kay reported that contrary to perceptions that there was little chance that sport organizations were adjusting and improving their approach to hiring women, "women have in fact been appointed in increasing numbers to senior jobs in sports governance" (2006, p. 465). In a tremendous sign of progress in gender equity in sport leadership, the London Organising Committee of the Olympic and Paralympic Games (LOCOG) led by Sebastian Coe made gender equity a primary guiding principle. Coe sought to have LOCOG membership be 50 percent female and 50 percent male (Roenigk, 2012). Men and women in German sport organizations have also evidenced gender differences in perceptions of power, prestige, and conflicts. According to Pfister and Radtke, "women not only experienced sex-specific discriminations but also showed a much higher emotional involvement in conflicts" (2006, p.

111). Chin, Henry, and Hong (2009) studied contrasting contexts in which the role of women is seen to be embedded in very different ideologies.

EXPLANATIONS FOR THE SCARCITY OF WOMEN WORKING IN CORPORATE SPORT

The scarcity of women working in leadership positions in the sport industry lends itself to three questions. First, what barriers exist for women pursuing sport careers in management? Second, how do women working in the corporate sport industry experience their work lives? And third, what do women need in order to experience initial success and get promoted within the sport industry? A growing body of research illuminates these questions to some degree.

Barriers to Women Pursuing Sport Careers in Management and Administration

One approach scholars have used in capturing the causes for the inequity women experience in the sport workplace is Kanter's 1977 concept of *homologous reproduction*. Proposed in the 1970s, Kanter used the term to describe the ways in which power elites maintain their positions of power. In everyday parlance, an example of homologous reproduction in sport is seen in the phenomenon of the good old boys' network (Acosta & Carpenter, 1990; Whisenant, Pedersen, & Obenour, 2002), where men protect the interests of each other; serve as gatekeepers by hiring men who reflect their style, image, and values; and create insular decision-making processes that elevate men who epitomize the system's ideals while restricting women in terms of numbers and roles. As demonstrated by Kane and Stangl (1991) in a study of female coaches of boy's teams, homologous reproduction in sport can occur through female tokenism or marginalization.

Tokenism occurs when women are hired in limited numbers, creating an appearance of change on the part of employers, when, in actuality, the small number of women in the system allows for minimal challenge to the status quo favoring men. Marginalization, on the other hand, is found in the gendered division of labor that tracks women into lower-level positions presenting the fewest prospects for future career growth and advancement.

Current hiring patterns offer examples of both. Whereas the sport industry is no longer exclusionary, it remains heavily skewed toward men. As a result, until the time women are equitably represented across the ranks of the sport industry, barriers to women's success will exist. Further, the likelihood that a balanced sport workforce will develop is diminished by the marginalization of women into positions of lower status.

The gendered power dynamics at play in hiring women are also found in the selection of women to national sport governing bodies. In interviews with male chairs and female board members, the issue of perceived fit was a key consideration in reaching a positive decision on female board candidates. Recruitment and selection hinged on finding women who did not threaten the male-dominated culture on the board while conveying a sense of assurance that female candidates valued the male culture as it was. Additionally, "women in their turn tend to negotiate their entry by distancing themselves from their gender and proving their 'fit'" (Claringbould & Knoppers, 2007, p. 495). And as women work to fit in, there is evidence that if sport organizations make a philosophical commitment to greater support of women through the creation of substantive human resource management programs, greater gender equity will be achieved, and there will be greater female representation in management positions (Moore, Parkhouse, & Konrad, 2000).

Inasmuch as there is evidence to support the conclusion that a pro-male bias exists in the sport industry that impairs the ability of women to be viewed as competent and credible, research suggests that some women may engage in self-limiting behavior by failing to see themselves as possessing the qualities and capabilities associated with sport leaders (Sartore & Cunningham, 2007). As Sartore and Cunningham explain, within the sport setting, female candidates may not seek advancement into upper-level positions as a result of being subjected to the appraisal of others who convey the belief that certain jobs are not appropriate for women (e.g., head coaches should not be female). In effect, in a sport system that subtly and straightforwardly undermines the value of women as leaders, it is not surprising that women would have a difficult time envisioning successful careers within it.

Experiences of Women Working in the Sport Industry

Most of what we know about women working in the corporate sector of the sport industry comes from anecdotal accounts. In one of the few studies focusing on women in this sector, conducted by Staurowsky, Brown, and Weider (2009), the majority of the 108 Women in Sports and Events (WISE)[7] female members responding indicated that they held positions at the supervisor, manager, or director level (55%). The next largest groups of responses came from women who worked at the levels of vice president (16%) and president or chief executive officer (11%). Only two women in the survey owned their own sport business. As a group, these women were well educated, with nearly 8 percent having taken some graduate school courses, 31 percent holding a master's degree (MBA, MD, or other), and just under 6 percent holding a law degree.

WISE women were generally satisfied with their experience working in sport, believing that they received good to excellent opportunities to succeed, and that they were given the resources necessary to be successful. Their satisfaction with working in sport seems to be supported by the fact that just 3 percent responded that they would not encourage women to pursue careers in sport.

Still, there was equivocation as to their commitment in continuing to work in the sport industry over the long term. Eleven percent were not sure how long they planned to remain in the industry and another third indicated that they were only somewhat committed to working long term in sport. And while the majority clearly expressed a belief that they were supported in their work, 20 percent indicated that they found it difficult to do their jobs because they did not have the staff or money and that they were blocked from professional development opportunities that would allow them to advance in their careers.

From the perspective of WISE women, the climate women encounter in the sport workforce does have its challenges. A large majority (nearly 70%) believed that there was a double standard for women in the sport industry that resulted in women having to work twice as hard to receive half the credit. They also indicated that there was a glass ceiling that prevented women from being promoted to upper-management positions (72%).

Career Advice From the WISE Women in Sport Survey

What do women need in order to experience initial success and get promoted within the sport industry? This open-ended question was asked of more than 100 women who were members of the organization Women in Sports and Events (Staurowsky, 2011. The advice listed below in their own words is a representative sampling of responses to that question:

- Approach sport as a business and develop a knowledge and skill base reflective of that.
- Broaden your educational base to include business management and finance courses.
- Learn how to negotiate.
- Be resilient; disappointments happen, but it's what happens after that makes all the difference.
- Understand that the sport industry is fast paced [and] competitive, and requires you to work hard.
- Do not mix business with pleasure, and understand that even when working events that are fun and social, you are still working.
- Cultivate strong relationships with male coworkers while carefully navigating the social scene.
- Do not date athletes.
- Develop a support network.

- Create your own personal advisory board.
- Network with men, network with women.
- Find a strong mentor.
- Be strategic in terms of career planning.
- Figure out what you want and what you need to do to get to your goals.
- Get as much exposure [or] experience as possible with the best people [and] properties in the industry.
- Dream big; it can happen.

IMPORTANCE OF STORIES ABOUT FEMALE EXECUTIVES IN SPORT

In a discussion regarding new paradigms of sport leadership, Maylon (2011) argued that the stories that are shared with students need to include stories about female leaders in sport, since students represent the future in terms of how leadership is conceived, employed, and exercised within sport organizations. By reexamining common understandings about who leads in sport, we have the opportunity to realize that leadership styles that may have been viewed as industry standards in previous generations may not be as effective in a new age. As more women move into leadership positions in sport, it is likely that the approach to leadership may change, as will conceptions of who sport leaders are. The heroic, masculine traits associated with sport leaders treat gender as neutral (Hovden, 2010) when the traits women may bring to the table simply go unrecognized or devalued. As Maylon pointed out, a quality that typically receives little attention but is evidenced among some female leaders in sport is empathy.

The importance of having those stories and what they mean to women working in the sport industry was reflected in the response WISE women gave when prompted in an open-ended question to identify the most visible women in the industry. In 2009, two names appeared more than any others—legend, advocate, and business woman Billie Jean King and then WNBA president, Donna Orender. When asked what strengths they associated with these women, some respondents thought it enough to simply write "Billie Jean King," as if there were no need to offer further elaboration. A legend, after all, is a legend. That being said, others wrote "leader and history maker," a "pioneer," and "an advocate for women in general." She was also recognized for her "constancy of commitment and devotion to equity for all." Donna Orender was lauded for her "knowledge of the business," "credibility," "energy/enthusiasm," "strong presence," "sense of humor," "fearlessness," "intelligence," and reputation as a "powerful, bottom line leader" (Staurowsky, 2011).

In a 2011 Turnkey Sports Poll, which included 1,100 senior-level sports executives, 49 percent indicated that they had, at some point during their professional careers, reported to a female supervisor ("Game Changers," 2011). And while the fact that more than half had not reported to a woman in their careers is troubling, it does signal a shift from a time when the reporting pipeline would have been exclusively male. Still, 54 percent of the senior-level sport executives (female and male) acknowledged in the poll that women face more challenges achieving success in the business of sports ("Game Changers," 2011).

Part of the story being told is playing out on the sports pages themselves as female executives emerge to run sport entities worth not only millions, but billions. In March of 2013, *Sports Illustrated* identified 10 of the most influential women in sport (Newman, 2013). They included the following:

- Sharon Byers, group vice president, and Alison Lewis, senior vice president for North America Marketing, Coca Cola North America (annual sports revenue: $260 million)
- Cindy Davis, vice president for Nike Inc., and vice president for Nike Golf (annual sports revenue: $623 million)
- Christine Driessen, executive vice president and chief financial officer for ESPN (annual sports revenue: $8.2 billion)
- Lesa France Kennedy, CEO of International Speedway (annual sports revenue: $750 million)
- Heidi Ueberroth, NBA president of international business operations (annual sports revenue: $300 million)
- Michelle Wilson, Chief Marketing Officer, WWE (annual sports revenue: $525 million)
- Denise DeBartolo York, former owner and current cochair of the San Francisco 49ers (annual sports revenue: $214 million)
- Rita Benson LeBlanc, part owner and vice chair of the board of the New Orleans Saints (annual sports revenue: $232 million)
- Stacey Allaster, CEO of Women's Tennis Association (annual sports revenue: $86 million)
- Kathryn Carter, president of Soccer United Marketing (annual sports revenue: $100 million)

If we return to Donna de Varona's story, all of these women have made a difference in changing the story around women's leadership in corporate sport at the professional and international levels, often times making inroads through changes in public and sport policy that has resulted in greater opportunities for women working in the sport industry. In the process, they have also changed the story of sport itself.

Learning Aids

Summary

For female executives in the sport industry, the workplace is a contradictory place, at times providing a firm platform for advancement and pursuing dreams, at others presenting women with quicksand that can slow them down, occasionally trap them, and sometimes keep them from moving forward. The percentages of women in executive leadership positions are clearly not where they should be. However, with each passing generation, more women are moving into the pipeline, supporting one another, and devising ways to lead the way. As that happens, the *she*, as Donna Orender (2015) would say, becomes the *we*, meaning that the sport industry itself changes, hopefully becoming more equitable, more inclusive, and more open to possibility.

Discussion Questions

1. In April of 2013, speculation arose that the Miami Dolphins (NFL) were considering the possibility of hiring their executive vice president of football administration, Dawn Aponte, as general manager (Florio, 2013). If she had been hired, she would have become the first female general manager in the sport of professional football and one of the only female general managers in all of professional sport. In the history of the NFL and other sport leagues, the pathway for women into the executive suite has often occurred because of family connections. How might hiring practices within the realm of professional sport be changed to make a more level playing field for women to be considered for executive-level positions?

2. Some believe that men gain entry and access to leadership positions in sport through their business experiences, contacts, and wealth, while women tend to come up through the ranks, starting out as athletes. If you go back and read the section on female leaders in the IOC, we see that there may be some truth to that observation. Research the backgrounds of female and male members of the IOC. Does this pattern exist? If there is a difference in the way that women and men become leaders in sport, what are the implications of that?

3. In April of 2015, *PBS News Hour* special correspondent John Carlos Frey did a story exploring the question, When will Major League Baseball hire its first female general manager? In the piece, he interviewed the woman whom some believe may be chosen when the time comes. That woman is Kim Ng, senior vice president of baseball operations at Major League Baseball. View the video at www.pbs.org/newshour/bb/will-major-league-baseball-hire-first-female-general-manager and then discuss when there will be a female general manager in the major leagues.

Learning Activities

1. Identify a woman working in a professional sport franchise, professional league office, or international sport organization. Research her background and conduct an interview to learn more about her career path and the steps she took to get the position she currently holds.

2. In 2013, Lydia Nsekera of Burundi became the first woman to be elected to FIFA. Research why it has taken so long for a woman to be included in the governance structure for a sport whose popularity has expanded exponentially worldwide because of the increasing number of women participating. Note: Two women were co-opted on to the FIFA governing board in the year previous to Nsekera's election (Hock, 2013).

3. Using the websites for the USOC, IOC, or IPC, determine which sports include more women in their leadership structures and which do not. Offer explanations for the various sports that are more inclusive of women, as well as reasons that might explain the exclusion of women in leadership in other sports.

Glossary

marginalization—Found in the gendered division of labor that tracks women into lower-level positions, which present the fewest prospects for future career growth and advancement.

pipeline—In a hiring context, this refers to the pool of individuals who are being prepared for positions in the future. Sometimes this is referred to as a *candidate pipeline*.

stereotype threat—A stereotype is an amplified set of characteristics that may or may not be true about a certain group. Stereotype threat can occur when someone feels that they have been put into situations where they risk confirming a negative stereotypical belief that affects them as a member of a social group.

terra firma—Information that has been firmly established about certain sectors of the sport industry.

terra incognita—Certain sectors of the sport industry that have not yet been explored relative to gender, hiring practices, and work climate.

tokenism—Occurs when women are hired in limited numbers, creating an appearance of change on the part of employers, when, in actuality, the small number of women in the system allows for minimal challenge to the status quo favoring men.

Notes

1. When de Varona returned from Tokyo, opportunities to swim at the college level were virtually absent. There were no scholarships available to female athletes.

2. Executives participating in the study represented companies from a wide range of sectors. Those who participated in the survey had annual revenues in excess of 250 million USD.

3. The Racial and Gender Report Card produced by Richard Lapchick at the University of Central Florida uses a standard that considers the percentage of female employees within a sport organization to determine a grade. An organization will receive a grade of A if 40 percent of employees are women, B for 32 percent, C for 27 percent, D for 22 percent, and F for anything lower than 22 percent.

4. While Lapchick, Lecky, and Trigg (2012) reported for the 2013-2014 season that nine female owners were high profile, it is notable that many of these women are related to ownership families. JoAnn, Jeanie, and Janie Buss are part of the ownership team of the LA Lakers; Helen, Elisabeth, Andrea, Maria, and Pamella DeVos are part of the ownership team of the Orlando Magic; and Colleen and Adrienne Maloof were part of the ownership team for the Sacramento Kings (before selling the team in 2013). Out of this group of female owners from ownership families, only one woman, Karen (Gail) Miller, is identified as a majority owner (for the Utah Jazz). Similarly, in 2013-2014, several teams had husband and wife minority owners—actors Jada Pinkett Smith and Will Smith for the Philadelphia 76ers; Popp Communications executive Bill Popp and his wife, Teri (Minnesota Timberwolves); and William Sexton, Old Northwest Company, and his wife, Joyce Sexton (Minnesota Timberwolves). Rita Benson LeBlanc (New Orleans Pelicans) is the granddaughter of owner Tom Benson. She had worked since 2001 with the NFL franchise he owned, the New Orleans Saints, and has

worked since 2012 with the Pelicans. A family dispute arose in December of 2014, when she was evicted from her office (Associated Press, 2015).

5. The IOC Executive Board is made up of the president, four vice presidents, and 10 members.

6. The inclusion of women in the IOC has been quite slow. The first women to be included as members were Pirjo Häggman and Flor Isava Fonseca in 1981. Isava Fonseca was elected to the executive board in 1990, and the United States' Anita DeFrantz was elected as the first female vice president in 1997.

7. WISE was selected for this study because it is perhaps the most representative group for women working in professional sport. As described on its website, "from its beginning in 1993, when a group of approximately sixty women met in a New York City restaurant, WISE has become the leading professional organization for women in the sports and sports events industry. As the leading voice and resource for women in the business, WISE now has chapters throughout the country; its membership spans a diverse spectrum in experience and area of expertise. In short, from entry level to C level, from the major professional sports leagues to consumer packaged goods and media, WISE provides an opportunity for women to meet, discuss career related issues and network" (Women in Sports and Events, n.d., para. 1).

CHAPTER 13

Female Leaders in High School and College Sport Workplaces

Ellen J. Staurowsky, EdD, Drexel University

Learning Objectives

In this chapter, you will learn about the following:

- The gendered nature of high school and college sport workplaces
- The wide range of jobs women perform in high school and college sport workplaces
- The degree to which women are represented as workers within high school and college sport settings
- Gendered division of labor in high school and college sport workplaces
- Factors that affect the hiring, retention, and advancement of women in high school and college sport workplaces
- The future for women in college and university workplaces

The sound a leather basketball makes as it rebounds off the polished hardwood floor of a court is unmistakable. So, too, is the sound of a high heel striking the same wood on the sidelines. If you listen carefully to a women's college basketball game, you'll hear both those sounds intermingle and intertwine, assuming the cadence and rhythm of the game itself as players handle the ball and female coaches patrol the perimeter. The split-second timing of a pass, pass, shoot, and score combination is accompanied by a tap, tap, tap, and *tap* of shoe on floor. The emphatic placement of a high heel can echo around an arena, a manifestation of myriad strategic decisions signaling shifts in defenses, changes in offensive schemes, exhilaration after an especially well-executed play, or the inconsolable frustration with an official's ill-timed and suspect call.

In March of 2012, high-heel-wearing women's basketball coaches from the Southeastern Conference (SEC) became a story at their own tournament, where they were featured along with their footwear. Louisiana State University (LSU) assistant coach Tasha Butts literally walked away with the Highest Heel award for her stylish black 6-inch (15 cm) stilettos (Kline, 2012). Six months later, history would be made when then North Carolina State head women's basketball coach Kellie Harper became the first female coach to wear her own collection of high heels—the signature line of Wolfpack Heels designed by a company called Fan Feet. Harper seems to have torn a page from the manual of her college coach at the University of Tennessee, the legendary Pat Summitt, who wrote in her memoir, "I remember standing on the sidelines and stomping my high heels on the hardwood so furiously it sounded like gunshots" (Summitt & Jenkins, 2013, p. 3).

In an industry where footwear is so important, the fact that some women wear high heels as part of the uniform for basketball coaching serves as a convergence point that illustrates tensions between societal expectations for women and the demands of the sport workplace. Anthropologist Kristal D'Costa wrote in *Scientific American*, "While it's true that an individual woman's presence is so much more than the footwear she has chosen for the day,

shoes can influence our interactions with others: they change how we walk, how we stand, and how others perceive us" (2012, para. 6). In 1988, Texas politician Ann Richards captured that sentiment in memorable fashion in her address to the Democratic National Convention. She observed that in 160 years of the party's existence, there had only ever been two women who delivered the keynote at the Convention, and she admonished the body to broaden its vision to include women more directly in leadership. She famously observed, "If you give us a chance, we can perform. After all, [dancer] Ginger Rogers did everything that [her dancing partner] Fred Astaire did. She just did it backwards and in high heels" (Richards, 1998, para. 3).

For women working in sport, where a premium is placed on moving freely without encumbrance to maximize strength, speed, power, and impact, the emblem of the high heel signals a conundrum of sorts. In a competitive environment where women labor for status and recognition, the multiple meanings of the high heel are in full view.

As a sort of power tool, the high heel is an enabler, a mechanism employed over centuries to level the playing field by allowing women to talk to their male counterparts eye to eye (Brockman, 2000).[1] Donna Lopiano, arguably one of the most influential forces in the development of women's sport in the United States, has referred to the high heel as a power shoe (Howard, 1994). The multitasking female coach may not detect the balancing act that is part of wearing the high heel within the range of everything else she gets done in a day. As an exercise in endurance and evidence of what women will put up with in order to prevail, it confirms in statistical form the degree to which women can withstand discomfort, as evidenced in the fact that 8 in 10 women admit to wearing shoes that hurt (D'Costa, 2012). The high heel has the capacity to offer an assurance that whatever career ambition a female coach has, she has not abandoned societal standards of womanly conduct and appearance. Marking a cultural space where fashion runway, Wall Street, and sport meet, the high heel may be a ready choice for the high-powered celebrity female coach who is navigating relationships

Nikki Caldwell, the head women's basketball coach at LSU, offers an example of how the high heel has gone from the runway to the sideline.

with television audiences, corporate sponsors, hometown crowds, program boosters, and her own team. Female coaches can also opt for the power flat in shoewear.[2]

Women who aspire to coach at the highest level can anticipate working in a financially rewarding profession. As LaVoi (2013) points out, college coaches in the most elite levels earn more than most U.S. citizens. During a time when salaries for the average American worker not only stalled but went down by 1.5 percent in the years following the economic downturn in 2008, college coaches benefitted from salary increases that outpaced those of any other sector in higher education (DeNava-Walt, Proctor, & Smith, 2012). In 2010-2011, while faculty salaries rose at a rate of 1.8 percent, their increases lagged behind the 3 percent increase in inflation. In contrast, coach salary increases improved by 9.5 percent, with football coach

salaries rising by 12 percent. To put this into tangible terms, an assistant coach of an NCAA Division I-A women's program made on average more than $51,000 (Equity in Athletics Disclosure Act Report, 2012), a salary that surpassed the median family income in the United States, which was just over $50,000 (DeNava-Walt et al., 2012).

While the coaching profession holds out the possibility of a good living for women, there remains the open question of whether subscribing to ultra-feminine societal norms such as the wearing of high heels in the most unlikely of places garners women further acceptance or merely serves to undermine their position as authorities within the sport realm. As a practical reality, the position of female workers in high school and college sport settings is hardly secure; women are generally outnumbered at a rate of eight to two in the head coaching ranks of all college sports (Acosta & Carpenter, 2012). And whether their feet are planted firmly on the ground or teetering slightly on the brink of their heels, female coaches equally share the dilemma that they are routinely compensated at rates that fall well short of their male counterparts (Gentry & Alexander, 2012; LaVoi, 2013).

As a case in point, Gentry and Alexander (2012) reported that the average salary for the coach of an NCAA Division I men's team in any sport between 2003 and 2010 increased by 67 percent to $267,007. The average salary for a coach of a women's team in the same division rose by only 16 percent during the same period of time, amounting to $98,106. And that analysis does not take into account money that coaches may receive from third parties that supplement their income considerably, such as appearance fees or endorsement contracts from athletic apparel companies. In the end, it is the male coaches in the polished loafers and classic Oxfords who have cashed in on lucrative athletic shoe contracts, not female coaches in high heels or flats.

During the past four decades, the school-based sport workforce has proliferated as the enterprise has grown. As Staurowsky, Murray, Puzio, and Quagliariello (2013) point out, the streamlined athletic departments of yester-year, where coaches and instructional staff

> *I remember every player—every single one—who wore the Tennessee orange, a shade that our rivals hate . . . to us the color is a flag of pride, because it identifies us as Lady Vols and therefore as women of an unmistakable type. Fighters. I remember how many of them fought for a better life for themselves. I just met them halfway.*
>
> Pat Summitt

outnumbered administrators by a wide margin, have morphed into multifaceted, sophisticated employment settings where coaches are surpassed in number by specialists providing services to support revenue generation, foster the development of athletes, encourage better athletic performance, ensure rules compliance across various regulatory schemes, and create, distribute, and manage information and content. Within that structure, more women than ever before are working in high school and college sport workplaces. At the same time, the transition into an employment area historically dominated by men has offered both opportunity as well as significant challenges for female workers because of the male-centric nature of the sport enterprise (Blom et al., 2011; Hoffman, 2011; Magnusen & Rhea, 2009; Wright, Eagleman, & Pedersen, 2011).

The remainder of this chapter examines the gendered nature of the athletic department workplace, the expanse of jobs women perform in school sport settings, and the degree to which women are represented as workers within the high school and college sport sectors. Following that overview, it pays attention to issues that affect the lives of working women in high school and college sport settings, including factors that affect the hiring, retention, and advancement of women. The chapter ends with a look at the future for women in high school and college sport.

GENDERED NATURE OF HIGH SCHOOL AND COLLEGE SPORT WORKPLACE SETTINGS

The incentives that might attract a woman to jobs in high school and college sport are probably as individual as the woman herself.

Surely, economic considerations play a role as do decisions regarding lifestyle, skill sets, and professional fit (Bracken, 2009; Schneider, Stier, Henry, & Wilding, 2010). A desire to work with young people and contribute meaningfully to their lives is often a driving consideration for those working in school-based sport settings. It is telling that after nearly 40 years of coaching, eight national championships, and a record 1,098 wins—accomplishments that place former University of Tennessee head women's basketball coach Pat Summitt in an echelon of achievement that no other coach, male or female, has attained—what she remembers most are her players. Even as she takes up the challenge of dealing with the onset of Alzheimer's, Summitt pointed out that the things that had faded from her memory were scores and statistics, but the relationships with her players remained vibrant (Summitt & Jenkins, 2013).

While the attractions may be obvious, the complexities of high school and college workplaces warrant consideration. There are few employment areas where gender dynamics play out in quite the way that they do in school-based sport workplaces due to sex-segregation of athletic teams, meaning there are separate teams for boys and girls, men and women. This gendered arrangement, which is permitted to exist under Title IX's conception of "separate and equal," has resulted in a system that maintains a **sex-segregated** infrastructure but demands that those playing and working within that structure be treated fairly and equitably.

At the time of Title IX's passage in 1972, separate programs for female and male athletes were run at the college level through department structures that were separate and associations that were single sex (Acosta & Carpenter, 2012; Grappendorf, Lough, & Griffin, 2004). On individual college and university campuses, male coaches and athletics directors ran programs for male athletes; female coaches and athletics directors created opportunities for female athletes, more often than not through physical education programs. With women's competitive teams just taking hold across the nation and the sport culture evolving to include women, there was the feel of a start-up about women's college sport during this era.

ESPN sportswriter Bonnie D. Ford offers a sense of what this time was like for female college athletes and coaches when she reflected on her experience playing basketball at Oberlin College in 1978. She pointed out that the Ohio Athletic Conference (OAC), a conference founded in 1902 that expressly prohibited women from competing under its umbrella, threatened to revoke Oberlin's membership because female athletes were competing on their previously all-male cross country team and were being encouraged to compete in exhibition races against OAC-member schools. Without the support of a league structure, scheduling of games was inconsistent, record keeping haphazard, and the playing experiences uneven. Ford recalled,

> The Oberlin women's basketball teams of my era . . . toiled through hodge-podge schedules made up of some comparable schools (Kenyon College) and some we probably had no business sharing a court with (Cleveland State). When I went looking for the trail we left behind, I found more cobwebs than statistics. (Ford, 2012, para. 13)

As women's college sport leaders moved forward into unchartered territory, the attempt to carve out a place for girls and women to compete in their own programs, while dealing with comparisons to fully developed and entrenched men's programs, presented challenges that have yet to be fully resolved. Just as the OAC predated emerging women's programs at Oberlin and other Ohio schools by 70 years, the all-male NCAA initially assumed a position of disinterest in women's sport, leaving the Association for Intercollegiate Athletics for Women (AIAW) to become the first national sports governing body for women's college sport.

According to Acosta and Carpenter, "the AIAW was a declaration that women leaders intended to fling open the gymnasium doors so female athletes could grow and benefit from full athletic participation" (2007, p. 49). Female college sport leaders rejected the male athletic model that emphasized the promotion of spectator sport for the purpose of drawing media attention, mass audiences, and revenue. Leaders in the AIAW viewed the concept of an athletic scholarship as a distortion of the relationship between student and school. Payment for athletic services rendered along with the attendant policies that needed to keep a system like that in place, most specifically intense recruiting of talent and rules to prevent athletes from switching schools, were perceived by AIAW leaders as tools of control that favored the interests of coaches and programs but not students. Placing a student philosophy at the center of their vision of intercollegiate athletics for women, the leadership of the AIAW sought to ground their association in a set of principles that honored the mission of higher education and created protections for athletes so as to ensure that they would be able to pursue their educations independent of their athletic commitments. In effect, attention was paid to athlete health and safety and moderating pressures associated with the conflicting demands of academics and athletics.

During its decade of existence, the AIAW progressively created the infrastructure that Ford (2012) noted was lacking in women's intercollegiate athletics. AIAW leadership also contributed to the national dialogue regarding the fair treatment of female students in schools as a result of Title IX's passage, a dialogue that the NCAA aggressively sought to silence by urging the U.S. Congress and the courts to remove athletics from Title IX enforcement. Failing that, and realizing that the AIAW was poised to become a more powerful force with access to its own financial resources through negotiated television contracts, the NCAA set about the task of absorbing women's college sport into its structure by offering national championships. The AIAW's leadership considered this a hostile takeover, but

> *Women have made strides. But there's still an old boys club. It's still a struggle to get women hired, and sometimes they have a tougher road when they get in. We're talking about a cultural shift. And those take time.*
>
> Patti Phillips, executive director, National Association of Collegiate Women Athletic Administrators

they were up against an opponent that had been around far longer and had far greater financial support; thus, the AIAW's control over women's sport ended a decade after it started.

With women's programs subsumed at the national level by the NCAA, individual athletic programs soon followed. At the high school level, school administrations copied what was happening at the college level, initiating **mergers** between boys' and girls' programs as well (Mather, 2007). When those mergers occurred, women were often left out of key decision-making positions. The legacy of those mergers is three distinct workforces operating within athletic departments: a men's sport workforce that is almost exclusively male, a women's sport workforce that has a mix of female and male employees, and an athletic administration workforce that should operate as a fully **sex-integrated** entity, but exhibits modes of operation and decision making that draw from the values of men's programs.

The submersion of girls' and women's programs under boys' and men's programs has had long-lasting effects on school-based sport employment settings in several ways. First, the decision to move women's programs under the existing men's athletic structure preserved the male status quo in interscholastic and intercollegiate athletics, setting the stage for women's programs to be measured according to a value system that was male dominated (Mather, 2007; Schneider et al., 2010). Second, while the women's sport workforce has become gender integrated, with men coaching female teams and running women's programs, the same movement toward gender integration has not occurred in

men's programs. Third, as school sport workplaces have become more complex with more support staff, a **gendered division of labor** has formed: Women are more limited in their career options, congregating in positions that do not pay as well and are not as likely to lead to career advancement. Before examining the issue of where female workers in school sport workplaces are found and how they are treated, an overview of the jobs in school sport settings available to women provides important context.

JOBS FOR WOMEN IN SCHOOL-BASED SPORT SETTINGS

The highly visible nature of athletic contests belies the number of people who work behind the scenes in school sport settings to create opportunities for athletes to play, spectators to cheer, and business entities to make money. In order to fully grasp the expanse of employment possibilities available in school-based sport, it is best to think of an athletic department as being one piece of a larger constellation of organizations that are interdependent and are designed to complement and support each other's efforts. Thus, jobs in high school and college sport can be found not only in individual athletic departments sponsored by schools but in these related organizations and associations (see table 13.1).

Responsibilities common to almost all school sport settings can be categorized into external affairs (athletic communications and sports information, fundraising and donor relations, marketing, merchandising, ticket sales, and sponsorships); athlete health, well-being, and development (academic-athletic counseling, coaching, mental training, strength and conditioning, sports medicine); and administration and management (budget and finance, compliance, facility and event management, human resources, legal, risk management, and security). Depending on the level of program organization and financial resources, jobs may be available in each of these specialized areas. In smaller and less funded athletic programs and organizations, job descriptions are typically less specialized, and people employed in these settings often take on a diverse set of responsibilities.

> You battle every day. Sometimes those battles are about gender. I'm sure to some degree decisions have been made or opinions formed around my gender. I can't worry about that. If there are barriers in the way, I've got to figure out how to get around them, either knock them down or take detours around them.
>
> Sandy Barbour, director of athletics, Penn State University

Table 13.1 Jobs in U.S. High School and College Sport

Area	Examples
National sports governing bodies	National Collegiate Athletic Association (NCAA), National Federation of State High School Associations (NFSHA)
Coaches associations	Women's Basketball Coaches Association (WBCA), Indiana Coaches of Girls Sports Association (ICGSA)
Athletic administrative organizations	National Association of Collegiate Directors of Athletics (NACDA), National Association of Collegiate Women Athletics Administrators (NACWAA)
Specific sport associations	College Football Association, United States Field Hockey Association
Specialized college sport associations	College Sports Information Directors Association (CoSIDA), National Association of Collegiate Marketing Administrators (NACMA)
College sport marketing firms	Active Imagination, Affinity Sports & Event Marketing, Front Row Marketing, GMR Marketing, IMG College, Nelligan Sports Marketing, Octagon
College sport consulting firms	Alden & Associates, Carr Sports Consulting, Collegiate Sports Associates, DHR International (Sports Division), Eastman & Beaudine, Korn/Ferry International, Parker Executive Search, Spencer Stuart, Westwood Partners, Witt/Kieffer
College sport networks and media support	Big Ten Conference, Longhorn Network, Pac-12 Enterprises, NeuLion, SEC Network, Sidearm Sports

WOMEN'S REPRESENTATION IN HIGH SCHOOL AND COLLEGE SPORT WORKPLACES

Despite the expansive range of jobs, and even as more female athletes than ever before participate in varsity sport programs all around the United States, research on the representation of women in school sport workplaces over the span of 40 years reveals that a similar increase in women represented in coaching, administration, and other roles has not been realized (see chapter 2 for information regarding the growth in sport participation opportunities for female athletes in colleges and high schools). Further, women are often concentrated in positions that typically carry less authority and less prestige.

In the school sport workplace, women remain in the minority in almost every job category calling for the assertion of authority, leadership, and vision. Among the college coaching ranks, taking into account all teams for male and female athletes, women make up 20 percent of the entire workforce. In the isolated sector

of women's teams, an area once virtually the exclusive domain of female coaches, Acosta and Carpenter (2012) noted that representation has fallen to 42.9 percent. As the gender integration of coaching staffs directing women's programs has occurred, the same phenomenon has not happened among men's teams, where male coaches continue to be represented at a rate of 98 percent, with the rare female coach typically coaching the individual sports of tennis, golf, or swimming.

A similar pattern of underrepresentation is found across the landscape. To illustrate, women hold 3 percent of athletic director positions within the NCAA's Football Bowl subdivision (the most competitive and financially lucrative), slightly more than 20 percent of all college and university athletic director positions, more than a third of head athletic trainer positions, less than 10 percent of head sports information director positions, and approximately a third of faculty athletics representative positions (Acosta & Carpenter, 2012; Lapchick, Farris, & Rodriquez, 2012). Notably, nearly 10 percent of all departments nationwide have no women in their administrative structure. No women serve as commissioners in the 11 most powerful conferences.[3] Within the NCAA itself, the higher the level of importance in the governance structure, the lower the percentage of women involved in leadership roles (Yiamouyiannis & Osborne, 2012). Women working at the NCAA are more likely to be found in director roles (47.3%), with 16.7 percent as managing directors and 23.5 percent in executive leadership positions (Yiamouyiannis & Osborne, 2012).

Among a select list of major sport marketing firms that service college and university athletic departments, 21 percent of principals identified on company websites were women. For identified college consulting and executive search firms, there was slightly better representation for women at 25 percent. Of that group of 16 college sport consulting and search firms, two were founded by women and another had two women as cofounders with two men (Staurowsky & Proska, 2013).

A close examination of patterns of employment for women in athletics reveals a division of labor where women are concentrated in positions that offer less pay and prestige. For example, according to the NCAA *Race and Gender Demographics Report* providing employment data for 2011-2012, 43 percent of workers in NCAA institutions across all divisions were women. The distribution of female workers within athletic departments reveals highest representation in support categories such as administrative assistant (92%), academic advisor or counselor (60%), compliance officer or coordinator (53%), life skills coordinator (69%), and business manager (60%). Comparing the employment patterns of women in athletic departments between 1995 to 1996 and 2011 to 2012, the positions realizing the greatest increases in female workers occurred in administrative assistant (82% to 92%), academic advisor or counselor (50% to 60%), business manager (45% to 60%), and compliance coordinator (46% to 53%). In positions characterized by levels of decision making, access to power, and revenue generation, women remain in the minority in positions such as athletic director (20%), associate athletic director (34%), assistant director of athletics (33%), fund-

raiser or development (32%), and promotions or marketing manager (34%). The largest number of jobs located in a single job category was that of administrative assistant, with 2,752 women serving in that capacity.[4] Women participating in internships within NCAA athletic departments increased by only four points between 1995-1996 and 2011-2012, going from 38 to 42 percent (Irick, 2012).

At the high school level in the United States, the representation of women is only slightly better. According to LaVoi (2013), 27 percent of all head coaches are women, while women made up less than 40 percent of the coaches working with female athletes. In contrast, 7.5 percent of coaches working with male athletes were female. In a study conducted by Whisenant, Miller, and Pedersen (2005) of high school athletic directors in 22 states, 13 percent were women. Tracking the gender breakdown of high school athletic directors within individual states, Barlow (1999) reported that female athletic directors made up 13 to 17 percent. The executive director for the National Interscholastic Athletic Administrators Association (NIAAA), Mike Blackburn, reported that in 2010, the national percentage of women working as high school athletic directors was 15 percent (White, 2012). Among executive directors overseeing state high school athletic associations in the United States during the 2012-2013 academic year, 94 percent were male and 6 percent were female. At the deputy executive, associate, assistant, and manager levels, women constituted 33 percent of the state high school association workforce. The only job categories where women dominated, at 95 percent, were administrative assistant, officials' secretary, and office manager (Staurowsky & Proska, 2013). At the board of director's level of the NIAAA in 2012, women made up 13 percent of the board (2 on a 15-member board).

HIRING, RETENTION, AND ADVANCEMENT OF WOMEN IN SCHOOL SPORT WORKPLACES

In 2009, Maria Shriver and the Center for American Progress documented dramatic changes in the U.S. workforce in the book *The Shriver Report: A Woman's Nation Changes Everything.* The driving force behind that report was the realization that women made up more than 50 percent of the American workforce. In the case of the leadership structures that have served to shape the experiences of girls, women, boys, and men competing within school-sponsored athletic system, the experience of women in the United States described by Shriver points to an inverse relationship between female athletic and leadership representation in the athletic community, which continues to be controlled and run primarily by men. Researchers speculate that this phenomenon, where female athletes become stronger on the field, court, and in the arena while female athletic administrators lose power in areas that affect decision making, may be due to a variety of factors, among them a wage gap that favors men, workplace barriers, and self-limiting behavior on the part of women.

For those who believe that the school-based sport workplace operates as a meritocracy, where people are hired on the basis of their qualifications, education, and accomplishments, gender-neutral explanations have been offered to explain the gap in representation of female employees and the representation of girls and women as athletes in the sport system. Some argue, for example, that women are simply catching up and that over time a workforce more reflective of the overall female population in sport and American society will occur. Others point to research that shows that there is a lack of fit between what women wish to do and the demands athletic departments put on workers. According to Bracken (2009), female athletes (N = 8,900) at the college level simply indicated that they had interests outside of intercollegiate athletics. She reported, "the desire for a higher salary, the required time requirements, and the preference of a nine-to-five position were factors cited by current female athletes for choosing not to pursue athletics careers" (p. 2). That said, female athletes who reported greater success as players exhibited greater interest in pursuing careers as coaches and administrators and working in exercise science professions.

Although female applicants for jobs in school-based sport may appear to be driven by these gender-neutral considerations, the preceding explanations for the gap in female representation in sport covers over the complexities that exist there for women, most specifically the systemic inequities that affect the work lives of women. It is not surprising, for example, that when female athletes are asked about whether they believe sex discrimination would be a deterrent in deciding about a career in athletics, they often state that they don't believe the college sport system is sex discriminatory. Women who work in that system, including coaches, athletics administrators, and athletic trainers, however, do consider that to be a legitimate factor (Schneider et al., 2010). Female coaches reported that their decision to accept a position and to continue in it was affected by the degree to which a university offers support for women's athletics. Eighty percent of female administrators working in college sport believed that "there are men in athletics administration who only hire men" (Bracken, 2009, p. 19).

Wage Gap for Women in the College Sport Workplace

Awareness regarding the wage gap for women in the college sport workplace is typically introduced through stories comparing the earnings of head coaches of men's basketball teams with those of head coaches of women's teams. In 2009-2010, the median salary for coaches of an NCAA Division I program was $329,300, a figure that was almost double the $171,600 salary earned by coaches of women's teams. In the sport of basketball over a four-year span of time (from 2006-2007 through 2009-2010), the median pay for coaches of men's basketball teams increased by 40 percent compared to a 28 percent increase for coaches of women's teams (Tyler, 2012).

At the NCAA Division I-A level, wage disparities between coaches of men's and women's teams were even more pronounced. According to EADA report data for the 2011-2012 academic year, the average salary for a head coach of a men's team exceeded the average salary for a head coach of a women's team by $372,047 (the average salary for a head coach of a men's team was $517,321; the average salary for a head coach of a women's team was $145,892) (U.S. Department of Education, 2012). Further, the average salary for a head coach of a men's team in NCAA Division I-A had more than doubled during the past seven years, increasing from $207,774 in 2003 to $517,321 in 2011. A similar rate of increase was not found for head coaches of women's teams, where the average salary increased from $93,486 in 2003 to $145,892 in 2010 (see figure 13.1). While the trend was not as pronounced for assistant coaches, there was a gap in the average salary there as well (see figure 13.2).[5]

Brook and Foster (2010) have argued that these kinds of gaps have been wrongly interpreted as reflective of systematic employer sex discrimination when they are merely the production of market forces. Controlling for program revenue generation, productivity, and coach experience, they determined that differences in salaries between coaches of men's and women's basketball teams were not in fact significant.

Brook and Foster are correct that despite the magnitude and persistence of these documentable disparities, the existence of a wage gap by itself is not sufficient evidence for reaching

a conclusion that sex discrimination in coach compensation is occurring. However, according to the Equal Employment Opportunity Commission (EEOC),

> These demonstrated pay disparities between the coaches of men's teams and women's teams are of concern . . . because the overall pattern of employment of coaches by educational institutions is not gender neutral. Women by and large have been limited to coaching women, while men coach both men and women. (Igasaki, 1997, para. 2)

Igasaki points to two flaws in the Brook and Foster analysis. First, the EEOC has been clear that market forces simply cannot be accepted superficially as a sign that sex discrimination is not going on any more than surface differences in pay can be used to prove sex discrimination. In a system where the gendered dynamics are as unique as they are in the college sport workplace, a question has to be asked about why men's programs have such a capacity to generate revenue. If an institution has not made similar efforts in the form of marketing the women's program to the same degree that it markets

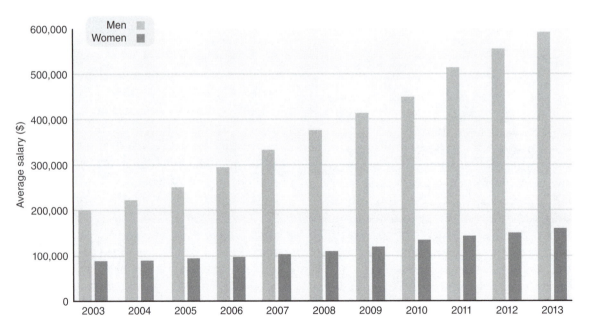

Figure 13.1 NCAA Division IA average head coach salaries, men's versus women's salaries, 2003-2013.

Created with data taken from the EADA analysis cutting tool located at http://ope.ed.gov/athletics.

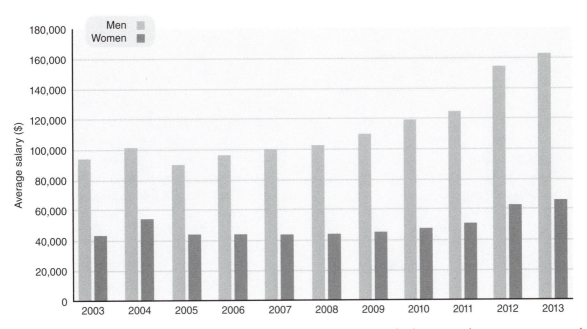

Figure 13.2 NCAA Division IA assistant coach average salaries, men's versus women's salaries, 2003-2013.

Created with data taken from the EADA analysis cutting tool located at http://ope.ed.gov/athletics.

the men's program or taken steps to allow the women's program to be successful, or if it has provided staffing to support marketing efforts for the men's program but not provided equitably for the women's program, then a market argument may not be defensible.

Second, while the isolated analysis of coaches of men's and women's basketball teams makes sense and speaks to issues associated with establishing a claim under the Equal Pay Act or Title VII, the propensity to pay coaches of women's teams less occurs throughout the entire college sport system. According to EADA data for 2011-2012, these disparities exist at every level, regardless of whether programs are revenue generating or revenue drain-

ing. Notice in table 13.2 that the average salaries for head coaches of men's teams surpass those for coaches of women's teams in every NCAA divisional affiliation.

This information supports why female coaches, administrators, and other workers in school sport settings cite salary issues and other forms of inequities as issues that affect job satisfaction. In a study of 406 senior female administrators working at NCAA institutions, the problem of inequitable salaries was determined to be among the top five discrimination factors that affect the advancement of women in athletic departments (Schneider et al., 2010). When asked about their perceptions of how satisfied they were with their own salaries, 33 percent

Table 13.2 Gendered Wage Gap in NCAA Institutions Across Division Affiliations

Division	Salary for male head coaches	Salary for female head coaches
NCAA DIA	$517,321	$145,892
NCAA DIAA	$125,507	$70,755
NCAA DIIF	$66,543	$53,040
NCAA DIINF	$55,299	$49,820
NCAA DIIIF	$59,610	$50,748
NCAA DIIINF	$47,019	$44,338

Created with data taken from the EADA analysis cutting tool located at http://ope.ed.gov/athletics.

of female college coaches expressed dissatisfaction with this aspect of their working lives, with 74 percent agreeing that the need for higher salaries was a reason contributing to the lack of representation of women in intercollegiate athletics coaching. Female coaches who had left the profession identified five areas of gender disparities that contributed to their decisions, including lack of adequate resources, discrepancies in compensation and job responsibilities, lack of administrative support, negotiations and gender hierarchy, and tendency of women to serve as primary caregiver at home (Kamphoff, 2010).

Workplace Barriers to Women's Advancement and Success

Beyond issues associated with program support and compensation, other barriers to women's advancement and success have been identified in school-based sport settings. In 2008, Rhode and Walker suggested that there were three broad reasons for the diminishing role of women in coaching, including work–home conflicts, adverse stereotypes (revealing racism, discrimination against sexual minorities, and ageism), and in-group favoritism.

For working mothers, the intersections between work and family life highlight the time-intensive and pressured environments that often characterize high school and college workplaces. In the absence of family-friendly policies, which recognize the extreme hours that athletic department employees can be called on to work through flex time and flexible boundaries that allow for children to be brought to work, working mothers are particularly taxed in terms of meeting caregiver responsibilities.

The lack of an inclusive and open climate within high school and college workplaces has also been found to be problematic for women of color (Kamphoff & Gill, 2008), sexual minorities, and young women just embarking on their careers. According to Sartore and Cunningham (2006), White raters of coaching applicants tended to rely on sport-related skill sets and racial stereotypes in evaluating and selecting promotable coaching candidates. Shedding light on the experiences of Black females coaches in collegiate basketball, Borland and Bruening

(2010) identified three impediments, including access discrimination, lack of support in terms of professional development, and stereotyping. Black women who aspire to be successful in the coaching ranks are often hired as assistant coaches to become "designated recruiters" of Black players. There is little opportunity within the scope of the job responsibilities in these roles to learn the expanse of skill sets needed to better position these women for career advancement. According to Lapchick, Agusta, Kinkopf, and McPhee (2013), African American female athletes accounted for 47.9 percent of Division I women's basketball players in 2011-2012, yet only 7.9 percent of the women's head coaching positions in those teams were held by African Americans.

In interviews with women who left coaching, Kamphoff (2010) found that the high levels of homophobia (fear of and intolerance for sexual minorities) among the collegiate coaching ranks negatively affected women throughout the system, most particularly lesbian coaches who felt they needed to conceal their sexual orientation. These women suffer the consequences of negative recruiting (a practice whereby the sexual orientation of a coach or members of team is used by opposing coaches to discourage athletes from attending a particular school) and regularly encounter discriminatory behavior in the form of jokes and comments about sexual minorities that are tolerated as normative.

Among young women just starting their careers, collegiate female athletic trainers have been seen to successfully disable gender bias before it can negatively affect their progress. Describing the sex discrimination they encountered in their first placements in athletic training, female athletic trainers reported that they needed to be assertive with coaches in order to establish their credibility and create a strong foundation so that they would not second guess their decision making when confronted by coaches who were operating with sexist stereotypes about women (Mazerolle, Borland, & Burton, 2012).

The gender bias witnessed by young women entering the profession distills at times into an expectation that women in athletic departments will remain compliant and will not raise issues associated with Title IX compliance, gender equity, and equal treatment. Recent studies of female head coaches and athletics administrators (Staurowsky & Weight, 2011, 2013) reveal a retaliatory culture that combines subtle pressure and outright threats to silence and control women in the athletic workforce, discouraging their advocacy on behalf of female athletes and themselves, undermining Title IX compliance efforts, and jeopardizing women's ability to succeed. This culture offers one plausible explanation as to why women's representation within athletic departments remains low after so many years.

Women in sport also encounter in-group favoritism, which in this context refers to male athletic directors being inclined to hire from within their established and familiar networks, which are composed primarily of male applicants and candidates. In their analysis of women's representation in athletics through the lens of homologous reproduction, Stangl and Kane (1991) concluded that the gender of the athletic director did have an effect on the hiring of women: Female athletic directors hired more women than did male athletic directors.

Self-Limiting Behaviors Among Women

In an environment where women receive mixed messages regarding their position, status, and worth, it is not surprising that women develop ambivalence about their own capabilities (at some level or another, whether consciously or unconsciously), adopting self-limiting behaviors and habits of mind. Evidence of this phenomenon has been found among both female athletes and coaches and athletics administrators (Greenawalt, Fleischman, & Smeaton, 2013). Examining how 144 NCAA Division I female athletes viewed male and female coaches, Greenawalt and colleagues reported that 81 percent expressed a preference for a male coach. Modern sexism in the form of a "think coach, think male" mind-set was found among the female athletes who expressed beliefs that male coaches were more credible, tougher, less likely to play head games, and less emotional than female coaches. One of the interviewed female athletes who had been coached by both men and women commented, "I love my female coach, but there's something about a

Women can help to influence the prevalence of women in sports within educational settings simply by not feeding into self-limiting behaviors like expecting that coaches *need* to be male.

male coach that demands a different level of respect."[6]

This tendency to self-limit carries over into the school-based sport system. Betsy Alden, founder of a college sport and executive search firm, has noted that women view themselves differently in the marketplace compared to men (Staurowsky, 2011). While men apply for positions that may be out of reach or require experience they do not yet have, women self-censor their application efforts, tending to apply only for positions where they can demonstrate that they have literally done everything listed in the job description. Nowhere is this evidenced more than in the fact that men apply for jobs throughout the college sport system while women typically restrict their applications to those areas where they have had direct experience. In keeping with a national trend, women in college sport are also less likely to negotiate for a higher salary, more benefits, or more resources to help them be successful at their jobs.

THE FUTURE FOR WOMEN IN HIGH SCHOOL AND COLLEGE SPORT WORKPLACES

In 2012, a record number of women were elected to the U.S. Congress, with an identifiable trajectory demonstrating a steady increase in the number of women's voices in the heart of the nation's lawmaking body, reminding us of how far the United States has come in affording women the opportunity to contribute in meaningful and important ways in society through avenues they were once prohibited from accessing (Hook, 2012). And even as barriers to women's access to employment and success in sport continue, promising events are occurring that may suggest that the collective efforts of everyone involved in school-based sport programs are moving toward equity.

In college sport, a number of significant firsts have occurred in the hiring of women into power positions. In June of 2013, former legal counsel for the NBA, founder of the WNBA, and president of USA Basketball Val Ackerman was chosen as the commissioner to lead a newly reconstituted Big East into the future (see sidebar).

Similarly, in the fall of 2015, Judy McLeod became the first woman to be named commissioner of one of the top 10 most elite conferences in the United States, Conference USA (Solomon, 2015). A few years earlier, Amy Huchthausen, who had worked at previously worked at the NCAA and in four Division I conferences in a variety of capacities, became the first woman to lead the America East Conference. In the process, she became the first woman of color to be named as a commissioner of a Division I conference ("Amy Huchthausen Named," 2011). And in March of 2012, Lisa Campos was selected as the vice president for intercollegiate athletics at Northern Arizona University, becoming the youngest person in the country to serve in such a capacity (Preuss, 2012).

At the high school level, some shifts in the athletic power structure seem to be occurring as well. In 2012, five women in school districts in the Houston (Texas) area were working as athletics directors (Barron, 2012). In school districts in Western Pennsylvania, seven female athletic directors were working at area high schools (White, 2012). In 2013, Diane Jordan was named as the first female athletic director in the Lehigh Valley Conference in Pennsylvania (Groller, 2013). For her work as the first female athletic director in Somerville High School history, Nicole Viele was named a recipient of an award from the Massachusetts Secondary School Athletic Directors Association recognizing athletic directors with five or fewer years of experience who have made significant contributions (Goisman, 2011).

Women have long led distinguished careers in high school and college sport settings. Their example, combined with what we know from research, offers helpful perspectives for the next generation of women who aspire to pursue a career in coaching, administration, or the array of other job opportunities in sport. University of Tennessee women's basketball coach Pat Summitt was known as a fierce competitor who had the capacity to challenge her players to be better. Above all else, women seeking jobs in school-based sport settings should be true to themselves. Cori Close, the head women's basketball coach who took over the reins of the women's basketball program at UCLA after Nikki Caldwell moved

Val Ackerman, Big East Commissioner

Ellen J. Staurowsky and Michael Proska

In June of 2013, the Big East hired Val Ackerman as the first commissioner of the newly reconstituted conference. A former basketball player with a law degree, she had previously served as an executive in the National Basketball Association (NBA), founding president of the WNBA, and the first female president of USA Basketball. Her corporate background, basketball credentials, and experience negotiating television contracts were considered ideal for a conference historically known for high-profile basketball teams such as Villanova and Georgetown.

When asked about the challenges that awaited her in the new role as Big East commissioner, Ackerman anticipated there would be many sleepless nights in order to create a model athletic conference. When asked about working in a male-dominated profession, she admitted that she "lacked the moral support that you often get from other women in the workplace who are experiencing the same thing" (Reynolds & Crockett, 2013, p. 2). When asked about advice she would offer to other women working in sport, she said, "I have found that to be a successful woman in the sport business takes a certain thickness of skin. You have to be really good at what you do. You have to roll with things at times, and have a sense of humor. You have to know at times when to pick your spots."

As a pioneer for women in the world of sports, Ackerman has helped to open doors for women. As a result of women like Ackerman, the sport world is not as lonely a place for women as it was when she started. In her new role in the Big East, her focus will be on opening as many doors for as many athletes, both female and male, as possible.

Michael Proska received his undergraduate sport management degree from Drexel in December 2014.

on to LSU, was questioned following her appointment about the fashion sense of her predecessor. In responding, Close said,

> One thing that Coach (John) Wooden has always taught me is to be yourself and to coach in a way that fits your personality. Even as much as I love Coach Wooden I can't coach like him. I have to coach in a way that pursues excellence that fits me. . . . I'm going to have to lead this program in a way that fits my personality and continues to move the program to its goals accordingly. (Reid, 2011, para. 5)

In her book *Lean In: Women, Work, and the Will to Lead*, executive Sheryl Sandberg offered career advice for women trying to balance work and home as they were breaking into new fields, some dominated by men. She admonished women to consider what they were afraid of that was holding them back and encouraged them to conquer that fear, to find a mentor who would offer sound guidance, and to **lean in**, meaning to step into new challenges with enthusiasm and energy. Sandberg wrote, "We can reignite the revolution by internalizing the revolution. The shift to a more equal world will happen person by person. We move closer to true equality with each woman who leans in" (2013, p. 11). Not all women agree with Sandberg's perspective on how women should approach their work lives. In fact, some have found it dismissive of perennial problems that women have faced. That said, as women continue to work toward accessing positions of power and influence in sport, it is worth contemplating what the school-based sport system would be like if women through the entire system leaned in.

In Pat Summitt's reflections about what she cherished most about her long career in coaching, she focused on memories of the young women she'd had the privilege of working with, recalling that they were fighters, young women who fought for better lives for themselves and their families. Women in sport have historically been fighters, women of conviction willing to step out of their comfort zone and test social boundaries. Women unafraid of shaking up the status quo in an effort to lead fulfilled lives of purpose have forged paths for other women to follow after them. Whether women walk or run down that path in high heels, high tops, running shoes, or power flats is of no consequence. The fact that they continue the journey celebrates those who came before and continues the work that still needs to be done.

Learning Aids

Summary

This chapter provides a broad overview of the status of women working through high school and college sport settings. It focuses on the expansive range of jobs that are available to women and the underrepresentation of women in sport leadership at the present time. It also explores possible explanations on why women are not represented in percentages in athletic workplaces that match either their participation as athletes or, more broadly, the percentage of women in the American workforce. It considers the wage gap that exists in school-based athletic programs, barriers to women's success, and the self-limiting behaviors that can undermine women as workers in school-sport settings. The chapter concludes with future possibilities for women and advice for advancing the interests of women.

Discussion Questions

1. Women typically do not coach traditional men's sports, specifically men's basketball and football. How would the athletic system change if the sex-segregated areas of the workforce no longer existed?

2. The path to athletic director positions at the high school and college levels are somewhat different. At the high school level, most athletic directors work their way up through the system as coaches and then move into administrative roles. At the highest levels of college sport, athletic directors are increasingly expected to have a business background. What are the implications of athletic directors being hired out of the corporate sector rather than coming up through the ranks as coaches who have spent time working in education?

3. Research Sheryl Sandberg's concept of *leaning in*. Debate whether women should lean in or whether the lean in approach just maintains the status quo and places the burden on women to resolve the myriad issues that prevent them from moving forward in their careers.

Learning Exercises

1. The blog *Women in Coaching* provides career advice and insights to women working in high school and college sports. Go the blog at http://stream.goodwin.drexel.edu/womenincoaching. Locate an article that addresses an issue discussed in the chapter and summarize it.

2. Using Storify or another multimedia format, identify a woman working in a leadership position in a high school or college sport setting. Find out about her

career path, the steps she took to be where she is, and what lessons can be learned from her life. In putting the story together, include photos, videos, interviews with the person you chose or with others who work with and for her, and other information in the public domain.

Glossary

gendered division of labor—An arrangement of jobs that is determined on the basis of gender rather than competence.

lean in—A phrase coined by COO of Facebook Sheryl Sandberg, who advises women trying to balance work and home to embrace work more enthusiastically and to accept that there will be tradeoffs that need not undermine a woman's career success. This concept has been accepted by some and has inspired controversy and concerns for others.

merger—In the context of this chapter, efforts made by colleges and universities to move women's athletic departments into men's departments in the 1970s and 1980s, with men in charge of both. The long-lasting effect of this has been a loss of representation of women in leadership in school-based athletic departments.

sex integrated—A workplace where men and women have an equal chance of being recruited, hired, and promoted.

sex segregated—A workplace that remains largely sex specific (in the case of athletics, men's sports are almost exclusively coached by men).

Notes

1. During the High Renaissance (1490s to mid-1500s), Venetian courtesans wore very high platform shoes that were called chopines. Chopines could be as high as 30 inches (76 cm), and a woman's social status was measured by the height of the platform. The higher the shoe, the more status a woman had (D'Costa, 2012).

2. In November of 2012, *Wall Street Journal* writer Christina Binkley reported on a shift from the power heel that had been the preferred shoe for female executives to the power flat inspired by menswear Oxfords.

3. In July of 2013, Val Ackerman, who had served as legal counsel for the NBA, the first president of the WNBA, and head of USA Basketball, was appointed commissioner of the Big East. Her hiring followed months of speculation about the fate of the Big East, which had experienced a complete breakdown in the fall of 2012 with Catholic institutions banding together to reform the conference, adding a few secular schools such as Butler University. Thus, at the time of this report, the status of the Big East as a major conference is up for debate. Whether it can reemerge as a significant force in college sport has yet to be determined.

4. Two other job categories had significant numbers for men, including graduate assistants at 2,128 and "other" at 2,763. Because of the vagaries of the "other" category and the part time nature of graduate assistantships, those were not included in the analysis.

5. According to Gentry and Alexander, for Division I basketball, "the median salary for coaches of a men's team in 2010 was $329,300, nearly twice that of coaches for women's teams, who had a median of $171,600. Over the past four years,

the median pay of men's head coaches increased by 40 percent compared with 28 percent for women's coaches" (2012, n.p.).

6. Not all studies have found this kind of prejudice on the part of female athletes toward female coaches, however. As Magnusen and Rhea (2009) reported, female athletes were comfortable with either male or female strength coaches. However, a barrier to success for female strength coaches was evidenced in the attitudes of football players, who expressed a clear and decisive preference for male strength coaches.

CHAPTER 14

Merchandising and Marketing Women's Sports

Corinne Farneti, PhD, Mount St. Mary's University

Learning Objectives

In this chapter, you will learn about the following:

- Women as sport consumers and fans
- Merchandising of sporting goods and apparel toward women
- Various approaches and specific efforts made toward the marketing of women's sport

Sixteen years ago, something happened that would alter the landscape of women's sport marketing forever. This something was the 1999 Women's World Cup final, an event hosted in the United States that drew record crowds and public attention in a way few had imagined could ever happen for a women's event. One would think that the event itself was sufficient to carve a special place in our memories. Members of the U.S. Women's Soccer team—Michelle Akers, Brandi Chastain, Julie Foudy, Kristine Lilly, Carla Overbeck, and Briana Scurry—captivated the United States with their winning ways and their winning personalities, so much so that on the day of the final, 90,000 spectators filled the Rose Bowl (Howard, 2011). If there was a star that shone just a little brighter in that constellation, it was Mia Hamm, the forward whose fierce competitiveness, grace under pressure, somewhat quiet demeanor, and surgical precision in shooting made her a celebrity and marketing icon for a time. While looking at an ad from that time that featured Hamm alongside NBA superstar Michael Jordan, an athlete who had a pretty good pedigree himself, the daughter of NFL quarterback Doug Flutie looked at her father and asked, "Who's that guy with Mia?"

What made a historic moment of national fervor for women's sport unlike any other witnessed heretofore, with 650,000 attending the 32 games leading up to the final and 40 million raptly watching the final on television, were the events that happened at the end of the hard-fought battle between Team USA and China. After regulation time had ended, penalty kicks were used to determine the winner of what had become an epic struggle on a global stage. And into that cultural space stepped charismatic Brandi Chastain. She was the player who managed to drill the ball past Chinese goalkeeper Gao Hong to win the game and the World Cup. Exuberant, Chastain circled away from the goal, ripped off her jersey in celebration, and executed a knee slide. The image of her savoring the moment of sheer triumph, her black sports bra and sculpted abs on display, was immortalized a few days later on the cover of *Sports Illustrated*.

I vividly remember the chills that ran through my body as I saw the game-winning shot hit the back of the net in the overtime shootout. At the time, I didn't think of anything but how much emotion and joy those women must have felt accomplishing the biggest feat of their athletic careers. Chastain ripping off her shirt seemed like a normal, spontaneous reaction to me. Men did it after nearly every goal. Why would it be different for a woman?

I was a naïve eighteen-year-old female athlete who had experienced the ups and downs of competitive sports her entire life. Little did I know that people weren't necessarily talking about the U.S. team's World Cup victory, but the tiny Nike swoosh on the black sports bra that Chastain had revealed in her celebration. The world was abuzz with opinions and questions. Was the celebration planned? Was Nike behind it? Did Chastain show too much skin?

Although these questions are debatable, one thing is for certain: This event and celebration served as the springboard for the marketing of female athletes and women's sport. Companies now realized that not only were women's sports visible (and popular) on a global scale, female athletes were actually marketable. The past decade and a half has seen women's sport grow, both on and off the field. In order to understand where the marketing of women's sport stands today, we must identify women as consumers and fans, along with the marketing strategies, approaches, and efforts of sport marketers in this ever-growing industry.

WOMEN AS CONSUMERS AND FANS

Women have more purchasing power than ever before. In fact, they now account for $7 trillion in consumer and business spending in the United States. Over the next decade, they will control two-thirds of consumer wealth. Additionally, women make or influence 85 percent of all purchasing decisions and purchase more than 50 percent of products traditionally bought by men, including home improvement products, automobiles, and consumer electronics (Krasny, 2012). In other words, women are the ones buying soft drinks, breakfast cereals, athletic shoes—and most other everyday items.

Despite these very telling statistics, various assumptions are made about female sport consumers and consumers of women's sport. For starters, marketing executives may consider women to be uninterested in sport, therefore concluding that targeting female consumers in sport sponsorship is ineffective (Ridinger & Funk, 2006). This assumption is unlikely true, considering that more than 43 percent of athletes who competed at NCAA institutions in 2011-2012, amounting to nearly 200,000, were women (Irick, 2012).

A second assumption is that men are not interested in women's sports. Contrary to this statement, SBRnet's annual Sports Fan/Social Media Report (2012) notes that almost 59 percent of the WNBA's viewing audience is male. Similarly, 63.4 percent of the LPGA's fan base is male ("Fans of PGA," 2011). While these statistics don't represent all women's sports, it is apparent that men do indeed watch women's sports with some regularity.

Also, there is the question of whether or not female sports fans are different from male sports fans. For example, one study revealed that men preferred watching combative sports while women preferred stylistic sports (Sargent, Zillmann, & Weaver, 1998). Similarly, when asked their favorite sports, men named more aggressive sports than women did (Wann & Ensor, 2001). However, other studies have found that female fans' interests actually coincide with those of their male companions (Farrell, Fink, & Fields, 2011; Whiteside & Hardin, 2011). Assuming this statement is true, wouldn't this mean women are watching just as much violent sport as their male counterparts? Other research found that male college students tend to be more involved with sport as spectators than female students. The men invested more time listening, watching, reading, and talking about sports, and were more emotionally involved (Bahk, 2000). Women place much more value on the social aspects of attending or being involved in a sporting event (Ridinger & Funk, 2006). Research has also indicated that male sports fans differ from female sports fans in their perceptions of pre-event influences (ticket prices, advertising), present behavior (merchandise purchases, wearing of team apparel, media consumption), and future behavior (loyalty, attendance intentions; Fink, Trail, & Anderson, 2002).

The fact that fans of women's and men's sports may differ in nature shouldn't be a death sentence for women's sport. In fact, marketing strategies should differ from sport to sport, since no one blanket approach exists that will effectively reach all sport fans and markets. Embracing the differences between sports and genders is the only way marketers will be successful in marketing a unique product.

MERCHANDISING AND SPORTING GOODS TARGETED TO FEMALE CONSUMERS

As female participation in sport has increased, so has the attention being paid to women's apparel and sporting goods. Women make the majority of the buying decisions in a household, as previously noted. It has also become evident that women are making decisions not only for their husbands and sons, but for themselves and their daughters as well. If you look around a typical sporting goods store, you now see that women have their own apparel and shoe section, with several different options, styles, and trends available. This has turned into a highly profitable business; women's athletic footwear alone brought in $4.8 billion in 2012 ("Footwear Industry Statistics," 2012). Apparel and merchandise manufacturers have come a long way in recognizing that women's bodies and tastes can be different than men's. Exploiting the influence the London 2012 Games had on women in sport, athletic apparel marketers have put their energy and dollars into this growing market. Adidas has recently started a big push in their women's running category, using social media to connect women from around the globe in sharing their athletic pursuits. Their goal is to inspire and celebrate women, allowing them to connect to their products and brand. Similarly, in 2013, Under Armour began using a social media campaign to help redefine the female athlete. This helped Under Armour better understand their consumer, and also allowed women to feel a connection with the brand (Joseph, 2013).

Nike's 2013 approach, a strategy they called Women's Amplify, was to market to the female consumer in a more unified manner. In other words, rather than speaking to her from each women's category (running, training, soccer, lifestyle), they marketed all sport as a connected women's brand. Their goal was to make a woman's shopping experience easier and more informed. The female consumer wants products to be both technical and designed for her—no more taking a man's product and lightly tweaking it to fit a woman. With this marketing strategy, Nike wanted women to see first that the products were truly designed for them (calling out different fits, showing prints and materials that speak to women). Once women got closer to the product and engaged with it, Nike made it easy for them to understand the technical benefits. This strategy is called "attract and engage" (attract from 10 to 20 feet [300-600 cm] away and engage at 1 to 5 feet [30-150 cm]).

Nike's Women's Amplify strategy recognized the modern need of female athletic consumers. A continued understanding of the women's athletic apparel and sporting goods market is necessary to take full advantage of the growing, active interest in sport. Research focusing on what women want has never been more important. As time goes by and trends change, so should campaigns and merchandising techniques. Companies now recognize that women are not just buying products to look good; they must be high quality, functional, and durable because women and girls are no longer just standing on the sidelines and cheering.

Sport organizations have also taken notice of women in the sports marketplace. The NFL has seen the percentage of female fans grow to become over 44 percent of its fan base, with 60 percent of girls and women over the age of 12 identifying themselves as NFL fans (Jessop, 2012). League executives have put time and money into researching just what women desire. In 2012, the NFL moved away from the "pink-it-and-shrink-it" approach and launched the "It's My Team" campaign. This promotion is based on the notion that women love mixing team apparel with everyday fashion. NFL market researchers also found that women don't like wearing the same thing to every game, which gave them ample opportunity to sell several different styles of products and apparel to women. Since the launch of the campaign, the NFL has

seen triple-digit growth (Jessop, 2012). Similar changes are occurring in many sport organizations, whose marketers hope to tap into their large female fan base.

APPROACHES TO WOMEN'S SPORT MARKETING

The marketing of women's sport has proven to be a challenge over the last several decades. While participation numbers of girls and women in sport have skyrocketed since the passage of Title IX, not as much progress has been made in the presentation and promotion of female athletes. Marketers have the seemingly complicated job of bringing attention to women in an arena that has been traditionally dominated by men and doing so in a way that both respects the talents of the athlete and draws attention from consumers. This section addresses reasons why the marketing of women's sport lags behind with a discussion on categories of gender and sexualization. It also addresses how this affects female athletes and how some women have taken the matter into their own hands.

Gender Schema Theory and Sexualization

Marketers handle promoting women's sport in several ways, and they are often guided (whether knowingly or not) by social phenomena. For example, often times we conform to gender stereotyping that regulates opportunities, relationships, and our overall place in society. This is the basis for something called **gender schema theory** (Bem, 1981). In other words, many people inherently try to put people and objects into two gender categories based on masculine and feminine traits. It can be as simple (and common) as giving blue gifts for a newborn boy and pink for a newborn girl. Society forms expectations of individuals and outcomes and if the norm doesn't occur, people may feel uneasy.

Over time, society has experienced a breakdown of the traditional views of sex and a rise of multiple categories of gender. We do not always see everything in black and white (or blue and pink) anymore. However, in the sports

A Long History of Utility Versus Fashion in Women's Sport

Lauren E. Brown, PhD, Assistant Professor of Sport Management, DeSales University

The All-American Girls Professional Baseball League (AAGPBL) was a league developed during World War II to keep baseball in the public eye while many male players were at war. The league was brought back into the minds of the American public with the release of the successful 1992 Columbia Pictures film *A League of Their Own*. While the plot was fictionalized, elements in the story built on the realities of the league and its players. One such example was the player uniforms. The leadership of the AAGPBL designed uniforms that included skirts instead of the pants worn by male baseball players. In the film, the AAGPBL players protest that they cannot slide in skirts, to which the league's general manager, Ira Lowenstein, responds that the uniforms were designed to attract spectators to the league, not for utility.

The exchange between Ira Lowenstein and the AAGPBL players regarding their uniforms calls attention to the evolution of apparel for female athletes. It is only during the last 30 years that manufacturers have mass-produced athletic shoes and clothing specifically designed for the utility of female athletes. What began as Reebok looking to capitalize on the popularity of aerobics among women in the 1980s evolved into a battle over this new market with Nike. The market has expanded exponentially over time, and even includes (though to a lesser extent) firms outside of the sports industry such as Ralph Lauren and Liz Claiborne.

Similar to the marketing of women's teams and athletes, women's athletic apparel can reinforce traditional gender norms and the sexualization of female athletes. From the prevalence of fitness skirts and dresses to short, tight shorts to the abundance of traditionally feminine colors such as pink and purple, today's women's athletic apparel can draw a fine line between selling utility and reinforcing stereotypes. Likewise, the market varies, with consumer priorities ranging from the style to the price of the apparel. In the interest of financial viability, firms must understand each of these different consumers in order to properly position the firm within this large, diverse market. Additionally, firms must be aware that marketing messages that overemphasize traditional gender roles and the sexualization of athletes may not be well received by all consumers, which could result in negative publicity.

context, this has been slower to occur. Researchers recently found that young adult viewers still strongly categorize sports into male and female (Hardin & Greer, 2009). For example, sports such as volleyball and gymnastics are seen as feminine sports, while basketball and rugby are categorized as masculine. So what is the market implication of this? Female leagues, teams, and athletes are put in a position where they must decide how to market themselves. Do they market themselves as women? Or do they market themselves as athletes, which society tends to categorize as masculine? Often times, they end up sending conflicting messages. For instance, McGinnis, Chun, and McQuillan (2003) cite the example that while the WNBA tries to empower and energize women, it also regresses when emphasizing the heterosexuality and family orientation of the players in its marketing campaigns and telecasts.

Frequently female athletes are feminized, putting emphasis on attractiveness to help draw in the casual fan. This has been the norm dating back to some of the first print advertisement studies in the 1970s (Belknap & Leonard, 1991). In present day, many marketing campaigns or advertisements feature women posed passively, while men are in active or athletic poses (McGinnis et al., 2003). For example, a female athlete may be shown lounging on a couch or standing with her hands on her hips while a male athlete may be shown mid jump or shot. In fact, scholars have found that if a female athlete is indeed actively engaged in an advertisement, it is in a leisure or recreational activity (Cuneen & Claussen, 1999). In one study, 81 percent of advertisements analyzed featured female athletes dressed suggestively or partially clad (Grau, Roselli, & Taylor, 2007).

While attractiveness may be a way to subconsciously grab a consumer's attention, blatant sexualization is a more overt strategy that some marketers use. Some feel that this strategy undermines players' achievements, inadvertently or otherwise. In June of 2011, the Badminton World Federation made a decree that stated that all female players must wear skirts on the court "to ensure attractive presentation of badminton" (Badminton World Federation, 2011, General Competition Regulation 19.2). Players and fans were not happy, and the rule was quickly overturned. In a *New York Times* interview shortly before the decision to shelve the rule was made, Paisan Rangsikitpho (American deputy president of the Badminton World Federation) defended the rule, saying BWF was not using sex to promote the sport: "We just

Golf Digest's History of Using Sex to Sell

Golf Digest is a 65-year-old monthly publication that offers its readers insight on golf courses, equipment, instruction, and news. Since 1969, 23 women have graced the cover of the magazine, drawing criticism for both the choice and portrayal of women.

In 2014, the daughter of hockey legend Wayne Gretzky and the fiancée of PGA Tour star Dustin Johnson, Paulina Gretzky, was featured. Many questioned why a non-golfer would be chosen over so many other qualified women. Posed leaning on an iron wearing white yoga pants and sports bra, Gretzky drew the ire of several female professional golfers. Stacy Lewis, ranked third in the world at the time, was asked by a *New York Times* reporter what she thought of the choice. She responded,

> It's frustrating for female golfers. It's the state of where we've always been. We don't get the respect for being the golfers we are. Obviously, *Golf Digest* is trying to sell magazines, but at the same time you like to see a little respect for the women's game.

Golf Digest used their own platform to explain the cover photo. Editor in chief Jerry Tarde responded to the controversy saying,

> Sports figures, celebrities and models have appeared on *Golf Digest* covers since the magazine's beginning. Paulina ranks at the high end of the golf celebrity scene today, and she has a compelling story to tell. She also might get some new people interested in the game.

The criticism did not dissuade *Golf Digest* from their "sex sells"–type covers. Their May 2015 fitness issue featured pro golfer Lexi Thompson posed in only black bottoms and a golf glove, with a white cloth draped over her breasts.

For a look at all *Golf Digest* issues with women on the cover, see www.golf-digest.com/magazine/golf-digest/2007-07/gdcovergirls_2#slide=1.

want them to look feminine and have a nice presentation so women will be more popular" (Longman, 2011, para. 11). Some other examples of sexualization of female athletes include the following:

- In 2004, FIFA president Sepp Blatter suggested "more feminine clothes" for women's soccer players. He said, "They could, for example, have tighter shorts" (BBC Sport, 2004, para. 3).

- The LPGA's first ad campaign after a four-year absence featured super-feminine player Natalie Gulbis. Ms. Gulbis was ranked #108 in the world at the time.

- In 2013, the Portland Thorns of the National Women's Soccer League sold merchandise with a catch phrase emblazoned in bold letters to help draw interest to their team: *Feeling Thorny?* The phrase was seen to be offensive and was pulled from stores.

- Many high schools, including Cascade High School in Everett, Washington, have banned cheerleaders from wearing their uniforms to school, citing the dress code policy. What's interesting here is that, in all of these cases, the short skirts were deemed acceptable to wear at games.

In one of their 2007 running ads, Nike used track and field star Lauren Fleshman to discredit the practice of sexualizing athletes. In the ad, Fleshman stands with her arms crossed, looking both strong and stern, with the copy daring the viewer in bold, capital letters: "Objectify me." While highlighting differences in the male and female body, Nike brags that they recognize and celebrate these differences in the products and technologies they offer.

Closely linked with the sexualization of women's sport is homophobia. Leagues, teams, and corporate partners alike try to shake the stigma of the lesbian bogeywoman or the underlying fear that participating in sports will encourage homosexuality and prevent women from fulfilling their stereotypical domestic role (Knight & Guiliano, 2003). Because female athletes often play aggressively, develop muscles, sweat, and have more masculine builds, they don't fit the norms of society (Krane, Choi, Baird, Aimar, & Kauer, 2004). Instead, we stereotype these "masculine" women as being mannish lesbians. Because of this, some female athletes find themselves overcompensating for their "masculine" behavior on the field by acting overly feminine outside of the game to appease marketers and society as a whole.

Some feel the need to present a heterosexual image to help relieve any underlying discomfort that some may have at the notion of women competing with the same intensity as men. For example, in 2011, five German professional female soccer players posed in their underwear in German *Playboy*. Midfielder Kristina Gessat said, "We want to disprove the cliché that all female footballers are butch" (Adams, 2011). Marketers are also afraid that consumers may view a female athlete as overly masculine and react negatively to the ad. To avoid this, models are sometimes used in advertisements to portray female athletes instead of sportswomen themselves (Grau et al., 2007).

Although these examples cite instances of homophobia and promotion of the heterosexual image, other marketers embrace their athletes and fan base as the people they are. Although this is not always the case for the WNBA, they recently decided it would be in their best interest to start marketing not only those who fit a traditional marketing profile, but its most talented athletes, like the Minnesota Lynx's heavily tattooed star Seimone Augustus. WNBA teams have also recognized and embraced their significant gay fan bases and the gay community as a whole (Rhoden, 2012). Not only are openly gay athletes being marketed, teams are hosting LGBTQ pride nights as well, with proceeds often going to local LGBTQ nonprofits.

Women as Success Stories and Role Models

As the women's sport has become more popular and more visible to the general public, college and professional female athletes have been thrust into the spotlight as role models. The term *role model* refers to anyone who is perceived as exemplary or worthy of identification or imitation (Yancey, 2008), and has a mix of desirable personal and professional qualities. Some of these qualities include technical skills, temperament, decision-making ability, work ethic, leadership qualities, moral standing, and self-confidence.

Athletes have long been seen as fitting this mold. If all (or most) of these characteristics are present, an athlete is very marketable. The Women's United Soccer Association (WUSA), formed after the wildly successful 1999 Women's World Cup, used this angle to market their league for their three years in existence. The women were seen as a group of strong individuals who trained hard and gave everything they had to the sport, and were the best in the world at what they did. Interestingly these elite athletes felt that their personality traits, such as a hard work ethic and positive outlook, were more important in their position as role models than their athletic skill (Guest & Cox, 2009).

No matter how sexily an athlete is portrayed or how good a role model she may be, a high skill level and success is the foundation necessary for respect. For example, racecar driver Danica Patrick has often been seen as playing up her sex appeal in GoDaddy.com commercials. While she doesn't mind using her sexuality, she has also acknowledged the importance of being successful in her sport in terms of being respected by her peers and the public (Ross, Ridinger, & Cuneen, 2009). Marketers recognize the importance of success of elite-level athletes in the mind of the public. That is often why we see successful athletes in ads more often than we see those who are not.

EFFORTS TO MARKET WOMEN'S SPORT

With the increase in participation at elite levels of sport, marketers have seen the need to promote their league, team, and athletes to the consumer. It would make sense that as participation increases, so does the desire to watch and associate with a team or athlete within a given sport. Therefore, marketers at all levels have made moves to grab the attention and dollars of these consumers. This section discusses specific efforts taken by both professional and collegiate sport marketers in the marketing of women.

Professional

The WTA is the gold standard for the marketing of female athletes. In 2013, they set new records in prize money, attendance, and viewership (WTA, n.d.). Part of this success is due to their active international marketing promotions. Along with their "40 Love" campaign, a 2013 promotion centered on their 40th year in existence, the WTA has also been actively marketing their athletes with an artful combination of glamour, action, and inspiration. The "Strong Is Beautiful" campaign features several WTA athletes in action poses while wearing dresses. The ads also feature soft feminine lighting, heavy makeup, and glitter. In conjunction with this promotion, the WTA has produced a series of related ads with celebrities stating what *strong* means to them. Use of nonathlete celebrities in sport ads usually indicate the team or league is stretching outside of their usual market demographic in hopes of gaining new fans.

From 2002 to 2007, the LPGA attempted to align sports with entertainment by utilizing a plan called the Five Points of Celebrity. This plan had the goal of increasing the marketability of LPGA athletes by elevating them to celebrity status through athlete assessment of their performance, approachability, passion and joy, relevance, and appearance (Sirak, 2008). The LPGA held the first-ever Players Summit, where athlete attendance was mandatory for training on the elements of the plan. While some players and experts felt this new approach was necessary for raising consumer awareness (and profitability potential) of the athletes and league as a whole, others were disappointed that appearance was such a focus of the plan. In fact, many felt that there was an underlying pressure for players to embody femininity (Wolter, 2010).

Collegiate

Collegiate women's sport has grown considerably since the passage of Title IX, in both participation and popularity. For example, NCAA women's basketball has increased its participation numbers from 9,000 student-athletes in 1982 to more than 15,000 in 2013 (Ackerman, 2013). While attendance has leveled off over the last few years, there was considerable growth

Serena Williams, seen here hitting a backhand at the U.S. Open, exhibits both the strength and beauty the WTA emphasizes in its "40 Love" and "Strong Is Beautiful" campaigns.

from 8.6 million in 2000 to more than 11 million fans per year in 2012 (National Collegiate Athletic Association, 2012). The period of growth spurred the NCAA to form the Division I Women's Basketball Issues Committee to focus on issues surrounding the marketing and promotion of women's basketball. In the mid-2000s, a series of focus groups were conducted to identify six or seven attributes unique to college women's basketball that could serve as the basis for a new branding effort (Lee, 2004). Specifically, the campaign developed tools and resources to assist institutions with their marketing and promotion efforts. It also instituted a national marketing initiative, with the following tagline for use by all NCAA schools: "All day. Every day. Our game." They realized that women's sport has its own set of valued characteristics and should be marketed as such.

According to Val Ackerman's (2013) white paper report to the NCAA on the state of

women's basketball, there is not currently a unified strategic approach to the marketing of women's college basketball. Also, the majority of nationwide corporate sponsorships are aimed at football and men's basketball, namely the men's basketball tournament. This may be related to the overarching feeling that women's college basketball sponsorships are hard sell to those wishing to reach the female audience due to the dominant male viewing base.

Some schools market their women's sports slightly differently than some of their men's sports, not necessarily because of gender, but because of revenue production. So while men's and women's soccer are marketed essentially the same way through autograph sessions, youth team discounts, free food for college students, and so on, the non-revenue sports (which includes all women's sports) are marketed differently than men's basketball and football. You see, it doesn't take as much outside incentive to get fans to a men's basketball or football game as it would to pack the stands at a women's lacrosse game. Marketers are tasked with the job of finding specific enticements, such as discounted food or a T-shirt giveaway, to get fans in the gate. Once fans are there, the quality of the sport and the entertainment of the experience will ultimately make them want to come back again and again.

Title IX has also had an influence on the marketing of collegiate sports. As part of the compliance criteria, program components that affect the quality of student-athlete experience are subjected to Title IX analysis. Included in this group of components is marketing. Each year, athletic departments set the budgets for each of its subdepartments, including the marketing department. It is up to the marketing department to allocate funds in a way that is relatively equal among athletic teams (see chapter 2). While some sport programs, such as football, may spend triple the amount of any other team on campus in a given year, the marketing dollars spent on both men's and women's sports teams should be reasonably equal if you look at the numbers over a handful of years.

College athletics marketing is unique in that the same group of marketers works with all of the sports teams in the athletic department.

The Marketing of Women's Basketball at the University of Kentucky

Nathan Schwake, Associate AD of Marketing and Promotions, University of Kentucky Athletics

At the University of Kentucky we've made a concerted effort to present our women's basketball players and staff as approachable and available. While our women's program is among the nation's elite, tickets are affordable, players are available after each game for autographs, and our fan base has access to a variety of events throughout the year that allows them to know the student-athletes on a more personal basis.

Famously it's been said that there are 24,000 coaches in Rupp Arena for every men's basketball game. Fans will yell (both positively and negatively) for coaches, players, and officials—using predominantly the name on the back of their uniform. On the women's side, it's more like we have 7,000 grandparents and cousins. While the passion is the same, the fans cheer for the women's team by first name, and we strive to give each player a platform throughout the season to enhance that. The entire team is featured on tickets and on the game program, and we accentuate the first name when referencing players in marketing collateral. Whenever possible, we seek out ways to show the players outside of just a uniform, as showcased by casual pictures in dress clothes in our media guides.

In addition to activities surrounding our games themselves, we actively present the women's basketball student-athletes as role models to local elementary and middle school students. Partnering with the local school district, we have an annual attendance challenge for elementary schools where we're also able to incorporate Coach Matthew Mitchell's winning tools of honesty, hard work, and discipline. By showing the successes of the student-athletes on and off the court, we're able to provide the kids and the staff of our partner schools with a real-world example.

In addition, we annually schedule a mid-day matinee game to allow for a field trip for local 6th graders to visit campus. To make it count, the 6th graders are dropped off on the opposite side of campus from our arena and led on a campus tour. For many, it's the first realization that college is more than just the football and basketball games they see on TV. Because of the nature of the brand of our women's basketball program, all these things are possible.

We've seen an increase in our women's basketball booster program over the last decade thanks in part to this presentation, the flexibility of our head coaches to be available to the public, and success on the court. That success has been helped in part by the family atmosphere that extends from the women's basketball staff to the fan base. When recruits come to a game for a visit they can see the types of relationships we're building and what our vision is for their future.

As the program grows, it becomes difficult to maintain a relatively close relationship between a student-athlete and a fan, but the idea is to allow that fan to develop the relationship through as many avenues as possible before ever meeting the player face to face.

238

The challenge is that many sports have different target markets. The first step in their marketing process is identifying these target markets, and then understanding how to reach them. For example, the University of Iowa's men's basketball fans (mainly college students and young to middle-aged adults) are primarily contacted through social media and e-mail with details about an upcoming game or promotion (L. Pearson, personal communication, July 9, 2013). Their women's basketball team, on the other hand, draws mainly families with young children and senior citizens. To reach the families, the marketing department goes through local schools to get kids excited about the game and to distribute information to parents. Senior citizens are targeted through direct mail and newspaper advertisements, since they prefer this method of communication rather than e-mail or social media.

Gender-specific promotions are also common. For example, Lisa Pearson, director of marketing at University of Iowa Department of Athletics, explains,

> Since we also see a lot of females attending women's basketball games, we'll do some promotions that are catered specifically to them. For example, we hosted a Girls Night Out that invited local salons to set up booths on the concourse during pregame where they offered free hairstyling, manicures, makeovers, and more for girls and women attending the game. We try to listen to the fans' interests. (personal communication, July 9, 2013)

SPORT MARKETING TACTICS

Along with the already-mentioned specific efforts, most levels of sport use many of the same general tactics to reach fans (or potential fans). These tactics have been successful in the marketing of men's sport, so one would think they would see comparable success in the marketing of women's sport. Unfortunately, that is not always the case. This section discusses the three popular strategies of word-of-mouth marketing, endorsements, and sponsorships. It specifically focuses on how these approaches are used and on the overall effectiveness in women's

sport. Missed marketing opportunities are also discussed.

Word-of-Mouth Marketing

Word-of-mouth (WOM) marketing or *buzz marketing* (Bush, Bush, Clark, & Bush, 2005) is creating hype about an event, team, or item. This has been recognized as a key component of marketing communication because it can be done in so many different ways (through peers, Internet portals, and celebrity endorsements). Research has revealed that word-of-mouth marketing may be even more effective among teenage girls since they rely heavily on their friends and the media to communicate, all while developing self-esteem and maturing (Bush, Martin, & Bush, 2004). Since the teenage years are an important time in a girl's life for developing team or athlete loyalty, marketers can use this to their advantage to specifically target this growing demographic.

Social media sites enable marketers to use WOM strategies to reach millions of consumers for very little or no money. Organizations (both leagues and teams) have fans at their fingertips through Facebook, Twitter, and Instagram, and have the power to shape the message being relayed. This is important, especially for women's sports, which don't get as much traditional media coverage as their male counterparts. For example, Nathan McCarter of *Bleacher Report* (2013) stated that the United States women's national soccer team (USWNT) is more popular than the men's national team largely because of their social media interactions with fans. Several of the USWNT members are avid Tweeters and Instagram users, as well as frequent posters of videos that show off their true personalities. Fans live for getting a peek at their favorite athlete in her everyday life or having fun with her teammate. Both athletes and marketers know that this is a necessity if they hope to see their sport to gain the attention (and consumer brand loyalty) it deserves.

Athletes are not just interacting with fans for the good of their sport or team. Individual athletes also promote their own brand through their personal social media accounts. While some leagues or organizations have rules regarding

> *We have campers coming from over 22 different states and a few from Canada. The furthest will win a prize! #abbywambach. com to register.*
>
> Abby Wambach, Twitter, July 2, 2013

when and what athletes can post, the majority of the content shared publicly is strictly an athlete's choice. Often times, an athlete will choose to promote her charitable foundation, host a Q&A session with fans, or simply send out a message about an upcoming game. All of these messages are seen by her followers, helping establish the foundation of fan identification that women's sports sometimes lack. The interaction between athlete and fan serves dual purposes in that it helps promote the athlete's own image, but also helps garner more interest in the league and in sport in general.

Endorsements

Product **endorsement** is one of the most common methods of sports marketing (Shank, 2008). Companies see great value in having athletes endorse their products and services, since it gains attention and generates publicity from a sports-crazed public. An endorser refers to any person who is publicly known to appear in advertisements with the purpose of promoting the product or service (McCracken, 1989) because of his or her expertise, attractiveness, or trustworthiness (Till & Busler, 2000). All three of these characteristics are related to source credibility, "a term commonly used to imply a communicator's positive characteristics that affect the receiver's acceptance of a message" (Ohanian, 1990, p. 41). Ohanian's research has shown that highly credible sources have been able to produce more positive attitude changes and induce behavior changes more often than less credible sources. For example, imagine seeing an athlete whom you deem credible (skier Lindsey Vonn, for instance) endorsing ski goggles. According to this research, your attitude would be positive about the athlete–product association, and you would be more apt to buy the goggles than if they were endorsed by an athlete you didn't deem credible. Marketers are

well aware of this, and do their best to find the athlete with high credibility.

As mentioned, three elements make up an endorser's credibility in the mind of the consumer. These are frequently discussed among scholars and professionals because they have come to be controversial in the world of women's sport. First let's focus on expertise. Often times, a company will use an athlete to endorse their product because of the athlete's life experiences. When watching your favorite professional athlete, most likely, you are admiring their skill set. You are in awe of, or you at least appreciate, the hard work they've put in to master their craft. Now imagine you see two identical tennis racquet commercials, one starring Serena Williams, the other featuring Bob from your father's rec league. Whose word would you put more credence in? Also, this expertise strategy is particularly effective if the product being endorsed has contributed to or is related to the endorser's celebrity status (Dyson & Turco, 1998).

The second characteristic, attractiveness, has proven to be a hot-button issue in regard to female athlete endorsements. While some may feel it is degrading and unnecessary for companies to rely on attractiveness or sexiness in athlete endorsements, research has proven that "physically attractive communicators are more successful at changing beliefs than are unattractive communicators" (Ohanian, 1991, p. 47). Ultimately, consumers are more swayed by attractive people than unattractive—regardless of celebrity status. Despite this, others have found that the degree of attractiveness necessary for effectiveness may depend on the product being endorsed. If the product is related to beauty, the use of an attractive celebrity endorser leads to more positive reactions in consumers than if the product had nothing to do with appearance (Kamins, 1990). For example, an attractive female athlete endorsing face lotion would lead to more positive feelings toward the product than if the same athlete were endorsing a cleaning product.

Findings are conflicted regarding whether attractiveness or expertise is more effective in piquing consumer interest. For example, several researchers (Fink, Cunningham, & Kensicki, 2004; Till & Busler, 2000) have found that expertise was significantly more important to product fit than attractiveness. Further, Till and Busler found that expertise was most closely related to intent to purchase the endorsed product. On the other hand, Cunningham, Fink, and Kenis (2008) stated that attractive athletes make better endorsers and are more likely to sell tickets to a sporting event.

Lastly, the trustworthiness of an endorser is also important to a consumer. If an athlete conducts herself well both on and off the field, this usually translates into a general likability by the consumer. On-field performance has been found to have a significant influence on athlete trustworthiness (Koo, Ruihley, & Dittmore, 2012). As an athlete performs better on the playing field, consumers will deem her as being an expert and trustworthy, and therefore a credible endorser. Also, female consumers have been shown to trust female athletes and endorsers, whereas male consumers trust male athletes (Grau et al., 2007). This is an interesting in that if product companies want to capture the female consumer's trust and purchasing dollars, they should use female athletes to get the job done.

Studies have shown that women have a bias toward purchasing products perceived to be more feminine, and female endorsers can increase the perceived femininity of a product. In fact, women prefer a spokesperson to be more similar to them (Antil, Burton, & Robinson, 2012). One would think this would be a marketer's dream—an easy way to reach female consumers. However, in spite of these factors favoring the use of female athletes, they are still relatively underutilized, especially in comparison with their male counterparts (Grau et al., 2007). Coinciding with his research, Professor John Antil of the University of Delaware described something called a "cycle of failure" that occurs with female athletic endorsements. He says that the way female athletes are being used as endorsers negatively influences their effectiveness and thus reduces further opportunities for other female athletes (Tippett, 2012).

That said, top female athletes are grabbing endorsement deals more frequently now than ever before. Maria Sharapova, one of the top women's tennis players in the world, makes about $22 million a year in endorsements, more

money than any other female athlete. Part of her allure is that she appeals to both men and women. According to Darren Rovell (2013), Sharapova has deals with Nike, Head, Cole Haan, Evian, Tag Heuer, and Samsung, and she recently became the first worldwide endorser for Porsche, male or female. Other big-time endorsement deals for female athletes include the following:

- In 2011, WNBA star (and former UCONN all-American) Maya Moore became the first woman to sign an endorsement deal with Jordan Brand.
- Tennis player Li Na is *so* big in Asia that Nike actually makes an exception for her that it won't make for anyone else: They allow her to wear non-Nike logos when she plays (On, 2012). Her other endorsement deals include Samsung and Mercedes-Benz.

Despite the increase in endorsement numbers and payouts, women still lag behind men. For example, Sharapova's $22 million in endorsements in 2013 is not even half of tennis star Roger Federer's endorsement earnings of $63.8 million. Further, between 1997 and 2009, 671 nationally televised ads were aired during the Super Bowl. Of those, 48 featured athletes, but only 4 (8%) used a sole female athlete (Antil et al., 2012).

Women have another barrier to overcome when it comes to being seen as effective endorsers. As previously discussed, female athletes go against the sex-typed gender schemas, which are well ingrained into many of our minds (Knight & Guiliano, 2001). We are presented with an inconsistent view of female athletes—one that is both athletic and feminine. This dynamic is difficult for many consumers to reconcile, which could be one reason female athletes aren't seen as quality endorsers. In other words, female athletes are portrayed as women first, athletes second, while male athletes are presented solely as athletes (Grau et al., 2007). Thus, male athlete endorsers are more easily and effectively associated with sport-related products than women.

Traditionally, female athletes in individual sports like golf and tennis (see Sharapova) have had much of the marketing success for women in terms of dollars and number of endorsements. According to Badenhausen (2012), the top-10 highest-paid female athletes in 2012 were all individual sport athletes. Bob Dorfman, writer of the *Sports Marketers' Scouting Report* (which analyzes athletes' endorsement potential), said he believed the lack of relevant team sports leagues was the chief reason the female athletes of team sports did not remain marketable outside of international competition like the Olympics or the World Cup that occur once every few years (Castillo, 2011). Why is this? Researchers McGinnis, Chun, and McQuillan (2003) may have an answer. They stated that some sports are considered more masculine and some more feminine. Generally, the individual sports (e.g., ice skating, gymnastics, tennis) are considered more feminine than most team sports. Their argument, based on the gender schema theory, points to our predilection for seeing feminine things paired with women (and masculine with men). In other words, female individual sport athletes are better endorsers because the public prefers seeing women who participate in sports that are traditionally more feminine.

So, does this mean that the sponsorship industry is biased against female athletes and sports? Perhaps. But there may be other reasons besides sexism. For example, Antil and colleagues (2012) stated that female athlete awareness is very low and likely due to the lack of consistent public attention necessary to create familiarity. Without familiarity, athletes are not recognized in an advertisement by a consumer, which renders the endorsement useless. Additionally, their research found that there seemed to be little interest in many female sports, and media attention given to these sports is also minimal. Michael Messner's 20-year study (2010) of television airtime revealed that coverage of women's sports decreased from nearly 9 percent of airtime in 1999 to only 1.6 percent in 2009. This is especially poignant considering how many more women participate in sport and compete at an elite level now than in the early years of Title IX.

As mentioned, media coverage has a direct effect on how women's sports are perceived. How are consumers supposed to be familiar with, and form opinions about, athletes whom they rarely (or never) see? Ultimately, companies are not going to pursue a female athlete to be their spokesperson if very few people know who she is, much less care to find out about her. The question is, who is to blame? Are marketers to blame for not exposing the public to women's sports? Or is it we, a group of sport consumers, who are guilty of not demanding or wanting more coverage of women's sports and athletes?

Sponsorships

Worldwide spending on sport sponsorship has continued to grow over the years. For our purposes, a **sponsorship** will be defined as an exchange of cash or in-kind products between a company and a sport league or team. Most of the time, the goal of the companies in these sponsorship agreements is to increase public awareness of their company or brand, change a brand's image, increase revenue through brand loyalty, and gain access to new markets (Maxwell & Lough, 2009). The key to an effective sponsorship is spectator recognition. In other words, if a fan at a softball game recalls that Progressive Insurance was a sponsor of the team, the company's goal is at least partially achieved. This recognition, or brand awareness, ideally would transfer into increased consumer purchase intentions of the company's products, thereby providing a return on their sponsorship investment.

Sponsorship decisions are most often made by senior managers in both sport and consumer-product organizations. As both continue to be dominated by masculine ideologies and networks, sponsorship agreements tend to be skewed this way as well. According to Shaw and Amis (2001), there are three interlinked reasons for the lack of women's sport sponsorships. First, the values and beliefs of decision makers (usually men) influence the choice of what to sponsor. Decisions are made based on prospective financial and social outcomes, including networking opportunities. In many cases, those making the decisions see men's sport, not women's, as a suitable venue to socialize and meet other corporate needs, such as promoting

By sponsoring this collegiate women's volleyball match, Wilson hopes their brand will be recognized by spectators, which will ideally lead to increased purchases.

themselves as a good corporate citizen through grassroots sport projects.

Second, media coverage (see chapter 11) has been cited as a major reason for involvement in sport sponsorship. Since men's sport is covered at a much higher rate, it would only make sense for the executives making sponsorship deals to choose this as a platform where they would get the most exposure and bang for their buck. Ultimately, women's teams aren't seen as capable of generating enough media coverage for executives to put the money into a sponsorship.

Finally, industry trends dictate sponsorship decisions. Sponsorships are a high-cost, risky investment, and executives want to make sure they are at least aware of what competitors are doing. Often executives will see another company do something that works well, and try to mimic it themselves. While it may not be the bold, groundbreaking move, it is the safe one. For example, if Companies A, B, and C recently signed sponsorship deals with men's minor league baseball teams, and all seem to be getting excellent exposure, the marketing exec for Company D is more likely to sign a sponsorship deal with another minor league team (or an equivalent sport) than invest money in a women's professional soccer event because of the known success rate of his peers.

MISSED OPPORTUNITIES TO MARKET WOMEN'S SPORT

Arguably the spectator event with the greatest influence for women's sports was the 1999 World Cup final, which claimed 40 million viewers and outdrew the men's World Cup in television ratings. But despite the booming popularity of this mega event and of soccer in general, the newly formed WUSA only survived three years, folding after the 2003 season. In a rebranding effort that included tempered attendance expectations, a second league, WPS, was formed five years later. Although soccer remained the most popular youth sport in the country and coverage of international women's soccer was at an all-time high, the WPS couldn't take advantage of it, and ceased operations prior to the 2012 season.

With the U.S. women's national team winning the 2012 Olympic gold medal, the United States Soccer Federation announced a newly formed eight-team league called the National Women's

Soccer League (NWSL) would begin play in 2013. The league's marketing campaigns have focused on star national team players, with an emphasis on fan interaction through social media. The league has signed national broadcasting deals with Fox Soccer, which televised nine games in the second half of the NWSL's inaugural season (National Women's Soccer League, 2013). It is too early to tell what the future holds for NWSL. That said, marketers should be able to learn from their predecessors' mistakes to improve the outlook of the league's position within the U.S. professional sports landscape.

The WNBA, started in 1996, is the most successful women's team sports league in American history. With top-level international talent and former college stars, the WNBA is in the position to dominate their May through September playing season. The timing, which is opposite all other college and professional basketball schedules in the United States, should prove to be beneficial in drawing in fans. Despite this, the WNBA has seen a recent decline in its regular-season attendance (7,318 in 2015), the lowest average since its inception in 1997. In fact, the league has not averaged more than 10,000 fans per game since 1999 (Rhoden, 2012). Additionally, the Los Angeles Sparks, who led the league in terms of average attendance in 2012 and 2013, are the only WNBA franchise with a paid local television contract. The other teams give the games away or pay a production fee to have their games televised. The reason for this is that television networks don't feel they can bring in the viewership numbers, and thus advertising dollars, from airing a game. Can you imagine an NBA team paying a network to broadcast a game?

Ultimately, these two examples of unreached potential have come down to marketing executives not understanding or catering to the target market. For example, while a good chunk of women's professional sport league fans come from the LBGTQ community, until recently, these fans weren't explicitly marketed to. In May of 2014, the WNBA finally announced a plan to directly target this group. Another opportunity lies in highlighting the difference between men's and women's sport. Most die-hard sports fans are engaged heavily in men's sports, and tend to compare women's sports to their male equivalent. If executives can positively emphasize the world-class talent and skill sets that lie in the women's game, they have a better chance of setting their franchise, league, or sport apart in the minds of *all* consumers. Unfortunately, lack of creativity and understanding, combined with unrealistic expectations, have caused women's professional leagues to struggle even though female team sport participation is booming.

> For us it's a celebration of diversity and inclusion and recognition of an audience that has been with us very passionately. This is one of those moments in the W where everybody comes together. It's taken the league 18 years to take the step, though it had discussions about the possibility previously. . . . We embrace all our fans and it's a group that we know has been very, very supportive.
>
> WNBA president Laurel Richie in describing the decision to market to LBGTQ fans

Learning Aids

Summary

The last decade and a half has seen the landscape of women's sport marketing and merchandising shift dramatically. Propelled by the United States' charismatic and victorious 1999 Women's World Cup team, the world began to recognize that female athletes were for real and that money could be made from the simultaneously growing female marketplace. Corporations and marketers began pumping more money and effort into the marketing and branding of both merchandise and the athletes themselves through sponsorships and endorsements.

While we as a society have come a long way in recognizing the talent and achievement of female athletes, we have yet to maximize their marketing potential. It's best to think of our current situation as a cycle. As we begin to market female athletes more consistently and with quality campaigns or strategies, women's sport will gain further interest from the public. This interest will, in turn, lead to more money being invested in women's sport from both consumers and advertisers. The more money and marketing effort put into women's sport will only further society's interest, completing the cycle.

Discussion Questions

1. What assumptions do people make about female sports fans and fans of women's sports? How should marketers go about reaching these fans?

2. Explain the gender schema theory. How can it be applied to women's sport today? How does this affect marketers?

3. What makes the marketing of college sport unique? What must college sport marketers do to maximize fan interest?

4. Why is word-of-mouth marketing especially important for women's sport? In your opinion, how can this practice become more effective?

5. Explain the various ways a female athlete can be presented in an advertisement or endorsement. Which way do you think would be the most effective? Why?

Learning Activities

1. Select a women's professional team and research their current season's marketing campaign. Consider all aspects of marketing, such as pricing and sponsorships, and include all media used to communicate the marketing themes (e.g., promotions, social media). Who is the team's target market? Does the campaign reflect traditional ideas of femininity? How so? Are there any changes you would make to the campaign?

2. Watch *Branded*, a documentary directed by Heidi Ewing and Rachel Grady as part of ESPN's *Nine for IX* series. The film focuses on the double standard placed on female athletes to be the best players on the field and the sexiest off the field. Do you think women can ever gain equal ground with their male counterparts? Or will sex appeal always be part of the equation?

Glossary

endorsement—An act of giving one's public approval or support to someone or something.

gender schema theory—Refers to the theory that people learn about what it means to be male and female from the culture in which they live, beginning at a young age. According to this theory, children adjust their behavior to fit in with the gender norms and expectations of their culture.

sponsorship—An exchange of cash or in-kind products between a company and a sport league or team.

word-of-mouth (WOM) marketing—Creating hype about an event, team, or item through consumer-to-consumer or marketer-to-consumer communication.

CHAPTER 15

Influence of Religion and Politics on Women's Sport

Carole Oglesby, PhD, Cochair, International Working Group on Women in Sport

Learning Objectives

In this chapter, you will learn about the following:

- The dichotomy of women's nature as defined by fundamentalist religious writers

- The influence of dualistic stereotypes of women in gaining and using political and organizational power and influence

- The dimensions of the underrepresentation of women in sport governance and possible relationships to male-only space in traditional religion and sport

- The legal, policy, and human rights bases for equitable representation of women in sport governance

- Strategies to move numbers of women into equitable power and leadership in sport

After reading this chapter, you could reasonably conclude that there is a discourse of *The more things change, the more they stay the same* in sport governance. A brief anecdote illustrates it. From 1972 to 1992, I served as women's representative from the **American Alliance for Health, Physical Education, Recreation and Dance** (now known as the Society of Health and Physical Educators) to the U.S. Collegiate Sports Council, which organized U.S. teams for the World University Games (WUG). The modern WUG began in 1959, and the unspoken tradition when I joined was that one official was sent in all sports in which the United States had athlete representation. There were no female officials (except occasionally in gymnastics), and women staffers were very rare. Imagine my surprise when (in 1987) I discovered that the regulations of FISU (translated to English, the International University Sports Federation) allowed a referee for each team entered. The United States had women's and men's basketball teams, so technically it was allowed to send two referees. I knew that one of my good old girl softball teammates, Darlene May, had international credentials. Another California connection, Dr. Karen Johnson, was the executive director for the National Association for Girls and Women in Sport (NAGWS) at the time, and together we were determined to get Darlene to WUG as the first woman to referee at this level on behalf of generally advancing women in officiating.

The men in charge would not send her, saying in effect it was "not an affordable or important expense." Through NAGWS, all the paperwork was submitted and the expenses paid. To make a long story short, Darlene May officiated! There was only one pool of officials for all basketball games at that time, and when FISU officials saw her competency, she was actually assigned to a men's game. A picture appeared on page 1 of the *New York Times* showing Darlene (all 5 feet, 10 inches) about to take a toss-up with two male players towering more than a foot above her. Great story, right? But I thought I must be in a time warp in the summer of 2013 when another situation crossed my desk through the **Women Sport International (WSI)** Task Force for Deaf and Hard of Hearing Women in Sport.

A woman referee was being denied the opportunity to officiate basketball at the Deaflympics (coincidentally both WUG 1987 and Deaflympics 2013 were held in Sofia, Bulgaria). She had the formal credentials and the international experiences in single-game competition. She had demonstrated leadership in both deaf sport and mainstream NCAA championship play. There had never been a woman basketball official in the Deaflympics, and the leadership was not going to allow her to officiate, although she maintained she was stonewalled as to why. Her struggle for the opportunity went on for more than a year as she went through all the proper grievance procedures for gaining entry. She paid her own way to the competition because her case was still ongoing, and she was committed to the end. She *was* successful in officiating one game, but she was not reimbursed for her travel and was not allowed to keep her officiating shirt as did all the male referees. This woman's name is Marsha Wetzel, and you can read her story (see the group "Support Deaf Women Basketball Referees" at www.facebook.com). This chapter makes clear some of the reasons that the men in sport governance power are adamant about their gatekeeper status and also how knowledge of political pressure and system operation can provide keys to opening the gates.

Individuals move on through careers, and yet our published words stand, and we are responsible or accountable for making sense of the distance between what was *then* and what is *now*. I first wrote about women in the sport governance system in 1974, more than 40 years ago. This chapter provides an opportunity to assess what stands and what has changed since 1974. I think it is helpful to visualize the sport governance context of this analysis as a community. Since 1974, the look of the community has changed and moved a great deal. Many more people have moved in; the structures (like houses and buildings) are different looking with elaborations of fashions and styles. But what about the ground beneath our feet? What about the nature of the very earth that undergirds it all and feeds its character into everything that is produced? My thesis is that the ground base has changed little and that those of us who desire significant transformation must adopt new assumptions and much different strategies in moving forward.

RELIGION, TRADITION, AND POWER POSITIONS FOR WOMEN IN SPORT GOVERNANCE

To develop new assumptions and understandings in sport, we can benefit from the analyses of religion and power from feminist scholars and authors. Whatever their differences in religion, cultural background, or academic training, they each can be seen to emphasize a common theme. They assert that the source of suppression for women is not a religion or all religions. It is a **patriarchal religious tradition** and interpretation that denies women full humanity.

In Rich's meticulous analysis of motherhood, she examined the treatment of women in ancient and medieval texts, concluding, "patriarchal monotheism did not simply change the sex of the divine presence; it stripped the universe of female divinity and permitted women to be sanctified only and exclusively as Mother" (Rich, 1986, p. 119). The psychologist Eric Neumann,

renowned student of Carl Jung, broadened the scope of this redefining of the duality of feminine nature to be characteristic of patriarchal cultures, including Judeo-Christian, Mohammedan, and Hindu (Neumann, 1955). Rich and Daly (1973), among others, have emphasized the power of the religious dichotomy of woman: (1) as impure, corrupt (Eve), unclean (site of bleeding and discharges), tempting, and dangerous, and (2) as Mother—sacred, pure, and nourishing (Mary, mother of God). The evil, impure, and dangerous manifestation must be controlled; the presence of woman is blocked from public life. The good and pure is exclusively seen in motherhood, family, and domestic life. These myths and stereotypes are spread widely through cultural traditions in all continents and all countries. Even in sport development work today, Meier (2005) describes how these cultural and religious traditions form obstacles in sport development work with girls—barriers that can barely be perceived because of how deeply they are embedded.

Perhaps one of the most striking examples of the global reach of the patriarchal and religious misappropriation of women's personhood is found in the writing of Benazir Bhutto. Bhutto

A symbol of empowerment to many Muslim women, the late Benazir Bhutto is revered by those who visit her shrine.

was Prime Minister of Pakistan 1988 to 1990 and 1991 to 1993, and was the first woman to lead a Muslim state. She was in exile from 1999 to 2007, when she returned home and was again poised to be elected head of state. There was an assassination attempt within hours of her arrival. Two months later, she was shot and killed. In the book she was finishing in her last months, she could not have been clearer about the manner in which extremist tribal elders were departing from the Holy **Quran**. She wrote, "Islam denounces inequality as the greatest form of injustice" (2008, p. 17). She further described these reactionary elements of her faith and homeland as having "gone astray from the right path" (2008, p. 19) through such acts as denying basic education to girls, blatantly discriminating against women and minorities, and ridiculing other cultures and religions. Bhutto described how discriminations against women are justified by tribal notions that men are superior to women. She stated unequivocally that these views are "repudiated in the Quran" (2008, p. 48). Her central conclusion seems to apply in much wider circles than her native Pakistan: "The battle for the heart and soul of Islam today is taking place between moderates and fanatics, democrats and dictators, those living in the past and those who adapt to the present and plan for a better future" (2008, p. 19).

These broad and theoretical musings concerning religion and cultural traditions can seem light years away from questions concerning women's power in the sport governance frame-

Resistance Coming From Religious, Political, and Other Cultural Influences

• Based on studies conducted in southern Africa, Fasting, Huffman, and Sand noted the following: "Culture plays a big role in preventing women from participating in sport. . . . clothing—it's difficult for parents and men to accept women in shorts. . . . Men are a problem—husbands are not happy to see their wives interacting with other men. Also there is competition for leadership; men don't think women can lead. And other cultural aspects such as religion and safety issues were mentioned [in the study] as reasons why there are not more women in sport" (2014, p. 15).

• In a study based in Kenya, Brady and Khan found similar limitations. "Typically the kinds of public spaces that are seen as legitimate venues for women—markets, health clinics—are those that enable women to fulfill their domestic roles as homemakers and mothers. In contrast, public spaces for males are less narrowly defined and not necessarily linked to their gender roles. . . . Females have a much more difficult time, and in some cases are completely excluded from, visiting spaces such as town halls, parks, sports stadiums unless accompanied by men" (2002, p. 2).

• "Women volleyball players at refugee camps for displaced Somalis in Kenya ran into intense negative community responses due to local dress codes. The UN High Commission for Refugees worked with Nike to design comfortable and practical sport apparel within the dress codes" (UNDAW, 2008, p. 15).

• In the Gender Equality Audit for the London 2012 Olympic Games, an incident in judo is described. One of the Saudi Arabian participants was informed by officials of the International Judo Federation that she could not wear the hijab that her national team had required. She was locked in a terrible situation. Finally a compromise was made, but study authors described this situation as the tip of the iceberg in regard to uniform issues (Donnelly & Donnelly, 2013).

work, but I believe that they are not. Freeman, Bourque, and Shelton (2001) identified four factors that limit women's political leadership in the United States today. The top two factors go directly to these same religion-infused images of women: a sexual division of domestic labor and the structure of work and the persistence of traditional sex role expectations. Both in the business world and in recent studies of women in coaching and sport administration, it is still the case that women are working two jobs: outside the home as a wage earner and inside it as primary caregiver and homemaker. If her husband participates in the latter, he is seen as helping her. Signs of these themes are seen in sport development work far afield from the contemporary United States. Meier described the long and arduous negotiations in less developed cultures to convince community elders to permit girls' sport programming, since elders insist that nothing should disrupt the traditional domestic responsibilities of young girls and teens, yet boys are allowed to play sports (2005).

In the United States, individuals and organizations advocating for a balanced sharing of home and family responsibilities so that women can move into and maintain careers (including in sport) encounter resistance from entrenched religious and political groups. See the sidebar Resistance Coming From Religious, Political, and Other Cultural Influences for examples of the resistance that women seeking sport careers come up against.

These conservative groups strongly oppose what they see as attempts to interfere with the family or traditional aspects of family life. Rich said that in the view of members of these groups, "a policy that enhances one member, in any way separate from the family entity, is a priori harmful" (1986, p. xvi).

As sport development programs proliferate and move beyond early-stage simplicity, it is accepted as a given, well stated by Meier: "A sustainable project for sport gender equity must take into account specific socio-cultural and socio-economic parameters including access to, and control over, resources, dynamics of local power and differing gender roles" (2005, p. 8).

Women and like-minded men have been at work on these issues in sport for decades. We still have a monumental task before us. Moving more women into power positions within the sport governance systems will help, but it is not the whole matter. On a global scale, women have not yet taken the strong stands necessary to ultimately solve the problem. The issues are complex, manifesting at policy and strategy levels (macro), professional and institutional levels (meso), and personal or social levels (micro) (Kirk, 2012). As Rich poetically describes, there is for women a cognitive enemy within: "God the Father—His word is Law and the idea of it is internalized as conscience, tradition, and our very morality" (1986, p. 67).

TRANSFORMATION OF GENDER POLITICS IN SPORT

Beginning in the writings of **second-wave feminism**, a long line of brilliant thinkers has spotlighted men's fear, dread, and hostility toward women, especially women who exercised or sought power (de Beauvoir, 1949/1989; Horney, 1967; Rich, 1986; Freeman et al., 2001). The sentiment is also succinctly captured in the oft-quoted line from Cardinal Richelieu, "intellect in a woman is unbecoming" (Bernstein, 2008, p. 201). If the depth of this antipathy is perplexing, equally so women's denial; psychoanalyst Karen Horney wrote, "It is almost more remarkable that women themselves have been so long able to overlook this" (1967, p. 67). Why is it that women continue to deny and ignore their own situation? Why is it that women appear so reluctant to claim institutional power even when it is their right? Is God the Father still laying down the law in women's own minds?

Women's participation in the leadership and governance of sport is extremely limited, as we see in other public realms such as religion and politics. In this chapter, I utilize the **International Olympic Committee (IOC)** as a key exemplar of what is wrong and as a context for transformative solutions. Just how bad is the situation? It is bad! It is not as if we don't have the answers before us. The Women's Sports Foundation of United States has published data on women in sport leadership (Smith & Wrynn, 2010a, 2010b). Other information from after 2010 is available on the Sydney Scoreboard website

Women in High-Level Governance of Sport

Because the absence of women from high-level governance of sport is taken for granted (thus unnoticed), during the past two decades, efforts have been made to publicize the data in order to catch public attention. In the United States, there are the well-known Acosta and Carpenter reports on levels of women in coaching, and the Women's Sports Foundation's Gender Equity Report Cards on women's participation and leadership involvement. The following two international efforts may be less well known:

• *Sydney Scoreboard* (www.sydneyscoreboard.org). As a legacy of the 2010 World Conference on Women and Sport in Sydney, Australia, a website was mounted to facilitate the collection and display of data by country in the five Olympic Regions in three leadership categories: executive boards of directors, chairpersons of boards of directors, and chief executive officers. The national data were reported from approximately 50 countries, and they focused on national governing bodies of sport and national Olympic committees. About 90 **International Federations (IFs)** added information on their chairs and CEOs. As you can see, less than half the national bodies chose to add their data. A thorough study reveals many interesting patterns; however, in a brief synopsis here, it is clear that these organizations do not come close to the modest targets suggested by the IOC. Only a handful of the groups have female representation around the 30 percent level, and the great majority of groups fall between 10 and 20 percent.

• *Gender Equality Audit of the 2012 London Olympic Games.* This report, written by Peter and Michelle Donnelly under the auspices of the University of Toronto, was dedicated to the search for the areas where work still needed to be done in relation to gender equality in these Games much heralded for their equity stance. The report focused almost all attention, and great detail, on the remaining issues in the structure of the Games but also, in many contexts, reminded readers how attaining equity in leadership would go a long way toward ironing out remaining competition issues. "It is no longer justifiable to maintain an Olympic Program where there are 30 more medal events for men than for women" (Donnelley & Donnelly, 2013, p. 6)

from the Fifth World Conference of the International Working Group (www.sydneyscoreboard.com). Additionally, the University of Toronto published the Gender Equality Audit following the 2012 London Olympic Games (Donnelly & Donnelly, 2013).

Perhaps women are lulled by the rhetoric from the IOC website and media (IOC Department of International Corporation and Development, 2013). For example, IOC mission statement 7 promises the complete commitment of the Olympic Movement "to encourage and support the promotion of women in sport at all levels and in all structures with a view to implementing the principle of equality of men and women" (International Olympic Committee, 2014, p. 15). Since the IOC positioned itself to be recognized by the United Nations by achieving official observer status in 2009, there is a great deal at stake for the IOC to be seen as a model of gender equality. What are the present facts about women's status in the Olympic Movement?

In 1994, an IOC study commission recommended a working group be created to suggest improvements in women's roles. By 1995, an IOC women's working group was established.

Despite numerous requests from the working group for formalization, it did not become a full-fledged commission until 2004.

Perhaps it is worth mentioning a few of the firsts for women that transpired decades before this IOC action and marking the IOC as late to the party!

- 1972: Title IX is passed in the United States.
- 1972: Woman director named to the N.Y. Stock Exchange.
- 1981: Sandra Day O'Connor is named to the Supreme Court.
- 1983: Sally Ride becomes the first U.S. female astronaut in space.
- 1989: Barbara Harris ordained as the first female bishop in the Episcopal church.
- 1993: Janet Reno named U.S. Attorney General.
- 1997: Madeleine Albright named U.S. Secretary of State.

The actions taken by the IOC in response to the decades-old call for women's equality have been decidedly underwhelming. The IOC promotes itself as engaged in gender mainstreaming (International Olympic Committee Department of International Cooperation and Development, 2013). The elements of their mainstreaming are activities such as the following:

- Seminars on women in sport in 18 countries in 10 years
- World conferences on women and sport every four years, with five held thus far
- Women in Sport Awards featuring six trophy winners, one from each continental region and an overall winner

Nothing is wrong with the IOC's efforts, but they are quite impotent in terms of changing the governance status quo. The seminars are publicized to "give visibility" and to "encourage NOCs to work harder on women's equality" (International Olympic Committee, 2014, p. 47). There is no requirement that women whose capacity has been enhanced by the seminars will have an opportunity to utilize their new skills. No data exist on the effects of participation on career

course. Several global women's groups hold global conferences as well, so, to women sport advocates, there is needless redundancy in the IOC conference efforts.

Perhaps most frustrating of all have been the self-acclaimed minimum targets for enhancing women's role in Olympic governance. The targets were set in 1996. By 2001, all elements of the Olympic Family were to achieve 10 percent women's involvement in leadership; by 2005, the target was 20 percent. The Loughborough gender equality and leadership study (Henry & Robinson, 2010) commissioned by the IOC further recommended adoption of stretch targets of 25 percent by 2014 and 30 percent by 2018!

In the first place, the size of these so-called targets must be called into question. Why did not women and fair-minded men respond with indignation that an international body, proclaiming itself to stand for gender justice, set a target of 20 percent female leadership participation for the year 2010?

Of course, of much greater concern is the issue of compliance. A quote from Women's Sports Foundation researchers speaks volumes: "The IOC rhetoric has only gained minimal response from NOCs, IFs, and the IPC, most of which still struggle to meet the IOC request that women be represented at a 20% standard" (Smith & Wrynn, 2010b, p. 2). The IOC targets are, in fact, requests. There is little beyond words for any group who fails the standard.

The International Olympic Committee Department of International Cooperation and Development (2013) stated the following:

- In 2013, the IOC membership hit 20 percent (the 2005 goal).
- Of 204 **national Olympic committees (NOCs)**, 11 had women presidents (5%).
- Of 87 IFs reporting, Summer Federations had two women presidents and three secretary generals.
- Winter Federations had one woman president and three secretary generals.

Smith and Wrynn (2010a, 2010b) stated the following:

- Of Winter Federations, 23 percent on the boards of directors were women.

- Of IOC Commissions, 7 of 25 met the 20 percent target.
- Of USOC, both the chair of the board and CEO were male.
- Of the 23 US NGBs, 16 met the 20 percent female target.

Sydney Scoreboard

The Sydney Scoreboard posts results from 45 countries with information requested on the representation of women on **national governing bodies (NGBs)**, IFs, and NOCs.

In the research commissioned by the IOC at Loughborough University (Henry & Robinson, 2010), only 110 of 204 NOCs replied to the survey requests. The units do not meet targets and they will not report significantly on progress. Clearly there is an unspoken norm that no repercussions will result from ignoring equality requests. This does not seem to be an issue that setting higher stretch targets will solve.

As in many other instances, it appears that the IOC believes if the appropriate words are spoken, that is enough. There is little, if any, consequence for failure to make good on promises. There is no sense of urgency that the mission is impaired or that the optimal accomplishment of the organization is affected by failure. If the targets really mattered, they would be accomplished.

KNOW THE SYSTEM

Women should be equally represented in all phases of the Olympic Movement. IOC Mission 7 makes that promise (International Olympic Committee, 2014). These, and other promises such as Title IX in United States, are hard-won equity victories for advocates, yet they are words that carry the burden of changing centuries of religious, political, and cultural marginalization. Women have developed, as athletes and sport leaders, through a different and complementary process as compared to men, and they bring a unique and valuable perspective. Daunting barriers to moving into leadership will not go away soon. How to overcome them? One crucial step is to study, observe, and develop a deep and comprehensive understanding of the system to be entered and its detailed operation.

The heart of this section is a functional analysis of the international Olympic sport governance system. The analysis identifies the essential components of this system, describes briefly the normative mission of the system, and identifies the complementary rights and duties of the component elements of the system. In this latter phase, we see the manner in which this governance structure must be understood as a system. Thus, organizational behavior cannot be understood as a single element, but must be regarded in the context of systemic functions.

My belief is that knowledge of the stated mission and functioning of the system produced by, and responsible for, both the Olympic Games and the Olympic Movement (Olympism) can facilitate action and programs for positive change within that system. Further, following similar principles and practices can be useful in facilitating progress in other institutionalized systems, such as the NCAA (in the United States), FISU (globally), or the **International Paralympic Committee (IPC)**. Figure 15.1 is a diagram of the structural components of the sport governance system.

The diagram was developed in 1974 in an attempt to illustrate the essential roles (rights and duties) of each component of this system, especially as they formed complementary relations with other system components. The two upper, horizontal levels of the diagram illustrate how the international realm has areas of dominance and power over the national structures. The vertical dimensions show how the multisport organizations have areas of dominance over the single-sport federations in this system.

The **local organizing committee of the Olympic Games (LOCOG)** has a very special relationship with the IOC, the supreme authority in the Olympic Movement. The LOCOG is given the responsibility of the manifestation of the Games. This manifestation has major financial implications, as well as the traditional and historic. Thus, the LOCOG is very influential for a given Games, but that structure is continually replaced, so the influence is fleeting.

When we speak the term *Olympics*, the connotation is often of the quadrennial event, a carnival of sport, tradition, and the proverbial

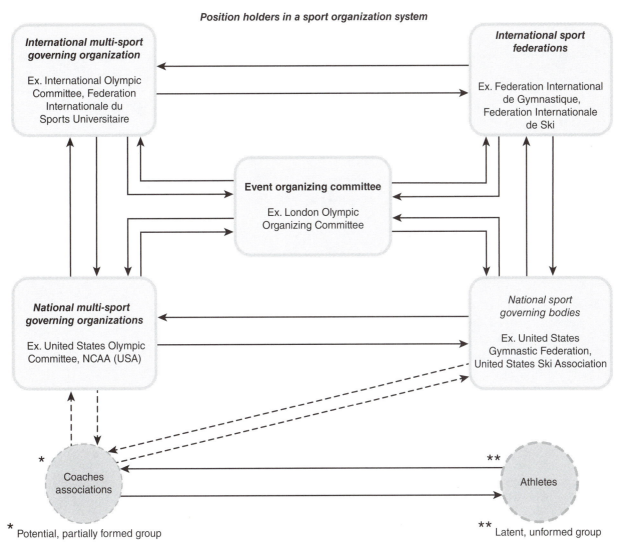

Position holders in a sport organization system

* Potential, partially formed group

** Latent, unformed group

Figure 15.1 The diagram of structural components of sport governance system shows the five basic components.

Reprinted, by permission, from C. Oglesby, 1974, "Social conflict theory and the sport organization system," *Quest* (22): 63-73.

thrill of victory and agony of defeat. Less recognized is the aspect of the Olympic Movement as a global multinational conglomerate. It is worth, and earning regularly, billions of dollars. It is recognized as a permanent observer at the United Nations (just as is the Holy See). The IOC is governed by its charter, a 107-page legal document of some heft. If we think about the globally televised announcement of the site of the next Olympic Games, it is not overstating to say that countries and leaders rise and fall with its operation. In the next section, we will try to navigate some of its intricacies, since I propose that if a woman seeks a powerful position within

the system (or if we seek to systematically bring numbers of women into this system), we need to understand the details. Many must be omitted due to space concerns, but hopefully the most crucial will stand out.

PRINCIPLES AND MISSION OF THE OLYMPIC MOVEMENT

Seven principles are found in a preamble to the Olympic Movement Charter. The principles are part history and part philosophy, and they paint a stirring portrait of the contribution of sport to "harmonious development; a peaceful society concerned with human dignity; a peaceful and better world by educating youth through sport practiced *without discrimination* of any kind" (italics mine; International Olympic Committee, 2014, Charter Fundamental Principles 2 and 4, p. 13). The principles are stated as follows:

Principles of Olympism

1. Olympism is a philosophy of life, exalting and combining in a balanced whole the qualities of body, will and mind. Blending sport with culture and education, Olympism seeks to create a way of life based on the joy of effort, the educational value of good example, social responsibility and respect for universal ethical principles.

2. The goal of Olympism is to place sport at the service of the harmonious development of humankind, with a view to promoting a peaceful society concerned with the preservation of human dignity.

3. The Olympic Movement is the concerted, organised, universal and permanent action, carried out under the supreme authority of the IOC, of all individuals and entities who are inspired by the values of Olympism. It covers the five continents. It reaches its peak with the bringing together of the world's athletes at the great sports festival, the Olympic Games. Its symbol is five interlaced rings.

4. The practice of sport is a human right. Every individual must have the possibility of practising sport, without discrimination of any kind and in the Olympic spirit, which requires mutual understanding with a spirit of friendship, solidarity and fair play.

5. Recognising that sport occurs within the framework of society, sports organisations within the Olympic Movement shall have the rights and obligations of autonomy, which include freely establishing and controlling the rules of sport, determining the structure and governance of their organisations, enjoying the right of elections free from any outside influence and the responsibility for ensuring that principles of good governance be applied.

6. The enjoyment of the rights and freedoms set forth in this Olympic Charter shall be secured without discrimination of any kind, such as race, colour, sex, sexual orientation, language, religion, political or other opinion, national or social origin, property, birth or other status.

7. Belonging to the Olympic Movement requires compliance with the Olympic Charter and recognition by the IOC.

Reprinted, by permission, from the International Olympic Committee, 2014 *Olympic charter.*

The principles outline the nature of the Olympic Movement through its philosophy (Olympism) and its manifestation (the Olympic Games). Chapter one of the Charter contains 16 mission statements that make the principles more concrete and programmatic.

Mission and Role of the IOC

1. to encourage and support the promotion of ethics and good governance in sport as well as education of youth through sport and to dedicate its efforts to ensuring that, in sport, the spirit of fair play prevails and violence is banned;

2. to encourage and support the organisation, development and coordination of sport and sports competitions;

3. to ensure the regular celebration of the Olympic Games;

4. to cooperate with the competent public or private organisations and authorities in the endeavour to place sport at the service of humanity and thereby to promote peace;

5. to take action to strengthen the unity of the Olympic Movement, to protect its independence and to preserve the autonomy of sport;

6. to act against any form of discrimination affecting the Olympic Movement;

7. to encourage and support the promotion of women in sport at all levels and in all structures with a view to implementing the principle of equality of men and women;

8. to protect clean athletes and the integrity of sport by leading the fight against doping and by taking action against all forms of

manipulation of competitions and related corruption;

9. to encourage and support measures relating to the medical care and health of athletes;

10. to oppose any political or commercial abuse of sport and athletes;

11. to encourage and support the efforts of sports organisations and public authorities to provide for the social and professional future of athletes;

12. to encourage and support the development of sport for all;

13. to encourage and support a responsible concern for environmental issues, to promote sustainable development in sport and to require that the Olympic Games are held accordingly;

14. to promote a positive legacy from the Olympic Games to the host cities and host countries;

15. to encourage and support initiatives blending sport with culture and education; and

16. to encourage and support the activities of the International Olympic Academy and other institutions which dedicate themselves to Olympic education.

Reprinted, by permission, from the International Olympic Committee, 2014 *Olympic charter*.

In viewing both the principles and the mission statement, there is no equivocation on the matter of gender equity. Mission 6 is a general no-discrimination statement, while 7 commits the IOC to "encourage and support the promotion of women in sport at all levels and in all structures and the principle of equality of men and women" (International Olympic Committee, 2014, p. 16). An interesting contrast could be suggested between the inaction of the IOC regarding mission 7 and the actions taken for mission 8, which commits the IOC to "fight doping." Where is the equivalent to the highly resourced and publicized World Anti-Doping Agency (WADA) in searching out those who ignore mission 7?

Chapters 1 and 2 of the Charter are explicit about the role of the IOC as the supreme authority of the Olympic Movement, while chapters 3 and 4 describe the interlocking responsibilities and actions of the IFs, NOCs, NGBs, and the LOCOG.

In order to increase the involvement of women in the Olympic system, each of us as advocates, and advocacy groups to which we belong, can benefit from studying the Charter and its operation with an eye to determine which individuals have the résumé to work into appropriate positions within the system. Each unit has a special sphere of authority. Lest there be any confusion, line 1 of chapter 1 states, "The IOC is the supreme authority of the Olympic Movement" (2014, p. 17). We might also say the buck stops here. The IOC is the body responsible for ensuring the Games occur, coordinating and organizing activities, and monitoring and administering the sale of the Games through TV and film rights, sponsorship, and the marketing of properties such as the Olympic rings, flags, stamps, emblem, motto, and torch. The Charter also confirms that the IOC may grant revenues gained back to the IFs, NOCs, and Olympic solidarity funds and to the LOCOG. In the sums of money for each unit we are dealing with, this potential revenue transfer results in enormous pressure to conform to IOC wishes and to keep all relations harmonious with tradition.

Rights and Duties of Other Main Actors in the Movement: IFs, NOCs, and NGBs

In regard to the IFs, their statutes, practices, and activities must be in conformity with the Charter. After those conditions are met, IFs are independent and autonomous in the administration of their sport. IFs are responsible for establishing and enforcing rules of the practice of the sport, developing the sport, establishing eligibility criteria, providing technical direction at the Games, and assisting NOCs and NGBs in solidarity projects.

NGBs act as technical resources for each sport within each country. The carrying out of functions differs from country to country, especially in regard to level of competition for that sport in the country.

NOCs have exclusive powers to represent the country in Olympic Games and at regional, continental, or world multisport competitions patronized by IOC. They are directed to take action against discrimination, but often do not do so in regard to women's leadership issues. Additionally, NOCs have the authority to designate the city that may apply to organize the Olympic Games (e.g., London 2012). Later in this chapter, I encourage women to organize themselves to advocate through the application of the system's own provisions. If a city attempting to win a bid opportunity was a highly appealing candidate, and it concurrently featured certain equity of opportunity regulations within the city government, then those regulations could become an integral feature of the Olympic bid. Opportunities for women and members of minority groups could be moved ahead with such regulations built into the bid. This is an example of using system knowledge and awareness to make a positive overall system change that is specifically mandated by system rules though not supported by ordinary system functioning.

Structural Evolutions, 1974 to 2010

Figure 15.2 illustrates what had and had not changed in the structural frame of the Olympic Charter in ensuing decades. The interlocking and interdependent framework of the IOC, IFs, NOCs, NGBs, and the LOCOG remains in place. This system, once long ago operated by volunteers, has become more massive, more elaborated, and more entrepreneurial. This chapter does not deal with economic factors directly, but one set of figures may aid in increasing a sense of the financial stakes. The IOC website presents a marketing and financial report stating that Olympic Market Revenues from 1993 to 1996 were 2.6 billion USD, while 2009 to 2012 came in above 8 billion USD.

Five specific elaborations (changes) in the governance configuration seem meaningful to point out in understanding structural patterns within this system:

- In the center of the structure remain the Games themselves. The sale of the

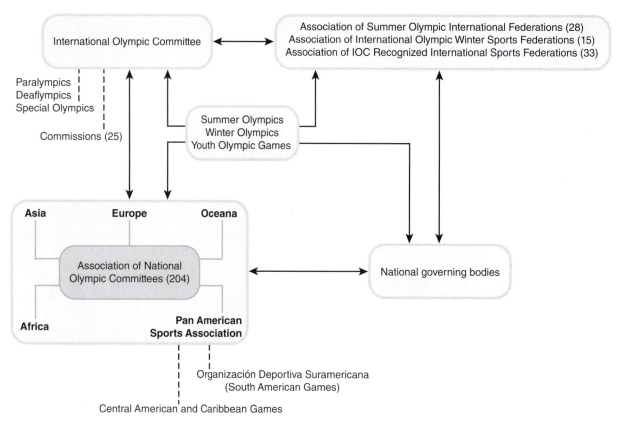

Figure 15.2 Updated structural diagram for a sport organization.

Games (leveraging of the Rings) is the principal revenue property of the IOC. The Games have gotten larger: more sports, events, and athletes. Possibly more importantly, at least one entirely new set of Games has been added: Youth Olympic Games, also to be held in quadrennial years. The first of these Games was Singapore 2010 (Summer), followed by Innsbruck 2012 (Winter), and Nanjing 2014 (Summer), with Lillehammer to come in 2016 (Winter).

- Other sets of multisport Games within the disability communities were pulled (or chose to move) much closer to the IOC. The multisport, international organizations that sponsored the Games were not new, but within the last decade they have moved to a special status with the IOC. The closest partner is the IPC with the Paralympic Games, which are now held directly after the Olympic Games and in the same facilities. Also moving closer is the Deaflympics, governed by the International Committee of Sports for Deaf and the Special Olympics and administered by Special Olympics International. These elaborations all involve greater financial revenues and expenses, as well as significant growth in staffing, technical leaderships, and policy.

- Additions have been made to the numbers of commissions that work with staff to guide and operate these massive enterprises. There are now 25 commissions. Women comprise only 17 percent of these bodies. The IOC can rightly say there are more women than ever before, but simple math shows that this is a weak claim. The great majority of the commissions have, at best, one woman among the group.

- One of the two more significant elaborations is in the International Federation category. At the time of the initial analysis, the IFs dealt formally as single units with the IOC. The power for each to maximize standing and support with IOC was limited. In the intervening years, the IFs have banded into associa-

tions of federations, recognized as such by the IOC. The Association of Summer Olympic International Federations has 28 members, the Association of International Olympic Winter Sports Federations has 15, and the Association of Recognized International Sports Federations has 33. These latter are sport federations waiting in the wings for Olympic program slots, and they include sports such as netball, cricket, motorcycle, dance, bowling, and bridge. At times, when the IFs are able to speak with one voice, they will now be much more likely to be heard.

- The last elaboration is found in the NOC categories. My speculation is that they also decided it was advantageous to increase power of their voices by speaking together. The NOCs have grouped into regional bodies to administer their own regional Games, and general affairs, in a more coordinated fashion. Together, all five of the regional associations are called the Association of National Olympic Committees. The regional body for the United States is the Pan American Sports Organization, with the Pan American Games also on the quadrennial schedule. Similar additions in sports, events, athletes, and grandeur have occurred with regional Games as with the Olympic Games. The bid process, the staff, the media, and the leadership have all increased exponentially, except for women's representation. In data from all sources, including the IOCs own commissioned research, the inclusion of women percentages for NOCs and the regional bodies is the lowest of all the structure categories.

The first takeaway from all of this is that the Olympic Games are the visible manifestation of the Olympic Movement. Each set of Games happens every four years. The public focus is primarily on athletic performances, and this is where female athletes maximize visibility. In London in 2012, women composed about 48 percent of the performances. The media sound bites all emphasized how close the Olympic

All of the pomp and circumstance of the Olympic Games can dazzle viewers without showing the inequality of the structure beneath.

Movement is to equity. Just underneath the surface, however, is the day-to-day reality of the work of the Movement. From the percentages of female coaches, officials, press, and the Olympic Family members in NOCs, NGBs, IF, LOCOG, and IOC, women stand around 20 percent inclusion at best. What would the Olympic Movement look like if women composed 48 percent in all categories? Why are women not there?

The second takeaway is that the process of winning positions in this massive system is, for now, a one-on-one struggle that can be achieved with difficulty, patience, and perseverance through a clear knowledge of system operation, obstacles, and potential allies. What is also needed is a clear knowledge of the legal and policy basis for women's inclusions. We close out the chapter with this last area of awareness building.

WOMEN'S PROGRESSING INFLUENCE OUTSIDE AND INSIDE SPORT

James F. Byrnes, former U.S. Secretary of State, famously said, "For men, power is never volun-tarily surrendered. It must be taken from them" (Miner & Rawson, 2006, p. 535). This maxim can certainly be applied to the IOC in regards to ceding space to women in the governance of sport. The pattern of begrudging inclusion can be seen even in the 1920s. The Olympic Games had no women's track and field competition at that time, yet there were women ready and willing to compete. A French woman, Alice Milliat, organized a women's sport federation that held their own event. Initially called the Women's Olympic Games, the first edition was held in Paris in 1922. There were 20,000 spectators. The second event in Sweden had a longer program and more spectators. By this time, the IOC was disturbed, and forced them to drop the word *Olympic* from the title. The 1930 Women's Games in Prague drew 200 competi-tors from 17 countries and 15,000 spectators. In order to regain control, the IOC struck an agreement with female leaders to incorporate a standard set of events for women in the Olym-pic program. The women's federation had held out for all of their more than 20 events to be moved over to the Olympic program, but in the end only 5 were included: 100- and 800-meter run, high jump, discus, and the 400-meter relay (Oglesby et al., 1998). It was a stirring example of the bravery of the women involved and the kind of tactics effective and necessary for opening space for women (Leigh & Bonin, 1977).

Wilma Scott Heide (second president of the National Organization of Women) described that progress for women's rights has never been accomplished by virtue of the passage of time alone (Oglesby, 1978). Progress must be made through advocacy such as the formation of Milliat's Federation. In the very recent past, this truth was demonstrated anew by the multipronged actions of the women's ski jumpers. The fight for inclusion in the Games went on for years, including a failed lawsuit in Vancouver (2010 Games) and a media blitz led by Women's Ski Jumping USA and Deedee Corradini, a former mayor of Salt Lake City. Corradini became engaged in this effort due to her observations at the Salt Lake City Olympic Games in 2002. The women who jumped in Sochi in 2014 were not allowed to compete in Nordic combined team events or jump on the big hill. Like Milliat, the jumpers took half a loaf for now.

Why are we seeing now certain advances for women, particularly in the athlete ranks? It is my thesis that the IOC has a large stake in the power politics game of recognition as a cultural contributor (and not a reactionary organization) on the world's widest stage: the United Nations.

Since the early 1990s, the women's sport international advocacy community had shown significant capacity to build bridges to the UN system women's units: **Convention on the Elimination of Discrimination Against Women**, the **Division for the Advancement of Women**, and the **Commission on the Status of Women**. Additionally, these same women's sport groups had shown capacity to build their own international networks. Because this work is largely unknown, especially in the United States, let me describe briefly how women's sport advocacy units operating inside and outside of sport were placing women's role in sport in a prominent public spotlight in the UN, with little contribution or role for the Olympic Movement until the very recent past.

Groups Outside of Sport

In 1995, the fourth World Congress on Women was held in Beijing, China. The first three Congresses—Mexico City 1975, Copenhagen 1980, and Nairobi 1985—had set powerful women's government and nongovernmental partnerships in motion, and the fourth Congress was a culmination event. The **Beijing Platform for Action** was a landmark document, eventually ratified by almost all UN-member countries. It was the first UN document to specifically single out contributions that women's sport could make in girls' and women's health and education and to address concerns of the girl child (UNDAW, 2008).

Five years later in 2000, sport and physical education for girls and women also appeared in specific text of the Beijing +5 document. The collaborations with the women's UN agencies came to fruition with the 2008 publication by the UN Division for the Advancement of Women of a monograph in its series: *Women Watch 2000: Women, Gender Equality and Sport*. This monograph was distributed through all usual UN sources, electronic and hard copy, in five languages. These advances—1995, 2000, and 2008—were all influenced and created by the women's sport advocacy groups, especially WSI, the Women's Sports Foundation USA, and the **International Working Group on Women and Sport (IWG)**. The IOC had no direct influence in these advances.

Groups Inside of Sport

During this time period, these same women's sport advocacy groups were mounting their own effective campaigns within sport. In 1994, the first Women's World Conference on Sport was held in Brighton, England. Two hundred eighty delegates participated, and the main outcome was a formal declaration on women's sport and the identification of a collaborative body (the IWG) that had the responsibility of gaining signatures (potential power) and monitoring and implementing the influence of the declaration.

Every four years since that time, conferences have been held with various outcomes leading to the expansion of the work and implementation of the declaration: Namibia 1998, Montreal

2002, Kumamoto 2006, Sydney 2010, and Helsinki 2014.

Today the Brighton Declaration remains a powerful document signed by 419 of the world's most important sports organizations, including the IOC, the IPC, WADA, Commonwealth Games Federation and the Commonwealth Sport Ministers, 20 International Sport Federations, and 71 National Olympic Committees, to name but a few. Signing the document represents a significant promise to the world's women. The ten areas covered are as follows (International Working Group on Women and Sport, 1994):

1. General equity in sport programs for men and women
2. Equity in facilities
3. Equity in school and junior sport
4. Development programs for women's sport
5. Equity in high-performance sport
6. Leadership opportunities
7. Equity in education, training, and development in all areas
8. Equity in sport information and media
9. Equity in resources and budgets
10. Extensive domestic and international cooperation to address barriers

As the rest of the chapter makes clear, these promises have been, for the most part, unmet. The various units of the Olympic Family have been persuaded to sign and subscribe to this foundation document for their own reason. Over the course of the nearly two decades described here, there have been many reasons for the IOC to move to retake the perceived leadership of the international governance frameworks in

My trainers taught me to believe in myself . . . . I was inspired and learned determination and discipline. . . . Sport allows you to get to know yourself.

Nawal El Moutawakel, first Olympic Gold medalist from Morocco, 1984 Olympic Games

regard to women's issues. Extensive and damaging charges have been leveled toward the IOC and the Movement that weaken the claims of the Olympism philosophy. It is well beyond the focus of this chapter to explore these many charges, such as bid city scandals and bribery, inability to control performance-enhancing drugs, heavy debt loads paid by taxpayers who could not then afford tickets to see events, Olympic venues trumping construction and environmental community and national needs, and the commodification of athletes and sports (see Jennings, 1996; Lenskyj, 2000). My point here is that the IOC has deep motivations for using new collaborative opportunities with the international UN, development, and philanthropic communities to deflect criticism over its practices and to enhance the image of the cultural contributions of the Movement in many areas, including gender justice.

The UN development agencies cannot fund the world's needed projects, and thus depend on effective and creative partnerships with financially endowed entities. The IOC has increasingly been successful at playing a role in terms of this need. In 2002, then Secretary General Kofi Annan created the UN Interagency Task Force on Sport for Development and Peace. From 2004 to 2008, the task force developed a report outlining sport development opportunities. In December 2008, General Assembly Resolution 63/135 was passed with the title Sport as a Means for Promoting Education, Healthy Development and Peace (United Nations, 2008).

The resolution also created a special advisor for sport, development, and peace who reports to the secretary general. In 2009, the IOC was granted observer status at the UN, primarily on the basis of its contributions to the UN's millennium development goals. A few of these refer directly to women's and children's health, and all of them apply generally to women's development. The IOC has a strong vested interest in its *appearance* as a gender-equitable organization and movement. It is well past the time when women and like-minded men should take steps to call out the Movement to more fully become what it appears to be.

Learning Aids

Summary

More than 20 years ago Dr. Rosabeth Kanter published a great deal of research on gender dynamics in groups, especially in the business world. Her research showed how the entry of one "other" (whom she dubbed the *O*) into an otherwise all-dominant group (the *X*s) had far-reaching consequences for all members. The typical discourse did not change, however, until a more balanced tipping point was reached. This chapter shows how far the global sport governance system is from gender balance in operation and representation. It identifies strategies in which organizing for political pressure and knowledge of system inner workings can lead to transformative change.

Discussion Questions

1. The chapter began with the observation that the more things change, the more things stay the same. One of the ways that change is being fostered—n terms of increasing the representation of women in leadership positions with national sport governing bodies, international federations, and national Olympic committees—is through the compilation of information on the Sydney Scoreboard site. How would you design a social media campaign that promoted that site and made that information available to journalists, legislators and policy makers, sport administrators, and athletes?

2. Earlier in the chapter you were introduced to the idea that cultural and religious traditions form obstacles in sport development work with girls. Compare and contrast two religious traditions and the way in which sport is thought of within those traditions. In your comparison, do you find evidence to support the conclusion that religious traditions form obstacles to sport development for girls? If so, in what ways?

3. Watch one of these short films and write a blog post reflecting on key points: *Sporting Sisters: Stories of Muslim Women in Sport* (www.youtube.com/watch?v=qOC7qfv90FE) or *Islam, Women, and Sport* (https://vimeo.com/108779707).

Learning Exercise

Identify a sport organization or group that you know well through affiliation or close observation. Describe where this group would fit in the sport governance system. As an example, you might select a local soccer team that has a link to USA Soccer (in turn affiliated with FIFA, the international federation for the sport). Identify how an athlete or coach or official might move up to a higher status in the organizational framework. Think about things like the following:

- Who is benefitted by such an advance and who might lose in some way?
- What would a new leader want to change or enhance about the operation of the team or club?
- Who, or what forces, might oppose any changes or new ways of operation, especially if the changes enhanced girls' or women's situations?
- How can the obstacles be removed or neutralized?

Glossary

American Alliance for Health, Physical Education, Recreation and Dance—
Umbrella of five distinct but related organizations devoted to meeting the needs of professional members serving in these fields. One of the organizations, National Association of Girls and Women's in Sport, focuses on women's issues. In 2013, the organization became the Society of Health and Physical Educators (SHAPE America).

Beijing Platform for Action—Document produced for the fourth World Conference on Women; also accepted by virtually all countries that are UN members.

Commission on the Status of Women—Appointed body of UN members meeting annually to review the status and progress of women's goals.

Convention on the Elimination of Discrimination Against Women—Treaty signed by virtually all UN member states; seeks to end all forms of discrimination.

Division for the Advancement of Women—Staffed unit of UN; in 2010, became UN Women.

International Federations (IFs)—Highest authority in regard to each sport discipline.

International Olympic Committee (IOC)—Supreme authority of the Movement, including Olympism (guiding philosophy of balanced and harmonious living) and the Olympic Games.

International Paralympic Committee (IPC)—Organizes Paralympic Games.

International Working Group on Women and Sport (IWG)—Global network of women's sport advocates whose aim is to develop a sporting culture that enables and values the full involvement of women in every aspect of sport.

local organizing committee of the Olympic Games (LOCOG)—Administers the Olympic Games in each host city.

national governing bodies (NGBs)—Highest authority in regard to each sport in each country.

national Olympic committee (NOCs)—Organization that represents the Movement and IOC country.

patriarchal religious tradition—The teaching of the world's major religions are patriarchal (men primarily occupy positions of power); founders and early leaders of Judaism, Christianity, Islam, Buddhism, and Chinese Philosophy are all men, and their influence has dominated belief and practice.

Quran—Central religious text of Islam; *Koran* is the anglicized form of the word.

second-wave feminism—The so-called first wave was the suffrage movement occurring in the late 19th and early 20th centuries; the second wave emerged in the 1960s and 1970s with a broader focus on liberation in roles relating to work, family, and sexuality.

Women Sport International (WSI)—Member organization devoted to evidence-based advocacy for girls and women's sport.

Epilogue

Glimpsing the Future for Girls and Women in Sport

Ellen J. Staurowsky, EdD, Drexel University

> *Our worth has nothing to do with what the world might say. We must each find our own voice, decide our own value, and then announce it to the world with all the pride and joy that is our birthright as members of the human race.*
>
> **Michelle Obama, first lady of the United States**

There is never a final chapter for girls and women in sport. The story unfolds generation to generation, written and rewritten by a cast of determined athletes, coaches, educators, executives, fans, journalists, parents, public policy makers, scientists, and visionaries. The inheritance that is left for girls and women who aspire to athletic greatness is rich with the accomplishments and sacrifices of those who came before. And the future shines bright with some possibilities envisioned long ago and other possibilities that have yet to be imagined.

In the vibrant present, there has never been a better time for girls and women in sport. In the vast multitude of opportunities in sport culture, girls and women have license to give expression to their passion and love of sport and to experience the joy of living life to the fullest, the thrill of rising to the occasion and overcoming, the comfort of teammates and family, the adulation that comes from competing with dignity and skill, and the livelihood that can be made by working in the sport industry.

The 21st century story of girls and women in sport is one of triumph, a resounding response that lays to rest a series of misconceptions about female inferiority that lasted for hundreds of years. Female athletes are stronger than they have ever been, and female fans are more numerous than ever before. The presence of female athleticism within the culture is more pronounced now than at any other time in history.

As the landscape of sport becomes more and more populated with a female presence, it tests the strength of the system of sex segregation that has been a defining aspect of sport participation for male and female athletes. Will the system hold the same power in this new century to shape how girls and women compete as it did in the previous one, or will there be greater emphasis on female and male athletes competing with and against each other on equal terms? While indicators suggest that given biological differences, separating girls from boys and men from women in the athletic realm is advisable, practical, and necessary, disintegrating gender boundaries and the fluidity of gender in its various manifestations argue for inclusive forms of sport.

What will be the most pressing questions to be confronted in order for girls and women to become fully enfranchised within the sport industry? What will it take for a woman to become commissioner of the NFL or MLB? How will sports broadcasting affect future generations of female athletes and viewers as the industry learns how to cover women's sport in respectful ways? Has research on the effects of high-level sport training on women focused on the right things in terms of the female athlete triad, female athlete susceptibility to knee injuries, and female athlete response to concussion? Will inherent sexism in sport become a thing of

> *I know women's sports will have made it when we start talking about "playing like a girl" and it's a compliment.*
>
> **Abby Wambach, U.S. women's national soccer team**

the past, so much so that there will be no need for Title IX? Or will the long reach of history continue to reinforce sexist ideologies, requiring ongoing vigilance in terms of Title IX? Will the phobias around sexual identity and orientation continue to lose their power to limit possibilities for the entire sport enterprise? Will intersections of race, gender, political ideology, religious background, ability, and sport become more fully recognized and understood to ensure that girls and women everywhere have equitable access to participate on their own terms?

Will the paradoxes that have been a hallmark of girls' and women's sport endure? Will women continue on a path of becoming stronger and more in control of their own lives and yet still experience the brutality of sexual violence in and outside of sport settings? Will the value systems that form the core of sport systems, which valorize the qualities of raw strength, speed, and size, traditionally thought of as

History, despite its wrenching pain, cannot be unlived but if faced with courage, need not be lived again.

Poet Maya Angelou

male, be reoriented to include a reverence for the feminine—balance, flexibility, and grace? Through advances in technology, will cyborg athletes render discussions about gender wholly irrelevant in a futuristic sport world?

As the next chapter awaits for girls and women, the words of feminist sport scholars Ellen Gerber, Jan Felshin, Pearl Berlin, and Wyneen Wyrick resonate: "What happens to women in sport will depend on the willingness of all those who have an interest in and concern for the American sportswoman to join in a unified, cooperative, intense effort on her behalf" (1974, p. 537).

References

Preface

Spence, B. (2009). Jesse Owens: One of the greatest athletes of all time. *Bleacher Report.* Retrieved from http://bleacherreport.com/articles/233873-jessie-owens-one-of-the-greatest-athletes-of-all-time

Introduction

Bem, S.L. (1993). *The lenses of gender: Transforming the debate on sexual inequality.* New Haven, CT: Yale University Press.

Cahn, S.K. (1994). *Coming on strong: Gender and sexuality in twentieth-century women's sport.* New York, NY: The Free Press.

Chalk, H.M., Miller, S.E., Roach, M.E., & Schultheis, K.S. (2013). Predictors of obligatory exercise among undergraduates: Differential implications for counseling college men and women. *Journal of College Counseling, 16*(2), 102-114.

Daniels, D.B. (2009). *Polygendered and ponytailed: The dilemma of femininity and the female athlete.* Toronto, Ontario, Canada: Women's Press.

Daniels, E. (2012). Sexy versus strong: What girls and women think of female athletes. *Journal of Applied Developmental Psychology, 33*(2), 79-90.

Eime, R.M., Harvey, J.T., Craike, M.J., Symons, C.M., & Payne, W.R. (2013). Family support and ease of access link socio-economic status and sports club membership in adolescent girls: A mediation study. *International Journal of Behavioral Nutrition and Physical Activity, 10*(1), 50-61.

Epstein, D. (2014, February 7). How much do sex differences matter in sports? *Washington Post.* Retrieved from www.washingtonpost.com/opinions/how-much-do-sex-differences-matter-in-sports/2014/02/07/563b86a4-8ed9-11e3-b227-12a45d109e03_story.html

Erskine, J. (Director/Writer), & Gregory, V. (Producer). (2013). *American masters: Billie Jean King* [Motion picture]. United Kingdom: Goldcrest Films and WNET.

Fausto-Sterling, A. (1993). The five sexes: Why male and female are not enough. *The Sciences, 33*(3), 20-25.

Henson, S. (2012, February 15). What makes a nightmare sports parent—and what makes a great one. *The Post Game. Yahoo Sports.* Retrieved from www.thepostgame.com/blog/more-family-fun/201202/what-makes-nightmare-sports-parent

Kane, M.J. (2013). The better sports women get, the more the media ignore them. *Communication & Sport, 1*(3), 231-236.

Knight, J.L., & Guiliano, T.A. (2003). Blood, sweat, and jeers: The impact of the media's heterosexist portrayals on perceptions of male and female athletes. *Journal of Sport Behavior, 26*(3), 272-284.

McArdle, W.D., Katch, F.I., & Katch, V.L. (2007). *Exercise physiology: Energy, nutrition, and human performance* (6th ed.). Baltimore, MD: Lippincott, Williams, and Wilkins.

Messner, M.A. (2002). *Taking the field: Women, men, and sports.* Minneapolis, MN: The University of Minnesota Press.

Munkwitz, E. (2012). Vixens of venery: Women, sport, and fox-hunting in Britain, 1860-1914. *Critical Survey, 24*(1), 74-87.

Rozsak, T. (1999). *The gendered atom: Reflections on the sexual psychology of science.* Berkeley, CA: Conari Press.

Sokolove, M.Y. (2008). *Warrior girls: Protecting our daughters against the injury epidemic in women's sports.* New York, NY: Simon and Schuster.

Stein, A. (Producer). (1987). *Shooting stars.* Montreal, Quebec, Canada: National Film Board of Canada. Retrieved from www.nfb.ca/film/shooting_stars

Terman, L.M., & Miles, C.C. (1936). *Sex and personality: Studies in masculinity and femininity.* New York, NY: McGraw-Hill.

Volner, D. (2014). ESPN's Beth Mowins reflects on growth of softball as WCWS finals begin. *ESPN Front Row.* Retrieved from www.espnfrontrow.com/2014/06/espns-beth-mowins-reflects-on-growth-of-softball-as-wcws-finals-begin

Chapter 1

Baker, J. (2013). *Amelia Bloomer and dress reform, or: How women came to wear pants.* Seattle, WA: Amazon Digital.

Cox, L. (2014, June 27). Alysia Montano completes 800 meter race while 8 months pregnant. *Hollywoodlife.com.* Retrieved from http://hollywoodlife.com/2014/06/27/alysia-montano-completes-800-meter-race-while-8-months-pregnant

Czajka, C. (n.d.). Frontier life: Homestead history. *PBS.org.* Retrieved from www.pbs.org/wnet/frontierhouse/frontierlife/essay10.html

Davis, L. (2014, April 17). No, corsets did not destroy the health of Victorian women. *IO9.com.* Retrieved from http://io9.com/no-corsets-did-not-destroy-the-health-of-victorian-wom-1545644060

Fee, E., & Brown, T.M. (2003). Bicycling for pleasure and power. *American Journal of Public Health, 93*(9), 1409.

Gerber, E., Felshin, J., Berlin, P., & Wyrick, W. (1974). *The American woman in sport.* Boston, MA: Addison-Wesley.

Gilman, S.L., King, H., Porter, R., Rousseau, G.S., & Showalter, E. (1993). *Hysteria beyond Freud.* Oakland: University of California Press.

Hoffman, A., Jette, S., & Vertinsky, P. (2009). "Skierinas" in the Olympics: Gender justice and gender politics at the local, national and international level over the challenge of women's ski jumping. *Olympika: The International Journal of Olympic Studies, 18,* 25-50.

Ikard, R.W. (2005). *Just for fun: The story of AAU women's basketball.* Little Rock: University of Arkansas Press.

Kimmel, M. (2012). *The history of men: Essays on the history of American and British masculinities.* Ithaca, NY: SUNY Press.

Lannin, J. (2000). *A history of basketball for girls and women: From bloomers to big leagues.* Minneapolis, MN: Lerner.

Lebing, W. (1987, February 9). The way it was when women were under wraps. *Sports Illustrated.* Retrieved from www.si.com/vault/1987/02/09/114853/the-way-it-was-when-women-were-under-wraps

Ley, T. (2014, August 13). *Fox & Friends* host has annoying question for Mo'ne Davis. *Deadspin.* Retrieved from http://deadspin.com/fox-friends-host-has-annoying-question-for-mone-davis-1621124476

Mann, B. (2005, November 14). Women lobby for Olympic ski jumping event. *National Public Radio.* Retrieved from www.npr.org/templates/story/story.php?storyId=5011904

Marks, P. (1990). *Bicycles, bangs, and bloomers: The New Woman in the popular press.* Lexington: University of Kentucky Press.

Melnick, R. (2007). *Senda Berenson: The unlikely founder of women's basketball.* Amherst: University of Massachusetts Press.

Ohikaure, J. (2013, July 29). How Sheryl Swoopes' pregnancy changed professional sports forever. *The Atlantic.* Retrieved from www.theatlantic.com/sexes/archive/2013/07/how-sheryl-swoopess-pregnancy-changed-professional-sports-forever/278168

Palmer, G. (1929). *Baseball for girls and women.* New York, NY: A.S. Barnes and Company.

Peavy, L., & Smith, U. (2008). *Full court quest: The girls from Fort Shaw Indian School, basketball champions of the world.* Norman: University of Oklahoma Press.

Pickup, O. (2012, July 25). London 2012 Olympics: Pregnant Malaysian shooter Nur Suryani Mohamad Taibi aiming for historic gold. *Telegraph.co.uk.* Retrieved from www.telegraph.co.uk/sport/olympics/news/9426433/London-2012-Olympics-pregnant-Malaysian-shooter-Nur-Suryani-Mohamad-Taibi-aiming-for-historic-gold.html

Popova, M. (n.d.). A list of don'ts for women on bicycles circa 1895. *Brain Pickings.* Retrieved from www.brainpickings.org/2012/01/03/donts-for-women-on-bicycles-1895

Sack, A., & Staurowsky, E.J. (1998).*College athletes for hire: The evolution and legacy of the NCAA amateur myth.* Westport, CT: Praeger Press.

Seelye, L.C. (1875). *Inauguration of Rev. L. Clarke Seelye as president of Smith College.* Pamphlet. Springfield, MA: Clark W. Bryan.

Smith-Rosenberg, C. (1972). The hysterical woman: Sex roles and role conflict in nineteenth century America. *Social Research, 39,* 562-583.

Steele, V. (2001). *The corset: A cultural history.* New Haven, CT: Yale University Press.

Travers, A. (2011). Women's ski jumping, the 2010 Olympic Games, and the deafening silence of sex segregation, whiteness, and wealth. *Journal of Sport and Social Issues, 35,*126-144.

Veblen, T. (1899). *The theory of the leisure class: An economic study of institutions.* New York, NY: MacMillan.

Wood, A.D. (1973). "The fashionable diseases": Woman's complaints and their treatment in nineteenth-century America. *The Journal of Interdisciplinary History, 4*(1), 25-52.

Chapter 2

Ali, R. (2010, April 20). *Intercollegiate athletics policy clarification: The three-part test—Part three.* U.S. Department of Education Office for Civil Rights. Retrieved from www2.ed.gov/print/about/offices/list/ocr/letters/colleague-20100420.html

Ali, R. (2011, December 2). *Dear colleague letter.* U.S. Department of Education Office for Civil Rights. Retrieved from www2.ed.gov/about/offices/list/ocr/letters/colleague-201111.html

American Bar Association. (2013). *Enrollment and degrees awarded: 1963-2012 academic years.* Washington, DC: American Bar Association.

Anderson, P. (2012). Title IX at forty: An introduction and historical review of forty legal developments that shaped gender equity law. *Marquette Sports Law Review, 22*(2), 325-391.

Anderson, P., & Osborne, B. (2008). Report: A historical review of Title IX litigation. *Journal of Legal Aspects of Sport, 127,* 127-168.

Bayh, B. (1971). Statement of Senator Birch Bayh. *Congressional Record.*

Bayh, B. (1972). Statement of Senator Birch Bayh outlining the sex discriminatory barriers to women encountered in higher education. *118 Congressional Record* 5804.

Biediger v. Quinnipiac University. (2013, March). Retrieved from www.nacua.org/documents/Biediger_v_QuinnipiacU_030413.pdf

Blumenthal, K. (2005). *Let me play: The story of Title IX.* New York, NY: Simon & Schuster.

Blumenthal, K. (2012, June 22). The truth about Title IX. *The Daily Beast/Newsweek.* Retrieved from www.thedailybeast.com/articles/2012/06/22/the-truth-about-title-ix.html

Bonnette, V.M. (2004). *Title IX and intercollegiate athletics: How it all works—In plain English.* San Diego, CA: Good Sports.

Brake, D., & Catlin, E. (1996). The path of most resistance: The long road toward gender equity in intercollegiate athletics. *Duke Journal of Gender, Law, & Policy, 51*(3), 5-25.

Bryant, A. (2012, June 27). Title IX at 40: Most schools aren't in compliance. *The Christian Science Monitor.* Retrieved from www.csmonitor.com/Commentary/Opinion/2012/0627/Title-IX-at-40-Most-schools-still-aren-t-in-compliance

Buzuvis, E. (2012, June 25). Celebrating Title IX, the little statute that could. *Education News.* Retrieved from www.educationnews.org/education-policy-and-politics/celebrating-title-ix-the-little-statute-that-could

Cantu, N. (1996). *Clarification of intercollegiate athletics policy guidance: The three-part test.* U.S. Department of Education Office for Civil Rights. Retrieved from www2.ed.gov/about/offices/list/ocr/docs/clarific.html

Cantu, N. (1998). Clarification regarding discrimination in the awarding of athletic scholarships in intercollegiate athletic programs. U.S. Department of Education Office for Civil Rights. Retrieved from www2.ed.gov/about/offices/list/ocr/docs/bowlgrn.html

Carpenter, L.J., & Acosta, R.V. (2005). *Title IX.* Champaign, IL: Human Kinetics.

Cohen, D. (2005). Gender equity in intercollegiate athletics: Where does Pennsylvania stand? *Women's Law Project.* Retrieved August 6, 2010, from www.womenslawproject.org/reports/GenderEquitySum.pdf

Golden, S. (2011). Getting in the game [Review of the book *Getting in the game: Title IX and the women's sports revolution,* by D.L. Brake]. *Inside Higher Education.* Retrieved from www.insidehighered.com/news/2011/01/28/new_book_on_title_ix_and_its_impact_on_college_sports

Hogshead-Makar, N. (2015, April). Highlighted projects . . . get involved! *Champion Women Newsletter. Champion Women Newsletter.*

Hosick, M.B. (2007, May 21). A force for equality. *NCAA News.* Retrieved from http://fs.ncaa.org/Docs/NCAANewsArchive/2007/Association-wide/a%2Bforce%2Bfor%2Bequity%2B-%2B05-21-07%2Bncaa%2Bnews.html

Hosick, M.B. (2010, April 20). OCR rescinds 2005 Title IX clarification. *NCAA News.* Retrieved from http://fs.ncaa.org/Docs/NCAANewsArchive/2010/aWide/ocr_rescinds_2005_title_ix_clarification.html

Irick, E. (2014). *Student-athlete participation 1981-1982–2013-14: NCAA sports sponsorship and participation rates report.* National Collegiate Athletic Association. Retrieved from www.ncaapublications.com/productdownloads/PR1314.pdf

Lhamon, C.E. (2015). *Protecting civil rights, advancing equity: Report to the President and Secretary of Education.* U.S. Department of Education Office for Civil Rights. Retrieved from www2.ed.gov/about/reports/annual/ocr/report-to-president-and-secretary-of-education-2013-14.pdf

Matthews, M., & McCune, S. (1975). *Title IX grievance procedures: An introductory manual.* Office of Education (Department of Health, Education, & Welfare). Retrieved from www.eric.ed.gov/PDFS/ED135296.pdf

Mellman Group. (2007, June 14). Memorandum written to "Interested Parties" regarding survey of attitudes towards Title IX. Retrieved September 1, 2007, from www.nwlc.org/details.cfmPid=3062&section=athletics

Meyer, R., & Nahra, J. (2012). Biediger v. Quinnipiac: What is a sport under Title IX? *Law 360.* Retrieved from www.law360.com/articles/384625/biediger-v-quinnipiac-what-is-a-sport-under-title-ix

Monroe, S. (2007, June 22). *35th anniversary of Title IX.* U.S. Department of Education Office for Civil Rights. Retrieved from www2.ed.gov/about/offices/list/ocr/letters/colleague-20070622.html

Monroe, S. (2008, September). *Clarification letter: How to determine which activities can be counted for the purpose of Title IX compliance.* U.S. Department of Education Office for Civil Rights. Retrieved from www2.ed.gov/about/offices/list/ocr/letters/colleague-20080917.pdf

Nash, M.A., Klein, S.S., & Bitters, B. (2007). The role of government in advancing gender equity in education. In S. Klein (Ed.), *Handbook for achieving gender equity through education* (pp. 63-101). Mahwah, NJ: Lawrence Erlbaum Associates.

National Center for Education Statistics (NCES). (2013). *Fact facts: Enrollment trends.* Retrieved from https://nces.ed.gov/fastfacts/display.asp?id=65

National Center for Educational Statistics (NCES). (2014). Bachelor's, master's, and doctor's degrees conferred by post-secondary institutions. *Digest of Education Statistics.* Retrieved from https://nces.ed.gov/programs/digest/d14/tables/dt14_318.30.asp

National Center for Education Statistics (NCES). (2015). *Public school enrollment.* Retrieved from http://nces.ed.gov/programs/coe/indicator_cga.asp

National Federation of State High School Associations (NFHS). (2014, October 30). High school participation increases for 25th consecutive year. *NFHSnews.com.* Retrieved from www.nfhs.org/articles/high-school-participation-increases-for-25th-consecutive-year

National Women's Law Center. (2012). *Title IX: 40 years and counting.* Retrieved from www.nwlc.org/sites/default/files/pdfs/nwlcathletics_titleixfactsheet.pdf

National Women's Law Center, & Piper, D.L.A. (2007). *Breaking down barriers: A legal guide to Title IX and athletic opportunities.* National Women's Law Center. Retrieved from www.nwlc.org/sites/default/files/pdfs/breaking_down_barriers_2007.pdf

NCWGE. (2007). Title IX timeline: Title IX at 35. Retrieved from www.ncwge.org/PDF/Title%20IX%20Timeline.pdf

New York Times. (2011, April 25). New York Times/CBS News Poll: Title IX. Retrieved from www.nytimes.com/interactive/2011/04/26/sports/26-poll-titleIX.html?ref=sports

Obama, B. (2012, June 23). Op-ed by President Obama: President Obama reflects on the impact of Title IX [Press release]. Retrieved from www.whitehouse.gov/the-press-office/2012/06/23/op-ed-president-obama-president-obama-reflects-impact-title-ix

Office of Civil Rights, U.S. Department of Education. (1979, December 11). A policy interpretation: Title IX and Intercollegiate Athletics. *Federal Register, 44*(239). Retrieved from www2.ed.gov/about/offices/list/ocr/docs/t9interp.html

Pemberton, C. (2012). More of the same—Enough already! *Marquette Sports Law Review: Title IX 40 Year Anniversary Symposium, 22*(2), 597-609.

Reynolds, G. (2003). *Further clarification of intercollegiate athletics policy guidance regarding Title IX compliance.* U.S. Department of Education Office for Civil Rights. Retrieved from www2.ed.gov/about/offices/list/ocr/title9guidanceFinal.html

Ruth, J.E. (2008). Patsy T. Mink papers at the Library of Congress. *The Library of Congress Manuscripts Reading Room.* Retrieved from www.loc.gov/rr/mss/mink/mink-about.html

Sandler, B. (1997, Spring). "Too strong for a woman"—The five words that created Title IX. *About Women on Campus* [former newsletter for National Association for Women in Education].

Sandler, B. (2002). How we got it and what a difference it made. *Cleveland State Law Review, 55,* 473-479.

Save Title IX. (2006, March). Title IX clarification: What's at stake? Save Title IX Coalition. Retrieved from www.titleix.info/Repository/Files/SaveTitleIXFactSheet.pdf

Simpson, J. (2012, June 11). How Title IX sneakily revolutionized women's sports. *The Atlantic.* Retrieved from www.theatlantic.com/entertainment/archive/2012/06/how-title-ix-sneakily-revolutionized-womens-sports/258708

Staurowsky, E.J., with Lawrence, H., Paule, A., & Reese, J. (2007). Travelers on the Title IX compliance highway: How are Ohio's colleges and universities faring. *Women in Sport and Physical Activity Journal, 16,* 46-83.

Staurowsky, E.J., & Weight, E.A. (2011). Title IX Literacy: What coaches don't know and need to find out. *The Journal of Intercollegiate Sport, 4*(2), 190-209.

Staurowsky, E.J., & Weight, E.A. (2013). Discovering dysfunction in Title IX implementation: NCAA administrator literacy, responsibility and fear. *Journal of Sport Administration and Supervision, 5*(1), 1-33.

Tolchin, S. (1976). *Women in Congress.* Washington, DC: Government Printing Office.

Wang, F. (2014, November 24). Hawaii's Patsy Mink honored with Presidential Medal of Freedom. *NBC News.com.* Retrieved from www.nbcnews.com/news/asian-america/hawaiis-patsy-mink-honored-presidential-medal-freedom-n248951

Ware, S. (2011). *Title IX: A brief history with documents* (The Bedford Series in History and Culture). New York, NY: Bedford.

Weitkamp, G. (Executive producer). (2012). *A sporting chance: The lasting legacy of Title IX* [Motion picture]. Indianapolis, IN: National Collegiate Athletic Association and Creative Street Entertainment.

Women's Sports Foundation. (2013, April 26). Women's Sports Foundation statement on Biediger v. Quinnipiac [Press release]. Retrieved from www.womenssportsfoundation.org/en/home/media-center-2/statements-and-media-responses/the-womens-sports-foundation-applauds-the-new-legal-precedents

Chapter 3

American Psychological Association (APA). (2013). Adolescent girls and physical activity—strengthening the mind, body and soul. *Raising Strong Girls Podcast Series.* Retrieved from www.apadivisions.org/division-35/news-events/news/physical-activity.aspx

Associated Press. (2013, July 28). Chess prodigy, 9, becomes youngest American to reach "expert" level. *Daily Mail Online.* Retrieved from www.dailymail.co.uk/news/article-2380425/Chess-prodigy-Carissa-Yip-9-youngest-American-reach-expert-level.html

Bickel, B. (2014, July 14). Matt Iseman on American Ninja Warrior: It's been the year of the women. Retrieved from http://kearth101.cbslocal.com/2014/07/14/matt-iseman-on-american-ninja-warrior-its-been-the-year-of-the-women

Bilalic, M., Smaldone, K., McLeod, P., & Gobet, F. (2008). Why are the (best) women so good at chess? Participation rates and gender differences in intellectual domains. *Proceedings of the Royal Society B: Biological Sciences, 276*(1659), 1161-1165. Retrieved from www.ncbi.nlm.nih.gov/pmc/articles/PMC2679077/#__ffn_sectitle

Boren, C. (2015, March 24). Meet the 35-month-old girl who is an archery prodigy in India. *Washington Post.* Retrieved from www.washingtonpost.com/blogs/early-lead/wp/2015/03/12/meet-the-35-month-old-toddler-who-is-an-archery-prodigy-in-india

Bradford, S.H., & Keshock, C.M. (2010). Athlete attrition and turnover: A study of Division I female athletes. *Psychology and Education: An Interdisciplinary Journal, 47*(3), 42-46.

Brekke, K. (2015, May 11). WNBA Skylar Diggins: You can be both a beauty and a beast. *Huffington Post.* Retrieved from www.huffingtonpost.com/2015/05/11/skylar-diggins-model_n_7244930.html

Broad, K.L. (2001). The gendered unapologetic: Queer resistance in women's sports. *Sociology of Sport Journal, 18*(2), 182-204

Burke, M. (2014, February 6). The men behind the Olympic curtain. *Huffington Post.* Retrieved from www.huffingtonpost.com/martha-burk/the-men-behind-the-olympi_b_4725449.html

Caggiano, J. (2010). Girls don't just wanna have fun: Moving past Title IX's contact sports exception. *University of Pittsburgh Law Review, 72*(1), 119-146.

Catanzaro makes history on American Ninja Warrior. (2014, July 14). *Towson Tigers.* Retrieved from www.towsontigers.com/ViewArticle.dbml?DB_LANG=C&ATCLID=209577078&DB_OEM_ID=21300

Chase, L.F. (2006). (Un)disciplined bodies: A Foucauldian analysis of women's rugby. *Sociology of Sport Journal, 23*(3), 229-247.

Chessmaniac.com. (2012, December 27). How many chess players? Retrieved from www.chessmaniac .com/how-many-chess-players

Cohen, A., Melton, N., & Peachey, J.W. (2014). Investigating a coed sport's ability to encourage inclusion and equality. *Journal of Sport Management, 28*(2), 220-235.

Conrod, M. (2014, April 7). Toy weapons for girls: Too violent, or too pretty? *Teaching Kids News.* Retrieved from http://teachingkidsnews.com/2014/04/07/1-toy-weapons-girls-violent-pretty

Davis-Delano, L.R., Pollock, A., & Vose, J.E. (2009). Apologetic behavior among female athletes: A new questionnaire and initial results. *International Review for the Sociology of Sport, 44*(2-3), 131-150.

Disney. (2012). Merida. *The Disney Wikia.* Retrieved from http://disney.wikia.com/wiki/Merida

Dolan, E. (2014, July 30). Meet Ronda Rousey: The woman who shattered the UFC's glass ceiling with an armbar. *The Raw Story.* Retrieved from www.rawstory .com/rs/2014/07/30/meet-ronda-rousey-the-woman-who-shattered-the-ufcs-glass-ceiling-with-an-armbar

Ezzell, M.B. (2009). "Barbie dolls" on the pitch: Identity work, defensive othering, and inequality in women's rugby. *Social Problems, 56*(1): 111-131.

Felshin, J. (1974). The triple option . . . for women in sport. *Quest, 21,* 36-40.

Festle, M.J. (1996). Playing nice: Politics and apologies in women's sports. New York, NY: Columbia University Press.

Fields, S. (2008). *Female gladiators: Gender, law, and contact sports in America.* Champaign, IL: University of Illinois Press.

Fields, S., & Comstock, D. (2008). Why American women play rugby. *Women's Sport and Physical Education Journal, 17*(2), 8-16.

Fink, J., & Maxwell, H. (2010). Challenging the gender binary: Male practice players' views of female athletes. Presentation at the North American Society for Sport Management, Tampa Bay, FL.

Friedman, H.L. (2013a). *Playing to win: Raising children in a competitive culture.* Oakland, CA: University of California Press.

Friedman, H.L. (2013b). Soccer isn't for girly-girls? How parents pick the sports daughters play. *The Atlantic.* Retrieved from www.theatlantic.com/sexes/archive/2013/08/soccer-isnt-for-girly-girls-how-parents-pick-the-sports-their-daughters-play/278386

Goyanes, C. (2012, March 21). This high school archer worthy of "Hunger Games." *ESPN.* Retrieved from http://espn.go.com/espn/page2/index?id=7718289

Hardy, E. (2015). The female "apologetic" behaviour within Canadian women's rugby: Athlete perceptions and media influences. *Sport in Society: Cultures, Commerce, Media, Politics, 18*(1), 155-167.

Henry, J.M., & Comeaux, H.P. (1999). Gender egalitarianism in coed sport: A case study of American soccer. *International Review for the Sociology of Sport, 34*(3), 277-290.

Holden, S., Keshock, C., Forester, B., Pugh, S., & Pugh, S. (2014, April 25). Athlete burnout: Is the type of sport a factor? *The Sport Journal.* Retrieved from http://thesportjournal.org/article/athlete-burnout-is-the-type-of-sport-a-factor

International Olympic Committee. (2014, May). Fact sheet—Women in the Olympic movement. Retrieved from www.olympic.org/Documents/Reference_documents_Factsheets/Women_in_Olympic_Movement.pdf

Jones, A., & Greer, J. (2011, December). You don't look like an athlete: The effects of feminine appearance on audience perceptions of female athletes and women's sports. *Journal of Sport Behavior, 34*(4), 358-377.

Kelley, B., & Carchia, C. (2013, July 11). "Hey data data—swing!" *ESPN.* Retrieved from http://espn.go.com/espn/story/_/id/9469252/hidden-demographics-youth-sports-espn-magazine

Krane, V., Choi, P.Y.L., Baird, S., Aimar, C.M., & Kauer, K.J. (2004). Living the paradox: Female athletes negotiate femininity and masculinity. *Sex Roles, 50*(5), 315-329.

Lawler, J. (2002). *Punch! Why women participate in violent sport.* Terre Haute, IN: Wish.

Martin, M. (2012, April). The (im)possible sexual difference: Representations from a rugby union setting. *International Review for the Sociology of Sport, 47*(2), 183-199.

McClain, D.L. (2011, December 17). Making the case, for and against, chess being an Olympic sport. *New York Times.* Retrieved from www.nytimes.com/2011/12/18/crosswords/chess/making-the-case-for-chess-as-an-olympic-sport.html?_r=0

McDonagh, E., & Pappano, L. (2012). *Playing with the boys: Why separate is not equal in sports.* New York, NY: Oxford University Press.

Messner, M. (2002). *Taking the field: Women, men, and sports.* Minneapolis: University of Minnesota Press.

Moore, J. (2011, January 26). Martial arts statistics and demographics: How many people and who in the US practice? *Maine Martial Arts.* Retrieved from http://mainemartialarts.com/martial-arts/martial-arts-statistics-demographics-people-practice

Mundo, N., & Croshere, R. (Directors). (2014, July 28). Rowdy Ronda Rousey. *ESPN.* Retrieved from http://espn.go.com/espnw/w-in-action/nine-for-ix/shorts/rowdy-ronda-rousey

National Collegiate Athletic Association. (2013). *NCAA sports sponsorship and participation report.* National Collegiate Athletic Association. Retrieved from https://www.ncaapublications.com/p-4334-1981-82-2012-13-ncaa-sports-sponsorship-and-participation-rates-report.aspx

National Federation of State High School Associations (NFHS). (2013). High school athletics participation data. Retrieved from www.nfhs.org/Participation Statics/ParticipationStatics.aspx

Riemer, B.A. & Visio, M.E. (2003). Gender typing of sports: An investigation of Metheny's classification. *Research Quarterly for Exercise and Sport, 74*(2), 193-204.

Riemer, B.A. & Wainwright, S. (2011, January). Ponytails and diamonds: The female apologetic in collegiate softball. Presented at the Fourth Annual Scholarly Colloquium on Intercollegiate Athletics in Conjunction with the NCAA Annual Convention. San Antonio, TX.

Ross, S.R., & Shinew, K.J. (2008). Perspectives of women college athletes on sport and gender. *Sex Roles, 58*(1-2), 40-57.

Rubin, C. (2012). "Hunger Games" makes archery hip. *Herald Tribune Health*. Retrieved from http://health.heraldtribune.com/2012/12/03/hunger-games-makes-archery-hip

Ryan, T.J., & Schwartz, N. (2013). NSGA sports participation report. *SGB Weekly, 1335*, 14-15.

Sabo, D., & Veliz, P. (2008). *Go out and play: Youth sports in America*. East Meadow, NY: Women's Sports Foundation.

Sabo, D., & Veliz, P. (2011). *The decade of decline: Gender equity in high school sports*. Ann SHARP Center for Women and Girls. Retrieved from http://irwg.research.umich.edu/pdf/OCR.pdf

Steinfeldt, J., Carter, H., Benton, E., & Steinfeldt, M. (2011). Muscularity beliefs of female athletes. *Sex Roles, 64*(7), 543-554.

Steinfeldt, J.A., Zakrajsek, R., Carter, H., & Steinfeldt, M. C. (2013). Conformity to gender norms among female student-athletes: Implications for body image. *Psychology of Men & Masculinity, 12*(4), 391-403.

Stout, H., & Harris, E.A. (2014, March 22). Today's girls love pink bows as playthings, but these shoot. *New York Times*. Retrieved from www.nytimes.com/2014/03/23/business/todays-girls-love-pink-bows-as-playthings-but-these-shoot.html

Thomas, L. (2014, April 24). Dana White co-signs Ronda Rousey, says Cyborg Justino once looked like "Wanderlei Silva in a dress and heels." *SBNation.com*. Retrieved from www.mmafighting.com/2014/4/24/5650584/dana-white-co-signs-ronda-rousey-says-cyborg-santos-once-looked-like

Thompson, R.A., & Sherman, R.T. (2010). *Eating disorders in sport*. New York, NY: Routledge.

U.S. Chess Federation. (2014). Top player list. Retrieved from www.uschess.org/component/option,com_top_players/Itemid,371

USA Gymnastics. (2013). *About USA Gymnastics*. Retrieved from https://usagym.org/PDFs/About%20USA%20Gymnastics/Statistics/MembershipInfo.pdf

Voepel, M. (2006, December 1). Male practice players cherish, grow from opportunity. *ESPN*. Retrieved from http://search.espn.go.com/male-practice-players/stories/mechelle-voepel/5-4294595284

Wachs, F. (2002). Leveling the playing field: Negotiating gendered rules in coed softball. *Journal of Sport and Social Issues, 26*(3), 300-316.

Wachs, F. (2005). The boundaries of difference: Negotiating gender in recreational sport. *Sociological Inquiry, 75*(4), 527-547.

Weil, E. (2015, March 4). Mary Cain is growing up fast. *New York Times Magazine*. Retrieved from www.nytimes.com/2015/03/08/magazine/mary-cain-is-growing-up-fast.html

Whitehead, S., & Biddle, S. (2008). Adolescent girls' perceptions of physical activity: A focus group study. *European Physical Education Review, 14*, 243-262.

Zucker, J. (2014, July 16). ESPYs 2014: Ranking nominees for best male and female athletes. *Bleacher Report*. Retrieved from http://bleacherreport.com/articles/2130933-espys-2014-ranking-nominees-for-best-male-and-female-athletes

Chapter 4

Appaneal, R., Levine, B., Perna, F.M., & Roh, J.L. (2009). Measuring postinjury depression among male and female competitive athletes. *Journal of Exercise Psychology, 51*(1), 66-76.

Audrain-McGovern, J., Rodriguez, D., Cuevas, J., & Sass, J. (2013). Initial insight into why physical activity may help prevent adolescent smoking uptake. *Drug and Alcohol Dependence, 132*(3), 471-478.

Brody, J.E. (2010, April 16). Personal health: Women and knee pain. *New York Times*. Retrieved from www.nytimes.com/specials/women/warchive/960814_1176.html

Brown, E., Spiller, L., Stiles, B., & Kilgore, L. (2013). Sexual coercion risk and women's sport participation. *Physical Culture and Sport Studies and Research, 57*(1), 5-11.

Carter, J.E., & Rudd, N.A. (2005). Disordered eating assessment for college student-athletes. *Women in Sport and Physical Activity Journal, 14*(1), 62-71.

Ciminera, J. (2011, October 21). Chiarelli comes back for 5th year. *The Triangle*. Retrieved from http://the triangle.org/sports/chiarelli-comes-back-for-5th-year

Coelho, G.M., Gomes, A.I., Ribeiro, B.G., & Soares, E. (2014). Prevention of eating disorders in female athletes. *Journal of Sports Medicine, 5*, 105-113.

Craft, L.L., & Perna, F.M. (2004). The benefits of exercise for the clinically depressed. *Primary Care Companion Journal of Clinical Psychiatry, 6*(3), 104-112.

Dams-O'Connor, K., Martin, J., & Martens, M.P. (2007). Social norms and alcohol consumption among intercollegiate athletes: The role of athlete and nonathlete reference groups. *Addictive Behaviors, 32*, 2657-2666.

Dawes, J.J., Dukes, R.L., Elder, C., Melrose, D., & Ocker, L.B. (2013). Attitudes of health club patrons toward the use of non-medical anabolic-androgenic steroids by competitive athletes versus recreational weightlifters. *Topics in Integrative Health Care, 4*(2).

Dharamsi, A., & LaBella, C. (2013, July 1). Prevention of ACL injuries in adolescent female athletes. *Contemporary Pediatrics.* Retrieved from http://contemporarypediatrics.modernmedicine.com/contemporary-pediatrics/news/prevention-acl-injuries-adolescent-female-athletes?page=full

Diehl, K., Thiel, A., Zipfel, S., Mayer, J., Litaker, D., & Schneider, S. (2012). How healthy is the behavior of young athletes? A systematic literature review and meta-analyses. *Journal of Sports Science and Medicine, 11*(2), 201-220.

Dodge, T., & Jaccard, J. (2002). Participation in athletics and female sexual risk behavior: The evaluation of four causal structures. *Journal of Adolescent Research, 17,* 42-67.

Donohue, B., Covassin, D., Lancer, K., Dickens, Y., Miller, A., Hash, A., & Genet, J. (2004). Examination of psychiatric symptoms in student athletes. *The Journal of General Psychology, 131,* 29-35.

Eitle, T.M., & Eitle, D.J. (2002). Just don't do it: High school sports participation and young female adult sexual behavior. *Sociology of Sport Journal, 19*(4), 403-418.

Eichelberger, C. (2013, July 17). Concussions among women exceed men as awareness is found lacking. *Bloomberg Business.* Retrieved from www.bloomberg.com/news/articles/2013-07-17/concussions-among-women-exceed-men-as-awareness-is-found-lacking

Elliot, D.L., Cheong, J., Moe, E.L., & Goldberg, L. (2007). Cross-sectional study of female students reporting anabolic steroid use. *Archives of Pediatric and Adolescent Medicine, 161*(6), 572-577.

Elliot, D.L., Moe, E.L., Goldberg, L., DeFrancesco, C.A., Durham, M.B., & Hix-Small, H. (2006). Definition and outcome of a curriculum to prevent disordered eating and body-shaping drug use. *Journal of School Health, 76*(2), 67-73.

Erkut, S., & Tracy, A.J. (2000). Protective effects of sports participation on girls' sexual behavior. Working Paper Series #301. Wellesley, MA: Center for Research on Women.

Fagan, K. (2015, May 7). Split image. *ESPN.com.* Retrieved from http://espn.go.com/espn/feature/story/_/id/12833146/instagram-account-university-pennsylvania-runner-showed-only-part-story

Farb, A.F., & Matjasko, J.L. (2012). Recent advances in research on school-based extracurricular activities and adolescent development. *Developmental Review, 32*(1), 1-48.

Fasting, K., Brackenridge, C.H., Miller, K.E., & Sabo, D. (2008). Participation in college sports and protection from sexual victimization. *International Journal of Sport and Exercise Psychology, 6*(4), 427-441.

Faurie, C., Pontier, D., & Raymond, M. (2004). Student athletes claim to have more sexual partners than other students. *Evolution and Human Behavior, 25*(1), 1-8.

Feldman, A., & Matjasko, J.L. (2005). The role of school-based extra-curricular activities in adolescent development: A comprehensive review and future directions. *Review of Educational Research, 75*(2), 159-210.

Fish, J. (2012, December 9). Performance enhancing supplements and drugs—why? *Philly.com.* Retrieved from www.philly.com/philly/blogs/sportsdoc/Performance-Enhancing-Supplements--DrugsWhy.html

Ford, J.A. (2007). Substance use among college athletes: A comparison based on sport/team affiliation. *Journal of American College Health, 55*(6), 367-373.

Franks, R.R. (2013, April 12). Why are concussions worse in females? *Philly.com.* Retrieved from www.philly.com/philly/blogs/sportsdoc/Why-are-concussions-worse-in-females.html

Giardina, E.V., Sciacca, R.R., Foody, J.M., D'Onofrio, G., Villablanca, A.C., Leatherwood, S., . . . Haynes, S.G. (2011). The DHHS Office on Women's Health Initiative to improve women's heart health: Focus on knowledge and awareness among women with cardiometabolic risk factors. *Journal of Women's Health, 20*(6), 893-900.

Gill, E.L. (2008). Mental health in college athletics: It's time for social work to get in the game. *Social Work, 53*(1), 85-88.

Greenleaf, C., Petrie, T.A., Carter, J., & Reel, J.J. (2009). Female collegiate athletes: Prevalence of eating disorders and disordered eating behaviors. *Journal of American College Health, 57*(5), 489-495.

Grossbard, J.R., Lee, C.M., Neighbors, C., Hendershot, C.S., & Larimer, M.L. (2007). Alcohol and risky sex in athletes and nonathletes: What role do sex motives play? *Journal of Studies on Alcohol and Drugs, 68*(4), 566-574.

Gruber, A.J., & Pope, H.G., Jr. (2000). Psychiatric and medical effects of anabolic-androgenic steroid use in women. *Psychotherapy and Psychosomatics, 69*(1), 19-26.

Habel, M.A., Dittus, P.J., De Rosa, C.J., Chung, E.Q., & Kerndt, P.R. (2010). Daily participation in sports and students' sexual activity. *Perspectives on Sexual and Reproductive Health, 42*(4), 244-250.

Hainline, B., Bell, L., & Wilfert, M. (n.d.). Mind, body and sport: Substance use and abuse. An excerpt from the Sport Science Institute's guide to understanding and supporting student-athlete mental wellness. *NCAA.* Retrieved from www.ncaa.org/health-and-safety/sport-science-institute/mind-body-and-sport-substance-use-and-abuse

Hammond, T., Gialloreto, C., Kubas, H., & Hap-Davis, H. (2013). The prevalence of failure-based depression among elite athletes. *Clinical Journal of Sports Medicine, 23*(4), 273-277.

Hanson, S.L., & Kraus, R.S. (1998). Women, sports, and science: Do female athletes have an advantage? *Sociology of Education, 71*(2), 93-110.

Hanson, S.L., & Kraus, R.S. (1999). Women in male domains: Sport and science. *Sociology of Sport Journal, 16*(2), 92-110.

Harmer, P.A. (2009). Anabolic-androgenic steroid use among young male and female athletes: Is the game to blame? *British Journal of Sports Medicine, 44*(1), 26-31.

Harmon, K.G., Drezner, J.A., Gammons, M., Guskiewicz, K.M., Halstead, M., Herring, S.A., . . . Roberts, W.O. (2013). American Medical Society for Sports Medicine position statement: Concussion in sport. *British Journal of Sports Medicine, 47*(3), 15-26.

Holmes, L., & Turgeon, J.K. (2015, June 3). What ESPN got wrong when reporting about Madison Holleran. *Huffington Post.* Retrieved from www.huffington post.com/lindsay-holmes/madison-holleran-suicide-what-espn-got-wrong_b_7454882.html

Huang, J.-H., Jacobs, D.F., & Derevensky, J.L. (2010). Sexual risk-taking behaviors, gambling, and heavy drinking among U.S. college athletes. *Archives of Sexual Behavior, 39*(3), 706-713.

IOC Medical Commission Working Group Women in Sport. (2006). *Position stand on the female athlete triad.* Lausanne, Switzerland: Author.

Isaac, L.G. (2010). *High-risk drinking on college campuses: College life and alcohol: Challenges and solutions: A resource guide.* Retrieved from www.rwjf.org/content/dam/farm/legacy-parents/high-risk-drinking-on-college-campuses

Iverson, G.L., Gerrard, P.B., Atkins, J.E., Zafonte, R., & Berkner, P.D. (2014). Concussion histories in high school girls are similar across sports. *American Journal of Physical Medicine & Rehabilitation, 93*(3).

Johnson, C., Powers, P.S., & Dick, R. (1999). Athletes and eating disorders: The National Collegiate Athletic Association study. *The International Journal of Eating Disorders, 26*(2), 179-188.

Kaczynski, A.T., Mannell, R.C., & Manske, S.R. (2008). Leisure and risky health behaviors: A review of evidence about smoking. *Journal of Leisure Research, 40*(3), 404-441.

Kaczynski, A.T., Manske, S.R., Mannell, R.C., & Grewal, K. (2008). Smoking and physical activity: A systematic review. *American Journal of Health Behavior, 32*(1), 93-110.

Kaufman, S.B. (2014, March 9). Are you mentally tough? *Scientific American.* Retrieved from http://blogs.scientificamerican.com/beautiful-minds/2014/03/19/are-you-mentally-tough

Kwan, M., Bobko, S., Faulkner, G., Donnelly, P., & Cairney, J. (2014). Sport participation and alcohol and illicit drug use in adolescents and young adults: A systematic review of longitudinal studies. *Addictive Behaviors, 39*(3), 497-506.

Lehman, S.J., & Koerner, S.S. (2004). Adolescent women's sports involvement and sexual behavior/health: A process-level investigation. *Journal of Youth and Adolescence, 33*(5), 443-455.

Lipscomb, S. (2006). Secondary school extracurricular involvement and academic achievement: A fixed effects approach. *Economics of Education Review, 26*(4), 463-472.

Lisha, N.E., & Sussman, S. (2010, May). Relationship of high school and college sports participation with alcohol, tobacco, and illicit drug use: A review. *Addictive Behavior, 35*(5), 399-407.

Loyola University Health System. (2014, April 30). Young female athletes suffering epidemic of ACL injuries. *Science Daily.* Retrieved from www.sciencedaily.com/releases/2014/04/140430091418.htm

Mallet, K. (2013, April 2). College athletes twice as likely to have depression than retired collegiate athletes [Press release]. Retrieved from http://explore.george town.edu/news/?ID=69971&PageTemplateID=295

Marar, M., McIlvain, N.M., Fields, S.K., & Comstock, R.D. (2012). Epidemiology of concussions among United States high school athletes in 20 sports. *American Journal of Sports Medicine, 40*(4), 747-755.

Mays, D., & Thompson, N.J. (2009). Alcohol-related risk behaviors and sports participation among adolescents: An analysis of 2005 Youth Risk Behavior Survey data. *Journal of Adolescent Health, 44*(1), 87-89.

Miller, K.E., Sabo, D.F., Melnick, M.J., Farrell, M.P., & Barnes, G.M. (2001). *The Women's Sports Foundation report: Health risks and the teen athlete.* East Meadow, NY: Women's Sports Foundation.

Miller, B.E., Miller, M.N., Verhegge, R., Linville, H.H., & Pumariega, A.J. (2002). Alcohol misuse among college athletes: Self-medication for psychiatric symptoms? *Journal of Drug Education, 32*(1), 41-52.

Miller, K.E., Hoffman, J.H., Barnes, G.M., Farrell, M.P., Sabo, D., & Melnick, M.J. (2003). Jocks, gender, race, and adolescent problem drinking. *Journal of Drug Education, 33*(4), 445-462.

Miller, K. E., Melnick, M., Barnes, G., Farrell, M., & Sabo, D. (2005). Untangling the links among athletic involvement, gender, race, and adolescent academic outcomes. *Sociology of Sport Journal, 22*(2), 178-201.

Morgan, W.P. (1980). Test of champions. *Psychology Today, 14*, 92-108.

Morgan, W.P., & Pollock, M.L. (1977). Psychologic characterization of the elite runner. *Annals of the New York Academy of Sciences, 301*, 382-403.

National Collegiate Athletic Association. (2007). *Managing student-athletes' mental health issues.* Indianapolis, IN: National Collegiate Athletic Association.

National Collegiate Athletic Association. (2009). *NCAA study of substance use trends among NCAA college student-athletes.* Indianapolis, IN: Author.

National Collegiate Athletic Association. (2012). *National study of substance use trends among NCAA college student-athletes.* Indianapolis, IN: Author.

National Collegiate Athletic Association. (2013). Trends in graduation-success rates and federal graduation rates at NCAA Division I institutions. Retrieved from www.ncaa.org/sites/default/files/GSR%2Band%2BFed%2BTrends%2B2013_Final_0.pdf

National Collegiate Athletic Association. (2014). *2013 NCAA national study of substance use habits of college student-athletes.* Preliminary data presented at the 2014 NCAA Convention, San Diego, CA. Retrieved from www.ncaa.org/sites/default/files/convention2014_drug-use-preliminary.pdf

National Eating Disorders Association. (2011). Coach and athletic trainer toolkit.

Neal, T.L., Diamond, A.B., Goldman, S., Klossner, D., Morse, E., Pajak, D., . . . Welzant, V. (2013). Inter-association recommendations for developing a plan to recognize and refer student-athletes with psychological concerns at the collegiate level: An executive summary of a consensus statement. *Journal of Athletic Training, 48*(5), 716-720.

Nichols, J.F., Rauh, M.J., Lawson, M.J., Ji, M., & Barkai, H.S. (2006). Prevalence of the female athlete syndrome among high school athletes. *Archives of Pediatric Adolescent Medicine, 160*(2), 137-142.

Noren, N. (2014). Taking notice of the hidden injury. *ESPN.com.* Retrieved from http://espn.go.com/espn/otl/story/_/id/10335925/awareness-better-treatment-college-athletes-mental-health-begins-take-shape

Pate, R.R., Trost, S.G., Levin, S., & Dowda, M. (2000). Sports participation and health-related behaviors among U.S. youth. *Archives of Pediatric and Adolescent Medicine, 154*(9), 904-911.

Pearson, J., Crissey, S.R., & Riegle-Crumb, C. (2009). Gendered fields: Sports and advanced course taking. *Sex Roles, 61*(7-8), 519-535.

Perkins, H.W., & Craig, D.W. (2012). Student-athletes' misperceptions of male and female peer drinking norms: A multi-site investigation of the "reign of error." *Journal of College Student Development, 53*(3), 367-382.

Petrie, T.A., Greenleaf, C., Reel, J., & Carter, J. (2008). Prevalence of eating disorders and disordered eating behaviors among male collegiate athletes. *Psychology of Men & Masculinity, 9*(4), 267-277.

Proctor, S.L., & Boan-Lenzo, C. (2010). Prevalence of depressive symptoms in male intercollegiate student-athletes and nonathletes. *Journal of Clinical Sport Psychology, 4*, 204-220.

Puffer, J.C., & McShane, J.M. (1992). Depression and chronic fatigue in athletes. *Clinics in Sport Medicine, 11*(2), 327-338.

Rodriguez, D., & Audrain-McGovern, J. (2004). Team sport participation and smoking: Analysis with general growth mixture modeling. *Journal of Pediatric Psychology, 29*(4), 299-308.

Sabo, D., Miller, K., Melnick, M., Farrell, M.P., & Barnes, G.M. (2005). High school athletic participation and adolescent suicide. *International Review of the Sociology of Sport, 40*(1), 5-23.

Severson, H.H., Klein, K., Lichtenstein, E., Kaufman, N., & Orleans, C.T. (2005). Smokeless tobacco use among professional baseball players: Survey results, 1998-2003. *Tobacco Control, 14*(1), 31-36.

Southall, R., Eckard, W., Nagel, M., Keith, E., & Blake, C. (2014). 2013-2014 adjusted graduation gap report:

NCAA D-I basketball. Retrieved from http://csri-sc.org/wp-content/uploads/2014/03/2013-14_MBB-WBB_AGG-Report_3-12-14.pdf

Staurowsky, E.J., De Souza, M.J., Miller, K., Sabo, D., Shakib, S., Theberge, N., . . . Williams, N. (2015). *Her life depends on it III: The importance of sport and physical activity in the lives of girls and women.* East Meadow, NY: Women's Sports Foundation.

Storch, E.A., Storch, J.B., Killiany, E.M., & Roberti, J.W. (2005). Self-reported psychopathology in athletes: A comparison of intercollegiate student-athletes and non-athletes. *Journal of Sport Behavior, 28*, 86-97.

Sundot-Borgen, J. (1993). Prevalence of eating disorders in elite female athletes. *International Journal of Sports Nutrition, 3*(1), 29-40.

Sundot-Borgen, J., & Torstveit, M. K. (2010, October). Aspects of disordered eating continuum in elite high-intensity sports. *Scandinavian Journal of Medical Science in Sport*, 112-120.

Terry, P. (1995). The efficacy of mood state profiling with elite performers: A review and synthesis. *The Sport Psychologist, 9*, 309-324.

Thomson, C.A., McCullough, M.I., Wertheim, C.A., Chelbowski, R.T., Martinez, M.E., Stefanik, M.L., . . . Newhouser, M.L. (2014). Nutrition and physical activity cancer prevention guidelines, cancer risk, and mortality in women's health initiative. *Cancer Prevention Research, 7*(1), 42-53.

Troutman, K.P., & Dufur, M.J. (2007). From high school jocks to college grads: Assessing the long-term effects of high school sport participation on females' educational attainment. *Youth and Society, 38*(4), 443-462.

Turrisi, R., Mallett, K.A., Mastroleo, N.R., & Larimer, M.E. (2006). Heavy drinking in college students: Who is at risk and what is being done about it? *Journal of General Psychology, 133*(4), 401-420.

U.S. Department of Health & Human Services. (2012). Women of color have more risk factors for heart disease [Press release]. Retrieved from www.hhs.gov/ash/news/2012/20120206.html

Veliz, P., & Shakib, S. (2014). Gender, academics, and interscholastic sports participation at the school level: A gender-specific analysis of the relationship between interscholastic sports participation and AP enrollment. *Sociological Focus, 47*(2), 101-120.

Verkooijen, K.T., Nielsen, G.A., & Kremers, S.P.J. (2008). The association between leisure time physical activity and smoking in adolescence: An examination of potential mediating and moderating factors. *International Journal of Behavioral Medicine, 15*(2), 157-163.

Volk, S. (2014, May 23). The tragedy of Madison Holleran and suicides at Penn. *Philadelphia Magazine.* Retrieved from www.phillymag.com/articles/penn-suicides-madison-holleran

Warren, J. (2013, August 20). Does exercise release a chemical in the brain? *Livestrong.com.* Retrieved from www.livestrong.com/article/320144-does-exercise-release-a-chemical-in-the-brain

276 References

Wichstrom, L., & Pedersen, W. (2001). Use of anabolic-androgenic steroids in adolescence: Winning, looking good or being bad? *Journal of the Study of Alcoholism, 62,* 5-13.

Wichstrom, T., & Wichstrom, L. (2009). Does sports participation during adolescence prevent later alcohol, tobacco and cannabis use? *Addiction, 104*(1), 138-149.

Wilson, G.S., Pritchard, M.E., & Schaffer, J. (2004). Athletic status and drinking behavior in college students: The influence of gender and coping style. *Journal of American College Health, 52*(6), 269-273.

Yang, J., Peek-Asa, C., Corlette, J.D., Cheng, G., Foster, D.T., & Albright, J. (2007). Prevalence of and risk factors associated with symptoms of depression in competitive collegiate student athletes. *Clinical Journal of Sport Medicine, 17*(6), 481-487.

Yusko, D.A., Buckman, J.F., White, H.R., & Pandina, R.J. (2008). Alcohol, tobacco, illicit drugs, and performance enhancers: A comparison of use by college student athletes and non-athletes. *Journal of American College Health, 57*(3), 281-289.

Zazzali, M. (2013, May 1). The female athlete: ACL injuries and prevention. *Huffington Post.* Retrieved from www.huffingtonpost.com/michael-zazzali/female-athletes-acl-injuries_b_3194815.html

Chapter 5

American Academy of Pediatrics (AAP). (1976). Fitness in the preschool child. *Pediatrics, 1,* 88-89.

American Psychological Association (APA). (2007). *Report of the APA Task Force on the sexualization of girls.* Retrieved from www.apa.org/pi/wpo/sexualization.html

Arabi, A., Tamim, H., Nabulsi, M., Maalouf, J., Khalifé, H., Choucair, M., . . . Fuleihan, G.E-H. (2004). Sex differences in the effect of body composition variables on bone mass in healthy children and adolescents. *American Journal of Clinical Nutrition, 80,* 1428-1435.

Arendt, E., & Dick, R. (1995). Knee injury patterns amongst men and women in collegiate basketball and soccer: NCAA data and review of literature. *American Journal of Sports Medicine, 23*(6), 694-701.

Astorino, T.A., Allen, R., Robertson, D., Jurancich, M., Lewis, R., McCarthy, K., & Trost, E. (2011). Adaptations to high-intensity training are independent of training. *European Journal of Applied Physiology, 111*(7), 1279-1286.

Bam, J., Noakes, T.D., Juritz, J., & Dennis, S.C. (1997). Could women outrun men in ultramarathon races? *Medicine and Science in Sports and Exercise, 29,* 244-247.

Barnett, A.G., & Dobson, A.J. (2010). *Analysing seasonal health data.* New York, NY: Springer.

Baxter-Jones, A.D. (1995). Growth and development of young athletes. *Sports Medicine, 20,* 59-64.

Baxter-Jones, A., & Mundt, C. (2007). The young athlete. In N. Armstrong (Ed.), *Pediatric exercise physiology: Advances in sport and exercise science* (pp. 299-324). Philadelphia, PA: Churchill Livingston Elsevier.

Benbow, D.H. (2014, September 16). Could high school sports be co-ed? *Indianapolis Star.* Retrieved from www.indystar.com/story/sports/high-school/2014/09/14/high-school-sports-coed/15645121

Bennett, S. (2007). Introducing freshman female athletes to strength and conditioning programs. *Strength and Conditioning Journal, 29,* 67-69.

Blanksby, B.A., Bloomfield, J., Elliott, B.C., Ackland, T.R., & Morton, A.R. (1986). The anatomical and physiological characteristics of pre-adolescent males and females. *Australian Pediatric Journal, 22,* 177-180.

Borms, J. (1986). The child and exercise: An overview. *Journal of Sports Sciences, 4,* 3-20.

Bouchard, C. An, P., Rice T., Skinner, J.S., Wilmore, J.H., Gagnon, J., . . . Rao, D.C. (1999). Familial aggregation of $\dot{V}O_2max$ response to exercise training: Results from the HERITAGE family study. *Journal of Applied Physiology, 87*(3), 1003-1008.

Brunet, M. (2010). *Unique considerations of the female athlete.* Clifton Park, NY: Delmar Cengage Learning.

Burgess, K.E., Pearson, S.J., & Onambele, G.L. (2009). Menstrual cycle variations in oestradiol and progesterone have no impact on in vivo medial gastrocnemius tendon mechanical properties. *Clinical Biomechanics, 24*(6), 504-509.

Buskirk, E.R., & Hodgson, J.L. (1987). Age and aerobic power: The rate of change in men and women. *Federation Proceedings, 46*(5), 1824-1829.

Campbell, B., & Spano, M. (Eds.). (2011). *NSCA's guide to sport and exercise nutrition.* Champaign, IL: Human Kinetics.

Campbell, K.L., Westerlind, K.C., Harber, V.J., Friedenreich, C.M., & Courneya, K.S. (2005). Associations between aerobic fitness and estrogen metabolites in premenopausal women. *Medicine and Science in Sports and Exercise, 37,* 585-592.

Carter, J.E. (1981). Somatotypes of female athletes. In J. Borms, M. Hebbelinck, & A. Venerando (Eds.), *The female athlete* (pp. 85-116). Basel, Switzerland: Karger.

Carter, J.B., Banister, E.W., & Blaber, A.P. (2003). The effect of age and gender on heart rate variability after endurance training. *Medicine and Science in Sport and Exercise, 35*(8), 1333-1340.

Chandler, T.J., & Brown, L.E. (2013). *Conditioning for strength and human performance* (2nd ed.). Philadelphia, PA: Lippincott Williams and Wilkins.

Chilibeck, P.D., Calder, A.W., Sale, D.G., & Webber, C.E. (1998). A comparison of strength and muscle mass increases during resistance training in young women. *European Journal of Applied Physiology and Occupational Physiology, 77*(1-2), 170-175.

Courteix, D., Lespessailles, E., Peres, S.L., Obert, P., Germain, P., & Benhamou, C.L. (1998). Effect of physical training on bone mineral density in prepubertal girls: A comparative study between impact-loading and non-impact-loading sports. *Osteoporosis International, 8*(2), 152-158.

Crampton, C.W. (1908). Physiological age: A fundamental principle. *American Physical Education Review, 8*(3), 141-154.

Croisier, J-L. (2004). Factors associated with recurrent hamstring injuries. *Sports Medicine, 34*(10), 681-695.

Daniels, E.A. (2009). Sex objects, athletes, and sexy athletes: How media representations of women athletes can impact adolescent girls and young women. *Journal of Adolescent Research, 24*, 399-422.

Daniels, E.A. (2012). Sexy verses strong: What girls and women think of female athletes. *Journal of Applied Developmental Psychology, 33*(2), 79-90.

Deschenes, M.R., & Kraemer, W.J. (2002). Performance and physiologic adaptations to resistance training. *American Journal of Physical Medicine and Rehabilitation, 81*(11), S3-S16.

Dewey, F.E., Rosenthal, D., Murphy, D.J., Jr., Froelicher, V.F., & Ashley, E.A. (2008). Does size matter? Clinical applications of scaling cardiac size and function for body size. *Circulation, 117*, 2279-2287.

Elosua, R., Molina, L., Fito, M., Arquer, A., Sanchez-Quesada, J.L., Covas, M.I., . . . Marrugat, J. (2003). Response of oxidative stress biomarkers to a 16-week aerobic physical activity program, and to acute physical activity, in healthy young men and women. *Atherosclerosis, 167*, 327-334.

England, S.J., & Farhi, L.E. (1976). Fluctuations in alveolar CO_2 and in base excess during the menstrual cycle. *Respiratory Physiology, 26*, 157-161.

Faigenbaum, A.D., Westcott, W.L., Loud, R.L., & Long, C. (1999). The effects of different resistance training protocols on muscular strength and endurance development in children. *Pediatrics, 104*(1), 1-7.

Fischer, D.V. (2005). Strategies for improving resistance training adherence in female athletes. *Strength and Conditioning Journal, 27*(2), 62-67.

Fleck, S.J., & Kraemer, W.J. (2004). *Designing resistance training programs* (3rd ed.). Champaign, IL: Human Kinetics.

Fortney, S.M., Turner, C., Steinmann, L., Driscoll, T., & Alfrey, C. (1994). Blood volume responses of men and women to bed rest. *Journal of Clinical Pharmacology, 34*(5), 434-439.

Fragala, M.S., Kraemer, W.J., Denegar, C.R., Maresh, C., Mastro, A.M., & Volek, J.S. (2011). Neuroendocrine-immune interactions and responses to exercise. *Sports Medicine, 41*(8), 621-639.

Frankovich, R.J., & Lebrun, C.M. (2000). Menstrual cycle, contraception, and performance. *Clinics in Sports Medicine, 19*(2), 251-271.

Fulco, C.S., Rock, P.B., Muza, S.R., Lammi, E., Cymerman, A., Butterfield, G., . . . & Lewis, S.F. (1999). Slower fatigue and faster recovery of the adductor pollicis muscle in women matched for strength with men. *Acta Physiologica Scandinavica, 167*(3), 233-240.

Gill, D.L. (2000). *Psychological dynamics of sports and exercise.* Champaign, IL: Human Kinetics.

Gonzalez, A.M., Hoffman, J.R., Townsend, J.R., Jajtner, A.R., Boone, C.H., Beyer, K.S., . . . & Stout, J.R. (2015). Intramuscular anabolic signaling and endocrine response following high volume and high intensity resistance exercise protocols in trained men. *Physiological Reports, 3*(7), 1-15.

Goodman, L.R., & Warren, M.P. (2005). The female athlete and menstrual function. *Current Opinion in Obstetrics and Gynecology, 17*(5), 466-470.

Grucza, R., Pekkarinen, H., Titov, E., Kononoff, A., & Hänninenet, O. (1993). Influence of the menstrual cycle and oral contraceptives on thermoregulatory responses to exercise in young women. *European Journal of Applied Physiology, 67*, 279-285.

Gurung, R.A.R, & Chrouser, C.J. (2007). Predicting objectification: Do provocative clothing and observer characteristics matter? *Sex Roles, 57*, 91-99.

Haff, G.G., & Triplett, N.T. (2015). *Essentials of strength training and conditioning* (4th ed.). Champaign, IL: Human Kinetics.

Häkkinen, K., Pakarinen, A., Kyröläinen, H., Cheng, S., Kim, D.H., & Komi, P.V. (1990). Neuromuscular adaptations and serum hormones in females during prolonged power training. *International Journal of Sports Medicine, 11*(2), 91-98.

Hannaford, P.C., & Webb, A.M.C. (1996). Evidence-guided prescribing of combined oral contraceptives: Consensus statement. *Contraception, 54*, 125-129.

Harput, G., Soylu, A.R., Ertan, H., Ergun, N., & Mattacola, C.G. (2014). Effect of gender on the quadriceps-to-hamstrings coactivation ratio during different exercises. *Journal of Sport Rehabilitation, 23*(1), 36-43.

Harris, G.R., Stone, M.H., O'Bryant, H.S., Proulx, C.M., & Johnson, R.L. (2000). Short-term performance effects of high power, high force, or combined weight-training methods. *Journal of Strength and Conditioning Research, 14*(1), 14-20.

Hazelhurst, L.T., & Claassen, N. (2006). Gender differences in the sweat response during spinning exercise. *Journal of Strength and Conditioning Research, 20*, 723-724.

Hewett, T.E., Ford, K.R., & Myer, C.D. (2006). Anterior cruciate ligament injuries in female athletes. *American Journal of Sports Medicine, 34*, 490-498.

Heywood, L., & Dworkin, S.L. (2003). *Built to win: The female athlete as cultural icon.* Minneapolis, MN: University of Minneapolis Press.

Holloway, J. B. (1998). A summary chart: Age related changes in women and men and their possible improvement with training. *Journal of Strength and Conditioning Research, 12*(2), 126-128.

Hunter, S.K., & Enoka, R.M. (2003). Changes in muscle activation can prolong the endurance time of a submaximal isometric contraction in humans. *Journal of Applied Physiology, 94*(1), 108-118.

Huston, L.J., & Wojtys, E.M. (1996). Neuromuscular performance characteristics in elite female athletes. *American Journal of Sports Medicine, 24*(4), 427-436.

Hutchinson, P.L., Cureton, K.J., Outz, H., & Wilson, G. (1991). Relationship of cardiac size to maximal oxygen uptake and body size in men and women. *International Journal of Sports Medicine, 12*, 369-373.

Hvid, I., & Andersen, L.I. (1982). The quadriceps angle and its relation to femoral torsion. *Acta Orthopaedica Scandinavica, 53*(4), 577-579.

Ireland, M.L., & Ott, S.M. (2004). Special concerns of the female athlete. *Clinical Sports Medicine, 23*, 281-298.

Janssen, I., Heymsfield, S.B., Wang, Z., & Ross, R. (2000). Skeletal muscle mass and distribution in 468 men and women aged 18-88 yr. *Journal of Applied Physiology, 89*(1), 81-88.

Juhas, I. (2011). Specificity of sports training with women. *Physical Culture, 65*, 42-50.

Kell, R. (2011). The influence of periodized resistance training on strength changes in men and women. *Journal of Strength and Conditioning Research, 25*(3), 735-744.

Kentta, G., Hassmen, P., & Raglin, J. (2001) Training practices and overtraining syndrome in Swedish age-group athletes. *International Journal of Sports Medicine, 22*, 460-465.

Kersey, R.D., Elliot, D.L., Goldberg, L., Kanayama, G., Leone, J.E., Pavlovich, M., & Pope, H.G. (2012). National athletic trainers' association position statement: Anabolic-androgenic steroids. *Journal of Athletic Training, 47*(5), 567-588.

Kibler, W.B., Chandler, T.J., Uhi, T., & Maddus, R.E. (1989). A musculoskeletal approach to the preparticipation physical examination. *American Journal of Sports Medicine, 17*, 525-531.

Kibler, W.B., Herring, S.A., Press, J.M., & Lee, P.A. (1998). *Functional rehabilitation of sports and musculoskeletal injuries.* Gaithersburg, MD: Aspen.

Kibler, W.B., Press, J., & Sciascia, A. (2006). The role of core stability in athletic function. *Sports Medicine, 36*(3), 189-198.

Knapik, J.J., Bauman, C.L., Jones, B.H., Harris, J.M., & Vaughan, L. (1991). Preseason strength and flexibility imbalances associated with athletic injuries in female collegiate athletes. *American Journal of Sports Medicine, 19*, 76-81.

Knechtle, B., Wirth, A., Baumann, B., Knechtle, P., Rosemann, T., & Oliver, S. (2010). Differential correlations between anthropometry, training volume, and performance in male and female ironman triathletes. *Journal of Strength & Conditioning Research, 24*(10), 2785-2793.

Kraemer, W.J., Rubin, M.R., Haäkkinen, K., Nindi, B.C., Marx, J.O., Volek, J.S., . . . & Ratamess, N.A. (2003). Influence of muscle strength and total work on exercise-induced plasma growth hormone isoforms in women. *Journal of Science and Medicine in Sport, 6*(3), 295-306.

Kraemer, W.J., Staron, R.S., Hagerman, F.C., Hikida, R.S., Fry, A.C., Gordon, S.E., . . . Hakkinen, K.

(1998). The effects of short-term resistance training on endocrine function in men and women. *European Journal of Applied Physiology and Occupational Physiology, 78*(1), 69-76.

Kvorning, T., Andersen, M., Brixen, K., & Madsen, K. (2006). Suppression of endogenous testosterone production attenuates the response to strength training: A randomized, placebo-controlled, and blinded intervention study. *American Journal of Physiology-Endocrinology and Metabolism, 291*(6), E1325-E1332.

Lebrun, C.M. (1994). The effect of the phase of menstrual cycle and the birth control pill on athletic performance. *Clinical Sports Medicine, 13*(2), 419-421.

Lebrun, C.M., McKenzie, D.C., Prior, J.C., & Taunton, J.E. (1995). Effects of menstrual cycle phase on athletic performance. *Medicine and Science in Sports and Exercise, 27*(3), 437-444.

Lebrun, C.M., Petit, M.A., McKenzie, D.C., Taunton, J.E., & Prior, J.C. (2003). Decreased maximal aerobic capacity with use of a triphasic oral contraceptive in highly active women: A randomized controlled trial. *British Journal of Sports Medicine, 37*, 315-320.

Lin, Y.C., Lyle, R.M., Weaver, C.M., McCabe, L.D., McCabe, G.P., Johnston, C.C., & Teegardena, D. (2003). Peak spine and femoral neck bone mass in young women. *Bone, 32*, 546-553.

Lipps, D.B., Oh, Y.K., Ashton-Miller, J.A., & Wojtys, E.M. (2012). Morphologic characteristics help explain the gender difference in peak anterior cruciate ligament strain during a simulated pivot landing. *American Journal of Sports Medicine, 40*(1), 32-40.

Liu, S.H., Al-Shaikh, R.A., Panossian, V., & Finerman, G.M. (1996). Primary immunolocalization of estrogen and progesterone target cells in the human anterior cruciate ligament. *Journal of Orthopedic Research, 14*, 526-533.

Maffulli, N., King, J.B., & Helms, P. (1994). Training in elite young athletes (the training of young athletes (TOYA) study): Injuries, flexibility and isometric strength. *British Journal of Sports Medicine, 28*(2), 123-136.

Maffulli, N., Margiotti, K., Longo, U.G., Loppini, M., Fazio, V.M., & Denaro, V. (2013). The genetics of sports injuries and athletic performance. *Muscles Ligaments and Tendons Journal, 3*(3), 173-189.

Malczewska-Lenczowska, J., Sitkowski, D., Orysiak, J., Pokrywka, A., & Szygula, Z. (2013). Total haemoglobin mass, blood volume and morphological indices among athletes from different sport disciplines. *Archives of Medical Science, 9*(5), 780-787.

Marsh, S.A., & Jenkins, D.G. (2002). Physiological responses to the menstrual cycle. *Sports Medicine, 32*, 601-614.

Marta, C., Marinho, D.A., Barbosa, T.M., Izquierdo, M., & Marques, M.C. (2013). Effects of concurrent training on explosive strength and $\dot{V}O_2$max in prepubescent children. *International Journal of Sports Medicine, 34*(10), 888-896.

Matos, N., & Winsley, R.J. (2007). Trainability of young athletes and overtraining. *Journal of Sports Science and Medicine, 6*, 353-367.

McArdle, W.D., Katch, F.I., & Katch, V.L. (2016). *Essentials of exercise physiology* (5th ed.). Baltimore, MD: Lippincott Williams and Wilkins.

McHugh, M.P., Magnusson, S.P., Gleim, G.W., & Nicholas, J.A. (1992). Viscoelastic stress relaxation in human skeletal muscle. *Medicine and Science in Sports and Exercise, 24*, 1375-1382.

Messner, M.A., & Cooky, C. (2010). *Gender in televised sports: News and highlights shows.* Los Angeles, CA: Center for Feminist Research, University of Southern California.

Mitchell, C.J., Churchward-Venne, T.A., Bellamy, L., Parise, G., Baker, S.K., & Phillips, S.M. (2013). Muscular and systemic correlates of resistance training-induced muscle hypertrophy. *PloS One, 8*(10), e78636.

Mueller, K., & Hingst, J. (2013). *The athlete's guide to sports supplements.* Champaign, IL: Human Kinetics.

Multer, C.E. (2001). Gender comparisons in neural, morphological and protein muscle markers of adaptation to acute resistance training [Dissertation]. University of Oregon.

National Federation of State High School Associations (NFHS). (2010). *2009-2010 high school athletics participation survey.* Retrieved from www.nfhs.org/content.aspx?id=3282&linkidentifier=id&itemid=3282

National Strength and Conditioning Association (NSCA). (1989). Position paper on strength training for female athletes: Part I. *NSCA Journal, 11*(5), 29-36.

Nichols, A.W., Hetzler, R.K., Villanueva, R.J., Stickley, C.D., & Kimura, I.F. (2008). Effects of combination oral contraceptives on strength development in women athletes. *Journal of Strength and Conditioning Research, 22*, 1625-1632.

Noakes, T. (2002). *The lore of running* (4th ed.). Champaign, IL: Human Kinetics.

Noyes, F.R., Barber-Westin, S.D., Fleckenstein, C., Walsh, C., & West, J. (2005). The drop-jump screening test: Difference in lower limb control by gender and effect of neuromuscular training in female athletes. *American Journal of Sports Medicine, 33*(2), 197-207.

Nunes, J.A., Crewther, B.T., Ugrinowitsch, C., Tricoli, V., Viveiros, L., de Rose, D., & Aoki, M.S. (2011). Salivary hormone and immune responses to three resistance exercise schemes in elite female athletes. *Journal of Strength and Conditioning Research, 25*(8), 2322-2327.

Paraskevas, G., Papadopoulos, A., Papaziogas, B., Spainidou, S., Argiriadou, H., & Gigis, J. (2004). Study of the carrying angle of the human elbow joint in full extension: A morphometric analysis. *Surgical and Radiologic Anatomy, 26*, 19-23.

Park, S-K., Stefanyshyn, D.J., Ramage, B., Hart, D.A., & Ronsky, J.L. (2009). Alterations in knee joint laxity during the menstrual cycle in healthy women leads to increases in joint loads during selected athletic movements. *American Journal of Sports Medicine, 37*(6), 1169-1177.

Poiss, C.C., Sullivan, P.A, Paup, D.C., & Westerman, B.J. (2004). Perceived importance of weight training to selected NCAA III men and women student-athletes. *Journal of Strength and Conditioning Research, 18*(1), 108-114.

Rechichi, C., & Dawson, B. (2009). Effect of oral contraceptive cycle phase on performance in team sports players. *Journal of Science and Medicine in Sports, 12*, 190-195.

Renstrom, P., Ljungqvist, A., Arendt, E., Beynnon, B., Fukubayashi, T., Garrett, W., . . . Engebretsen, L. (2008). Non-contact ACL injuries in female athletes: An International Olympic Committee current concepts statement. *British Journal of Sports Medicine, 42*, 394-412.

Riggs, B.L., Khosla, S., & Melton, J.L. (2002). Sex steroids and the construction and conservation of the adult skeleton. *Endocrine Reviews, 23*, 279-302.

Ristolainen, L., Heinonen, A., Waller, B., Kujala, U.M., & Kettunen, J.A. (2009). Gender differences in sport injury risk and types of injuries: A retrospective twelve-month study on cross-country skiers, swimmers, long-distance runners and soccer players. *Journal of Sports Science and Medicine, 8*, 443-451.

Roberton, M.A., & Halverson, L.E. (1984). *Developing children: Their changing movement.* Philadelphia, PA: Lea & Febiger.

Ruby, B.C., & Roberts, R.A. (1994). Gender differences in substrate utilization during exercise. *Sports Medicine, 17*, 393-410.

Schoene, R.B., Robertson, H.T., Pierson, D.J., & Peterson, A.P. (1981). Respiratory drives and exercise in menstrual cycles of athletic and nonathletic women. *Journal of Applied Physiology, 50*, 1300-1305.

Shultz, S.J., Levine, B.J., Nguyen, A-D., Kim, H., Montgomery, M.M., & Perrin, D.H. (2010). A comparison of cyclic variations in anterior knee laxity, genu recurvatum, and general joint laxity across the menstrual cycle. *Journal of Orthopaedic Research, 28*(11), 1411-1417.

Shultz, S.J., Sander, T.C., Kirk, S.E., & Perrin, D.H. (2005). Sex differences in knee joint laxity change across the female menstrual cycle. *Journal of Sports Medicine and Physical Fitness, 45*(4), 594-603.

Shultz, S.J., Schmitz, R.J., & Nguyen, A.D. (2008). Research retreat IV: ACL injuries—The gender bias. *Journal of Athletic Training, 43*, 530-537.

Sutton, K.M., & Montgomery Bullock, J. (2013). Anterior cruciate ligament rupture: Differences between males and females. *Journal of American Academic Orthopedic Surgery, 21*(1), 41-50.

Szivak, T.K., Hooper, D.R., Dunn-Lewis, C., Comstock, B.A., Kupchak, B.R., Apicella, J.M., . . . Kraemer, W.J. (2013). Adrenal cortical responses to high-intensity, short rest, resistance exercise in men and women. *Journal of Strength and Conditioning Research, 27*(3), 748-760.

Tan, K.S., McFarlane, L.C., & Lipworth, B.J. (1997). Modulation of airway reactivity and peak flow variability in asthmatics receiving the oral contraceptive pill. *American Journal of Respiratory and Critical Care Medicine, 155*(4), 1273-1277.

Tarnopolsky, M.A. (2008). Building muscle: Nutrition to maximize bulk and strength adaptations to resistance exercise training. *European Journal of Sports Science, 8*(2), 67-76.

Thompson, W.R. (2013). Now trending: Worldwide survey of fitness trends for 2014. *ACSM's Health and Fitness Journal, 17*(6), 10-20.

Thomsen, S.R., Bower, D.W., & Barnes, M.D. (2004). Photographic images in women's health, fitness, and sports magazines and the physical self-concept of a group of adolescent female volleyball players. *Journal of Sport and Social Issues, 28*, 266-283.

Tse, M.A., McManus, A.M., & Masters, R.W. (2005). Development and validation of a core endurance intervention program: Implications for performance in college-age rowers. *Journal of Strength and Conditioning Research, 19*(3), 547-552.

Uchida, M.C., Crewther, B.T., Ugrinowitsch, C., Bacurau, R.L., Moriscot, A.S., & Aoki, M.S. (2009). Hormonal responses to difference resistance exercise schemes of similar total volume. *Journal of Strength and Conditioning Research, 23*(7), 2003-2008.

Vingren, J.L., Kraemer, W.J., Hatfield, D.L., Volek, J.S., Ratamess, N.A., Anderson, J.M., . . . & Maresh, C.M. (2009). Effect of resistance exercise on muscle steroid receptor protein content in strength-trained men and women. *Steroids, 74*(13), 1033-1039.

Vingren, J.L., Kraemer, W.J., Ratamess, N.A., Anderson, J.M., Volek, J.S., & Maresh, C.M. (2010). Testosterone physiology in resistance exercise and training: The upstream regulatory elements. *Sports Medicine, 40*(12), 1.

Volek, J.S., Forsythe, C.E., & Kraemer, W.J. (2006). Nutritional aspects of women strength athletes. *British Journal of Sports Medicine, 40*(9), 742-747.

Wang, H-K., & Cochrane, T. (2001). Mobility impairment, muscle imbalance, muscle weakness, scapular asymmetry and shoulder injury in elite volleyball athletes. *Journal of Sports Medicine and Physical Fitness, 41*, 403-410.

West, D.W., Burd, N.A., Churchward-Venne, T.A., Camera, D.M., Mitchell, C.J., Baker, S.K., . . . & Phillips, S.M. (2012). Sex-based comparisons of myofibrillar protein synthesis after resistance exercise in the fed state. *Journal of Applied Physiology, 112*(11), 1805-1813.

Williams, C.A., Armstrong, N., Kirby, B., & Welsman, J. (1995). Is there a relationship between children and adolescents' anaerobic and aerobic performance? *Medicine and Science in Sports and Exercise, 27*(5), S639.

Wojtys, E.M., Huston, L.J., Boynton, M.D., Spindler, K.P., & Lindenfeld, T.N. (2002). The effect of the menstrual cycle on anterior cruciate ligament injuries in women as determined by hormone levels. *The American Journal of Sports Medicine, 30*(2), 182-188.

Women's Sport and Fitness Foundation (WSFF). (n.d.). Female physiology and considerations for coaching practice. Retrieved from www.wsff.org.uk/system/1/assets/files/000/000/319/319/959f0f1f0/original/female_psychology_and_considerations_for_coaching_practice_2771.pdf

Yang, N., MacArthur, D.G., Gulbin, J.P., Hahn, A.G., Beggs, A.H., Easteal, S., & North, K. (2003). ACTN3 genotype is associated with human elite athletic performance. *American Journal of Human Genetics, 73*(3), 627-631.

Zatsiorsky, V., & Kraemer, W. (2006). *Science and practice of strength training* (2nd ed.). Champaign, IL: Human Kinetics.

Chapter 6

Abney, R. (2007). African American women in intercollegiate coaching and athletic administration: Unequal access. In D. Brooks and R. Althouse (Eds.), *Diversity and social justice in college sport: Sport management and the student athlete* (pp. 51-75). Morgantown, WV: Fitness Information Technology.

Alsharif, A. (2012, February 29). Saudi women push for the right to play sports. Retrieved from www.reuters.com/article/2012/02/29/us-saudi-women-sport-idUS-TRE81S1BX20120229

Andrews, E. (2009, June 29). Wimbledon says looks important in deciding who plays on Centre Court. *The Courier Mail.* Retrieved from www.adelaidenow.com.au/news/wimbledon-says-looks-important-in-deciding-who-plays-on-centre-court/story-e6frea6u-1225744058152

Benn, T., & Dagkas, S. (2013). The Olympic movement and Islamic culture: Conflict or compromise for Muslim women? *International Journal of Sport Policy and Politics, 5*, 281-294.

Black Women in Sport Foundation. (n.d.). The BWSF story. Retrieved from www.blackwomeninsport.org/about-bwsf

Brake, D.L. (2010). *Getting in the game: Title IX and the women's sports revolution.* New York, NY: New York University Press.

Bruening, J. (2000). Phenomenal women: A qualitative study of silencing, stereotypes, socialization, and strategies for change in the sport participation of African American female student-athletes [Doctoral dissertation]. Retrieved from OhioLINK (osu1392903455).

Bruening, J. (2005). Gender and racial analysis in sport: Are all the women white and all the Blacks men? *Quest, 57*, 340-359.

Bruening, J., Armstrong, K.L., & Pastore, D.L. (2005). Listening to the voices: The experiences of African American female student athletes. *Research Quarterly for Exercise and Sport, 76*(1), 82-100.

Butler, J., & Lopiano, D. (2003). *The Women's Sports Foundation report: Title IX and race in intercollegiate sport.* East Meadow, NY: Women's Sports Foundation.

Cahn, S.K. (1994). *Coming on strong: Gender and sexuality in twentieth-century women's sport.* Cambridge, MA: Harvard University Press.

Carter, A. (2008). Negotiation identities: Examining African American female collegiate athlete experiences in predominantly White institutions [Unpublished dissertation]. University of Georgia.

Carter, A.R., & Hawkins, B.J. (2011). Coping strategies among African American female collegiate athletes in the predominantly white institution. In K. Hylton, A. Pilkington, P. Warmington, & S. Housee (Eds.), *Atlantic crossings: International dialogues in critical race theory* (pp. 61-92). Birmingham, England: Sociology, Anthropology, Politics (C-SAP), The Higher Education Academy Network.

Carter-Francique, A.R., & Flowers, C. (2013). Intersections of race, ethnicity, and gender in sport. In E. Roper (Ed.), *Gender relations in sport* (pp. 73-94). Rotterdam, The Netherlands: Sense.

Carter-Francique, A.R., & Regan, M. (2012). Power and politics. In G.B. Cunningham & J.N. Singer (Eds.), *Sociology of sport and physical activity* (2nd ed., pp. 373-396). College Station, TX: Center for Sport Management Research and Education.

Chase, C. (2011). Henin is sorry for the Serena hand incident . . . but not really. Retrieved from http://sports.yahoo.com/tennis/blog/busted_racquet/post/Henin-is-sorry-for-the-Serena-hand-incident-?urn=ten-325848

Clark, C., & Arboleda, T. (1999). *Teacher's guide for "In the shadow of race: Growing up as a multiethnic, multicultural, and 'multiracial' American."* Mahwah, NJ: Lawrence Erlbaum Associates.

Coakley, J. (2007). *Sports in society: Issues and controversies* (9th ed.). Boston, MA: McGraw-Hill.

Cohen v. Brown University, 101 F.3d 155 (1st Cir. 1996).

Collins, P. (2000). *Black feminist thought: Knowledge, consciousness, and the politics of empowerment.* New York, NY: Routledge.

Combahee River Collective. (1995). A black feminist statement. In B. Guy Sheftall (Ed.), *Words of fire: An anthology of African-American feminist thought* (pp. 231-240). New York, NY: The New Press.

Corbett, D., & Johnson, W. (2000). The African-American female in collegiate sport: Sexism and racism. In D. Brooks (Ed.), *Racism in college athletics: The African-American athlete's experience* (pp. 179-204). Morgantown, WV: Fitness Information Technology.

Couch, G. (2011, June 24). Serena's court 2 placement raises racism, sexism suspicions. *Sporting News.* Retrieved from www.sportingnews.com/sport/story/2011-06-24/serenas-court-2-placement-raises-racism-sexism-suspicions

Crenshaw, K. (1991). Mapping the margins: Intersectionality, identity politics, and violence against women of color. *Stanford Law Review, 43*(6), 1241-1299.

Crenshaw, K. (1993). Beyond racism and misogyny: Black feminism and 2 Live Crew. In M. Matsuda, C.

Lawrence, R. Delgado & K. Crenshaw (Eds.), *Words that wound: Critical race theory, assaultive speech, and the First Amendment* (pp. 111-132). Boulder, CO: Westview Press.

Csizma, K.A., Wittig, A.F., & Schurr, K.T. (1988). *Journal of Sport and Exercise Psychology, 10,* 62-74.

Cunningham, G.B. (2011). *Diversity in sport organizations* (2nd ed.). Scottsdale, AZ: Holcomb Hathaway.

Dagkas, S., & Benn, T. (2006). Young Muslim women's experiences of Islam and physical education in Greece and Britain: A comparative study. *Sport, Education & Society, 11*(1), 21-38.

Davis, F.J. (1991). *Who is Black? One nation's definition.* University Park, PA: The Pennsylvania University.

Davis, L.R., & Harris, O. (1998). Race and ethnicity in US sport media. In L. Wenner (Ed.), *Media sport* (pp. 154-169). London, England: Routledge.

Dees, A.J. (2008). Access or interest: Why Brown had benefited African-American women more than Title IX. *University of Missouri Kansas City Law Review, 76,* 625-641.

DeGraffenreid v. General Motors Assembly Division, St. Louis, 558 F.2d 480 (1977).

de Tarczynski, S. (2010, May 3). Australia: Hijab-wearing footballers oppose FIFA ban. *Interpress Service.* Retrieved from www.ipsnews.net/2010/05/australia-hijab-wearing-footballers-oppose-fifa-ban

Douglas, D. (2005). Venus, Serena, and the Women's Tennis Association: When and where "race" enters. *Sociology of Sport Journal, 22,* 256-282.

Drucker, J. (2009, March 11). What happened at Indian Wells? *ESPN.* Retrieved from http://sports.espn.go.com/sports/tennis/columns/story?columnist=drucker_joel&id=3952939

Evans, T. (1998). In the Title IX race toward gender equity, the black female athlete is left to finish last: The lack of access for the invisible woman. *Howard Law Journal, 42*(1), 105-128.

Eyler, A., Baker, E., Cromer, L., King, A., Brownson, R., & Donatelle, R. (1998). Physical activity and minority women: A qualitative study. *Health Education Behavior, 25,* 640-652.

Foster, K.M. (2003). Panopticonics: The control and surveillance of black female athletes in a collegiate athletic program. *Anthropology & Education Quarterly, 34*(3), 300-323.

Gathers, R.C., & Mahan, M.C. (2014). African American women, hair care, and health barriers. *The Journal of Clinical and Aesthetic Dermatology, 7*(9), 26-29.

Gibson, A. (2000). Sports. In R. Newman (Ed.), *African American quotations* (p. 344). New York, NY: Oryx Press.

Gibson served as role model for Williams sisters. (2003, September 28). *ESPN.* Retrieved from http://espn.go.com/classic/obit/news/2003/0928/1625394.html

Gibson, A., & Curtis, R. (1968). *So much to live for.* New York, NY: G.P. Putnam's Sons.

Giddings, P. (1984). *When and where I enter: The impact of Black women on race and sex in America.* New York, NY: William Morrow.

Gill, E. (2011). Rutgers women's basketball & Don Imus controversy (RUIMUS): Privilege, new racism, and the implications for sport management. *Journal of Sport Management, 25,* 188-130.

Green, T., Oglesby, C.A., Alexander, A., & Franke, N. (1981). *Black women in sport.* Reston, VA: American Alliance for Health, Physical Education, Recreation and Dance.

Hall, R.R., Francis, S., Whitt-Glover, M., Loftin-Bell, K., Swett, K., & McMichael, A.J. (2013). Hair care practices as a barrier to physical activity in African American women. *JAMA Dermatology, 149*(3), 310-314.

Hancock, A.M. (2007). When multiplication doesn't equal quick addition: Examining intersectionality as a research paradigm. *Perspectives on Politics, 5*(1), 63-79.

Haslam, S.A., Oakes, P.J., Reynolds, K.J., & Turner, J.C. (1999). *Personality and Social Psychology Bulletin, 25*(7), 809-818.

High cost of youth sports. (2013, June 21). *Huffington Post Parents.* Retrieved from www.huffingtonpost.com/visualnewscom/high-cost-of-youth-sports_b_3469012.html

Hogshead-Maker, N., & Zimbalist, A. (2007). *Equal play: Title IX and social change.* Philadelphia, PA: Temple University Press.

hooks, b. (2000). *Feminist theory: From margin to center* (2nd ed.). Cambridge, MA: South End Press.

Irick, E. (2014). NCAA Race and Gender Demographics, 1995-2014 (United States) [Data file]. Retrieved from http://web1.ncaa.org/rgdSearch/exec/saSearch

Jenkins, B. (2013, March 12). It's time for Williams sisters to return to Indian Wells. *Sports Illustrated.* Retrieved from www.si.com/tennis/2013/03/12/williams-sisters-indian-wells-venus-serena

Jinxia, D. (2003). *Women, sport and society in modern China.* London, England: Frank Cass.

Johnson, R. (2015, April). Queen of the court. *Vogue Magazine,* 242-247.

King, D. (2007). Multiple jeopardy, multiple consciousness: The context of Black feminist ideology. In B. Landry (Ed.), *Race, gender and class: Theory and method of analysis* (pp. 16-38). Upper Saddle River, NJ: Pearson Education.

Laboy, S. (2015, March 12). Saudi girls *still* can't play sports in public schools. *Fusion.* Retrieved from http://fusion.net/story/102498/saudi-girls-still-cant-play-sports-in-public-schools

Lapchick, R., Aristeguieta, F., Bragg, D., Clark, W., Cloud, C., Florzak, A., . . . Vinson, M. (2011). *The complete racial and gender report card.* Retrieved from http://dl.dropbox.com/u/11322904/RGRC/2011_RGRC_FINAL.pdf

Lapchick, R., Fox, J., Guiao, A., & Simpson, M. (2015, March 3). *The 2014 racial and gender report card: College sport.* Orlando, FL: The Institute for Diversity and Ethics in Sport, University of Central Florida.

McCall, L. (2005). The complexity of intersectionality. *Journal of Women in Culture and Society, 30*(3), 1771-1800.

McDowell, J., & Cunningham, G.B. (2009). Personal, social, and organizational factors that influence black female athletic administrators' identity negotiation. *Quest, 61,* 202-222.

Murphy, C. (2009, March 17). Girls' sports opportunities MIA in city schools. *WeNews.* Retrieved from http://womensenews.org/story/090317/girls-sports-opportunities-mia-in-city-schools#.UiKS02wo7IU

Muslim group slams female Indian tennis star Sania Mirza for wearing revealing clothing. (2005, September 9). *CBS Sports.* Retrieved from www.cbssports.com/tennis/story/8822682

National Collegiate Athletic Association (NCAA). (2015). Sport Sponsorship, Participation and Demographics Search [Data file]. Retrieved from http://web1.ncaa.org/rgdSearch/exec/sponSearch

NCAA emerging sports timeline. (n.d.). Retrieved from www.ncaa.org/sites/default/files/Emerging%2BSports%2BHistory.doc

Nichols, R.A. (2002, September 7). Sensational siblings; Serena, Venus Williams reach U.S. Open final. *The Washington Post,* p. D1.

Oakes, P.J., Haslam, S.A., & Turner, J.C. (1994). *Stereotyping and social reality.* Cambridge, MA: Blackwell.

Off-court distractions: Racism charges swirl as Williams sisters advance. (2001, March 27). *Sports Illustrated.* Retrieved from http://sportsillustrated.cnn.com/tennis/news/2001/03/26/ericsson_open_ap

Philip, R. (2002, July 5). Sister act "sad for women's tennis" says Mauresmo. *The Telegraph.* Retrieved from www.telegraph.co.uk/sport/main.jhtml?xml=/sport/2002/07/05/stphil05.xml

Pickett, M.W. (2009). The invisible black woman in the Title IX shuffle: An empirical analysis and critical examination of gender equity policy in assessing access and participation of black and white high school girls in interscholastic sports [Doctoral dissertation]. *Open Access Dissertations* (Paper 288).

Roberts, S. (2002, June 24). Tennis seeks a foil to stop another all-Williams final. *New York Times,* p. D3.

Rodrick, S. (2013, June 18). Serena Williams: The great one. *Rolling Stone Magazine.* Retrieved from www.rollingstone.com/culture/news/serena-williams-the-great-one-20130618

Sabo, D., & Veliz, P. (2008). *Go out and play: Youth sports in America.* East Meadow, NY: Women's Sports Foundation.

Safire, W. (1988, Nov. 20). On language; people of color. *New York Times.* Retrieved from www.nytimes.com/1988/11/20/magazine/on-language-people-of-color.html

Saudi female athletes: Heroes in London, "prostitutes of the Olympics" at home. (2012, August 12). Retrieved from http://rt.com/news/saudi-female-athletes-prost itutes-olympics-494

Sellers, R.M., Kuperminc, G.P., & Damas, A. (1997). The college life experiences of African American women athletes. *American Journal of Community Psychology, 25*(5), 699-720.

Singer, J.N., & Carter-Francique, A.R. (2012). Representation, participation, and the experiences of racial minorities in college sport. In G. Sailes (Ed.), *Sports in higher education: Issues and controversies in college athletics* (pp. 113-138). San Diego, CA: Cognella.

Sinha, S. (2014, Aug. 20). 3 reasons Mo'ne Davis' *Sports Illustrated* cover is an even bigger deal than you realize. *Mic.* Retrieved from http://mic.com/articles/96654/3-reasons-mo-ne-davis-sports-illustrated-cover-is-an-even-bigger-deal-than-you-realize

Sloan Green, T. (2007). My letter to Traci. *Title IX, 35*, 25-28.

Smith, Y. (1992). Women of color in society and sport. *Quest, 44*(2), 228-250.

Smith, Y. (2000). Sociocultural influences of African American elite sportswomen. In D. Brooks and R. Althouse (Eds.), *Racism in college athletics: The African American athlete experience* (2nd ed., pp. 173-197). Morgantown, WV: Fitness Information Technology.

Staurowsky, E. (2005). SuAnne Big Crow: Her legend and legacy. In R. King (Ed.), *Native athletes in sport and society* (pp. 189-210). Lincoln, NE: University of Lincoln Press.

St. Jean, Y., & Feagin, J. (1998). *Double burden: Black women and everyday racism.* Armonk, NY: M.E. Sharpe.

Suggs, W. (2001, November 30). Left behind. *The Chronicle of Higher Education*, A35.

Suggs, W. (2005). *A place on the team: The triumph and tragedy of Title IX.* Princeton, NJ: Princeton University Press.

Sylwester, M. (2005, March 29). Hispanic girls in sports held back by tradition. *USA Today*, p. A1.

The story of my life. Serena struggles to deal with harsh treatment from crowd. (2003, June 5). *Sports Illustrated.* Retrieved from http://sportsillustrated.cnn.com/tennis/2003/french_open/news/2003/06/05/serena_distraught_reut

Vecsey, G. (2003, June 26). Theories about Paris from Serena's mother. *New York Times*, p. D1.

Versey, H.S. (2014). Centering perspectives on Black women, hair politics, and physical activity. *American Journal of Public Health, 104*(5), 810-815.

Vertinsky, P., & Captain, G. (1998). More myth than history: American culture and representations of the black female's athletic ability. *Journal of Sport History, 25*(3), 532-561.

Wiggins, S.K. (2008). Title IX and African American female athletes. In M. Lomax & K. Shropshire (Eds.), *Sports and the racial divide: African American and Latino experience in an era of change* (pp.126-145). Jackson, MS: University Press of Mississippi.

Williams, S., & Paisner, D. (2009). *On the line.* New York, NY: Grand Central.

Women's Sports Foundation (WSF). (2011). *Foundation's position on race and sport.* East Meadow, NY: Author.

Chapter 7

American Psychological Association (APA). (2008). *Answers to your questions: For better understanding of sexual orientation and homosexuality.* Washington, DC: Author. Retrieved from www.apa.org/topics/sorientation.pdf

Athlete Ally. (2013a). Heather O'Reilly. Retrieved from www.athleteally.org/allies/heather-oreilly

Athlete Ally. (2013b). Meleana Shim. Retrieved from www.athleteally.org/allies/meleana-shim

Banda, P.S. (2013, February 27). Coy Mathis, Colorado transgender girl, not allowed to use school bathroom. *Huffington Post.* Retrieved from www.huffingtonpost.com/2013/02/27/coy-mathis-colorado-trans_n_2776472.html

Birkett, M., Espelage, D.L., & Koenig, B. (2009). LGB and questioning students in schools: The moderating effects of homophobic bullying and school climate on negative outcomes. *Journal of Youth & Adolescence, 38*, 989-1001.

Blatt, J. (2006). "I was kicked off my team for being 'gay.'" *Cosmo Girl, 8*(9), 96.

Buzinski, J. (2005, November 3). Rene Portland targeted with legal complaint. *Outsports.* Retrieved from www.outsports.com/2013/2/20/4010880/rene-portland-targeted-with-legal-complaint

Buzinski, J. (2013, July 25). Rutgers athletic director Julie Hermann reveals she is lesbian. Retrieved from www.outsports.com/2013/7/25/4557326/rutgers-athletic-director-julie-hermann-reveals-gay-lesbian

Coleman, E., Bockting, W., Botzer, M., Cohen-Kettenis, P., DeCuypere, G., Feldman, J., . . . Zucker, K. (2011). Standards of care for the health of transsexual, transgender, and gender-nonconforming people, version 7. *International Journal of Transgenderism, 13*, 165-232.

D'Augelli, A.R., Grossman, A.H., & Starks, M.T. (2006). Childhood gender atypicality, victimization and PTSD among lesbian, gay and bisexual youth. *Journal of Interpersonal Violence, 21*, 1462-1482.

DeFrancesco, D. (2013, May 8). Volleyball eases transgender player's transition. *USA Today.* Retrieved from www.usatoday.com/story/sports/college/volleyball/2013/05/08/taylor-edelmann-purchase-college-mens-volleyball-transgender-player/2144599

Drescher, J., & Byne, W. (2012). Gender dysphoric/gender variant (GD/GV) children and adolescents: Summarizing what we know and what we have yet to learn. *Journal of Homosexuality, 59*, 501-510.

Edwards-Leeper, L., & Spack, N.P. (2012). Psychological evaluation and medical treatment of transgender youth in an interdisciplinary "gender management service" (GeMS) in a major pediatric center. *Journal of Homosexuality, 59*, 321-336.

Edwards-Stout, K. (2012, Sept 11). The mother of a transgender child speaks out. *Huffington Post.* Retrieved from www.huffingtonpost.com/kergan-edwardsstout/the-mother-of-a-transgender-child-speaks-out_b_1868029.html

Enke, A.F. (2012). Note on terms and concepts. In A. Enke (Ed.), *Transfeminist perspectives: In and beyond transgender and gender studies* (pp. 16-20). Philadelphia, PA: Temple University Press.

Espelage, D.L., Aragon, S.R., Birkett, M., & Koenig, B.W. (2008). Homophobic teasing, psychological outcomes, and sexual orientation among high school students: What influence do parents and schools have? *School Psychology Review, 37*, 202-216.

Fink, J.S., Burton, L.J., Farrell, A.O., & Parker, H.M. (2012). Playing it out: Female intercollegiate athletes' experiences in revealing their sexual identities. *Journal for the Study of Sports and Athletes in Education, 6*, 83-106.

GLSEN. (2011). *The 2011 national school climate survey: The experiences of lesbian, gay, bisexual and transgender youth in our nation's schools.* Retrieved from www.glsen.org/binary-data/glsen_attachments/file/000/002/2105-1.pdf

GLSEN. (2013). *The experiences of LGBT students in school athletics (research brief).* Retrieved from www.glsen.org/binary-data/glsen_attachments/file/000/002/2140-1.pdf

GLSEN. (n.d.). About the project. Retrieved from http://sports.glsen.org/about-the-project

Grossman, A.H., & D'Augelli, A.R. (2006). Transgender youth: Invisible and vulnerable. *Journal of Homosexuality, 51*, 111-128.

Grossman, A.H., D'Augelli, A.R., & Frank, J.A. (2011). Aspects of psychological resilience among transgender youth. *Journal of LGBT Youth, 8*, 103-115.

Haas, A.P., Eliason, M., Mays, V.M., Mathy, R.M., Cochran, S.D., D'Augelli, A.R., . . . Brown, G.K. (2011). Suicide and suicide risk in lesbian, gay, bisexual, and transgender populations: Review and recommendations. *Journal of Homosexuality, 58*, 10-51.

Haywood, M. (2013, May 9). California transgender student has to quit basketball team, but keeps passion for the sport. Retrieved from www.glaad.org/blog/california-transgender-student-has-quit-basketball-team-keeps-passion-sport

IOC. (2003). *Statement of the Stockholm consensus on sex reassignment in sports.* Retrieved from www.olympic.org/Documents/Reports/EN/en_report_905.pdf

Ionnatta, J.C., & Kane, M.J., (2002). Sexual stories as resistance narratives in women's sports: Reconceptualizing identity performance. *Sociology of Sport Journal, 19*, 347-369.

Kauer, K.J. (2009). Queering lesbian sexualities in collegiate sporting spaces. *Journal of Lesbian Studies, 13*, 306-318.

Kauer, K.J., & Krane, V. (2006). "Scary dykes" and "feminine queens": Stereotypes and female collegiate athletes. *Women in Sport & Physical Activity Journal, 15*(1), 43-55.

Kauer, K.J., & Krane, V. (2013). Sexual identity and sport. In E. Roper (Ed.), *Gender relations in sport* (pp. 53-71). Boston, MA: Sense.

Krane, V., & Barber, H. (2005). Identity tensions in lesbian intercollegiate coaches. *Research Quarterly for Exercise and Sport, 76*, 67-81.

Krane, V., Surface, H., & Alexander, L. (2005). Health implications of heterosexism and homonegativism for girls and women in sport. In L. Ransdall & L. Petlichkoff (Eds.), *Ensuring the health of active and athletic girls and women* (pp. 327-346). Reston, VA: National Association for Girls and Women in Sport.

Krane, V., & Symons, C. (2014). Gender and sexual orientation. In A. Papaioannou & D. Hackfort (Eds.), *Fundamental concepts in sport and exercise psychology* (pp. 119-135). Abingdon, England: Taylor & Francis.

Lapauw, B., Taes, Y., Simoens, S., Van Caenegem, E., Weyers, S., Goemaere, . . . T'Sjoen, G.G. (2008). Body composition, volumetric and areal bone parameters in male-to-female transsexual persons. *Bone, 43*, 1016-1021.

Ljungqvist, A., & Genel, M. (2005). Essay transsexual athletes—When is competition fair? *Lancet, 366*, S42-S43.

Lovett, I. (2013, May 6). Changing sex, and changing teams. *New York Times.* Retrieved from www.nytimes.com/2013/05/07/us/transgender-high-school-students-gain-admission-to-sports-teams.html?pagewanted=all&_r=0

Lucas-Carr, C.B., & Krane, V. (2011). *What is the T in LGBT?* Supporting transgender athletes via sport psychology. *The Sport Psychologist, 4*, 532-548.

McGuire, J.K., Anderson, C.R., Toomey, R.B., & Russell, S.T. (2010). School climate for transgender youth: A mixed method investigation of student experiences and school responses. *Journal of Youth and Adolescence, 39*, 1175-1188.

Mueller, A., Zollver, H., Kronawitter, D., Oppelt, P., Claassen, T., Hoffmann, I., . . . Dittrich, R. (2011). Body composition and bone mineral density in male-to-female transsexuals during cross-sex hormone therapy using gonadotrophin-releasing hormone agonist. *Experimental and Clinical Endocrinology & Diabetes, 119*, 95-100.

Mustanski, B.M., Garofalo, R., & Emerson, E.M. (2010). Mental health disorders, psychological distress, and suicidality in a diverse sample of lesbian, gay, bisexual, and transgender youths. *American Journal of Public Health, 100*, 2426-2432.

National Collegiate Athletic Association (NCAA). (2009). Current NCAA position regarding transgender student-athlete participation and resource list. Retrieved from www.ncaa.org/wps/wcm/connect/0eece8804378fefdbaecba6bcdc87ae7/NCAA+TSA+Issues+Resource.pdf?MOD=AJPERES&CACHEID=0eece8804378fefdbaecba6bcdc87ae7

NCLR. (2005, October 11). National Center for Lesbian Rights asks Penn State to stop decades of anti-gay harassment by women's basketball coach Rene Portland [Press release]. Retrieved from www.clubs.psu.edu/up/psupride/articles/NCLR%20Press%20Release%2010112005.pdf

Nikki. (2013, May 1). Nikki's Story. *Go! Athletes.* Retrieved from http://goathletes.org/go-athletes-blog/116-nikki-s-story.html

Osborne, B. (2007). "No drinking, no drugs, no lesbians": Sexual orientation discrimination in intercollegiate athletics. *Marquette Sports Law Review, 17,* 481-501.

Russell, S.T., Ryan, C., Toomey, R.B., Diaz, R.M., & Sanchez, J. (2011). Lesbian, gay, bisexual, and transgender adolescent school victimization: Implications for young adult health and adjustment. *Journal of School Health, 81*(5), 223-230.

Spack, N.P., Edwards-Leeper, L., Feldman, H.A., Leibowitz, S., Mandel, F., Diamond, D.A., & Vance, S.R. (2012). Children and adolescents with gender identity disorder referred to a pediatric medical center. *Pediatrics, 129,* 418-425.

Stieglitz, K.A. (2010). Development, risk, and resilience of transgender youth. *Journal of the Association of Nurses in AIDS Care, 21,* 192-206.

Stoelting, S. (2011). Disclosure as an interaction: Why lesbian athletes disclose their sexual identities in intercollegiate sport. *Journal of Homosexuality, 58,* 1187-1210.

Tony Zamazal, Texas transgender student, wins right to wear dress and heels to prom [Blog post]. (2013, April 5). Retrieved from www.huffingtonpost.com/2013/04/05/tony-zamazal-transgender-prom_n_3021109.html

Torre, P.S., & Epstein, D. (2012, May 28). The transgender athlete. *Sports Illustrated, 116*(22). Retrieved from http://www.si.com/vault/2012/05/28/106195901/the-transgender-athlete

Transgender Law & Policy Institute. (2009). *Guidelines for creating policies for transgender children in recreational sports.* Retrieved from www.transgenderlaw.org/resources/TLPI_GuidlinesforCreatingPoliciesforTransChildreninRecSports.pdf

Understanding gender. (2013). *Gender Spectrum.* Retrieved from www.genderspectrum.org/understanding-gender

Van Caenegem, E., Wierckx, K., Taes, Y., Dedecker, D., Van de Peer, F., Toye, K., . . . T'Sjoen, G. (2012). Bone mass, bone geometry, and body composition in female-to-male transsexual persons after long-term cross-sex hormonal therapy. *Journal of Clinical Endocrinology and Metabolism, 97,* 2503-2511.

Wallien, M.S.C., & Cohen-Kettenis, P.T. (2008). Psychosexual outcome of gender-dysphoric children. *Journal of American Academy of Child Adolescent Psychiatry, 47,* 1413-1423.

Women's Sport Foundation. (2011). Recruiting—Negative recruiting/slander based on sexuality: The Foundation position. Retrieved from www.womenssportsfoundation.org/home/advocate/foundation-positions/lgbt-issues/negative_recruiting

Woog, D. (2013, March 7). US soccer, and all that trans Jazz. *Between the Lines.* Retrieved from www.pridesource.com/article.html?article=58803

Zeigler, C. (2013, May 8). Taylor Edelmann is trans volleyball player at Purchase College. *Outsports.* Retrieved from www.outsports.com/2013/5/8/4312770/taylor-edelmann-transgender-volleyball-purchase-college

Zhao, Y., Montoro, R., Igartua, K., & Thombs, B.D. (2010). Suicidal ideation and attempt among adolescents reporting "unsure" sexual identity or heterosexual identity plus same-sex attraction or behavior: Forgotten groups? *Journal of the American Academy of Child and Adolescent Psychiatry, 49,* 104-113.

Chapter 8

Administration on Aging. (2013). Profile of older Americans 2013. Retrieved from www.aoa.gov/Aging_Statistics/Profile/index.aspx

Anderson, K. (2008, August 25). One for the aged. *Sports Illustrated, 109*(7), 74-77.

Associated Press. (2015, May 31). 92-year-old becomes oldest woman to complete marathon after finishing race in San Diego. *U.S. News.* Accessed from www.usnews.com/news/sports/articles/2015/05/31/92-year-old-seeks-to-become-oldest-woman-to-finish-marathon

Berkley, N. (2013). How many golfers in the U.S.? *Berkley Golf Consulting.* Retrieved from http://nancyberkley.com/771810.html

Borzi, P. (2007). Grannies are flexing their muscles, gently. *New York Times.* Retrieved from www.nytimes.com/2007/02/21/sports/othersports/21granny.html?pagewanted=alland_r=0

Boyd, T. (2006). *Report on demographic and consumption behaviors of USMS members.* United States Masters Swimming. Retrieved from www.usms.org/admin/surveys/May2006/consumption_report.pdf

Bruce, D.G., Devine, A., & Prince, R.L. (2002). Recreational physical activity levels in healthy older women: The importance of falling. *Journal of the American Geriatric Society, 50*(1), 84-89.

Carmichael, F., Duberley, J., & Szmigin, I. (2014, July). Older women and their participation in exercise and leisure-time physical activity: The double edged sword of work. *Sport in Society: Cultures, Commerce, Media, Politic, 18*(1), 1-19.

Clift, E. (2011, August 18). Finishing strong—older women athletes show the way. *Women's Media Center.* Retrieved from www.womensmediacenter.com/feature/entry/finishing-strongolder-women-athletes-show-the-way

Cooper, P. (1998). *The American marathon.* Syracuse, NY: Syracuse University Press.

Cousins, S. (2000). "My heart couldn't take it": Older women's beliefs about exercise. *Journal of Gerontology, Behavior Psychology, and Social Science, 55*(5), 283-294.

Dara Torres: The new beauty myth. (2008, August 8). *The-F-Word*. Retrieved from http://the-f-word.org/blog/index.php/2008/08/08/dara-torres-the-new-beauty-myth

Daughtery, C., Vowels, N., & Black, G. (2011). *United States Masters Swimming survey* [Unpublished report]. U.S. Masters Swimming. Retrieved from www.usms.org/admin/surveys/2011/full_member_survey_web version.pdf

Doi, T., Ono, R., Ono, K., Yamguchi, R., Makiura, D., & Hirata, S. (2012). The association between fear of falling and physical activity in older women. *Journal of Physical Therapy Science, 24*(9), 859-862.

Dunbar, B., Beach, R.E., Spannuth, J., & Wilson, M. (2012). *Masters swimming for life—from the beginning*. Presented at International Aquatic History Symposium and Film Festival, May 9-12, Fort Lauderdale, FL. Retrieved from www.usms.org/hist/40yrsofusms.pdf

Franks, J. (2012, August 18). American Diana Nyad starts latest Cuba-U.S. swim attempt. *Chicago Tribune*. Retrieved from http://articles.chicagotribune.com/2012-08-18/business/sns-rt-cuba-swim-tvpix l2e8ji1tm-20120818_1_shark-cage-unassisted-open-ocean-cuba

Geoghegan, T. (2011). Why do Americans die younger than Britons? *BBC News*. Retrieved from www.bbc.com/news/world-us-canada-14070090

Grierson, B. (2010, November 25). The incredible flying nonagenarian. *New York Times*. Retrieved from www.nytimes.com/2010/11/28/magazine/28athletes-t.html?_r=0

Ha, T.T. (2014, June 26). Olga Kotelko, a Canadian track star well into her 90s, has died. *The Globe and Mail*. Retrieved from www.theglobeandmail.com/news/national/senior-athlete-olga-kotelko-dead-at-95/article19329789

Harsbarger, R., & Jacobsen, J. (2013). *National running survey*. Retrieved from www.runningusa.org/national-runner-survey

Harvard Health Publications. (2014). Simple exercises to prevent falls. *Harvard Women's Health News, 2*(11), 6.

Henderson, K.A. (2010). Women, gender, and leisure matter. *Journal of Zhejiang University, 40*(2), 117-124.

Heo, J., Culp, B., Yamada, N., & Won, Y. (2013, August). Promoting successful aging through competitive sports participation: Insights from older adults. *Qualitative Health Research, 23*(1), 105-113.

House, C. (2003, January 7). June Krauser gets her own lane: 2001 masters swimmer of the year. Biography. *U.S. Masters Swimming*. Retrieved from www.usms.org/articles/articledisplay.php?aid=1402

Howard, J. (2010, August 19). Diana Nyad: Back to the sea again. *ESPN.com*. Retrieved from http://sports.espn.go.com/espn/commentary/news/story?page=howard/100819

Julian, S. (2015, May 31). Fit@50: Mountain-climbing motivational speaker shares her best training tips. *AARP.com*. Accessed from www.aarp.org/health/healthy-living/info-2015/fitness-tips-susan-ershler.html

Kelley, K., Little, S., Lee, J.S., Birendra, K.C., & Henderson, K. (2014). Articulating meanings of positive adjustment to aging through physical activity participation among older adults. *Journal of Park and Recreation Administration, 32*(1), 63-79.

Kirby, J.B., & Kluge, M.A. (2013). Going for the gusto: Competing for the first time at age 65. *Journal of Aging and Physical Activity, 21*(3), 290-308.

Litchfield, C., & Dionigi, N. (2013). Rituals in Australian women's veteran's field hockey. *International Journal of Sport & Society, 3*(3), 171-189.

National Senior Games Association. (2013). National Senior Games results book. Retrieved from www.nsga.com/media/documents/national-results/2013/Results-Book2013.pdf

Nyad, D. (1978). *Other shores*. New York, NY: Random House.

Nyad, D. (2011). Swimming toward a lifetime goal. Retrieved from www.aarp.org/personal-growth/life-stories/info-07-2010/diana_nyad_firstperson.html

Oghene, P.O. (2013). Understanding the meanings created around the aging body and sports by masters athletes through media data [Unpublished master's thesis]. Sudbury, CA: Laurentian University.

Palowski, A. (2014, January 20). What makes Olga run? Lessons from a 94-year-old track star. *Today Health and Wellness*. Retrieved from www.today.com/health/what-makes-olga-run-lessons-94-year-old-track-star-2D11947816

Pfister, G. (2012). It's never too late to win—sporting activities and performances of ageing women. *Sport in Society, 15*(3), 369-385.

Running USA. (2013). 2013 state of the sport—Part III: U.S. race trends. Retrieved from www.runningusa.org/state-of-sport-2013-part-III

Serra, M. C., McMillin, S. L., & Ryan, A. S. (2012). Aging in women athletes. *An International Perspective on Topics in Sports Medicine and Sports Injury*, 131-144. Retrieved from http://cdn.intechopen.com/pdfs-wm/28446.pdf

Sharples, M. (1989). *If Madge can do it*. London, England: MRG.

Sims, S.T., Larson, J.C., Lamonte, M.J., Michael, Y.L., Johnson, K.C., Sarto, G.E., & Stefanik, M.L. (2012, January). Physical activity and body mass: Changes in younger versus older postmenopausal women. *Medical Science and Sports Exercise, 44*(1), 89-97.

Sloane, M., Hanna, J., & Ford, D. (2013, September 3). "Never, ever give up": Diana Nyad completes historic Cuba-to-Florida swim. *CNN.com*. Retrieved from www.cnn.com/2013/09/02/world/americas/diana-nyad-cuba-florida-swim

Smith, C. (2012, August 21). Diana Nyad photos show how badly attempted Cuba-to-Florida swim ravaged her features. *Yahoo Sports*. Retrieved from http:// sports.yahoo.com/blogs/olympics-fourth-place-medal/ diana-nyad-photos-show-just-badly-attempted-cuba-200627924--oly.html

Smith, K.L., Carr, K., Wiseman, A., Calhoun, K., McNevin, N.H., & Weir, P.L. (2012). Barriers are not the limiting factor to participation in physical activity in Canadian seniors. *Journal of Aging Research*, 1-9.

Staton, R. (2014, May 4). Granny basketball game photos. *City of Georgetown Website*. Retrieved from https://georgetown.org/2014/05/03/granny-basketball-game-photos

Staurowsky, E. J., DeSousa, M. J., Miller, K. E., Sabo, D., Shakib, S., Theberge, N., . . . Williams, N. (2015). *Her life depends on it III: Sport, physical activity, and the health and well-being of American girls and women*. East Meadow, NY: Women's Sports Foundation.

Stephan, Y., Boiché, J., & Le Scanff, C. (2010). Motivation and physical activity behaviors among older women: A self-determination perspective. *Psychology of Women Quarterly, 34*(3), 339-348.

Stein, J. (2011, August 10). Diana Nyad's Cuba-to-U.S. swim has lessons for us all. *Los Angeles Times*. Retrieved from http://articles.latimes.com/2011/aug/10/news/la-heb-diana-nyad-20110810

Stewart, J. (2014). "Just get out there and move" master athlete Olga Kotelko leaves gold legacy. *Friesen Press*. Retrieved from http://friesenpress.com/blog/2014/6/27/master-athlete-olga-kotelko-leaves-gold-legacy

Strawbridge, M. (2001). Current activity patterns of women intercollegiate athletes from the 1960s and 1970s. *Women in Sport and Physical Activity Journal, 19*(1), 55-68.

Sun, Q., Townsend, M.K., Okereke, O., Franco, O.H., Hu, F.B., & Grodstein, F. (2010). Physical activity at midlife in relation to successful survival in women at age 70 years or older. *Archives of Internal Medicine, 170*(2), 194-201.

Syeed, N. (2007, January 14). More senior women stay fit playing hoops. *Washington Post*. Retrieved from www.washingtonpost.com/wp-dyn/content/article/2007/01/14/AR2007011400388.html

Tahmaseb-McConatha, J., Volkwein-Caplan, K., & DiGregorio, N. (2011). Culture, gaining and well-being: The importance of place and space. *The International Journal of Sport and Society, 2*(2), 41-48.

USA Volleyball. (2013, March 1). *USA Volleyball demographics*. Colorado Springs, CO: Author.

U.S. Department of Health & Human Services. (2010). *Healthy people 2020*. Washington, DC: Author.

Vertinsky, Patricia. (2000). A woman's place in the marathon of life: Feminist perspectives on physical activity and aging. *Journal of Aging and Physical Activity, 8*, 386-406.

Vertinsky, P. (2002). Sporting women in the public gaze: Shattering the master narrative of aging female bodies. *Canadian Women's Studies, 21*(3), 58-63.

Walker, L. (2012). *Aging with strength*. Waialua, HA: Author.

Weil, E. (2008, June 29). A swimmer of a certain age. *New York Times*. Retrieved from www.nytimes.com/2008/06/29/magazine/29torres-t.html?pagewanted=all and_r=0

Weil, E. (2011, December 1). Marathon swimmer Diana Nyad takes on the demons of the sea. *New York Times*. Retrieved from www.nytimes.com/2011/12/04/magazine/marathon-swimmer-diana-nyad.html?_r=0

Women's Health USA. (2010). *Health status—Health behaviors*. Retrieved from http://mchb.hrsa.gov/whusa10/pdfs/w08hshb.pdf

Chapter 9

About Linda. (n.d.). Retrieved from www.lindamastandrea.com/About-Linda.html

About Tatyana. (n.d.). Retrieved from http://tatyanamcfadden.com/about-tatyana

Active Policy Solutions. (2013). Q and A: Disability in sport Dear Colleague Letter. Washington, DC: Author.

Benjamin, A. (2001). *Making an entrance: Theory and practice for disabled and non-disabled dancers*. New York, NY: Routledge.

Biography: Aimee Mullins. (n.d.). Retrieved from www.aimeemullins.com/about.php

Blaze Sports America. (2013). Our purpose. Retrieved from www.blazesports.org/about/our-purpose

Brittain, I. (2012). The role of gender in participation in disability sport. Retrieved from http://paralympicanorak.wordpress.com/2012/06/07/the-role-of-gender-in-participation-in-disability-sport

Clifford, J. (2011). The UN disability convention and its impact on European equality law. *The Equal Rights Review, 6*, 11-25.

Cody, A. (n.d.). *Gender issues in disability sport: Strategies for engaging girls and women in sport and physical activity*. Decatur, GA: Blaze Sports America.

Division of Disability Resources & Educational Services, University of Illinois. (n.d.). Stephanie Wheeler. Retrieved from www.disability.illinois.edu/athletics/coaches/stephanie-wheeler-0

Equity in sport. (n.d.). Retrieved from www.tatyanamcfadden.com/equity-in-sports.html

Grinberg, E. (2012). Ending the R-word: Ban it or understand it. Retrieved from http://edition.cnn.com/2012/03/07/living/end-r-word

Harpur, P., & Bales, R. (2010). Positive impact of the Convention on the Rights of Persons with Disabilities: A case study on the South Pacific and lessons from the U.S. experience. *Northern Kentucky Law Review, 37*(4), 363-388.

Hums, M.A., Wolff, E.A., & Morris, A. (2009, January). *Implementation of Article 30.5 of the Convention on the Rights of Persons with Disabilities*. Presented at the Boston University Law School Disability in Sport Symposium, Boston, MA.

Illinois Legal Aid. (2005). *Disabilities guidebook: Section 504: Education in schools receiving federal funds.* Retrieved from www.illinoislegalaid.org/index.cfm?fuseaction=home.dsp_content&contentID=228

International Olympic Committee. (2011). *The Olympic charter.* Lausanne, Switzerland: Author.

International Paralympic Committee (IPC). (n.d.-a.). History of the movement. Retrieved from www.paralympic.org/TheIPC/HWA/HistoryoftheMovement

International Paralympic Committee (IPC). (n.d.-b). London 2012. Retrieved from www.paralympic.org/paralympic-games/london-2012

International Paralympic Committee (IPC). (n.d.-c.). Record number of females to take part in London 2012. Retrieved from www.paralympic.org/news/record-number-females-take-part-london-2012

International Paralympic Committee (IPC). (2010). *IPC women in sport leadership toolkit.* Bonn, Germany: Author.

International Paralympic Committee (IPC). (2013). *International Paralympic Committee annual report 2012.* Bonn, Germany: Author.

McCallum, J. (2008, December 8). Small steps, great strides. *Sports Illustrated.* Retrieved from www.eunicekennedyshriver.org/bios/si

Milestones in APA and sport for people with disabilities. (n.d.). *International Platform on Sport and Development.* Retrieved from www.sportanddev.org/en/learnmore/sport_and_disability2/background___sport___disability/milestones_in_apa_and_sports_for_people_with_disabilities_

Moorman, A.M., & Hums, M.A. (2010, September). Analysis of the UN Convention on the Rights of Persons with Disabilities and US disability discrimination laws. Presented at the annual Congress of the European Association for Sport Management, Prague, Czech Republic.

Moorman, A.M., & Hums, M.A. (2013, March). Summary and discussion of the Department of Education guidance document clarifying legal obligations of schools to provide equal opportunity for students with disabilities in extracurricular activities. Presented at the annual conference of the Sport and Recreation Law Association, Denver, CO.

Moorman, A., & Masteralexis, L. (2001, June 11-17). *PGA-Martin* ruling's a verdict for inclusion, not doom. *Street & Smith's Sports Business Journal, 4*(8), 32.

Paralympic record breaker, Aimee Mullins seeks to redefine the word "disabled." (2012). *Epic Victories.* Retrieved from http://epicvictories.com/athlete-and-actor-aimee-mullins-seeks-out-to-redefine-the-word-disabled-she-instead-is-differently-abled

Special Olympics. (n.d.-a.). Demographics. Retrieved from http://resources.specialolympics.org/Topics/Research/Program_Research_Toolkit/Demographics.aspx

Special Olympics. (n.d.-b). International Women's Day: Celebrate the females of Special Olympics and help get more involved. Retrieved from http://specialolympicsblog.wordpress.com/2013/03/08/international-womens-day-celebrate-the-females-of-special-olympics-help-us-get-more-involved

Staurowsky, E.J. (2013, March 21). New guidance from the Office for Civil Rights regarding athletes with disabilities. *College Sports Business News.* Retrieved from http://collegesportsbusinessnews.com/issue/march-2013/article/new-guidance-from-the-office-for-civil-rights-regarding-athletes-with-disabilities

United Nations. (2006). *Convention on the Rights of Persons with Disabilities and Optional Protocol.* Geneva, SUI: Author.

United Nations Enable. (n.d.). Fact sheet on persons with disabilities. Retrieved from www.un.org/disabilities/default.asp?id=18

United Nations Human Rights. (2013). International human rights law. Retrieved from www.ohchr.org/en/professionalinterest/Pages/InternationalLaw.aspx

United States Department of Justice. (2009). A guide to disability rights laws. Retrieved from www.ada.gov/cguide.htm

United States Olympic Committee (USOC). (n.d.). Stephanie Wheeler. Retrieved from www.teamusa.org/Athletes/WH/Stephanie-Wheeler.aspx

White House Task Force on Childhood Obesity. (2010). V. Increasing physical activity. In *Solving the problem of childhood obesity within a generation* (pp. 65-85). Washington, DC: Author.

Women's Sports Foundation. (2007). *What is the Women's Sports Foundation?* East Meadows, NY: Author.

Chapter 10

Acosta, V., & Carpenter, L. (2012). *Women in intercollegiate sport: A longitudinal national study. Thirty-five year update. 1977-2012.* Retrieved from http://acostacarpenter.org/AcostaCarpenter2012.pdf

Ali, R. (2010, October 26). *Dear colleague letter.* U.S. Department of Education, Office for Civil Rights. Retrieved from www2.ed.gov/about/offices/list/ocr/letters/colleague-201010.pdf

Ali, R. (2011, April 4). *Dear colleague letter.* U.S. Department of Education, Office for Civil Rights. Retrieved from www2.ed.gov/about/offices/list/ocr/letters/colleague-201104.html

Brackenridge, C.H. (1997). Understanding sexual abuse in sport. In R. Lidor & M. Bar-Ell (Eds.), *Proceedings of the IX World Congress of Sport Psychology* (pp. 142-144). Netanya, Israel: Ministry of Education, Culture, and Sport.

Brackenridge, C.H., Bishop, D.T., Moussali, S., & Tapp, J. (2008). The characteristics of sexual abuse in sport: A multidimensional scaling analysis of events described in media reports. *International Journal of Exercise and Sport Psychology, 6,* 385-406.

Brake, D. (2012). Going outside Title IX to keep coach-athlete relationships in bounds. *Marquette Sports Law Review, 22*(2), 395-491.

Buchwald, M.E. (2008). Sexual harassment in education and student athletics: A case for why Title IX sexual harassment jurisprudence should develop independently of Title VII. *University of Maryland Law Review*, *67*(3), 672-724.

Burton Nelson, M., & Brake, D. (2012). *Staying in bounds: An NCAA model policy to prevent inappropriate relationships between student-athletes and athletics department personnel*. National Collegiate Athletic Association. Retrieved from www.ncaa.org/sites/default/files/Staying+in+Bounds+Final.pdf

Christiansen, S., Hubbell, K., Lee, C., O'Brien, E., & Staurowsky, E.J. (2010). Of orange pride and prejudice: An examination of host/hostess groups in college recruiting. Presented at College Sport Research Institute Conference, University of North Carolina, Chapel Hill, NC.

Chuchmach, M., & Patel, A. (2010, April 9). ABC News investigation: USA swimming coaches molested, secretly taped dozens of teen swimmers. *ABC News*. Retrieved from http://abcnews.go.com/Blotter/abc-news-investigation-usa-swimming-coaches-raped-molested/story?id=10322469#.UchrmZxc2pI

Crossett, T., Ptacek, J., McDonald, M.A., & Benedict, J.R. (1996). Male student athletes and violence against women. *Violence Against Women, 2*(2), 163-179.

Diamond, M. (2011, December 16). NBA official allegedly fired for reporting sexual harassment against female employees. *Think Progress*. Retrieved from http://thinkprogress.org/justice/2011/12/16/390943/nba-official-allegedly-fired-for-reporting-sexual-harassment-against-female-employees

Distant, D. (2013, June 19). Serena Williams on Steubenville rape: "Shouldn't have put herself in that position." *The Christian Post*. Retrieved from www.christianpost.com/news/serena-sorry-for-steubenville-rape-comments-williams-contacting-victims-family-98350

Elendu, I.C., & Umeakuka, O.A. (2011). Perpetrators of sexual harassment experienced by athletes in southern Nigerian universities. *South African Journal for Research in Sport, Physical Education and Recreation, 33*(1), 53-63.

Fasting, K., Brackenridge, C., & Sundgot-Borgen, J. (2000). *Females, elite sports, and sexual harassment: The Norwegian Women's Project*. Oslo, Norway: Norwegian Olympic Committee.

Fasting, K., Brackenridge, C., & Walseth, K. (2007). Women athletes' personal responses to sexual harassment in sport. *Journal of Applied Sport Psychology, 19*(4), 419-433.

Fasting, K., & Knorre, N. (2005). *Women in sport in the Czech Republic: The experience of female athletes*. Oslo, Norway, & Prague, The Czech Republic: The Norwegian School of Sport Sciences and Czech Olympic Committee.

Fejgin, N. and Hanegby, R. (2001). Gender and cultural bias in perceptions of sexual harassment in sport. *International Review for the Sociology of Sport, 36*(4): 459-478.

Forbes, G.B., Adams-Curtis, L.E., Pakalka, A.H., & White, K.B. (2006). Dating aggression, sexual coercion, and aggression-supporting attitudes among college men as a function of participation in aggressive high school sports. *Violence Against Women, 12*(5), 441-454.

Gregoire, C. (2012, April 9). Rape statistics: Over 17 percent of high school-age girls in Indiana experience sexual assault. *The Huffington Post*. Retrieved from www.huffingtonpost.com/2012/04/09/indiana-sexual-assault-17_n_1412507.html

Hartill, M. (2013). Concealment of child sexual abuse in sports. *Quest, 65*(2), 241-255.

Hill, C., & Kearl, H. (2011). *Crossing the line: Sexual harassment at school*. Washington, DC: American Association of University Women.

Humphrey, S.E., & Kahn, A.S. (2000). Fraternities, athletic teams, and rape: Importance of identification in high risk groups. *Journal of Interpersonal Violence, 15*(12), 1313-1322.

Kirby, S., Greaves, L., & Hankivsky, O. (2000). *The dome of silence: Sexual abuse and harassment in sport*. London: Zed Books.

Krebs, C., Lindquist, C.H., Warner, T.D., Fisher, B.S., & Martin, S.L. (2007). *The campus assault (CAS) study*. National Institute of Justice. Retrieved from www.ncjrs.gov/pdffiles1/nij/grants/221153.pdf

LaVoi, N. (2013, May 28). Female coaches in high school sports: Data released. *Women in Coaching Blog*. Retrieved from www.nicolemlavoi.com/female-coaches-in-high-school-sports-data-released

Lyndon, A.E., Duffy, D.M., Smith, P.H., & White, J.W. (2011, December 14). The role of high school coaches in helping prevent adolescent sexual aggression: Part of the solution or part of the problem? *Journal of Sport and Social Issues*, 1-23. DOI: 10.1177/019372351/0193723511426292

Macur, J., & Schweber, N. (2012, December 16). Rape case unfolds on web and splits city. *New York Times*. Retrieved from www.nytimes.com/2012/12/17/sports/high-school-football-rape-case-unfolds-online-and-divides-steubenville-ohio.html?pagewanted=all&_r=0

McMahon, S. (2010, July/August). Rape myth beliefs and bystander attitudes among incoming college students. *Journal of American College Health, 59*(1), 3-11.

Moynihan, M.M., Banyard, V.L., Arnold, J.S., Eckstein, R.P., & Stapleton, J.G. (2010). Engaging intercollegiate athletes in preventing and intervening in sexual and intimate partner violence. *Journal of American College Health, 59*(3), 97-204.

Noveck, J. (2013, March 19). In Steubenville case, social media is a double-edged sword. *Akron Beacon Journal*. Retrieved from www.ohio.com/news/break-news/in-steubenville-case-social-media-is-a-double-edged-sword-1.382772

Ove, T. (2013, March 15). Teen testifies under immunity that he videotaped Steubenville assault. *Pittsburgh Post-Gazette*. Retrieved from www.post-gazette

.com/local/region/2013/03/15/Teen-testifies-under-immunity-that-he-videotaped-Steubenville-assault/stories/201303150269

Pedersen, P., Lim, C.H., Osborne, B., & Whisenant, W. (2009). An examination of the perceptions of sexual harassment by sport print media professionals. *Journal of Sport Management, 23*(3), 335-360.

Ressler, T.C. (2013, April 23). Michigan high school chooses to protect star basketball player instead of his rape victim. *Think Progress*. Retrieved from http://thinkprogress.org/health/2013/04/23/1907651/michigan-high-school-rape-culture

Rios, C., & Clancy, C. (2013). No more Steubenvilles: Educate coaches about sexual assault. Retrieved from www.change.org/p/no-more-steubenvilles-educate-coaches-about-sexual-assault

Rodriguez, E.A., & Gill, D.L. (2011). Sexual harassment perceptions among Puerto Rican female former athletes. *International Journal of Sport and Exercise Psychology, 9*(4), 323-337.

Sawyer, R.G., Thompson, E.E., & Chicorelli, A.M. (2002). Rape myth acceptance among intercollegiate student athletes: A preliminary examination. *American Journal of Health Studies, 18*(1), 19-25.

Shulman, L.B., & Clifton, G.E. (2011). Sexual harassment and professional sports organizations. *Professional Sports and the Law, 1*(6), 1-3.

Starr, K. (2013, January 16). Breaking down sexual abuse in sports. *Huffington Post*. Retrieved from www.huffingtonpost.com/katherine-starr/breaking-down-sexual-abus_b_2500956.html

Steinbach, P. (2012). Abuse victim Katherine Starr launches Safe4Athletes. *Athletic Business*. Retrieved from www.athleticbusiness.com/athlete-safety/abuse-victim-katherine-starr-launches-safe4athletes.html

Toftegaard-Nielsen, J. (2001). The forbidden zone: Intimacy, sexual relations and misconduct in the relationship between coaches and athletes. *International Review for the Sociology of Sport, 36*(2), 165-182.

USA Gymnastics. (2013, May). Permanently ineligible members. Retrieved from http://usagym.org/pages/aboutus/pages/permanently_ineligible_members.html

USA Swimming. (2013). Individuals permanently suspended or ineligible. Retrieved from www.usaswimming.org/ViewMiscArticle.aspx?TabId=1963&mid=10011&ItemId=5107

Volkwein, K.A.E., Schnell, F.I., Sherwood, D., & Livezy, A. (1997). Sexual harassment in sport: Perceptions and experiences of American female student-athletes. *International Review for the Sociology of Sport, 32*(3), 283-297.

Welsh-Huggins, A. (2013, May 24). Grand jury resumes investigating Steubenville rape case. *The Columbus Dispatch*. Retrieved from www.dispatch.com/content/stories/local/2013/05/24/grand-jury-resumes-investigating-case.html

Wetzel, D. (2013, March 13). Steubenville rape trial divides Ohio town. *YahooSports.com*. Retrieved from http://sports.yahoo.com/news/highschool--steubenville-rape-trial-divides-ohio-town-052958178.html

Willmsen, C., & O'Hagan, M. (2003). Coaches continue working for schools and private teams after being caught for sexual misconduct. *Seattle Times*. Retrieved from http://seattletimes.com/news/local/coaches/news/dayone.html

Women's Law Project. (2012). The impact of sexual victimization on women's and girls' health. In *Through the lens of equality: Eliminating sex bias to improve the health of Pennsylvania's women*. Philadelphia, PA: Women's Law Project. Retrieved from www.womenslawproject.org/resources/TLE_Chapter3B.pdf

Chapter 11

Ain, M. (2012). The body issue: Hope Solo. *ESPNW*. Retrieved from http://espn.go.com/espnw/body-issue/6974155/hope-solo

Association for Women in Sports Media (AWSM). (2013, April 29). AWSM responds to Cherry's comments about women in locker rooms. Retrieved from http://awsmonline.org/awsm-response-to-cherry-comments

Barnett, B. (2013). The babe/baby factor: Sport, women, and mass media. In P. Pedersen (Ed.), *Routledge handbook of sport communication* (pp. 350-358). New York, NY: Routledge.

Billings, A.C., Angelini, J.R., & Eastman, S.T. (2005). Diverging discourses: Gender differences in televised golf announcing. *Mass Communication & Society, 8*(2), 155-171.

Brennan, C. (2012, July 25). Finally: It's all about the women at the London Olympics. *USA Today*. Retrieved from http://usatoday30.usatoday.com/sports/story/2012-07-25/London-Olympics-Brennan-women/56488526/1

Bruce, T., & Hardin, M. (2014). Reclaiming our voices: Sportswomen and social media. In A.C. Billings & M. Hardin (Eds.), *Routledge Handbook of Sport and New Media* (pp. 774-795). New York, NY: Routledge.

Byerly, C.M. (2011). Global report on the status of women in the news media. International Women's Media Foundation. Retrieved from http://iwmf.org/pdfs/IWMF-Global-Report.pdf

Chambers, D., Steiner, L., & Fleming, C. (2004). *Women and journalism*. New York, NY: Routledge.

Clavio, G., & Eagleman, A.N. (2011). Gender and sexually suggestive images in sports blogs. *Journal of Sports Management, 25*(4), 295-304.

Cooky, C., & LaVoi, N.M. (2012). Playing but losing women's sports after Title IX. *Contexts, 11*(1), 42-46.

Cooky, C., Messner, M.A., & Musto, M. (2015). "It's dude time!": A quarter century of excluding women's sports in televised news and highlight shows. *Communication & Sport*, 1-27.

Creedon, P. (1994a). From whalebone to spandex: Women and sports journalism in American magazines, photography and broadcasting. In P. Creedon (Ed.),

Women, media, and sport: Challenging gender values (pp. 108-158). New York, NY: Sage.

Creedon, P. (1994b). Women in toyland: A look at women in American newspaper sports journalism. In P. Creedon (Ed.), *Women, media, and sport: Challenging gender values* (pp. 67-107). New York, NY: Sage.

Eastman, S.T., & Billings, A.C. (2000). Sportscasting and sports reporting. *Journal of Sport and Social Issues, 24*, 192-224.

Fink, J.S., & Kensicki, L.J. (2002). An imperceptible difference: Visual and textual constructions of femininity in *Sports Illustrated* and *Sports Illustrated Women*. *Mass Communication & Society, 5*(3), 317-339.

Fitz-Gerald, S. (2013, April 27). Don Cherry on female reporters: "I don't believe women should be in the male dressing room." *National Post*. Retrieved from http://news.nationalpost.com/sports/nhl/don-cherry-on-female-reporters-i-dont-believe-women-should-be-in-the-male-dressing-room

Goldstein, R. (2008, Sept. 22). Mary Garber, sportswriter, dies at 92. *New York Times*. Retrieved from www.nytimes.com/2008/09/23/sports/23garber.html?_r=0

Hardin, M., & Shain, S. (2005a). Female sports journalists: Are we there yet? "No." *Newspaper Research Journal, 26*(4), 22-35.

Hardin, M., & Shain, S. (2005b). Strength in numbers? The experiences and attitudes of women in sports media careers. *Journalism & Mass Communication Quarterly, 82*(4), 804-819.

Hardin, M., Shain, S., & Shultz-Poniatowski, K. (2008). "There's no sex attached to your occupation": The revolving door for young women in sports journalism. *Women in Sport and Physical Activity Journal, 17*(1), 68-79.

Hardin, M., & Whiteside, E. (2006). Fewer women, minorities work in sports departments. *Newspaper Research Journal, 27*(2), 38-51.

Hardin, M., & Whiteside, E. (2009). Token responses to gendered newsrooms: Factors in the career-related decisions of female newspaper sports journalists. *Journalism, 10*(5), 627-646.

Hardin, M., & Whiteside, E. (2014). From second-wave to poststructuralist feminism: Evolving frameworks for viewing representations of women's sports. In A.N. Valdivia & E. Scharrer (Eds.), *The International Encyclopedia of Media Studies, Vol III* (pp. 116-136). Oxford, England: Blackwell.

Hatton, E., & Trautner, M.N. (2011). Equal opportunity objectification? The sexualization of men and women on the cover of *Rolling Stone*. *Sexuality & Culture, 15*(3), 256-278.

Herman, R. (2013, July 16). How far have we really come? *espnW*. Retrieved from http://espn.go.com/espnw/w-in-action/nine-for-ix/article/9481107/espnw-how-far-female-journalists-really-come

Horky, T., & Nieland, J.-U. (2011). *First results of the International Sports Press Survey 2011*. Cologne, Germany:

German Sport University. Retrieved from www.playthegame.org/fileadmin/image/PTG2011/Presentation/PTG_Nieland-Horky_ISPS_2011_3.10.2011_final.pdf

Jones, A.H. (2011). Visual and verbal gender cues in the televised coverage of the 2010 Winter Olympics. *The International Journal of Interdisciplinary Social Sciences, 6*(2), 199-216.

Jones, R., Murrell, A.J., & Jackson, J. (1999). Pretty versus powerful in the sports pages print media coverage of U.S. women's Olympic Gold Medal winning teams. *Journal of Sport & Social Issues, 23*(2), 183-192.

Kane, M.J. (2011, July 27). Sex sells sex, not women's sports. *The Nation*. Retrieved from www.thenation.com/article/162390/sex-sells-sex-not-womens-sports#

Kane, M.J., LaVoi, N.M., & Fink, J.S. (2013). Exploring elite female athletes' interpretations of sport media images: A window into the construction of social identity and "selling sex" in women's sports. *Communication & Sport, 1*(3), 269-298.

Kaszuba, D. (2003). They are women, hear them roar: Female sportswriters of the roaring twenties [Doctoral dissertation]. The Pennsylvania State University. Retrieved from https://etda.libraries.psu.edu/paper/6174/1455

Knoppers, A., & Elling, A. (2004). "We do not engage in promotional journalism": Discursive strategies used by sport journalists to describe the selection process. *International Review for the Sociology of Sport, 39*(1), 57-73.

Krane, V., Ross, S.R., Miller, M., Rowse, J.L., Ganoe, K., Andrzejczyk, J.A., & Lucas, C.B. (2010). Power and focus: Self-representation of female college athletes. *Qualitative Research in Sport and Exercise, 2*(2), 175-195.

Lapchick, R., Burnett, C., Farris, M., Gossett, R., Orpilla, C., Phelan, J., . . . Snively. D. (2013, March 1). The 2012 Associated Press sports editors racial and gender report card. Retrieved from www.tidesport.org/RGRC/2012/2012_APSE_RGRC.pdf

Messner, M.A., & Cooky, C.A. (2010). Gender in televised sports, news and highlights shows, 1989-2009. Los Angeles, CA: Center for Feminist Research, University of Southern California.

North, L. (2007). "Just a little bit of cheeky ribaldry"? *Feminist Media Studies, 7*(1), 81-96.

Nylund, D. (2007). *Beer, babes, and balls: Masculinity and sports talk radio*. Albany, NY: State University of New York Press.

Pedersen, P., Lim, C.H., Osborne, B., & Whisenant, W. (2009). An examination of the perceptions of sexual harassment by sport print media professionals. *Journal of Sport Management, 23*, 335-360.

Riley, L. (2013, July 13). Claire Smith's locker room exile a reminder of how far we've come. *The Courant*. Retrieved from http://articles.courant.com/2013-07-13/sports/hc-riley-column-0714-20130713_1_san-diego-padres-espn-documentary-claire-smith

Rowe, D. (2007). Sports journalism: Still the "toy department" of the news media? *Journalism, 8*(4), 385-405.

Walsh-Childers, K., Chance, J., & Herzog, K. (1996). Sexual harassment of women journalists. *Journalism & Mass Communication Quarterly, 73*(3), 559-581.

Whiteside, E., & Hardin, M. (2010). Public relations and sports: Work force demographics in the intersection of two gendered industries. *Journal of Sports Media, 5*(1), 21-52.

Whiteside, E., & Hardin, M. (2012). On being a "good sport" in the workplace: Women, the glass ceiling, and negotiated resignation in sports information. *International Journal of Sport Communication, 5*(1), 51-68.

Chapter 12

Acosta, V., & Carpenter, L. (1990). *Women in intercollegiate sport: A longitudinal study, thirteen-year update, 1977-1990* [Unpublished report]. Brooklyn, NY: Brooklyn College.

Associated Press. (2015, June 3). Rita LeBlanc testifies of grandfather Tom Benson's unsound mind. *ESPN.* Accessed from http://espn.go.com/nfl/story/_/id/13007327/granddaughter-new-orleans-saints-new-orleans-pelicans-owner-tom-benson-concludes-testimony

Bergeron, D.M., Block, C.J., & Echtenkamp, B.A. (2006). Disabling the able: Stereotype threat and women's work performance. *Human Performance, 19,* 133-158.

BLS Reports. (2013, February). *Women in the labor force: A databook.* Washington, DC: U.S. Bureau of Labor Statistics.

Burstyn, V. (1999). *The rites of men: Manhood, politics, and the culture of sport.* Toronto: University of Toronto.

Chin, Y.W., Henry, I., & Hong, F. (2009, March). Gender, interculturalism, and discourses on women's leadership in the Olympic Movement. *International Journal of the History of Sport, 26*(3), 442-464.

Claringbould, I., & Knoppers, A. (2007). Finding a "normal" woman: Selection processes for board membership. *Sex Roles, 56*(7), 495-507.

Daddario, G. (1997). Gendered sports programming: 1992 Summer Olympic coverage and the feminine narrative form. *Sociology of Sport Journal, 14*(1), 103-120.

Di Giorgio, M. (n.d.). Golf for business for career and business success. *Par Excellence Magazine.* Retrieved from www.parexcellencemagazine.com/business-golf-for-women-golfers/massmutual-promotes-successful-women.html

Disch, L., & Kane, M. J. (1996). When a looker is a real bitch: Lisa Olson, sport, and the heterosexual matrix. *Signs, 2*(12), 278-308.

Ernst & Young. (2013, May). Women athletes business network. Retrieved from www.ey.com/BR/pt/About-us/Our-sponsorships-and-programs/Women-Athletes-Global-Leadership-Network---perspectives-on-sport-and-teams

Ernst & Young. (2014, October). Female executives say participation in sport helps accelerate leadership and career potential. Retrieved from www.ey.com/GL/en/Newsroom/News-releases/news-female-executives-say-participation-in-sport-helps-accelerate--leadership-and-career-potential

Espinosa, P. (2012). Golden girl: Olympic champion Donna de Varona champions others. Retrieved from www.wagmag.com/golden-girl

Florio, M. (2013, April 4). Aponte could be on track to become NFL's first female GM. *NBC Sports.* Retrieved from http://profootballtalk.nbcsports.com/2013/04/14/aponte-could-be-on-track-to-become-nfls-first-female-g-m

Game changers: Women in sports business. (2011). *Street & Smith's SportsBusinessJournal.* Retrieved from www.sportsbusinessdaily.com/Journal/Issues/2011/10/10/Game-Changers/Intro.aspx

Hall, M.A. (1996). *Feminism and sporting bodies: Essays on theory and practice.* Champaign, IL: Human Kinetics.

Hardin, M., & Whiteside, E. (2006, Spring). Fewer women, minorities work in sports departments. *Newspaper Research Journal, 27*(2), 38-51.

Heilman, B. (1962, April 16). Still on top at 14. *Sports Illustrated.* Retrieved from http://sportsillustrated.cnn.com/vault/article/magazine/MAG1073687/

Henry, I.P., & Robinson, L. (2010). *Gender equality and leadership in Olympic bodies: Women, leadership and the Olympic Movement, 2010.* Lausanne, Switzerland: International Olympic Committee.

Hock, L. (2013, June 14). Lydia Nsekera becomes first women elected to FIFA executive board. *The S.H.E. Network.* Retrieved from www.womenssportsfoundation.org/en/sitecore/content/home/she-network/sports/lydia-nsekera-becomes-first-woman-elected-to-fifa-executive-board.aspx

Hovden, J. (2010, July). Female top leaders—prisoners of gender? The gendering of leadership discourses in Norwegian sports organizations. *International Journal of Sport Policy, 2*(2), 189-206.

Kane, M. J., & Stangl, J. (1991). Employment patterns of female coaches in men's athletics: Tokenism and marginalization as reflections of occupational sex-segregation. *Journal of Sport & Social Issues, 15*(1), 21-41.

Kanter, R.M. (1977). *Men and women of the corporation.* New York, NY: Basic Books.

Knoppers, A., & Anthonissen, A. (2005). Male athletic and managerial masculinities: Congruencies in discursive practices? *Journal of Gender Studies, 14*(2), 123-136.

Kuttler, H. (2014, August 14). For ex-WNBA chief Donna Orender, NBA breakthrough for women a show of respect. *JTA.com.* Retrieved from www.jta.org/2014/08/14/arts-entertainment/for-ex-wnba-chief-donna-orender-nba-breakthrough-for-women-a-show-of-respect

Lapchick, R., Domingues, J., Haldane, L., Loomer, E., & Pelts, J. (2014). *The 2014 racial and gender report card: Major League Soccer.* Retrieved from www.tidesport.org/Final%202014%20MLS%20RGRC.pdf

Lapchick, R., Donovan, D., Loomer, E., & Martinez, L. (2014). *The 2014 racial and gender report card: National*

Basketball Association. Retrieved from www.tidesport .org/The%202014%20Racial%20and%20Gender%20 Report%20Card-%20NBA.pdf

Lapchick, R., Donovan, D., Rogers, S., & Johnson, A. (2014). *The 2014 racial and gender report card: National Football League.* Retrieved from www.tidesport .org/The%202014%20NFL%20Racial%20and%20 Gender%20Report%20Card2.pdf

Lapchick, R., Johnson, A., & Yacaman, A. (2014). *The 2014 Women's National Basketball Association racial and gender report card.* Retrieved from www.tidesport .org/The%202014%20Racial%20and%20Gender%20 Report%20Card-%20NBA.pdf

Lapchick, R., Lecky, A., & Trigg, A. (2012). *The 2012 racial and gender report card: National Basketball Association.* Retrieved from www.tidesport.org/ RGRC/2012/2012_NBA_RGRC%5B1%5D.pdf

Lapchick, R., & Salas, D. (2015). *The 2015 racial and gender report card: Major League Baseball.* Retrieved from www.tidesport.org/Ammended%20-%20The%20 2015%20MLB%20Racial%20&%20Gender%20 Report%20Card.pdf

Mathis, K. (2015, February 23). First Coast success: Donna Orender connects to reach her goals. *Daily Record.* Retrieved from www.jaxdailyrecord.com/ showstory.php?Story_id=544942

Maylon, H. (2011). Leadership, women in sport, and embracing empathy. *Advancing Women in Leadership,* *31*(1), 160-165.

Messner, M. (2002). *Taking the field: Women, men, and sports.* St. Paul, MN: University of Minnesota Press.

Messner, M., & Sabo, D. (1990). *Sport, men, and the gender order: Critical feminist perspectives.* Champaign, IL: Human Kinetics.

Messner, M., & Solomon, N.M. (2007). Social justice and men's interests: The case of Title IX. *Journal of Sport and Social Issues, 31*(2), 162-178.

Moore, M., Parkhouse, B., & Konrad, A.M. (2000). Women in sport management: Advancing the representation through HRM structures. *Gender in Management: An International Journal, 25*(2), 104-118.

National Collegiate Athletic Association. (2014). *NCAA race and gender demographics database: Student-athlete data.* Indianapolis, IN: Author.

Newman, E. (2013, March 8). Ranking the 10 most influential women in sport. *Sports Illustrated.* Retrieved from http://sportsillustrated.cnn.com/more/ news/20130308/women-sports-power-list

Orender, D. (2015, March). A conversation about gender equity. *Gen W Now.* Retrieved from www.genwnow .com/author/donna-orender

Pfister, G., & Radtke, S. (2006). Dropping out: Why male and female leaders in German sports federations break off their careers. *Sport Management Review, 9*(2), 111-139.

Riley, L. (1999, November 4). de Varona still a pioneer. *The Courant.* Retrieved from http://articles.courant .com/1999-11-04/sports/9911040073_1_female-athletes womensports-celebration-women-s-sports-foundation

Rogers, P. (2000, May 15). Making waves: Olympian Donna De Varona charges ABC fired her because of her age. *People.* Retrieved from www.people.com/ people/archive/article/0,,20131248,00.html

Roenigk, A. (2012, February 17). Sebastian Coe a champion for women. *ESPNW.* Retrieved from http://espn. go.com/espnw/olympics/article/7588059/sebastian- coe-champion-women

Rossingh, D. (2013, March 8). Former Olympian de Varona spearheading women's network. *Bloomberg.* Retrieved from www.bloomberg.com/news/2013-03- 08/former-olympian-de-varona-spearheading-women- s-network.html

Sartore, M.L., & Cunningham, G.B. (2007). Explaining the under-representation of women in leadership positions of sport organizations: A symbolic interactionist perspective. *Quest, 59*(2), 244-265.

Shaw, S., & Hoeber, L. (2003). "A strong man is direct and a direct woman is a bitch": Gendered discourses and their influence on employment roles in sport organizations. *Journal of Sport Management, 17*(4), 347-375.

Smith, M.M., & Wrynn, A.M. (2009). *Women in the 2000, 2004 and 2008 Olympic and Paralympic Games: An analysis of participation and leadership opportunities, a Women's Sports Foundation research report.* New York, NY: Women's Sports Foundation.

Smith, M.M., & Wrynn, A.M. (2010). *Women in the 2002, 2006 and 2010 Winter Olympic and Paralympic Games: An analysis of participation and leadership opportunities, a Women's Sports Foundation research report.* New York, NY: Women's Sports Foundation.

Smith, M.M., & Wrynn, A.M. (2013). *Women in the 2012 Olympic and Paralympic Games: An analysis of participation and leadership opportunities, a Women's Sports Foundation research report.* New York, NY: Women's Sports Foundation.

Staurowsky, E.J. (2011). *The WISE/Ithaca College Status of Women in Sport Industry Survey findings* [Unpublished report].

Staurowsky, E.J., Brown, K., & Weider, N. (2009). *Women's reflections on working in the sport in the sport industry.* Paper presented at the To Remember Is to Resist Conference, Toronto, Ontario, CANADA.

Tahmincioglu, E. (2012, June 29). Playing youth sports helps women in their careers. *USA Today.* Retrieved from www.today.com/money/playing-youth-sports- helps-women-their-careers-853207

Wentworth, C. (2009). The role of collegiate sports participation in preparing women for executive leadership [Doctoral dissertation]. Retrieved from http:// athenaeum.libs.uga.edu/handle/10724/11744

Whisenant, W. A., Pedersen, P. M., & Obenour, B. (2002). Success and gender: Determining the rate of advancement for intercollegiate athletic directors. *Sex Roles, 47*, 485-491.

White, M., & Kay, J. (2006). Who rules sport now? White and Brackenridge revisited. *International Review for the Sociology of Sport, 41*(3), 465-473.

Women in Sports and Events (WISE). (n.d.). Our History. Retrieved from http://wiseworks.org/about/history

Chapter 13

Acosta, V., & Carpenter. L. (2007). Intercollegiate sports. In M.A. Hums, G.G. Bower, & H. Grappendorf (Eds.), *Women leaders in sport: Impact and influence* (pp. 45-62). Oxon Hills, MD: AAHPERD.

Acosta, V., & Carpenter, L. (2012). *Women in intercollegiate sport. A longitudinal, national study. Thirty-five year update. 1977-2012* [Unpublished report]. Retrieved from http://acostacarpenter.org/AcostaCarpenter2012.pdf

Amy Huchthausen named conference's fourth commissioner [Press release]. (2011, December 8). *American East Communications*. Retrieved from www.americaeast.com/ViewArticle.dbml?DB_OEM_ID=14000&ATCLID=205304418

Barlow, K.A. (1999). Factors that impact the present and future of women high school athletic directors. *Dissertation Abstracts International, 59*(7).

Barron, D. (2012, February 13). Five women ADs in area proof of change in high school athletics. *Houston Chronicle*. Retrieved from www.chron.com/sports/highschool/article/5-women-ADs-in-area-proof-of-change-in-high-3357536.php

Blom, L.C., Abrell, L., Wilson, M.J., Lape, J., Halbrook, M., & Judge, L.W. (2011). Working with male athletes: The experiences of U.S. female head coaches. *The ICHPER-SD Journal of Research in Health, Physical Education, Recreation, Sport & Dance, 6*(1), 54-61.

Borland, J., & Bruening, J.E. (2010). Navigating barriers: A qualitative examination of the under-representation of Black females as head coaches in collegiate basketball. *Sport Management Review, 13*(4), 407-420.

Bracken, N. (2009). *Gender equity in college coaching and administration: Perceived barriers report.* Indianapolis, IN: NCAA.

Brockman, E. (2000, March 5). A woman's power tool: High heels. *New York Times*. Retrieved from www.nytimes.com/2000/03/05/weekinreview/a-woman-s-power-tool-high-heels.html

Brook, S.L., & Foster, S. (2010). Does gender affect compensation among NCAA basketball coaches? *Journal of Sport Finance, 5*(2), 96-106.

D'Costa, K. (2012). Power, confidence, and high heels. *Scientific American*. Retrieved from http://blogs.scientificamerican.com/anthropology-in-practice/2012/01/13/from-the-archives-power-confidence-and-high-heels/?print=true

DeNava-Walt, C., Proctor, B.D., & Smith, J.C. (2012). *Income, poverty, and health insurance coverage in the United States: 2011.* Washington, DC: United States Census Bureau.

Equity in Athletics Disclosure Act Report 2011-2012. (2012). U.S. Department of Education. Retrieved from http://ope.ed.gov/athletics

Ford, B. (2012, March 26). Fruit punch, basketball, and a desire to improve. *espnW*. Retrieved from http://espn.go.com/espnw/title-ix/article/7728181/bonnie-ford-playing-women-basketball-oberlin-college-title-ix

Gentry, J.K., & Alexander, R.M. (2012, April 2). Pay for women's basketball coaches lags behind that of men's coaches. *New York Times*. Retrieved from www.nytimes.com/2012/04/03/sports/ncaabasketball/pay-for-womens-basketball-coaches-lags-far-behind-mens-coaches.html

Goisman, M. (2011, June 8). Somerville High AD Nicole Viele. Retrieved from http://mgoisman.sportsblognet.com/2011/06/08/somerville-high-ad-nicole-viele-%E2%80%98our-program-is-so-much-bigger-than-wins-and-losses%E2%80%99

Grappendorf, H., Lough, N., & Griffin, J. (2004). Profiles and career patterns of female NCAA Division I athletic directors. *International Journal of Sport Management, 5*(3), 243-261.

Greenawalt, N., Fleischman, R., & Smeaton, P. (2013). Modern sexism and preference for a coach among select National Collegiate Athletic Association Division I female athletes: A quantitative and qualitative analysis. Paper presented at the North American Society for Sport Management Conference, Austin, TX.

Groller, K. (2013, July 9). Diane Jordan is ready for the challenge as Freedom's new athletic director. *The Morning Call*. Retrieved from http://articles.mcall.com/2013-07-09/sports/mc-aroundthevalley-0708-20130709_1_assistant-ad-new-ad-sam-senneca

Hoffman, J. (2011). Inside the huddle: Gender stereotyping work among senior level women athletic administrators. *International Journal of Sport Management, 12*(3), 255-274.

Hook, J. (2012, November 8). Another "Year of the Woman" in Congress. *The Wall Street Journal*. Retrieved from http://online.wsj.com/article/SB10001424127887324073504578107342686881904.html

Howard, J. (1994). Donna Lopiano and the art of reform. In R. Rapoport (Ed.), *A kind of grace: A treasury of sportswriting by women* (pp. 37-43). Bandon, OR: Zenobia Press.

Igasaki, P. (1997). *EEOC notice: Enforcement guidance on sex discrimination in the compensation of sports coaches in educational institutions.* Equal Employment Opportunity Commission. Retrieved from www.eeoc.gov/policy/docs/coaches.html

Irick, E. (2012). *NCAA sports sponsorship and participation rates report 1981-1982–2011-2012.* Indianapolis, IN: National Collegiate Athletic Association.

Kamphoff, C. (2010). Bargaining with patriarchy: Former female coaches' experiences and their decision to leave collegiate coaching. *Research Quarterly for Sport and Exercise, 81*(3), 360-372.

Kamphoff, C.S., & Gill, D. (2008). Collegiate athletes' perceptions of the coaching profession. *International Journal of Sports Science and Coaching, 3*(1), 55-72.

Kline, K. (2012, March 9). High heeled affair for SEC coaches. *Full Court.* Retrieved from www.fullcourt.com/kelly-kline/5533/high-heeled-affair-sec-coaches

Lapchick, R., Farris, M., & Rodriquez, B. (2012, November 28). *Mixed progress throughout collegiate athletic leadership: Assessing diversity among campus and conference leaders for Football Bowl Subdivision (FBS) schools in the 2012-2013 academic year* [Unpublished report]. Retrieved from www.tidesport.org/Grad%20Rates/2012_D1_Leadership_Report.pdf

Lapchick, R., Agusta, R., Kinkopf, N., & McPhee, F. (2013). *The 2012 racial and gender report card: College sport* [Unpublished report]. Retrieved from http://tidesport.org/RGRC/2012/2012_College_RGRC.pdf

LaVoi, N. (2013, May 23). Female coaches in high school sports: Data released. *Women in Coaching Blog.* Retrieved from www.nicolemlavoi.com/female-coaches-in-high-school-sports-data-Released

Magnusen, M.J., & Rhea, D.J. (2009). Division I athletes' attitudes toward and preferences for male and female strength and conditioning coaches. *Journal of Strength and Conditioning Research, 23*(4), 1084-1090.

Mather. M. (2007). Interscholastic sport. In M.A. Hums, G.G. Bower, & H. Grappendorf (Eds.), *Women leaders in sport: Impact and influence* (pp. 25-44). Oxon Hill, MD: AAHPERD.

Mazerolle, S.M., Borland, J.F., & Burton, L.J. (2012). The professional socialization of athletic trainers: Navigating experiences of gender bias. *Journal of Athletic Training, 47*(6), 694-703.

National Collegiate Athletic Association. (2012). Race and gender demographics report. Retrieved from http://web1.ncaa.org/rgdSearch/exec/instSearch

Preuss, A. (2012, March 31). Lisa Campos hired to replace Jim Fallis at NAU. *PHXFan.* Retrieved from http://phxfan.com/2012/03/lisa-campos-hired-to-replace-ad-jim-fallis-at-nau

Reid, S.M. (2011, April 21). UCLA basketball: Close will lead in her own way. *Orange County Register.* Retrieved from www.ocregister.com/ucla/strong-462371-close-ucla.html

Reynolds, R., & Crockett, R.O. (2013, April 2). Leadership in the field: Interviews with global leaders: Val Ackerman. Retrieved from www.russellreynolds.com/sites/default/files/rr_video_series_v3.pdf

Rhode, D., & Walker, C. (2008). Gender equity in college athletics: Women coaches as a case study. *Stanford Journal of Civil Rights and Civil Liberties, 4,* 1-50.

Richards, A. (1988, July 19). Address to the Democratic National Convention. *New York Times.* Retrieved from www.nytimes.com/1988/07/19/us/text-richards.html

Sandberg, S. (2013). *Lean in: Women, work, and the will to lead.* New York, NY: Random House.

Sartore, M., & Cunningham, G. (2006). Stereotypes, race, and coaching. *Journal of African American Studies, 10*(2), 69-83.

Schneider, R.C., Stier, W.F., Henry, T.J., & Wilding, G.E. (2010). Senior women administrators' perceptions of factors leading to discrimination of women in intercollegiate athletic departments. *Journal of Issues in Intercollegiate Athletics, 3,* 16-34.

Shriver, M. (2009). *The Shriver Report: A woman's nation changes everything.* Washington, DC: Center for American Progress.

Solomon, J. (2015, October 26). New C-USA commish Judy McLeod breaks female barrier; more must fall. *CBSSports.com.* Retrieved from www.cbssports.com/collegefootball/writer/jon-solomon/25354623/new-c-usa-commish-judy-macleod-breaks-female-barrier-more-must-fall

Stangl, J.M., & Kane, M.J. (1991). Structural variables that offer explanatory power for the underrepresentation of women coaches since Title IX: The case of homologous reproduction. *Sociology of Sport Journal, 8*(1), 47-60.

Staurowsky, E.J. (2011, September). Traversing the gender tightrope: Reflections from the NACWAA Convention. *College Sports Business News.* Retrieved from http://collegesportsbusinessnews.com/issue/october-2011/article/traversing-the-gender-tightrope-reflections-from-the-2011-nacwaa-convention

Staurowsky, E.J., Murray, K., Puzio, M., & Quagliariello, J. (2013). Revisiting James Madison University: A case analysis of program restructuring following so-called Title IX cuts. *Journal of Intercollegiate Sport, 6*(1), 96-119.

Staurowsky, E.J., & Proska, M. (2013, July 15). Gender equity at the high school level. *Women in Coaching Blog.* Retrieved from http://stream.goodwin.drexel.edu/womenincoaching/2013/07/15/gender-equity-at-the-high-school-level/#more-3948

Staurowsky, E.J., & Weight, E. (2011, December). Title IX literacy: What coaches don't know and need to find out. *Journal of Intercollegiate Sport, 4*(2), 190-209.

Staurowsky, E.J., & Weight, E. (2013). Discovering dysfunction in Title IX implementation: NCAA administrator literacy, responsibility, and fear. *Journal of Applied Sport Management: Research That Matters, 5*(1), 1-30.

Summit, P., & Jenkins, S. (2013). *Sum it up: A thousand and ninety-eight victories, a couple of irrelevant losses, and a life in perspective.* New York, NY: Random House.

Tyler, G. (2012, December). The pay gap between men's and women's sports lives on 40 years after Title IX. *The Sport Digest.* Retrieved from http://thesportdigest.com/2012/12/the-pay-gap-between-mens-and-womens-sports-lives-on-40-years-after-title-ix

U.S. Department of Education. (2012). The Equity in Athletes Data Analysis Cutting Tool. Retrieved from http://ope.ed.gov/athletics

Whisenant, W., Miller, J., & Pedersen, P. (2005). Systemic barriers in athletic administration: An analysis of job descriptions for interscholastic athletic directors. *Sex Roles, 53*(1), 911-918.

White, M. (2012, October 5). A new direction: Women athletic directors on the rise. *Pittsburgh Post Gazette.* Retrieved from www.post-gazette.com/stories/sports/high-school-other/varsity-xtra-the-changing-face-number-of-women-ads-rising-sharply-656292

Wright, C., Eagleman, A.N., & Pedersen, P.M. (2011). Examining leadership in intercollegiate athletics: A content analysis of NCAA Division I Athletic Directors. *Choregia, 7*(2), 35-52.

Yiamouyiannis, A., & Osborne, B. (2012, May). Addressing gender inequities in collegiate sports: Examining female leadership representation within NCAA sport governance. *Sage Open.* Retrieved from http://sgo.sagepub.com/content/2/2/2158244012449340.full.pdf+html

Chapter 14

Ackerman, V. (2013, July 5). Division I women's basketball white paper. *NCAA.* Retrieved from www.ncaa.org/wps/wcm/connect/public/ncaa/pdfs/2013/ncaa+division+i+womens+basketball+white+paper+2013

Adams, W.L. (2011, July 2). Game, sex, and match: The perils of female sports advertising. *Time.* Retrieved from www.time.com/time/business/article/0,8599,2081209,00.html

Antil, J., Burton, R., & Robinson, M.J. (2012). Exploring the challenges facing female athletes as endorsers. *Journal of Brand Strategy, 1*(3), 292-307.

Badenhausen, K. (2012, July 30). Olympic stars top list of the 10 highest-paid female athletes. *Forbes.* Retrieved from www.forbes.com/sites/kurtbadenhausen/2012/07/30/seven-london-olympic-athletes-among-the-worlds-highest-paid-female-stars

Badminton World Federation. (2010/2011). *BWF handbook II (laws of badminton & regulations).* Retrieved from www.worldbadminton.com/rules/documents/bwfHandbook2010.pdf

Bahk, C.M. (2000). Sex differences in sport spectator involvement. *Perceptual and Motor Skills, 91*(2), 79-83.

BBC Sport. (2004, January 16). Women footballers blast Blatter. Retrieved from http://news.bbc.co.uk/sport2/hi/football/3402519.stm

Belknap, P., & Leonard, W. (1991). A conceptual replication and extension of Erving Goffman's study of gender advertisements. *Sex Roles, 25*, 103-118.

Bem, S.L. (1981). Gender schema theory: A cognitive account of sex typing. *Psychological Review, 88*, 354-364.

Bush, A.J., Martin, C.A., & Bush, V.D. (2004). Sports celebrity influence of behavioral intentions of Generation Y. *Journal of Advertising Research, 44*, 108-118.

Bush, V.D., Bush, A.J., Clark, P., & Bush, R.P. (2005). Girl power and word-of-mouth behavior in flourishing sports market. *Journal of Consumer Marketing, 22*(5), 257-264.

Castillo, J. (2011, August 7). The marketing of Moore is a team challenge. *New York Times.* Retrieved from www.nytimes.com/2011/08/08/sports/basketball/maya-moores-deal-with-jordan-brand-could-be-breakthrough.html?pagewanted=all&_r=0

Cuneen, J., & Claussen, C. (1999). Gender portrayals in sports product point-of-purchase advertising. *Women in Sport and Physical Activity Journal, 8*(2), 73-102.

Cunningham, G., Fink, J.S., & Kenis, L.J. (2008). Choosing an endorser for a woman's sporting event: The interaction of attractiveness and expertise. *Sex Roles, 58*(5/6), 371-378.

Dyson, A., & Turco, D. (1998). The state of celebrity endorsement in sport. *Cyber Journal of Sport Marketing, 2*(1).

Fans of PGA, LPGA tours continue to skew older, have high incomes. (2011, July 28). *SportsBusiness Daily.* Retrieved from www.sportsbusinessdaily.com/Daily/Issues/2011/07/28/Research-and-Ratings/Golf-demos.aspx?hl=Scarborough%20Properties&sc=0

Farrell, A., Fink, J.S., & Fields, S. (2011). Women's sport spectatorship: An exploration of men's influence. *Journal of Sport Management, 25*, 190-201.

Fink, J.S., Cunningham, G.B., & Kensicki, L.J. (2004). Using athletes as endorsers to sell women's sport: Attractiveness vs. expertise. *Journal of Sport Management, 18*, 350-367.

Fink, J.S., Trail, G.T., & Anderson, D.F. (2002). Environmental factors associated with spectator attendance and sport consumption behavior: Gender and team differences. *Sport Marketing Quarterly, 11*(1), 8-19.

Footwear industry statistics. (2012). Statistic Brain Research Institute. Retrieved from www.statisticbrain.com/footwear-industry-statistics

Grau, S.L., Roselli, G., & Taylor, C.R. (2007). Where's Tamika Catchings? A content analysis of female athlete endorsers in magazine advertisements. *Journal of Issues & Research in Advertising, 29*(1), 55-65.

Guest, A.M., & Cox, S. (2009). Using athletes as role models? Conceptual and empirical perspectives from a sample of elite women soccer players. *International Journal of Sports Science & Coaching, 4*(4), 567-581.

Hardin, M., & Greer, J.D. (2009). The influence of gender-role socialization, media use and sports participation on perceptions of gender-appropriate sports. *Journal of Sport Behavior, 32*(2), 207-227.

Howard, J. (2011, June 23). Twelve years later, still the best. *ESPN.* Retrieved from http://sports.espn.go.com/espn/commentary/news/story?page=howard-110623

Irick, E. (2012). *NCAA sports sponsorship and participation rates report: 1981-1982 to 2011-2012.* National Collegiate Athletic Association. Retrieved from www.ncaapublications.com/productdownloads/PR2013.pdf

Jessop, A. (2012, November 26). How new marketing approaches helped the NFL achieve triple-digit growth in women's apparel sales. *Forbes.* Retrieved from www.forbes.com/sites/aliciajessop/2012/11/26/how-new-marketing-approaches-helped-the-nfl-achieve-triple-digit-growth-in-womens-apparel-sales

Joseph, S. (2013, March 25). Sports brands to go beyond pink to woo women. *Marketing Week*. Retrieved from www.marketingweek.co.uk/news/sports-brands-to-go-beyond-pink-to-woo-women/4006092.article

Kamins, M.A. (1990). An investigation into the match-up hypothesis in celebrity advertising: When beauty may only be skin deep. *Journal of Advertising, 19*(1), 4-13.

Knight, J.L., & Guiliano, T.A. (2001). He's a Laker; she's a looker: The consequences of gender-stereotypical portrayals of male and female athletes by the print media. *Sex Roles, 45*, 217-229.

Knight, J.L., & Guiliano, T.A. (2003). Blood, sweat, and jeers: The impact of the media's heterosexist portrayals on perceptions of male and female athletes. *Journal of Sport Behavior, 26*(3), 272-284.

Koo, G.Y., Ruihley, B.J., & Dittmore, S.W. (2012). Impact of perceived on-field performance on sport celebrity source credibility. *Sport Marketing Quarterly, 21*, 147-158.

Krane, M.J., Choi, P.Y.L., Baird, S.M., Aimar, C.M., & Kauer, K.J. (2004). Living the paradox: Female athletes negotiate femininity and muscularity. *Sex Roles, 50*(5/6), 315-329.

Krasny, J. (2012, February 17). Infographic: Women control the money in America. *Business Insider*. Retrieved from www.businessinsider.com/infographic-women-control-the-money-in-america-2012-2#ixzz1mtTRybbl

Lee, J. (2004, July 19-25). NCAA panel wants branding for women's hoops. *SportsBusiness Journal, 7*(12), 6.

Longman, J. (2011, May 26). Badminton's new dress code is criticized as being sexist. *New York Times*. Retrieved from www.nytimes.com/2011/05/27/sports/badminton-dress-code-for-women-criticized-as-sexist.html?pagewanted=all&_r=0

Maxwell, H., & Lough, N. (2009). Signage vs. no signage: An analysis of sponsorship recognition in women's college basketball. *Sport Marketing Quarterly, 18*, 188-198.

McCarter, N. (2013, January 4). 5 reasons why Americans' favorite team is USWNT, not USMNT. *Bleacher Report*. Retrieved from http://bleacherreport.com/articles/1468184-5-reasons-why-americans-favorite-team-is-uswnt-not-usmnt

McCracken, G. (1989). Who is the celebrity endorser? Cultural foundations of the endorsement process. *Journal of Consumer Research, 16*, 310-321.

McGinnis, L., Chun, S., & McQuillan, J. (2003). A review of gendered consumption in sport and leisure. *Academy of Marketing Science Review, 5*, 1-24. Retrieved from www.amsreview.org/articles/mcginnis05-2003.pdf

Messner, M. (2010, June 3). Dropping the ball on covering women's sports. *Huffington Post*. Retrieved from www.huffingtonpost.com/michael-messner/dropping-the-ball-on-cove_b_599912.html

National Collegiate Athletic Association (NCAA). (2012). Women's basketball attendance. Retrieved from www.ncaa.org/wps/wcm/connect/public/NCAA/Resources/Stats/W+Basketball/attendance.html

National Women's Soccer League (NWSL). (2013, April 18). NWSL, FSMG announce national TV agreement. Retrieved from http://nwslsoccer.com/home/711844.html

Ohanian, R. (1990). Construction and validation of a scale to measure celebrity. *Journal of Advertising, 19*(3), 39-53.

Ohanian, R. (1991). The impact of celebrity spokespersons' perceived image on intention to purchase. *Journal of Advertising Research, 31*(1), 46-54.

On, E. (2012, August 15). The 9 highest paid female athletes of 2012. *Total Pro Sports*. Retrieved from www.totalprosports.com/2012/08/15/highest-paid-female-athletes-of-2012/#9

Rhoden, W.C. (2012, October 7). Amid successes, WNBA is still facing challenges. *New York Times*. Retrieved from www.nytimes.com/2012/10/08/sports/basketball/amid-successes-wnba-is-still-facing-challenges.html?pagewanted=all&_r=0

Ridinger, L.J., & Funk, D.C. (2006). Looking at gender differences through the lens of sport spectators. *Sport Marketing Quarterly, 15*, 155-166.

Ross, S.R., Ridinger, L.L., & Cuneen, J. (2009). Drivers to divas: Advertising images of women in motorsport. *International Journal of Sports Marketing & Sponsorship, 10*(3), 204-214.

Rovell, D. (2013, April 22). *Maria Sharapova, Porsche reach deal*. Retrieved from http://espn.go.com/tennis/story/_/id/9198876/maria-sharapova-inks-3-year-endorsement-deal-porsche

Sargent, S.L., Zillmann, D., & Weaver, J.B. (1998). The gender gap in the enjoyment of televised sports. *Journal of Sport & Social Issues, 22*(1), 4-64.

Shank, M.D. (2008). *Sports marketing: A strategic perspective* (4th ed.). Upper Saddle Ridge, NJ: Prentice-Hall.

Shaw, S., & Amis, J. (2001). Image and investment: Sponsorship and women's sport. *Journal of Sport Management, 15*, 219-246.

Sirak, R. (2008, February 8). The LPGA's new money game: Endorsements spread rapidly as firms capitalize on circuit's global reach. *Golf Digest*. Retrieved from www.golfdigest.com/golf-tours-news/2008-02/gw20080208sirakbunker

Sports fan/social media report. (2012). *Sports Business Research Network*. Retrieved from www.sbrnet.com/fanreports

Till, B.D., & Busler, M. (2000). The match-up hypothesis: Physical attractiveness, expertise, and the role of fit on brand attitude, purchase intent, and brand beliefs. *Journal of Brand Advertising, 29*(3), 1-14.

Tippett, A.B. (2012, July 30). Star power squandered. *UDaily*. Retrieved from www.udel.edu/udaily/2013/jul/study-female-athletes-073012.html

Wann, D.L., & Ensor, C.L. (2001). Family motivation and a more accurate classification of preferences for aggressive sports. *Perceptual and Motor Skills, 92*(2), 603-605.

Whiteside, E., & Hardin, A. (2011). Women (not) watching women: Leisure time, television, and implications for televised coverage of women's sports. *Communication, Culture, & Critique, 4*(2), 122-143.

Wolter, S. (2010). The Ladies Professional Golf Association's five points of celebrity: "Driving" the organization "fore-ward" or a snap-hook into the next fairway? *International Journal of Sport Communication, 3*(1), 31-48.

WTA. (n.d.). Strong is beautiful. Retrieved from www.wtatennis.com/strong-is-beautiful

Yancey, A. (2008). Role models. In W. Darity, Jr. (Ed.), *International Encyclopedia of the Social Sciences* (pp. 273-275). Detroit, MI: Macmillan Reference.

Chapter 15

Acosta, V., & Carpenter, L. (2012). *Women in intercollegiate sport: A longitudinal, national study. Thirty-five year update. 1977-2012* [Unpublished report]. Retrieved from http://acostacarpenter.org/AcostaCarpenter2012.pdf

Bernstein, C. (2008). *A woman in charge: The life of Hillary Rodham Clinton.* New York, NY: Vintage Books.

Bhutto, B. (2008). *Reconciliation: Islam, democracy and the West.* New York, NY: Harper Perennial Press.

Brady, M., & Khan, A. (2002). *Letting girls play: The Methare Youth Sport Association's football program for girls.* New York, NY: The Population Council.

De Beauvoir, S. (1949/1989). *The second sex.* New York, NY: Vintage Books. (Original work published in French.)

Donnelly, P., & Donnelly, M. (2013). *The London 2012 Olympics: A gender equality audit.* Toronto, Ontario, Canada: University of Toronto Center for Sport Policy Studies.

Daly, M. (1973). *Beyond God the Father: Toward a philosophy of women's liberation.* Boston, MA: Beacon.

Fasting, K., Huffman, D., & Sand, T. (2014). *Gender, participation, and leadership in sport in southern Africa: A baseline study.* Oslo, Norway: The Norwegian Olympic and Paralympic Committee and Confederation of Sports.

Freeman, S., Bourque, S., & Shelton, C. (2001). *Women on power: Leadership redefined.* Boston, MA: Northeastern University Press.

Henry, I., & Robinson, L. (2010). *Gender equality and leadership in Olympic bodies: Women, leadership and the Olympic Movement.* Lausanne, Switzerland: International Olympic Committee.

Horney, K. (1967). *Feminine psychology.* New York, NY: W.W. Norton.

International Olympic Committee (IOC). (2014). *Olympic Charter.* Retrieved from www.olympics.org/Documents/olympic_charter_en.pdf

International Olympic Committee, Department of International Cooperation and Development. (2013).

Olympism in action: Sport serving humankind. Lausanne, Switzerland: International Olympic Committee.

International Working Group on Women and Sport. (1994.) *The Brighton Declaration on women and sport.* Retrieved from http://iwg-gti.org/?s=brighton+declaration

Jennings, A. (1996). *The new lords of the rings.* London, England: Pocket Books.

Kirk, D. (2012). *Empowering girls and women through physical education and sport: Advocacy brief.* Bangkok, Thailand: UNESCO.

Leigh, M.H., & Bonin, T.M. (1977). The pioneering role of Madame Alice Milliat and the FSFI in establishing track and field competition for women. *Journal of Sport History, 4*(1), 72-83.

Lenskyj, H. (2000). *Inside the Olympic industry: Power, politics and activism.* Albany, NY: State University of New York Press.

Meier, M. (2005). *Gender equality, sport and development.* Biel, Switzerland: Swiss Academy for Development.

Miner, M., & Rawson, H. (2006). *The Oxford dictionary of American quotations.* New York, NY: Oxford University Press.

Neumann, E. (1955). *The great mother: Analysis of the archetype* (R. Manheim, Trans.). Princeton, NJ.: Princeton University Press.

Oglesby, C. (1974). Social conflict theory and the sport organization system. *Quest, 22,* 63-73.

Oglesby, C. (1978). *Women and sport: From myth to reality.* Philadelphia, PA: Lea & Febiger.

Oglesby, C., Greenberg, D., Hall, R., Hill, K., Johnston, F., & Ridley, S. (1998). *Encyclopedia of Women and Sport in America.* Phoenix, AZ: Oryx Press.

Rich, A. (1986). *Of woman born: Motherhood as experience and institution.* New York, NY: W.W. Norton.

Smith, M., & Wrynn, A. (2010a). *Women in the 2010 Olympic and Paralympic Winter Games: An analysis of participation and leadership opportunities.* East Meadow, NY: Women's Sports Foundation.

Smith, M., & Wrynn, A. (2010b). *Women in Olympic and Paralympic Games: An analysis of participation and leadership opportunities.* Ann Arbor, MI: SHARP Center for Women and Girls.

UNDAW. (2008). *Women 2000 and beyond: Women, gender equality and sport.* New York, NY: Division for the Advancement of Women of the United Nations Secretariat.

United Nations. (2008). *Resolution 63/135. Sport as a means to promote education, health, development and peace.* Retrieved from www.un.org./wcm/webdav/site/sport/shared/sport/pdfs/Resolutions/A-RES-63-135/2008-12-11_A-RES-63-135_EN.pdf

Epilogue

Angelou, M. (1993). The inauguration: Maya Angelou—On the pulse of the morning. *New York Times.* Retrieved from www.nytimes.com/1993/01/21/us/the-inauguration-maya-angelou-on-the-pulse-of-morning.html

Gerber, E., Felshin, J., Berlin, P., & Wyrick, W. (1974). *The American woman in sport.* Boston, MA: Addison-Wesley.

Obama, M. (2014). Remarks by the First Lady at memorial service for Dr. Maya Angelou. Retrieved from www.whitehouse.gov/the-press-office/2014/06/07/remarks-first-lady-memorial-service-dr-maya-angelou

O'Neill, T. (2015, June 4). Abby Wambach's big goals: Win the World Cup and change FIFA forever. *Rolling Stone.* Retrieved from www.rollingstone.com/sports/features/abby-wambachs-big-goals-win-the-world-cup-change-fifa-forever-20150604

Index

Note: The letters *f* and *t* after page numbers indicate figures and tables, respectively.

About the Editor

Ellen J. Staurowsky, EdD, is a professor in the Department of Sport Management at Drexel University. She is renowned as an authority on the business of college athletics, college student-athlete rights, and Title IX and gender equity. Staurowsky has been featured in numerous national media outlets and served as an expert witness in the historic antitrust case *O'Bannon v. NCAA*. Staurowsky draws from more than 30 years of experience as both a practitioner and scholar, having served as a collegiate athletic director at multiple colleges as well as a coach at the collegiate level of field hockey, women's lacrosse, and men's soccer. Prior to her appointment at Drexel in 2011, she was a professor at Ithaca College, where she worked for nearly two decades. Staurowsky teaches courses in Women and Sport, Gender Issues in Sport, Legal Foundations of Title IX, and courses in the Sociology of Sport. She is a member of the College Sport Research Institute advisory board, the Ursinus College Board of Trustees, and various professional organizations, having previously served as president of the National American Society for the Sociology of Sport. She is co-author of *College Athletes for Hire: The Evolution and Legacy of the NCAA Amateur Myth* and is lead author of *Big Time Athletes, Labor, and the Academy* (forthcoming).

About the Contributors

Dunja Antunovic, PhD, is an assistant professor of sports communication at Bradley University's Charley Steiner School of Sports Communication. Her research focuses on issues of gender in sports media, including representation of female athletes, status of women in journalism, and female fans. Her work has previously appeared in journals such as *New Media & Society* and *International Review for the Sociology of Sport*. She earned her PhD in mass communications, with a minor in women's studies, at Pennsylvania State University.

Akilah Carter-Francique, PhD, is an assistant professor of sport management in the Department of Health and Kinesiology at Texas A&M University. Her research scholarship, teaching, and service focus on the historical and contemporary experience of participants in sport and physical activity, experiences of Black female and male students and staff in educational institutions (K-20), and health and well-being for women of color. Because she is a former collegiate athlete and sport administrator, her work is shaped by current issues of diversity and social justice, participation and representation, and access and opportunity. She has published numerous book chapters and journal articles on the experiences of women and people of color in sport and physical activity. Carter-Francique is on the executive committee for the North American Society for the Sociology of Sport (member at large) and on the editorial board for the *Journal of Issues in Inter-*

collegiate Athletics. Lastly, Carter-Francique is the cofounder (with Deniece Dortch, MA) and director of Sista to Sista, a cocurricular leadership development program that fosters a sense of connectedness among Black female collegiate athletes.

Dayna B. Daniels is an emeritus professor of women and gender studies and of kinesiology at the University of Lethbridge in Lethbridge, Alberta, Canada. Dayna is a life-long participant in many sports and physical activities as a participant, coach, administrator, and volunteer. She dedicated her professional endeavors to improving sporting opportunities for girls and women throughout the lifespan and in all aspects of sport and physical activity involvement. Dr. Daniels is the author of *Polygendered and Ponytailed: The Dilemma of Femininity and the Female Athlete*.

Corinne Farneti, PhD, is an assistant professor of sport management at Mount St. Mary's University. She has published and presented nationally in areas of sport personnel management, media representation of gender, fantasy sport, and team dynamics. Her current research interests include NCAA regulation and social capital in community recreation. She earned her doctorate at Ohio State University after receiving her master's degree from the University of Georgia and her bachelor's degree from Ithaca College.

Marie Hardin, PhD, is a professor of journalism and dean in the College of Communications at Pennsylvania State University. Her research, published in communication and sport-related journals, has focused primarily on issues of gender in the sports media workplace. She served as associate director of the John Curley Center for Sports Journalism at Penn State between 2005 and 2014 and is a co-editor of the 2014 *Routledge Handbook of Sport and New Media.*

Mary A. Hums, PhD, is a professor in sport administration at the University of Louisville. She holds a PhD in sport management from Ohio State University, an MA in athletic administration and an MBA from the University of Iowa, and a BBA in management from the University of Notre Dame. In 2009, Hums was selected as the North American Society for Sport Management's Earle F. Zeigler lecturer, the organization's most prestigious academic honor. In 2014, she received the North American Society for Sport Management's Diversity Award. In 2008, Hums was an Erasmus Mundus visiting international scholar at Katholische Universiteit in Leuven, Belgium. In 2006, she was selected by the United States Olympic Committee to represent the United States at the International Olympic Academy Educators Session in Olympia, Greece. She worked as a volunteer for the 1996 Summer Paralympic Games in Atlanta, the 2002 Winter Paralympic Games in Salt Lake City, the 2010 Winter Paralympic Games in Vancouver, and the 2015 Para-Pan American Games in Toronto. In 2004, she lived in Athens, Greece, working both the Olympic (softball) and Paralympic (goalball) Games.

Vikki Krane, PhD, is a professor of teaching excellence in the School of Human Movement, Sport, and Leisure Studies at Bowling Green State University, where she also is an affiliated faculty member with the Women's, Gender, and Sexuality Studies and American Culture Studies programs. Her teaching and scholarship are focused on sport psychology and gender and sexuality in sport. She has been the editor of *The Sport Psychologist* and the *Women in Sport and Physical Activity Journal,* and she currently is on the editorial boards of *The Sport Psychologist* and *Psychology of Sport and Exercise.* She is a certified consultant through the Association of Applied Sport Psychology and a fellow of the National Academy of Kinesiology and the Association for Applied Sport Psychology. She earned her doctorate at the University of North Carolina at Greensboro after receiving her master's degree from the University of Arizona and her bachelor's degree from Denison University.

Jacqueline McDowell, PhD, is an assistant professor in the School of Recreation, Health, and Tourism at George Mason University. She holds a PhD in kinesiology with an emphasis in sport management from Texas A&M University. McDowell's research focuses on issues of diversity and inclusion in sport and recreation organizations, with a particular emphasis on investigating and developing strategies and programs that can be implemented to remove barriers to participation. Her emerging research stream investigates the utility of sports and sport programs in reducing health risks.

Carole Oglesby, PhD, has been in the professoriate for more than 40 years. She earned a PhD in kinesiology at Purdue University in 1969 and a PhD in counseling at Temple University in 1999. Carole's scholarly career has been devoted to growth and development in two areas: women's and gender studies in sport and sport psychology. She has held major leadership positions in the National Association of Girl's and Women's Sport, Women's Sport Foundation, WomenSport International, the Association for Applied Sport Psychology, and the International Working Group for Women in Sport.

Sharon Phillips, PhD, is an assistant professor of specialized programs in education at Hofstra University. Prior to coming to Long Island, she was living abroad and working as a lecturer in the Sport and Leisure Studies Department at the University of Waikato in New Zealand. Phillips' research focuses on student attitudes toward physical education and teaching and learning in physical education. One of the highlights of her career is when, as a public school teacher, she was awarded Teacher of the Year for her excellence in teaching physical education. Outside of her career, Phillips has founded the Christopher and Susan Phillips Foundation, raising scholarship money in honor and memory of her mother and brother.

Katie Sell, PhD, CSCS*D, TSAC-F, ACSM EP-C, is an associate professor in the department of health professions at Hofstra University, where she coordinates the undergraduate exercise science program. She teaches undergraduate and graduate courses in exercise physiology, physical fitness assessment, and the interpretation of research. Her primary research interests are in physical fitness assessment in wildland firefighters and collegiate student-athletes. She is on the NSCA Tactical Strength and Conditioning SIG Executive Council, which focuses on disseminating information on physical training for tactical athletes (military personnel, firefighters, law enforcement agents, and emergency first responders).

Maureen Smith, PhD, is a professor in the Department of Kinesiology and Health Science at California State University Sacramento, where she teaches sport history and sport sociology. Smith is a past president of the North American Society for Sport History, and is also an active member in the North American Society for the Sociology of Sport and Western Society for the Physical Education of College Women. She has been a member of ISHPES for 10 years, and she served on the ISHPES council for several years before being elected as one of the vice presidents. Smith is a fellow of the National Academy of Kinesiology. Her work has been published in the *Journal of Sport History*, the *International Journal of the History of Sport*, and the *Journal of Sport and Social Issues*, as well as in a number of edited collections. Smith's interests are varied, ranging from gender participation in the Olympic and Paralympic Games, racial issues in post–World War II America, sporting statues, as well as media and sport. She earned her PhD in cultural studies of sport at The Ohio State University.